PUNCH, OR THE LONDON CHARIVARI.—June 7, 1862.

THE "SENSATION" STRUGGLE IN AMERICA.

3092

That New Metallic Currency

Civil War Encased Stamps

The Issuers and Their Times

Comprising a History, Merchant Chronicle
Catalog, Auction Summary and Counterfeit Guide
to John Gault's Patent
Mineral and Metal Store Card
Emergency Money of 1862

By Fred L. Reed III, NLG

BNR Press

Civil War Encased Stamps

This volume is the first title in a planned seven-volume series entitled, "A Numismatist's Perspective of the Civil War."
Portions of this book have been previously published in *Coin World*

and separately as *Civil War Encased Stamps: Auction Census Data, 1891-1988*

Library of Congress Cataloging-in-Publication Data
Reed, Fred L. III. 1948-
Civil War Encased Stamps, the Issuers and Their Times
Includes bibliographical references and index.
ISBN 0-931960-43-6 : $59.95 (hard bound)
560 p. 16 X 23 c.m. Includes Dust Jacket
1. United States – History – Civil War, 1861-1865 – Economic aspects.
2. United States – History – Civil War, 1861-1865 – Social aspects.
3. Economics – United States – Civil War, 1861-1865
4. Paper Money – United States – Catalogs.
I. Author. II. Title. III. Title: Civil War Encased Stamps. 973.7

ISBN: 0-931960-43-6 (hard bound)
Library of Congress Catalog Number: 94-96886
American Numismatic Association Library Catalog Number: US-50/R-4
First Edition, First Printing December 1994
Revised First Edition, July 1995
Third Printing, August 1995

This book is also available in CD-ROM, inquire of the Author at the address below

Published by **BNR Press**
132 East Second Street, Port Clinton, Ohio 43452-1115
Manufactured in the United States of America

Address all correspondence, corrections, criticisms or commentary to the Author at P.O. Box 118162, Carrollton, Texas 75011-8162.

Civil War Encased Stamps

By Fred L. Reed III, NLG

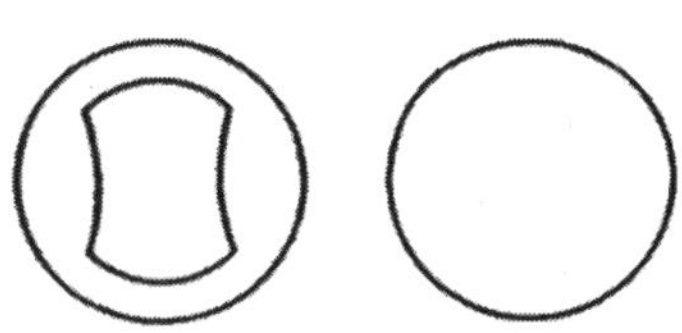

Design for Postage Stamp Case
Patented Aug. 12. 1862.

John Gault

Dedication

This book is dedicated to my loving family without whose support it would not have been possible: to my father Fred L. Reed Jr., who taught me the love of collecting; to my mother Maria A. Reed, who believed I could become a writer; to my patient and supportive wife Patricia K. Reed, who has encouraged me to do both; to our children Rebecca Reed Cornelius and Fred L. Reed IV, both of whom literally grew up while this work was in progress, and to my brother Michael S. Reed, for his lifelong friendship. To all of you, who showed marvelous forbearance and understanding as days became weeks, then months, and ultimately years, "Thanks, our *Big Book* is finally done."

Contents

Frontispiece: *Twins representing competing combatants struggle mortally on the precipice of bankruptcy, as the stability of The Union shatters; "The 'Sensation' Struggle in America,"* Punch, or the London Charivari, *June 7, 1862*

End Papers: *"Broadway at City Hall Park from Barnum's Museum" by Mathew Brady, 1862. (From original glass plate, collodion negative in the possession of Mr. Philip B. Kunhardt Jr.)*

Foreword

When I first wrote about Encased Postage Stamps for national philatelic publications, like *The Blue and the Gray* and *Linn's Weekly Stamp News*, during the Civil War Centennial three decades ago, I was amazed at the lack of attention given to this remarkable series. The Civil War is the most minutely dissected of all American experiences. Sometimes it seems as if each bullet of that sad conflict has been chronicled many times over. But it is not only the military aspects that have attracted such rapt attention. The political, biographical, judicial, social, civil rights, business and economic spheres have each attracted their serious students and able pens. Broad, scholarly and well-written works abound in all these fields.

Yet for the most part, despite the active collector interest of several generations, numismatic insights into this era were still in their primitive, somewhat pre-historic stage, as lamented then by the founding editor of *Coin World*, D. Wayne Johnson. Why was this so? Numismatists and philatelists, generally, are among the most detailed students in any discipline. Their love for their material – what I like to call the collector's heart – imbues their investigations with an intensity of purpose that neither mere scholarship nor pecuniary considerations alone could readily sustain.

A decade later, when I turned serious scholarly attention to Civil War numismatics, the situation had not much improved during the intervening years. Although national, Confederate and fractional currencies, Civil War bank and merchant scrip, tokens and store cards had all risen in stature with the celebration of the Civil War Centennial, these encased stamps continued to languish. Although frightfully imprecise, my juvenile efforts were still practically "state of the art."

The same few facts, guesses, and fables continued to be repeated by more or less able pens as were posited in earlier generations by Messrs. Ben Green and John Jones. Few addi-

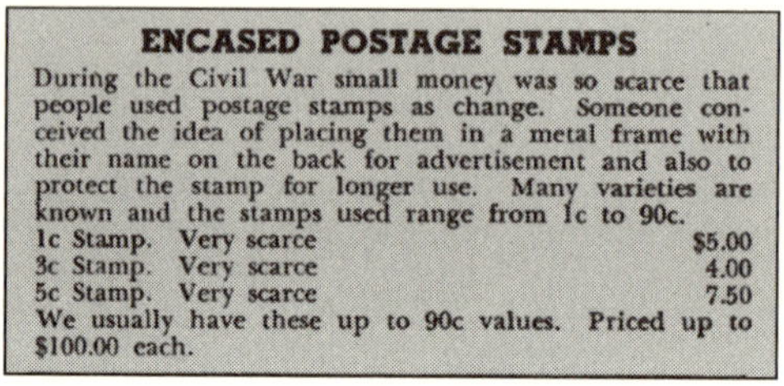
ENCASED POSTAGE STAMPS

During the Civil War small money was so scarce that people used postage stamps as change. Someone conceived the idea of placing them in a metal frame with their name on the back for advertisement and also to protect the stamp for longer use. Many varieties are known and the stamps used range from 1c to 90c.

1c Stamp. Very scarce	$5.00
3c Stamp. Very scarce	4.00
5c Stamp. Very scarce	7.50

We usually have these up to 90c values. Priced up to $100.00 each.

Figures 6a, b

Tatham Stamp & Coin Co. of Springfield, Massachusetts, was the author's gateway into the mysteries and joys of encased stamp collecting. Specimens were available for $4-$5 each. Lookalike stamp label and ad. (Both, Author's collection)

tional, individual contributions to encased stamp study of genuine merit had appeared, although insights by Arnold Perl, Herman Herst, John J. Ford, Q. David Bowers and Arlie Slabaugh were original and thought-provoking during my high school and collegiate days.

Such brief waftings from other interested parties kept alive my youthful interest in these remarkable stamp-coins, which had been sparked originally by my father and his stamp dealing buddies in New England and the northeast generally, who offered hundreds of such treasures for mere pittances in the late Fifties.

In 1973 after a three-year Army stint as a military newspaper editor, I returned to graduate school to remedy my defective knowledge of encased stamps in particular, and of other aspects of Civil War economics and finance generally which mirrored by collecting passions. A dream was conceived to write the record right and eventually prepare a comprehensive "Numismatist's Perspective of the Civil War." I spent nearly three years reading through the daily newspapers of that era in leading publications from Chicago, New York, New Orleans, Richmond, Cincinnati.

Fortunately, I also came under the influence of able Civil War scholar Dr. LeRoy Fischer in perfecting proper research methods. Tens of thousands of resources are available. So simultaneously I was exposed to the broadest possible background training in other primary and secondary literature. Over that period, I digested literally thousands of government documents, personal diaries, compilations of letters, autobiographies, biographies, regional histories, economic, political and social commentaries, specialized journal articles and the like. My note card file grew to stupendous proportions. I quit counting after the 20,000 reference note file figure was reached. My bibliography eventually became book-length in itself.

Leaving school for employment was both fortuitous and necessary. In mid-1975 I was employed as staff writer, then news editor of *Coin World*. I was very fortunate to spend nearly six years immersing myself in the literature of numismatics and philatelics, and especially in meeting a great many collectors as avid as myself with whom it was possible to broaden one's vision, sharpen one's skill and improve one's collection.

It was also the occasion for several converging episodes which reignited encased stamp interest: discovering in the New York Public Library that the encased stamp inventor survived the Civil War; purchasing a check he had written; and engaging in dialogues with two prominent dealers, one of whom told the author it had long been an open invitation by a certain dealer for encased stamp fragments to reassemble obscure varieties, and the reminiscence of another dealer of breaking open (for reasons unclear) encased stamp mounts only to find Scott catalog numbers *already* penciled on the backs of the stamps inside.

It was plain that there was much more to the story of Civil War Encased Stamps. Yet, the "Numismatist's Perspective of the Civil War" might have remained only a dream. Instead of a multi-volume set of books on specialized aspects of this field, my research might have been packed away in my garage had not a change in careers afforded me the opportunity and incentive to mine this load: two dozen cardboard boxes filled with note cards, photocopies, clippings and growing personal libraries and collections.

In 1981 the impetus was provided by Bob Lemke, then editor of *Bank Note Reporter* and *Coins* magazine at Krause Publications. Bob suggested I pen several articles on encased stamps for his publications. A hectic month of labor produced a 100-page manuscript of unpublished material on this subject – hardly a magazine article, yet not quite a book.

It became apparent that the latter alternative was a possible though distant objective. So work was begun in earnest with a view of producing the first book-length treatment ever afforded this series. Much of that research became the basis for the merchant chronicles this author provided in 1984 for the James F. Ruddy collection auction catalog, which was subsequently incorporated into *The Standard Catalogue of Encased Postage Stamps (1989)*. There are books, of course, and then there are books. The book in the reader's hands now is the result of many additional years of eye-blearying research, back-breaking writing, re-writing, corresponding, collecting, checking and cross-checking.

Many years ago the late Robert Friedberg lamented: "At present, there is no current numismatic book that catalogues the entire series of Encased Postage Stamps." Although aspects of historical accident and delayed expectations have intervened and Friedberg's concern is no longer the case, this book finally answers that crying need well. Now there is one.

Let the historian or the critic read with his special prejudices in mind, but let the collector be the judge of this present effort. This book is by a collector for collectors. May it at once inform and entertain.

Fred L. Reed III
Dallas, Texas
Thanksgiving, 1994

Figure 8a

The Civil War brings forth an array of diverse images depending on the experience and interests of an individual. Although neglected, certainly the economics and social climate of those tumultous years are interesting – even exciting – in their own rights. Items for the cover photo were selected with those special interests in mind. This assemblage, from the collections of Bob Kincaid and the author, were photographed during a two-day photo shoot by a Dallas professional photographer. Included are a Civil War soldier's tintype, uniform buttons and .58 caliber bullets, an 1862 Boston almanac, a soldier's letter, and an advertising trade card. Also shown are the postage stamps, Postage Currency, merchant cardboard and paper scrip, U.S. fractional coins and cents, merchant store cards, tokens, and an assortment of John Gault's New Metallic Currency with which military and civilian, great and small, transacted their daily business during the dark days of the war. (Jay Bitzer photo)

Acknowledgements

One of the most remarkable aspects of the highly remarkable story of John Gault and his patent emergency money is that it has taken fully six-score and thirteen years to tell it in any detail. His very name *Gault* (from Gald, Galt, Galte) signifies "the stranger or foreigner" in its original Scots-Irish usage. And so he has remained down to this day, an enigmatic and obscure figure, in short a stranger. But as revealed in the pages that follow, the canvas on which the story of this inventor, his associates and clients can be sketched is a very broad one indeed. It covers the gamut of American history in the century of this great continent's coming of age. It involves tales of amazing ingenuity, energy and good fortune, while boasting a broad spectrum of leading players, cameo roles, and scalawags, alike.

Writing such a history would have been much, much easier only two generations ago. Although the principals had passed from this earthly scene, many second-hand accounts could have been assembled with relative ease compared to the avenues left to my collaborators and myself. An earlier writer specifically rejected the challenge of producing such a work. Writing on the golden anniversary of Gault's patent, Ben Green opined, "A history [would be] interesting, but probably not pertinent at this time." This lapse is regrettable. When he was writing, 10 of the issuing firms were still in existence and Green was personally acquainted with several of the original issuers.

A generation later, John Jones lamented his inability "to find the evidence needed on many points of interest," despite what he termed diligent efforts to do so. He blamed the intervening years, lost records, and lapsing memories due to time. Even then, such a work as this would have been much easier than the present effort proved. Arlie Slabaugh's pamphlet and the Hodder-Bowers compilation referenced above have successfully broken the ground for a collecting community dedicated to preserving "even the smallest of things."

However, the very enormity of performing this task comprehensively, involving as it does serious research across broad geographical and topical ranges, as well as other physical, financial and practical constraints, necessitated a unique strategy before ultimately becoming the book in the reader's hands. No such effort would have been possible without the considerable cooperation of literally hundreds of individuals over the years. This book is a unique collaboration of collectors, dealers, archivists, historians, descendants of the principals and numerous other interested parties. Many such contributors are recognized directly in text or figure captions, notes or bibliographical references, and a special section "About the Author/Contributors" in the back of the book. These last referenced individuals deserve a thank you up front, too. They are Wayne Homren, Bill Gibbs, Wally Lee, Bob Gardner, Bob Kincaid and George Cuhaj. Certain Friedberg catalog numbers (EP numbers) are used with the permission of Arthur Friedberg, The Coin and Currency Institute, New York. Other Friedberg catalog numbers (postage stamp envelope numbers) are used with permission of M. R. Friedberg, Pepper Pike, Ohio. Scott catalog numbers are used with the permission of James B. Hatcher, Scott Publishing Co. (then of New York, now a division of Amos Press, Sidney, Ohio). Krause-Lemke catalog numbers are used with the permission of Bob Lemke, Krause Publications, Iola, Wisconsin. Hessler catalog numbers are used with the permission of Gene Hessler, St. Louis. Rulau catalog numbers are used with the permission of Russ Rulau, Iola, Wisconsin. Schenkman catalog numbers are used with the permission of David Schenkman, Bryans Road, Maryland. Special notes of thanks must go to several coin, stamp, check, currency and other specialized dealers who have assisted the author over the years. Two principally stand out: Tom DeLorey and David T. Alexander, both former colleagues at *Coin World*, and since for many years successful professional numismatists in Chicago and New York City, respectively. Both contributed directly and indirectly in many ways. Most recently, Tom critiqued and proofread galleys of this book. To James F. Ruddy, formerly a principal with Bowers and Ruddy Galleries, and to Q. David Bowers, his former partner now with Bowers and Merena Galleries, go my sincere appreciation for the use of Ruddy's fine encased stamp collection as the basis to illustrate this book. To Dave, also, goes appreciation for providing additional photographic resources and critiquing portions of this work in manuscript form. Special thanks also to Maureen Clark, who photographed the Ruddy collection.

Sincere thanks also must go to Art Kagin, Don Kagin and George Fuld, all formerly of Kagin's Numismatic Investment Corp. Don and George permitted the author to examine the entirety of Don's enormous collection, dispersed in 1988, supplied photographs of every piece from that collection, and critiqued various parts of this work in manuscript form. Art Kagin, in his role as Governor of the American Numismatic Association, was largely responsible for catching the vision for this book and successfully filibustering the ANA Board into funding a significant research grant which materially aided in the evolution of this work. The ANA's action was both unprecedented and helpful. Others connected with the ANA are to be commended for their actions regarding the awarding of that grant. Ruth Ann Brettell and Ken Bressett, then in positions of administering educational resources for the organization, examined the 1,000-page manuscript and photographic resources, and avidly recommended that the board vote favorably on the measure. Board members in addition to Kagin responding favorably to that recommendation and voting in favor of the grant were Bob Medlar, Florence Schook, Ken Hallenbeck, Harry X Boosel, and Kurt Krueger. Their foresight is a shining example of the cooperation possible among various elements of the hobby-science-industry of numismatics. It is also splendid affirmation that ANA can rise affirmatively to fulfill the mandate of its Congressional Charter to further the educational aspects of numismatics. As well, I would like to thank those board members who – while not supporting the grant – never-the-less spurred lively debate on the matter by voicing their opinions and permitting the matter to be openly debated at the ANA Mid-Winter

Convention in San Antonio in 1985. These were John Jay Pittman, and Steven Taylor, who voted against the measure, and Q. David Bowers, who abstained. ANA Counsel George Hatie has been the principal point of contact between the author and the ANA in intervening years. Edward C. Rochette and Robert J. Leuver, in their executive roles with the ANA, have been supportive. My special thanks regarding this matter are extended to *Coin World* editor Beth Deisher, and professional numismatist Michael Haynes, who as ANA members witnessed the several hours of spirited debate, provided emotional support, and were in fact the first people to congratulate the author following the affirmative ANA board vote. Additionally since then Beth wrote a strong editorial commending the ANA on their progressive action, published 13 articles based on this book's research, provided photographic support, and permitted access to a variety of the *Coin World* resources enumerated in various parts of this book.

The author wishes to especially thank several past and present colleagues for their able assistance. Dr. James Beckett kindly and generously permitted the author access to his technological resources, and at various times provided such additional benefits as furthered the course of this book. Therese Bellar ably designed the book, selected type faces, and provided the *Colophon*. Reed Poole and Airey Baringer skillfully solved production dilemmas which would have thwarted less talented and dedicated publishing professionals. Sara Jenks Maneval contributed original illustrations of Arthur M. Claflin, Patrick Drake and George G. Evans especially for this book based on materials provided her. Jay Bitzer spent two laborious days arranging, lighting, and ultimately capturing the cover photo. Mary Gonzalez-Davis spent tireless hours electronically imaging virtually all of the illustrations in this book. Kaki Matheson designed the EPS logo reminiscent of Gault's patent design that is used throughout the text. Richard Olivieri and Teri McGahey excelled in database preparation and performed the mathematical modelling based on the Auction Census Database. Ricky Harrison, John Patneau, Bruce Smith, and Stephen Moore provided assistance in the book's timely publication. Omar Mediano, Paul Kerutis, and Fred Schwan provided additional electronic images. More should be said about Carlton Fred Schwan, a real publisher and real "Fred." Schwan, a friend of nearly 20 years standing, a significant currency book publisher and a fine researcher and author in his own right, provided great impetus for this work over many, many years. First, he clearly foresaw and predicted the emergence of the new technology which would make massive desktop efforts such as this one possible. Second, he convinced the author to follow through on his commitment to see this work to its conclusion and successful publication over a period spanning a decade since an agreement was reached with BNR Press to publish the work. Third, although he erred in dissuading the author from publishing in short form a rarity guide and catalog in pamphlet form in the mid-Eighties (opening the door to a competing work), he never-the-less stood steadfastly by the original vision for this book. His unfailing support is much appreciated. No author could ask for more.

Descendants of the Ayer, Buhl, Bussing, Burnett, Cook and Schapker families provided personal recollections and photographs, as did friends of the Claflin, Cook, and Drake families. Principally contributing in this regard were: Henry A. Schapker, grand nephew of Bernard S. Schapker; Francis J. Rikhoff, great grandson of Bernard S. Schapker; and J. G.

Schapker; John D. Bussing, grandson of John W. Bussing; and Marilyn Bussing Oldenburg, great granddaughter of John W. Bussing, who supplied the pictures of John W. and Wilhelmina B. Bussing; Lois A. Bussing, widow of a grandson (W. C. Bussing Sr.) of J. W. Bussing; Wayne Spiller and Hardin Jones, friends of descendants of H. A. Cook, including Heather Anne Cook; Ruth Ellen Patton Totten, granddaughter of Frederick Ayer; Robert Burnett and James Bishop, descendants of Joseph Burnett; friends of Walter Drake, a descendant of John B. Drake; and Wayne Huff, David Robb, Bob and Marian Branan, friends of the Claflin family. All of the still existing firms who issued encased stamps provided willing and notable assistance. The author thanks especially the management of Shillito's who provided historical and illustrative material. Public Relations Director JoAnn Bongiorno of The Drake provided accommodations, photographic and archival material. Roy Clymer, advertising director and vice president of McAlpin's, as well as Fred W. Schneider, assistant to the McAlpin's president, provided archival material on their firm. Paul W. Thurston, vice president of the Insignia Department of Bailey Banks & Biddle Co. provided a great deal of background, and illustrative material. PR Director Peggy Kaufman of Lord & Taylor did likewise for her fine company. Additionally, I would like to thank the management of Chicago's Tremont Hotel; Debra Kabacinski, manager of corporate communications at Manhattan Life Insurance Co.; and Martin J. Kunberger, regional sales director of North American Life and Casualty Company.

Any large work, covering as this does such wide-ranging and diverse aspects, could not have been accomplished solely by the dedication and industry of even the exemplary group named thus far. At the risk of failing to mention others who provided assistance, many individuals provided details which helped make this book a better effort. Richard C. Eckebrecht provided material on the Chicago issuers. Warren Baker and William H. MacDonald added to information on William Weir. Gary Pipher aided research on Patrick Drake. John W. Wilson helped considerably in rounding out the chapter on Sands' Ale. Former *Coin World* editor Margo Russell provided the photo of Millie Gault, use of her private correspondence, and access to *Coin World* archival material. Ann Lainhart, Michael Lewis Cook and Edwin F. Lochner, able genealogists, provided background material based on their research. David Schenkman researched leads in Baltimore for the author and provided the McAlpen (sic) sutler's store card. Many unfortunately now deceased individuals contributed in major ways. Amon Carter Jr., the author's great benefactor and generous friend in the late Seventies and early Eighties, opened many doors. Dealer Herb Melnick was unflaggingly interested in the author's research. Collector and writer Fay C. Smith assisted in research and critiqued the author's early writings. Matt Rothert, past ANA president and who (along with Margo Russell) sponsored the author's membership to ANA in 1964, assisted the author in numerous other ways. Past Civil War Token Society President John Canfield, whose support helped land the author his job at *Coin World*, proved a grand friend in his remaining years, as did Ray Byrne, a great collector.

A host of research professionals provided extensive and courteous service in the performance of their official duties. I'd like to thank especially Roger D. Bridges, director of research at the Illinois State Historical Library, who provided microfilm periodicals of the Civil War era on an almost weekly basis for three years, 1972-1975. Others to whom I owe thanks are Martin Gengerke, currently of Stack's, for photographic support; Steve Ivy; Joe Schmidt; Joe Kinney, photo archivist Society of Paper Money Collectors; Louis Hornberger, philatelic department of Harmer's of New York; John Sicker, *Linn's Stamp News;* Sandra Roff, New-York Historical Society; Donna Caccamesi, research assistant Boston Public Library; Ernie Keusch; Bill Christensen; Kevin Foley and Milt Friedberg for illustrations of stamp envelopes; Clifford Cole supplied the excellent photos of the Series 1861 U.S. Postage Stamps; Mary Jane Sharpe, circulation manager American Philatelic Research Library; Gordon Blueler; Thomas M. Denly, shared his views on variety rarities and values; Edmund B. Sullivan; Dennis Forge for illustrations; Dr. Richard Doty and L. W. Vosloh, Smithsonian Institution; Benj. Fauver and Roy Van Ormer, who provided examples of the Evans' store cards; Richard Riley, who provided the Mustang Bank note; John F. Walter, who provided information on the 38th Massachusetts Volunteer Regiment; Joanne Lavell, Charlton Publishing, Inc.; Willard Mumford, then editor of the *Copperhead Courier*, Journal of the Civil War Token Society; Cheryl Maisch, then librarian of the Token and Medal Society; and Herman Herst. Also, Jack Stewart and Bill Crouse, who proved good personal friends at critical times in the development of this book; Dennis Forgue; David Gladfelter; John J. Ford; Len Glazer, who provided encased stamps for study, provided photographs, answered questions and critiqued the author's views, provided use of his extensive collection of "Romain" specimens, shared his views on variety rarities and values; Dana Linett, who provided extensive photographic support, shared his views on variety rarities and values; Neil Shafer; Philip B. Kunhardt Jr.; Wayne Kroll; James W. Slaten, who helped me track down the patent model to John Gault's sewing machine; Kermit Pike, director Western Reserve Historical Society Library; Frances Forman, reference librarian Cincinnati Historical Society; Gordon Harris, who provided the Sands' scrip; Wendell Wolka, who provided the Cook scrip; Russell Kaye, who provided the Claflin scrip; Robert H. Lloyd; David L. Ganz; J. Arthur Wenzel; Ellen Murphy, assistant to the Commissioner of Internal Revenue for Public Affairs, who provided the photograph of George Boutwell; Constance H. Andrews, Providence Public Library; Betsy Hine, archivist, University of Evansville Library; Nancy Machura, Jane Stevens, Larry Viskochil and Clarence Clark, Chicago Historical Society; Gary Pipher; Danny Stephens who shared his enthusiasm and collection of pre-1900 bottles; Charles W. Cooney Jr., Milwaukee County Historical Society; Dr. Herbert W. Rice, Milwaukee Public Library; Robert N. Andersen, Rensselaer County Historical Society; and Jennifer Bright, photo librarian, Museum of the City of New York.

Others who assisted were Jean Springer, executive director Cincinnati Mercantile Library; Helena Zinkham, New-York Historical Society; J. Graham Esler, Bank of Canada and curator of the Canadian National Currency Collection, who supplied the Weir bank notes; Lloyd Bockstruck, Genealogy Collection, Dallas Public Library, who proved to be exceptionally resourceful and helpful in a variety of ways; Charles Durden and Harriet Mador, Dallas Public Library (Casa View branch); Martina Luebbers, Independent Township Library, Claflin, Kansas; Jeanette M. Ellsworth, director Hopkinton, Massachusetts, Public Library; Mary Crowther, Salina, Kansas, Public Library; Joan M. Elliott, Willard Library, Evansville, Indiana; Alice C. Dalligan, Burton Historical Collection, Detroit Public Library; Patience A. Nauta, registrar Detroit Historical Museum;

Mark E. Neely, Jr., director, Louis A. Warren Lincoln Library and Museum; Mrs. W. A. Caddick; Michael Lewis Cook; Jean R. Acker, Troy Public Library; Robert N. Andersen, Rensselaer County Historical Society, Troy, N.Y.; Diane L. Nicholson, St. Mary's Medical Center, Evansville, Indiana; Joyce Johnson, Peoria Public Library; Sheila Schmick, Cemetery Service Corporation, Peoria; Miss G. Van Spall, secretary to William H. McDonald; Louise McNamara, Ethnography Museum, Le Chateau Ramezay; Cynthia England, Boston Athenaeum Library; and Bill Welch, editor of *American Philatelist*. Also, Margaret Cushing, West Orange Free Public Library; Larry Adams, formerly president Society of Paper Money Collectors; G. Frederick Kolbe, who contributed to my understanding of Evans' U.S. Mint guide; Dick Sine, former editor of *American Philatelist*, editor of *Scott's Monthly Journal*; Mary K. Rider, Frances Forman, Steven W. Plattner, and Dorothy Babbs, Cincinnati Historical Society; James F. Krejci, who provided his extensive collection for study, added to the auction census data, as well as photographing varieties, notably the die states of the ASMD pieces; Marcia Hill; Frank J. Katen; Susan Embree, The National Portrait Gallery; Francis D. Campbell Jr. and Margaret D'Ambrosio, American Numismatic Society; John W. Adams; Charles R. Hoskins and Francis "Skip" Fazzari, International Numismatic Society Authentication Bureau; Constance H. Andrews, Providence Public Library; Frank D. Chandler, Willard Library, Evansville; Mark Neely, director of the Louis A. Warren Lincoln Library; Martha Mayo, University of Lowell Library Special Collections; Linda Sturdevant, who supplied the unpublished diary of her Civil War ancestor; and Walter Hickey, Donna Mailloux, David Gomes, Samuel S. Pollard Memorial Library, Lowell, Massachusetts. Special thanks to Dr. Larry D. Sall, Ralph Smith, Leona Caudle and Mary Caspari, Wineburgh Philatelic Research Library, University of Texas at Dallas, for their unfailing courtesy, helpful suggestions and interest in my work; Judith N. Williams, Southborough Library; Elaine Killam, library assistant Newport News Mariners Museum; Bill J. Castenholz; Erna Mausolf, Barton County, Kansas, Historical Society; Jane Nokes, archivist, The Bank of Nova Scotia, Toronto; Gordon McHenry; Eric Jackson; Michael E. Aldrich; David L. Ganz; Lloyd Ostendorf; Richard LaSusa; Eric P. Newman; C. and D. Gale; James Milgram; Jack Gilbert; Jim Johnson; H. Joseph Levine, who supplied several photographs; Mark Katz; Larry Parks; Bruce Hagen of R. M. Smythe; R. E. Wallace; Steve Shreve, then of Steve Ivy Philatelic Auctions; and John Koza, Stephen Phillips librarian, Peabody Essex Museum. And not the least of which, although they are credited appropriately elsewhere, the author is clearly indebted to the spirits of four earlier writers on encased stamps from the past whose spirit clearly inhabits the pages of this study. They are Ben Green, John Jones, Arlie Slabaugh and Arnold Perl. Collectors such as these, who clearly enjoy their investigations and go to the additional troubles to share the fruits of their knowledge, can never be thanked enough. Although this rather large cast has freely shared views and expertise with the author, I alone accept responsibility for the conclusions drawn.

Then finally, I would like to say a special thanks to former colleague Joan Dodds, whose quizzical "Who is John Gault?" kept this project going at a time when I didn't know the answer and feared I might not find out. To all of you, now we all know.

Thank you, all.

Introduction

A generation ago a novelist invented a fictional character as the protagonist in her highly acclaimed (and vilified!) book, *Atlas Shrugged*. Ayn Rand endowed her fictional character with vision, fierce independence, broad-ranging creativity and a sense of destiny. She named her creation John Galt, and opened her masterpiece with the book's first sentence: "Who is John Galt?"

In nearly 1,000 pages Ms. Rand answered her question. Readers familiar with *Atlas Shrugged* know that the book is built on the premise that rugged American individualism, self-determination and genius bring progress to society. In her highly dramatic narrative way, she demonstrates that individual self-interest is of paramount importance. The aggregate of individual betterment is a better society. This was a practical outworking of her personal philosophy of Objectivism. Gary Cooper, himself the epitome of rugged self-determination, could have played Galt in a movie version of the novel.

The central figure of the present book, John Gault, shares uncanny resemblance to that novelist's fictional creation. He is an inventor, a man who asks "Why? of the universe and lets nothing stand between the answer and his mind," to borrow a line from Rand's fictional biography. "He was green eyed, with russet hair and a crystal-clear gaze. . . ."

Facts and interpretation. Research and analysis. "Facts and interpretation," an old history professor stressed in this author's formative post-graduate years. "History is nothing but . . . facts and interpretation." There are facts aplenty in the pages that follow, and interpretation surely. It's high time for a new fable about John Gault and his New Metallic Currency. It's time for the recreation of John Gault's novel invention. . . . He *was* green-eyed, thinning russet-haired with a crystal-clear gaze. He needn't be the stranger any longer.

THE COMING MAN'S PRESIDENTIAL CAREER, *à la* BLONDIN.

Figure 16a

A traditional view of the Civil War centers on President Abraham Lincoln's delicate balancing act on the racial question. This book focuses on the resultant financial struggle of the fratricide which dissolved the union as depicted by the book's frontispiece. Above, Cartoon, Harper's Weekly, *August 25, 1860, p. 544. (Author's collection)*

Who is John Gault?
Chapter I

On Friday evening, December 8, 1848, the Boston *Evening Transcript* was aglow with reports of "The Gold Excitement" in faraway California. These accounts transcended "passages from the Arabian Nights," the newspaper informed its readers:

> What a spectacle, that the whole villages being deserted, and citizens and squatters, soldiers and sailors, black and white, men women and children, rushing pell mell, away into the interior, over mountains, through forests, across rivers, into the newly discovered mine region!

Riches were there for the taking. "No other implements are necessary than an ordinary

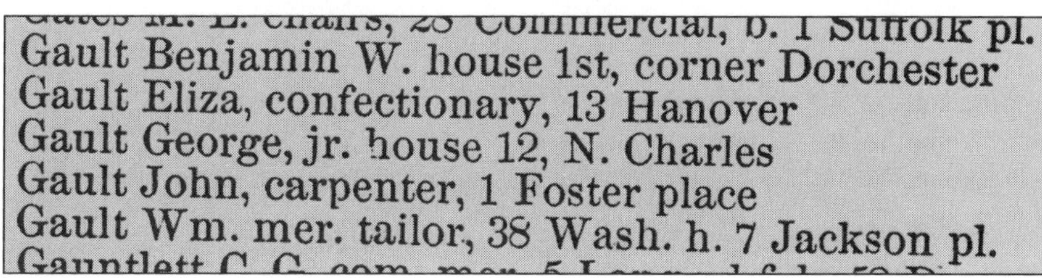
Gault Benjamin W. house 1st, corner Dorchester
Gault Eliza, confectionary, 13 Hanover
Gault George, jr. house 12, N. Charles
Gault John, carpenter, 1 Foster place
Gault Wm. mer. tailor, 38 Wash. h. 7 Jackson pl.

Figure 17a

Irish immigrant John Gault plied his carpentry trade in Baltimore and Boston prior to the Civil War. Within the month of the appearance of this listing, he died. He was the father of the encased stamp inventor. Adams's *(sic)* Boston Directory, 1847-July-1848, *p. 108. (Author's collection, ex-A. & A. S. Reed & Co., grain dealers, 6 Lincoln St., Boston)*

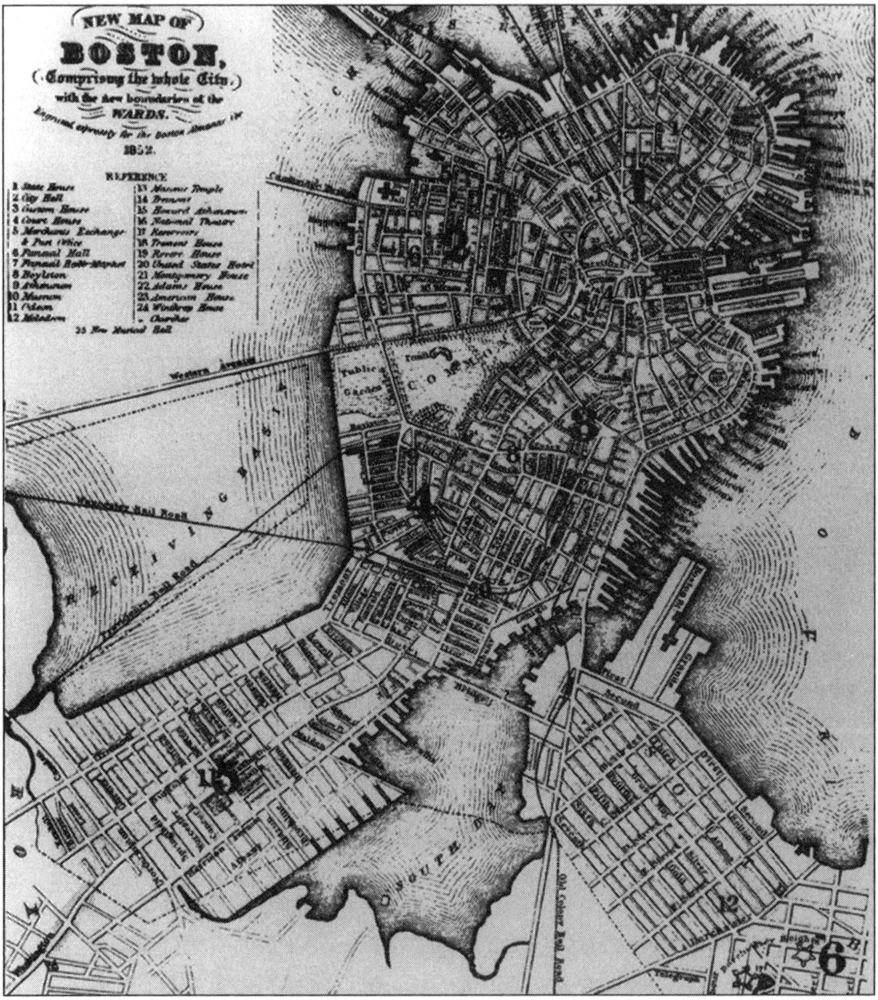

Figure 18a

The City of Boston, 1852. John Gault and his family lived in a succession of residences in Wards 1, 3 and South Boston. The Boston Almanac, *1852, tipped in. (Author's collection, Coin World photo)*

sheath knife, to pick the gold from the rocks," reliable sources reported. No other implements are necessary . . . an El Dorado after all . . . gold is picked up in pure lumps . . . the ground is represented to be one vast gold mine . . . Everybody, by the accounts, is getting money . . . $1,500 . . . $1,800 in a single day . . . already fifteen millions . . . other reports cascaded in. Gold fever was breaking on the eastern coastline.

Even President Polk was convinced. Only three days earlier had he not addressed the

Figure 19a

Visionary inventor and entrepreneur, John Gault witnessed the exciting events of 19th century America up close. Son of immigrant parents, he trekked to California's gold fields, buried a younger brother as a casualty of the Civil War, and achieved a measure of economic success plying the bar trade in New York. He also left a small testament in his New Metallic Currency – a splendidly ingenious solution to a wartime plight of both the great and the small. Previously unpublished Albumin Silver Print. Copyright © 1994 Fred Reed. All Rights Reserved. (Author's collection)

Congress of the United States on this very subject in glowing terms? "The accounts of the abundance of gold in that territory are of such an extraordinary character as would scarcely command belief were they not corroborated by the authentic reports of officers in the public service who visited the mineral district and derived the facts which they detail from personal observation," Polk told an excited Congress.

What a beacon-light these tales must have been to a fatherless, 16-year-old man-child that cold, bleak, late autumn, New England evening. Men were crowding out in the streets exchanging information, excitement, plans. To an Irish son of immigrants, we can little imagine what temptation such hysterium must have served, what rising adventurism and boyhood fancy such proceedings must have surely kindled, but for John Gault as for so many other young men of all ages that mid-century day we do know what happened soon after: he joined the mass exodus that answered the siren's call. As the newspapers continued to fan the flames of excitement by painting renewed visions of El Dorado, none other than editor Horace Greeley proclaimed the new *Age of Gold*: "the youth of the world was on the move, headed for San Francisco. The stampede was on."

Gold mania was gripping the imaginations of all alike, but it was the youthful, "bursting with unproved confidence and bravado," who were especially tempted by the "irre-

BUSINESS DIRECTORY.

Perry W. S., Lehigh, near Lincoln	Gault John, 19 Harvard
Porter & Darrow, Lewis, c. Marg'l	Globe Locomotive W'ks, First,
Pope Wm. & Sons, 280 Harr. ave.	Harwood B. R. 18 Avery
Rankin & Piper, Albany, c. Lehigh	Haskell Edward, 22 Hawley
Roberts D. B. 418 Federal	Haskell J. A. 8 Court avenue

Figure 20a

Returning from the California gold fields, John Gault established himself in his hometown as a machinist, one of 60 such firms listed in the city directory for 1857. The Boston Almanac, *1857, p. 135. (Author's collection)*

sistible opportunity for adventure, for successful action." Opportunity. Riches. Adventure. Thousands of young men like Gault answered Greeley's challenge: "Who should go to California?" Greeley asked in his *Tribune*. Single young men of moderate means and resolute energies, was the visionary editor's answer. "Give the first chance at the gold region to those who have as yet had no chance elsewhere," he said. Go West, young man. Go, West.

So, to the strains of "Oh, Susanna," "Sweet Betsy from Pike," or in Gault's case, "Coming Around the Horn," El Dorado lay only 18,000 miles and five arduous months away. Young John Gault enlisted into the exodus and shipped out from his native Boston to follow his dreams for riches and fame. It was to be the first of several such rainbows he would chase during his eventful lifetime . . . finding eventually a measure of both.

The world knows little of John Gault.

Who is, or was, he?

"One of the lost men of American History," says one. A "genius," replies another. "An almost lost American," retorts a third. "An advertising guru," "a Yankee entrepreneur," "a Boston sewing machine salesman," remark passersby in the cocktail party conversations of History. For a century now, collectors have pondered the simple metal and mineral stamp cases bearing his testament: "PAT AUG 12, 1862. // J. GAULT." and speculated in true cocktail party repartee. Clever words in place of insights. While John Gault, the man, languished as a blank page . . . an uninvited guest at a party thrown in his honor.

The pieces themselves, his encased stamps, demand that John Gault emerge from obscurity, a well-rounded figure. What needs to be done is to put a face to the character of a man capable of such notable, if minor, achievement.

What we can find emerges. Gault was a man of good character, sympathetic and family-oriented. He was intelligent. Opportunistic. He lived a life caught up in the great currents of his times, the 19th century. His father died when he was in his teens. His mother, whom he took care of, died of melancholia. His brother died the wounds of war. He married a widow woman late in life and provided for her two young sons, both of whom died. Ultimately, he too died. He provided well for his survivors. His wife passed away too, and the surviving heirs squabbled over the remains.

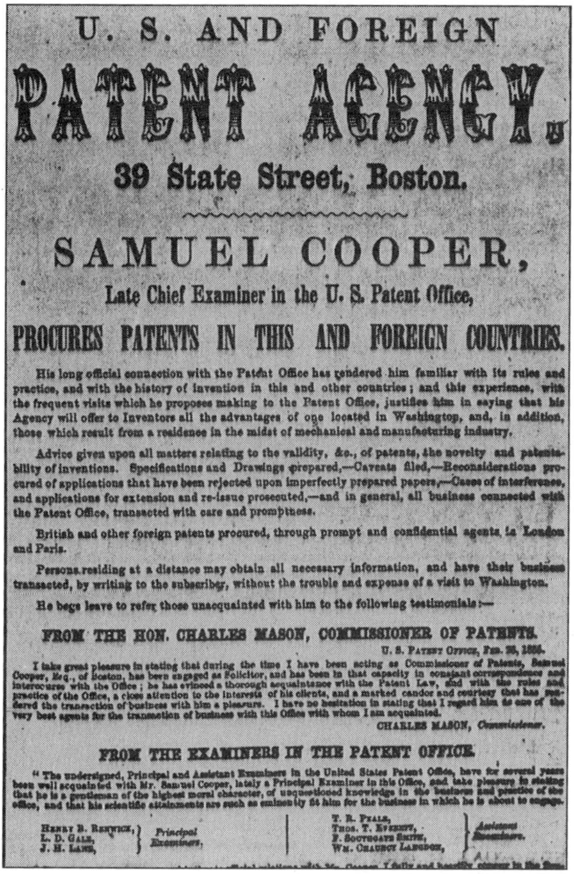

Figure 21a

The Boston patent agency of Samuel Cooper assisted Gault with his early inventions. Boston General Advertiser, *1856, p. 5. (Dallas Public Library)*

Gault was a minor swimmer in the great currents of his age. He didn't create the tides. He was forced to swim in their waves. A youthful visionary, he joined a Massachusetts mining company and set off for California. He returned a realist to face the unraveling of the Union. A tinkerer with mechanical ability, he invented a series of ingenious devices: principally a sewing machine to knit its parts together, his encased postage stamp device to remedy its financial problems, and a series of exploding artillery shells to silence its rebellion. In true objectivist fashion, however, his own station was his primary interest. And so, his interests not greatly successful, he ultimately turned to selling his generation whiskey and commiserating with others similarly passed by in the Great Stream of Life.

As much as anything it is his brass and mica case which is the key to unlocking a studied response to the question, "Who is John Gault?" It would be too much to call John Gault a figure or representative of his age. He is not that important. His accomplishments are not that significant. But what emerges from the pages of History is a portrait that definitely defines a man of his age.

Gault attached himself to men of true genius. Gault associated with men of driving

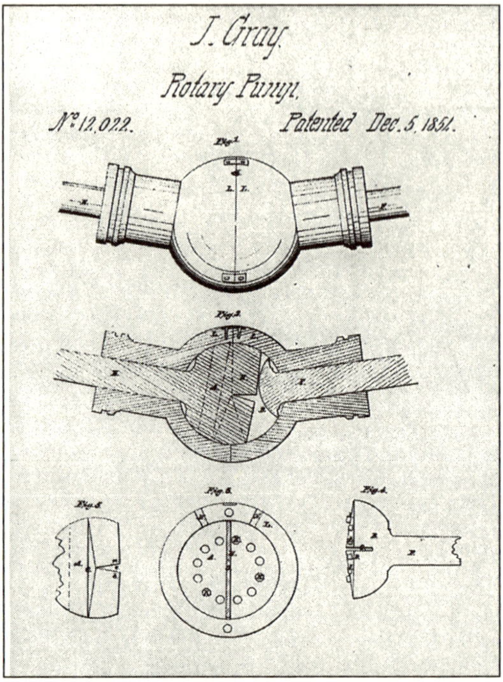

Figure 22a

Swan Court machinist Joshua Gray developed numerous lines of advancing technology in Boston during the 1850s before the younger inventor, John Gault, approached him for assistance with his sewing patent. Patent No. 12,022, December 5, 1854. (U.S. Patent Office)

entrepreneurship. It was men such as purchased stamp cases from Gault who are perhaps the best witnesses from whom to summon an answer to the defining question of this chapter. Their own lives are testimonies in this courtroom of history, more so surely than cocktail punditry which masquerades as knowledge or insight. Gault knew men of true vision. Men who were rich already, and getting richer saw in Gault's creative and fertile inventiveness the flickering glow of attraction. And so their own stories become as much a part of the answer as the biographical narrative attached to Gault, himself. Men of achievement, powerful men who really did help forge the last three-quarters of the 19th century gave Gault a sterling endorsement by buying space on the simple backs of his stamp money.

As the threads of their lives weave together, a picture of John Gault emerges. His customers were competitive businessmen, among the most astute of eager men out to make their marks, their own reputations, and secure their own fortunes. They were looking for every competitive edge. Gault's success lies not in his ability to quickly sign up several dozen businesses to his change-making scheme. He could have thrown a stone into the street and hit many more prospective customers than that. Besides, his success was not so quick, nor so great (as we shall see). His success was that successful men of his own age recognized this genius in this emergency money and originally purchased those small change substitutes which collectors have inherited. *Parva ne pereant.*

Irish men, and Irish women too, had a rough time of it. As the 18th century became the 19th lives languished under overcast skies and shortened horizons. Three thousand, six

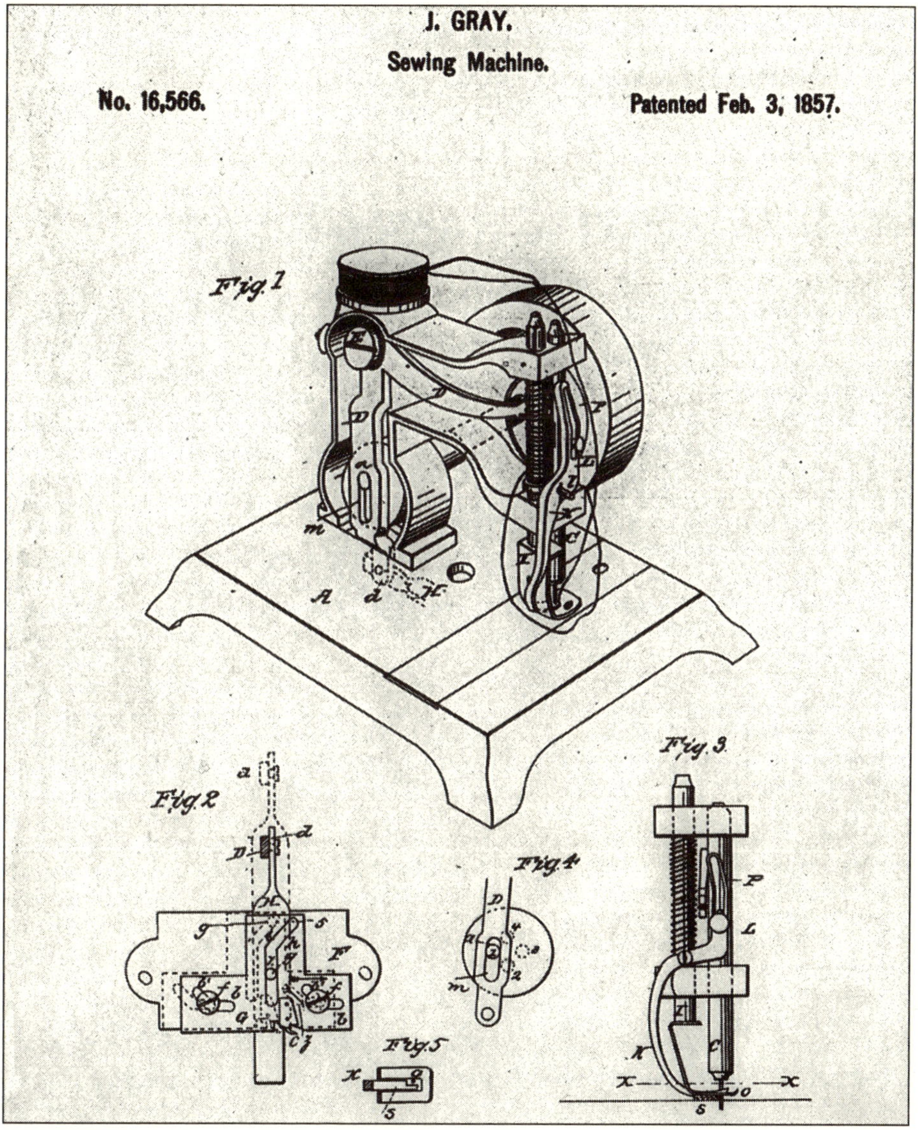

Figure 23a

Joshua Gray was a machinist and inventor of considerable renown. He patented several improvements to the sewing machine, which was revolutionizing the domestic textile manufacturing industry of New England at the time. For example, a gentlemen's shirt sewn by hand took a skilled seamstress 14 hours and 26 minutes to produce. Conversely a machine-stitched garment could be completed in one hour and 16 minutes. Patent No. 16,566, February 3, 1857, by John Gault, assigned to Joshua Gray and himself. (U.S. Patent Office)

Figure 24a

Patent Model of John Gault's lock-stitch sewing machine. Fewer than 300 production models were built, and the company ceased when sued by the Sewing Machine "Combination." (Smithsonian Institution photo, neg. 36102-C)

hundred and fourteen of them immigrated to the United States seeking better lives in 1820. Fifteen hundred-eighteen, the following year. Two thousand, two hundred and sixty-seven came in 1822. Nineteen hundred-eight in 1823. Two thousand, three hundred and forty-five came in 1824. Wave upon Wave. And then, these seekers of renewed expectations really began to pour in: Forty-eight, eighty-eight; Fifty-four, oh-eight, annually. These "old immigrants" were among the first to feel the lure of the New World. For the large bounty of 10-12 Pounds Sterling, steerage class from British ports to these United States meant the opportunity of the Promised Land. The Irish were not alone, of course; they were merely the most numerous of that day.

We know about some among those faceless numbers. It was March 31, 1823, when the elder John Gault, a 24-year-old carpenter, disembarked the schooner *Maria* at Newburyport, Massachusetts, "to become [an] inhabitant" of this brave, new world. Armed with that resolute intention and not much else, Gault came well equipped for opportunity in this continent's coming of age. Born late the prior century, this John Gault was a risker and a skilled tradesman, eager to wade into the hurly-burly swirl of New England's maelstrom. America welcomed such strong swimmers in time. In fact, 30 months later, it similarly embraced a 24-year-old orphan girl, who clambered over the side of an anonymous vessel at the port of

Figure 25a

Joshua Gray and partner, Thomas Grace, produced a small number of medium-priced sewing machines prior to the Civil War at their shop in Boston's Eighth Ward. The Boston Almanac and Directory, *1860, p. 74. (Dallas Public Library)*

Baltimore, Maryland. She possessed a similar eager desire to become "inhabitant thereof." She was Mary Ann McGee.

Mary McGee was a domestic, a common and decent enough task for young women in a new land. The young carpenter had been a brewer in his native Dublin. Of independent Scots-Irish heritage, he had perfected his carpentry skills building casks for his family's brewing and malting business. It is not known when or how they met, or if indeed they had known each other in the Old Country, because as will happen in the rushing streams of history, this pair was quickly swallowed up by their new surroundings. She made her way to Boston, where John was plying his trade as a housewright in Boston's Ward 1 near the Charles River Bridge. They wed there May 4, 1826, in Christ Church, Reverend Asa Eaton officiating. A son, Henry, was born the following year. A daughter, Ann Jane, the next. Both were duly baptized, according to the rites of the Episcopal church. They changed residences annually.

Opportunity beckoned the carpenter, but seizing opportunity involves risk. He removed to Baltimore in spring 1830 leaving his wife and young children behind. It took a while to reestablish himself. Finally he sent for them and the family was reunited. It was only fitting. She had conceived and soon bore him another son. Six days prior to Christmas, 1831, in Baltimore the John Gault of this history was born. But steady work proved difficult to maintain. The elder John Gault returned to Boston with his family the following year, only to see his wife and kids return to Baltimore once again. Mary Ann took up the trade of tailoress. As her children grew during the remainder of the decade, Mary Ann Gault supplemented her husband's wages with her seamstress trade. At length, by their hard work and perseverance, conditions bettered for the Gault family. A fourth child was born two years later. Their family was complete, they named the offspring after her father, Samuel, biblical meaning "gift from God." The Gaults were still in Baltimore when the census taker arrived.

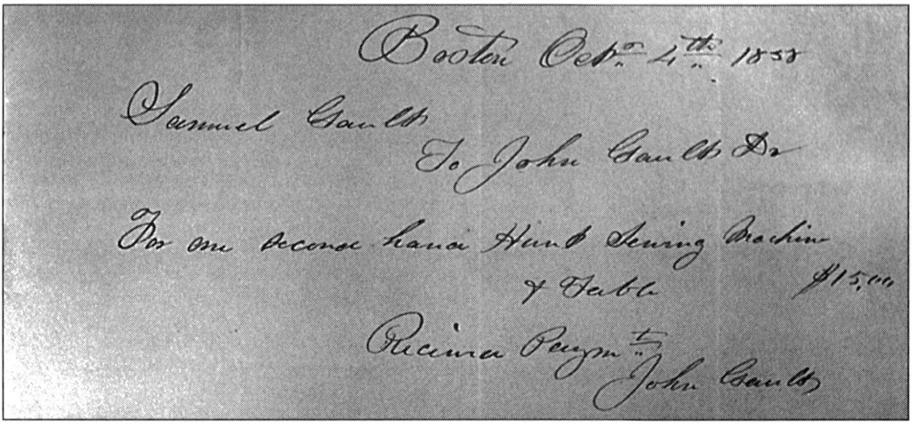

Boston Octr. 4th. 1858
Samuel Gault
To John Gault Dr
For one second hand Hunt Sewing Machine
& Table $15.00
Received Paymt.
John Gault

Figure 26a

Several selections of Gault family correspondence have been discovered in the past three decades. This hand receipt records John Gault's sale of a used sewing machine to his younger brother Samuel in 1858 for their mother's use. Autograph Receipt Signed, October 4, 1858. (Dr. Robert D. Gardner collection, Dabney C. Jackson photo)

They had taken in a female boarder and the elder Gault was supplementing his income in some form of agriculture.

The Gaults returned to Boston in 1841. The decade of the Fourties proved good to the Gault family of Boston. As the directories evidence, there were a great many newcomers making good their opportunities in this new land. Carpentry was a necessary trade. Hundreds of framing carpenters were so employed. New residences were being thrown up at a rapid rate. John Gault, housewright, had steady employment. His young boys became gifted with their hands. Ann Jane learned her mother's skills as seamstress. Henry, John and Samuel were introduced to mechanics and invention. Yankee ingenuity was the very real stuff of everyday life. Newer, better, faster were not goals, but means to improving one's lot and achieving those goals. The middle boy especially shared more than his father's name. Although we have no evidence of any great formal education, the younger John Gault understood intuitively his parents' skill of bringing into being that which existed not yet. Their tools differed greatly. Hammers and saws. Needles and threads. Drills and awls. All stitched together a home, a future, and a hope through two decades of struggling Irish immigrants seeking to make their personal way in good health and good fortune. The family changed residences constantly, moving deeper and deeper into the bustling region of South Boston. They arrived at 1 Foster place in late 1846.

Their world turned on end July 25, 1847. John Gault, Carpenter, 1 Foster place, died. His namesake was 15 years old. Evidence shows that Mary Ann McGee Gault was stricken. The family moved once again, this time to 1 Harrison avenue, corner of Essex Street. The eldest son, Henry, found employment as a machinist. Within six months gold was discov-

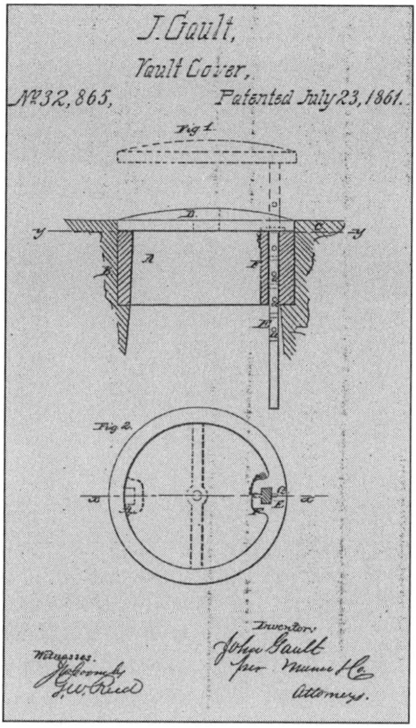

Figures 27a, b

Coal was a principal fuel in mid-19th century America. Gault's swivelling vault cover permitted ease of unloading by horse drawn delivery wagons. It also prevented theft of the covers or a person accidentally falling into the hole. This was one of several patents the prominent New York firm of Munn & Co. handled for the Boston inventor. He paid the firm a $5 fee and the $15 patent application fee during mid-June, 1861. Gault then assigned the patent to William A. Moore of Lowell, Massachusetts, to develop. Patent No. 32,865, July 23, 1861. (U.S. Patent Office)

ered near Sacramento in far off California. By year's end all the world knew the exciting news, including young John Gault. He boarded the bark *Edward Fletcher* on March 5, 1849, all of seventeen years old. The three-masted *Edward Fletcher* was a single deck, 111 feet in length and weighed 265 tons. Only six months old, it had recently returned from its maiden voyage to the Italian States of Genoa and Palermo under its Master, Aaron Holbrook. The following morning the ship sailed from Boston Harbor. One of the "Argonauts of '49," Gault was a member of the *Edward Fletcher* Company, 30-strong, mostly Boston men. These New England companies favored the long sea route around the tip of South America. They were familiar with the sea and it was cheaper. Even then, how this young man raised the $150 passage paid to ship's owner Henry W. Fletcher is something of a mystery. Perhaps his older brother staked him. The bylaws of Gault's company forbade strong liquor, and prescribed fines for such offenses as swearing or gambling. Care was exercised in the selection of company members to assure men of good character, who could be an asset to the enterprise. Gault had what the mining companies were looking for. He was young, resolute, and single. Also, Gault's mechanical ability was much prized.

The youth of the world was on the move, headed for San Francisco. The stampede was on. Gault's passage took longer than normal. "The trip usually began as an adventure, settled quickly into tedium broken by spurts of conflict, and deteriorated into dreary ordeal," according to a gold rush historian. Quarters were cramped beneath deck. Days were long topside. In Gault's case, the tedium lasted half a year, following stops at places like Rio de

Figure 28a

Munn & Co. virtually monopolized patent office filings in the antebellum period. As publisher of Scientific American *it was in the business of promoting client's inventions to the trade, the public, and to potential capital investors. They also were successful in securing foreign rights for American inventors. Their preeminence continued after the Civil War.* Harper's Weekly, *May 1, 1869, p. 288. (Author's collection)*

Janeiro and the Falkland Islands. In Brazil, he experienced the shock of a Portuguese culture after six or seven weeks shipboard. "Lively Rio assaulted their senses. The long silence of the sea gave way to a babel of sound," according to one account. But the city beneath Sugar Loaf Mountain was also beautiful and exotic. When Gault arrived, it was also a city full of Americans like he was headed for California, and enchanted by a culture ruled by an emperor only slightly older than he was himself. Rounding the feared Cape Horn, Gault's company stopped additionally on the west coast of South America midway along the Chilean coast for water on their northward swing. Most ships also stopped at San Juan del Sur, Nicaragua. Whether Gault's did or not, that last 40 days of the voyage was enlivened a bit by a challenge race with the Old Harvard Company, aboard the *Duxbury*. The *Duxbury* had left Boston shortly before Gault's group. The two companies had recently been in Rio at the same time. Alas, the Harvard boys outran the *Edward Fletcher*, "passing her to the tune of 'Yankee Doodle.'" Gault and the rest of the *Edward Fletcher* Company finally made San Francisco in late September after a passage of 189 days.

Passing through San Francisco's Golden Gate on the *Edward Fletcher* was only part of the way to El Dorado, though. The gold fields lie inland and upland, in the gilded valleys of the Sierra Nevada range. After outfitting himself, Gault traveled up the Sacramento River most likely on a barge through its break in the Coastal Ranges and on to Sacramento. There he would have shifted his gear to wagon for his nearly 60 mile trek up the American River to where the action was. Passing by such picturesque locales as Negro Bar, Texas Hill, and Salmon Falls, Gault climbed the golden sluice toward James Marshall's discovery zone. Just past Michigan Bar and the big bend where the South Fork of the American River angles southwest toward the falls, he put up stakes. The routine was backbreaking and slow. Pay dirt was hauled by hand to the river, where it was washed in cradles or rockers. Many miners eventually equipped themselves with the so-called Holland Yoke, a ten-gallon cask sawed in two mounted at the ends of a pole. "The process was slow and laborious, and became more and more so as the claims were worked back from the water," a contemporary observed.

About the same time John arrived in California, his sister, Ann, married a Boston cabinet maker, George Rutledge. Within six months in the field, John Gault had made something of a strike himself. He purchased a family cemetery plot June 24, 1850, in Cambridge,

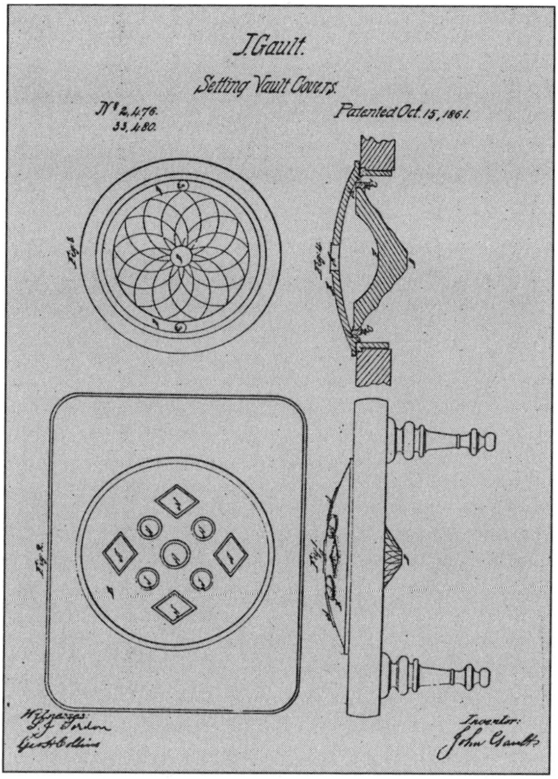

Figure 29a

Gault's fruitful imagination allowed him to progressively tinker with his ideas. This improvement to his coal hole cover permitted sunlight to penetrate the dark subterranean cavities. Patent Nos. 2476 and 33,480, October 15, 1861. (U.S. Patent Office)

Massachusetts, with the proceeds he sent home from his gold digging. The federal census taker caught up with Gault in Union Town, El Dorado County, California on October 25, 1850. Union Town was on the South Fork of the American River, a mile-and-a-half below Gold Hill and Coloma, site of Sutter's Mill and the original gold strike. Union Town was a rude shack town with ten or twelve boarding houses and several stores. A thousand miners like Gault were working the digs there. Gault was one of 13 residents in one of the hotels. Besides the three Rhode Islanders who kept the boarding house, there were six miners, two butchers and two laborers. All were males. Most were in their 20s and 30s. They came from New York, Ohio, New Hampshire, in addition to Massachusetts. Gault was one of those miners, and a successful one at that. According to the government's record keeper, he was averaging $8 in gold per day, about double the average take per man daily in that district. Although not quite 19 years old, he is recorded as 22.

That's probably because the census taker didn't get his information directly from Gault, himself. Doubtless Gault was off at the digs, and the informant was the hotelkeeper. Gault looked and acted the part, so 22 he was. Gault's gold take represented half an ounce of precious metal per day. That sum was generally recognized as the minimum amount necessary to keep a miner going, after paying exorbitant prices for food and supplies, lodging, and setting aside a little nest egg. Many miners fell far short of that amount and left the fields for

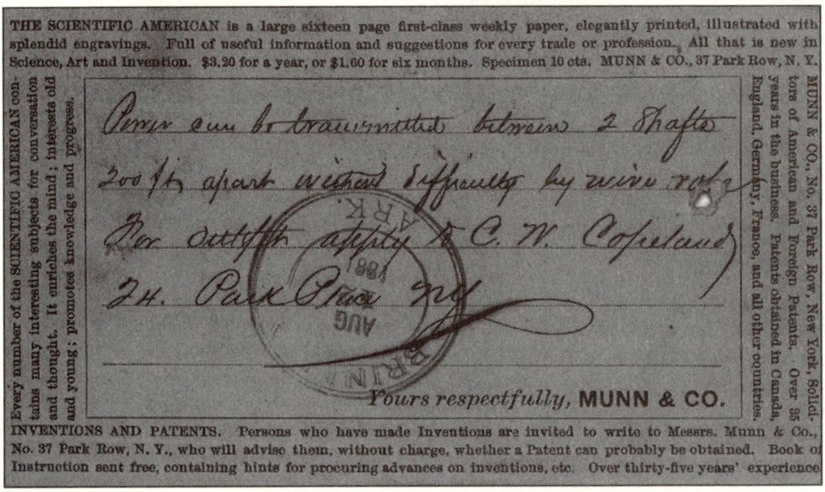

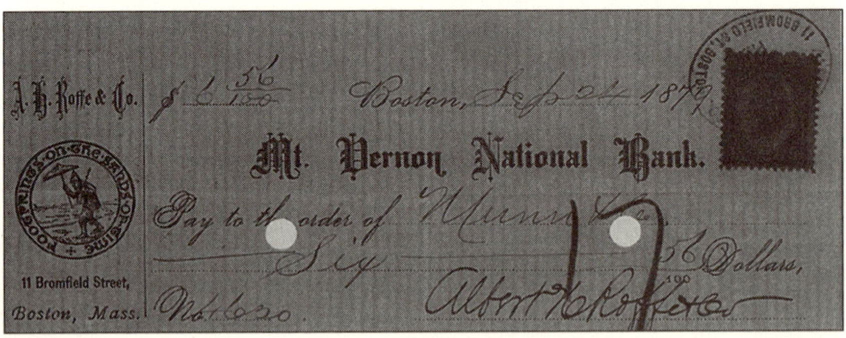

Figures 30a, b, c, d

Top, in the post-Civil War period, Munn & Co. continued to dominate its field. In addition to publishing the most influential technology journal of its day, Scientific American, *and extensive advertising in the popular press, in 1868 it issued a brass embossed store card. (Bowers and Merena photo); and in 1881 it corresponded with a Brinkley, Ark., firm on the back of a U.S. postal card turned into an advertising trade card. (Author's collection) At bottom, in 1879 Albert H. Roffe & Co. paid fees to the company through its Nassau Bank account. (Author's collection)*

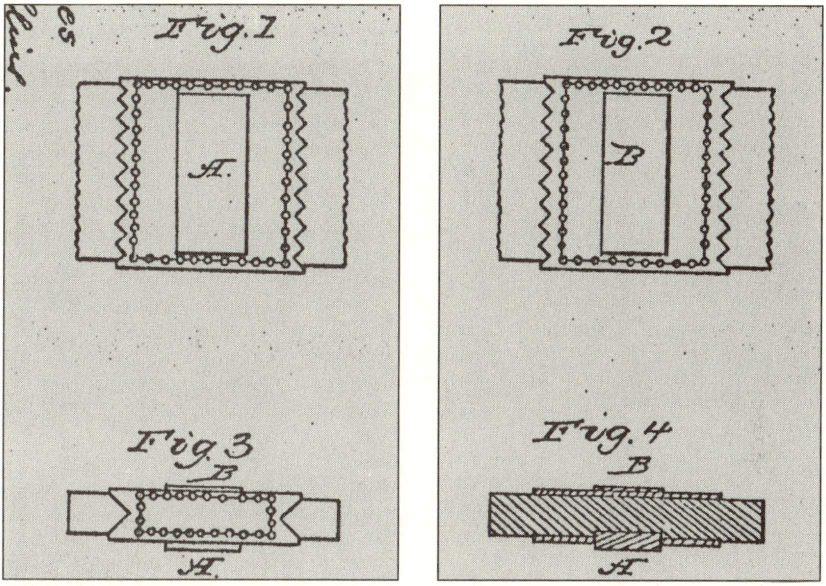

Figure 31a

Gault's eraser sharpener was a minor fruit of his fertile imagination. Patent No. 33,304, September 16, 1861. (U.S. Patent Office)

other lines of work, or left the gold fields for good. Gault stayed around. Although the state census taker missed him in 1852, we know he was still there in June. He may not have been still engaged in mining though. Among family papers which were discovered in the 1960s was an invoice indicating that Gault ordered 105 quarts of milk that summer. He paid five cents a quart for a total of $5.25. Since dairying was a necessary and profitable venture in California in those days, it seems he was engaged in some kind of commercial pursuit.

John Gault returned to Boston after five years out west. A youth no more he moved into his mother's Harrison avenue home which she shared with his younger brother, Sam. He took up his older brother Henry's profession of machinist. There are 60 machine shops listed in the city directory for 1855. Boston machine shops were no mean propositions. It was from them and the fertile mechanical genius of young Yankee tinkerers that the Industrial Revolution was springing forth in this country. A principal beneficiary of this mechanical enterprise was the New England textile industry. Sewing machine manufacturers were revolutionizing this trade and becoming rich in the process.

Gault soon threw in with Nesbitt D. Stoops, a machinist at 19 Harvard place. After a little over a year, Stoops sold his interest to Gault, who took up with Joshua Gray at the same location. Wages of a typical machinist were about $2 a day, not exactly a princely sum compared with the $8 a day Gault had earned in California. But Gault was not content to merely while away his time on other people's projects. His mother and sister had been seam-

Figure 32a

New York steel plate engraver George E. Perine's vibrant depiction of the opening of Civil War hostilities captured the horror of wartime artillery bombardment for readers of Abbott's Civil War, *Vol. I, 1863, facing p. 88. (Author's collection)*

stresses. New and improved sewing machines were being produced in his own neighborhood. He understood their challenges. Despite the progresses of the name sewing machine makers, Howe and Singer, no one as yet had really solved the problems of unraveling caused by inexpensive chain-stitching machines. If one stitch tore, the seam was soon gone, too. Gault was one of those who turned his attention to perfecting a lock-stitch mechanism. The prize to the winner would be riches surely, and possibly fame, too.

Gault's solution was patented February 3, 1857. He assigned the patent to his partner, Gray, and himself. The original patent model survives to this day. It was a somewhat inelegant solution, but it worked. Several movable plates and a vibrating bar attached to the

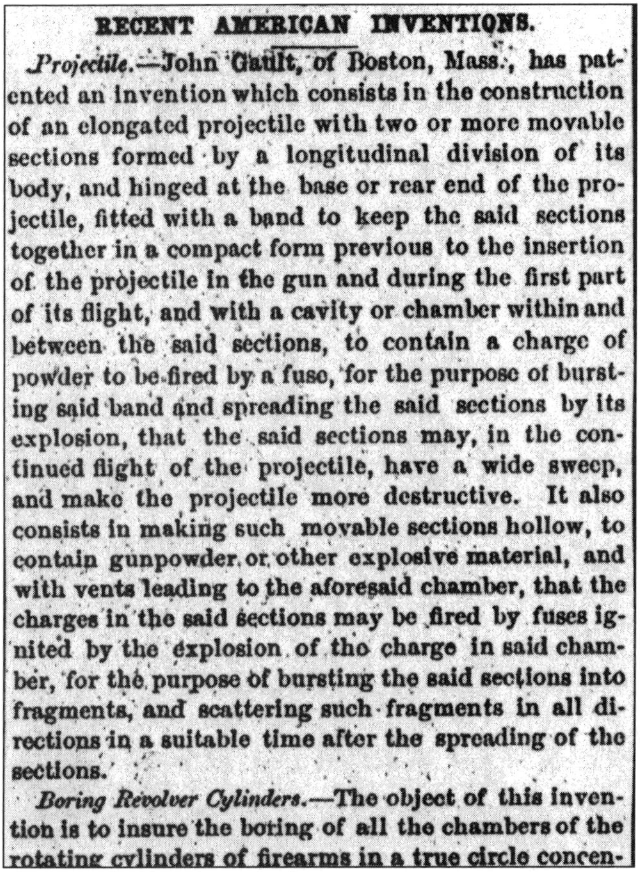

RECENT AMERICAN INVENTIONS.

Projectile.—John Gault, of Boston, Mass., has patented an invention which consists in the construction of an elongated projectile with two or more movable sections formed by a longitudinal division of its body, and hinged at the base or rear end of the projectile, fitted with a band to keep the said sections together in a compact form previous to the insertion of the projectile in the gun and during the first part of its flight, and with a cavity or chamber within and between the said sections, to contain a charge of powder to be fired by a fuse, for the purpose of bursting said band and spreading the said sections by its explosion, that the said sections may, in the continued flight of the projectile, have a wide sweep, and make the projectile more destructive. It also consists in making such movable sections hollow, to contain gunpowder or other explosive material, and with vents leading to the aforesaid chamber, that the charges in the said sections may be fired by fuses ignited by the explosion of the charge in said chamber, for the purpose of bursting the said sections into fragments, and scattering such fragments in all directions in a suitable time after the spreading of the sections.

Boring Revolver Cylinders.—The object of this invention is to insure the boring of all the chambers of the rotating cylinders of firearms in a true circle concen-

Figure 33a

The editors of Scientific American *at Munn & Co. noted John Gault's exploding artillery shell in the publication's "Recent American Inventions" columns. Such a plug was guaranteed to bring the projectile to the notice of both capitalists and military procurement officers seeking new fodder for the machineries of war.* Scientific American, *July 27, 1861, p. 55. (Dallas Public Library)*

under surface of the machine operated in concert with the vibrating needle to lock the stitch. A further refinement was made later that year. Gray put the moderately-priced machine into production. With his share of the proceeds, John Gault moved out of his mother's house and into a home of his own at 3 Fuller street. He took in his widowed mother and his younger brother as boarders. Gault's business was located near Old South Church. Next door, Charles and Andrew Spring manufactured sewing machine needles. On the opposite side Thomas A. Branigan and John Cuddy had their glassworks. It was a neighborhood of small merchants. As Gault's business prospered, he moved to a better location on Water street selling sewing machines in addition to his tinker's trade. Eventually he moved to a better house, too. In 1860 he removed to 3 Grenville place, and still a bachelor, he again took his mother and brother with him.

The *Scientific American* classed the sewing machine as "the most useful article in the house, next to the cradle, and no less indispensable than that." A religious publication of the day recommended that one set up one's household around the family Bible and the sewing machine. None other than Henry Ward Beecher was widely quoted as offering the

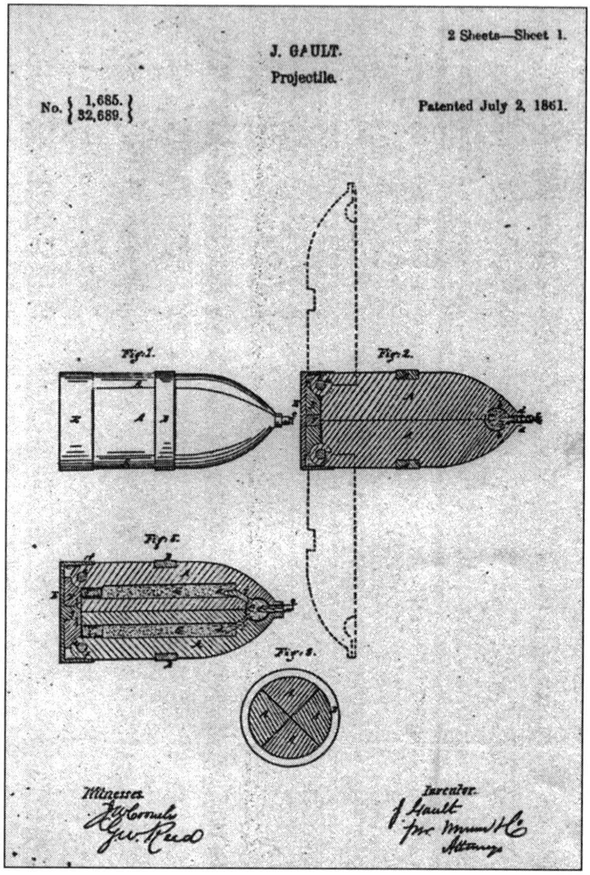

Figure 34a

Gathering war clouds attracted the interest of New England inventors rushing to supply the burgeoning appetites of both militarists and industrialists. To promote his initial foray into artillery shell design, John Gault turned to his patent attorney George Reed at Munn and Co., which maintained large offices in both New York and Washington, D.C., for just those purposes. Note, Gault acquired both design and manufacturing patents. Patent Nos. 1685 and 32,689, July 2, 1861, sheet 1. (U.S. Patent Office)

opinion that "the needle has slain more than the sword of war." In explaining his hyperbole, the good reverend surmised, "I pity those women whose staff is their needle, for when they lean on it, it pierces not their side, but their heart." New and improved machines streamed from the factories of Wheeler and Wilson, Grover and Baker, Singer, Howe, Wilcox and Gibbs. Their names were becoming well known in homes throughout the land. Thousands of machines were pouring out, and at $30 and $40 a clip, the money was pouring back in. Hundreds of small, independent companies, like Gault's were attempting to compete with the Sewing Machine "Combination" that had a virtual stranglehold on production. John Gault was not so fortunate with his device. The firm of Gray and Grace, that he licensed his improvement to produced only about 300 machines before it too was put out of business by the "Combination." According to a leading authority, the firm would not have lasted long anyway. The machine was poorly made. Yet today, it carries a collector value of $1,500 to $2,000.

Eighteen-sixty was a watershed year in the history of this country. It had been only

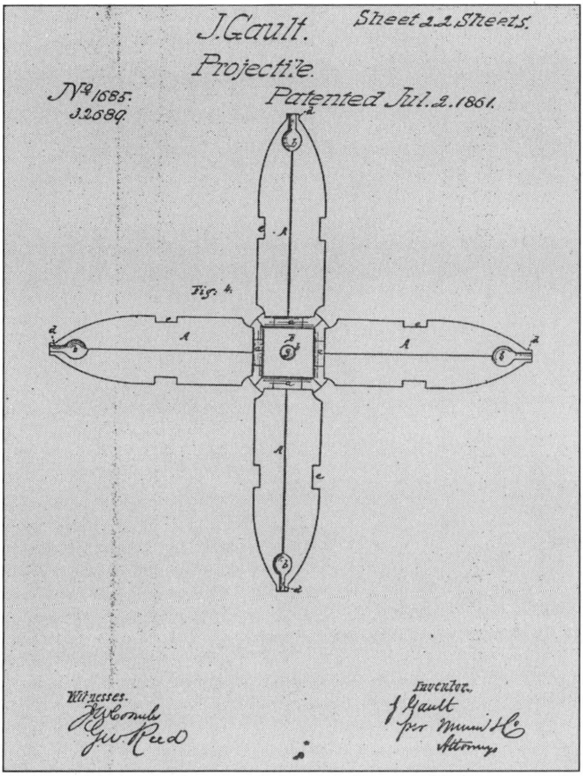

Figure 35a

The destruction radius of Gault's spinning, exploding projectile may be seen in this heads-on view, the idea of which – of course – was to inflict maximum damage on an adversary. Patent Nos. 1685 and 32,689, July 2, 1861, sheet 2. (U.S. Patent Office)

four-score and four years since representatives North and South had pledged their lives, fortunes, and sacred honors to one another and their posterities. Yet those descendants were having difficulty maintaining those covenants. With the nation coming apart at the seams, not even an improved lock-stitch device could rejoin the dividing remnant of the parting fabric of American society. With the calls to secession echoing through the state houses of the South, it would take more than needle and thread to implement the federal administration's determination to bind up the Union. It would take the sinews of war – money and arms – to resolve this forbidding crisis. Before the conflict would be resolved, John Gault would turn his inventive eye to perfecting both: money and armaments.

Reverend Beecher's flowery phrases notwithstanding, the relative merits of the needle and the sword, the nation's attention was quickly riveted on the battlefields by the strange events in obscure places like Fortress Monroe and Bull Run. Thousands of young men massed under arms to perform the duty of the day. When the sectional divisions broke out into armed conflict, John Gault answered the siren's call to national service, but he did not enlist in one of the volunteer companies being raised around Boston. The War of the Rebellion was unprecedented in many respects, not the least of which was the increasing effectiveness of its machineries of war. Military inventiveness was not only confined to the battlefield. The country experienced a proliferation of military-related inventions. Patents

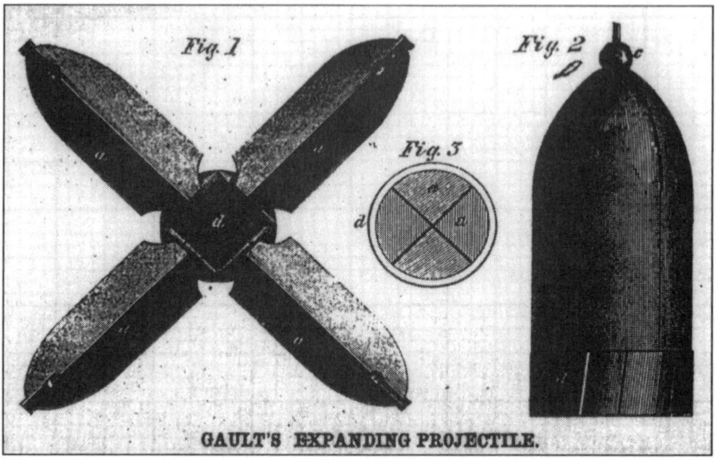

GAULT'S EXPANDING PROJECTILE.

Improved Expanding Projectile.

New ideas in regard to weapons of war continue to come forth from the fertile brains of our thinking people in vast numbers. The novel invention here illustrated is but one of the many which have been developed by the war. A shot is made in four sections, hinged at the breech, and carrying a fuse with a charge of powder so arranged that at the proper time in the flight they will be thrown apart in the form represented in Fig. 1; thus increasing the breadth of their destructive track.

The four sections, *a a a a*, Fig. 1, are made of cast iron, and are connected by simple hinges to the breech-piece; *b*, also of cast iron. When brought together they form the acorn-shaped shot represented in Fig. 2; the button, *c*, being screwed around the projections on their ends to hold them together. They are also further confined by the soft metal cup, *d*, around the base, this cup serving to fill the rifling, thus closing the windage and giving the spiral motion to the shot. A cavity, *e e e e*, is formed in the shot near its apex to receive a charge of powder, which is connected with a fuse leading outward to be fired at the discharge; kindles the fuse and this conveys the fire to the central charge, exploding the shell. Fig. 3 is a cross-section of the projectile, showing the shape of the sections. The shell may be made in 2, 3, 4, or more sections; and the lengths of the fuses must be adjusted to the times of flight.

It will be seen that this shot cleaves the air with the ease of the ordinary elongated projectile; at the desired point in its flight throws out its wings, cutting a wide path of destruction; and finally explodes into a multitude of fragments, scattering death in every direction. A shot 4 inches in diameter measures 20 inches when expanded.

The patent for this invention was granted to the inventor, John Gault, of Boston, Mass., through the Scientific American Patent Agency, July 2, 1861; and further information in relation to it may be obtained by addressing George R. Jackson & Co. (to whom an interest in the invention has been assigned) at their iron works, 201 Center street, New York. This firm is prepared to manufacture the projectiles in any quantity.

Figures 36a, b

Scientific American *reported extensively on advances in technology and mechanics, which blossomed during the dark days of the Civil War. In addition to short notices, its editors frequently published roundup articles addressing the principal advances in the various areas of invention. One such article appearing early in the war took particular note of Gault's expanding projectile and its manufacture at the New York iron works of George R. Jackson & Co. Gault engaged Munn & Co. to market the invention.* Scientific American, *September 14, 1861. p. 168. (Dallas Public Library)*

granted for canon, projectiles, small arms, cartridges and related items totalled into the thousands. Before the smoke cleared from the nations battlegrounds in 1865, both Gray and

Patents for New Inventions.

Messrs. MUNN & CO., Proprietors of The Scientific American, No. 37 Park Row, New York, continue to solicit Patents in the United States, and in all foreign countries, on the most reasonable terms. Consultations and pamphlets of advice in English and German free on application to the office.

Read what the

Hon. Joseph Holt,

the great patriot, says:

Messrs. MUNN & Co.: It affords me much pleasure to bear testimony to the able and efficient manner in which you have discharged your duties of Solicitors of Patents while I had the honor of holding the office of Commissioner. Your business was very large, and you sustained (and, I doubt not, justly deserved) the reputation of energy, marked ability, and uncompromising fidelity in performing your professional engagements.

Very respectfully,
Your obed't serv't, J. HOLT.

Messrs. MUNN & CO. have been engaged in soliciting Patents for over sixteen years, and more than Fifteen

NEW INVENTIONS.

MUNN & COMPANY,

Proprietors of the SCIENTIFIC AMERICAN, and Agents for procuring American and Foreign

PATENTS,

WITH SIXTEEN YEARS' EXPERIENCE IN THE BUSINESS,

Refer to Hon. Judge MASON, Hon. JOSEPH HOLT, Hon. W. D. BISHOP, Ex-Commissioners of Patents, and to more than FIFTEEN THOUSAND INVENTORS who have had business done through Munn & Co.'s Patent Agency.

PAMPHLET OF ADVICE sent free by mail.

Offices, No. 37 Park Row, New York, and Washington.

Figures 37a, b, c, d

Scientific American *is still published today. Its masthead, top, in 1862 depicted the U.S. Patent Office building, opposite which its Washington, D.C., branch office was located.* Scientific American, *June 21, 1862, p. 385. (Author's collection) Typical solicitations in the leading periodicals of the day, at center, relied heavily on endorsements of past Patent Commissioners.* Harper's Weekly *issues September 28, 1861, p. 624, and June 21, 1862, p. 400. (Oklahoma State University Library) At bottom, half a century later, the company was still meeting needs of American inventors. Cover, September 21, 1915. (Author's collection)*

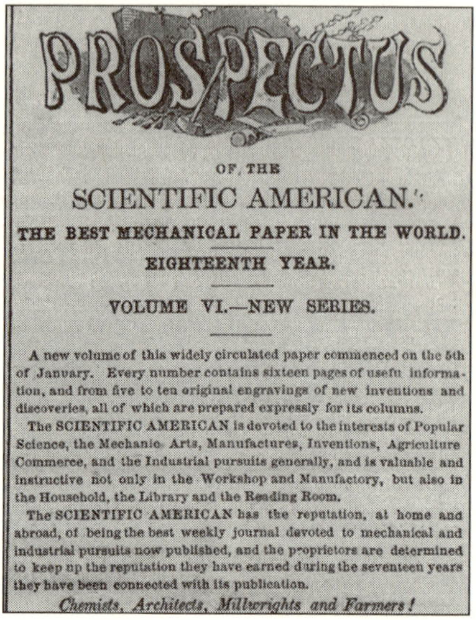

PROSPECTUS

OF THE

SCIENTIFIC AMERICAN.

THE BEST MECHANICAL PAPER IN THE WORLD.

EIGHTEENTH YEAR.

VOLUME VI.—NEW SERIES.

A new volume of this widely circulated paper commenced on the 5th of January. Every number contains sixteen pages of usefu informa-tion, and from five to ten original engravings of new inventions and discoveries, all of which are prepared expressly for its columns.

The SCIENTIFIC AMERICAN is devoted to the interests of Popular Science, the Mechanic Arts, Manufactures, Inventions, Agriculture Commerce, and the Industrial pursuits generally, and is valuable and instructive not only in the Workshop and Manufactory, but also in the Household, the Library and the Reading Room.

The SCIENTIFIC AMERICAN has the reputation, at home and abroad, of being the best weekly journal devoted to mechanical and industrial pursuits now published, and the proprietors are determined to keep up the reputation they have earned during the seventeen years they have been connected with its publication.

Chemists, Architects, Millwrights and Farmers!

Figure 38a

The purpose and scope of Scientific American *was outlined in a "Prospectus" published during the Civil War. "No person engaged in any of the mechanical pursuits should think of doing without" it, the publication editors wrote. In fact, the assistance of its good offices and influential connections was of great benefit to individual inventors such as John Gault, seeking to prosper from the fruits of their industry and labor.* Scientific American, *May 31, 1862, p. 352. (Author's collection)*

Gault would turn their inventive intelligences to perfecting the weapons of war.

On the eve of the Civil War, the United States Army could muster only 163 pieces of field artillery of all types. Nearly a quarter of these were lost when the Confederates seized the Federal armories in the South. Now 31, a seasoned John Gault quickly turned his attention to this arena. Gault was one of the first northern inventors to seize upon the events of the day. After the hostilities broke out in South Carolina, his was the second recorded artillery patent, July 2, 1861. His plan was right out of today's headlines with its multiple warhead missiles. Gault's idea for a breech loading artillery shell of last century was to split the shell into sections held together by a band of soft metal and hinged at the rear. The hollow cavity within the shell was filled with gunpowder and vented for a fuse. When the shell was fired at the enemy, its fuses were ignited by the explosion which propelled the shell from the gun's barrel. The gunpowder charge would break the shell open in several directions, yet still fused at its rear would give the shell a "wide sweep, and make the projectile more destructive" in the opinion of its inventor. His unique shell would still be accurate, but due to its expanded radius its destructiveness would be enormous, Gault contended.

To register his patent claim, Gault employed the services of Munn & Co., No. 37 Park Row. As proprietors of the influential *Scientific American*, this firm had by then become the leading patent firm of its day, securing thousands of American and foreign patents to its clients in the previous decade. Like others with inventive acumen, Gault supplied the idea, the design and the rationale; Munn & Co. prepared the specifications, drawings, caveats and all other patent necessities, which it would then register with the District Court in New York City on its client's behalf. Initially Gault paid Munn & Co. $5 in late March to conduct a preliminary search of Patent Office records on the patentability of his proposed design. This patent search was conducted by staff at the firm's Washington, D.C. branch office, located at the corner of F and 7th Streets. Gault traveled to New York a month later

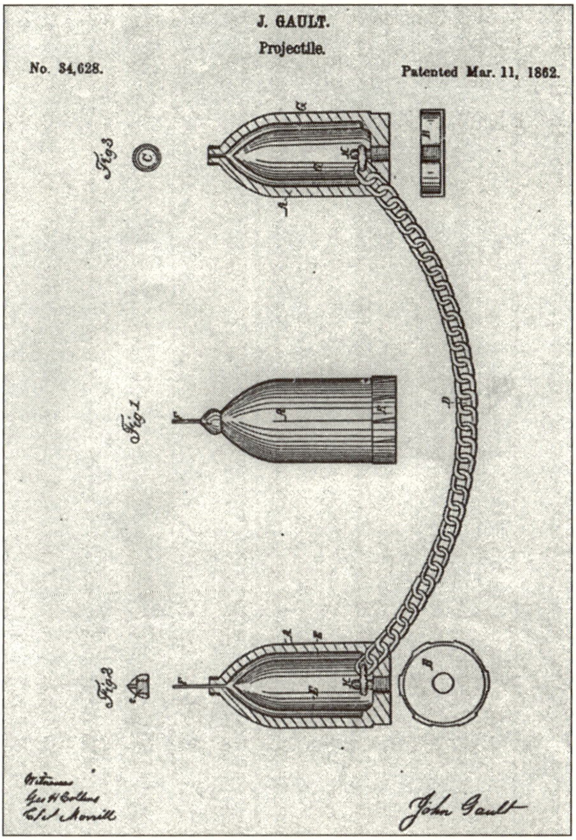

Figure 39a

Gault's second foray into designing a practical expanding artillery shell employed a chain to hold the exploded segments together during flight. This greatly expanded the shell's effective diameter with minimal additional weight or air resistance. Apparently, however, Gault elected not to use Munn & Co. in filing his patent papers. Patent No. 34,628, March 11, 1862. (U.S. Patent Office)

to engage the firm to assist him in his enterprise. At that time he paid Munn & Co. an additional $30, half for the patent application fee and the other half for their services. After filing, the patent papers would then be forwarded to Washington, D.C. where in due course a patent would be granted, which Munn & Co. would publicize in the pages of its journal and help the inventor capitalize or market, for the appropriate fees, as such needs arose. Munn & Co. completed their work and filed Gault's patent application, specifications, drawings and patent model during the week May 29-June 5, 1861. Less than a month later, Gault was in business. The patent was granted, and with Munn & Co.'s assistance plus another $45 fee paid the week following the filing of the application, Gault's projectile was put into production at the New York iron works of George R. Jackson & Co.

Military officials, however, were not generally impressed with such novel munitions. They were seeking to standardize armaments, not diversify their arsenal. Press and public alike complained about the lack of success on the battlefield. "Artillery and cool weather," one pundit explained, "are the two things that the government is waiting for before sending its great military expeditions against the secessionists at the south." Undeterred, less than a year later, Gault provided another exploding projectile for the north's panoply of war. As

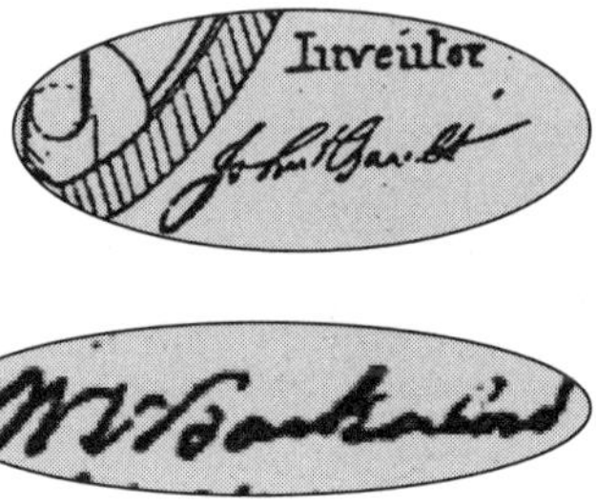

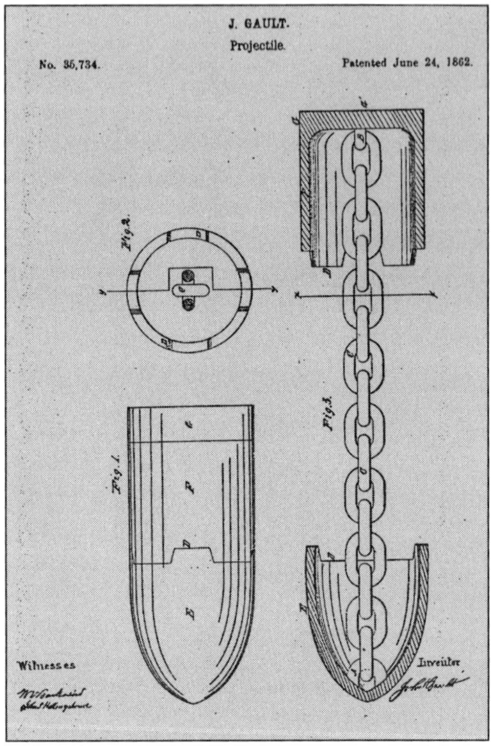

Figures 40a, b, c

Gault's final attempt to capitalize on the military exigency was another chain link exploding artillery shell. This variant employed a longitudinal (transversal) rather than lateral chain to hold the shell case together prior to impact. Significantly, his partner in this venture was New Yorker W. V. Barkalow, who also witnessed the patent. Patent No. 35,734, June 24, 1862, and (detail) signatures. (U.S. Patent Office)

the *Scientific American* reminded its readers, there has been "no diminution in the line of warlike inventions." On March 11, federal officials granted him a patent for one of several improvements in chain shot ordnance granted on the same day George McClellan was relieved of command of the Union armies. Again the exploding projectile was ignited by a fuse breaking a band uniting its sections. This time a chain connected the shell sections. The whole, he contended, would be given a "wide sweep, thereby making it more destructive in its continued flight." Three months later Gault, then residing in New York, paid Munn & Co. to assist him with his third solution to the killing equation. He paid Munn & Co. a $15 fee for the patent that was granted on June 24, 1862. Gault was joined in this claim by New Yorker William V. Barkalow. His new exploding shell remedied prior problems of inaccurate fuses. It separated on impact and ricocheted through fortifications, its inventor contended. It was one of his "clear the way" weapons, Gault said, designed to open breaches in fortifications and artillery lines.

As can be easily demonstrated, Gault's entire attention was not directed solely to military exigency. Concurrently he developed several civil patents to remedy other deficiencies. It was into this non-military sphere that he was to make his most lasting contribution, his encased postage stamp.

Civil War Change Crisis
Chapter II

Figure 41a
Punch, or The London Charivari, *June 7, 1862. (Author's collection)*

Figures 42a-e

In 1862 the U.S. Mint, above, was hard pressed to meet small change needs of the country. Engraving. Harper's New Monthly Magazine, *Dec.1862, p. 3. (Author's collection) Due to the specie premium, it virtually suspended silver coinage such as that at right. 1862 25 cents and dollar coins. (Bowers and Merena photos)*

In summer 1862 a cartoon appeared in the British publication *Punch* which epitomizes the financial circumstances of the time. It shows a rebel dragging his brother over the precipice, the ties of Union snapped and the gloomy abyss of bankruptcy below. Both figures are teetering on the brink as the two wage mortal combat. The rebellious brother grasps his sibling in a head lock, steely-eyed ready to land a mortal blow to his brother's midsection. The brother simultaneously readies to plunge his knife decisively into the back of the usurper. The cartoonist's perception that this mortal struggle would soon plunge both parties into insolvency was shared by the American public at large.

PLEASANT.

Under the above Circumstance, you are called upon to pay your Fare—and, hurry up! You have only Postage Stamps in your pocket; and the Old-Fashioned sticky ones, at that!

Figures 43a, b

Top, Confederate note facsimilist and proprietary medicine vendor, Sam Upham lampooned banking, political and military crises on his patriotic envelope. (Author's collection) While, above, the very real plight of public and merchant fell under the purview of sharp editorialist Thomas Nast. Harper's Weekly, *August 9, 1862, p. 512. (Author's collection and Wineburgh Philatelic Library)*

Figures 44a-d

The U.S. postage stamps pressed into service as small change were a colorful lot. Engraved and printed by the bank note companies for the government, this fine series debuted in August, 1861, replacing the former issues which were demonetized because of the war. The blue one-cent depicts Benjamin Franklin (Scott 63); the rose three-cent, George Washington (Scott 65); the red brown five-cent, Thomas Jefferson (Scott 75); and the yellow green ten-cent, Washington (Scott 68). (Clifford Cole photos)

Fearing the worst, people were doing their best to conserve their resources against that dark day of financial embarrassment. Specie, that is coinage, was hoarded and began to com-

Figures 45a-d

The black twelve-cent (Scott 69), red lilac twenty-four cent (Scott 70) and blue ninety-cent (Scott 72) have three fine engravings of Washington, while the orange thirty-cent depicts Franklin (Scott 71). (Clifford Cole photos)

mand a premium in relation to paper money. Such paper currency was of two basic types: (1) notes issued by state chartered banks; and (2) notes which began to be issued by the federal government a year earlier in response to the need to raise funds to finance the war. Brokers quoted the premium at 4-3/4 percent in early February, 1862. By June this premium had doubled. As the disparity between this paper currency and specie escalated, not only the

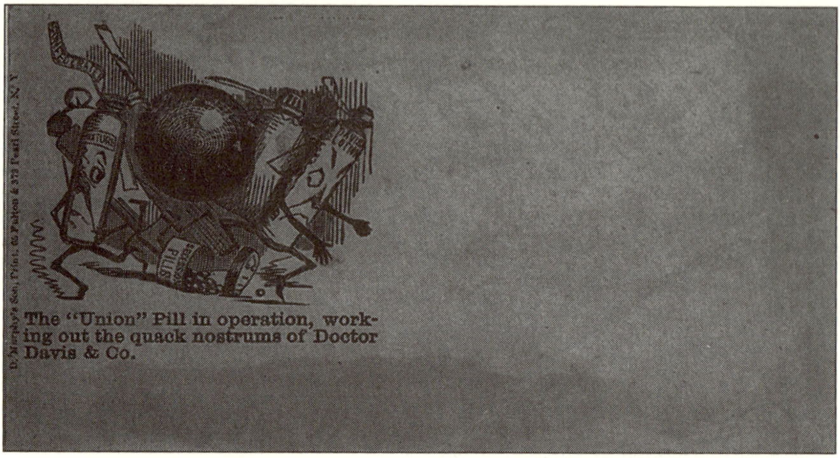

Figures 46a, b

Top, New York City stationers and patriotic envelope makers such as W. H. Murphy on Pearl Street rushed out smaller envelopes, right, to contain and protect government stamps from abuse while in circulation. (Above, Author's collection; right, Milton R. Friedberg)

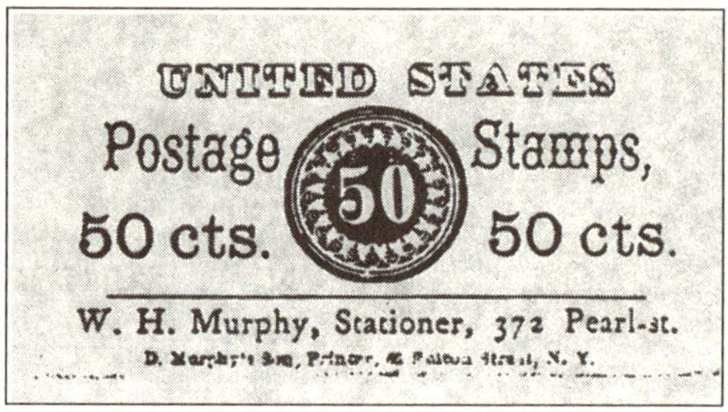

valuable gold and silver coinage, but ultimately even the copper nickel cents disappeared from circulation.

Almost over night $25 million in small change disappeared from the channels of commerce. Although many people had coins stashed away, they were reluctant to spend them even at the advanced price the coins brought in the marketplace fearing additional inflation would drive the coins' value higher and they would lose out. Brokers competed with one another to purchase up additional amounts.

Amid the myriad military exigencies, the general government failed to supply this want efficiently. Financial disarray was widespread. Public hoarding of small change reached overwhelming proportions. Much has been written about the difficulties in making purchases. Even in our increasingly cashless society, we can well imagine what our lives would be like today without small change. In 1862 it was much worse. Prices were fractions of what they are today for most items. A quarter was a good deal of money. Three cents would buy a newspaper or a stage ride. Five cents would buy a glass of beer and a lunch. Not getting one's change from even a small purchase was intolerable.

The Mint at Philadelphia turned its coining presses to copper-nickel cents almost exclusively. The public on its side turned to the only generally available medium at hand and seized upon the postage stamps for small change. Merchants were forced to accept this

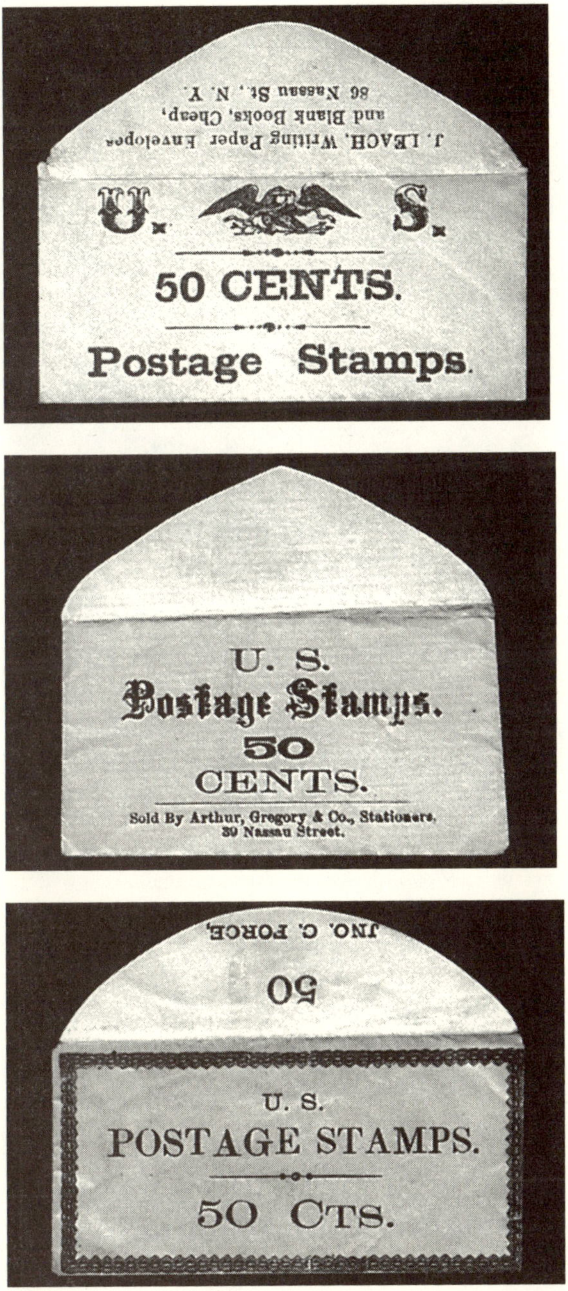

Figures 47a, b, c

Fifty cents was a common denomination for the postage stamp envelopes, although 5-, 10-, 12-, 13-, 15-, 20-, 24-, 25-, 30-, 60-, 75-cent and undenominated values are known. Thus far collectors have identified more than 200 distinct varieties. (Kevin Foley photos)

substitute. The lower stamp values were similar to the lately circulating coinage denominations: 1-, 3-, 5-, and 10-cents. Even the irregular 12-, 24-, 30- and 90-cent stamp values

Figures 48a, b

Inexpensive to produce but very functional, the stationers soon found a ready market for the diminutive postage stamp envelopes which they would customize to clients' needs. Below, Ads soliciting this trade soon appeared in the press. Chicago Evening Journal, *August 1, 1862, p. 4. (Right, Kevin Foley photo; below, Illinois State Library)*

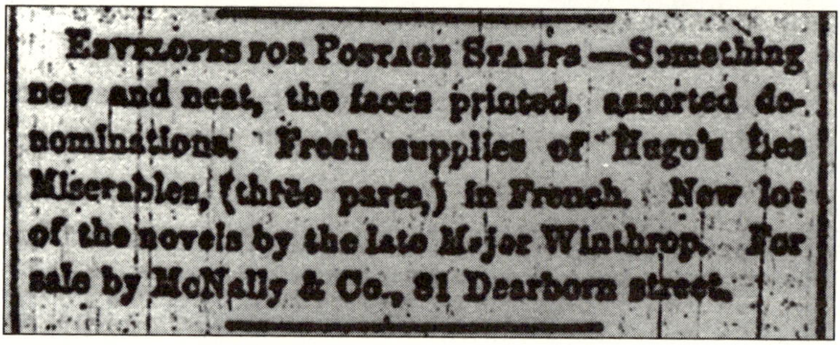

ENVELOPES FOR POSTAGE STAMPS —Something new and neat, the faces printed, assorted denominations. Fresh supplies of Hugo's Les Miserables, (three parts,) in French. New lot of the novels by the late Major Winthrop. For sale by McNally & Co., 81 Dearborn street.

were better than most other substitutes or, worse yet, no change at all.

The tenor of the times required some accommodation to the needs of the public. As 1862 wore on shopkeepers posted signs such as "postage stamps received for goods and given in change for current money." Others advertised stamps for sale. The practice had become general by the time the leading publications began urging the federal government to sanction this practice. With silver commanding 12% premium compared to currency, it's easy to see why.

Public response was to run on the post offices, depleting available quantities and taxing the Post Master General's ability to supply the calls for postal purposes. This only exacerbated an already difficult situation since a year earlier the outbreak of war had caused the government to repudiate its then current postage stamps necessitating their replacement, and the enacting of internal revenue acts to help finance the war had called for supplies of additional stamps for those purposes. The government contractors were unable to supply all these requirements.

Sticky adhesive stamps changing hands in the market place soon soiled and collected in messy wads in the bottoms of pockets and purses. A contemporary observer, certainly not given to hyperbole, characterized the distress in the market place as the most important problem of the day. He said the small change panic "apparently absorbs the entire attention

Figures 49a-e

Left, Merchants realized the virtues of the small envelopes for change and advertising purposes. (Kevin Foley photos) Below, a Philadelphia merchant pasted stamps on thin cardboard with his business opposite the stamp. A. M. Kagin collection. (Fred Schwan electronic imaging) This made the stamp somewhat durable, but destroyed any future postal value. Bottom, another solution affixed stamps to slips of printed paper with the same downside. ex- H. K. Crofoot collection, courtesy Matt Rothert.

(Smithsonian Institution)

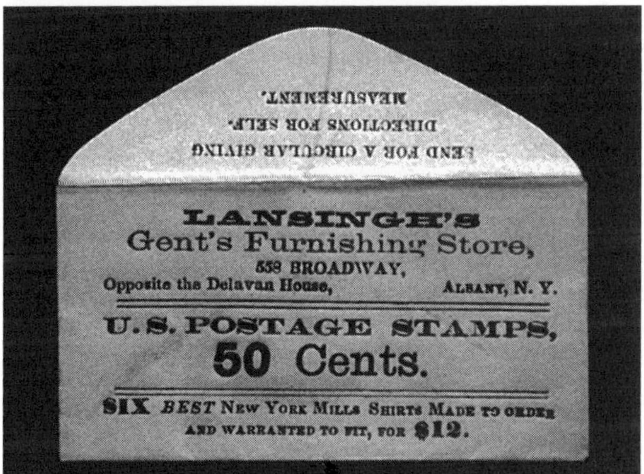

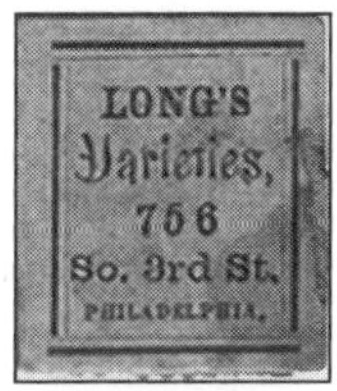

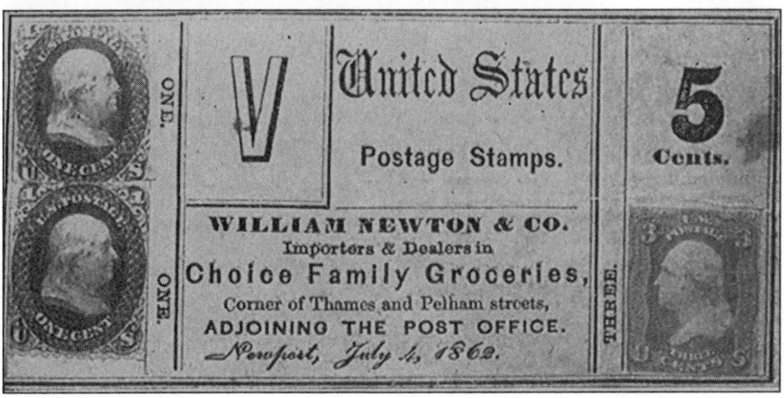

of the people to the exclusion of the war, the condition of the army, the new call for troops, the doings of Congress, or even the policy to be pursued with regard to the Negro."

Figures 50a, b, c

The national government was hamstrung by the breadth and severity of the small change crisis, which necessarily took a back seat to the many other exigencies of war. The solution finally adopted was to print impressions of the postage stamps monetized by the Act of July 17, 1862 on small slips of bank note paper. Above, is a sample of the proposed change notes. ex- H. K. Crofoot collection, courtesy Matt Rothert. (Smithsonian Institution) This Postage Currency not only bore facsimile impressions of the stamps, but the early issues were also perforated like stamps. (Len Glazer photos) The appearance of this new currency occasioned advertising such as appears below. Harper's Weekly, *1862. (Author's collection)*

$50 per week net profits.—NEW ARTICLE. Everybody must have it. Retails for $1 00. Exclusive rights for sale low. For terms, &c., address BALLOU & SON. Haverhill, Mass. ☞ P. S. Samples for Agents sent by mail for 30 cents, Postage Currency. Address as above.

Other expedients arose. Private individuals and merchants as well as municipalities and merchant associations began issuing scrip in small values. The New York *Times* remonstrated against both the private shinplasters and the circulation of postage stamps, which it

Figures 51a, b, c

Postage Currency presented a neat and attractive appearance, but unfortunately was slow to appear as trade and commerce ground to a small change standstill. Those notes that did reach circulation were reluctantly parted with as even these small notes went to a premium. This premium was not simply a matter of convenience. Close reading of the reverse obligation on the notes will show why: In small quantities they were unfortunately made the equivalent of specie since they were payable for ALL DUES to the central government, including customs. Hence they were the legal equivalent of gold. This defect in their issue was remedied by subsequent small denomination note issues, styled Fractional Currency. (Len Glazer photos)

termed "an annoyance, particularly in these dog days." Secretary of the Treasury, Salmon P. Chase, reluctantly addressed the matter in a letter to Congress July 14. He recommended "receiving of postage and other stamps in payment of the fractional parts of a dollar." Congress remained in session an extra day to provide for the remedy. In one of its last acts before adjournment for its summer recess, it passed the legislation monetizing stamps. President Abraham Lincoln signed the legislation immediately on July 17, authorizing the Secretary of the Treasury to furnish postage and other stamps for use as currency in payments to the United States less than $5.

Despite its earlier outrage against this minute stamp currency, the *Times* reacted favor-

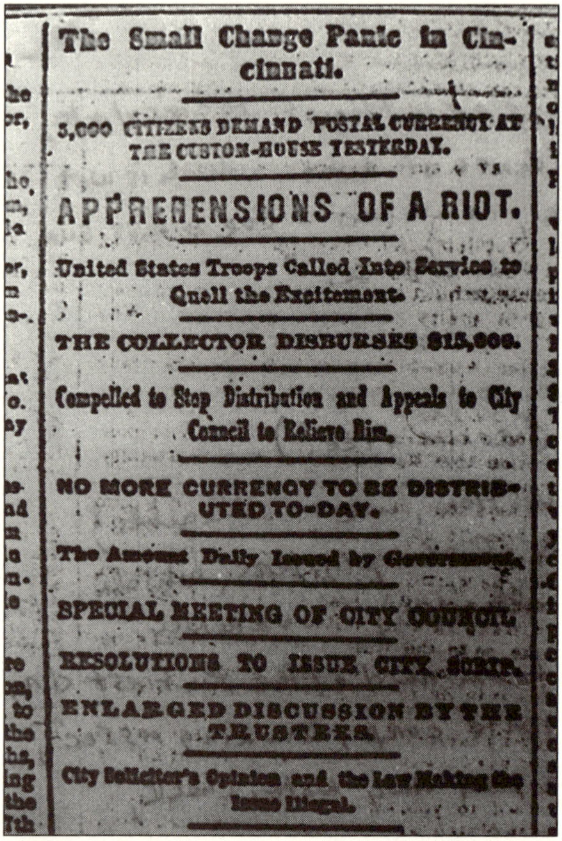

The Small Change Panic in Cincinnati.

5,000 CITIZENS DEMAND POSTAL CURRENCY AT THE CUSTOM-HOUSE YESTERDAY.

APPREHENSIONS OF A RIOT.

United States Troops Called Into Service to Quell the Excitement.

THE COLLECTOR DISBURSES $15,000.

Compelled to Stop Distribution and Appeals to City Council to Relieve Him.

NO MORE CURRENCY TO BE DISTRIBUTED TO-DAY.

The Amount Daily Issued by Government.

SPECIAL MEETING OF CITY COUNCIL.

RESOLUTIONS TO ISSUE CITY SCRIP.

ENLARGED DISCUSSION BY THE TRUSTEES.

City Solicitor's Opinion and the Law Making the Issue Illegal.

Figures 52a, b, c, d

Above, delays in the release of the government Postage Currency in 1862, especially in the hinterlands, gave rise to emergency store cards such as Fuld NY-695A-1a. (Author's collection) Dribbles of notes were dispatched to post offices and subtreasuries for disbursement, but long lines of overcharged customers and inadequate supplies created a riot situation in Cincinnati. Above right, Cincinnati Daily Enquirer, *November 5, 1862, p. 3. (Illinois State Library) In New York City rationing was imposed. Permit. (Ernie Keusch photo)*

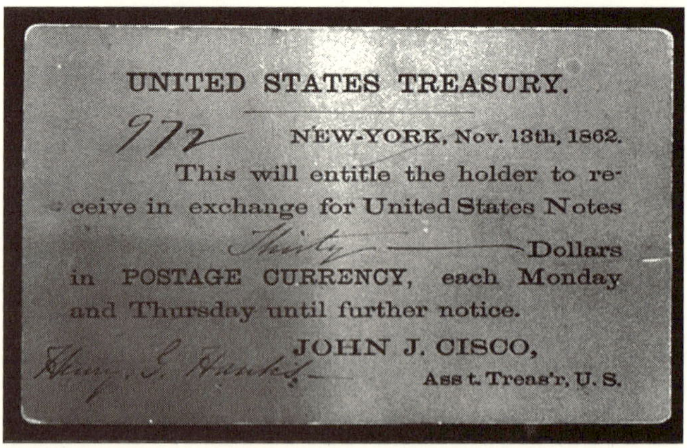

UNITED STATES TREASURY.

972 NEW-YORK, Nov. 13th, 1862.

This will entitle the holder to receive in exchange for United States Notes Thirty Dollars in POSTAGE CURRENCY, each Monday and Thursday until further notice.

JOHN J. CISCO,
Ass't. Treas'r, U. S.

ably. It hailed the passage of the stamp act "as THE (emphasis given in the original) solution to the problem." Even though the act required the Treasury Department to furnish the

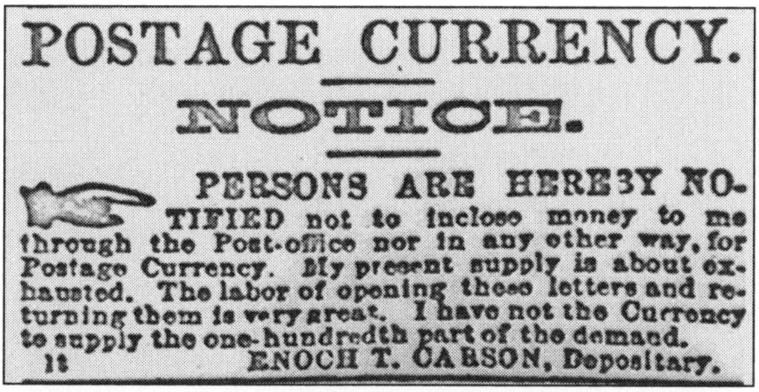

POSTAGE CURRENCY.

NOTICE.

PERSONS ARE HEREBY NOTIFIED not to inclose money to me through the Post-office nor in any other way, for Postage Currency. My present supply is about exhausted. The labor of opening these letters and returning them is very great. I have not the Currency to supply the one-hundredth part of the demand.

1t ENOCH T. CARSON, Depositary.

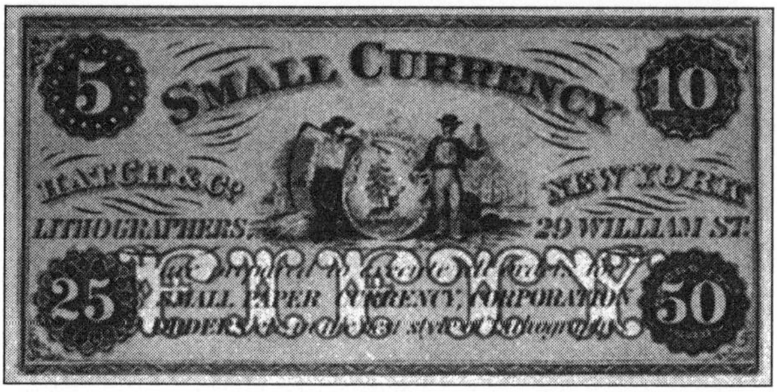

Figures 53a, b

An exasperated U.S. paymaster, Depositary Enoch T. Carson, complained that he had not one percent of the demand for Postage Currency at hand. Left, Cincinnati Daily Enquirer, *November 7, 1862, p. 2. (Illinois State Library) In the meantime, private entrepreneurs like the lithography firm of Hatch & Co. solicited merchants and others to place orders for their own "small paper currency" prepared in the best style. (Herb Melnick, NASCA photo)*

public stamps, it did not make them payable for dues to the government until August 1. The public, however, immediately descended *en masse* upon the Post Office. Horace Greeley's *Tribune* reported that "no sooner was the passage of the act known than a rush for postage stamps began. Whereas stamp sales in New York on a normal day prior to the act's passage was about $3,000, the day after [passage] sales jumped to $10,000. The following day sales in New York hit $16,000 and three days later $24,000!"

In its optimism and hysteria to employ the stamps in its purchases, the public had rushed thousands of dollars of these miniature "gum backs" into circulation despite their obvious disadvantages. "To hand a New York stage driver his fare of two three-cent postage stamps on a wet day, to buy a newspaper on a windy street corner, to make change hurriedly doing the sums necessary in the ordinary affairs of life with the intrusion into the decimal system of such odd sums as those represented by the stamps only increased the vexations of life," and marked the stamps as the "worst circulating medium ever known in the United States," according to one observer.

The public's euphoria of the day passed quickly. The grave draw backs of such a poor change substitute became quickly apparent, especially to those concerns which were ultimately paid in this motley currency. Within two days of the stamp act, Harnden's Express urged in the New York *Herald* that the stamps be placed in small, neat envelopes especially made for this purpose, with the sum of the stamp denominations printed on the outsides of the envelopes. On August 3rd Murphy's, a New York printer, advertised it would supply postage stamp envelopes for 75 cents per thousand. Other printers in New York, Brooklyn, Jersey City and elsewhere quickly offered such envelopes for sale. One type was printed by T. R. Dawley of New York, who advertised he could supply "envelopes of all sizes, styles and

Figures 54a, b, c

Printers in all the major cities, and plenty of minor ones too, vied for the burgeoning traffic in printing small change notes. Anyone who could pay the printing bill was a candidate for this unregulated issue of money. Two prominent firms in this trade were Prang of Boston and Mayer of New York City. Ads. Top, Boston Commercial Advertiser, *December 26, 1862; right,* New York *Times, November 19, 1862, p. 3. (Illinois State Library) Ferd. Mayer Shinplaster Bank Advertising Note, c. 1862. (Author's collection)*

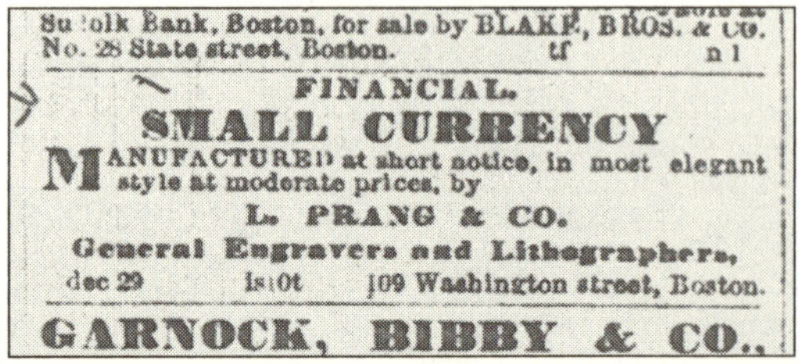

Suffolk Bank, Boston, for sale by BLAKE, BROS. & CO. No. 28 State street, Boston. tf n1

FINANCIAL.

SMALL CURRENCY

MANUFACTURED at short notice, in most elegant style at moderate prices, by

L. PRANG & CO.

General Engravers and Lithographers,

dec 29 [illegible] 109 Washington street, Boston.

GARNOCK, BIBBY & CO.,

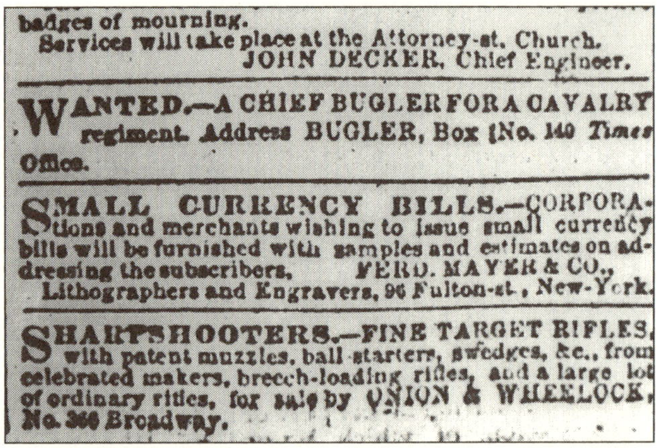

badges of mourning.

Services will take place at the Attorney-st. Church.

JOHN DECKER, Chief Engineer.

WANTED.—A CHIEF BUGLER FOR A CAVALRY regiment. Address BUGLER, Box No. 140 Times Office.

SMALL CURRENCY BILLS.—CORPORATIONS and merchants wishing to issue small currency bills will be furnished with samples and estimates on addressing the subscribers. FERD. MAYER & CO., Lithographers and Engravers, 96 Fulton-st., New-York.

SHARPSHOOTERS.—FINE TARGET RIFLES, with patent muzzles, ball starters, swedges, &c., from celebrated makers, breech-loading rifles, and a large lot of ordinary rifles, for sale by UNION & WHEELOCK, No. 366 Broadway.

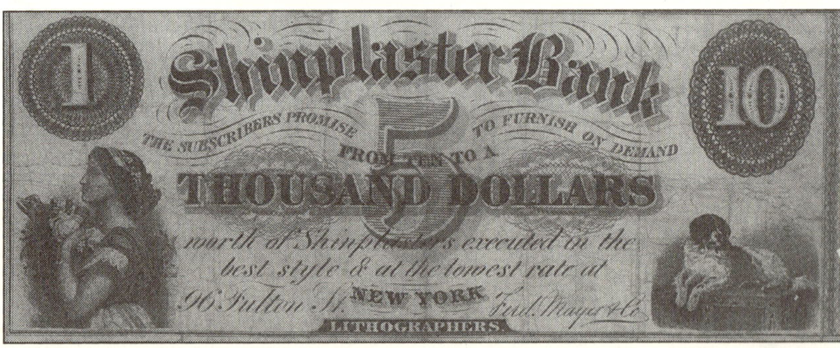

colors, for enclosing the 'Sticking Plaster Currency.'" Such envelopes were convenient, but ultimately failed to keep the stamps clean. No prudent soul could fail to open the envelope and count out the stamps. Another makeshift, pasting stamps on folded slips of paper such as Harvey Gridley Eastman and others did, destroyed their future postal value.

The runaway stamp sales could not continue indefinitely and Postmaster General Montgomery Blair urged local postmasters to restrict sales to the "normal levels existing" prior to the run on stamps. Even so, less than a week after the passage of the stamp monetizing act, the New York postmaster was ordered by Washington officials to cease supplying the stamps for currency, which he did on July 23. Even for postal purposes, patrons were restricted to no more than $10 worth of stamps. Soon large retailers were offering premiums to

Figures 55a-g

Thousands of small denomination notes sprang up almost overnight, initially bringing some relief to change-strapped commerce. But soon the bewildering mass of questionable notes brought cries for suppression of such shinplasters. (All specimens, Author's collection, except one-cent Walton, below, Neil Shafer collection)

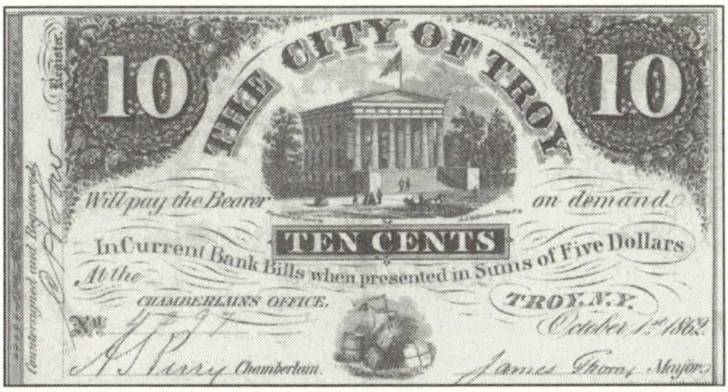

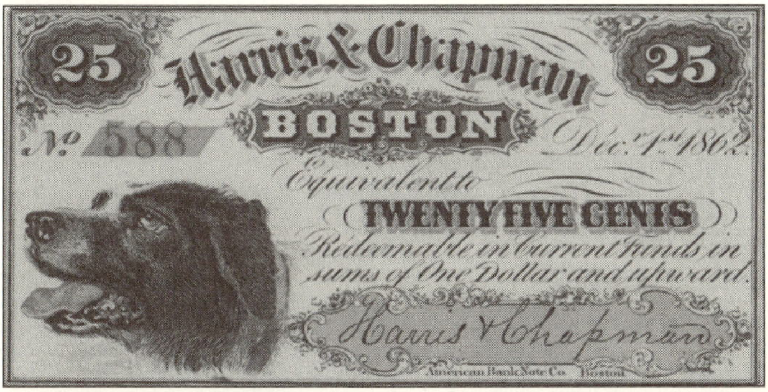

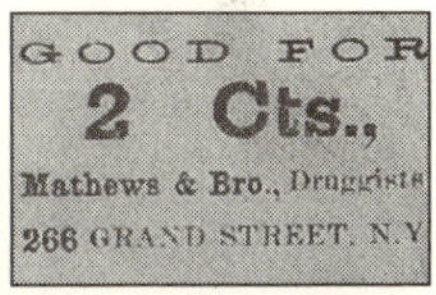

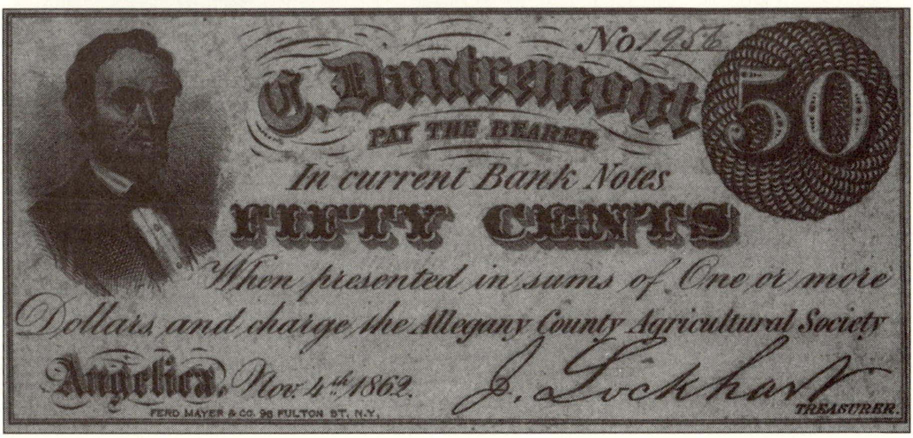

Nickel Cents.

The *United States Gazette* (Philadelphia) says :—

"The mint is now running its entire force upon nickels. The cost of making this insignificant coin is nearly as much as the cost of making double-eagles. The only difference is that the latter coin is weighed and adjusted, piece by piece. The nickels are exempt from any such close manipulation. The labor daily done at the mint, if expended upon double-eagles, would produce $40,000 per day. Upon nickels, as it is now expended, the results are but about twenty-five hundred dollars per day in nickel. When the currency question is regulated and specie comes forth from its many hiding-places, nickel cents will be like the locusts of Egypt. They will be so abundant as to constitute a nuisance. Except for convenience in doing retail business, they are of small value. In small sums each nickel represents the hundredth part of a dollar, yet it is not intrinsically worth even that. Nickels cannot be used as legal tender, nor for exportation, yet a fictitious value is given to them by speculation that is really culpable. To produce them in sufficient quantities, the nickel-coining machinery of the United States mint is running even into over-hours."

Figures 56a, b, c

Unable to coin silver and gold for circulation, the U.S. Mint turned its entire attention to the copper nickel one-cent coin. Although prodigious efforts were expended to produce these pieces, they scarcely met demands. Scientific American, *March 21, 1863, p. 187. (Dallas Public Library) Soon even these pieces were bringing a premium in the market-place, one percent by summer 1862, although their intrinsic value was much less than their face. This was a convenience premium. Once again merchants rushed into the void and issued copper and brass store cards. Convenience in trade and advertising suitability combined to make these pieces popular choices for thousands of merchants. Scovill-made 1862 store card, Fuld NY-770B-2b. Note spelling error, NI. (Author's collection)*

obtain stamps in quantity for use as change. The *Times* reported on July 24 that a restaurateur was offering three percent premium for stamps. Although it was illegal to charge a premium for stamps, other firms responded by advertising their sale for currency purposes, too.

John Gault
Chapter III

Despite the constant warnings that stamps needed to be kept clean so as to remain suitable for prepayment of postage, one can visualize the impossibility of actually doing so. Stamps were crammed into pockets, stuck to the palm of one's hand or to each other. In addition to the small envelopes, some firms adopted the practice of pasting them on sheets of paper folded in half or on small cardboard chits. A stationer, Leeds & Franklin at 112 Broadway, New York City, sold mounted stamps on cards of its own design. "These stamps are inserted in inclosed cards, with raised rims around the edge of each stamp, which effectually protects them from wear and tear, and make them very convenient to handle," according to a newspaper report. The stamps were offered to merchants at premiums ranging from one percent to two and one-half percent. Although these measures provided modest protection, such stamps were rendered postally useless. If for this reason and no other, these practices were not nearly so widespread as the use of the small stamp envelopes.

Most stamps, however, continued to be simply passed from hand to hand. With no intrinsic value of their own, this stamp currency depended for its acceptance and circulation

Figure 57a

Reed JG10 obverse, PAT AUG 12, 1862. // J. GAULT. By law Gault was required to stamp or engrave the precise date the patent was granted upon each article of manufacture. He was not required to put his name on the piece, although it was customary to do so. ex-James F. Ruddy specimen. (Bowers and Merena photo)

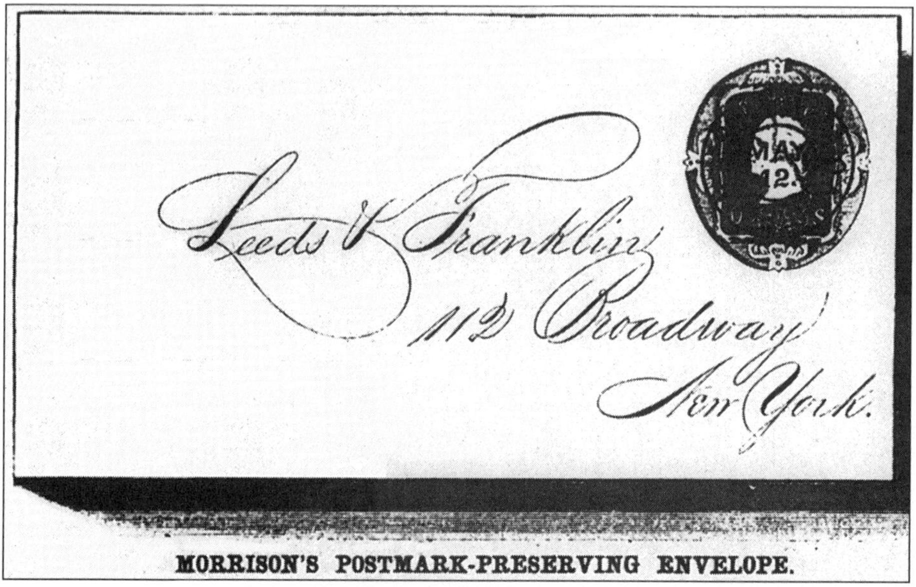

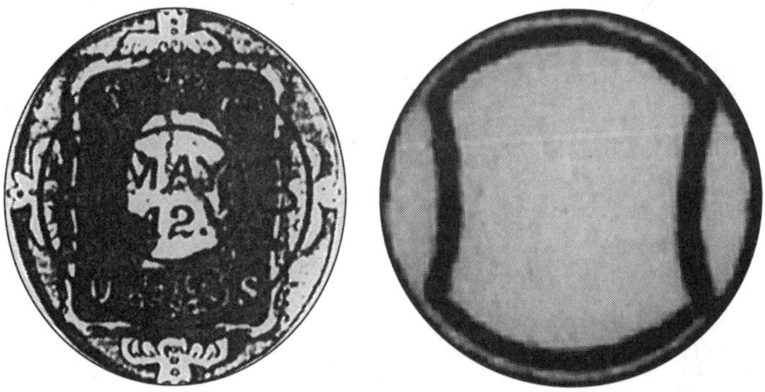

Figures 58a, b, c
L. W. Leeds purchased Benjamin Morrison's die cut patent envelope which presaged John Gault's encased stamp design. Scientific American, *July 12, 1862, p. 32. (Dallas Public Library)*

on its ultimate availability for use for its intended postal purpose. Soon stamps were proven to be a wretched and unfit currency substitute for small change. The federal government responded by printing specially prepared small notes with stamps as part of their designs. This Postage Currency, however, was much delayed, too. Wags of the day joked: "Can't change a dollar bill, eh? Well, I'm glad of that. I've had thirty-six drinks on it in three days, and it may stand a good deal of wear and tear yet."

The humor of this situation was lost on most people. Those caught up in the throes of the situation understood the climate precipitating the *Times* story headlined, "An amusing quarrel concerning paper change." What happened was a broker refused to accept postage stamps in change from the driver of an omnibus. The pair argued and being unable to resolve the difficulty, the driver headed off in the other direction, eventually pulling up in front of City Hall. The driver took his case to the City Marshal. The rider contented that

Figure 59a

Left, Cabinet card. Previously unpublished photograph. Copyright © 1994 Fred Reed. All Rights Reserved. (Author's collection) Above, autograph. (Author's collection)

since the driver had a sign posted refusing stamps for fares, the prohibition should work both ways. The marshal took the side of the driver, and the rider took the stamps under protest. The rider threatened to sue the marshal and demanded to be transferred to his original destination for the fare he had already paid. The driver would not allow him to reenter the stage and drove off. The broker's loud protestations as he tried unsuccessfully to climb back into the stage drew a crowd of people in front of City Hall and a reporter from the adjacent *Times* Building. The Times editor found the situation amusing. It's doubtful the participants did.

The quarrel took place in City Hall Park, immediately across Broadway from the Park Place Hotel, where John Gault already had a room by early summer 1862. Perhaps he was one of the amused bystanders. Maybe not, but it is certain that Gault was already in New

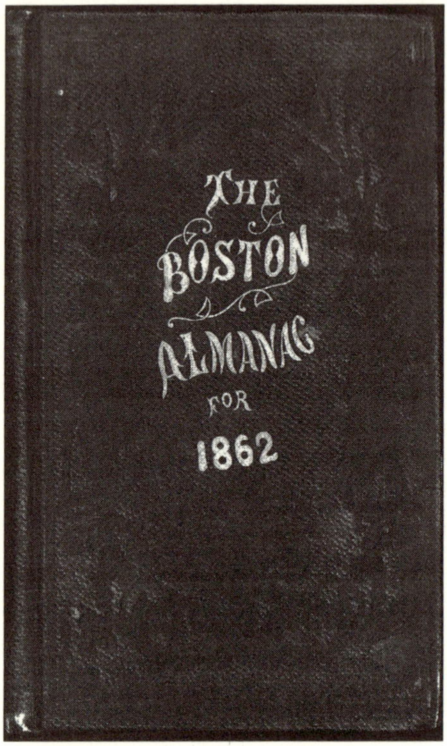

Figure 60a

John Gault's Boston in 1862 was a heady place of activity and opportunity. It was also a place that was recognizing the stark realities of war. The Boston Almanac for 1862 *reflects the exigencies of its era. The greater portion of the book is a regimental listing of Massachusetts and other New England military units with a great deal of advertising. (Author's collection)*

York *before* receiving the encased stamp patent. He had set up shop at No. 1 Park Place seeking his fortune with his military-related patents and his newfound business relationships with the other driven young men ensconced there.

Obviously aware of the commercial difficulties of his time, Gault conceived his ingenious solution to the small change crisis in July. As we have seen times over, John Gault was insightful in anticipating needs. He was a quick study, decisive, in short, a man of action. Among the Gault family papers is a key missive, which he dispatched to his brother Henry explaining that he would not be available to spend the July 4th weekend with family members in Boston. It is dated July 1st and headed "1 Park Place." Gault writes: "Dear Brother [Henry], I have been travelling so much lately getting my new business started that I don't feel able to go to Boston as I expected to spend the 4th. . . . Yours, John." This letter was written in the week following the granting of the patent he shared with William V. Barkalow. Barkalow had sights on being a prime military contractor. He had designs on Gault's exploding artillery shells, and the pair was out to convince military procurement officials of the superiority of their designs.

Simultaneously his new enterprise – supplying a neat and efficient alternative for the hoarded government small change to merchants for a modest fee – was conceived, patented and launched. It was icing on the cake. The Patent Law had been recently modified to expedite processing of design patents to encourage improvements in matters of "taste, form and

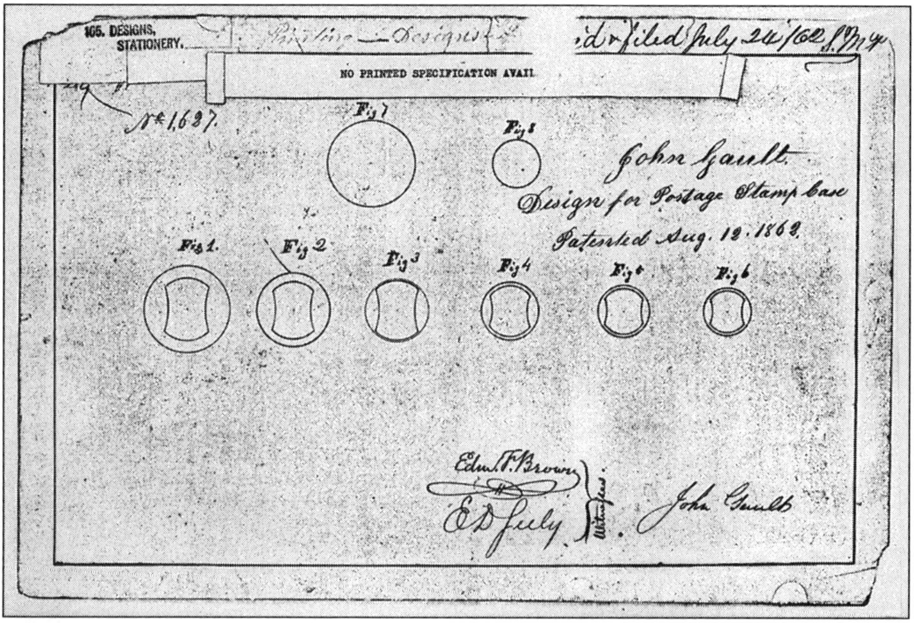

Figure 61a

The original design registration sheet for John Gault's encased stamp bears the written notation that it was received and filed in the Southern District of New York (New York City) on Thursday, July 24, 1862. It also bears the hand written notation that it was originally classified as a Printing Design and a label that it was subsequently reclassified as a Stationery Design. It was, of course, neither use that Gault anticipated with his multiform design when he affixed his signature to his patent application. Patent No. 1,627, August 12, 1862. (U.S. Patent Office)

artistic skill." Gault worked quickly. During the week prior to Wednesday, July 23, 1862, he met with O. D. Munn and his staff at *Scientific American* to iron out the details of his plan. A brief stroll across City Hall Park from his office at 1 Park Place brought him to their offices at 37 Park Row. It was relatively simple to obtain a Design Patent. His drawing was witnessed by Ed Brown and E. D. July. Gault paid Munn & Co. $35 for their services on July 22. Thirty dollars was for the patent itself; the remainder for Munn & Company's services. On July 23rd. *Scientific American* published receipt of the funds, and Munn & Co. registered his patent design claim in the District Court in New York City. According to the records of the U.S. Patent Office itself, Gault's claim to his unique invention was filed July 24. Gault claimed to have invented "a circular metallic case, to contain a postage or government stamp, to be used for currency, the configuration of the open face plate being as described and represented." Three weeks later on Tuesday, August 12, he was granted a design patent, number 1627, for his "Design for Encasing Government Stamps." The patent was good for 14 years. Gault was not required to submit a model for his design patent, just two copies of the drawings. However, he went to the extra trouble. The patent model he devised is simi-

DESIGNS.

1,624.—S. D. Arnold (assignor to P. & F. Corbin), of New Britain, Conn., for Design for Lifting Handle Plate for Coffins, &c.

1,625.—J. W. Burt, of New York City, for Design for Ornamental Anklet.

1,626.—T. W. Evans, of Philadelphia, Pa., for Design for a Trade Mark.

1,627.—John Gault, of Boston, Mass., for Design for Postage Stamp case.

1,628.—Constant Hesdra, of Brooklyn, N. Y., assignor to W. H. Core and A. Lorenz, of New York City, for Design for the Base of a Show Case.

1,629.—H. G. Tyer, of Andover, Mass., for Design for Trade Mark.

1,630 to 1,649.—E. J. Ney, of Lowell, Mass., assignor to The Lowell Manufacturing Company, for twenty Designs for Carpet Patterns :

Figure 62a

As a publication of record, Scientific American *published brief notices of all patent applications as they were approved. In that era, incidentally, all patents were granted on Tuesdays. Gault's encased stamp patent, No. 1627, was a design patent numbered independently from mechanical patents granted that same day, August 12, 1862.* Scientific American, *August 30, 1862, p. 141. (Dallas Public Library)*

lar, of course, to the designs illustrated on his filing papers. Its obverse (merchant side) bears the engraved message: "JOHN GAULT // BUSINESS // CARD. Its reverse (stamp side) has a 10-cent green Washington Stamp (Scott 68) in a frame with thicker rims and tabs than the issued pieces. It most closely approximates Figure 2 on the design sheet Gault submitted. Its existence has been known at least since 1959.

Let's examine Gault's novel idea. The construction of his encased stamps is interesting. As virtually any item of manufacture, it consists of several parts. In this instance five distinct elements are joined together to form the encased stamp. These are:

(1) an outer, wrap-around frame of thin brass with an opening in its center;

(2) a thin piece of mica;

(3) a cardboard circle around which the corners of the stamp is wrapped;

(4) a circular disc of thicker brass on which a message is embossed;

(5) a U.S. postage stamp.

Photo buttons, of the type patented by Humphrey Copeley and R. E. Hitchcock, and marketed ubiquitously by Abbott & Co for Scovill were already a common item of commerce, having been frequently employed during the presidential campaign of 1860 and thereafter. Holding small tintype pictures or engravings, such brass containers frequently

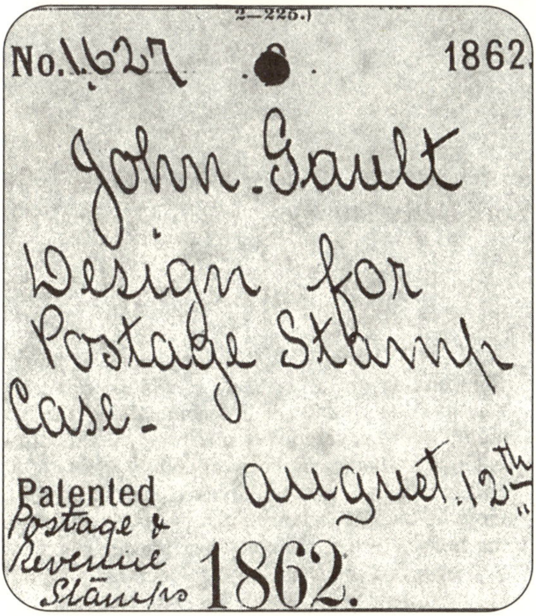

Figures 63a, b, c

John Gault // Business // Card is engraved on the obverse of the original patent model for his encased stamps. This custom made stamp enclosure differs significantly from the mass-produced pieces. It is approximately 10 percent larger in diameter, with thicker tabs and frame rims. Although the law specified "postage and other stamps" of the U.S., someone has written "Postage & Revenue Stamps" on the Form 2-225. (Bowers and Merena photos)

were holed for suspension, studded for use as buttons, or fastened by pins as decorations. Gault's case is not much dissimilar from such photo buttons. His claim was not for a button *per se*, but rather he claimed "an invention new and original [for] a circular metallic case, to contain a postage or government stamp, to be used for currency." The precise wording of his claim shows the influence of the Munn & Co. patent attorneys, reflecting as it does the precise wording of the July 17th law which monetized "postage and other stamps." These "other" stamps might have included the Revenue Stamps authorized by the Internal Revenue Act of July 1. Although no regular issue encasements contain these revenue stamps, their absence is due to their unavailbility at the time of encased stamp manufacture. The Revenue Act also limited, a sanction not lifted until December 25, 1862, use of these stamps to payment of the tax upon the particular article or instrument specified on the

Figure 64a

Within weeks of its patenting, Editor Horace Greeley took notice of Gault's invention, calling the small change substitute "not a bad" idea. New York Daily Tribune, *August 30, 1862. (Illinois State Library)*

City Items

A SUBSTITUTE FOR COIN -- A friend has shown us a light circular metallic sheath of white metal for postage stamps of large and small denominations, the face of the stamp being covered with a transparent sheet of mica. It is slightly smaller in diameter than a quarter of a dollar, and is designed to take the place of small silver coin. The metallic back is to be stamped with the advertisement of the houses ordering them. Their price to purchasers is $20 or less a thousand; to the general public, only the value of their face. The idea is not a bad one.

stamps' face. Bids to supply the revenue stamps were not advertised for until August and the contract printer, Butler and Carpenter of Philadelphia, did not supply many of these issues until late in the year, 1862, with large quantities becoming available only still later the following year.

Gault's "Stationery Design" as it was later classified by a Patent Office clerk, was for a metal frame similar to those devised by Copeley, Hitchcock and others, except for the single opening through which the stamp was visible under a mica pane which kept the stamp clean and safe. Mica is not familiar to most modern readers, but it was a commonly employed mineral at that time. Sometimes incorrectly called isinglass, its chief use was in heat resistant window panes in the stoves of that day. Because of this mineral's perfect cleavage, mica "books" could be split cleanly into sheets or layers. These clear sheets of paper thick mineral were durable, flexible and elastic enough to serve Gault's purposes well.

Since no back opening was necessary (unlike the political pieces which permitted depicting a vice presidential running mate in the 1860 political pieces), a plain brass disk was all that was necessary for the closure. In this configuration Gault's encased stamp cases resemble the gilt buttons produced by Scovill Manufacturing Co. and other large button companies for military and similar uses. A quick comparison with any of the multitude of different Scovill-made buttons of that day will quickly confirm this. This led an earlier writer to wax eloquently: "by comparing the backs of encased stamps with the backs of their [Scovill's] large buttons, we find the same smooth, round folding of the front disk over the back – evidence of perfect, well-finished work by the same machine, the same workmen, and the same firm." This can be observed perfectly well by the several examples of Scovill buttons shown.

Gault's design patent illustrates six similar obverses in as many sizes, all with similar shield-shaped openings and wing tabs to left and right. His two reverses are plain. It is likely Gault anticipated various sizes for his denominations not unlike the displaced coinage. However, all the issued pieces are approximately 24 millimeters in diameter, including the full range of denominations he had made up for himself. The issued stamp cases are slightly smaller than a quarter dollar in diameter and thickness, but weigh much less. The quarter is 24.3 mm in diameter. In thickness, 16 encased stamps stack to an inch, compared to 14-15

Figures 65a-h

Presenting a uniform "neat and handy" appearance, a denominational typeset of Gault's small change store cards display Benjamin Franklin on one- and thirty-cent values, George Washington on three-, ten-, twelve-, twenty-four-, and ninety-cent denominations, and Thomas Jefferson on the five-cent issue. (Dr. Wallace Lee photos)

quarters. A dozen encased stamps weigh an ounce. So they are much lighter than a quarter. Slightly over 4.5 quarters weigh an ounce.

The press employed to manufacture Gault's encasements has been described as an "old fashioned flat-button machine." The press forced the thin brass wrap-around frame to encircle the edge of the advertising disc, securing it solidly. It is interesting to note a contemporary account of such a machine process employed at that time by Scovill:

> The melted red-hot liquid is turned into molds, making narrow plates say 15 or 18 inches long, 4 to 5 inches wide and half or 3/4 inch in thickness. These plates are then rolled down to the proper thickness for buttons between cylinders which are nearly a foot in diameter. Then the buttons are cut out. Then the buttons are stamped in a mold [embossing die]. The mold [embossing die] gives the figures, letters, or whatever is desired for the outside of the buttons, and gives them the flat, convex or concave shape. ... They are then gilded by dipping them in an amalgam of gold and mercury or quicksilver and then made smooth and bright. Everything is done by machinery. Every process upon the buttons is done in an instant, as it were.

Figures 66a, b

Slightly smaller than a quarter dollar, the advertising side of the store card is more properly called its obverse than the stamp or "heads" side. Reed JG30. (Bowers and Merena photos)

Substitute stamp case for button, silvering for gilding, allow for the insertion of the cardboard spacer, stamp, and mica disc, and one has a good understanding of how Gault's patent cases were produced.

Another contemporary view of the Scovill operation pegged its production capacity at 216,000 brass buttons daily. Employment was 53 persons in the brass rolling mill and about three times as many in their brass products department. It is thus clear that Gault's specialized button product would not have taxed the manufacturer overly much. Production of the encased stamps, however, could not have proceeded nearly so rapidly as military buttons due to the fragility of the mica insert, and the stamp/cardboard insert. It seems reasonable that the cardboard may have served as a "shock absorber" to protect the mica from the shock of the case closing as much as in holding the stamp in place.

The encased stamps present two distinct types of obverses (advertising side of the encased stamps). The initial pieces circulated by John Gault, as well as those subsequently produced for John I. Brown and the Irving House, have plain borders. This is the Type I obverse. The Type II obverse is used on all other issues, and is differentiated primarily by a border of approximately 100 raised balls surrounding the advertisement, set within the recessed ring at the circumference of the advertiser's metallic disc.

Likewise the issued pieces present two distinct types of reverses (stamp side). These are the normal or "plain" (flat) wrap around design and the so-called "ribbed" or grooved wrap around. Much useless speculation has appeared concerning the purpose of the ribs or grooves. As can be readily seen from Scovill buttons of the period, such parallel corduroy patterns were normal for backgrounds on military buttons of that period. On the shiny military buttons, these grooves presented a less reflective (hence darker) background for the main button device, setting it off aesthetically. A similar artistic treatment is common to engravings for dark backgrounds. On encased stamps such grooves serve no similar purpose. Pieces displaying these grooves (Type A reverses, i.e. stamp side of the encasements) were merely punched from leftover rolled, brass button stock. (Note: the grooves appear over the entire face of the wraparound, not just on the half moon tabs as some authors have erroneously stated). Once Gault's product got into general production, flat, rolled brass stock

He has undergone close imprisonment for six months, and a part of the time in a crowded dungeon, and deprived of light and air.

A New Currency.—A new plan for obviating the small change trouble has been suggested and is being carried out by parties in Connecticut, which seems about the best expedient to adopt until we come back to the good old times of gold and silver. The small stamps now in use are incased in a small white metal covering, with a mica face, so that their denomination is easily seen. The whole is then of exactly the same shape, though not as large or thick as a quarter dollar: and is as handy in every respect as ordinary silver change. It can be furnished at about five per cent. premium. An effort is to be made to induce the Treasury Department to adopt this style of currency, in preference to the small bills, which, it is argued, being printed on inferior paper, will soon become dirty and ragged.

Scarcity of Currency.—Philadelphia, it seems, is not only afflicted with a scarcity of small change, but has but little currency of any denomination below twenty dollar bills in circulation. The *Ledger* says: "One of our greatest inconviences in trade now, and for some weeks past, is the almost universal scarcity of currency—not the fractional parts of a dollar, but currency of all denominations up to $20. The banks have it not, and to meet the demand existing for it several of our prominent brokers

Figures 67a, b, c
By mid-October Gault had been joined by Joseph Kirkpatrick. By remarkable coincidence articles appearing in the Chicago and New York papers on October 18 indicate that the federal government was considering adopting his patent encased stamps. Above left, "Parties in Connecticut" refers to Scovill Manufacturing Co. a large button and brass stamping firm in Waterbury. Chicago Evening Journal, *October 18, 1862, p. 1. (Illinois State Library) Above, if Scovill had issued encased stamps on its own account, they might have looked like its corporate seal. (Author's collection) Left, Treasury Secretary Chase expected a great deal in a short time from Revenue Commissioner George S. Boutwell. How Gault's encased stamps came to his attention is a mystery.* New York Times, *October 18, 1862. (Illinois State Library)*

THE PROPOSED STAMP AND MICA CURRENCY -- The Commissioner of Internal Revenue, after an examination of the mica and metal cases for revenue stamps, designed to facilitate their use as currency, is disposed to believe them well suited for the purpose intended, and sufficiently cheap to justify the Government in their adoption. They are but little larger than the nickel cent, and very clean and beautiful in appearance. The only question, except that of cheapness, is as to their durability, and even if the mica should occasionally break, the value of the stamp is not impaired for the use originally intended. *Washington, Oct. 17*

was used for these (Type B) wrap arounds.

Some pieces are also found silvered and this has also caused additional useless speculation in the past. It was normal for brass military buttons to be gilded or silvered, although not all buttons were produced so expensively. Initially Gault felt it necessary to silver his

Figures 68a, b

Brass buttons were produced by embossing dies in which positive and slightly larger negative dies created thin brass shells which were fastened by a forming press. (Source unknown)

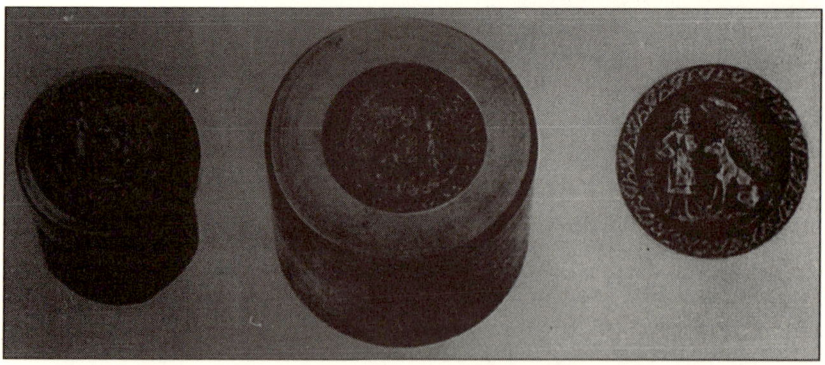

encased stamps, too, since both sides were silvered. He felt this made them look more like the silver change for which they were a ready substitute. Since the silvering wore off quickly he soon concluded that such a costly process was unnecessary.

Figures 69a, b

Scovill was a principal producer of military buttons for federal and state regiments during the Civil War. Except for their high relief and shanks, their similarity in design and workmanship to Gault's encasements cannot be missed. Several of the U.S. Army, U.S. Navy and Massachusetts brass buttons shown, above, also are silvered like some of the encased stamps. Additionally, one is gilded. (All specimens from the Author's collection)

It is plain that once Gault's patent was issued, he wasted no time securing his first order. Horace Greeley, who had originally urged use of stamps for small change but reversed

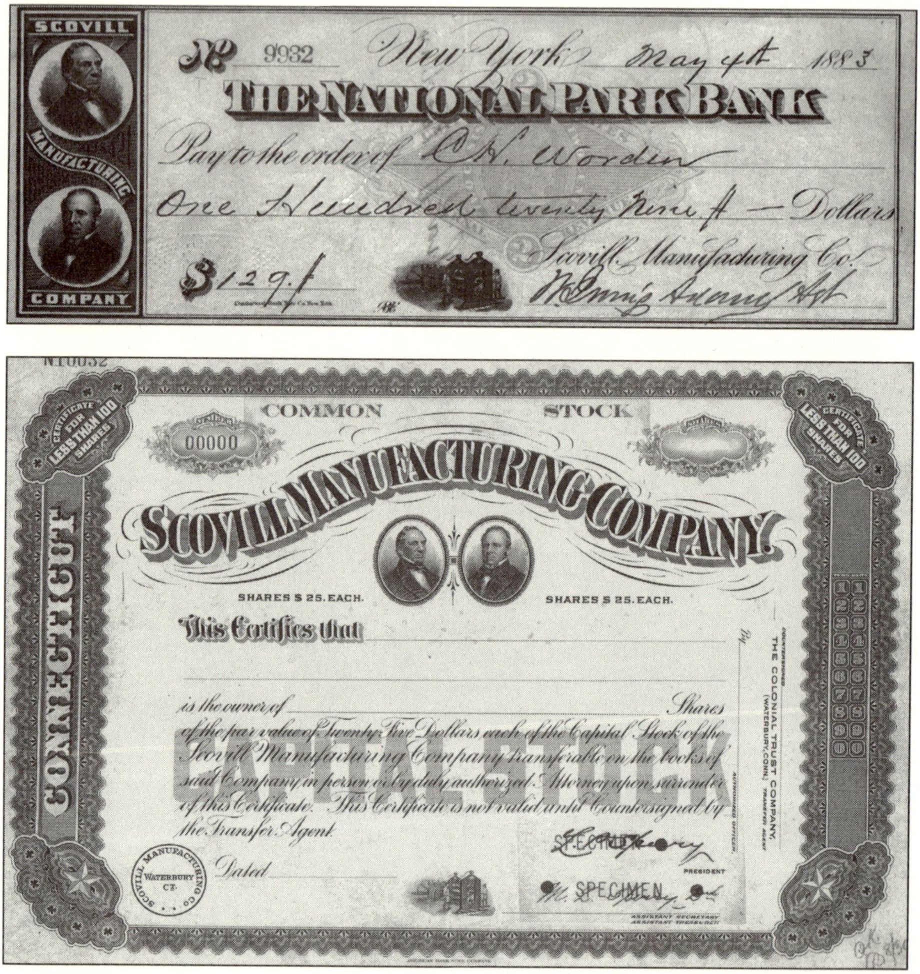

Figures 70a, b

Token collectors (exonumists) have long been familiar with the products of Scovill Manufacturing Co., but check and bond collectors (scripophilists) also have good reason to pursue mementoes of this firm, especially since engravings of founders J. M. L. and W. H. Scovill often appear on its emissions. Issued check, May 4, 1883, and specimen stock certificate, 1946. This company is still in business as a subsidiary of Hamilton Beach (Both from Author's collection)

his position when the fate of that medium in actual circulation became manifest, was quick to acknowledge the benefits of Gault's New Metallic Currency. On August 19, only a week after the government issued Gault's patent, Greeley's New York *Tribune* took notice of Gault's plan. He called the encased stamps a "happy solution to our common plight." *Scientific American* published the granting of Gault's patent August 30. That same day,

Figures 71a, b, c, d

Collectors have long expressed puzzlement over the so-called "ribbed frames" of some encasements. These parallel grooves cover the entire wrap around stamp frame (not just the tabs as some authors state). They were machined, sheet brass stock prepared for button manufacture (detail from Scovill scrip), common on military and other buttons the company produced during the period. On buttons the grooves added aesthetic depth to the design; on Gault's pieces they are merely ornamental. (At top, Dr. Wallace Lee and Bob Kincaid photos; center and above, Author's collection)

Greeley called attention once again to encased stamps in circulation and reprised their virtues for his readers.

Figure 72a

Press reports indicate the possibility of the Federal Government adopting Gault's expedient for remedying the small change crisis was real. Was it? Perhaps the notation on Gault's Patent Form 2-225, "Postage & Revenue Stamps," is a clue. Chicago Evening Journal, *October 31, 1862, p. 2. (Illinois State Library)*

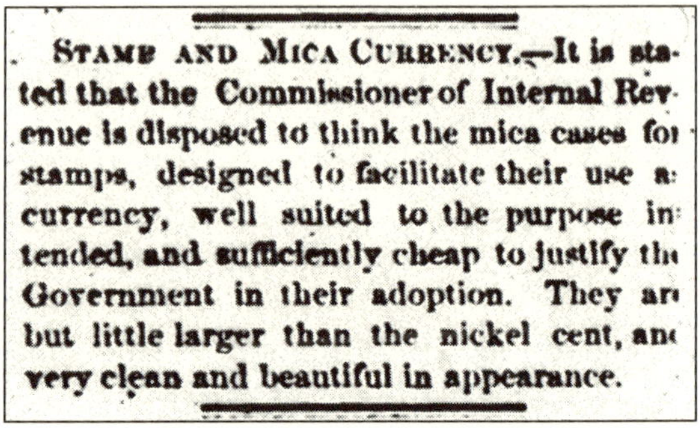

STAMP AND MICA CURRENCY.—It is stated that the Commissioner of Internal Revenue is disposed to think the mica cases for stamps, designed to facilitate their use as currency, well suited to the purpose intended, and sufficiently cheap to justify the Government in their adoption. They are but little larger than the nickel cent, and very clean and beautiful in appearance.

Such commendation from the influential New York daily newspaper editor is interesting. The same law of July 17 which monetized stamps for use in payment of dues to the United States from and after August 1, also should have prohibited the competitors to Gault's "New Metallic Currency" The precise language of the law reads: "That from and after the first day of August, 1862, no private corporation, banking association, firm, or individual shall make, issue, circulate or pay any note, check, memorandum, token, or other obligation, for a less sum than one dollar, intended to circulate as money or to be received or used in lieu of lawful money of the United States." On conviction, the penalties provided by the statute were a fine up to $500 and/or imprisonment up to six months.

It seems clear that Congress intended to prohibit the fractional shinplasters and the proliferating tokens and store cards. What is arguable is whether Congress would have considered the very kind of currency issue Gault contemplated forbidden. Sanctioning circulating stamps is one thing. Circulating stamp tokens with private advertising messages would appear to be another thing entirely. Yet Gault received the government's tacit approval when his patent was granted less than four weeks later. Gault wasted little time in instituting his plan once his patent was granted.

In addition to the military buttons Scovill was turning out by the thousands, the firm was also producing a wealth of photo medals marketed through Abbott & Co. in New York City and throughout the country via advertisements in the prominent periodicals of the day. These were the natural offspring of the popular campaign ferrotypes the firm had produced for the 1860 general election. The popular subjects of the day were George Washington and various of the Northern generals. In size, shape, and design they are very similar to Gault's encased stamps. It was easy for them to convert machinery and dies to Gault's product.

John Gault's initial output had grooved frame, Type A wrap arounds. This first emission was overwhelmingly five- and ten-cent ribbed (grooved) stamps: i.e. Reed JG05RB and Reed JG10RB. Although three-cent and one-cent stamps were the most commonly available, he practically eschewed these denominations. He was creating small change for circulation. Replacements for those two denominations were the most critical. Although silver three-cent coins and copper-nickel one-cent coins were becoming scarce, they were the last to be hoarded and bore the smallest premiums. These small government coins were the less "dear" in practical terms.

Figure 73a
Commissioner of Internal Revenue George S. Boutwell was a political ally of James C. Ayer, and also a former patent attorney. Either connection could have sparked interest in Gault's invention. (Internal Revenue Service, Del Ankers photo, 74-11132)

Gault's initial August output of this first order was about 25,000 pieces, which Gault offered to the public on a cost-plus basis. The convenience of Gault's medium appealed universally. The stamps expressed a recognized value. The public was already conditioned to accept this substitute and had shown it would also accept its limitations. Now, in Gault's stamp cases, the stamps were protected from deterioration. Their denominations were still clearly seen. The cases were uniform and round, and of a convenient size to facilitate their use in trade. In their silvered, brass cases Gault's coinage substitute was every bit equivalent to the hoarded government coinage. Whether their issue was prohibited by the strict construction of the act monetizing postage and other stamps was a moot point considering the financial dislocation of the day. Gault's substitute was much preferred to the heterogeneous paper scrip of questionable value being passed off on the public. Gault's case preserved the stamp's integrity as a postal document better than the other makeshifts as yet supplied. In the absence of the yet unavailable federal Postage Currency, they perfectly remedied the absence of the hoarded coinage.

The public's reaction to this neat and clean coinage substitute was the same as the

Figures 74a, b, c

Enigmatic pieces exist with non-standard stamps to perplex and delight collectors and historians. This ten-cent Gault encasement with an 1857 stamp (probably Scott Nos. 32, 33, or 35) is one such piece. It has been labeled a "trial" piece, but even if genuinely produced, why Gault would employ a demonetized stamp to produce such a queer duck remains speculative at best. Reed JG10'57. (Kagin's Numismatic Auctions photos)

newspaperman's. These stamp store cards were readily accepted as change and merchants offering them stood an excellent chance of being patronized. Is it any wonder that Gault was hailed for his ingenuity and that his new metallic currency was readily embraced? Is it any wonder the encased stamp won the sobriquet as the "happy solution to our common plight"? Gault's five- and ten-cent encased stamps were natural sellers. When he first sought to market his small change, he had no further to look than his own doorstep. He produced pieces in large quantities for sale to merchants at a premium as a convenience money with which to transact their commercial business. He had solved the chief drawbacks of the sticky gum backs.

Careful analysis demonstrates Gault's business plan:

(1) he produced JG05RB and JG10RB for sale at a premium (August)
(2) he produced IH05RB and IH10RB for sale to Irving House
(3) he urged public support of his plan in the press
(4) he produced BT03, BT05, BT10
(5) he produced AC03LA and AS03LG
  he produced AS SM (1-, 3-cents)
  he produced AC SA (1-, 3-cents), AP (1-, 3-cents), AS MD (1-, 3-cents)
(6) he produced JG05 and JG10 (September)
(7) he produced KG05 and KG10 (October)
(8) he urged IRS adoption of his plan
(9) he advertised encased stamps in newspapers (November)
(10) he produced the other encased stamps (various dates)
  5-, 10-cents for change-making (CO, EM, IH, JG, KG, SA, TH)
  3-, 5-, 10-cents balanced issue (BC, BE, BK, BT, BU, LT, ME, SB)
  1-, 3-cents for advertising (DO, DR, EV, TA, WH)
  1-cents for maximum exposure (AB, BA, CL, NA, ST)
  HO03, MI05, NO, PE03-05, SH03-05, WL10

> PROPOSED NEW POSTAL CURRENCY.—A Washington correspondent says that parties in New England propose a new style of postal currency. It is to inclose the Post Office (or postal currency) stamp in a circle of white metal, covered by a piece of mica making a circular metallic case with the stamp protected from the wear and tear of use. It has been approved by all who have seen it. It is stated that, at the present rate of issue of the postal currency, it will take eight years to bring out the fifty millions authorized by Congress. The inventors of this new style of currency propose to get up the stamps themselves at their own cost if allowed to issue these metallic currency. They think that by employing the button factories of New England they can very nearly supply the demand at such an advance as will be satisfactory to the bankers and to the public.

Figure 75a
It is likely that the "Washington correspondent" was a Munn & Co. staff lawyer who had approached the IRS Commissioner on Gault's behalf. Scientific American, *October 25, 1862, p. 259. (Dallas Public Library)*

The response to Gault's initial order was phenomenal. His September reorder of his own encased stamps (Reed JG05 and Reed JG10) was upwards of 100,000 pieces. While the intricacies of the customer orders are described in detail in the chapters devoted to each, it is worthy examining the possible scenario that the U.S. government might have been induced to adopt Gault's small change measures. As incredible as that sounds, notices in the press indicate that such a "trial balloon" went up for at least several weeks during the fall of 1862. This may be the most incredible part of the unfolding encased stamp saga. One wonders what the government might have chosen to advertise: INSURRECTIONS ARRESTED AT EARLIEST POSSIBLE OPPORTUNITY! In autumn 1862, the public wouldn't have believed it!

The first notice that something of the sort was under consideration was the Oct. 17 report out of Washington published in the New York *Times* the following day. Sourced to the *Times* Washington correspondent, it appears to indicate that federal officials were examining Gault's proposed currency as an alternative to the small fractional bills which were then being issued by the government. The notice is shown as Figure 67c. Precisely how the encased stamps came to the attention of the federal official, Revenue Commissioner George S. Boutwell may never be precisely known. Although fellow Massachusetts residents, a search of the IRS correspondence during the time in question revealed no extant record of correspondence directly between Gault and Boutwell.

A former patent attorney, Boutwell was a close friend and political ally of James Cook Ayer, Gault's principal client in the encased stamp venture. He had a long and distinguished public record, including two terms as Governor of Massachusetts. With his background and experience, Boutwell was an excellent choice to examine Gault's small change expedient on behalf of the government. As has been noted, the Internal Revenue Service was created by

Figure 76a

By fall Kirkpatrick & Gault were in high gear touting their small change substitute, as Editor Henry Raymond noted in his influential newspaper. New York *Times, October 8, 1862, p. 2. (Illinois State Library)*

NEAT AND HANDY – Messrs. Kirkpatrick & Gault, of this City, have struck upon a plan for the assistance of our currency-mud stuck people which is most neat & handy. It consists of an ingenious fixed arrangement of stamps in a circular frame with a mica covering, which can be used without detriment to the stamp & with convenience by the people. The cost will be but a trifle above the par value of the stamp, & much less than that of silver change.

the Act of July 1st. Boutwell entered upon his duties as commissioner July 12. His first responsibility was to set up the bureau. His immediate problems were myriad. His duties included carrying out the newly enacted laws and supplying brand new stamps for the multitude of documents and articles requiring payments. These were onerous enough without multiplying his obligations to include solving the change shortage, too!

From the very beginning, however, he had also been tasked by Secretary of the Treasury, Salmon P. Chase, to work out the details for implementing the legislation of July 17 which monetized stamps. Chase, too, had a million problems, of which "small change" was – well – simply "small change." With runs on postal stamp supplies, the lethargy in introducing the Postage Currency, and the squabbling going on between his department and Postmaster General Montgomery Blair's, Chase assigned Boutwell the equivalent task of a "quick fix." On his part, Boutwell considered his midwestern boss rather dull witted, slow of mind and rather preoccupied. Boutwell had a much higher opinion of himself.

If the *Times* report is to be believed the matter in question before Boutwell concerned the sanction of encasing revenue stamps. It is extremely intriguing that the report should specifically note "metal cases for revenue stamps" since the patent office tagging accompanying Gault's patent model makes reference to revenue stamps directly, too, and the act monetizing stamps passed on July 17 did indeed embrace "postage and other stamps of the United States." It is also known that at the time in question, the Treasury department was indeed considering aborting the paper fractional currency project and supplanting the Postage Currency "with a currency based on the issue of revenue stamps," at the suggestion of Secretary Chase. Such an issue would serve several purposes. It would disentangle the fractional currency from involvement with the Post Office both in the public's and official mind, and it would reaffirm the government position that paper currency was a means of raising revenue to prosecute the war effort. Of course, the idea was ultimately abandoned in favor of new legislation passed March 3, 1863, which provided for the issue of the Fractional Currency.

The Ayer connection is worth exploring. The Revenue Acts placed taxes on a wide variety of articles. In fact the greatest portion of Boutwell's time and energy in late summer and fall 1862 was formulating the schedules and determining rates for the various classes of goods. Manufacturers and merchants were in a real quandary over how much excise was to be exacted on the various items. Newspapers of the day are replete with numerous items list-

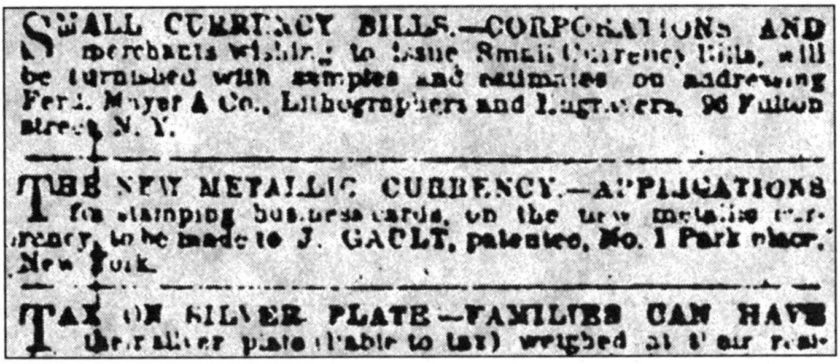

SMALL CURRENCY BILLS.—CORPORATIONS AND merchants wishing to issue Small Currency Bills, will be furnished with samples and estimates on addressing Ferd. Mayer & Co., Lithographers and Engravers, 96 Fulton street, N.Y.

THE NEW METALLIC CURRENCY.—APPLICATIONS for stamping business cards, on the new metallic currency, to be made to J. GAULT, patentee, No. 1 Park place, New York.

TAX ON SILVER PLATE—FAMILIES CAN HAVE their silver plate (liable to tax) weighed at

Figure 77a
Gault placed ads in strategic newspapers in the northeast and midwest soliciting clients. New York Herald, *November 6, 1862, p. 8. (Omaha Library)*

ing the tax decisions of the Treasury agents. As one of the leading vendors of taxable articles, James Cook Ayer of Lowell, Massachusetts, was most interested in these proceedings. His factory turned out millions of bottles of sarsaparilla, boxes of pills and other remedies that were required to bear tax stamps. His mills produced enormous quantities of yard goods. He was already engaged in other far-flung aspects of his growing financial empire. Each check or other official document associated with one of his enterprises required still more revenue stamps. It meant a great deal of money to this merchant capitalist. His renown and financial standing alone would have gained him a hearing with Washington bureaucrats on these matters. But he had much more going for him. Ayer was a close personal friend and Republican political ally of the very man whose job it was to implement the wide-ranging revenue laws. They were the same age and had many common interests. In prior years, Boutwell had represented the district in which Ayer lived in the Massachusetts legislature. In fact, when Boutwell eventually moved upstairs to the Secretary's job in Grant's Treasury Department, it was Ayer who vied for Boutwell's vacated U.S. congressional seat. Ayer's encased stamps were already in circulation. Is it so unreasonable an hypothesis that it was Ayer who interested Boutwell in Gault's stamp cases? We know from Boutwell's own testimony that he valued Ayer's opinions on public questions. Boutwell esteemed Ayer's industry and business acumen. Ayer was forthright and frank in making his ideas known. Boutwell recalled his friend's advice as "sound, frank, resolute and consistent."

However, an alternately strong case can be made for the patent office connection. Prior to his appointment as Commissioner of Internal Revenue, Boutwell had been a patent attorney with considerable experience. His familiarity with the patent system would have left him friends there and it would have been natural for him to be apprised of the new stamp case invention in his new official capacity. However, another notice in the press seems to offer testimony in this regard (see Figure 75a). A remarkable article appeared in *Scientific American* on October 25, 1862. By 1862 Munn & Co. had acted as patent attorneys for more than 17,000 inventors, including John Gault on several occasions. Their influence was considerable and highly regarded at the Patent Office. Former Commissioner Joseph Holt, praised the company's energy and uncompromising fidelity in working in its clients' best interests. Its weekly periodical, *Scientific American*, was the publication of record in its field. According to an insider, "It not unfrequently (sic) happens that after having procured a patent for an inventor, he comes to them for advice as to the best plan to realize (make money from) it." Munn & Co. had influence with the Patent Office examining corps, the same source adds. We know Munn & Co. were assisting Gault with his artillery shell venture. We also know that he had enlisted their aid in connection with his encased stamp patent. Of course, neither hypothesis is mutually exclusive. Other circumstances may also have contributed. At this very time Holt himself was in the process of evaluating Gault's partner William Barkalow's contracts with the government regarding importation of British rifles. He ultimately decided in Barkalow's favor and extended the terms of his contract with the government. A Gault family friend named Conant was one of the insiders at the Patent Office. Allegedly Gault gifted President Lincoln with a gold-plated set of encased stamps in the full range of values. Prominent Republican newspaper editors endorsed the proposal in their columns. Additional circumstances, not yet known, may have intervened.

Although such circumstantial evidence is not conclusive, what is clear from the range of press reports, however, is that for two weeks in October 1862, the Federal government was considering adopting John Gault's metal and mica emergency money. He could have indeed made a million dollars, as he later purportedly alleged. How close he may actually have been to achieving such patriotic and commercial success by having his patent currency become the primary circulating medium of the change-strapped country may never be known. Ultimately the very independent and assertive Boutwell KO'd the complicated scheme of printing stamps and then enclosing them in die struck brass and mineral containers for use as change. It is clear from Treasury records that he was ultimately and solely responsible for settling the issue. His boss' standing advice upon any inquiry from Boutwell was "decide for yourself." No matter what pressures were brought to bear on him from outside, the very independent-minded public servant knew his own mind on the matter. He considered himself an excellent judge of mechanics and invention. His long past experience had exposed him to the whims and caprice of inventors and had left him suitably able to judge the relative merits of such a proposal. Apparently he did and turned Gault down. Soon thereafter, Boutwell was elected to the U.S. House of Representatives, although he filled out his term at IRS until he took his seat in Congress March 3, 1863. At the top of the agenda: passage of the Fractional Currency bill. The United States embarked on a remedy of small fractional notes and die struck brass (bronze) and copper-nickel token coinage to solve its change woes. John Gault was out of the picture.

Is it any coincidence, then, that immediately his advertisements began appearing in newspapers in New York City, Chicago and elsewhere? Encased stamps were still a good idea and a government remedy was months, even years off in getting control of the matter. The problem didn't go away just because a Washington official had acted. There was still money to be made for a bright, aggressive inventor named Gault.

Auction Census Data Summary, 1891-1994

	1	2	3	5	10	12	24	30	90	Total	Pct
JG	45	18	44	185	259	93	92	63	43	842	
JG RB	11		13	110	71	12	11	9	1	238	
JG '57					1					1	
Blank	3		2	1						6	
	59	**18**	**59**	**296**	**331**	**105**	**103**	**72**	**44**	**1087**	**12.1%**

Irving House
Chapter IV

After securing his patent, John Gault sought out clients for his "New Metallic Currency." Already ensconced in New York City promoting his artillery shells with his partner William V. Barkalow, he had no further to look than down Broadway to the elegant Irving House. The hotel had recently come under the new management of George W. Hunt and Charles W. Nash. The hotel's proprietors were well aware of the small change shortage. They were already circulating the small stamp envelopes in amounts of 10-cents (cf. Figure 84a) and possibly other values as well. Gault, eager for a quick sale, demonstrated the superiority of his product sharing samples of his five- and ten-cent encased stamps with the merchants. He quickly struck a bargain with these progressive innkeepers who were trying to put their best feet forward in the competitive New York hotel trade. As Gault's first customer, the design of their unique advertising message was problematical. There was no precedent. They settled on a virtual copy of the message on their stamp envelopes: i.e. in descending order (1) the hotel's name, IRVING HOUSE; (2) its location, [NEW YORK] BROADWAY & 12TH ST.; (3) its terms, EUROPEAN PLAN; and (4) its management, HUNT & NASH PROPT. The contents message about stamps and denomination was unnecessary (Gault's unique case took care of that), so the bottom third of the stamp case contains Gault's patent information. The design is unique in that Gault's information is presented in a type style and size commensurate with the other items on the piece. This was a

Figure 79a
Reed IH05 obverse, ex-James F. Ruddy specimen. (Bowers and Merena photo)

Figure 80a

The Irving House was an imposing structure on Broadway at the corner of Chambers Street, opposite the forerunner of today's Tiffany jewelers. Outside antebellum Broadway teemed with a parade of horse drawn vehicles and pedestrian traffic. Woodcut. Gleason's Pictorial Drawing-Room Companion, *March 11, 1854. (Dallas Public Library)*

real coup for Gault, and became a virtual advertising piece for the patent holder as well as for the proprietors of the hotel.

Hunt's and Nash's order was a large one, a thousand dollars. Gault raced to Waterbury to have the pieces struck. The order called for about 10,000 encased stamps, equally split between five- and ten-cent values. The cost to Hunt and Nash was $750 face value for those stamps, $200 for the cases at $20/1000, and probably about $10 die cutting charges. Gault also delivered a small number of pieces in the other values to round out the order. Scovill filled the order with wrap around rims cut from the grooved button stock, and silvered just like Gault's pieces. These are the fairly common varieties collectors know today as Reed IH05RB and Reed IH10RB. These are the *only* encased stamps, other than Gault's initial, August output to be issued with the grooved (ribbed) wrap-around frames. The "New Metallic Currency" was an instant hit with the hotel's proprietors and clientele. They were proud to see their store cards in circulation – after all the next city business directory would not be out for nearly a year. After a time the initial amount was put into circulation, and Hunt and his partner placed a second order with Gault. The second order was for a like number of plain frame (Type B) pieces, but this time the hotel proprietors desired a wider assortment of face values for their stamp cards. The order was filled with significant numbers of three- and twelve-cent stamps and a smattering of the others, too, although the largest quantities were again the five- and ten-cent workhorse change-making values (Reed IH05 and Reed IH10).

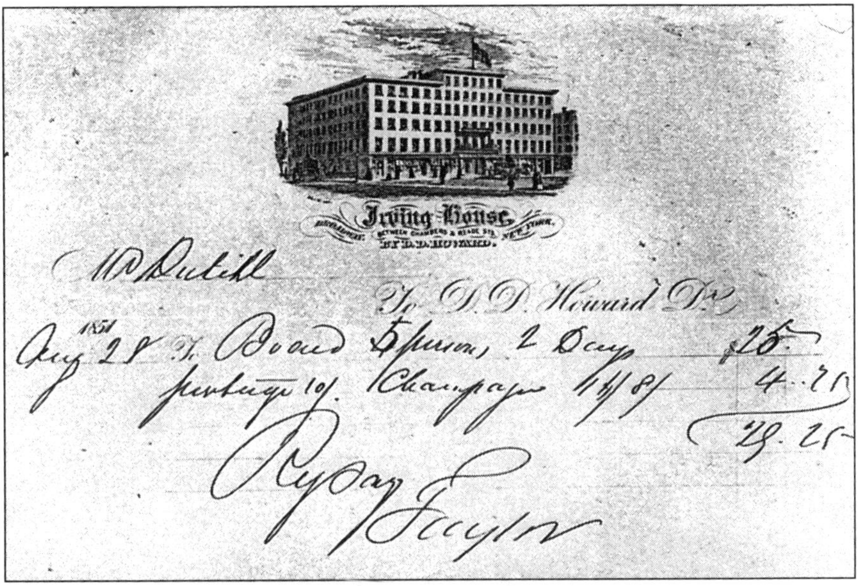

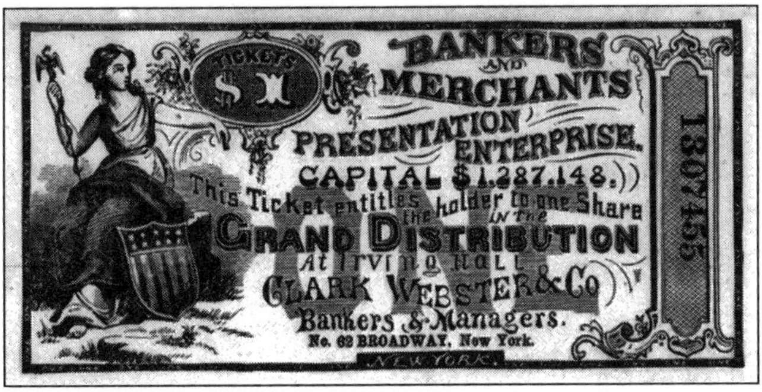

Figures 81a, b

In 1851, five people could board two days and drink Champagne for $30, a month's income for many. (New-York Historical Society) A day's wages could.buy a lottery ticket in the hotel arcade. (Author's collection)

Irving House was one of a series of fine hotels on Broadway's west side opposite City Hall and its park. Also located there were the famous Astor House, the North American Hotel and the Park Place Hotel. The Irving House, in the block between Reade and Chambers Streets, was the last large hotel to be built in the city in the first half of the 19th century. Capt'n Dan Howard, who had cashed in his chips on the Howard Hotel earlier, constructed and outfitted the hotel lavishly. Fixtures reportedly cost $150,000 alone. Among Howard's innovations were the city's first bridal suite. A contemporary account called these chambers "love bowers where Eve might have whispered love to Adam after she was expelled from paradise, without regretting the change." At its center the hotel was six stories high; its wings were one story less. The facade was occupied by small merchants, including a pharmacy, a book seller, and a tailor, all of whom benefitted from the immense Broadway pedestrian traffic. The hotel had a splendid second-story balcony facing Broadway.

Figure 82a

On December 6, 1851, a grand reception parade was held for Hungarian dissident Louis Kossuth, shown in progress passing before the Irving House. Brown and Severin lithograph, the Edward W. C. Arnold collection, Metropolitan Museum of Art. (Museum of the City of New York photo)

Named for America's first distinguished man of letters, Washington Irving, the hotel played host to visiting foreign and local dignitaries who were attracted by its fashionable halls, salons and rooms. Jenny Lind lodged there when she came to New York from Europe in 1850. She was feted by her host P. T. Barnum. Within 10 minutes of her arrival at the Irving House, a crowd estimated at 20,000 people congregated along Broadway outside the hotel. An eye witness recorded the scene for posterity:

> Jenny Lind has arrived, and was received with such a spontaneous outbreak of rushing, and crowding, and hurrahing, and serenading as this city has never seen before. The streets round the Irving House [are] blocked up with a mob night and day; horses hardly [are] permitted to carry her through the streets. So vehemently did the mob thirst for the honor of drawing her carriage, and so on. A great chorus urged her to appear on the balcony. At nightfall a 200-piece band, accompanied by 300 uniformed firemen carrying lit torches, arrived to serenade the singer. Barnum escorted his starlet onto the Irving House balcony amid a thunderous applause. The mania continued for weeks.

The next year a similar outpouring greeted Louis Kossuth's arrival following the Hungarian Revolution and consequent political turmoil. "Magyar-mania" gripped New Yorkers who streamed around his headquarters at the Irving House for a glimpse of the exile. Kossuth's purpose was fund raising to back his political movement. A contemporary lithograph of his public reception indicates the extent to which the Hungarian's struggle for

Figures 83a, b

John L. Tucker preceded Hunt and Nash as proprietor of the Irving House and instituted the "European Plan" which he brought from Boston's famed Tremont House. He was related by marriage to the Gage brothers, proprietors of Chicago's Tremont House. Southworth and Hawes daguerreotype. The Metropolitan Museum of Art, gift of I. N. Phelps Stokes, Edward S. Hawes, Alice Mary Hawes, Marion Augusta Hawes, 1937. (Metropolitan Museum of Art photo) Ad, *below,* Cowell's New York Business Directory, *1861, p. 118. (New-York Historical Society photo)*

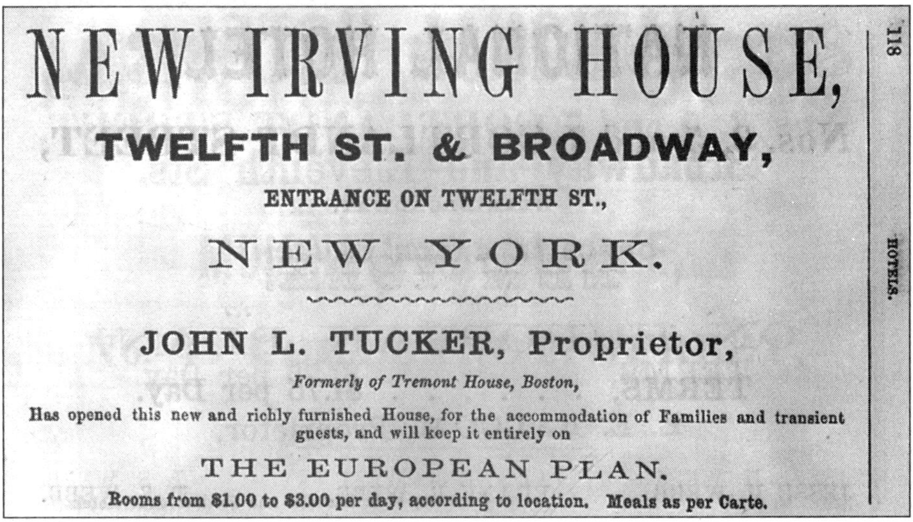

political independence from Austria excited the democratic sympathies of the American people as he toured the U.S. "There was no other person of a foreign race and language of whose name and career as much was known," a contemporary observed.

A bill from that era indicates five people boarded at the hotel for two nights for $25 in August, 1851. Later in the decade the New Irving House was relocated farther north on Broadway at 12th Street, just south of Union Square, then one of the finest residential dis-

Figure 84a
In 1862 Hunt and Nash seized upon the advantages of the small stamp envelopes in promoting their hotel. The relatively small value of this envelope, 10-cents, indicates that advertising promotion was paramount in ordering this medium. Friedberg No. 69. (Milton R. Friedberg)

tricts in town. The hotel came under the management of Boston's revered inn keeper John L. Tucker, formerly of Boston's famous Tremont Hotel. As host of that prestigious Boston showplace, Tucker was a popular figure in that city for a tenure spanning two decades. During that time he played host to Dickens, Andrew Jackson, Thackeray, de Tocqueville and similar luminaries. He introduced such innovations as private, locking rooms, gas lighting and bathrooms with running water. Upon his retirement in 1851 a lavish party was thrown in his honor.

What lured him out of retirement was the challenge and opportunity the Irving House afforded. Hotel keeping in New York was a profitable venture since the city had the largest transient population of any city in the country. "Thousands come and go daily, and they all pour a constant stream of money in the coffers of the hotels," a contemporary observed. Tucker brought his successful principles of hotel management with him to New York. These included the so-called "European Plan," which Tucker had first introduced in Boston. This plan consisted of separate charges for room and board in contrast to the standard of the day which entitled the guest to literally all the food he could eat – all day long. Under Tucker's plan, an *a la carte* dining service replaced the smorgasbord *table d'hote*. Meals were served in Irving Hall, which also was the site for a local lottery.

In summer 1862, in the middle of the small change crisis, Tucker turned over the reigns of the hotel to George W. Hunt. Tucker's departure left big shoes to fill. Lured by the lucrative opportunities for large profits and the small risks entailed by taking over an established venture, Hunt must have felt good about his chances. To secure his future, however, Hunt enticed local restaurateur Charles W. Nash into co-management of the hotel. Nash had been the proprietor of a successful eating-house on Nassau Street for several years. The pair quickly seized upon the small stamp envelopes to publicize their joint proprietorship of the hotel. This was important since a new business directory was many months away. As indicated by both the stamp envelope and the New Metallic Currency they ordered from John Gault, the new proprietors continued the European Plan, which well served their divisions of labor. Hunt received proceeds from daily and weekly rentals of the parlors and sleeping apartments, while Nash received revenues from the food service.

The mica and brass store cards they purchased from Gault were of prestige as well as

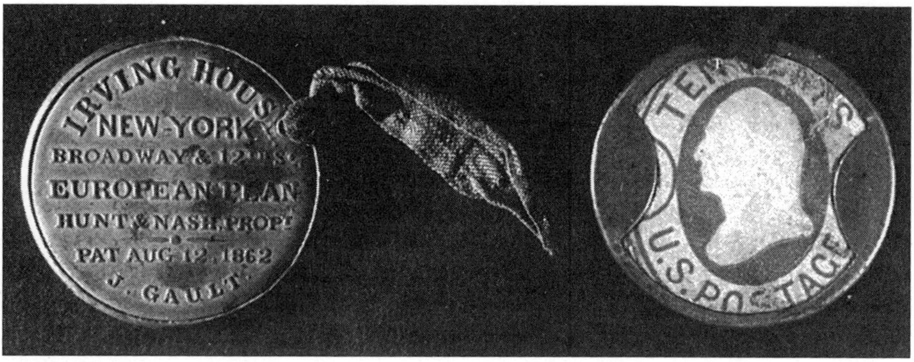

Figures 85a, b

As Gault's first customer, the obverse (merchant) design for his encased stamps was not yet standardized. Interestingly, the design chosen for the IH issue mirrors closely that which Hunt and Nash had employed on their postage stamp envelopes, shown on the opposite page. The enigmatic piece, above, contains an 1861 ten-cent envelope stamp (Scott No. U34) and was holed for suspension. Reed IH10ES. (Dr. Robert D. Gardner collection, Dabney C. Jackson photos)

advertising value. In a city famous for its public houses, Hunt and Nash were only too happy to put their names on the pocket change of every man and woman in town. Hunt continued to manage the hotel through the war years, during which he prospered greatly. Shortly following cessation of the hostilities, he remodeled and enlarged the hotel. The Broadway entrance thereafter became the principal portal for guests. In July 1868, New York's Tammany Hall played host to the national Democratic Party nominating convention. The nearby Irving House was reportedly a "hot-bed of button-holing, political arm-twisting, horse-trading and other hyphenated bargaining." Shortly thereafter, Hunt resigned from management of the hotel. He continued to remain prominent, however, and when he died in July 1877, the New York *Times* carried obituaries of him on consecutive days.

Charlie Nash was quite a bit younger than his partner, Hunt. He was only connected with the Irving House management for a short period, leaving the hotel in spring 1863. At that time he also closed down his restaurant on Nassau Street, which he had continued to operate. Apparently he took up arms and served in the northern Army two years. When he returned to New York in April, 1865 he opened a saloon in the *Tribune* building. The following year, he was admitted to partnership in the restaurant firm of Crook, Fox and Nash, a favored rendezvous for the midday crowd. This enterprise thrived in the post-war years. It was so well patronized that late comers were turned away at the door regularly.

By 1872 Nash had succeeded his former partners. The successor firm of Nash and Fuller was among the best restaurants in the city. According to a contemporary view:

> Some of the best restaurants in the city are those in which a lady is never seen. It must not be supposed that they are disreputable places. They are entirely the opposite. They are located in the lower part of the city, often in some by-street of the heavy business section, and are patronized chiefly by merchants and clerks, who come here to get lunch and dinner. The fare is excellent and the prices are reasonable.

That source calls Nash's one of the very best of this type of eatery, but he was progressive,

Figures 86a, b

Unlisted, Reed IH12RB with an 1851 12-cent black stamp (Scott 17). This enigmatic piece sports a demonetized stamp. (Kagin Numismatic Auctions photo)

too. Going a step farther than most of his competitors, he offered, in addition to his main dining room, a separate facility for ladies, whether dining alone, in groups or accompanied by an escort. He had operated such a Ladies Dining Hall at the Irving House to good advantage. This innovation proved popular here, too. Nash prospered greatly and lived to an advanced age.

George P. Harlow managed the Irving House after George Hunt left. In the 1870s, although it would still be recalled as "fashionable," by then the city's horsey trade had bid the Irving adieu. Larger, more sumptuous hotels were the order of the day and New York was blessed with many new "models of their kind." A guidebook to the city written in 1872, for example, failed to even mention the Irving House, although literally dozens of other hotels were commented upon favorably.

As noted, the Irving House encasement is highly individualistic in style. Several difficulties in the letter punches are apparent. Among these, the ampersand and at least the "1" of "12th" are repunched, as is the "U" in GAULT. In addition to the regular encased stamp issues, a series of curious pieces exists. These include pieces with the demonetized one-, three-, ten- and twelve-cent stamps of the Series of 1851, as well as with the two-cent Internal Revenue Stamp, and three- and ten-cent envelope stamps. A highly distinctive piece belonged to Ben Green. When his large collection of encased stamps was displayed at the 1911 convention of the American Numismatic Association, Edgar Adams commented: "One of the oddities was issued by Hunt and Nash . . . which contains an unused brick-red one-penny English stamp." This anomaly is encased in a grooved (ribbed) frame.

Auction Census Data Summary, 1891-1994

	1	**2**	**3**	**5**	**10**	**12**	**24**	**30**	**90**	**Total**	**Pct**
IH	9		20	37	33	22	12	9		142	
IH RB	3		5	80	73	5	5			171	
IH '51	1									1	
IH '51 RB						1				1	
IH '61 ES					2					2	
	13		**25**	**117**	**108**	**28**	**17**	**9**		**317**	**3%**

John I. Brown
Chapter V

Arguably, Gault could have sold additional merchants on the virtues of his New Metallic Currency prior to leaving New York City, however apparently he did not. His next customized pieces were for legendary Boston pharmacist John I. Brown. Once again, the parties borrowed the design for the encased stamp store card directly from an already created advertising piece which the merchant favored. Trademarks and trade styles were even then deemed very important in business, especially with literacy less than universal. So for Brown's order Gault delivered encased stamps patterned largely from the trade mark for his famous Bronchial Troches. As may be readily seen on the several trademarks reproduced on various products in this chapter, the sans serif lettering with the rolling BRONCHIAL is virtually identical to the styles shown in Figures 90b and 93a. The message is identical to the later. As happened when preparing the earlier Irving House piece, the letter cutter had difficulty positioning his message: FOR and AND are oddly out of place. The addition of Gault's patent information is largely an afterthought on the Type I (plain, without the 100+ raised balls around the border) merchant obverses. All wrap-arounds are plain (Type B).

The Brown order was a large one, probably in excess of 20,000 pieces in all. Unlike the new proprietors of the New York City hotel, the Boston pharmacist was already well known and his product was already universally familiar. Thus his order is more well-rounded than the Irving House order, meaning a more even distribution of denominations (i.e. Reed

Figure 87a

Reed BT05 obverse, ex-James F. Ruddy specimen. (Bowers and Merena photo)

Figures 88a, b, c

Ad, right, Adams's (sic) Boston Directory, 1848 - July -1849. *(Dallas Public Library). Below, the evolution of Brown's cough drops appears on package labels. The product's trade name changed from Brown's Bronchial Troches, the product's style at the time Brown used Gault's encased stamps. Ad detail from* Boston Sights and Strangers Guide, *1856, p. [257]. (Author's collection) Later it became Brown's Troches due to greater scrutiny of advertising claims in a later era. Label, c. 1930. (Author's collection)*

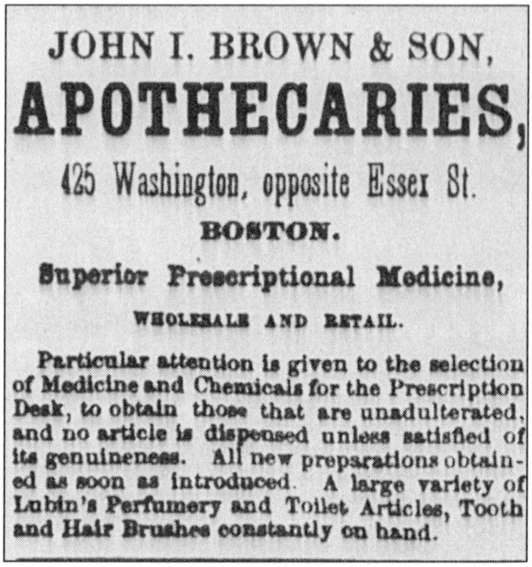

JOHN I. BROWN & SON,

APOTHECARIES,

425 Washington, opposite Essex St.

BOSTON.

Superior Prescriptional Medicine,

WHOLESALE AND RETAIL.

Particular attention is given to the selection of Medicine and Chemicals for the Prescription Desk, to obtain those that are unadulterated, and no article is dispensed unless satisfied of its genuineness. All new preparations obtained as soon as introduced. A large variety of Lubin's Perfumery and Toilet Articles, Tooth and Hair Brushes constantly on hand.

BT03, BT05 and BT10 are evenly distributed, with much smaller amounts of one- and twelve-cent values).

By the time he purchased space on the back of John Gault's New Metallic Currency, John Isaac Brown and Son was regarded as one of Boston's venerable tradesmen. According to the Boston *Journal* of the day, Brown stood among the first rank of chemists in that city. The firm's stock in trade, its Brown's Bronchial Troches for Coughs and Colds was a widely used throat lozenge of its day. The cough drops can correctly be pronounced either tro-kees or troshes. The common folk of that era probably preferred the latter. Brown introduced this medication in 1850 and they became immensely popular in the years before the war, although they were only sold in prepackaged small quantities at 25 cents a box. Brown was a heavy advertiser for his era relying on personal endorsements from those reliant upon their voices, largely ministers, teachers, singers, lawyers and lecturers. He took every advantage he could to make his product visible. In this regard his interest in Gault's store cards was natural.

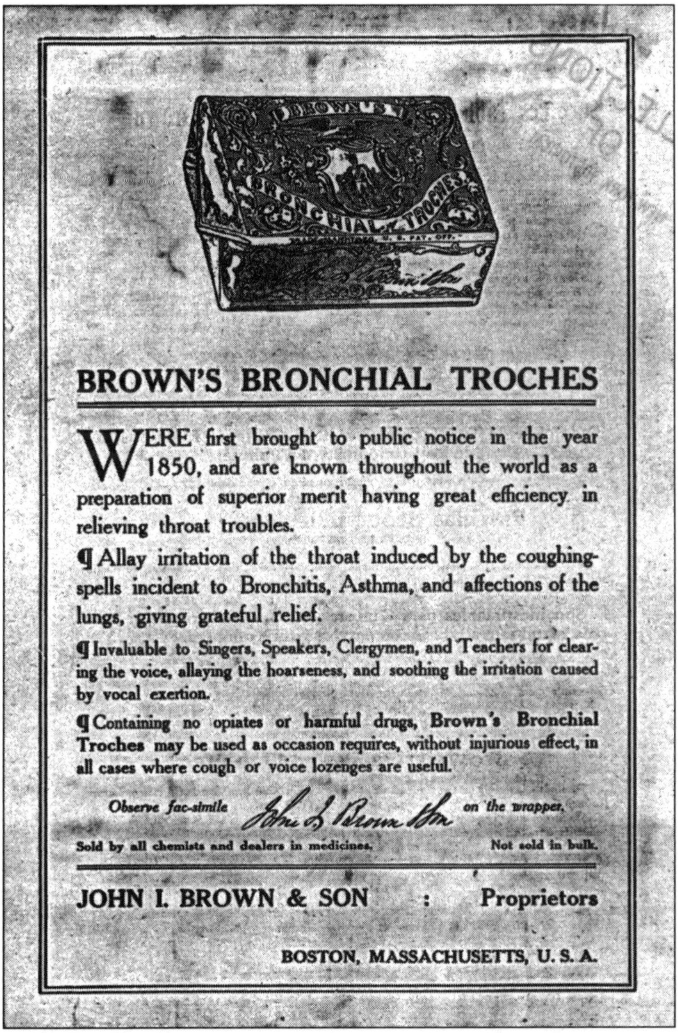

Figures 89a, b
Left, Brown's Bronchial Troches was a staple over the counter cough remedy for nearly a century. It contained licorice, cubebs, conium, gum arabic and sugar. Advertising handbill. (New-York Historical Society) Below ad, Boston Daily Evening Transcript, *February 3, 1853, p. [4] (Author's collection)*

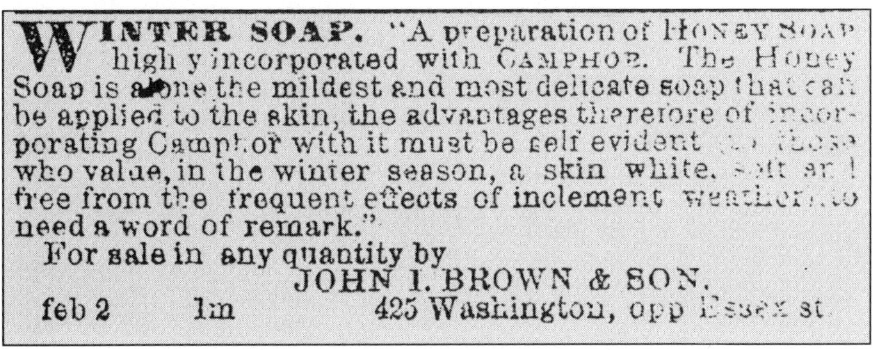

"Brown's Bronchial Troches."—Rev. Charles S. Robinson, late of Troy, now of Brooklyn, N. Y., writes of *Brown's Bronchial Troches*; "Rev. Mr. Booth gave me two or three from his pocket, a few years ago, recommending me to make a trial of them, for he had found them beneficial. I have kept them on hand ever since, and found them very serviceable after the weariness of speaking, as well as allaying the irritation consequent on a cold."

Figures 90a, b
Testimonial advertising was a cornerstone of Brown's success. Top, ad, New York Times, *April 18, 1864, p. 5. (Illinois State Library) The inspiration for the design of the BT issue is clear. Brown's logo was copied on his encased stamp, down to the rolling lettering of* BRONCHIAL. *There was good reason for Brown to prefer that design for his encased stamps. He trademarked his logo in 1856 and had spent time and money to build its franchise. Metallic pill box. (Dr. Robert D. Gardner collection, Dabney C. Jackson photo)*

Unlike many of his competitors his troches contained no opiates. His advertising is understated for his era, making few of the wild claims we associate with nostrums of the mid-19th century. Brown himself wanted it that way, according to an insider. Brown's ads are invariably small and often used a cut or picture, which was not characteristic of his competitors. But Brown's ads were well placed and widely dispersed in the periodicals of his day. Typical of his techniques was the ad which appeared during the Civil War in the New York *Times*:

> Reverend Mr. (William) Booth gave me two or three [Brown's Bronchial Troches] from his pocket, a few years ago, recommending me to make a trial of

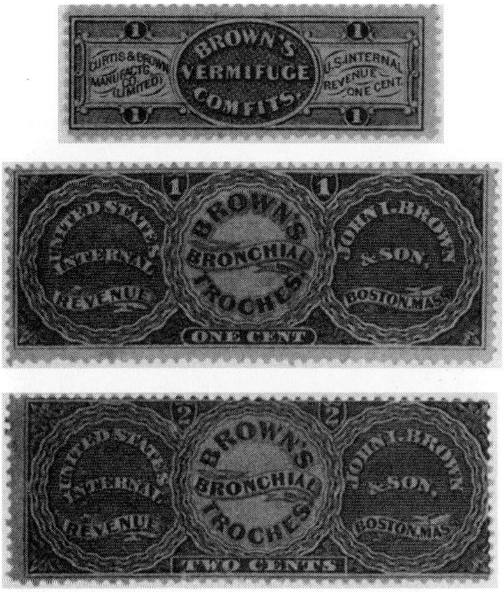

Figures 91a, b, c

The Revenue Acts passed to finance the Civil War included taxation on many objects, proprietary medicines being prime examples. Private die medicine stamps affixed to bottle tops or package seals attested to payment of these fees. Attractive, and collectable in their own rights, the John I. Brown issues feature the logos of his principle products. From top, Scott Nos. RS71, RS39, RS40. (All specimens, Author's collection)

> them, for he had found them beneficial. I have kept them on hand every since, and found them very serviceable after the weariness of speaking, as well as allaying the irritation consequent on a cold.

The practice of obtaining endorsements from prominent ministers in that era was equivalent to today's practice of signing sports heroes as spokesmen. Ads of that period appearing in periodicals give endorsements from ministers in Illinois, New York, Massachusetts and elsewhere. Academics, editors, and even Christian periodicals endorsed the troches. Thespians, too, could be counted on to endorse such a wonderful product. In the era before microphones and surround sound, the voice was even more critical to the success of a stage performer. A highly individualistic poster depicts Adah Isaacs Menken, one of last century's most illustrious femme fatales, in her memorable climactic scene from her rendition of Byron's play, "Mazeppa," touting Brown's troches. So universally popular it was, yet so mild, that even children and babies were said to benefit from the lozenges' effects, Brown affirmed.

But we have more than such self-interested candor by which to judge Brown's product, however trustworthy and upstanding the principled men (and women) who endorsed these troches were. Brown's remedy, it seems, achieved the status worthy of being copied. If imitation is indeed the sincerest form of flattery, Brown may have taken some solace in the left-handed compliment handed him and his troches by a New York City apothecary in 1863. Early that year, Brown advised his customers of this unsavory turn of affairs. "The good effects resulting from the use of the Troches, and their extended use, has caused them to be counterfeited," Brown exclaimed. "Be sure to guard against worthless imitations," he warned. The medicine's proprietor may have been flattered, but that did not keep him from pressing suit against William Leith, a drug broker of New York, charging him with counterfeiting and imitating, and selling spurious imitations of the articles bearing "the trade mark, labels, wrapper, box & c. of Brown's Bronchial Troches." Leith was arrested in December of

Figure 92a

The reverse of this attractive advertising trade card for Brown's dentifrice includes health tips on what to do until the doctor arrived. Maladies covered were sunstroke, choking and fainting. "Keep this handy, it may save a life," the card urges. (Author's collection)

that year, and convicted in the Court of General Sessions the following spring. He was sentenced to nine months in the penitentiary. As a drug broker, Leith was well able to judge which preparations were most worthy (and profitable!) to imitate. So well known was Brown's preparation that the story of Leith's conviction made front page news as far away as Cincinnati.

After winning his case in court, Brown made hay of the skullduggery practiced by the miscreant drug broker. Brown turned the counterfeiting brouhaha to his own distinct advantage by thereafter proclaiming that his troches must be good to be counterfeited. A handbill at the New-York Historical Society is particularly piquant in this regard. On it Brown warns in four languages – English, French, Spanish, and Dutch – not to accept substitutes. "Buy only those boxes bearing the facsimile [signature of] John I. Brown & Son on the wrapper," the handbill cautions.

The originator of this product, John I. Brown was born October 31, 1790 in Little Compton, R.I. At 17 years of age, he took employment with Dr. Stephen Thayer in Boston. Reaching majority in 1811, he remained a clerk in Thayer's employ for an additional year before buying out his mentor, thus becoming the first of four siblings to pursue the pharmaceutical trade in Boston. He married Rebecca Miller in 1824, and established his firm as John I. Brown, Druggist the following year at the 425 Washington Street address he was to occupy for many years. During the ensuing years he took several of his sons into his employ. These along with additional pharmacists trained by his brothers during the period created a

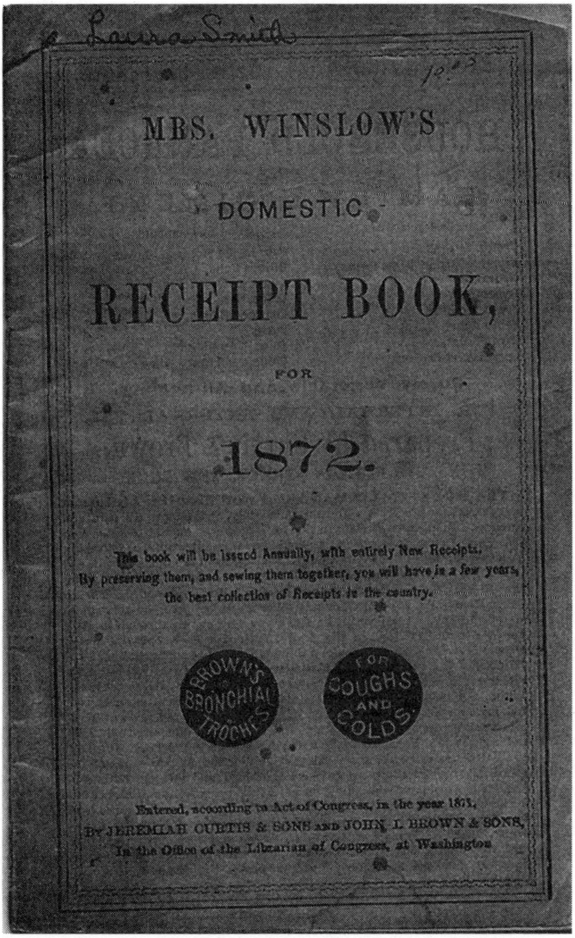

Figure 93a
In the parlance of its times, Mrs. Winslow's Domestic Receipt *(sic)* Book *was produced to appeal to mothers, who would purchase Mrs. Winslow's Soothing Syrup and other products in Brown's pharmacopoeia. Today, we would call such a publication a recipe book, filled as it was with culinary tips laced with advertising pitches.* *(Author's collection)*

veritable army of younger disciples in the city's drug trade. Brown retired from his firm in 1870 after 63 years as a druggist, and died at age 92 as "the oldest apothecary in Boston," according to his obituary. He died of gangrene of the foot. His eulogies were many and splendidly wrought. He was commended for the excellence of his character, his mild-mannered disposition, and his civic attitudes. A large crowd turned out to pay their respects.

With the passing of the firm's founder, the younger members of the firm merged interests with the Curtis brothers of Brooklyn. "The two drug firms came to be associated by marriage much in the way feudal kingdoms and European empires had been linked in a matrimonial knot," a contemporary observed. Their joint venture eventually became the Anglo American Drug Co. The Curtis brothers were proprietor to many products including the infamous Mrs. Winslow's Soothing Syrup. The product's namesake was purportedly a pediatric physician with 30 years experience. Due to extensive advertising her name became so widely known that other products pirated her identity. Unfortunately, this product with the

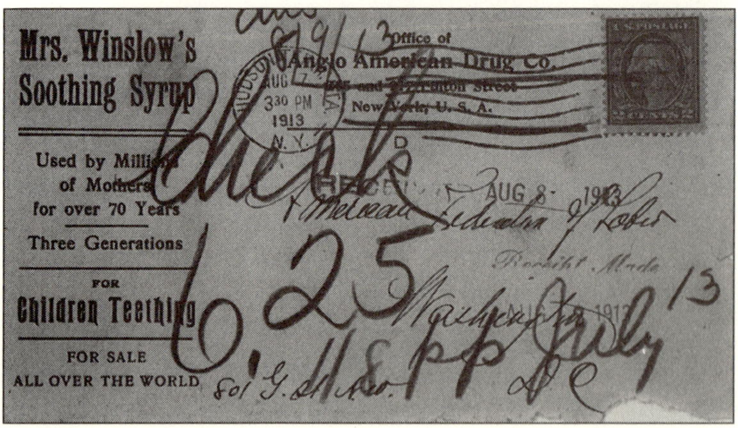

Figures 94a, b, c
Brown inherited a public relations disaster when Mrs. Winslow's tonic was subjected to the sharp pen of the muckraking press. Although Brown changed the constituents of the medication, the bad press led to the product's demise. Proprietary die revenue stamp (Scott RS68), advertising trade card, advertising cover: ex-Samuel Gompers, American Federation of Labor correspondence. (All, Author's collection)

mild sounding name became one of the most vilified of its era leading to disgrace for the Brown connection to it. Advertised widely as the ideal product to comfort crying infants, it was in reality based on an opium derivative, containing both morphine and alcohol. The alcohol content alone was 60 percent, or 120 proof, a stiff beverage by any standard. Infant deaths resulted. Over time such occurrences came to the attention of the popular press. Soon parents became irate over these "baby killing medicines" and many drug stores refused to carry such a product. "Patent medicines are poisoning people throughout America today,"

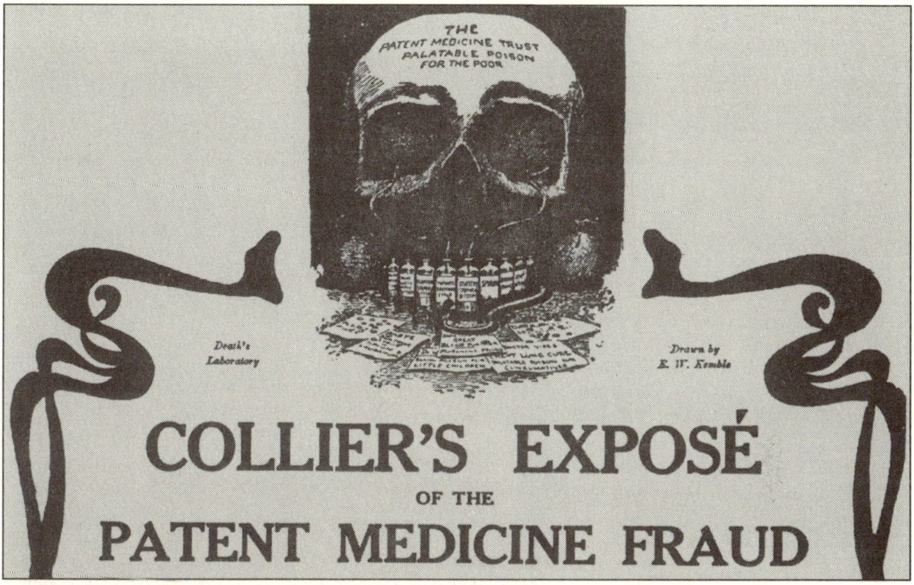

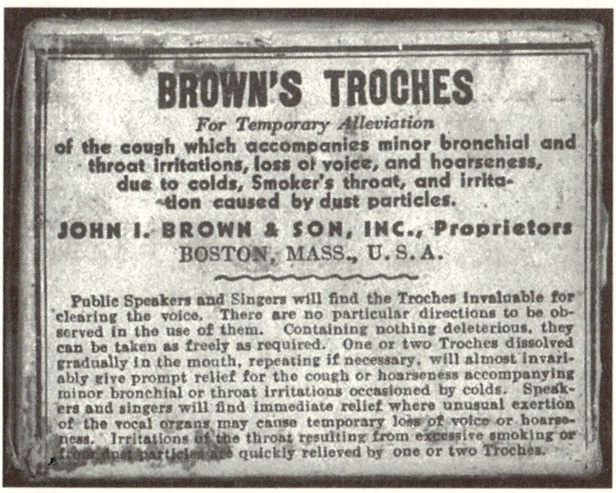

Figures 95a, b

Above, muckraking journalists called public attention to the unwholesome effects of some proprietary medicines. Collier's, 1906. *(Texas Christian University Library) In 1906, the Pure Food and Drug Act brought changes to both Mrs. Winslow's teething syrup and Brown's cough drops. Left, Brown's lozenges sold for 35 cents a box when this box of troches was sold. (Author's collection)*

Samuel Hopkins Adams charged in an influential expose in *Collier's* magazine. "Babies who cry are fed laudanum under the name of syrup." Federal authorities charged the Anglo-American Drug Co. with mislabeling on June 12, 1915. Its label claimed only five percent alcohol. Convicted, 10 months later, the company was fined $100. Shortly thereafter the alcohol and opiates were removed. Ironically, the version of Mrs. Winslow's sold in Great Britain never did contain the morphine because stricter British laws would have required the word POISON to be stamped on such a preparation.

As was the case with Irving House, the hand cut die here upon close inspection reveals a great degree of recutting, especially around the W of BROWN'S, the H of BRONCHIAL, the C of TROCHES, the Cs of both COUGHS and COLDS and especially around AND.

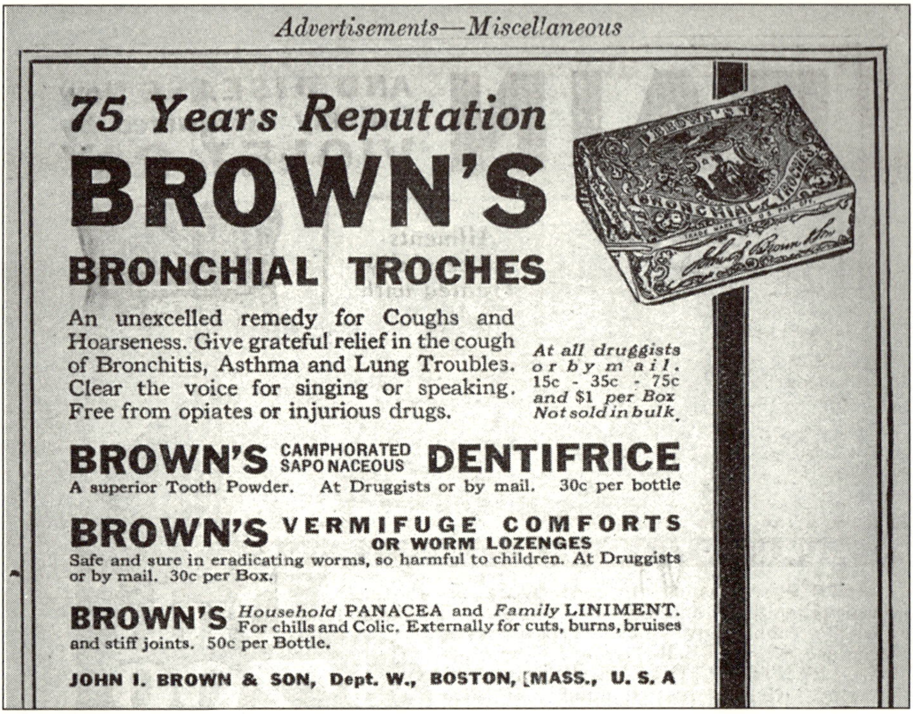

Figure 96a

The troches continued to headline Brown's product line well into this century. Ad, World Almanac, *1929, p. 914. (Author's collection)*

Auction Census Data Summary, 1891-1994

	1	2	3	5	10	12	24	30	90	Total	Pct
BT	16		70	80	63	18	3	3		253	3%
	16		**70**	**80**	**63**	**18**	**3**	**3**		**253**	**3%**

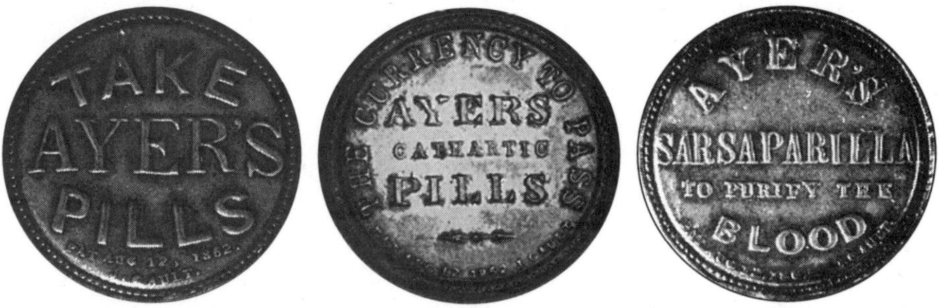

James C. Ayer
Chapter VI

Although not his first customer, James Cook Ayer proved to be John Gault's best customer. In fact, if Ayer had been Gault's *only* customer the venture would have been a success. Ayer's pharmaceutical empire was located in Lowell, Massachusetts, an industrial mill town located 26 miles northwest of Boston. For a year John Gault had been in a business relationship with William Moore of Lowell. Moore was in the process of developing Gault's coal hole cover patent. Shortly following the creation of the BT issue for Boston pharmacist John I. Brown, Gault signed Lowell merchant Ayer as a customer, too. Ayer was a major advertiser in several media. So it is not surprising that he was a major advertiser on John Gault's New Metallic Currency also. Ayer was more interested in additional exposure than in furnishing small change. He placed an order of 20,000 pieces. Virtually all of them were small denominations. During the next few months the enthusiastic Ayer doubled and redoubled his initial order. Again, and again, he ordered small denomination pieces. Ultimately Gault delivered 200,000 pieces to the Lowell merchant.

Consequently, most of Ayer's varieties are still quite common today. Since the Ayer issues are the most commonly seen of all the stamp encasements, they are most often the first introduction to the New Metallic Currency for numismatist and philatelist alike. They are also the most commonly encountered pieces outside the numismatic and philatelic

Figures 97a, b, c

From left, Reed AP03 obverse. (Dr. Wallace Lee photo) Reed AC03LA obverse, ex-James F. Ruddy specimen. (Bowers and Merena photo) Reed AS05MD obverse (Jim Krejci photo)

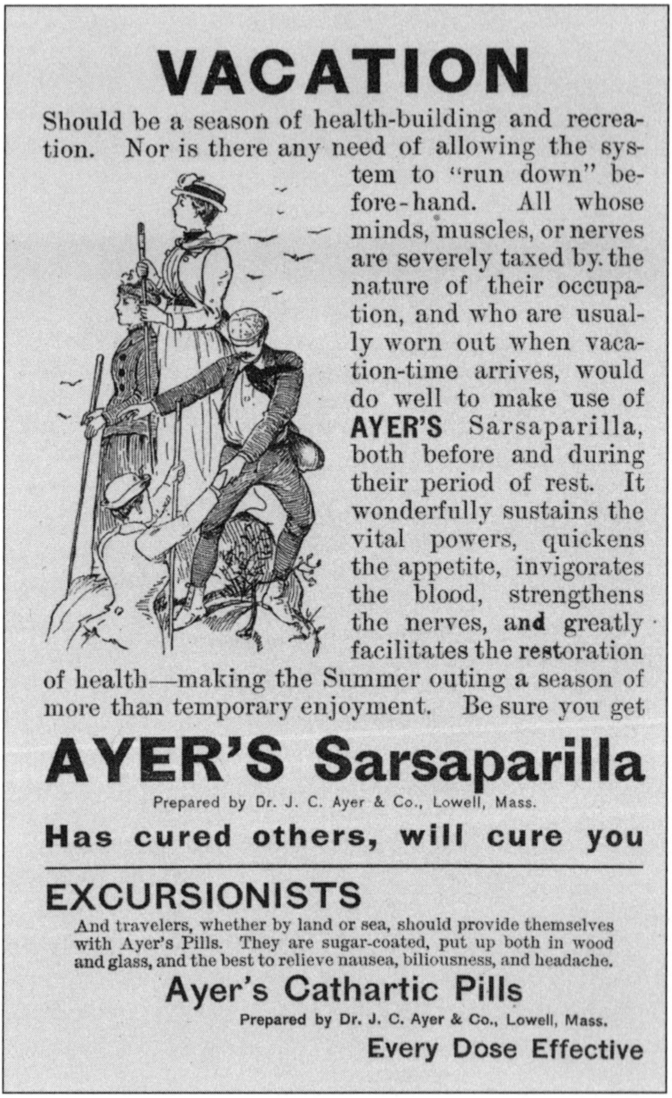

Figure 98a

Ayer's famous proprietary medicines – his sarsaparilla and cathartic pills, as advertised on his encased stamps – were still popular a generation after appearing on the New Metallic Currency he purchased from John Gault during the Civil War. Advertising circular, c. 1890. (Author's collection)

mainstream. For many readers, coming to this series and this book from outside the collecting mainstream, the other merchants discussed in this book may be quite surprising. Rampant speculation surrounds the extent of Ayer's issue. So common are they, in fact, that many collectors and even a few dealers seem puzzled. Opinions abound. One numismatic dealer very familiar with the encased stamp series has come to the conclusion after many years of handling these pieces that Ayer may have been responsible for upwards of a third of Gault's output. Another, who also has handled many encased stamps over the years, estimates that "far over 50 percent of the extant pieces are Ayers. . . . I had always thought that

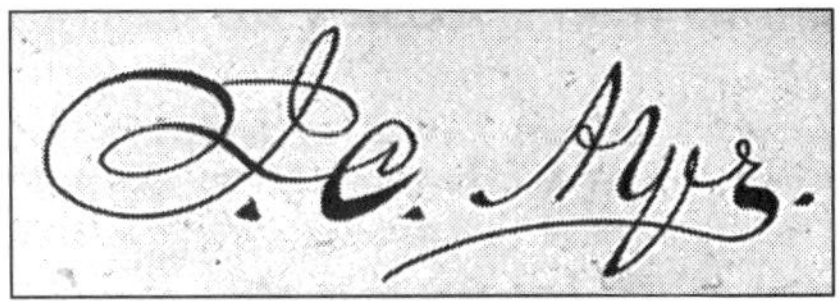

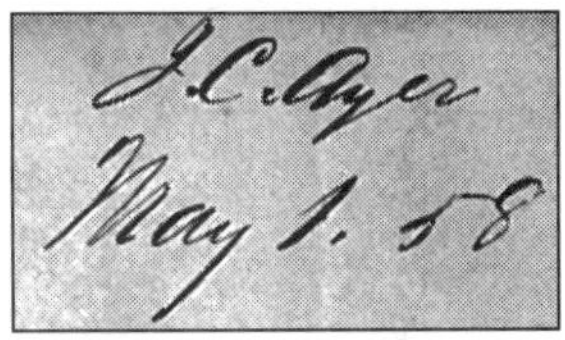

Figures 99a, b, c

J. C. Ayer was a driving entrepreneur whose proprietary medicine business fueled a succession of other ventures. His stylized signature, top, bears some semblance to his autographed signature, above. Engraving and facsimile signature, The Reminiscences of Frederick Ayer, *1923, plate op. p. 65. (Rare Book Division, New York Public Library, Astor, Lenox and Tilden Foundations) Autograph. (Author's collection)*

their original order was probably half or more of the total pieces," he wrote this author several years ago. Writer Arlie Slabaugh, one of the most original thinkers ever to write about Gault's New Metallic Currency, has gone so far as to conjecture that had history been kinder to Gault's idea and the encasements achieved a longer period of circulation, Ayer would likely have purchased or leased Gault's patent rather than pay Gault's premium. Given Ayer's proclivities (He was a major advertiser in all the media available to him in his day – often buying into the medium, thus exacting cheaper rates and paying himself to boot!), Slabaugh is probably right. Gault probably would not have been adverse to the idea either. He typically sold, licensed, or partnered his ideas to others with capital to develop.

It appears, after considerable study and computer modeling, that Ayer's large output probably did account for 25-30 percent of Gault's business. In addition to their very numbers, the great number of types and minor varieties support such a conclusion. The Ayer issue is the most complex of the encased stamp series. At least 50 varieties exist, several quite rare, in fact. No author has clearly and sufficiently illustrated and described these vari-

Figures 100a, b

Ayer's earliest success stemmed from his remedy for coughs and colds. His Cherry Pectoral received widespread approval parlayed via testimonial advertising. Trade card and bottle. (Both, Author's collection, electronic imaging by Mary Gonzalez-Davis)

eties before. As the illustrations in this chapter show, the series can be parsed effectively.

All of this has obscured a relatively simple emission. In fact, what emerges from concentrated study is the very clear direction Ayer took in issuing his pieces. He clearly understood the value of this New Metallic Currency. Let's take the series apart and understand his goals in placing his orders. Ayer had a simple message to deliver. It appears over and over again in periodical advertising and prodigious amounts of directed advertising via his almanacs and other sales literature. In a marketplace congested with competing health aids and remedies, buy his product. They work. His method was to saturate the public with his franchise name. Unlike many of Gault's clients, Ayer was not a newly established merchant or marketing a new product or service. Everyone already knew his products. Most had probably already purchased them and experienced their effectiveness at one time or another. He was merely interested in keeping his name always at hand, always in the public's awareness. Although other merchants could have similar goals, Ayer was blessed with both the wherewithal and the desire to actually follow though.

His purpose required inexpensive media, widely distributed, and always at hand. Daily newpapers and helpful daily almanacs fit his purposes quite naturally. What better ancillary

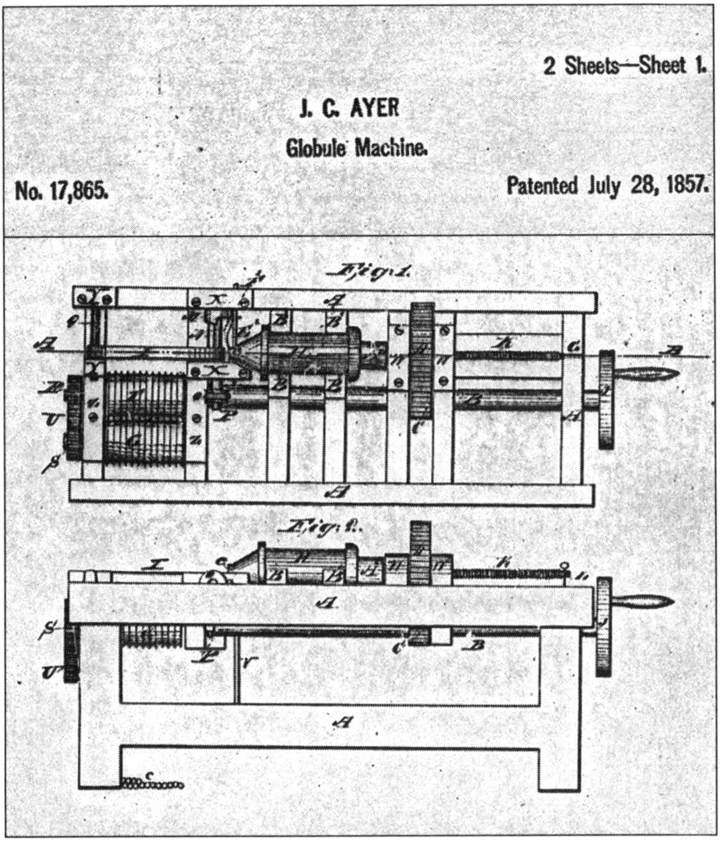

Figure 101a
The demand for his cathartic pills was created by Ayer's ubiquitous advertising, and supplied by technological innovations such as his patent pill machine. Ayer patented (but did not invent) this sophisticated pill machine developed in his factory to crank out his "globules." U.S. Patent No. 17,865, July 28, 1857, Sheet 1. *(U.S. Patent Office)*

Figures 101b
If Munn & Company, which assisted J. C. Ayer in securing his pill machine patent, had followed his lead in issuing encased stamps, its issue might well have mimicked its own logo, left, the design of which suggests the beaded border and circumferential design of many of the encased stamp obverses. Logo. Scientific American, *June 21, 1862, p. 399. (Author's collection) Six years later, of course, Munn & Company did issue the brass embossed store card, shown at Figures 30a, b.*

medium than the country's small change to reinforce his franchise? To do so, Ayer needed the broadest possible distribution and the smallest possible price. Unlike Gault, Hunt and Nash and John I. Brown before him (all of whom to a greater or lesser extent preferred the

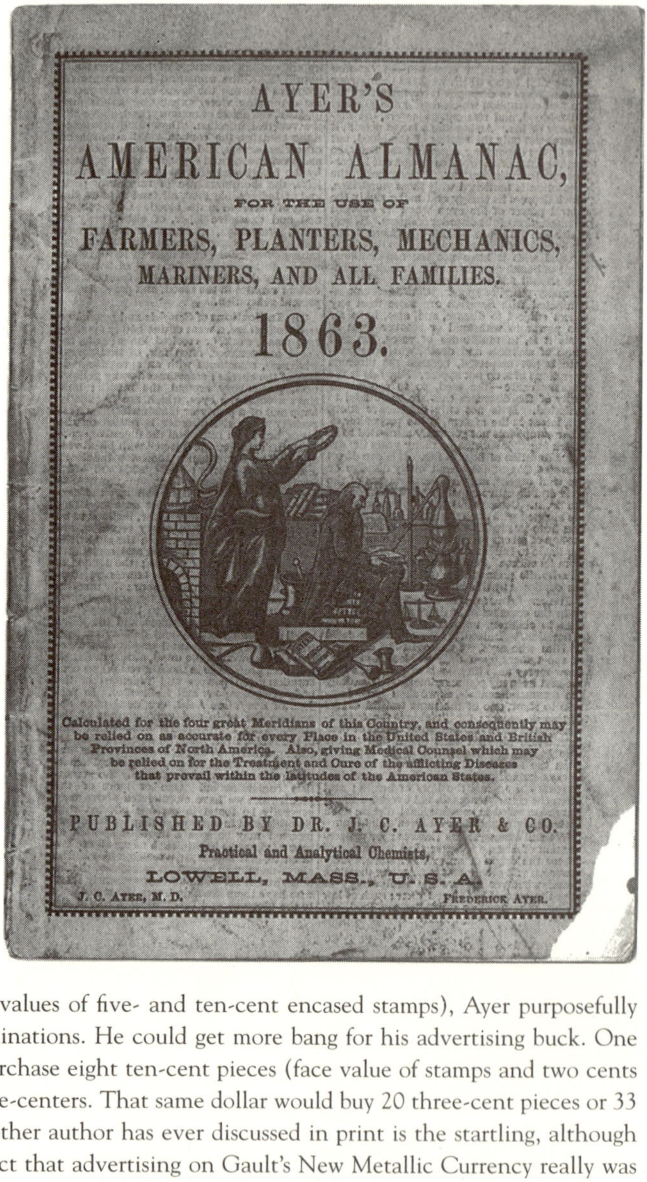

Figure 102a

Ayer's American Almanacs *were among the most prolifically issued of this type of commercial literature. His 1863 edition appeared contemporaneously with his encased stamps in fall 1862, both kinds of advertising intended to draw the public's attention and patronage to his proprietary medicinal empire. (Author's collection)*

workhorse change making values of five- and ten-cent encased stamps), Ayer purposefully selected the smaller denominations. He could get more bang for his advertising buck. One advertising dollar would purchase eight ten-cent pieces (face value of stamps and two cents each for the cases) or 14 five-centers. That same dollar would buy 20 three-cent pieces or 33 one-cent issues. What no other author has ever discussed in print is the startling, although it should be self-evident, fact that advertising on Gault's New Metallic Currency really was an expensive proposition because of the manufacturing premium. This premium varied from 66 percent on the one-cent store card to slightly over two percent on the highest, 90-cent stamp/coin.

This built in "overhead" for materials and manufacture delimited the usefulness of the product. With silver coins available in the marketplace for the specie premium of about 20 percent during the period Gault was peddling his New Metallic Currency, a merchant

Figures 103a-d

A variety of non-standard issues dot the Ayer encased stamp landscape. This is not surprising considering the multitudinous Ayer issue. Top, Reed AP02RS with Two-cent Internal Revenue Stamp, Scott Type R2 (Dana Linett photos); Bottom, Reed AS01'51 with 1851 series stamp, probably Scott 7 (Kagin's Numismatic Auctions photos)

needed to envision a great value in purchasing Gault's change. John Gault's medium was not for everybody, but shrewd businessmen could employ it to good advantage.

James Cook Ayer was one such perceptive individual. As outlined in the earlier chapter on John Gault (cf. page 74), Ayer selected the saturation coverage provided by the smallest value stamps. Small values turn over quicker because they are useful in a greater number and variety of purchases. Also small values represent the largest measure of exposure for his franchise. Thus, *ALL* his types, regardless which product or what die is employed, are predominantly one- and three-cent store cards. This propensity for the smallest of small change values – giving him the widest circulation for his gross expenditure on his advertising message – parallels Ayer's demonstrated purposes in the other media in which he advertised. It also has for too long obscured the *relative* scarcity of Ayer's five-and ten-cent pieces.

Aside their very numbers, multiple styles and differing denominational preferences, Ayer's encased stamps differ from the earlier issuers' emissions in other important ways. They are the first to employ the Type II (beaded obverse) advertising insert, which thereafter becomes the norm for all of Gault's subsequent clients. This design consists of 100+ beads or balls around the circumference of the advertising side of the store card. Artistically, Ayer's designs are also better and more professionally die sunk than Gault's products for the New York innkeepers, the Boston cough drop merchant, or even his own pieces. We would expect Ayer to demand such a professionally-turned product. Given Ayer's financial clout, it was very much in John Gault's best interests to provide him what he wanted.

Modern accounts of James Cook Ayer are mixed. Numismatist Slabaugh calls him "important" and "interesting," while a chronicler of American folk literature finds Ayer

Figures 104a-d

The Ayer's (AYERS, sic) Cathartic Pills issue was an extremely large one. Two major varieties are recognized by collectors, illustrated at top by Reed AC10SA and Reed AC03LA, Short Arrows and Long Arrows varieties respectively, and easily distinguishable in the comparative photos, above. (Dana Linett photos)

somewhat of a scoundrel with a low profile. However, the latter author is very disparaging of the "patent" medicine vendors and their associated literature. His research methods are also somewhat suspect. For instance, he states, "I find no mention of him in the books to which one usually refers for 19th century biographical information." That author's belligerence toward Ayer is mystifying, as is his unwarranted assertion to the lack of public recognition or appreciation for Ayer. As can be seen, J. C. Ayer lived continually in the public eye, and those who knew him well liked him best. His benefactions were exemplary and the recognition he achieved was widespread. Furthermore, the Ayer family had a real historical consciousness and several books by family members are readily available to anyone who really *wants* to find out about Ayer. That tradition of literate endeavor continues down to the present. The writer's statements are simply unfair.

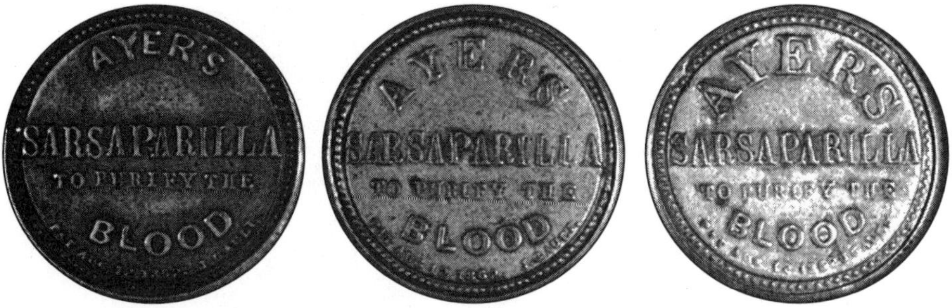

Figures 105a, b, c

Ayer's Sarsaparilla is the most complex issue of encased stamps. Three major varieties exist: Small AYER'S, Medium AYER'S, and Large AYER'S. These are easily distinguishable in the comparative photos, above. From left, Reed AS03SM, Reed AS03MD, and Reed AS03LG obverses. (Len Glazer photos)

What is fair to say, however, is that James Cook Ayer and his younger brother Frederick literally built an empire on the constitutional frailty of their fellow men. A town, Ayer, Massachusetts, was named in his honor. In his day, Dr. Ayer (the medical doctorate was earned, unlike some of his competitors – notably Patrick Drake) came to be the "King of Patent Medicines." The moniker stuck, even though most – including Ayer's – preparations never were patented because to do so their constituents would have had to be publicly revealed. The proper terminology is *proprietary* medicines.

This proprietor of these famous health aids did not arrive on this early scene in such an auspicious manner, however. Born May 5, 1818 in Ledyard, Connecticut, he was named after a maternal uncle James Cook, who was an early mayor of Lowell, Massachusetts, a town which his namesake would make world-famous within his lifetime. Ayer's lineage was old line New England. His grandfather had been a privateer during the Revolutionary War, was captured and taken prisoner by the British. His father, Frederick Ayer, was a veteran of the War of 1812. The father owned a saw and grist mill. He was also the local blacksmith, wheelwright, and produced the town's cider. Frederick Ayer had married Persis Cook and sired five offspring, three of whom survived. When Frederick died at age 33, only four days before Christmas in 1825, the family was dispersed and the homestead sold. His seven-year-old son, James, was then the oldest son surviving infancy.

The widow and her children moved in with her parents. Young James came under the influence of his maternal grandfather, who operated a flannel mill and exposed the boy to the intricacies of machinery and mechanics. The youth worked long hours in his grandfather's employ for three years. According to his biographer, this often involved 20-hour days for the princely sum of four cents per hour. However, this early training produced a man steeled to hard work, self-discipline, and a desire to get ahead. Combined with "his native energy and shrewdness," Ayer was able "to advance in the world rapidly and surely," according to a later writer. Evidence of both aspects of Ayer's character is revealed by an anecdote recorded in Ayer's biography: As an 11-year-old, he saved $14 out of his salary, loaned the

Figures 106a, b, c

Part of the reason for three distinctive obverse dies for the AS issue was the die disintegration evidenced by the emerging lengthy die break which destroyed the Medium Letters variety die as illustrated by these specimens. Reed AS05MD obverses showing three die states. (James F. Krejci photos)

money back to his grandfather at interest, and then presented the note to his mother as a gift.

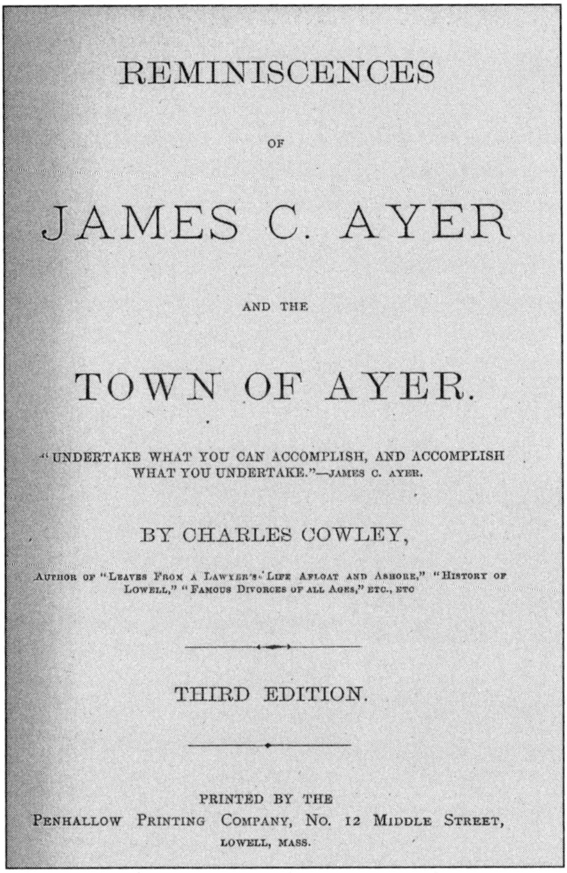

REMINISCENCES

OF

JAMES C. AYER

AND THE

TOWN OF AYER.

"UNDERTAKE WHAT YOU CAN ACCOMPLISH, AND ACCOMPLISH WHAT YOU UNDERTAKE."—JAMES C. AYER.

BY CHARLES COWLEY,

AUTHOR OF "LEAVES FROM A LAWYER'S LIFE AFLOAT AND ASHORE," "HISTORY OF LOWELL," "FAMOUS DIVORCES OF ALL AGES," ETC., ETC

THIRD EDITION.

PRINTED BY THE
PENHALLOW PRINTING COMPANY, NO. 12 MIDDLE STREET,
LOWELL, MASS.

Figure 107a
A great deal of information, much of it suspect, is contained in Charles Cowley's paean to James C. Ayer, Cowley's benefactor. The book, although enjoyable, must be read with a certain detachment and some skepticism. It is very interesting, never-the-less. Title Page, Reminiscences of James C. Ayer and the Town of Ayer. *(Book courtesy John J. Ford)*

As might be expected, young Ayer was not content with his hard lot. "When twelve years old, his hunger and thirst for learning became uncontrollable. . . . Again and again he threatened to run away, unless his mother did something to secure an education for him," the biographer records. His mother finally consented and permitted him to attend school for six months. During that time, he clerked in a country store. While in his teens, Ayer was shuffled among his relatives. Fortunately his uncle, after whom he was named, took a fancy to him. So in 1835, J. C. Ayer first came to Lowell under his uncle James Cook's tutelage. His uncle and aunt treated him like a son, and he responded in like manner towards them. They permitted him to attend Wexford Academy, where a classmate was Benjamin F. Butler, later a governor, congressman and Civil War general. While in school Ayer clerked in a dry goods store. Upon finishing high school his great ambition was to go on to college, but no one would aid him with finances. So Ayer sought an appointment to the military academy at West Point, but again failed. "How the heart of the widow's son sank within him as he realized, at length, that for him the doors of Yale and Dartmouth and the gates of West Point were closed and barred forever," Charles Cowley wrote.

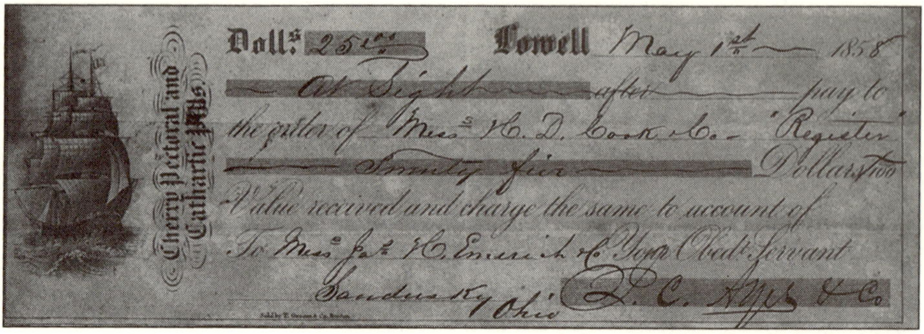

Dolls 25 00/100 Lowell May 1st 1858

At Sight after pay to

the order of Mess. H. D. Cook & Co. - Register

Twenty five Dollars 00/100

Value received and charge the same to account of

To Mess. Jas. H. Emerich & Co. Your Obedt. Servant

Sandusky Ohio J. C. Ayer & Co.

Cherry Pectoral and Cathartic Pills

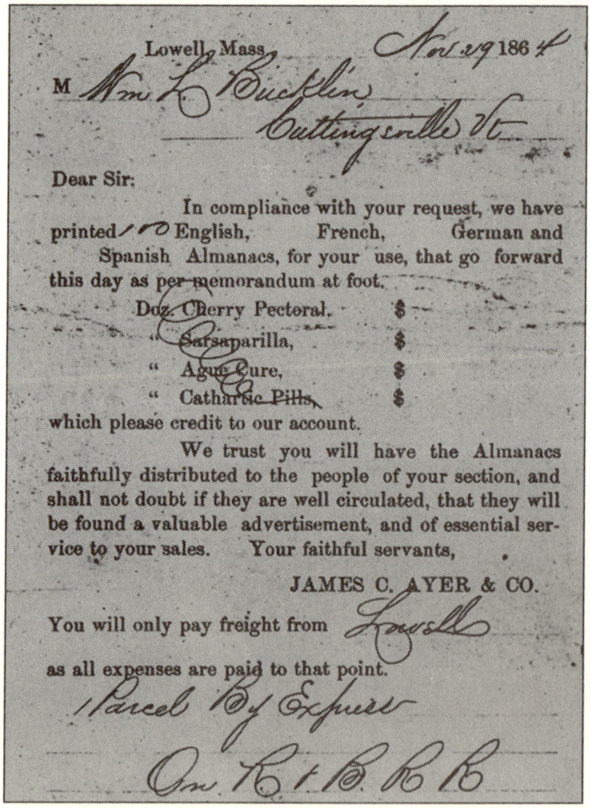

Lowell, Mass., Nov 29 1864

M Wm L Bucklin

Cuttingsville Vt

Dear Sir:

In compliance with your request, we have printed 100 English, French, German and Spanish Almanacs, for your use, that go forward this day as per memorandum at foot.

Doz. Cherry Pectoral, $

" Sarsaparilla, $

" Ague Cure, $

" Cathartic Pills, $

which please credit to our account.

We trust you will have the Almanacs faithfully distributed to the people of your section, and shall not doubt if they are well circulated, that they will be found a valuable advertisement, and of essential service to your sales. Your faithful servants,

JAMES C. AYER & CO.

You will only pay freight from Lowell

as all expenses are paid to that point.

1 Parcel By Express

On R & B R R

Figures 108a, b

A sight draft, above, in favor of Ayer's western salesmen advertises his Cherry Pectoral and Cathartic Pills. Sight Draft, May 1, 1858. (Author's collection) Ayer custom printed advertising on the cover of his annual almanacs for his customers to distribute in their local areas. The receipt at right acknowledges an order and shipment of 100 almanacs to a Vermont patron. Invoice, Nov. 29, 1864. (New-York Historical Society)

This unfortunate turn or affairs was really opportunity in disguise. Ayer apprenticed to a leading local apothecary, Jacob Robbins, in summer 1838. He quickly mastered the drug trade, both its commercial and chemical aspects, and Robbins left for Europe leaving the entire enterprise in Ayer's capable, willing hands. The young man soon became the confidant of the local physicians. This "gave James a rare opportunity . . . and many of them

Figures 109a, b

Ayer's "travellers" like Carlos A. Cook, above, fanned across the landscape. Copy photo. Wineburgh Philatelic Research Library collection, University of Texas at Dallas. (Rick Biddenstadt photo) The dirt road to the historic Concord bridge was typical scenery for Ayer's travelling salesmen. Albumin silver print. (Author's collection)

became interested in him to the extent of taking him with them if they had unusual cases or operations." In one recorded case, Ayer's knowledge of chemistry led him to find the source of lead contamination, which had led to the deaths of several children of a friend. Another time, he scientifically investigated the cause of a potato blight. In those days the relationship of local doctors and apothecaries was a close one since custom-compounded medicines

Figure 110a

Fortunately for collectors of Ayer's brand of New Metallic Currency, his sales literature and commercial paperwork is nearly as plentiful as pieces of his encased stamps. Such items, variously referred to as "go-withs" or association items, give insights into his business practices a century or more ago. Receipt, November 24, 1875. (Wayne Homren collection)

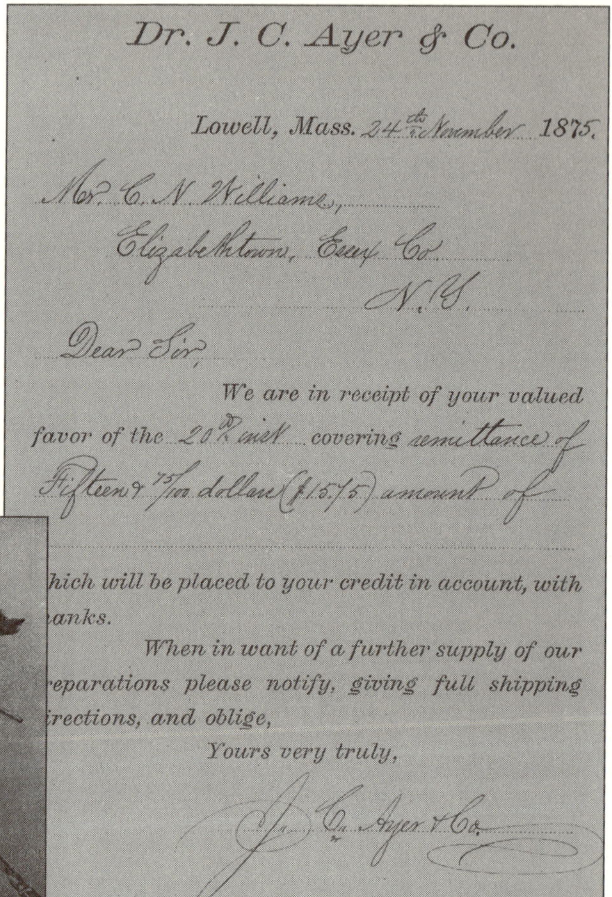

Dr. J. C. Ayer & Co.

Lowell, Mass. 24th November 1875.

Mr. C. N. Williams,
Elizabethtown, Essex Co
N. Y.

Dear Sir,

We are in receipt of your valued favor of the 20th inst covering remittance of Fifteen & 75/100 dollars ($15.75) amount of

hich will be placed to your credit in account, with anks.

When in want of a further supply of our eparations please notify, giving full shipping irections, and oblige,

Yours very truly,

J. C. Ayer & Co

Figure 110b

Left, very colorful and popular card extolling the virtues of Ayer's pills metaphorically depicts "The Fight for the Standard" in military terms. The Ayer's proponent rides a white steed and raises aloft a red, white and blue standard (flag). The reverse could be customized for the local pharmacist's name and address. (Author's collection)

were the general rule. Young Ayer commenced the study of medicine with Dr. Samuel Dana, a local practitioner. Eventually, Ayer was awarded an M. D. degree by the University of Pennsylvania, dated July 23, 1860, but he never practiced medicine. Given his immense success as a practical and analytical chemist, however, one biographer has affirmed that "had he elected to follow that profession [he] would have attained eminence beyond a doubt." Ayer also studied in a variety of other fields with tutors from Harvard.

Figures 111a, b

Ayer's trade cards are plentiful and relatively inexpensive. Their subject matter runs the gamut of popular appeal. Compare the gentle, domestic card at left to the military scene opposite. Trade card. (Author's collection) Below, a payment to Ayer following the Civil War. Check, April 19, 1867. (Author's collection)

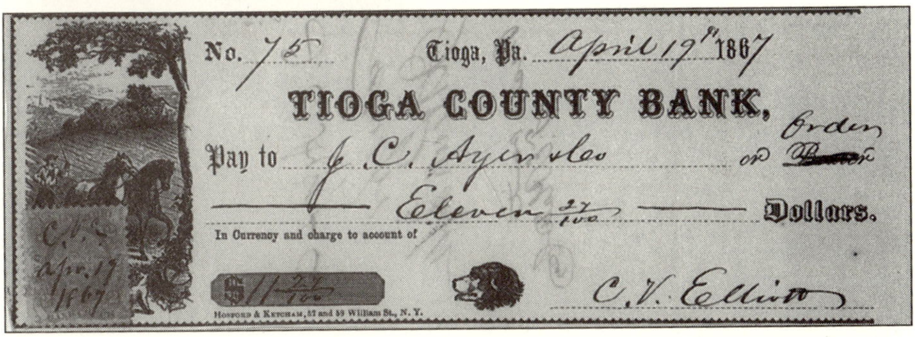

Purportedly, Ayer's personal credo was "Undertake what you can accomplish, and accomplish what you undertake." His personal string of successes certainly underscores that theme. He set out on that road in April 1841, then age 22, when he bought out the Robbins drug store for $2,486.61 borrowed from his uncle. A contemporary estimated his chances of success at one-in-a-hundred, but he quickly repaid the five-year note in three years. His early success was derived from the sale of a home remedy which he devised while in Robbins' employ. From his close association with physicians, he conceived the idea that a standard remedy for coughs and colds was highly desirable. Styled "Ayer's Cherry Pectoral,' the syrup was intended for victims of pulmonary difficulties by serving as an expectorant. Ayer induced physicians to try his product, and the "favorable reports he received con-

Figures 112a, b, c

Ayer's pills came packaged in oval wooden boxes, (below) and glass vials (right) to insure freshness for sales in the tropics. Labeled package and trade card. (Both, Author's collection) Bottom, Ayer's proprietary medicine stamp for his boxes and bottles of pills, Scott RS4. (Author's collection)

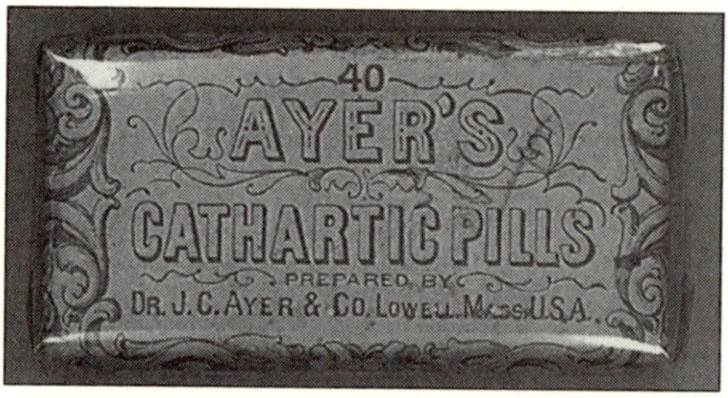

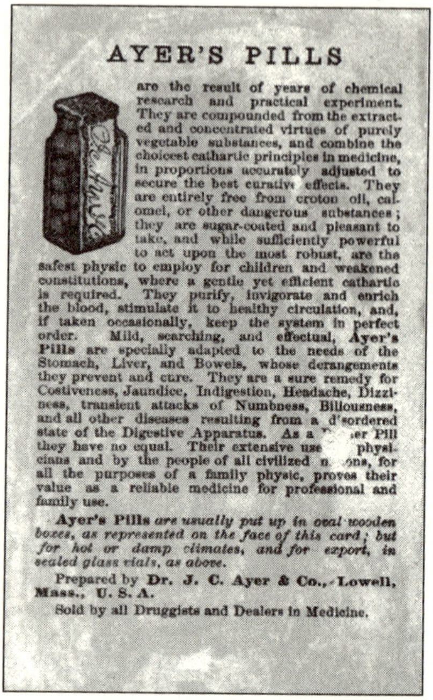

vinced him that he had found a valuable remedy." Reflecting on his success, he wrote: "Diseases of the throat and lungs are so prevalent in our ever-changing climate. . . . This medicine acts with certainty; it strikes at the very foundations of disease, and is, withal, absolutely harmless."

Given the endorsements of prominent clergymen and physicians, sales of the product took off. With its success, its fame grew. The syrup was more than a cherry-flavored cough syrup, though, since it contained a derivative of opium, too. In later years as the laws became stricter and labels were required to supply the ingredients of their contents, Ayer unfailingly printed the proportion of heroin in contained. In contrast to dreadfully awful-tasting medicines associated with its time, Ayer's cherry-flavored syrup was a delightful contrast. A contemporary records:

> There is a memory of the presence in the house of a bottle containing a liquid of a golden pomegranate color, enclosed in a paper wrapper somewhat approaching the same shade, the taste of the liquid suggesting something akin to the flavor of the meats in the black cherry stones with which a country boy was likely to be acquainted on account of their close connection with a delicacy known as cherry rum.

To preserve its flavor, the product's wrapper advised keeping the bottle in a dark place. As

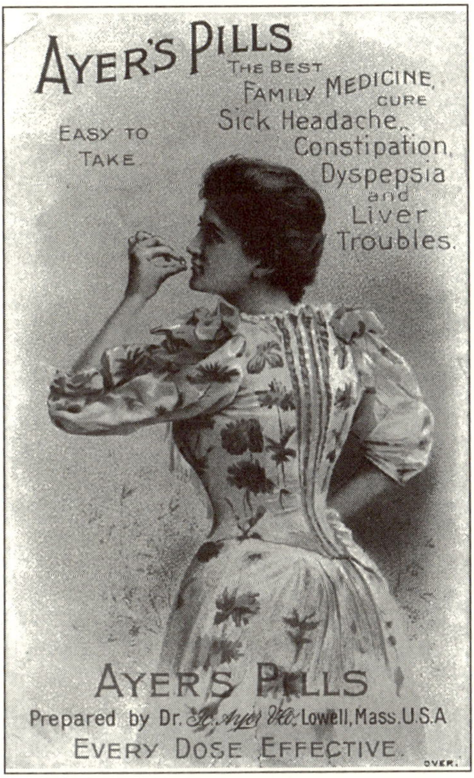

Figure 113a

Ayer's pills were sugar-coated and easy to take according to this large-sized trade card. His medicine was also unequalled, the card claims. Trade card. (Author's collection)

demand for the Cherry Pectoral skyrocketed, more and more of Ayer's time was absorbed in filling the "needs of the trade." So he brought his cousin Carlos A. Cook into the firm as a partner to run the drug store.

Right from the beginning "printer's ink found in him an ardent advocate, and even in those early years he made liberal appropriations for advertising," an historian records. Quickly discovering that advertising pays and a great deal of advertising pays greatly, Ayer reinvested the receipts of his growing bank balance popularizing his tonic. Eventually, he became the most successful advertiser in a field noted for its practitioners of this craft. It was said by an insider in the ad game, George P. Rowell, that Ayer outspent his nearest rivals $10-to-$1 promoting his remedies. In newspapers as far away as Memphis, Richmond and New Orleans, this "practical and analytical chemist," as he liked to call himself, ballyhooed the desirability of his cherry-flavored syrup as a rapid and sure cure for a host of ailments including catarrh (nasal or head cold), influenza, whooping cough, croup, asthma, coughs, hoarseness, bronchitis, diphtheria and "incipient consumption." "It saved my life," was a frequent component of the testimonies Ayer assembled to promote the syrup.

A student of this field has attributed the phenomenal development of advertising during the last half of the 19th century "almost exclusively . . . to the patent and proprietary medicine industry," which he calls the "principal support of most magazines and newspa-

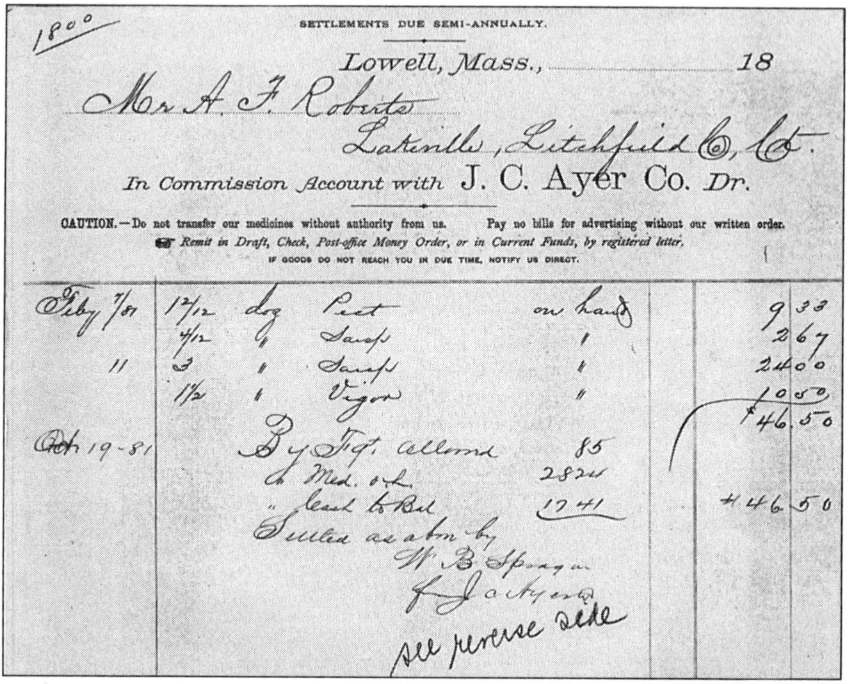
1800

SETTLEMENTS DUE SEMI-ANNUALLY.

Lowell, Mass., ... 18

Mr A. F. Roberts

Lakeville, Litchfield Co, Ct.

In Commission Account with J. C. Ayer Co. Dr.

CAUTION.—Do not transfer our medicines without authority from us. Pay no bills for advertising without our written order.

Remit in Draft, Check, Post-office Money Order, or in Current Funds, by registered letter.

IF GOODS DO NOT REACH YOU IN DUE TIME, NOTIFY US DIRECT.

Feby 7/81	12/12 doz Pect	on hand		9 33
	4/12 " Sarsp	"		2 67
11	3 " Sarsp	"		24 00
	1½ " Vigor	"		10 50
				46 50
Oct. 19-81	By Fgt. allowd	85		
	" Med. o.h.	28 24		
	" Cash to Bal	17 41		46 50

Settled as above by
W. B. Sprague
for J. C. Ayer Co.
see reverse side

Figures 114a, b

For some reason it took eight months in 1881 to fill the pharmacist's order, at top, for Cherry Pectoral, Sarsaparilla and Hair Vigor. Invoice, October 19, 1881. (New-York Historical Society) The packing crew for Ayer's Pill boxes, above, however was decidedly young and spontaneous. They were also quite diminutive. Compare the wrapped box at Figure 112a. (Author's collection)

Figures 115a, b

Ayer's Hair Vigor was not advertised on his encased stamps, a seemingly incomprehensible oversight. Since it was a well-established brand by then, and Ayer was willing to procure large supplies of encased stamps, a plausible explanation is that Ayer did not feel it needed the additional marketing exposure of his newer brands. At left, a bottle with full labeling – a very rare specimen – and below an advertising trade card. Bottle and Trade Card. (Both, Author's collection, electronic imaging by Maria L. Gonzalez-Davis)

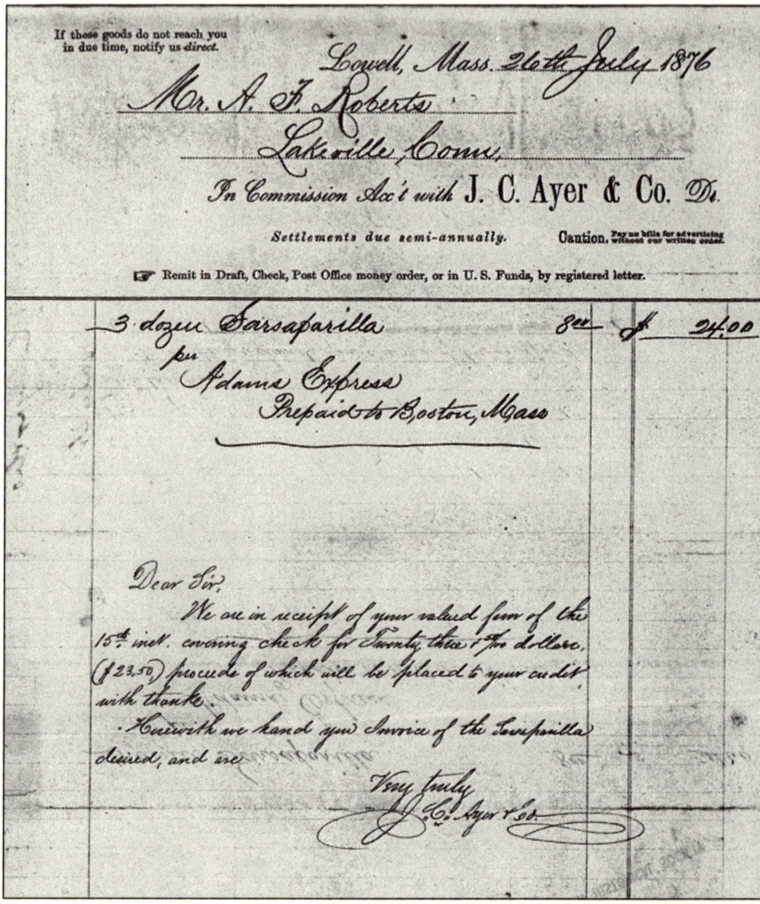

If these goods do not reach you in due time, notify us *direct*.

Lowell, Mass. 26th July 1876

Mr. A. F. Roberts

Lakeville, Conn.

In Commission Acc't with J. C. Ayer & Co. Dr.

Settlements due semi-annually. Caution. Pay no bills for advertising without our written order.

Remit in Draft, Check, Post Office money order, or in U. S. Funds, by registered letter.

3 dozen Sarsaparilla per Adams Express Prepaid to Boston, Mass	8.00	$	24.00

Dear Sir;

We are in receipt of your valued favor of the 15th inst. covering check for Twenty three & 50 dollars, ($23.50) proceeds of which will be placed to your credit with thanks.

Herewith we hand you Invoice of the Sarsaparilla desired, and are

Very truly

J. C. Ayer & Co.

Figure 116a

Interestingly, the terms Ayer offered his customers was net 180 days. Invoice, July 26, 1876. (New-York Historical Society)

pers." Collectors today certainly have little trouble finding Ayer's ads in virtually any publication of that era in which they choose to look. With every new remedy, Ayer is said to have redoubled his advertising. By 1870 he had signed advertising contracts with 1,900 newspapers annually. His competence in the advertising field, coupled with his business acumen generally, assured the success of his product line. A competitor describes his practices glowingly: "He required a newspaper to place his advertising according to specifications and received allowance for all shortcomings. . . . Dr. Ayer had the best corps of advertising men that ever traveled in the interest of patent medicine, and, although they never paid a newspaper any too much money for a service to be rendered, they gave as much flattery and soft soap as the publisher could make use of. The great Trinity Building on Broadway, in

Figures 117a, b, c, d
Ayer's star burst proprietary medicine stamp (Scott R59a) for his bottles is a unique design of that attractive series. Ayer's bottles are collectible in their own rights. Four-cent stamp and Bottles. (All, Author's collection, electronic imaging by Maria L. Gonzalez-Davis and Omar Mediano)

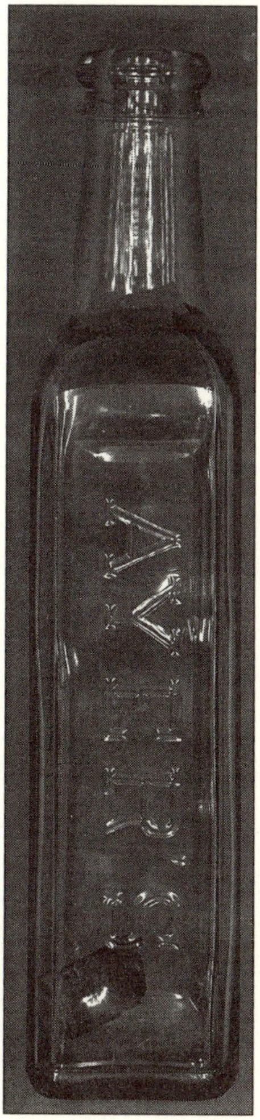

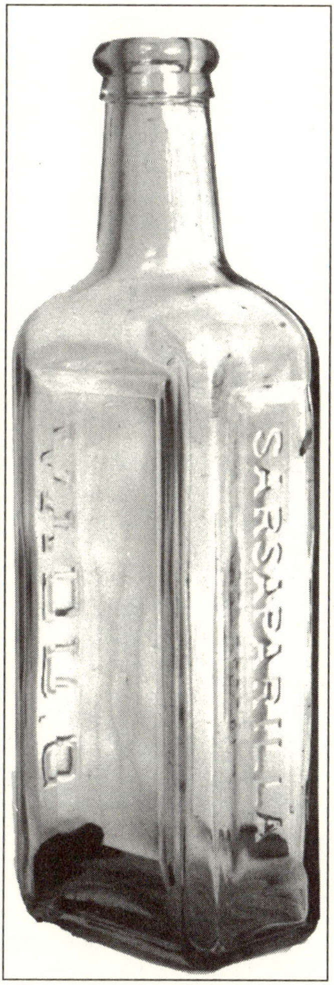

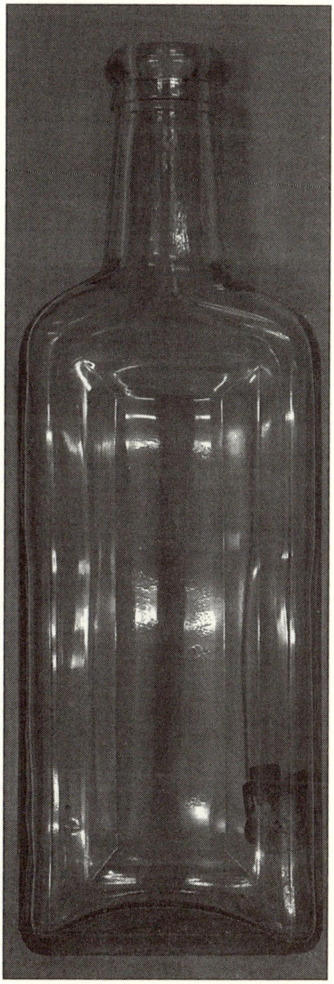

Figure 118a

This is the author's favorite Ayer trade piece, although not technically an Ayer trade card at all. Actually it is a theatrical card advertising a play entitled, "A Rag Baby" by Charles H. Hoyt. Characters included Old Sport, the Three Tramps, the Three Innocents, the Fresh Druggist, Handsome – the homeliest dog alive, and of course the Three Terribles, according to the stage manager Ed Murphy who issued this card. B[eaver] Falls, September 23, 1883. (Author's collection)

New York, is only one of numerous existing monuments that testify to Dr. Ayer's ability as a moneymaker."

In the early years, out-go outstripped in-come. Ayer borrowed frequently from family members until his fledgling operation turned the corner about 1850. Eventually he outgrew the Robbins building, and then a succession of expanded locations until eventually his company became the largest non-textile industry in Lowell. Along the way, by constant experimentation Ayer sought to develop a pill for general use. In 1854 he devised his sugar-coated pill, which he advertised the following decade on his encased stamps. The following year, after "much labor, investigation, experimentation and study," he added his famous compound extract of sarsaparilla, also appearing on the advertising store cards he ordered from John Gault. By 1856, he employed 150 people and revenues topped the half million dollar mark. In that year, Ayer shipped three doses of his medications for every man, woman and child in the United States.

Ayer, himself, attributed his success in no small measure to his successful marketing of his remedies in concert with the western expansion of the United States. "They are for sale at every Indian agency, military station, trader's camp, and mining settlement in the far west," he wrote. "If any emigrant has located where [the preparations] are not to be found, let him write us, and we will supply him by mail or otherwise," he promised. An able student of the changing times, Ayer early recognized that the frontier movement left Americans dis-

Figure 119a

This widely circulated card speaks for itself. Theatrics was alive and well a century ago, too. Issued in several sizes, shown approximately half size, this has been reproduced in modern "antique" plaques. A 7X13-inch chromo lithograph of this card along with a set of album cards was offered to the public for a dime. (Author's collection)

persed, not living in tightly knit communities with doctors in their midst. Of necessity such settlers needed the wherewithal to doctor themselves. Even on horseback, doctors needed easily dispensed, already-compounded medications with simple directions for their continued use. Ayer supplied such remedies, he had testimonies to prove it. "During the 25 years I have lived on the frontier," Colorado pioneer John McDowall wrote:

> Ayer's Pills have been my best friend. I have lived mostly where I had no doctor

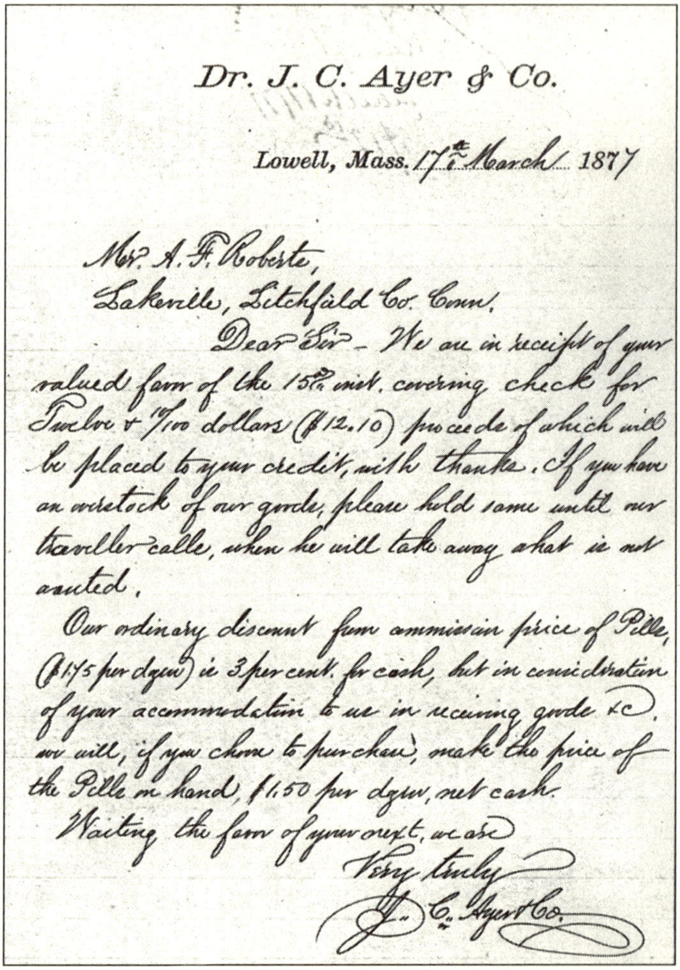

Dr. J. C. Ayer & Co.

Lowell, Mass. 17th March 1877

Mr. A. F. Roberts,
Lakeville, Litchfield Co. Conn.

Dear Sir – We are in receipt of your valued favor of the 15th inst. covering check for Twelve & 10/100 dollars ($12.10) proceeds of which will be placed to your credit, with thanks. If you have an overstock of our goods, please hold same until our traveller calls, when he will take away what is not wanted.

Our ordinary discount from commission price of Pills, ($1.75 per dozen) is 3 per cent. for cash, but in consideration of your accommodation to us in receiving goods &c. we will, if you choose to purchase, make the price of the Pills in hand, $1.50 per dozen, net cash.

Waiting the favor of your next, we are

Very truly
J. C. Ayer & Co.

Figure 120a

Ayer's company instructed the settling of an account with a client in Connecticut. Mention is made of the Ayer "traveller" or outside sales person (travelling salesman) in modern terminology, such as the one shown at Figure 109a. (New-York Historical Society)

> within 20 miles, and I have been hard sick several times; but I have always kept your medicines on hand, and with them and your almanac have pulled through.

In his position as Ayer "traveller" in the western U.S. Carlos A. Cook was principally responsible for building this large western trade. Eventually Cook settled in Chicago and built a large reputation and fortune for himself in the advertising business.

Ayer blanketed the country with his medicines and his advertising, but there were other worlds to conquer. He set his sights on achieving a worldwide reputation and Great Britain, France, and the German States quickly came to know the benefits of his various preparations. As early as 1856, he launched a campaign to take his remedies around the globe. He presented cases of his medicines to heads of states of many foreign lands through the good offices of the American ambassadors in those countries. Quickly the emperors of Japan, China and Brazil, the kings of Norway, Denmark, Portugal and Siam, the queen of

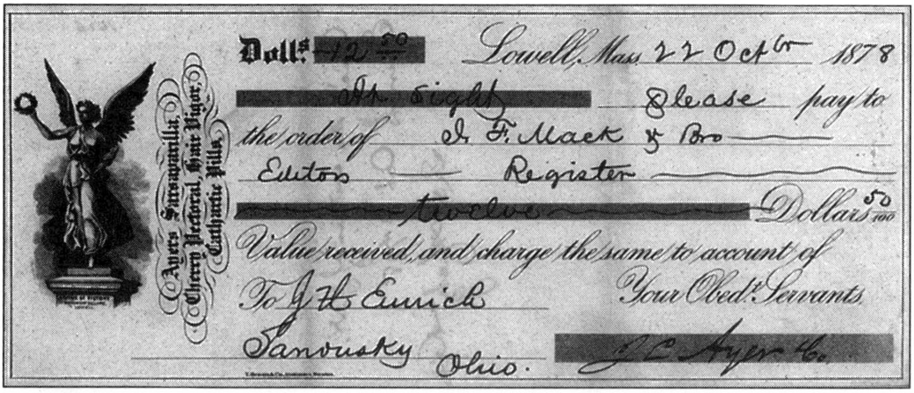

Figures 121a, b

At top, Ayer paid for advertising in an Ohio newspaper. Sight Draft, October 22, 1878. (Author's collection) Above, Ayer received a large payment from a New York City firm. Check, September 11, 1879. (Author's collection)

Spain, the shah of Persia, the sultan of Turkey, the czar of Russia, the iman of Muscat, and the presidents of Mexico, Chile, New Granada and Peru were added to the roll of Ayer fanciers.

By 1859 Ayer took up the location at 165 Market Street which it occupied at the time it issued its multitudinous stamp encasements. This four-story, red brick factory was one of the largest of its kind in the world and was magnificently equipped. In August, 1864, the firm survived an extensive fire, expanding in 1866, 1872 and again in 1874. Such constant growth is evidence of greatly increasing sales fueled by his ubiquitous and very effective advertising campaigns.

The question emerges why Ayer chose to advertise his pills and sarsaparilla and not his other best-selling preparation, his Cherry Pectoral, on his encased stamps. Since the cough syrup was nearly a generation old by that time, but these other medicines were only several years old in 1862, Ayer evidently calculated that the extra measure of public exposure via

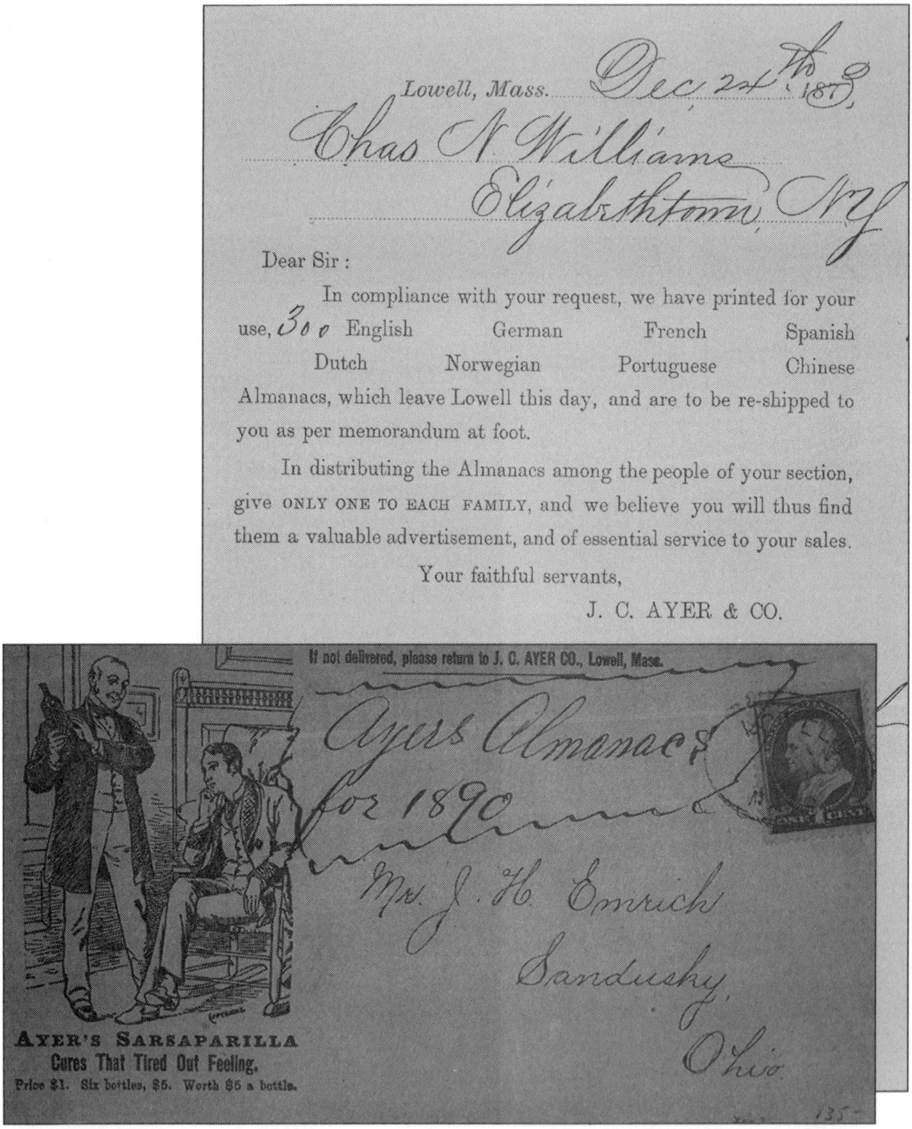

Lowell, Mass. Dec 24th 1873

Chas N Williams
Elizabethtown NJ

Dear Sir :

In compliance with your request, we have printed for your use, 300 English German French Spanish Dutch Norwegian Portuguese Chinese Almanacs, which leave Lowell this day, and are to be re-shipped to you as per memorandum at foot.

In distributing the Almanacs among the people of your section, give ONLY ONE TO EACH FAMILY, and we believe you will thus find them a valuable advertisement, and of essential service to your sales.

Your faithful servants,

J. C. AYER & CO.

Figures 122a, b

At top, Ayer's Almanacs were offered in various linguistic editions annually. Memorandum, December 24, 1873. (Wayne Homren collection) Above, an advertising cover used to send almanacs to an Ohio client in 1890. (Author's collection)

Gault's New Metallic Currency would better serve the newer products. It surely couldn't have been the expense.

Figures 123a, b, c

In the family-owned company, J. C. Ayer's younger brother, Frederick, rose to prominence and consequently great prestige and riches in the community as well. Eventually he became a mainstay of the Beacon Hill society set. Young portrait from The Reminiscences of Frederick Ayer, *1923, plate opposite p. 34. (Rare Book Division, New York Public Library, Astor, Lenox and Tilden Foundations) Below, Mature Portrait engraved by A. H. Ritche and facsimile autograph,* History of Middlesex County, Massachusetts. *(University of Lowell Library)*

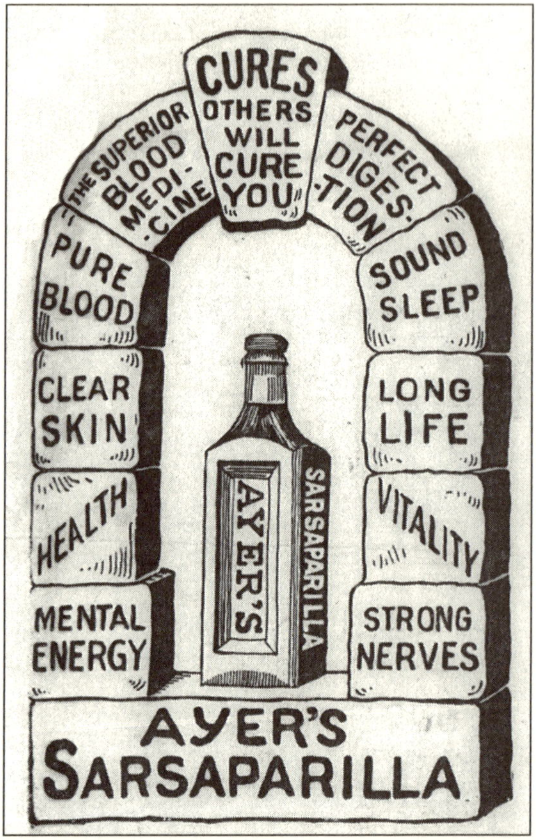

Figures 124a, b

Right, the keystone of promises which bolstered Ayer's Sarsaparilla sales was "cures others, will cure you." Illustration, Lowell of Today, *1893. Below, a visual pun as revealed on the card's reverse: "Without doubt, the Discovery of America is Ayer's Sarsaparilla." Trade card. (Author's collection)*

Ayer's Cathartic Pills were touted as a wonderful remedy for a variety of ailments stemming back to derangements of the stomach, liver and bowels. Magical purgative preparations are older than recorded history. The pun on the Ayer's Cathartic Pills (Reed AC) emission, "The Currency to Pass," was intended. Although its humor seems to have been

Figures 125a, b

Left, in his old age, Ayer's economic interests spanned the globe. The sun never set on the British Empire nor Ayer's Sarsaparilla. Engraving. (University of Lowell photo) Below, the Ayer company was a massive enterprise in the late 19th century. (University of Lowell, Special Collections photo A-9037)

Figures 126a (above), and 127a (opposite)

The model for this attractive card was the young girl in Frederick Ayer's lap, his daughter Beatrice. Trade card. (Author's collection) At right, this emotive, previously unpublished portrait graced the mantlepiece of a Beacon Hill mansion for generations, until it was graciously loaned to the author for reproduction in this book by the young girl's sister. (Photo courtesy Ruth Ellen Patton Totten)

lost on much of the present generation, this pun was obviously not lost upon the Ayer contemporary suffering from constipation. These sugar-coated pills in their small oval, wooden

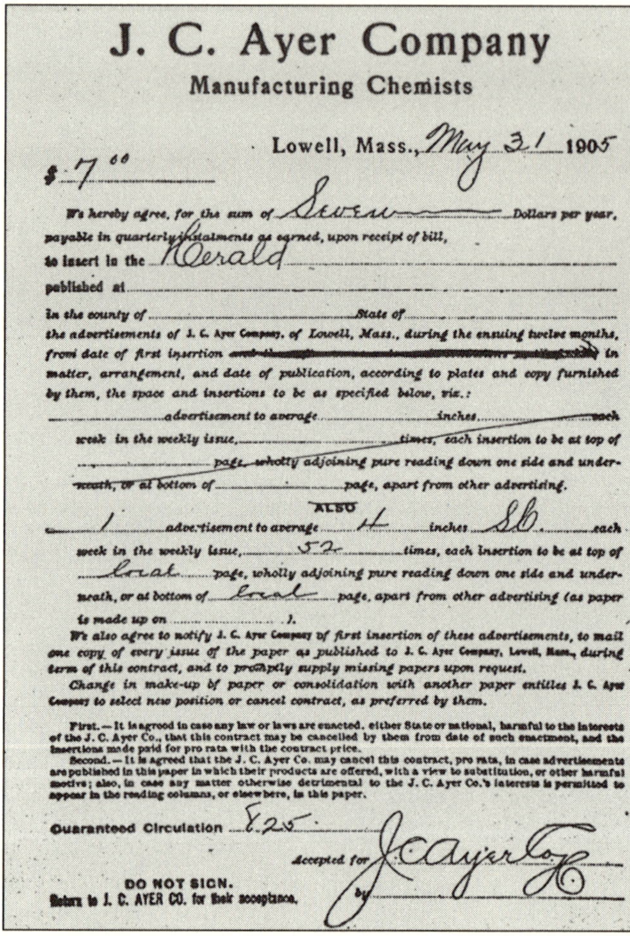

J. C. Ayer Company

Manufacturing Chemists

Lowell, Mass., May 31 1905

$ 7.00

We hereby agree, for the sum of Seven Dollars per year, payable in quarterly instalments as earned, upon receipt of bill, to insert in the Herald published at ________ in the county of ________ State of ________ the advertisements of J. C. Ayer Company, of Lowell, Mass., during the ensuing twelve months, from date of first insertion ~~[struck out]~~ in matter, arrangement, and date of publication, according to plates and copy furnished by them, the space and insertions to be as specified below, viz.:

~~________ advertisement to average ________ inches ________ each week in the weekly issue, ________ times, each insertion to be at top of ________ page, wholly adjoining pure reading down one side and underneath, or at bottom of ________ page, apart from other advertising.~~

ALSO

1 advertisement to average 4 inches SC. each week in the weekly issue, 52 times, each insertion to be at top of local page, wholly adjoining pure reading down one side and underneath, or at bottom of local page, apart from other advertising (as paper is made up on ________).

We also agree to notify J. C. Ayer Company of first insertion of these advertisements, to mail one copy of every issue of the paper as published to J. C. Ayer Company, Lowell, Mass., during term of this contract, and to promptly supply missing papers upon request.

Change in make-up of paper or consolidation with another paper entitles J. C. Ayer Company to select new position or cancel contract, as preferred by them.

First.—It is agreed in case any law or laws are enacted, either State or national, harmful to the interests of the J. C. Ayer Co., that this contract may be cancelled by them from date of such enactment, and the insertions made paid for pro rata with the contract price.

Second.—It is agreed that the J. C. Ayer Co. may cancel this contract, pro rata, in case advertisements are published in this paper in which their products are offered, with a view to substitution, or other harmful motive; also, in case any matter otherwise detrimental to the J. C. Ayer Co.'s interests is permitted to appear in the reading columns, or elsewhere, in this paper.

Guaranteed Circulation 825.

Accepted for J. C. Ayer Co.

by ________

DO NOT SIGN.

Return to J. C. AYER CO. for their acceptance.

Figure 128a

The standard advertising contract with Ayer restricted the press' ability to investigate claims against the pharmaceutical giant, whose advertising supported hundreds of newspapers and other periodicals across the country. Contract, May 31, 1905. Collier's *magazine, 1905, p 131. (Texas Christian University Library)*

boxes were a welcome addition to sideboards and medicine cabinets across the country. To understand the reception of such cathartic remedies, one need go no farther than the laxative shelves on which such preparations still abound today. More than a century ago, with the operations of proper diet and alimentary canal function less well understood, the necessity and popularity of such preparations was even more widespread.

The other preparation touted on his New Metallic Currency was Ayer's Sarsaparilla "to purify the blood." It was a dollar a bottle in 1859 and the same price 25 years later. The sarsaparilla was obviously intended to be more than a refreshing drink. Originally Ayer said he acquired his sarsaparilla roots from Russia (surely a curious place for a tropical plant), but eventually he turned south of the border and contracted with the Nicaraguan government for a steady supply. Popularly known as "sweetroot," the word *sarsaparilla* means "thorny vine" in Spanish. It was originally introduced into Europe as a remedy for syphilis, but soon proved worthless in that regard. By the mid-19th century it was experiencing a resurgence of

Figure 129a, b
Frederick Ayer's son, George Frederick Ayer, was responsible for orchestrating the Ayer company's successful stranglehold on newspaper advertising at the turn of the century. Steel engraved portrait and facsimile signature. History of Middlesex County, Massachusetts. *(University of Lowell Library)*

popularity, and Ayer specifically laid claim to its efficacy as a cure for that social disease. Today's western, comedy cliche of the dude sauntering up to the bar and ordering a cool sarsaparilla instead of vile red eye would have fallen flat on a real western saloon room. Sarsaparilla did indeed grace the back bars of such establishments, but its common use was to fend off the dread disease and hardly to simply oil a rusty throat.

During the war, Ayer continued to trade with the South where he owned property. His political ambivalence on the slave issue caused the radical wing of his party to abandon him in his several bids for Congress following the war. In 1874 Ayer had a nervous breakdown, followed two years later by mental collapse. The end came July 3, 1878, although family members continued the firm under the Ayer name for nearly two additional generations.

Collectors should keep in mind that modern, counterfeit ASMD and AP obverses exist, and that sets of fakes in a full range of denominations were produced. See chapter on "Collecting Encased Stamps" for details.

Figure 130a

J.C. Ayer's Lowell mansion on Pawtucket Street is an imposing structure, serving the community in a variety of roles after passing from family hands. It still stands. (Lowell Cultural Resources Inventory photo)

Auction Census Data Summary, 1891-1994

	1	2	3	5	10	12	24	30	90	Total	Pct
AC SA	107		133	31	53	9	9	5		347	
AC LA	7		187	19	18	11	3	1		246	
AP	96		229	38	48	22		3	6	442	
AP RB	1		1	7						9	
AP '51		1								1	
AP RS		1								1	
AS SM	75		102	4	24	3				208	
AS MD	257	2	267	59	62	22	14	11	6	700	
AS MD RB			7		6					13	
AS MD CD	1		1							2	
AS MD '51	1									1	
AS LG	11		139	12	11	3	1			177	
AS LG RB										0	
AS LG '51	1									1	
	557	**4**	**1066**	**170**	**222**	**70**	**27**	**20**	**12**	**2148**	**24%**

Joseph L. Bates
Chapter VII

Explaining Joseph L. Bates' interest in John Gault's New Metallic Currency is strictly circumstantial. He was neither a new merchant nor was he in a new line of business. He was a longtime neighbor of John I. Brown and a former neighbor of machinist John Gault. None of this provides palpable evidence, of course, but it does provide clues for his fairly large issue of store cards. What is not circumstantial is a projected issue in excess of 20,000 pieces with a clear predominance of one-cent values. Nearly two-thirds of Bates' issue were cent pieces. Clearly the FANCYGOODS (Reed FG varieties) were issued first and when Bates discovered that Gault's die sinker had misspelled his stock in trade, Gault supplicated the venerable merchant by having a corrected die (two words, Reed F/G varieties) made to complete the issue.

By the Civil War, Bates was a legend among Boston merchants, having been in business for nearly as long as Brown. Both merchants were mainstays of the fashionable Washington Street business district, with businesses dating back a generation prior to the war. Bates commenced business as an importer and manufacturer of musical instruments, umbrellas and parasols, and "turner of ivory and wood," and added to his product line through the years. *Fancy Goods* for those unfamiliar with the term included various classes

Figures 131a, b

Left above, Reed BA01FG obverse, ex-Bruce Minevitz specimen. (Dana Linett photo) Right, Reed BA01F/G obverse, ex-James F. Ruddy specimen. (Bowers and Merena photo) The two word variety is correct.

Figures 132a, b (right) 133a, b (opposite)
Bates commenced business as an artisan and developed a stock-in-trade of diverse specialty wares. Top, ad Boston Annual Advertiser, *1828, unnumbered ad page. From the beginning his ads show effective advertising. In an era of classifieds, his multiple insertions and illustrative "cuts" foreshadow his experimentation with Gault's change medium. Ads right,* Boston Daily Evening Transcript, *February 3, 1853. p. [2]. (Author's collection). Opposite, top, Bates demonstrates a stereopticon to three Boston women on a unique advertising trade card. Stereopticon trade card, 1860s. (Author's collection) Below, Bates' store stood nearly opposite Old South Church on bustling Washington Street. Engraving by John Andrew.* Boston Sights and Strangers Guide, *1856, p. 22. (Author's collection)*

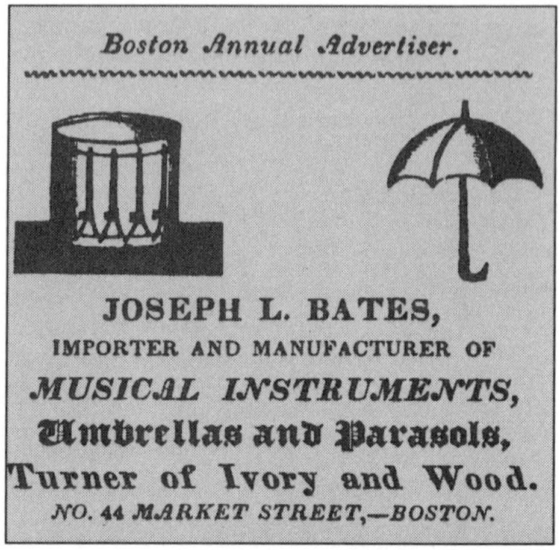

LARGE SIZE BACKGAMMON BOARDS—for sale by JOSEPH L. BATES, 129 Washington st. tc jan 28

WOODROFFE'S LONDON THERMOMETERS—for sale by JOS L. BATES, 129 Washington street. tc jan 28

HORN PUFF COMBS, of the largest size. This desirable article for sale by JOSEPH L. BATES, 129 Washington st. tc feb 3

SPANISH FANS of all qualities—received today and for sale at low prices by JOSEPH L. BATES. 129 Washington st. tc feb 3

SHELL PUFF COMBS—Of the best quality and finish—for sale by JOSEPH L. BATES, jan 22 tc 129 Washington st.

BATCHELOR'S HAIR DYE—The best yet invented, is constantly for sale at the manufacturer's wholesale and retail prices, by JOSEPH L. BATES, 129 Washington st. tc jan 22

of small items including pocket books, writing lap desks, card cases, money belts, toilet articles, buttons, combs, hosiery, jewelry, gold pens, ivory chess boards and the like. He stocked luxury goods according to the manner of the times and dealt with the first class clientele of a city known for its patrician attitudes.

Bates was born c. 1807 and took up the import business in his early twenties. After several relocations he came to the 129 Washington street location touted on his New Metallic Currency. Washington was a busy commercial street as contemporary engravings reveal. His store appears in a panoramic view in Gleason's Pictorial Drawing-Room companion. Nearby were several other merchants familiar to numismatists today, including the brush manufactory of J. J. Adams and H. B. Stanwood's jewelry store. Bates lived for many years at 57 Allen Street as a confirmed bachelor. The census of 1850 credited him with a large portfolio

STEREOSCOPIC
VIEWS
STEREOSCOPIC
STEREOSCOPIC
VIEWS
STEREOSCOPIC

TEA
130
T.B. SKINNER
JOSEPH L. BATES

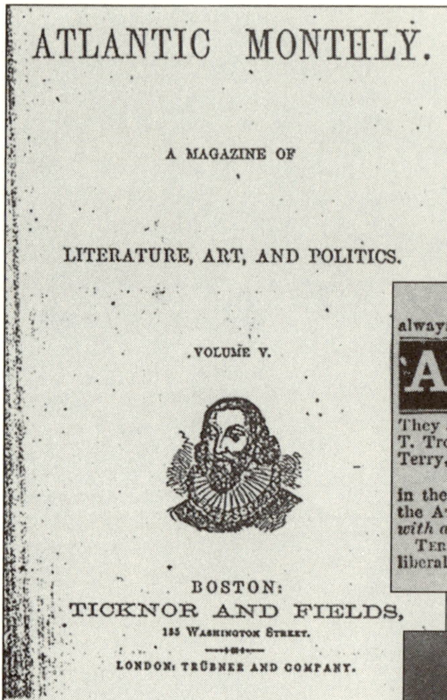

ATLANTIC MONTHLY.

A MAGAZINE OF

LITERATURE, ART, AND POLITICS.

VOLUME V.

BOSTON:
TICKNOR AND FIELDS,
135 WASHINGTON STREET.
LONDON: TRÜBNER AND COMPANY.

GOOD STORIES
always form a part of the contents of the
Atlantic Monthly
They are supplied by such writers as Harriet Prescott, J. T. Trowbridge, Caroline Chesebro, Bayard Taylor, Rose Terry, and other contributors of eminent ability. Some of
THE BEST STORIES
in the language have been written for and published in the ATLANTIC MONTHLY. *Subscriptions may begin with any number.*
TERMS. $3 00 a year, 30 cents a number. Clubs at a liberal reduction. Address the publishers,
TICKNOR & FIELDS, Boston.

Figures 134a, b, c

Boston was "the hub of the universe" in mid-19th century American letters, science, scholarship, and manners. To many, Ticknor and Fields' offices were "the hub of the hub." Atlantic Monthly, *published by Ticknor and Fields, was a focal point for New England's intelligentsia. Its pages are replete with the essays, literature, articles, and poetry that define the flourishing spirit of mid-19th century New England Enlightenment. Physician and Harvard professor Dr. Oliver Wendell Holmes (right) was a patriarch of the movement and frequent visitor to the publisher's offices. Holmes also frequented Bates' and Burnett's shops and developed friendships and business relationships with them.* Atlantic Monthly, *Vol. V, 1860, title page. (Author's collection)* Ad, Harper's Weekly, *August 6, 1864, p. 512. (Author's collection) Portrait, right, Albumin Silver Print. (Author's collection)*

of real estate. At the time he was responsible for his elderly mother, his widowed sister and her son.

In addition to his importing business, which stocked the best of Parisian and other European elegant items (fancy goods), from the earliest days Bates also manufactured much of his stock, particularly delicate shell combs. He also offered "articles for presents, for the

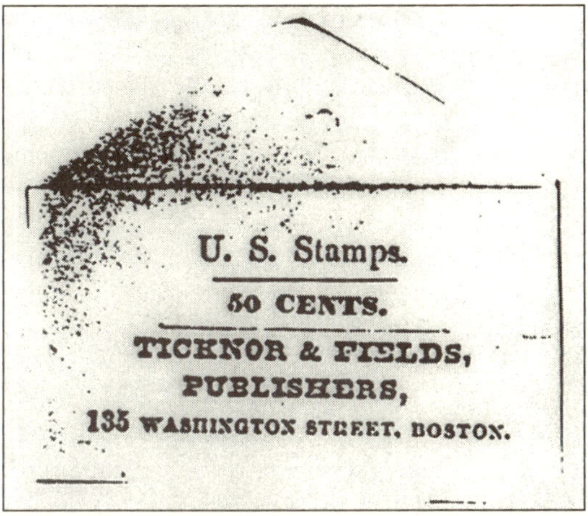
U. S. Stamps.

50 CENTS.

TICKNOR & FIELDS,
PUBLISHERS,
135 WASHINGTON STREET, BOSTON.

Figures 135a, b

Ticknor and Fields' location, corner of School and Washington streets, was just three doors down from Bates' store, both depicted here in a winter scene, below. The publisher was a natural to adopt the postage stamp envelopes which predated Gault's encased stamps as an advertising and small change medium. Envelope. (Milton R. Friedberg illustration) Below, W. S. Peirce Woodcut, Ballou's Pictorial, *February 21, 1857. (Dallas Public Library)*

use of travellers, or utility, taste and ornament," according to a trade notice.

Through the years he added other lines to his trade, notably stereo views and other photographic images during the 1860s. This was largely due to the proximity of Joseph Ward, a photographer next door, and especially to his friendship and partnership with literary lion Oliver Wendell Holmes. Bates store was three doors from the publishing house of William Ticknor and James T. Fields. In 1857, Holmes, James Russell Lowell, Longfellow, Emerson and others had launched a magazine dedicated to bringing "the literary influence of New England to aid the anti-slavery cause." Christened the *Atlantic Monthly* magazine at Holmes' suggestion, the periodical was published by Ticknor and Fields, Bates' neighbors for a decade by that time. Bates and his longtime neighbors were well acquainted long before the magazine commenced, but as it picked up steam and the publishing house became a mecca for New England literati, they also came to frequent Bates' shop regularly.

In its day the *Atlantic* was a national institution of a scope hard to grasp by the current

Fancy Goods.

JOSEPH L. BATES,

129 Washington Street, ... Boston,

FOUR DOORS NORTH OF SCHOOL STREET,

IMPORTER OF AND DEALER IN

EUROPEAN AND AMERICAN

FANCY GOODS,

Perfumery, Umbrellas, Parasols, Brushes, Cutlery, Stationery, Toilet Articles, Games, and

HORN AND SHELL COMBS.

Articles for Presents; for the use of Travellers; of Utility, Taste, and Ornament,—constantly for sale at the lowest prices.

☞ New PARIS GOODS, of the latest and most fashionable description, received by every arrival.

Figures 136a, b

Bates imported luxuries for the genteel Boston society set: wealthy, influential and worldly. Ad, above, The Boston Almanac, *1862, p. 305. (Author's collection) His principal trade in the post-war years, however, became stereopticon photographs and viewers. These three-dimensional photos were pioneered in America by Dr. Holmes as an offshoot of his interest in 3-D microscopy. Holmes invented an improved viewer (left above) which Bates further refined (right above). Woodcuts,* The American Photographer. *(Author's collection)*

mind. *All* the best essayists, poets and fiction writers appeared in its pages, and Ticknor's became the practical center of a literary/philosophical movement nearly religious in its fervor. Its influence was not just regional. In a very real sense the *Atlantic* and Ticknor's was the hub of the national cultural spirit which defined the new social and intellectual horizons of its age. The magazine extended a national focus out to hamlets across the country through the writing of the likes of Emerson, Longfellow, Whittier, Hawthorne, Howells,

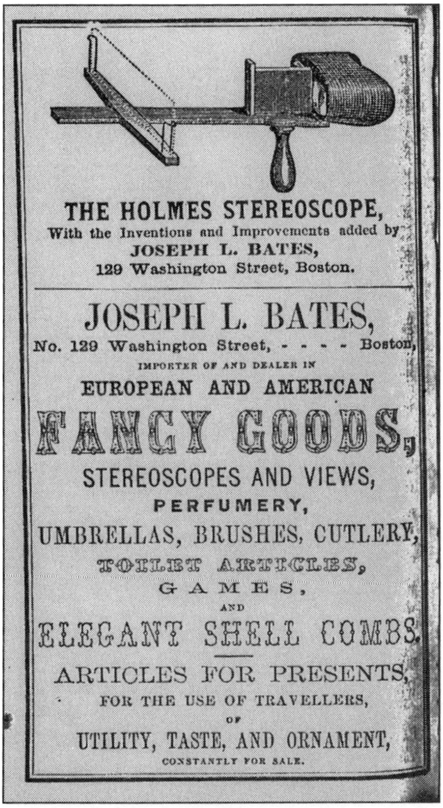

Figures 137a,b

Bates relationship to the eminent Dr. Holmes is an interesting one. Holmes interest in 3-D photography was a scientific and academic one. Bates interest was a commercial one. Bates developed a much improved photo mount, which he patented, produced and sold in great quantities. The fad swept the country bringing the mysteries of the Orient, Europe and Africa into the parlors of America. By the time the ad at left appeared in the city directory, his improved Holmes stereoscope dominated his trade. Ad, The Boston Almanac and Directory, *1869, facing p. 186. (Author's collection) Bates sold a great variety of stereo photos. Below, the great Niagara Falls frozen solid in winter was a favorite of photographers and viewers. Stereopticon Card. (Author's collection)*

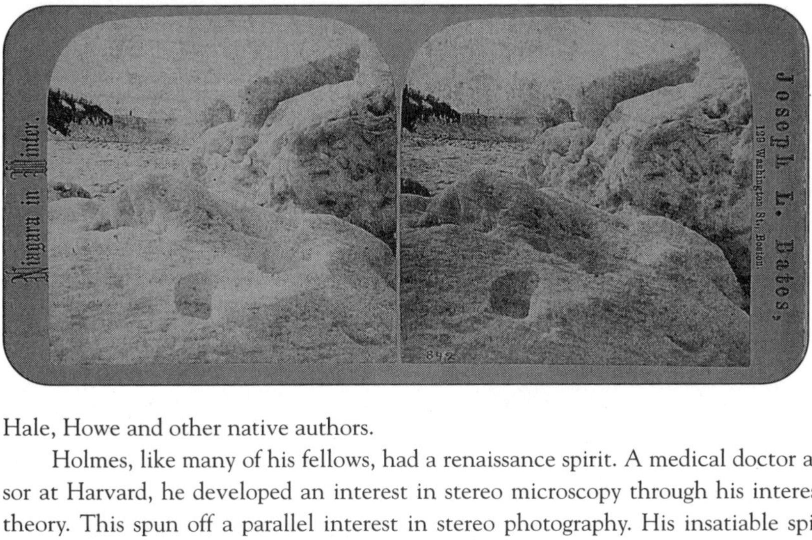

Hale, Howe and other native authors.

Holmes, like many of his fellows, had a renaissance spirit. A medical doctor and professor at Harvard, he developed an interest in stereo microscopy through his interest in germ theory. This spun off a parallel interest in stereo photography. His insatiable spirit caused

UNITED STATES PATENT OFFICE.

JOSEPH L. BATES, OF BOSTON, MASSACHUSETTS.

IMPROVEMENT IN PICTURE-HOLDERS FOR STEREOSCOPES.

Specification forming part of Letters Patent No. 151,745, dated June 9, 1874; application filed May 13, 1874.

To all whom it may concern:

Be it known that I, JOSEPH L. BATES, of Boston, of the county of Suffolk and State of Massachusetts, have invented a new and useful Improvement in the Stereoscope; and do hereby declare the same to be fully described in the following specification and represented in the accompanying drawings, of which—

Figure 1 is a top view, Fig. 2 a side elevation, and Fig. 3 a perspective view, of a stereoscope having my improvement.

My invention relates to the picture-slide, which, heretofore, has consisted of a single bar of wood and two wire staples projecting up from it near its ends, each staple near its upper end being bent over at a right angle to the vertical parts of the legs. Such a slide is usually calculated for supporting at once but one picture, which has to be inserted into the staples or withdrawn from them vertically. My improved slide or picture-supporter is calculated to support at once a pack of pictures, and to admit of each of them to be withdrawn from it, or placed upon it, endwise, such being much more convenient to an observer while using the instrument.

In the drawing, A denotes the bar; B, the lens-carrier; C, the eye-shield; D, the handle, and E the screen, applied and arranged as in most stereoscopes. F is the picture supporter or slide, which, in this case, consists of a horizontal plate or board, *a*, a vertical board or rest, *b*, and a wire, *c*, all being arranged as shown. The said wire, bent at right angles and inserted at one end in the board *b*, and at the other in the plate *a*, at or in close proximity with their two next adjacent ends, answers as a gage or stop for the pictures, which, when in proper positions, will at one end of each abut against the horizontal part of the wire. The said slide straddles the bar A, and is provided with a friction-spring, *d*, having a knob, *e*, all being such as are commonly used with the slides of stereoscopes.

I claim—

In the stereoscope, the improved picture slide or supporter F, composed of the two boards *a b* and the single gage *c*, arranged as specified and represented.

JOSEPH L. BATES.

Witnesses:

LANGDON S. WARD,
J. R. SNOW.

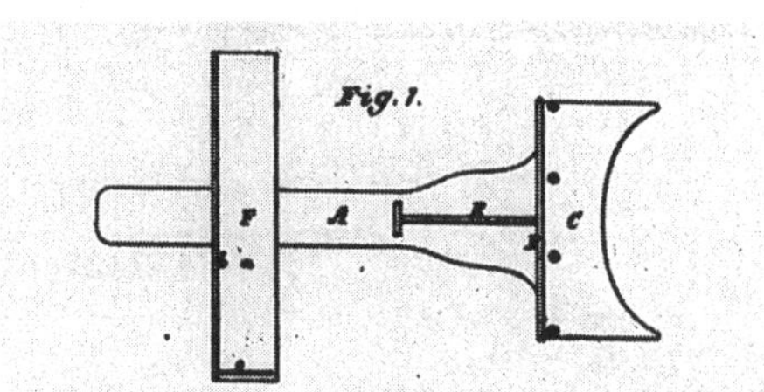

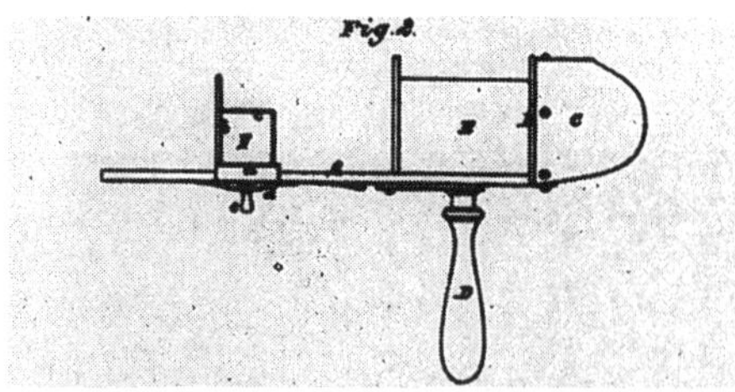

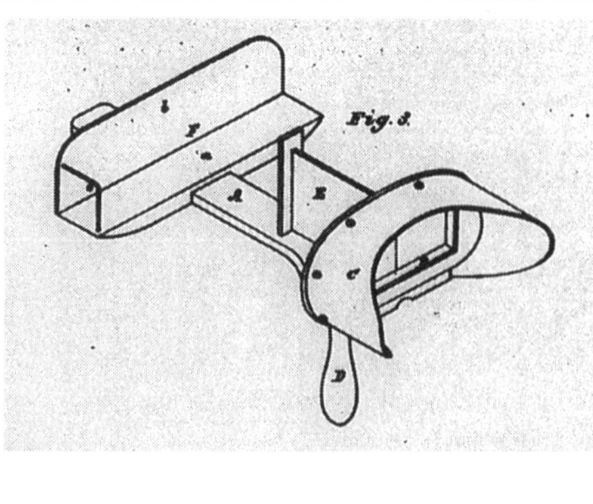

Figures 138a-d

Bates' sliding carrier was easier to use than Holmes' fixed holder. A later improvement added a stand to the viewer freeing the hands. Patent No. 151,745, June 9, 1874. (U.S. Patent Office)

Figures 139a, b

Above, a remarkable photograph shows Joseph L. Bates in the doorway with his next door neighbor, photographer Joseph Ward. Photo. (The Bostonian Society, Old State House, Neg. No. 2319) At left, is Ward's copy of the famous Anthony Berger photo of Lincoln and his son Tad examining a volume of cartes de visite. It was common practice during that era for photographers to re-release other's work under their own imprint. Carte de Visite Photo (detail). (Author's collection)

him to develop a practical stereo viewer for the stereo photographs just coming into vogue on the heels of the Civil War. A patrician to the core and hardly given to developing his

Figures 140a, b

Above, 1870s model of Bates' stereo viewer. (Author's collection, electronic imaging by Omar Mediano) Right, in later years images dominated Bates' trade. Trade Card. (Dr. Robert D. Gardner collection, Dabney C. Jackson photo)

invention, Holmes gave his idea to Bates, who for years was practiced in manufacturing small items. Bates' improved upon Holmes' overall design and added several additional improvements, including a sliding carrier which made focusing simpler and a stand for the viewer which freed up the hands. Increasingly his business in stereo views and stereo viewers grew, eclipsing his trade in the other small luxury items he had dealt in for most of his adult life.

Following the Great Boston Fire of 1872 and the economic distress of 1873, Bates retired from retail activity briefly. He spent his time perfecting his stereo apparatus and in 1874 was granted an additional patent for an improved picture slide that permitted "cards to be slid laterally, and a number to be successively used without displacing any." This was an important commercial patent which must have been worth considerable sums. He reopened for commercial business at 7 Beacon Street, and still later at 13 1/2 Bromfield Street. Judging from the viewers still extant employing his patent, he should have prospered. He

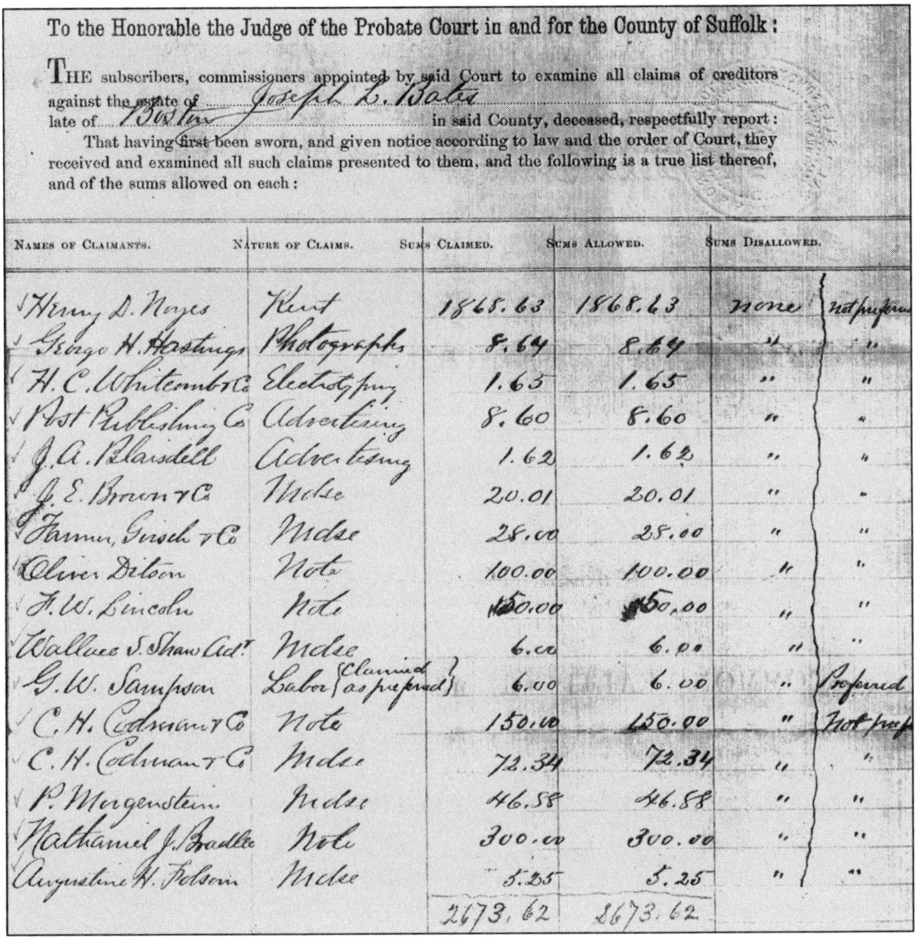

To the Honorable the Judge of the Probate Court in and for the County of Suffolk:

THE subscribers, commissioners appointed by said Court to examine all claims of creditors against the estate of Joseph L. Bates late of Boston in said County, deceased, respectfully report:

That having first been sworn, and given notice according to law and the order of Court, they received and examined all such claims presented to them, and the following is a true list thereof, and of the sums allowed on each:

Names of Claimants.	Nature of Claims.	Sums Claimed.	Sums Allowed.	Sums Disallowed.	
Henry D. Noyes	Rent	1868.63	1868.63	none	not preferred
George H. Hastings	Photographs	8.64	8.64	"	"
H. C. Whitcomb & Co	Electrotyping	1.65	1.65	"	"
Post Publishing Co	Advertising	8.60	8.60	"	"
J. A. Blaisdell	Advertising	1.62	1.62	"	"
J. E. Brown & Co	Mdse	20.01	20.01	"	"
Farmer, Gersh & Co	Mdse	28.00	28.00	"	"
Oliver Ditson	Note	100.00	100.00	"	"
F. W. Lincoln	Note	150.00	150.00	"	"
Wallace J. Shaw Adm'r	Mdse	6.00	6.00	"	"
G. W. Sampson	Labor (Claimed as preferred)	6.00	6.00	"	Preferred
C. H. Codman & Co	Note	150.00	150.00	"	Not pref
C. H. Codman & Co	Mdse	72.34	72.34	"	"
P. Morgenstein	Mdse	46.88	46.88	"	"
Nathaniel J. Bradlee	Note	300.00	300.00	"	"
Augustine H. Folsom	Mdse	5.25	5.25	"	"
		2673.62	2673.62		

Figure 141a

Bates' estate was a simple one. His debts recorded above indicate he lived simply. Virtually all these entries are connected to his retail business. (Suffolk County Probate Court)

continued in the stereo business until 1886, when at the advanced age of 79 business and life caught up with him.

He died March 2, 1886 of what was believed to be heart disease. He did not leave a will, nor much in the way of an estate. What happened to his prewar portfolio of real estate or to the profits from his active trade in photographs and viewers remains a mystery. The court appointed a nephew as administrator of the meager estate. Bates left no real estate and a mere $345.84 in personal property. Debts totalling nearly ten times that amount were established. For his contributions to photographic history, Bates rates passing mention in that science's literature, which credits the much more famous Holmes with most of Bates'

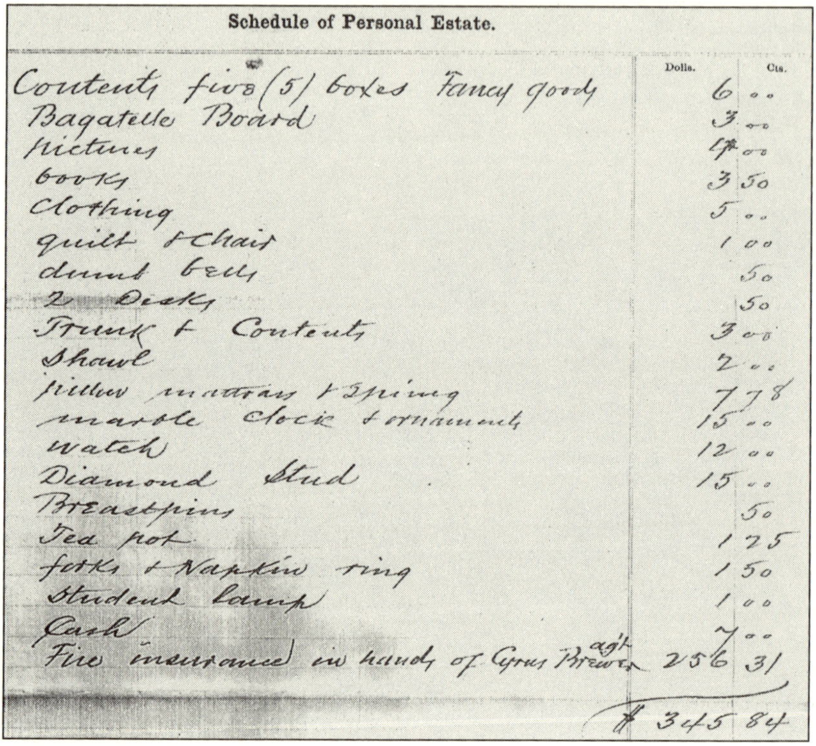

Schedule of Personal Estate.

	Dolls.	Cts.
Contents five (5) boxes Fancy goods	6	00
Bagatelle Board	3	00
Pictures	4	00
books	3	50
Clothing	5	00
quilt & chair	1	00
dumb bells		50
2 Desks		50
Trunk & Contents	3	00
Shawl	2	00
pillow mattress & spring	7	78
marble clock & ornaments	15	00
watch	12	00
Diamond Stud	15	00
Breastpins		50
Tea pot	1	75
forks & Napkin ring	1	50
Student lamp	1	00
Cash	7	00
Fire insurance in hands of Cyrus Brewer agt	256	31
	$345	84

Figure 142a

A summary of the personal assets of Bates' long career is short: a little bit of jewelry and not much else. (Suffolk County Probate Court)

contributions. Unfortunately we may never be able to set the record straight.

Bates' principal legacy aside from his stereo items remains his encased stamps, which are fairly plentiful. His proclivity for one-cent pieces (Reed BA01FG and BA01F/G) indicates a desire for a large number of pieces for a minimal outlay. Even so, the large order must have lasted quite a while for a small retail merchant. Perhaps he considered the pieces novelties, a trinket among his luxury goods. Perhaps he gave them out as pocket pieces. Bates' location is now a parking garage. Ticknor & Field's building, however, still stands housing "The Olde Corner Bookstore." Its publishing imprint was recently folded into Houghton Mifflin's juvenile titles.

Auction Census Data Summary, 1891-1994

	1	2	3	5	10	12	24	30	90	Total	Pct
BA FG	68		2	5	11	0				86	
BA FG RB	1			5	3					9	
BA F/G	103		16	13	23	16	2			173	
	172		**18**	**23**	**37**	**16**	**2**			**268**	**3%**

Joseph Burnett
Chapter VIII

Another of the Boston apothecaries, Joseph Burnett, also became a principal user of John Gault's New Metallic Currency. While not ordering anything approaching the numbers of pieces purchased by J. C. Ayer, his expenditure on Gault's small change store cards was considerable, nevertheless. We may realistically determine that Burnett purchased about 60,000 pieces of encased stamps in fall 1862. These are of two types reflecting the duality of his business at the time. One advertises his line of food additives, his Standard Cooking Extracts (Reed BE). The second touts three of his other products, a line of personal grooming aids: his Cocoaine, his Kalliston, and his Toilet Sets (Reed BK). This latter piece is commonly referred to in the trade as the Cocaine (sic) Kalliston issue, a clear misapprehension of the products. The piece has nothing to do with cocaine, the drug. Burnett's Cocoaine was a cocoa nut oil-based hair tonic, and his Kalliston was a skin lotion. The third item, toilet sets, were other small necessities associated with personal hygiene.

Total numbers of pieces produced for the two lines are roughly comparable, although more Reed BE pieces are extant today. Like Ayer, Burnett ordered a wide range of denominational values, although principally concentrated in the four workhorse denominations: i.e. one-, three-, five- and ten-cents. Unlike Ayer, who showed a decided preference for the lower two denominations, Burnett's preference was clearly in favor of the two higher valued

Figures 143a, b

Above, left, Reed BE10 obverse, ex-James F. Ruddy specimen. (Bowers and Merena photo)
Right, Reed BK10 obverse. (Dana Linett photo)

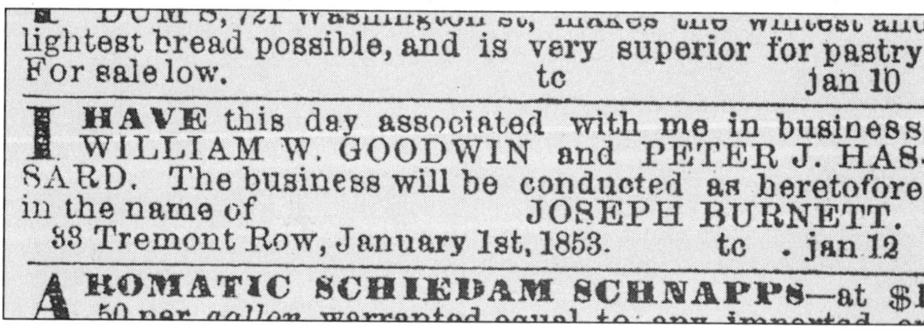

lightest bread possible, and is very superior for pastry. For sale low. tc jan 10

I HAVE this day associated with me in business, WILLIAM W. GOODWIN and PETER J. HASSARD. The business will be conducted as heretofore, in the name of JOSEPH BURNETT.
33 Tremont Row, January 1st, 1853. tc . jan 12

AROMATIC SCHIEDAM SCHNAPPS—at $1

Figures 144a, b

Joseph Burnett's storefront, c. 1850. Woodcut. Gleason's Pictorial Drawing Room Companion, *1857. (Boston Athenaeum) Bottom, a legal notice published to indicate Burnett had brought two partners into his business. Legal Notice, Boston* Daily Evening Transcript, *February 3, 1853, p. [4] (Author's collection)*

pieces. Thus Burnett's expenditure was proportionally lower than Ayer's, clearly showing Ayer's advertising liberality in comparison. It also illustrates well the simple fact that Ayer did not conduct a retail trade, but Burnett did so, in addition to his manufacturing business, and so he also needed small change in his cash box for retail customers.

In its day the manufacturing chemists Joseph Burnett & Co. enjoyed a solid reputation, richly deserved, based on the quality of their products. It was also fostered by cunningly-worded advertising, so Burnett knew what to expect when he succumbed to John Gault's sales' pitch. "Whatever Dr. Burnett makes is the best of its kind," a contemporary observed.

Figures 145a, b, c

Young, handsome, and full of dedication, Burnett posed for this daguerreotype sometime in the 1850s. Copy of a Daguerreotype, probably by Southworth and Hawes. (Photograph courtesy of Robert Burnett) Left below, a cut signature of Burnett. (Courtesy of Robert Burnett) Bottom, a secretarial signature of Joseph Burnett & Co. from the reverse of a check payable to the company. (Author's collection)

That view was self-serving, of course. It appeared in a Burnett ad. Such a high opinion, unfortunately, has not uniformly prevailed down to the present day. Fishing for his own advertising copy to help sell a Burnett Extracts encased stamp some years ago, a modern copy writer – who misunderstood the nature of the product completely – leaped to an ignoble conclusion and termed the product as sounding "like some left-over sludge at the bottom of the pan!" So much for the intellectual skills of an average cataloger. In fact, Burnett's advertising practices, including brief notices "in every conceivable journal, published in every conceivable place," fueled an economic empire which was already quite well advanced

THE SAN FRANCISCO DAILY HERALD.

SAN FRANCISCO: SUNDAY MORNING, APRIL 1, 1855.

Superior Dentifrice;
Fine Pomades, and other articles for the Toilet;
Cologne Water, of our own make, in large Hock

STANDARD FAMILY MEDICINES.

BURNETT'S KALLISTON.—THIS EMULSIVE lotion for improving the complexion and removing freckles, rendering the skin soft, fair and delicate, is without a rival. Prepared only by
JOSEPH BURNETT,
39 Tremont st., Boston.
And for sale by KEITH, HASSARD & CO.,
d24tf Montgomery street, corner Clay.

ORIENTAL TOOTH WASH—FOR CLEANSING and preserving the Teeth from Caries, Toothache, Neuralgia, etc., the accumulation of Tartar. Also for purifying and preserving the durability of all kinds of Artificial Teeth. Prepared only by BURNETT, 39 Tremont street, Boston.
Sold by KEITH, HASSARD & CO.,
d24tf Montgomery street, corner Clay.

BURNETT'S SUPERIOR EXTRACTS OF Lemon, Vanilla, Rose, Nectarine, Bitter Almond, and Cinnamon, prepared from fruits of the best quality, and highly concentrated Sold by
KEITH, HASSARD & CO.,
d24tf Montgomery street, corner Clay

THE SUBSCRIBERS HAVING BOUGHT the SIERRA NEVADA MILLS, have appointed Mr. B. GALUSHA their Agent, who alone is authorized to transact business for the same.
As usual, Extra Superfine Family FLOUR will be constantly kept on hand, in lots to suit purchasers.

Figures 146a, b

Above, Burnett was a prolific user of advertising on a national scale. Ads, San Francisco Daily Herald, *April 1, 1855, p. 1. (James Bishop collection) Right, The keystone to Burnett's incredible success was his vanilla extract, which even a century later was a ready seller for its superior quality and delicate aroma. Twentieth century ad slick. (Courtesy James Bishop)*

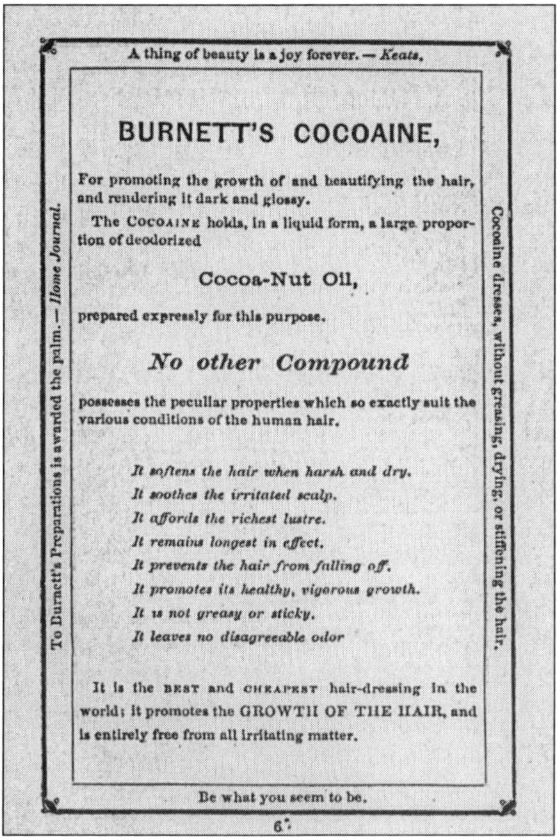

Figure 147a

Burnett followed the accepted practice of his day in publishing a wealth of advertising literature which also offered enough other information to be useful to the recipient. The material would thus be kept close at hand – where the customer would receive additional reinforcement from his advertising pitches. The page facing his Cocoaine pitch, for example, provides poetical sentiments on the "meaning" of various flowers as gifts as well as scriptural paraphrases. Burnett's Floral Hand Book, *1872, p. 6. (The New-York Historical Society)*

by the time his space ads appeared on the backs of Gault's New Metallic Currency.

The originator, chief architect, and principal benefactor of this commercial success, Joseph Burnett, was born in Southborough, Massachusetts, November 11, 1820. He was the fourth of five children of Charles Burnett, a yeoman and rope maker, and Keziah Pond Burnett. Young Joseph was educated in the district schools and subsequently in the English and Latin Schools of Worchester. He worked in the latter community for two years. In 1837, at age 17, Burnett came to Boston, finding employment as a clerk in the successful drug business of Theodore Metcalf. He was admitted into partnership and remained there until 1854, principally engaged in the manufacture of perfume. It was said that he studied medicine, but he never practiced that art, although he went by the title "Doctor."

In addition to his trade in fragrances for his employer Metcalf, young Burnett developed a sideline on his own which was to make his fortune in the ensuing years. In 1845 a cosmopolitan woman came into the Metcalf drug store and requested a vanilla flavoring such as she had enjoyed while traveling in France. Her request was a challenge for the young pharmacist, since extracting such a flavoring from the vanilla bean was a difficult and

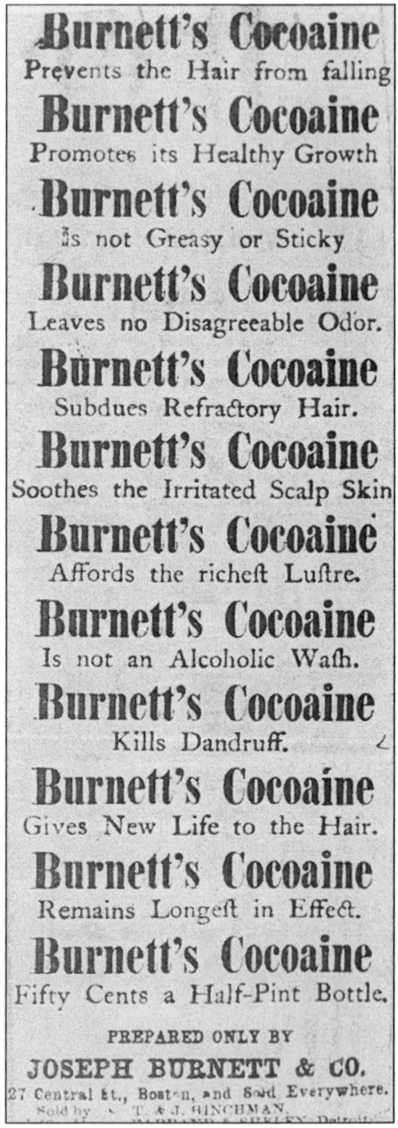

Figures 148a, b

Burnett's ads employed repetition to achieve brand identification, an almost cheerleader approach. An outstanding example appears at right. The product's name is drummed at the reader and reinforced by his efficacy claims. This message was further reinforced by repeated re-exposure. An advertising code (de18eod4w) at the bottom of the ad indicates it was to run in the publication every other day for a month. Detroit Advertiser, *December 18, 1862. (Bob Kincaid) Below, facsimile labels.* Burnett's Floral Hand Book, *1875, p. 6. (Author's collection)*

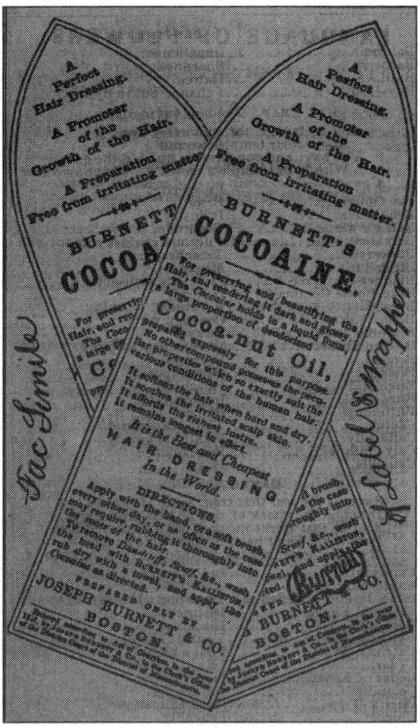

time-consuming procedure. "The cooks of that day who wanted a vanilla flavor were accustomed to soaking the vanilla bean in alcohol to draw out the flavor – a method which didn't always prove satisfactory. In those days such a plea to a druggist . . . was far more astounding than can be realized today," a writer suggests. But Burnett stuck to the task. Eventually he produced the required bottle of vanilla extract. The woman was delighted. She spread news of Burnett's success by word of mouth and sent her friends to the pharmacist. In short time, he was in the flavoring business full time.

Figures 149a, b

Burnett was a major advertiser in many media. He was the largest advertiser in Jewett's Boston Sights and Strangers Guide, *published a few years before the Civil War. He pitched his Kalliston as "Oriental Water" offering an exotic elixir for ailments or irritations of the skin. He showed its label so a prospective buyer would already be familiar with it when out shopping. The bottle's labeling was in keeping with this mystique, as shown at left. Ad (detail).* Guide to Boston and Suburbs, *1856, p. [240] (Author's collection) Below, Invoice for a dozen Cocoaine bottles, Sept. 27, 1857. (The New-York Historical Society)*

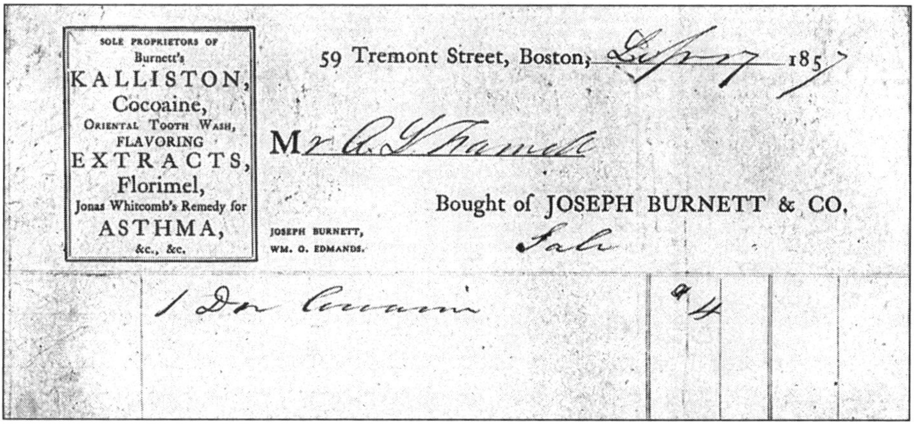

Burnett sold his interest in Metcalf's perfume business and formed a partnership with William O. Edmands, called Joseph Burnett & Co., occupying several different premises as the success of the venture grew. In 1858, the firm moved to 27 Central, where it was located at the time of the small change panic and where it remained for several additional decades.

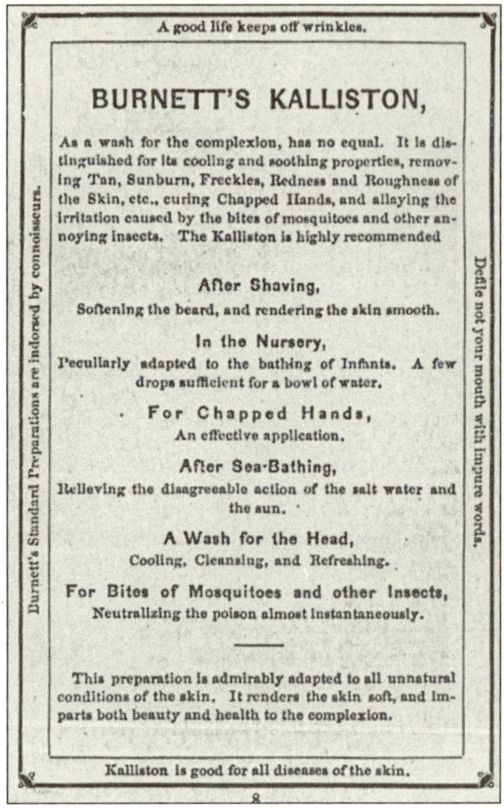

A good life keeps off wrinkles.

Burnett's Standard Preparations are indorsed by connoisseurs.

BURNETT'S KALLISTON,

As a wash for the complexion, has no equal. It is distinguished for its cooling and soothing properties, removing Tan, Sunburn, Freckles, Redness and Roughness of the Skin, etc., curing Chapped Hands, and allaying the irritation caused by the bites of mosquitoes and other annoying insects. The Kalliston is highly recommended

After Shaving,
Softening the beard, and rendering the skin smooth.

In the Nursery,
Peculiarly adapted to the bathing of Infants. A few drops sufficient for a bowl of water.

For Chapped Hands,
An effective application.

After Sea-Bathing,
Relieving the disagreeable action of the salt water and the sun.

A Wash for the Head,
Cooling, Cleansing, and Refreshing.

For Bites of Mosquitoes and other Insects,
Neutralizing the poison almost instantaneously.

This preparation is admirably adapted to all unnatural conditions of the skin. It renders the skin soft, and imparts both beauty and health to the complexion.

Defile not your mouth with impure words.

Kalliston is good for all diseases of the skin.

8

Figure 150a

In the much looser commercial codes prevailing in mid-19th century, Burnett could claim his Kalliston "is good for all diseases of the skin," hyperbole he would not be allowed today. Never-the-less his product must have been efficacious judging by its enormous sales over many, many years. Its high alcohol content (11 percent) provided its cooling effect. Burnett's Floral Hand Book, *1872, p. 8. (The New-York Historical Society)*

The enterprising Burnett saw the value of a flavoring business, "If one flavor made business good, additional flavors could make business better." By the Civil War, he had a dozen different flavorings. The diminutive size of the stamp cases only allowed him to specifically list four. He continued to add additional extracts until eventually 30 different flavors bore his famous label. Highly concentrated, they "won universal approval," and no well ordered kitchen would be without them, Burnett contended.

Burnett's Cocoaine was invented in November 1856 to compete with the harsh alcohol hair dressings which burned the scalp and the greasy preparations made from animal oils and fats which could not be absorbed by the skin. His coconut oil dressing won quick acceptance from his female clients. "No other preparation so exactly suits the various conditions of human hair," its inventor proclaimed. Like other purveyors of proprietary products, Burnett backed up his claims with effusive testimonials. Most, like the testimonials of New York publisher Frank Leslie, are run of the mill for the times. Burnett went one better, however, by widely circulating the tale of an 82-year-old bald man, a William S. Eddy, who claimed a new dark growth of hair "where [he] had been bald for years" following his introduction to the product. Eddy was not the only bald man benefitted. A D. T. Merwin headlined a national advertising campaign claiming a similar cure from Burnett's hair oil.

Figures 151a, b

Original package wrappings for Burnett's products are rare. These fine examples belong to a descendant of Burnett, who graciously made them available especially for this book. (James Bishop photos)

The strength of such advertising claims was not lost on Burnett's competitors. Approximately two years after introducing his hair tonic, a spurious imitation was brought out in New York City seeking to capitalize on its name and reputation. Burnett won his suit in April 1859 before New York Superior Court Justice Pierrepont, who ruled that the New Yorker's *Cocoine* was a illegal attempt to capitalize on Burnett's success. On appeal, the decision was upheld by the New York Court of Appeals in July, 1867. The case would seem to offer ample proof that Slabaugh is correct in the pronunciation of this product, i.e. *coco-ine*. Thereafter Burnett vigorously defended this and his other trademarks against illegal infringement, too.

Kalliston was simply "the best cosmetic in the world" as a sunburn restorative, tan and freckle remover, and complexion builder. The produce dates at least from 1854, and marks that century's desire for a clear and fair complexion as the height of beauty and female

Figure 152a

Another hallmark of Burnett's ad campaigns, still very much used today, was testimonial. This particular pitch for his line of food flavorings relied on positive comments from some of the leading inn keepers of their day from across the country. It has particular relevance for this book, however, because the proprietor of Chicago's Sherman House was another of Gault's customers, David A. Gage, a former resident of Boston himself. Burnett's Floral Hand Book, *1872, p. 10. (The New-York Historical Society)*

adornment. The Kalliston contained a "peculiar erasive property which [removes] those disagreeable stains . . . and renders the complexion clear and beautiful," Burnett's pitchmen claimed. It was also useful as an antidote to shaving burn, rash, chapped hands, insect bites and other skin irritations. Included in the Toilet Sets were Burnett's Oriental Tooth Wash, "a superior dentifrice," his Florimel, "an exquisite handkerchief perfume," as well as cologne, and cod liver oil. He also marketed, but did not advertise on his stamp cases, Jonas Whitcomb's Remedy for Asthma, which became very popular when it was touted unsolicited in the extremely popular biography, *The Life of Washington Irving*. Interestingly, the rights to this product were given to Burnett by longtime friend, Dr. Oliver Wendell Holmes.

Burnett was well able to judge the merits of John Gault's New Metallic Currency as an advertising medium. He took a personal, active interest in the public presentation of his products. Although Burnett's notices are almost invariably small, they are particularly well-placed, according to a contemporary ad man. Often they are but two or three lines at the end of a column of type, occupying a prominent location before the reader adjusted his gaze to the next column or story. Burnett's advertising staff, headed by Lyman D. Morse, was tenacious. "No man," competitor George Rowell wrote, "ever worked more faithfully, more

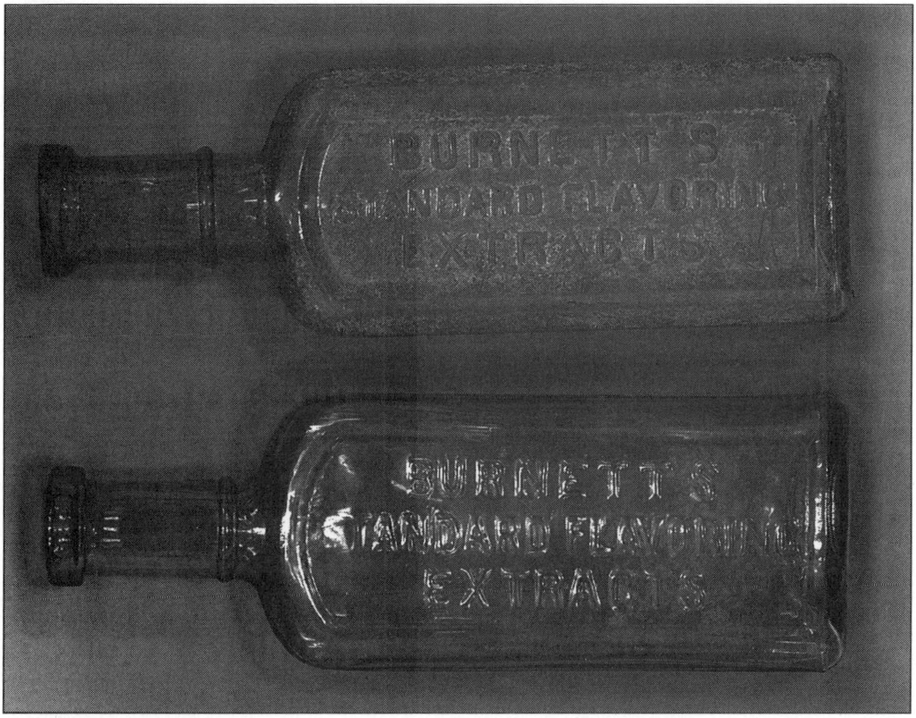

Figures 153a, b

Burnett's Flavoring Extracts bottles are fairly common and inexpensive at antique shows and shops. Frequently flea market specimens will be found in "as dug" condition, with the corrosion prominent on the top specimen, above. Burnett's Standard Flavoring Extracts Bottles. (Author's collection)

tirelessly to get a low rate, an extra concession, and a position nobody else could secure." Rowell continued:

> Time was no object. If a small concession was all that could be had that was better than nothing. No matter how good the terms that were offered Morse was never quite satisfied. He was always in earnest, never laughed. He had no sense of humor, but held the dollar very close to his eye.

Burnett also had a good eye for the benefits of free advertising. He quickly recognized the benefits and desirability of designing his own private die, proprietary medicine revenue stamp for his preparations. If such excise taxes had to be paid to help finance the war and stamps had to be affixed on the bottles to prove that the tax had been paid, well then his stamps should be the best one. Clearly, amid the proliferation of odd styles adopted by many of his competitors, his classic style stands out. His stamp was so effective, he believed, that in later years when such duties were no longer required, he redesigned the stamp without the words U.S. INTER. REV. // FOUR CENTS and the "4" counters. Bearing instead TRADE MARK and rosettes, he continued to use the device as a label.

Additional products followed. At the Centennial Exposition in 1876, the firm was

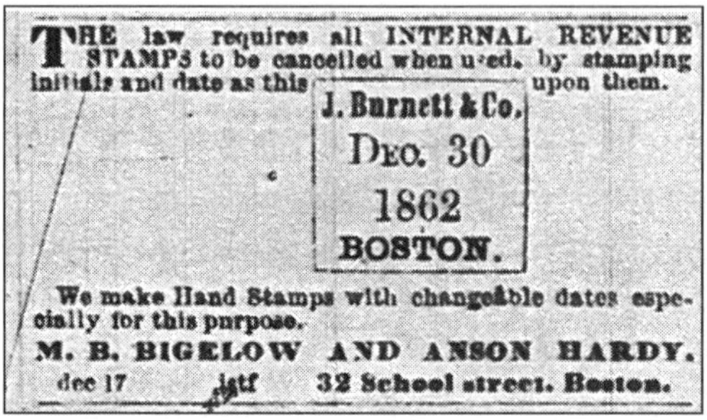
THE law requires all INTERNAL REVENUE STAMPS to be cancelled when used, by stamping initials and date as this upon them.

J. Burnett & Co.
DEC. 30
1862
BOSTON.

We make Hand Stamps with changeable dates especially for this purpose.
M. B. BIGELOW AND ANSON HARDY.
dec 17 istf 32 School street. Boston.

Figures 154a, b, c, d

Burnett's endorsement, above left, was beneficial. This device would cancel government Revenue Stamps required by war tax legislation. Boston Commercial Advertiser, *December 17, 1862. (Bob Kincaid) Due to production delays on government stamps, private merchants were permitted to execute stamps of their own design for prepackaged proprietary medicines. Burnett's design, top and right (detail) highlights this series for the author (Scott No. RS46). Above, Check payable to Joseph Burnett & Co., December 27, 1876. (Specimens, Author's collection)*

awarded a medal for its colognes and fragrances. Special food colors were also introduced for cakes, and about 1890 for ice cream, too. About the time of the Second World War, Burnett's name also graced pie crust and muffin mixes. The firm was very progressive for its times. It also experimented successfully in packaging, offering for instance several sizes of all products, and multiplying packaging.

As he prospered, Burnett developed other interests. He "lived like a gentleman and associated with gentlemen." In 1850 he built Deerfoot Farm in his birthplace,

Figures 155a, b

Joseph Burnett was already a prosperous and influential member of the community long before the outbreak of the Civil War. A real patrician, he built the fine residence, below, in 1849-50, one of his many visible and lasting contributions to his era. Photos left and below. (University of Texas at Dallas and Boston Historical Society)

Southborough. There he pioneered the importation and raising of Jersey cattle from the Channel Islands. An ardent churchman, he built Southborough's Episcopal Church in 1862

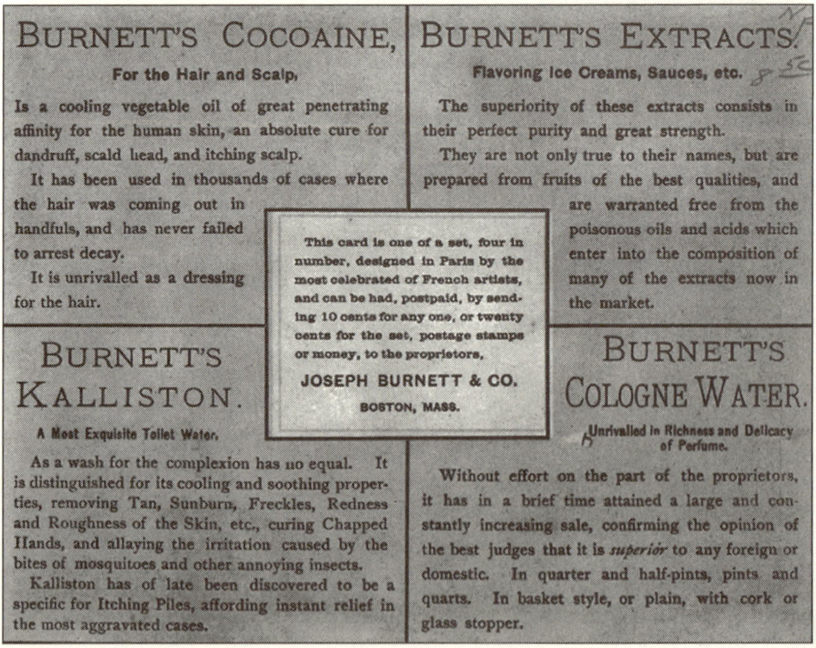

BURNETT'S COCOAINE,

For the Hair and Scalp,

Is a cooling vegetable oil of great penetrating affinity for the human skin, an absolute cure for dandruff, scald head, and itching scalp.

It has been used in thousands of cases where the hair was coming out in handfuls, and has never failed to arrest decay.

It is unrivalled as a dressing for the hair.

BURNETT'S EXTRACTS.

Flavoring Ice Creams, Sauces, etc.

The superiority of these extracts consists in their perfect purity and great strength.

They are not only true to their names, but are prepared from fruits of the best qualities, and are warranted free from the poisonous oils and acids which enter into the composition of many of the extracts now in the market.

This card is one of a set, four in number, designed in Paris by the most celebrated of French artists, and can be had, postpaid, by sending 10 cents for any one, or twenty cents for the set, postage stamps or money, to the proprietors,

JOSEPH BURNETT & CO.

BOSTON, MASS.

BURNETT'S KALLISTON.

A Most Exquisite Toilet Water.

As a wash for the complexion has no equal. It is distinguished for its cooling and soothing properties, removing Tan, Sunburn, Freckles, Redness and Roughness of the Skin, etc., curing Chapped Hands, and allaying the irritation caused by the bites of mosquitoes and other annoying insects.

Kalliston has of late been discovered to be a specific for Itching Piles, affording instant relief in the most aggravated cases.

BURNETT'S COLOGNE WATER.

Unrivalled in Richness and Delicacy of Perfume.

Without effort on the part of the proprietors, it has in a brief time attained a large and constantly increasing sale, confirming the opinion of the best judges that it is *superior* to any foreign or domestic. In quarter and half-pints, pints and quarts. In basket style, or plain, with cork or glass stopper.

Figures 156a, b

Except for cologne water, each product on this trade card was also advertised on Burnett's encased stamps. Trade card, front and back, c. 1875. (Author's collection)

Figures 157a, b

Left, a principal advertising vehicle for Burnett's products was his Burnett's Floral Hand Book, *which itself was popularized by colorful lithographic trade cards. Trade card, 1881. (Author's collection) Burnett's food flavorings were popular well into this century, when these bottles, below, were sold. (James Bishop photo)*

out of his own resources and presented it to the parish. He stipulated that the church be open to all "with no distinction as to wealth, color, race, or station." His desire to provide

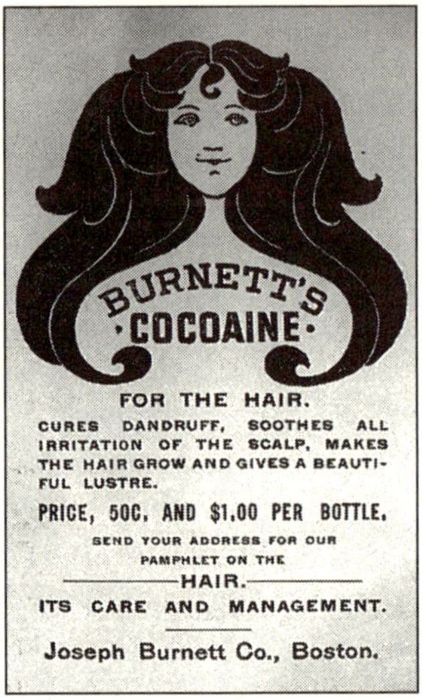

Figures 158a, b, c

Burnett's empire may be traced by its extant sales literature, which is plentiful. Above, a 20th century take on Burnett's Cocoaine offers a hair care booklet. Ad from The Cosmopolitan, *c. 1900. (James Bishop photo) Above right, another of Burnett's helpful booklets: his* Burnett's Floral Hand Book and Ladies' Calendar, *1875. (Author's collection) As may be seen by the ad, at right, Burnett eventually expanded his line of fragrances. Ad,* Life *magazine, December 19, 1889. (Author's collection)*

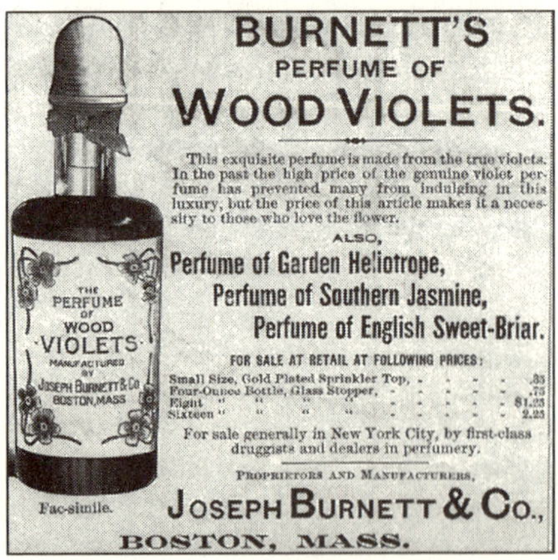

his sons a Christian education and his immense financial resources, then allowed, him to lead in the establishment of St. Mark's School, which quickly became a leading college prep school. In both enterprises, he actively participated in the institution's activities and upkeep. He maintained an active public life setting his hands to a variety of civic tasks and impressing all who knew him with his generosity and gentle spirit. His sterling reputation was such that not even his competitors had occasion to speak ill of him.

Burnett was still active when the end came, August 11, 1894 and he was buried in the church yard of the stone church he had built and contributed to liberally for many years.

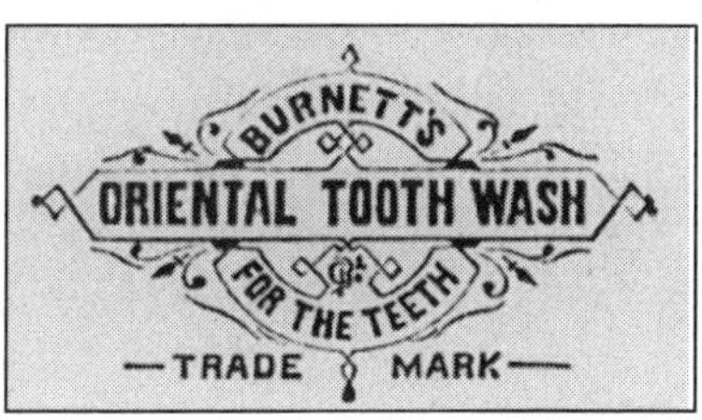

Figures 159a-i

Burnett vigorously protected his trade marks. He won a landmark infringement case in New York Superior Court in 1859, a verdict upheld eight years later in the New York Court of Appeals. He continually reminded competitors of his willingness to prosecute, and used past incidents as tacit testimonials of the superiority of his product line. Eventually he owned a shelf full of valuable properties, a testimony to his long and successful career as a manufacturing chemist. Trade marks. (James Bishop illustrations)

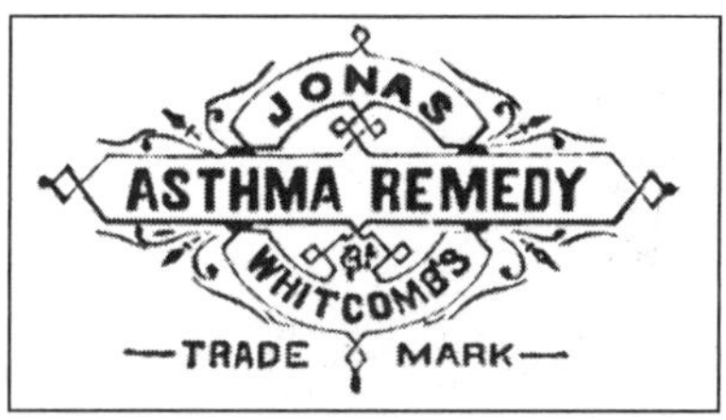

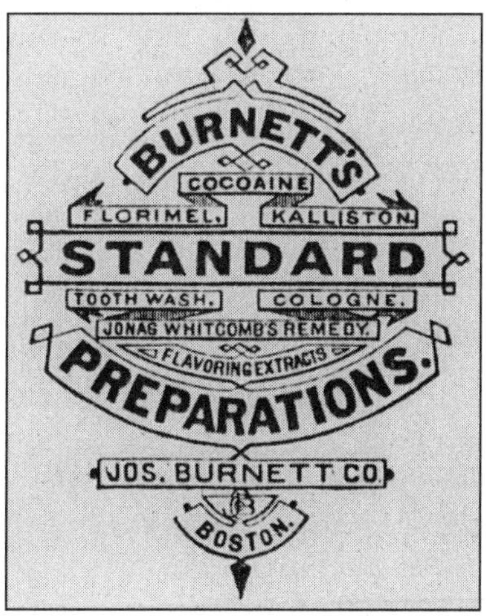

Figure 160a

The financial strength afforded by his pharmaceutical empire allowed Joseph Burnett to diversify into additional ventures. One of his principal achievements was the importation and breeding of Jersey cattle at his famous Deerfoot Farm. (Photo courtesy of Robert Burnett)

Burnett was the unfortunate victim of an accident. An electric trolley spooked his carriage horse. He was thrown to the pavement and never regained consciousness. By a simple operation of fate, also dying that day was prominent numismatist Matthew A. Stickney. The company Burnett founded celebrated its centennial in 1945. The following year it was purchased by General Foods.

Auction Census Data Summary, 1891-1994

	1	2	3	5	10	12	24	30	90	Total	Pct
BE	54		78	99	97	22	7	8	3	368	
BE RB					10					10	
BK	50	1	56	70	101	16	5	7	3	309	
	104	**1**	**134**	**169**	**208**	**38**	**12**	**15**	**6**	**687**	**8%**

Arthur M. Claflin
Chapter IX

Hopkinton and Lowell are both in Middlesex County, Massachusetts, which possibly accounts for the purchase of a small amount of John Gault's New Metallic Currency by Arthur M. Claflin in the autumn of 1862. Surely the purchase could not have amounted to more than 2,500 pieces, making Claflin one of Gault's smallest customers. Of this small number, the extant population of pieces suggests that preference was given to one-cent pieces (Reed CL01) and relatively fewer five-cent issues (Reed CL05) were ordered. This issuer has long been cited as the "rarest of the rare" in the encased stamp series and thus a great deal of interest has been attached to him. It's remarkable, given this general interest that it took investigations associated with this book to properly place the location of his dry goods store in Massachusetts. Today, Hopkinton is perhaps best known as the starting line for the Boston Marathon, but in Claflin's day it was one of the thriving New England factory towns that grew up along the region's abundant, rushing rivers. Hopkinton's specialty was the manufacture of boots and shoes. Although Arthur M. Claflin's family was intimately connected with this industry, he had a broader vision for his life's goal.

Claflin's parents were old New England stock. They married in 1829 and six children followed. The third child, Arthur Melville, was born January 23, 1836. His father, Lowell, was a Middlesex farmer, the kind of solid individual to whom Paul Revere made his historic ride at the beginning of the Revolutionary War. The small family farm produced hay, pota-

Figure 161a

Reed CL01 obverse, ex-James F. Ruddy specimen. (Bowers and Merena photo)

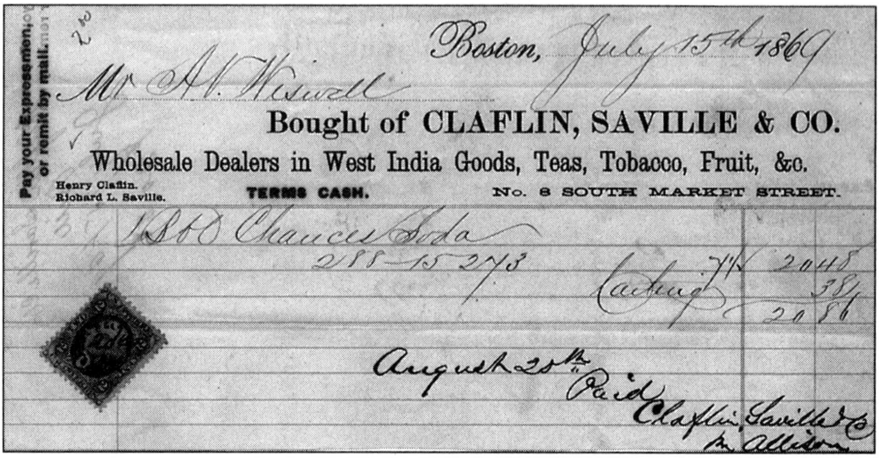
Pay your Expressmen, or remit by mail.

Boston, July 15th 1869

Bought of CLAFLIN, SAVILLE & CO.

Wholesale Dealers in West India Goods, Teas, Tobacco, Fruit, &c.

Henry Claflin.
Richard L. Saville.

TERMS CASH.

No. 8 SOUTH MARKET STREET.

August 20th
Paid
Claflin, Saville & Co

Figure 162a

Arthur M. Claflin came from a long line of successful New England merchant capitalists. His cousin Henry, for whom he worked as a bookkeeper, schooled Claflin for a life of success. Political sentiment and wanderlust took the younger Claflin to the Kansas frontier, and sentimental affection caused him to return there following a brief sojourn in nearby Hopkinton selling clothing as advertised on his encased stamps. Invoice, July 15, 1869, Scott R15. (Author's collection)

toes, Indian corn, grain, fruit and milk. During the 1840s and '50s, the population of Hopkinton doubled because of great growth in the foot trade, led by Lee Claflin, a relative. About 1848 his father also left the farm for the boot factory. He moved his family into town, where the following year he was elected as a Free-Soiler to represent Hopkinton in the state legislature. By 1850, the elder Claflin's personal estate was valued at $3,500. Three children, including a teenaged Arthur were still living at home.

In spring 1856, 20-year-old Arthur went to Boston to keep books for a wholesale clothier and fancy goods merchant. He also clerked at the grocery store operated by another relative, Henry Claflin, in exchange for room and board. But this occupation was short-lived. Late that year, A. M. headed west to Kansas Territory for "health reasons." Whether young Claflin was really sickly is difficult to know. More probably this explanation is euphemistic. As students of history know, Kansas in the 1850s was called "Bleeding Kansas," a microcosm of the sectional strife that was tearing at the fabric of the nation as a whole. The Kansas-Nebraska Act two years earlier had provided for inhabitants to choose whether they would be admitted as slave or free states. By 1856 extremists of both North and South were encouraging young men to emigrate to Kansas and purchase land to keep it out of the hands of the opposing side. Thus Claflin joined an exodus of solid, straight forward, Bunker Hill types who were thronging the territory seeking cheap land, and the furtherance of abolition sentiments.

The question must arise, what was a New England abolitionist doing in a hotbed of slavery and secession? The logical answer is that he was part of the Free Soil movement that

Figures 163a, b

Left, Claflin was a man of deep civil convictions and great moral passions. He was also a man of great civic responsibility who put his money where his mouth was time after time, leaving a legacy of merit and honor. Original pen, ink, charcoal and wash drawing especially for this book by Sara Jenks Maneval. *(Author's collection) Below, in addition to encased stamps, Claflin experimented with scrip during the change crisis. 25-cent Scrip, December 20, 1862. (Russell Kaye collection)*

was sweeping the territory and eventually carried the day. This border war was a prelude to the Civil War to come. At times the political rhetoric boiled over into armed conflict as ruffians played on the political and social unrest to mask their banditry. For a Yankee seeking to regain his health, there was much to be watchful of even if he were not directly involved in the social unrest.

Circumstances suggest he was looking for more than favorable weather conditions. His father was only a minor figure in the Free Soil movement, but his family as a whole were rabid abolitionists. Several of his relatives were prime movers and financiers of the New England Emigrant Aid Company, which enlisted Eastern capitalists in financing land pro-

Figure 164a

Claflin stands in the doorway of his Salina, Kansas, general store. An unidentified man stands at right. c. 1870s. Edith Dow collection (Dale Weis photo)

motion in Kansas in the interests of abolition and profit. Convinced of their moral rectitude and the opportunities for financial gain, the company helped finance the northern exodus to the territory where it laid out towns, established depots, built hotels, sawmills and grist mills. One of Claflin's kin intimately associated with this movement was New York merchant Horace B. Claflin. He subscribed $6,000 in 1856 and made a profit several times that much on the goods he shipped west to sell to the settlers.

The year 1856 was pivotal in the affairs of the Emigrant Aid Company, which stepped up its support by sending additional money and supplies to the Kansas Territory. In addition to land speculation, and abolition principles, there were also charitable considerations. In the fall of that year especially, Boston merchants supplied enormous amounts of clothing for the relief of destitute Northern settlers. Working for a wholesale clothier at the time, Claflin may have accompanied these shipments in October. If not, he almost certainly came west two months later, when the boot manufacturers subscribed $20,000 to the Emigrant Aid Company. As a principal contributor, another of A. M. Claflin's kin, William Claflin, was honored by having a new town in Bourbon County named for him. Because of their large financial backing, the New Englanders sent by the company exerted tremendous influence in the burgeoning territory. They became the important leaders and influential businessmen

Figure 165a

Claflin's big financial windfall came as a railroad land agent in the settlement of the Kansas plains. This closeup of his storefront (Claflin is the elder gentleman at right) also advertises his position as Union Pacific agent. c. late 1880s. Edith Dow collection. (Dale Weis photo)

in the towns that were established. Although only a youth, Claflin was buoyed by his family connections, and he was no younger than many of the other adventurers. He took up residence in Sumner in the northeast part of the state and soon became an important figure in his adopted hometown. This new company town was just across the river from Missouri's slave belt, whose emigrés had set up the nearby town of Atchison as a hotbed of pro-slavery rhetoric and agitation. Sumner, on the other hand, was thrown up by young Massachusetts men, who like Claflin

> were imbued with the spirit of creed and cant, self-reliance and fanaticism that could have been born only on Plymouth Rock. They had come to the frontier to make Kansas a free state and to build a city within whose walls all previous conditions of slavery should be disregarded and where all men born should be regarded equal. The time – 1856 – was auspicious. Kansas was both a great political and military battlefield, upon which the question of the institution of slavery was to be settled for all time.

Claflin threw in quickly with another young Massachusetts enthusiast, John P. Wheeler, an attorney and budding capitalist who had founded Sumner as a forwarding point on the Missouri River for men and materiél of the Yankee persuasion. By September, 1857, young Claflin had established himself as a "general land agent, forwarding and commission agent." Both activities would have been especially helpful in furthering his family's commer-

Figure 166a

Claflin was a frugal Yankee. His well furnished (by south plains standards certainly) apartment was above his general store. Edith Dow collection. (Dale Weis photo)

cial interests. He was also Wheeler's partner in the local lumber business operated in conjunction with the Sumner Town Company. These businesses and Wheeler's brick yard provided a virtual monopoly on town development and construction in the area. Sumner blossomed and quickly outstripped its rival, Atchison. On February 1, 1858, acting military governor General James W. Denver appointed Claflin as notary public for Atchison County. Claflin no doubt received his commission – a political plum – through the intercession of Wheeler, who was serving in the territorial legislature.

Conditions in Kansas were both primitive and hostile. The settlers suffered from what historian Carl Becker has called "an almost unparalleled succession of special calamities." Even town folk suffered. If Claflin didn't return to Massachusetts in April 1859, when his mother died, or 12 months later when his sister married, he almost surely left shortly thereafter. From mid-June 1859 until November 1860, not one good rain or snow fell. It was "the great dry year," according to a local historian. "Day after day the burning rays of the sun beat mercilessly down on a dry and parched land. . . . The slavery struggle died out and a struggle for existence took its place. Bleeding Kansas became starving Kansas," a centennial historian wrote. Most settlers were reduced to a dollar and a bushel of corn. Thousands departed. Kansas lost a third to half of its white population. "Settlers in the territory were able to fight border ruffians with more courage than they could endure starvation," an early commentator records.

Such hardships were not confined to farmers. Sumner was hard hit by the drought, too.

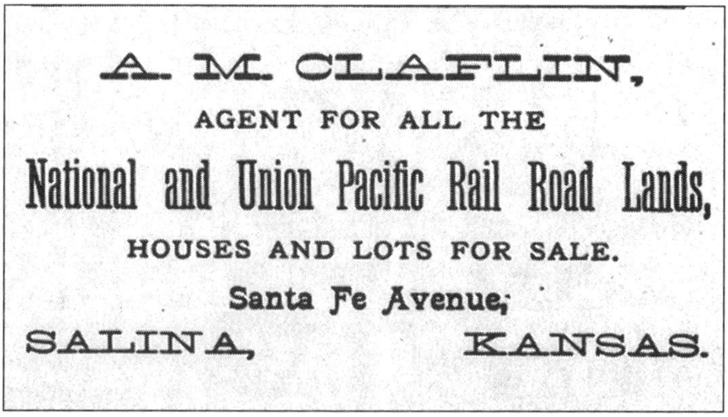

Figures 167a, b
Left, Claflin prospered as land agent. Ad. Edwards' Atlas of Saline County, *1884, p. 32. (Salina Public Library) Below, he stands on the balcony of the Kansas Pacific building. (Dale Weis photo)*

Then in June 1860, a "cyclone struck the town and either blew down or damaged nearly every building." What was left was wiped off the map in September "by a visitation of grasshoppers." Some residents moved to Atchison. Claflin was one who left, taking his profits with him. His "health" must have improved by then because he had returned to Hopkinton before January 1861, when – mission accomplished – Kansas was admitted as a Free State.

His stint on the prairie had given a matured Claflin the wherewithal to start up a store in his home town, Hopkinton. Claflin's New Metallic Currency was purchased from John Gault the following year, soliciting customers for his new clothing business. It's clear from

Figures 168a, b

As a director and officer of the National Bank of America in Salina, right, Claflin promoted the economic growth of his adopted home town. Ad, Chittenden's Directory of Salina, *1898. (Salina Public Library) His Victorian, below, residence stood in Salina as a landmark until recently. (Dale Weiss photo)*

SALINA, KAN.

W. W. WATSON, President,
A. M. CLAFLIN, Vice-President,
FRANK HAGEMAN, Cashier,
M. C. STEVENSON, Assistant Cashier.

DIRECTORS.

W. W. Watson,	B. L. Wilson,	J. H. Wolsieffer,
A. M. Claflin,	H. H. F. Sudendorf,	L. A. Will,
Wm. Muir,	W. H. Winterbotham,	Frank Hageman.

the timing and his interest in low-valued pieces that publicizing his store was his principal desire in purchasing these advertising store cards. We have second-hand testimony about that transaction. At the 1912 American Numismatic Association convention, Chicago coin dealer Ben Green, who had known Claflin a decade earlier, reported that the merchant ordered "several hundred dollars worth" of the encased stamps. There is good reason to conclude that, speaking from memory, Green was talking "off the cuff." Nevertheless, a good estimate based on mathematical modeling indicates that \$170-\$190, or about \$200 should not be far off the mark. As such, the Hopkinton dry goods merchant's order was one of Gault's smallest, amounting to something like 2,500 pieces. Presumably one of Gault's first customers, these pieces were placed into circulation at the height of the public small change

Figure 169a

The grave stone of Claflin and his wife attest to their high adventure on the plains of 19th century Kansas. (Bob Kincaid photo)

panic in the fall of 1862. He paid a heavy advertising premium for his small change substitute, about 100 percent. Remembering that silver change could be purchased from brokers for one-fifth that markup, this frugal Yankee merchant decided that the name recognition value and good will for his new enterprise was worth this premium. However, his clear insights are reflected in the distribution of his order. Although he ordered some pieces in all the lower denominations, his preference of one-cent values (Reed CL01) to three-cent pieces and substitutes for half dimes (Reed CL05) to dimes clearly gave him more pieces to distribute for his limited funds than the other way around. The change-hungry public would have benefitted greatly from Claflin's metallic currency, and its use would have accelerated Claflin's new business affairs. Again, according to Green, Claflin paid out every piece except for a single specimen he had retained as a souvenir.

Packing his bags at war's end, Claflin, age 29, returned to Kansas and married Lucretia Archibald at Salina on November 29, 1865. His bride, also 29, was one of the few white women there among the few dozen families who shared the land with the roving bands of Indians. Claflin brought his bride back to Massachusetts the following year when his widower father remarried. The couple took up residence permanently in Salina about 1870. The railroad had reached the town on its way west. The town was booming with opportunity. Both his sisters and their husbands also resided there. Times were still crude, however, and the town's main street "was axle deep mud, all but impassable." According to the press of the day, it was often said, "There is no Sunday west of Junction City and no God west of Salina."

However, the situation was ripe for an industrious and hard working merchant. He

Figure 170a

Claflin was a great philanthropist and benefactor of civic causes. On his death, his widow memorialized him by constructing Claflin Hall in the city's principal park. Shown is a turn of the century Chatauqua event. Copy photo of real photo postcard, Salina Public Library. (Dale Weis photo)

opened a general store and through his brother-in-law, a sibling of railroad promoter Jay Gould, became general land agent for eastern Kansas. Claflin was responsible for locating hundreds of settlers upon the Kansas railroad lands. His administration of these duties was marked with sobriety and honesty. The town of Claflin, Kansas, was named in honor of his sister Delia by her second husband, a founder of the town. Arthur Claflin prospered greatly. He ventured into banking and became a great public benefactor. Expressing his moral upbringing and heritage, he supported a variety of educational enterprises. His abolitionism showed itself in his support of the Freedmen through the African Methodist Episcopal Church. Leaving no heirs, he died November 6, 1904, "the most kindly spirit that ever moved."

Auction Census Data Summary, 1891-1994

	1	2	3	5	10	12	24	30	90	Total	Pct
CL	22		3	12	3	5				45	<1%
	22		**3**	**12**	**3**	**5**				**45**	**<1%**

Kirkpatrick & Gault
Chapter X

By mid-Summer 1862 New York was awash with paper trash, and the public was already becoming short-fused on the issue. Regarding the opinions of the man on the street on the course of the war effort, a contemporary devalued one to the level of the other. "People's speculations," he wrote in his diary, "are not worth a damaged Delmonico shinplaster." (see Figure 413a) John Gault was familiar with New York City, of course, when he took up his business dealings at No. 1 Park Place in June, 1862. He had commuted to New York regularly during the previous several years in his business dealings with Munn & Co. His military patents, especially, had brought him there since his patented artillery shells were being produced at a New York City foundry. As we have seen, it was through these military patents that Gault became acquainted with William V. Barkalow. Barkalow was actively procuring military weapons for the Army from his office at No. 1 Park Place.

Barkalow had taken up residence in New York in 1859. By summer 1861, he had moved his place of business from 39 Park Place several doors to the east to the six-story building denoted on Gault's New York City encased stamp. Barkalow listed his business as commission merchant. In other words, he was a broker. Commission merchants sold goods consigned to them by outsiders. Generally, such brokers specialized. Typical specialties of the day included dry goods, flour, hardware, or the like. However, most dealt in any product that promised to turn a profit. Generally the commission broker did not purchase the goods

Figure 171a
Reed KG05 obverse, ex-James F. Ruddy specimen. (Bowers and Merena photo)

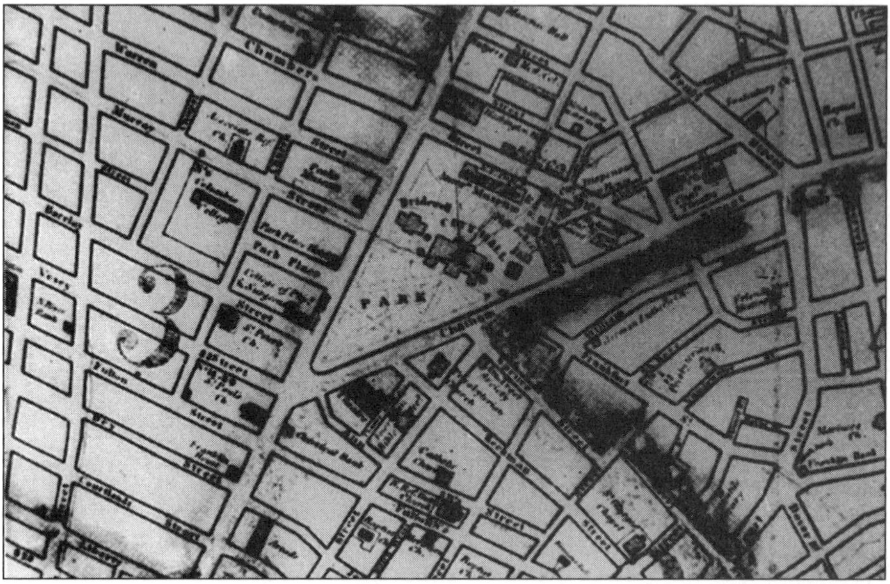

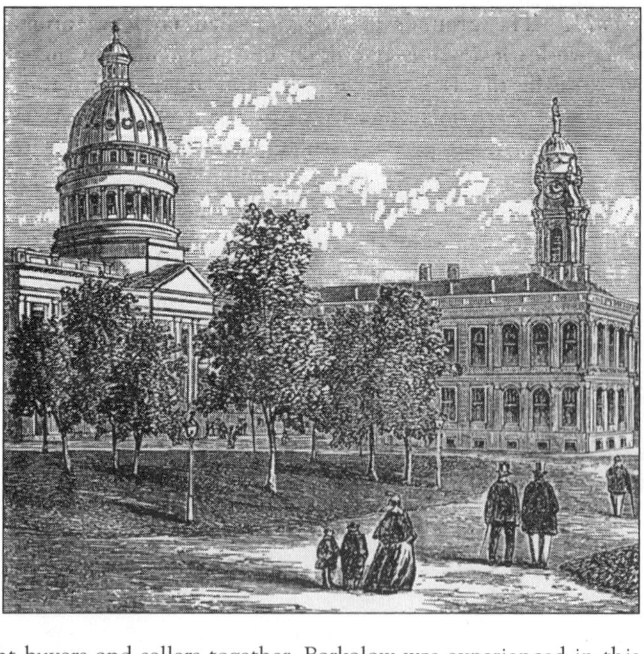

Figures 172a, b

Lower Manhattan was the center of Gault's enterprise and location of many clients. Park Place had been an approach to Columbia College. The City Hall Park, right, was a lovely reprieve from bustling Broadway, the unnamed thoroughfare traversing the map segment, above, from top to bottom. Map. (New-York Historical Society) Engraving, Lights and Shadows of New York Life, *1872, p. 198. (Author's collection)*

outright, but merely brought buyers and sellers together. Barkalow was experienced in this trade. He had been operating as Eastern agent for the Cincinnati firm of Ellis, McAlpin & Co. for several years in both New York City and Philadelphia. It was common practice for western merchants to secure goods from the East through such brokers. This readily explains

Figure 173a

The southern end of City Hall Park looking across Ann and up Broadway, taken from Barnum's American Museum in 1862, and oriented as the map opposite. The Astor House is at left. This was the environment into which Bostonian John Gault brought his mica and brass small change in the late summer of that year. These are the people whose clamoring need his encased stamps filled. No. 1 Park Place is less than two blocks north and but two doors west of the beer and sarsaparilla stand at right. Eight of Gault's clients had shops in the vicinity. Copy photograph from original Mathew Brady negative in the possession of Philip B. Kunhardt. (Author's collection)

Figure 174a

Proceeding up Broadway to a point in the park looking down Park Place. Facing west, No. 1 Park Place is on the right (north) side of the street immediately behind the six story building on the corner. Woodcut. Gleason's Pictorial Drawing Room Companion. *(Dallas Public Library)*

how the encased stamps came to Cincinnati several months hence.

But Barkalow's attention in 1862 was fixed higher than yard goods or encased stamps, for that matter. He was one of several New York importers who were busily engaged in importing British Enfield rifles for sale to the U.S. government. Initially Barkalow contracted to supply 26,000 long rifles at $20 each. The Queen's embargo, however caused him to partially default. Federal officials agreed to take 8,000 of the weapons for the pro rata price of $160,000. He returned from England and delivered on the contract between April 26 and July 18, 1862. His rifles arrived on the Inman line of propeller steamships. On November 2nd, he contracted to supply for a like amount another 8,000 long Enfields, all of which he made good on. Such Enfields were one of the best of the foreign arms supplied to Federal infantrymen. His interest in Gault's artillery shells was a natural extension.

It was Barkalow who introduced Joseph Kirkpatrick to Gault. Kirkpatrick was an express agent, who by the summer of 1862 also had officed at No. 1 Park Place for several years. Kirkpatrick fancied himself something of a broker, too, and in fact was a bit player in the import rifle trade. His sources were much less fruitful than Barkalow's. On September 12, 1862, he sold 80 long Enfields to federal officials at about $16 each.

The No. 1 Park Place address was a six-story office building adjacent to Bixby's Boarding House (Park Place or Brandreth Hotel), No. 239 Broadway. As shown in contemporary lithographs, it was a plain building, three shuttered windows wide with a single entrance stairway and a basement level. What it lacked in ambience, it more than made up for with location. Directly across Broadway was City Hall Park, a center of New York civic life. Across the park was "Publisher's Square," home of the influential periodicals of the day,

Figure 175a

Entering Park Place, the broad thoroughfare (exaggerated in this illustration) teemed outside No. 1 Park Place. Facing the north side of the street, Gault and Kirkpatrick's encased stamp business was located in the six-story office building adjacent to the taller six story corner building. Gault's office building is distinguishable in this illustration by the dual chimneys on its west side. Lithograph by William Buell (detail), 1855. (The New-York Historical Society, No. 49904)

including the *Times*, the *Tribune*, the *World*, *Scientific American*, the *Sun*, and other publications. Gault would have looked out on what is today the Woolworth Building. Then it was a five-story Berkshire Life Insurance Building, erected in 1852. Its first floor was occupied by the Broadway Savings Bank (see Figure 55b). One block south down Broadway was the famous Astor House, the city's leading downtown hotel. Directly beyond that rose St. Paul's Chapel, which dated from before the American Revolution. Across from St. Paul's was Barnum's American Museum.

Barnum's was the center of the city's thriving public entertainment halls. Located at the corner of Broadway and Ann Street, it was the most widely acclaimed mecca for entertainment, and "America's Number One Place of Amusement," according to its proprietor. It was world famous for its circus freaks and curiosities from all parts of the globe. That summer the stars of Barnum's show were his "Esquimaux (Eskimo) Indians which have just arrived in this country, from the Arctic Regions." Others on the bill were Commodore Nutt, the Madagascar Albino family, performing bears, wax figures, colored tropical fish, "monster snakes, and a million other wonders." A French drama was playing in its auditorium. A

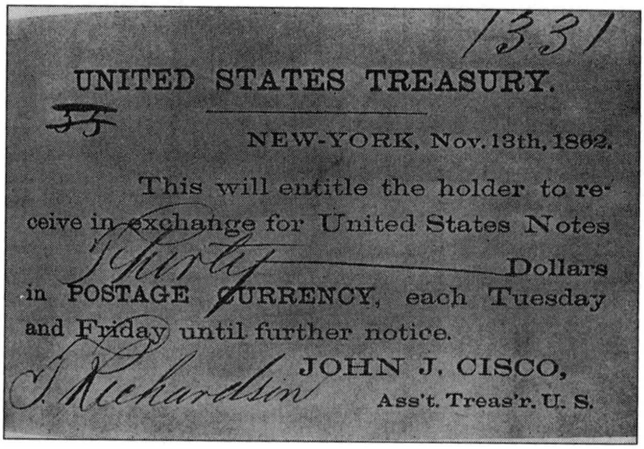

1331

UNITED STATES TREASURY.

NEW-YORK, Nov. 13th, 1862.

This will entitle the holder to receive in exchange for United States Notes Thirty Dollars in POSTAGE CURRENCY, each Tuesday and Friday until further notice.

JOHN J. CISCO,
Ass't. Treas'r. U. S.

Figures 176a, b, c
Gault and Kirkpatrick offered a simple product customized for their clients. Right is their advertising insert, an embossed brass disc pitching their product. KG obverse insert, front and back. (Author's collection, ex-George Fuld) Right, a pass issued for fractional currency distribution in New York demonstrates that rationing of the government small change medium left room for the circulation of Gault's change substitute well into Autumn, 1862. Compare with Figure 52b. U.S. Treasury pass, November 13, 1862. (Coin World photo)

quarter would gain admittance. For children under 10, fifteen cents would suffice. On its first floor was the White Hatter, soon to be one of Gault's customers.

Broadway was a constant beehive of activity. Rimmed with its five-story commercial buildings, the sky-scrapers of their day, its 80-foot width had long since become congested with traffic. The sides of its horsecars were painted gaily by the well known artists of the day. An estimated 17,000 vehicles plied the stretch alongside the park each day. "Over all and around all there was the daytime noise of a street crowded with people, working people and people at leisure, with lumbering wagons, scurrying carts, hurrying carriages, thundering omnibuses," a witness wrote. Broadway, of course, was the great thoroughfare for the march of business up Manhattan island. The center of the area was the marble-faced City Hall, acclaimed as one of the finest municipal structures in the country. City Hall was surrounded by its park, the fountain of which had long been a focal point of busy city life. During the war, the park also became a staging ground and embarkation point for Union troops being shipped to the theaters of war. At its southern end, an Army barracks had been erected. "No wonder," an historian records, "an enterprising vendor selected this spot to sell his sarsaparilla and beer at three cents per glass." As the Mathew Brady photo reproduced on this book's endpapers (and in part on page 173) clearly shows, the boardwalk across Ann Street was a constant swirl of pedestrian traffic. How many times John Gault passed this very spot in ensuing years is anybody's guess. Perhaps he appears in the photo after all.

"THE NEW METALLIC CURRENCY."—Applications for stamping business cards on the new metallic currency to be made to J. GAULT, Patentee, No. 1 Park Place, N. Y.

WIGS—WIGS—WIGS.
HAIR DYE—HAIR DYE.
HAIR DYEING—ALL COLORS.
MOLDAVIA CREAM,
For PRESERVING, BEAUTIFYING, and FORCING THE HAIR TO GROW.—All these articles in the greatest perfection, at
W. A. BATCHELOR'S celebrated establishment,
No. 16 Bond-st., N. Y.

WOULD you call the bloom of health to the cheeks of that pale-faced girl, buy her a CANTERING LOCOMOTIVE HORSE, on which she can have the most delightful out-door exercise. They are sold by STEPHEN WM. SMITH, at No. 498 Broadway.

1,000 TO 3,000 CANAL WHEELBARROWS and TRAYS constantly on hand; cheap for cash, at GALE'S, No. 207 Greenwich-st.

250 RARE RECEIPTS—Including things to do about home, whereby several dollars a week can be made by any active person, boy or girl. Book sent free by mail on receipt of 12 cents. Agents wanted by STAFFORD & Co., Publishers, 442 Broadway, N. Y.

Figure 177a

Failing to induce the government to adopt his emergency "coinage," Gault advertised his "New Metallic Currency" in local newspaper classified ads, along with such other items as the wigs, rocking horses, wheelbarrows, and work-at-home money-making schemes of other entrepreneurs. New York Tribune, *November 6, 1862, p. 3. The New Metallic Currency ads which appeared in known sources do not mention Joseph Kirkpatrick, indicating the relationship may have been short-lived. (Coin World archives)*

Gault's encased stamps were proclaimed by Horace Greeley the "happy solution to our common plight" only a week after they were patented. Shortly thereafter, the editor published an extended item in his city notes column, which is reproduced as Figure 64a. It is important for several respects:

(1) Obviously the piece examined by Greeley was the J. GAULT issue, which must have been produced between the August 12 patent date and the August 30 column date;

(2) It is described as white metal, indicating that Gault's initial procedure was to silver both sides imitating silver coinage;

(3) It was meant to house stamps of "large and small denominations";

(4) Customer advertisements were a part of Gault's original plans;

(5) Their price wholesale was $20 or less a thousand.

Furthermore, Greeley liked the idea.

The Kirkpatrick and Gault piece was likely issued in October. Stylistically it is the Type II obverse, with the difference, of course, in the location of the patent information. Kirkpatrick's purpose in the partnership has been speculated at *ad nauseum*. Many have suggested that he was a capital source for Gault. Since he was an express agent, recently authors have favored his role as a source of stamps for Gault. One author, however, has suggested the equally plausible view that he may have been the shipping agent for Gault to forward his product to western concerns. Although any or all of these are possible, the present author favors his role as broker. That is a role we know he was embracing in summer and fall 1862, and it fits with what we know about John Gault's myriad other business relationships.

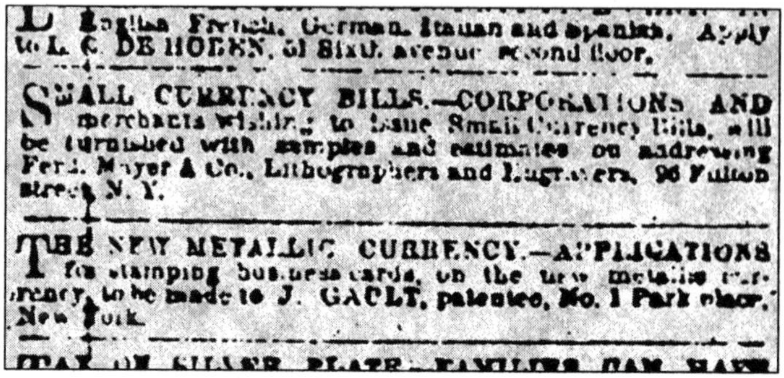
English, French, German, Italian and Spanish. Apply to L. C. DE HOBEN, 61 Sixth avenue, second floor.

SMALL CURRENCY BILLS.—CORPORATIONS AND merchants wishing to issue Small Currency Bills, will be furnished with samples and estimates on addressing Ferd. Mayer & Co., Lithographers and Engravers, 96 Fulton street, N. Y.

THE NEW METALLIC CURRENCY.—APPLICATIONS for stamping business cards, on the new metallic currency, to be made to J. GAULT, patentee, No. 1 Park place, New York.

Figure 178a
Gault was competing for small change business with vendors of scrip like Ferd. Mayer. Ad. New York Herald, *November 6, 1862, p. 8. (Omaha Public Library)*

Such a role specifically explains the Ellis, McAlpin and other issues in Cincinnati. It also helps explain in a general way the predominance among Gault's western customers of dry goods, periodical and similar vendors of articles produced in the east, since "by express" was the standard mode of conveying these items to midwestern retailers.

Certainly their business relationship was cemented by early October. The KG issue mimics the original JG issue to an outstanding degree, and both are atypical of the series in general. It will be remembered that although all eight stamp values are represented, the JG issue is predominantly five-and-dime oriented. In fact, high values are more plentiful than low values. This is certainly a differing mode of emission from the entire encased stamp series taken as a whole. Since it was true of both the Type A reverses (ribbed or grooved) and Type B (flat) reverses, it clearly represents Gault's desire to supply useful change for commerce. The KG emission pattern is virtually identical, although all pieces were Type B (flat) wrap-arounds. The size of the output was approximately 35,000 pieces, and the shift from ten-cent predominant (JG issues) to five-cent dominance shows Gault's increased interest in the advertising value of the KG emission in soliciting new business, even while presenting workhorse change-making pieces for retail sale for commercial transactions. We should make nothing of the order of their surnames. It was simply a matter of fitting a great deal of type on a small circular disc. Clearly Gault was still calling the shots. The first notice that the partnership had been established is Editor Henry Raymond's mention in his New York *Times*, labeled "NEAT AND HANDY" (see Figure 76a), which appeared October 8th. Ads appeared within a month, failing to mention Kirkpatrick at all, leading to speculation that the partnership was short-lived.

Collectors should keep in mind that modern, counterfeit Kirkpatrick & Gault obverses exist, and that sets of fakes in a full range of denominations were produced. See chapter on "Collecting Encased Stamps" for details.

Auction Census Data Summary, 1891-1994

	1	2	3	5	10	12	24	30	90	Total	Pct
KG	25	1	33	123	69	32	49	60	20	412	4.7%
KG RB					0	0					
	25	**1**	**33**	**123**	**69**	**32**	**49**	**60**	**20**	**412**	**4.7%**

Aërated Bread
Chapter XI

Not nearly so imposing a commercial concern was the new venture touted by Stephen F. Ambler on his pieces of Gault's New Metallic Currency. Ambler purchased a small quantity, estimated at about 6,000 pieces of one-cent store cards (Reed AB01), from Gault soon after Gault commenced selling the currency substitutes to New York City merchants. Ambler was decidedly interested in the publicity value of these pieces. For less than $200 he obtained the maximum quantity of this neat and handy image-builder for his new enterprise. Ambler shared more than an interest in encased stamps with their inventor, however. He also acquired a patent on August 12, 1862, the very day on which Gault's postage stamp case received its approval from Patent Office officials. These circumstances suggest a Munn & Co. connection, which may or may not have happened. The plausibility of the patent connection notwithstanding, the pieces themselves argue for an early connection of Ambler to Gault. The piece mirrors a newspaper advertisement of early November, precisely the time Gault abandoned his hopes of convincing the government to adopt his small change expedient in favor of direct canvassing of the merchants themselves.

Readers today would be unfamiliar with the term "aërated" bread. They needn't be ashamed. Ambler's prospective clients were unfamiliar with it too, hence, the felt need to use such an unorthodox advertising vehicle as Gault's cent pieces. For the benefit of the modern reader, aërated bread was "clean, pure and sweet" to borrow Ambler's phraseology:

Figure 179a

Reed AB01 obverse, ex-James F. Ruddy specimen. (Bowers and Merena photo)

Figures 180a, b

Stephen F. Ambler was industrious and shrewd. His patent for aërated bread was one of many interests. Coincidentally, this patent for making unfermented bread was granted on the same day as Gault's encased stamp patent. U.S. Patent No. 36,134, August 12, 1862. (U.S. Patent Office). His principal activity, however, was as a mining engineer. Earlier that year he patented a device to separate silver and gold ore from alluvial sand. Publication of Patent No. 34,286, notice, Scientific American, *February 22, 1862, p. 124 (Dallas Public Library)*

UNITED STATES PATENT OFFICE.

STEPHEN F. AMBLER, OF BROOKLYN, NEW YORK.

IMPROVEMENT IN THE MANUFACTURE OF AERATED BREAD.

Specification forming part of Letters Patent No. **36,134**, dated August 12, 1862.

To all whom it may concern:

Be it known that I, STEPHEN F. AMBLER, of Brooklyn, Kings county, State of New York, have invented, made, and applied to use certain new and useful Improvements in the Manufacture of Unfermented Bread; and I do declare the following to be a full, clear, and correct description of the same.

The nature of my invention consists in the use or employment in the manufacture of unfermented bread of carbonic-acid gas made by fermentation from saccharine or farinaceous matter, as hereinafter fully described, by the use of which the bread is rendered cheaper, lighter, and whiter, and its cost of manufacture is considerably reduced.

To enable those skilled in the arts to make and use my invention, I will proceed to speak of the same.

Prior to my invention the carbonic-acid gas used in the manufacture of unfermented bread was made from sulphuric acid and the carbonate of lime or carbonate of soda. The objection to the use of carbonic-acid gas thus made is its high cost and the fact that in its manufacture other injurious gases are frequently formed.

My process may be thus described: I place any desired quantity of farinaceous or saccharine matter in a vessel, and in the case of the farinaceous matter treat it as follows: Cornmeal used is first heated to 180° Fahrenheit, and cooled by stirring to 160° Fahrenheit, when rye-meal and malt are added; then cooled to 65° to 70° Fahrenheit, and the yeast is added; then placed in a tight vessel, in which vessel is inserted a pipe conducting the gas as formed to a gasometer or gas-holder. In case saccharine matter be used, the molasses is diluted by adding a quantity of water, is cooled to from 65° to 70° Fahrenheit, when the yeast is added, and the process first described is repeated. The gas thus formed is passed from the gasometer or gas-holder to the necessary vessels.

By making carbonic-acid gas as described not only the quality of the gas formed is improved, but the alcohol remaining in the farinaceous or saccharine matter pays the cost of the farinaceous matter or saccharine matter used.

While my improvement is particularly applicable to unfermented bread, it will be found equally useful in the manufacture of soda-water, to which I have applied it.

Having thus described my invention, what I claim therein as new, and desire to secure by Letters Patent, is—

In the manufacture of unfermented bread, the use or employment of the carbonic-acid gas made as herein fully described, for the purposes specified.

STEPHEN F. AMBLER.

In presence of—
A. TURNER,
A. SIDNEY DOANE.

34,286.—S. F. Ambler, of Brooklyn, N. Y., for Improved Amalgamator:

I claim, first, Giving to the pan, D, the shaking and vibratory motions for the purpose described.

Second, The combination of the agitating board, H, constructed as shown, with the pan, D, for the purpose specified.

Third, Placing the discharge openings, O, upon the side of the pan, D, for the purpose set forth.

"No hand touches the dough. It is free from all deleterious ingredients. It never sours. No change of climate affects it," he affirmed. The bread was produced by forcing carbonic acid gas into the flour and water at the moment of their mixture. This process eliminated the timely, arduous, and largely unsanitary (at that time) requirements of kneading the dough to get it to rise. This English process invented in 1856 was just then sweeping this country. Articles touting the new procedures appeared in newspapers as far away as San Francisco. But it was also expensive. The chief difficulty was in generating the carbonic acid gas. It was principally produced from sulphuric acid and carbonate of lime or soda. The process was both expensive and dangerous. *Scientific American* had challenged American inventors several times to develop a better way to produce the gas. The most recent of these articles appeared in early spring 1862.

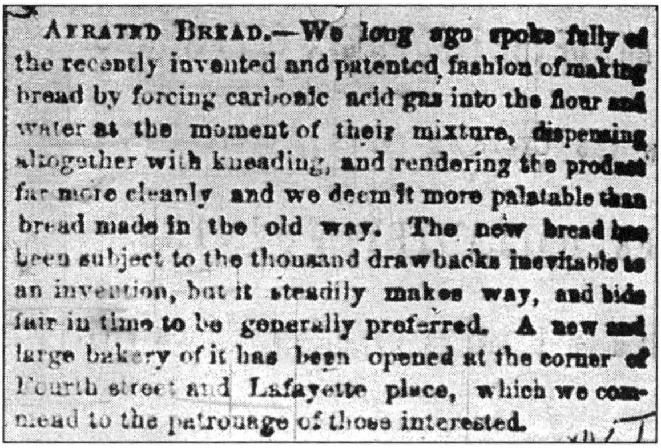

AERATED BREAD.—We long ago spoke fully of the recently invented and patented fashion of making bread by forcing carbonic acid gas into the flour and water at the moment of their mixture, dispensing altogether with kneading, and rendering the product far more cleanly and we deem it more palatable than bread made in the old way. The new bread has been subject to the thousand drawbacks inevitable to an invention, but it steadily makes way, and bids fair in time to be generally preferred. A new and large bakery of it has been opened at the corner of Fourth street and Lafayette place, which we commend to the patronage of those interested.

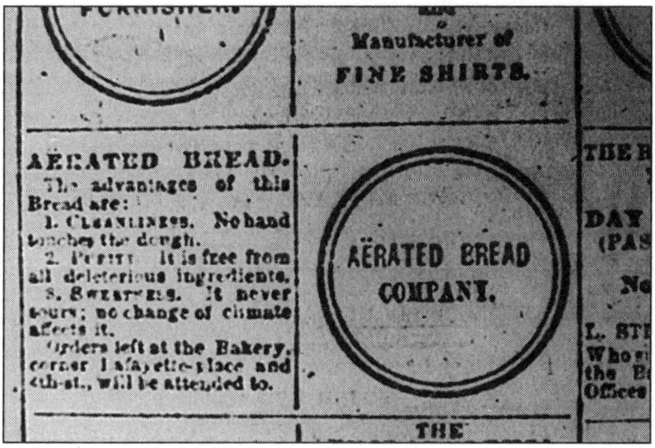

Manufacturer of
FINE SHIRTS.

AËRATED BREAD.
The advantages of this Bread are:
1. CLEANLINESS. No hand touches the dough.
2. PURITY. It is free from all deleterious ingredients.
3. SWEETNESS. It never sours; no change of climate affects it.
Orders left at the Bakery, corner Lafayette-place and 4th-st., will be attended to.

AËRATED BREAD COMPANY.

THE

Figures 181a, b

Unfermented bread was something of a health food fad in 1862. Horace Greeley took note of Ambler's bakery in a City Items column in his newspaper shortly after Ambler purchased encased stamps from Gault. New York Tribune, *December 13, 1862. p. 2. (Illinois State Library) Ambler's use of encased stamps to advertise his bakery was presaged somewhat by his checker board ad, left, which bears resemblance to the AB design. New York* Times, *November 1, 1862, p. 8. (Illinois State Library)*

The proprietor of the aërated bread bakery, Ambler, took up *Scientific American's* challenge literally. An upstate New Yorker by birth and son of a farmer, he had first tried the trade of shoemaking. Forty-four, married with a daughter, Ambler was recently arrived to Brooklyn when he read the challenge. An inventor by profession, with deep family credentials especially in mining and metallurgy, the process he developed was sufficiently unique to warrant patent protection. Ambler was rewarded U.S. Patent No. 36,134 for a process which produced the desired result by fermenting "saccharine or farinaceous matter." Ambler's idea was to heat cornmeal, add rye-meal and malt, allow to cool and then add yeast. Bang, there you have it. His process was a good one. Horace Greeley said so. Ambler opened a "new and large bakery" at the corner of Fourth Street and Lafayette Place, to produce his bread. With such good press clippings, his neat and handy stamp cards, and an excellent light and white product, his future looked great.

But alas, something came a cropper. Even Gault's advertising store cards could not avail Ambler. The bakery was short-lived, lasting only a little more than a year. Thereafter Ambler returned to his primary interests, mining. Returning to the metallurgical trades, he

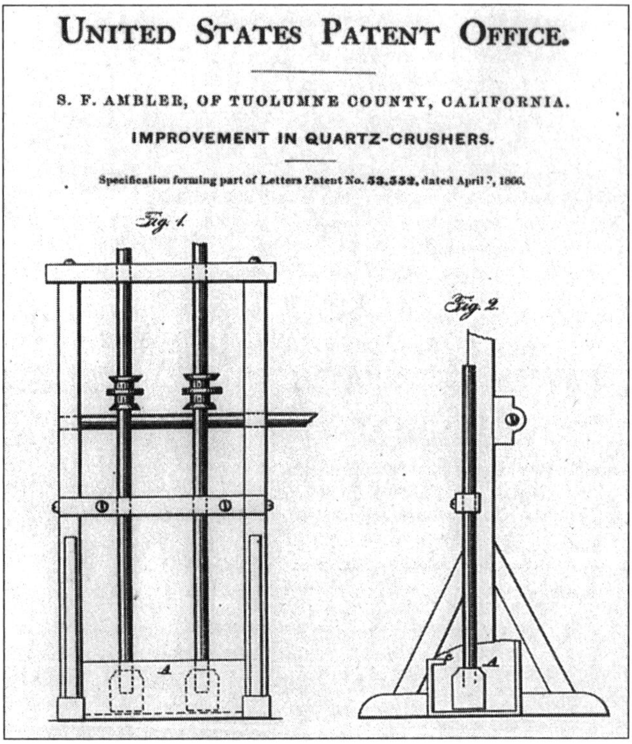

Figure 182a

Ambler was well connected. His father perfected several mining technology improvements during the California gold rush in connection with the Sutter claim. In Spring 1866, Ambler and a brother went to California where they contributed additional innovations to the mining business. Right is one of Ambler's several post-war mining machines. Patent No. 53,552, April 2, 1866. (U.S. Patent Office.

continued working in New York in professions variously listed as refiner or miner. In Spring 1866 he and a brother went west to California, where they contributed innovations to the mining business.

The die sinking on the Ambler piece is distinctive. The umlaut on the letter "e" suggests that the die sinker was German, since Ambler did not use that diacritical mark in any of the other literature associated with his product except the checker board ad which patterns his stamp case. It is also punch-linked to the Irving House pieces (an obviously early emission) and the Bailey & Co. issue, suggesting that it too was one of the early pieces.

Auction Census Data Summary, 1891-1994

	1	2	3	5	10	12	24	30	90	Total	Pct
AB	56			4						60	<1%
	56			**4**						**60**	**<1%**

Dougan the Hatter
Chapter XII

John A. Dougan, a New York hatter, has proved as elusive as any of John Gault's clientele. Very little, in fact, has been learned about this man, who was located for many years at 102 Nassau Street, corner of Ann Street. This address was close to Gault's New York City address, except that Dougan was on the other side of City Hall Park. Dougan purchased about 10,000 pieces from Gault in the four lowest values, although he too showed a decided preference for one-cent (Reed DO01) and three-cent (Reed DO03) denominations. True to his heritage, he was a frugal Scotsman. And as a small merchant he was looking for the broadest possible circulation of his store cards for his several hundred dollar expenditure.

It appears Dougan was an immigrant from Glasgow, Scotland, arriving on the ship *Madawaska* at the port of New York on November 8, 1848. At that time he was 20 years old, and he gave his trade as "dyer." He did not stay long in New York, however. A little over a year later he boarded another vessel for the trip to the California mine fields. Unlike John Gault and other venturesome souls headed for the west coast, Dougan did not have the sea legs of some of the New England adventurers. Upon arriving in Central America, instead of continuing on the long sea voyage around South America, he instead chose land passage across Panama to reach its Pacific coast. Such a passage was filled with its own share of difficulties, no doubt, but Dougan successfully made the passage from Chagres to Panama City. Arriving at the isthmus' west coast, he booked passage on the steamer *Northerner* on July 31,

Figure 183a
Reed DO03 obverse, ex-James F. Ruddy specimen. (Bowers and Merena photo)

1850. The intercoastal run along the baja to the Golden Gate required only 16 days, and Dougan arrived at San Francisco on August 15th. Where he headed is open to speculation. He was not necessarily heading for the gold fields. A skilled tradesman looking for opportunity, he could have remained in the bay area or passed on to any of the other larger communities. The California census that year apparently missed him, and he remains in obscurity until his return to New York in 1854.

He worked briefly as a tailor. Evidently he worked out of his residence. Again his stay in New York was of short duration. Where he went is open to speculation, but he returned about the end of the decade. By summer 1861 he had taken up his hat trade at the Nassau Street location. He resided uptown on West 33rd Street. By the time the city swooned under the pressure of its small change crisis, his budding enterprise was only a year old. New York's hat trade was a highly competitive endeavor. The wars among the established hatters fashionably located along Broadway south and east of the park are legendary. Dougan's location was strictly "low rent" fashionwise for his era. Nassau Street was a warren of mixed activity north of Wall Street. A narrow street running parallel to Broadway for about half a mile, it was "one of the narrowest and most inconvenient streets in the city," according to a contemporary account, "yet the truth is that it is one of the most important streets in the city in respect to the amount and variety of the traffic carried on within its limits." In Dougan's era his neighbors included lawyers, publishers, artists, engravers, restaurant keepers, matrimonial agents, book sellers, jewelers and fruit merchants. "Every device of the sign maker has been exhausted here," a contemporary of Dougan's observed.

The city's hatters were especially competitive and any little distinguishing tidbit was a leg up. Dougan was resourceful. He was the only one of Gault's merchants to express a desire for an emblem on his store cards. As the "new kid on the block," Dougan felt he needed any advertising advantage he could muster, however small. He had a hat sign outside his doorway. He wanted a hat on his encased stamp store card. Gault obliged him by providing the distinctive hat which marks his pieces of New Metallic Currency. The device is very effective. One could not help but wish others of Gault's clients would have demanded as much.

Dougan may have been new and small when he purchased rights to Gault's store cards, but his hats and business practices must have been excellent. In his adopted country, Dougan also developed a staunch patriotism and republican sentiment. He continued to operate his hat shop on Nassau at least through 1876 during the United States Centennial celebration. In that year he circulated a lithographed trade card, an example of which is in the collection of the New-York Historical Society. The card shows the ornate Horticultural Hall at the Centennial Exhibition in Philadelphia. Later that year, Dougan again issued an innovative trade item, a small folding note pad. The piece dates from the Tiden-Hayes presidential campaign. One side proclaims: "Dougan Leader of Fashions in Gentlemen's Hats, 102 Nassau Street, Fine Hats of Every Description at Moderate Prices." The other side gives the electoral vote by state in Grant's 1872 reelection victory over Horace Greeley, with space to fill in the tallies for the Centennial year aspirants. In doing so, he was rubbing Democrats' and fellow New Yorker, editor Horace Greeley's noses in their loss. Greeley failed in his presidential bid despite the schism in the Republican Party, which saw its liber-

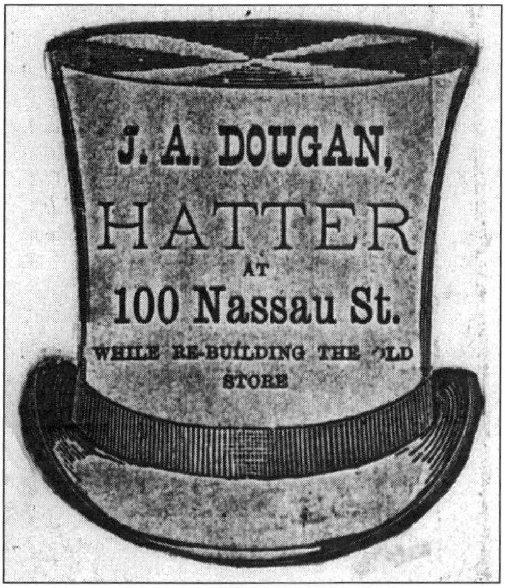

Figures 185a, b, c

Dougan's hat not only graced his encased stamp (above, detail), but also an inventive die cut advertising card. Trade Card. (The New-York Historical Society) Another Dougan ad card, below, illustrated Horticulture Hall at Centennial Fair in Philadelphia. Trade Card, 1876. (The New-York Historical Society)

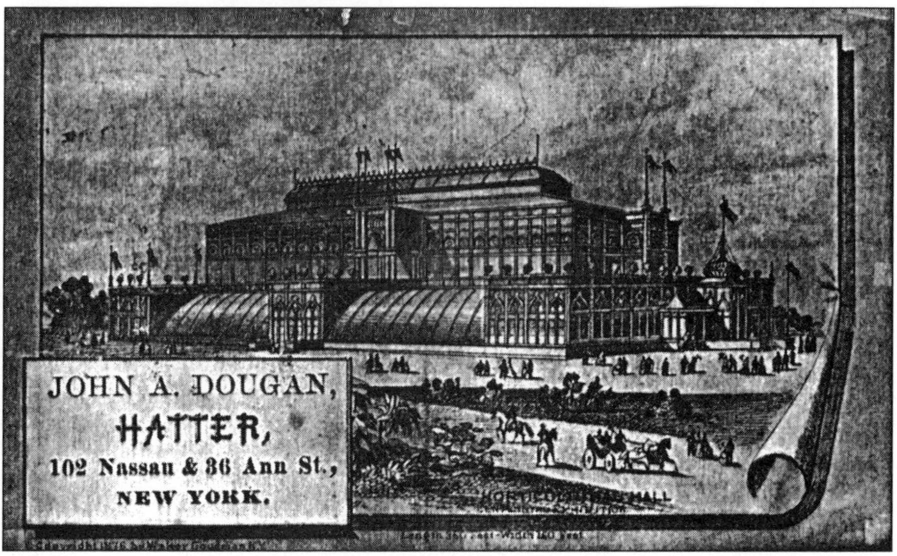

al wing join the Democrats in Greeley's support under the banner of "Revenue Reform, Universal Amnesty, and Impartial Suffrage." This excellent piece also resides in the New-York Historical Society collection.

A third Dougan trade card is also known. In it the hat emblem which decorated his encased postage has found its close kin through a die cut trade card issued in the shape of a hat, itself. The piece is of an uncertain date, but bears the interesting message: "J. A. Dougan, Hatter at 100 Nassau St. while re-building the old store." It is not known whether

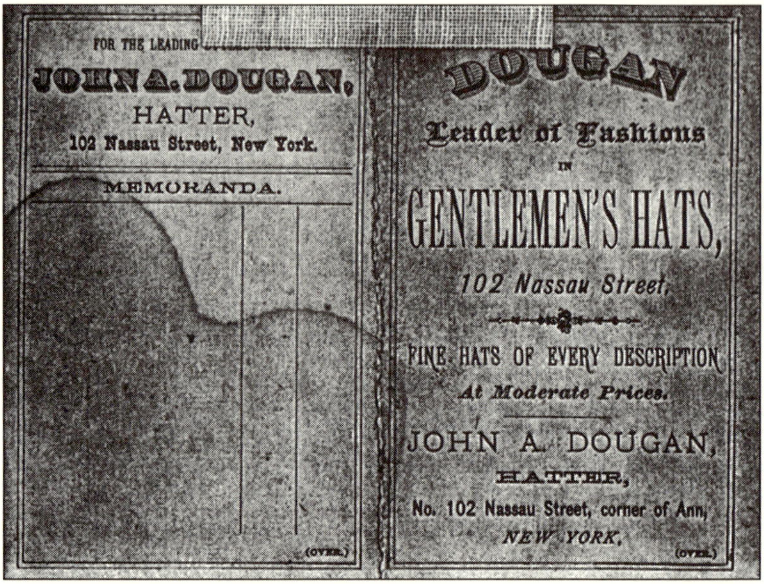

Figure 186a *A folding note pad given away by Dougan to his customers in 1876. (The New-York Historical Society)*

the rebuilding was due to renovation or calamity.

In addition to his hat trade, Dougan embarked on an unrelated sideline following the Civil War. In 1867 he opened an eating house at 144 Ninth Street. The following year he moved this establishment to 78 East Ninth, but closed down in 1870. Two years later, still pursuing his hat business, he moved his residence from 113 Macdougal to 103 Clinton Place.

Auction Census Data Summary, 1891-1994

	1	2	3	5	10	12	24	30	90	Total	Pct
DO	40		40	21	11					112	1%
	40		**40**	**21**	**11**					**112**	**1%**

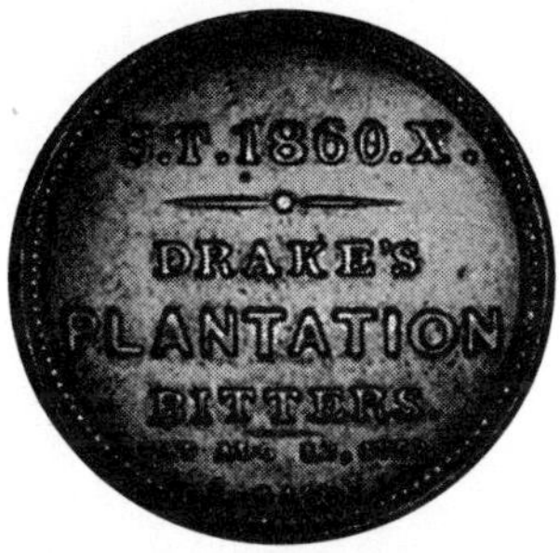

P. H. Drake
Chapter XIII

One of the more flamboyant and larger users of the New Metallic Currency was Patrick H. Drake, ofttimes called Doctor, sometimes called Colonel, but in truth neither. It's no coincidence that the major advertisers on Gault's stamp money were the proprietary medicine merchants. As a whole they were among the biggest advertisers in any media throughout that period. Drake's relationship to Gault was certainly no exception. Reliably, he ordered 45,000 of Gault's change checks, of all denominations but with a decided preference for one- (Reed DR01) and three-cent (Reed DR03) values. For comparison purposes, Drake's order approximated the quantity J.C. Ayer ordered for his TAKE AYER'S PILLS (Reed AP) alone. Nevertheless, the Drake order was significant to Gault, representing gross sales of approximately $4,000. It was a good deal for Drake, too. His advertising premium on the deal to pay Gault for the cost of manufacture was 22.5 percent, just about what a like amount of silver change would have cost him at the broker's, and with Gault's substitute he got his name and bitters stamped on the coin of the realm to boot. The large numbers of pieces in his secondary circulation, five- and ten-cent pieces (Reed DR05 and DR10 respectively) helped drive down this premium when compared to another large issuer such as Ayer. Stylistically, they appear to be an early emission.

The subject of this chapter was an astute businessman to be sure. In the small space of a decade he went from a canal toll taker to nearly the pinnacle of the proprietary medicine

Figure 187a

Reed DR10 obverse, ex-James F. Ruddy specimen. (Bowers and Merena photo)

Figure 188a
The base for Drake's bitters was St. Croix rum, made from sugar cane, right, on that tropical paradise. STX, Drake's anagrammatical logo, about which so much speculation has ensued, is merely a short hand notation for St. Croix (or cross) Woodcut. (Author's Collection)

business, a very lucrative business all in all. Drake was originally from Binghamton, N.Y., where on January 22, 1856, he was appointed collector of tolls upon the canal there. The following year he associated with Jerome B. Brown in the firm of Brown and Drake, makers of Catawba Bitters. After several years the partners went their separate ways: Brown became a cigar maker; Drake switched the base of his bitters from wine to rum and developed a surefire prescription to boost sales of his bitters. He devised and patented his figural bottle in the shape of a log cabin. The patent (on the bottle, not its contents) was granted on February 18, 1862. Shortly thereafter, he moved his operation to New York City. As the new man in town, Drake needed a base of operations and the support of one of the city's large drug wholesalers to market his bitters. Almost immediately, he came under the wing of Demas Barnes, "then the leading institution in that line in the United States." Thus began an eight-year association that brought both men millions in revenue and spread their names far and wide.

Drake established himself quickly at Barnes "great medicine warehouse," two blocks south of City Hall Park where at 202 Broadway Barnes superintended his wholesaling operations and at 47 Dey Street, a manufacturing and bottling plant. In the transaction, Barnes acquired a half interest in what Drake was then calling his Plantation Bitters, although they were marketed under the style of P. H. Drake & Co. Demas Barnes & Co. owned all or part of a great many other trademarks. Barnes acquisition of half interest in Drake's bitters was significant, because according to Barnes himself ownership of a trademark was worth the gross amount of three year's sales. In the case of a popular preparation, such as Drake's proved to be, that amount could be enormous.

The bitters tonic was based on St. Croix rum. In fact the cryptic STX is a shorthand for

Figures 189a, b, c,d

Drake was a dapper dude as this original pen and ink drawing, made expressly for this book, shows. Illustration by Sara Jenks Maneval. Copyright © 1994 Fred Reed. All Rights Reserved. (Author's collection) Below, Secretarial Autograph from

check. Compare to Drake's facsimile signature, below left. (Both from Author's collection) Below, preparing and cleaning bottles. His initials PHD (Ph.D.) were the only claim to a doctorate the good Dr. Drake had. Woodcut. Morning, Noon and Night, *1871. (Bowers and Merena)*

UNITED STATES PATENT OFFICE.

P. H. DRAKE, OF BINGHAMTON, NEW YORK.

DESIGN FOR A BOTTLE.

Specification forming part of Design No. 1,538, dated February 18, 1862.

To all whom it may concern:

Be it known that I, P. H. DRAKE, of Binghamton, in the county of Broome and State of New York, have invented or produced a new and original Design for a Bottle; and I do hereby declare that the following is a full, clear, and exact description of the same, reference being had to the accompanying drawings, making a part of this specification, said drawings being a perspective view of the design.

The design of the bottle is a log cabin or cottage, in which the neck A of the bottle is the chimney. The bilge or portion B, which forms the connection between the neck and body of the bottle, is the roof, which has four inclined sides to give the pitch and is so molded or formed that it will represent thatch.

C is the body of the bottle, which is of rectangular form and is so molded or formed that it will represent logs *a*, placed one over the other and lapped at their ends, as shown at *b*.

The neck A, it will be seen, has a smooth surface, is of slightly-conical form, and is provided with the usual knob around its upper end or orifice.

The thatch of the roof B is represented by corrugations *c*, which are at right angles to horizontal shoulders or projections *d*. The corrugations *c* represent the straw and the shoulders or projections *d* represent the layers of thatch or the lower ends of the same, which project or lap over the upper parts of the layers below them.

Having thus described my invention, what I claim as new, and desire to secure by Letters Patent, is—

The general configuration of the parts herein shown and described to represent a log cabin or cottage and constitute a new and original design for a bottle.

P. H. DRAKE.

Witnesses:
JAMES LAIRD,
EDWARD W. HODGSON.

Figure 190a

Drake's claim to his log cabin-shaped bottle was perfected before he moved from upstate New York to New York City in 1862. Patent No. 1538 Specification, February 18, 1862. (U.S. Patent Office)

St. Croix (or cross). Although Drake denied it to keep the public guessing, the 1860 in the enigmatic anagram is literally the year he acquired rights to the product from his former partner Brown. Drake's bitters were potent. A chemist of that era tested the popular brands. At 76 proof, Drake's beverage contained 38.24 percent alcohol. To this over the years he claimed to add a host of esoteric and medicinal herbs, berries and other expensive ingredients. Principal ingredients included Peruvian Bark (calisaya) a source of quinine, Cascarilla Bark (a bowel stimulant), and a host of flowers including dandelion, chamomile, lavender, and aromatics such as wintergreen and anise. He flavored the potion with clove buds, orange, caraway, coriander and snake root. It is known that some such bitters can increase gastric and salivary secretions stimulating taste buds and improving appetites. Any other medicinal value is apt to be psychological. That was probably the "secret" ingredient he

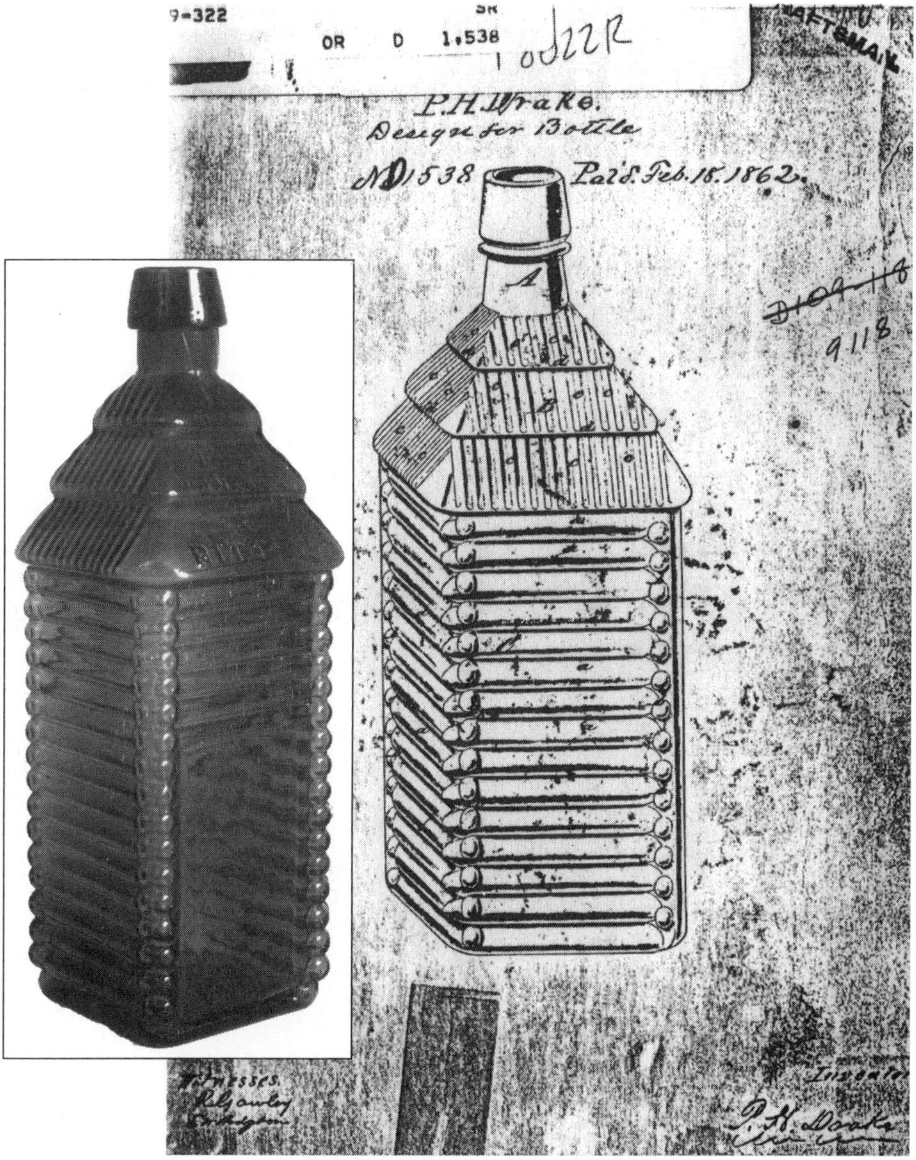

Figures 191a, b

Most so-called "patent" medicines of the Civil War era are properly termed proprietary medicines. In order to patent an elixir, its recipe would have had to be revealed. A recognizable bottle design, like Drake's, however, was a useful marketing tool worth patent protection. Original Drake Patent design, Patent No. 1538, February 18, 1862, bearing Drake's Autograph. (U.S. Patent Office) Inset photo. Plantation Bitters Bottle. (Author's collection, Omar Mediano electronic imaging)

Figures 192a-c
Drake's success is due in no small measure to 19th century advertising genius George P. Rowell, whom he re-signed as his ad agent shortly after the Civil War, at top. Letter, P. H. Drake & Co. to Geo. P. Rowell & Co. September 18, 1868, The Men Who Advertise, *p. 40. (Texas Christian University Library) Rowell was no slouch advertising his services. Currency Lookalike Coupon, May 1868. (Author's collection) He specialized in placing notices, such as at right, in newspapers across the country. Ad,* Harper's Weekly, *September 25, 1862. (Author's collection)*

OFFICE OF P. H. DRAKE & CO., NEW YORK, Sept. 18, 1868.
MESSRS. GEO. P. ROWELL & CO., 40 PARK ROW, NEW YORK:

Gents: Having compared your figures with those furnished us by other advertising agencies and with the terms obtained from publishers direct, for the insertion of advertisements of Plantation Bitters and Magnolia Water, we find them satisfactory, and accept your contract as given in your letter of this date. Oblige us by causing the advertisements to appear without unnecessary delay. Your bills for the amount, forty-three thousand, seven hundred and seventy-six dollars and twenty-six cents, will be paid in accordance with the terms proposed. Yours, very respectfully,
P. H. DRAKE & CO.

S.-T.-1860-X.

DRAKE'S PLANTATION BITTERS

Invigorates, strengthens, and purifies the system; is a perfect appetizer, and Nature's great restorer. It is composed of pure St. Croix Rum, the celebrated Calisaya Bark, roots and herbs. Particularly adapted to weak and delicate persons, and can be relied upon for its purity. It cures Dyspepsia, is a gentle tonic, and is just the thing for changes of the seasons. Sold by all Grocers, Druggists, Hotels, and Saloons. P. H. Drake & Co. 202 Broadway, New York. s26 6ms

never did reveal. Drake's secret ingredient was "faith." Drake maintained otherwise claiming a host of positive health values for his concoction. Among the check list of ailments the Plantation Bitters would cure, according to Drake, were "weakness, dullness, constipation, dyspepsia, sour stomach, liver complaint, nervous affections, fever, ague, diarrhea, jaundice and general debility."

Drake's public exaggerations and publicity skills seemingly knew no bounds (nor shame). Not content to confine his claims to the pages of virtually all the leading publications (and many more of the minor ones) of the day, he found it expedient to stamp his message on the face of nature itself. Drake painted his mystical trade symbol S.–T.–1860–X. on the sides of barns and taverns. He painted the cabal on tree trunks, big rocks at roadsides,

Figures 193a, b

Fueled by plentiful advertising and its unique log cabin bottle, Drake's bitters required an extensive and elaborate manufacturing facility to supply accounts worldwide. Drake was justifiably proud of the building, which appears on some of the company's proprietary medicine revenue stamps. Left, detail from four-cent medicine stamp, Scott RS83a. (Author's collection) Drake's building was a beehive of activity. Below, workers prepare more advertising material. Woodcut. Morning, Noon and Night, *1871. (Bowers and Merena)*

Figures 194a, b, c

Drake availed himself of the opportunity to issue his own medicine stamps, above left, which as today were affixed to bottle tops, right. Above, the bottle label depicted the hypothetical plantation or old homestead which gave the bitters its name. Revenue Stamp, Scott RS83a. (Author's collection). Woodcuts of bottle and label (detail). Morning Noon and Night, *1871. (Bowers & Merena)*

and "surfaces that must have seemed inaccessible to an astonished traveler." An English clergyman recorded:

> Every prominent rock, not only in the White Mountain district but along the beautiful banks of the Hudson and in every place where travelers must congregate, is carefully painted in large letters with the name of some specific or other – the most persistently obtrusive being the Plantation Bitters. . . . If you stand by the Profile Mountain to gaze on the wonderful old stone face, your eye is arrested by Drake's Plantation Bitters.

Perhaps Drake's most audacious act was to cut down an entire forest so that he could adver-

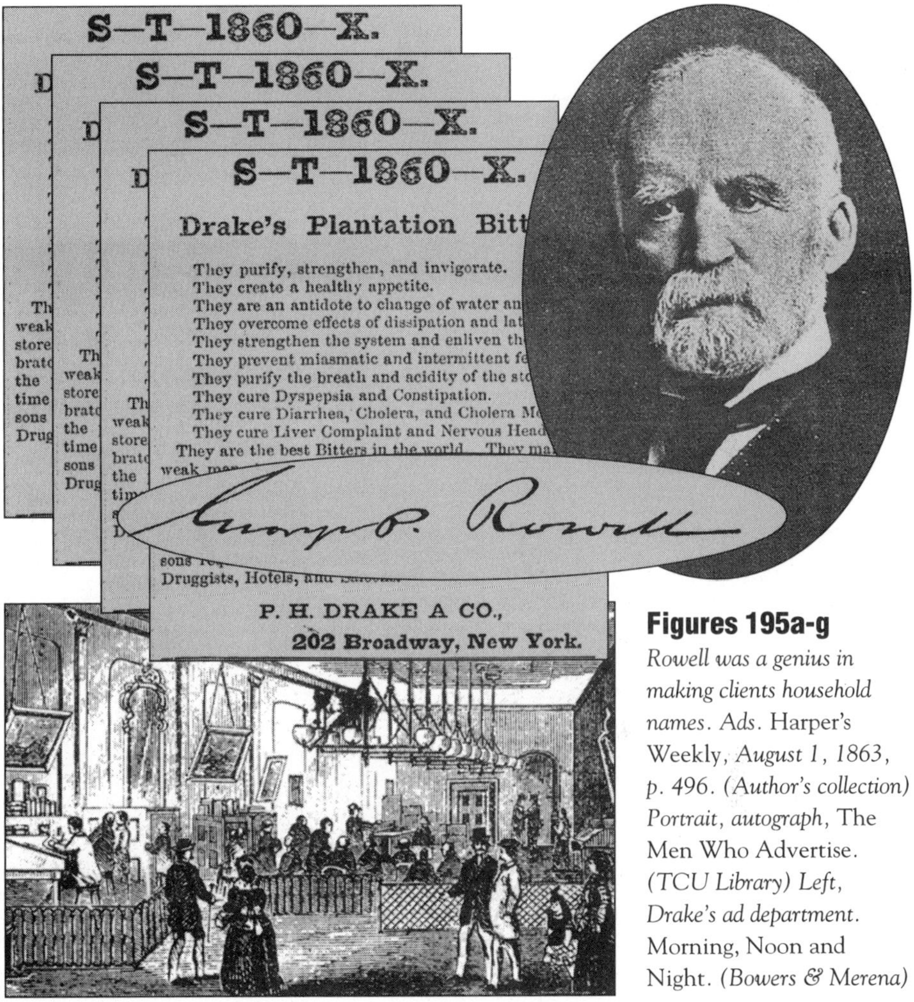

Figures 195a-g

Rowell was a genius in making clients household names. Ads. Harper's Weekly, *August 1, 1863, p. 496. (Author's collection) Portrait, autograph,* The Men Who Advertise. *(TCU Library) Left, Drake's ad department.* Morning, Noon and Night. *(Bowers & Merena)*

tise to the passengers of the Pennsylvania Railroad "in letters four hundred feet tall." It's probably apocryphal, however, that Drake sent forth crews to append his label to such foreign attractions as the Sphinx and Mount Ararat. Such huckstering brought the opprobrium of foreign visitors such as Robert Louis Stevenson. It also caused *Scribner's* magazine to speculate on the "Future of Scenery," and to publicize "The Fight Against Public Disfigurement," while *The Atlantic Monthly* publicly railed against the "Abuse of Public Advertising." It was such activity that led the New York legislature to pass the first outdoor advertising legislation in the country. On March 28, 1865, they proscribed such "Wanton Defacement of Public Scenery." Unfortunately the passage of a law did not stop the practice.

Drake's Plantation Bitters were available at virtually all druggists, grocers, hotels,

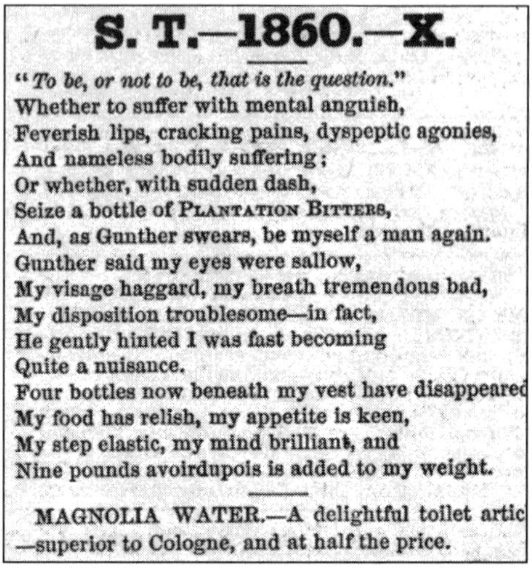

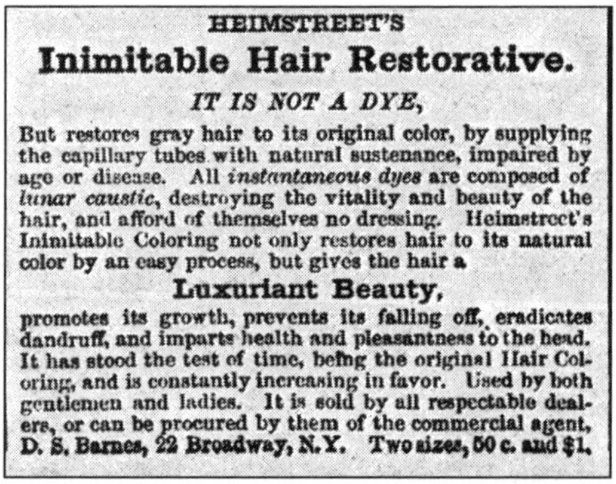

Figures 196a, b

A measure of the success of Drake's ad campaigns was the brand identification value of his enigmatic S. T. – 1860. – X. So prevalent was the awareness of it from Rowell's periodical advertisements that within a few years, that alone was deemed sufficient to buoy sales. Top, Harper's Weekly, *May 16, 1868, p. 318. (Author's collection) Drake's partner D. S. Barnes promoted various proprietary medicines, too. Heimstreet's hair preparation was one such product. Note, the typographical error, 22 (sic) Broadway in the ad. Right,* Harper's Weekly, *January 24, 1863, p. 64. (Author's collection)*

saloons, steamboats, country stores and restaurants. Every bottle bore the facsimile signature of the proprietor on its label. The label was intricately engraved and more than once records show that it was passed off as a piece of currency. One such instance was during the height of the small change crisis when a Drake's label found its way to a church collection plate in Chicago at Thanksgiving time.

The biggest calling card was Drake's unique quart bottle. These bottles come in several color, height, and log configurations. They are avidly collected today and several specimens have long graced this author's office. Although collectors today invariably regard the bottle as a log cabin (it fits in well with the "Age of Lincoln"), from the first Drake maintained that it also could represent a "Swiss Cottage" or chalet. "They are an adornment to the sideboard," Drake claimed, "since they are put up in Patent Bottles, representing a Swiss Cottage." Most were produced at Whitney Glass Works in New Jersey. Normally they are dark to shield the contents from harmful sun rays. His bottle was such a calling card that during the war when devising his own proprietary medicine stamps for his bottles Drake opted for a depiction of the bottle rather than his own picture, unlike his partner Barnes.

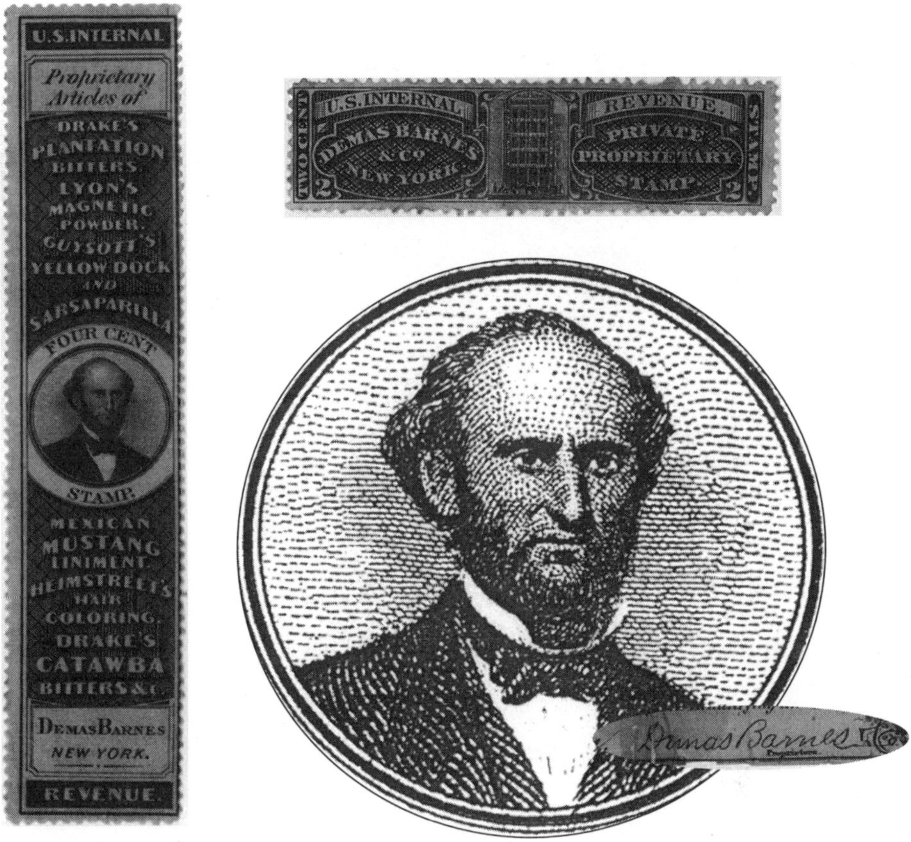

Figures 197a, b, c

Demas Barnes, a grand promoter and shrewd businessman himself, was a perfect counterpart for Drake when the later removed to New York City. They formed a formidable alliance which prospered greatly during the war and thereafter, ultimately forming the basis for a pharmaceutical dynasty which far outlived its progenitors. Barnes was vain. Whereas Drake depicted his patented log cabin bottle on his medicine stamps, Barnes depicted himself, left, or their building (as Drake did also). The detail portrait from the stamp, above, shows the fine engraving of their expensively produced stamps. (All specimens, Author's collection)

Drake's advertising successes were managed by George P. Rowell, who became a legend in the ad biz in New York City. A contemporary of the issuers of Gault's New Metallic Currency, he knew many of them personally. For many years Drake was Rowell's largest client. During his 40-year career Rowell not only led his own advertising agency but established his *American Newspaper Directory*, which was the first serious attempt to gather and publish circulation statistics of all American periodicals. Rowell also founded *Printer's Ink*, the first advertising journal and still a potent trade publication. He also left two highly lucid

Figures 198a, b

Females pack cases of bitters on an assembly line. Source unknown. (Author's collection) Below, currency lookalikes were primary ad vehicles for Drake and Barnes. Imitation $100 The Plantation Bank, c. 1863. (Author's collection)

accounts of his career, from which much of the advertising insights in this book are gleaned. Rowell specialized in saturation advertising, signing lengthy contracts with hundreds of periodicals. Just after the Civil War ended, Rowell records:

> In those days, a $50,000 contract was unheard of, but he [Drake] gave me an order one day amounting to $46,000. That kind of money could buy a lot of publicity in those days.

As Drake knew advertising pays. Princely advertising pays, well, princely. Sales were so plentiful that in the first year in New York, Drake reportedly purchased $50,000 in revenue stamps required to appear on each bottle. At two cents per bottle, that's 2.5 million! Of course, the revenue act was only in operation for part of that year. Sales continued to skyrocket. At the height of the Civil War, Drake supplied nine wholesalers in Cincinnati, alone. Later, Drake claimed to have sold 179 miles of his bottled bitters in a single year. Since his log cabin bottles were about three and a quarter inches wide, mathematics says the good doctor claimed sales of about 3.6 million bottles that year.

To supply such an immense craving for his rum toddy, Drake's production facility was enormous. A contemporary describes it as "a great institution . . . a six story building in Dey Street, from cellar to garret, is occupied as a laboratory for producing this single medicine." Only six months after arriving in New York when he purchased his encased stamps, Drake employed 40 people to operate his factory. In 1868, sales of nearly five million bottles were

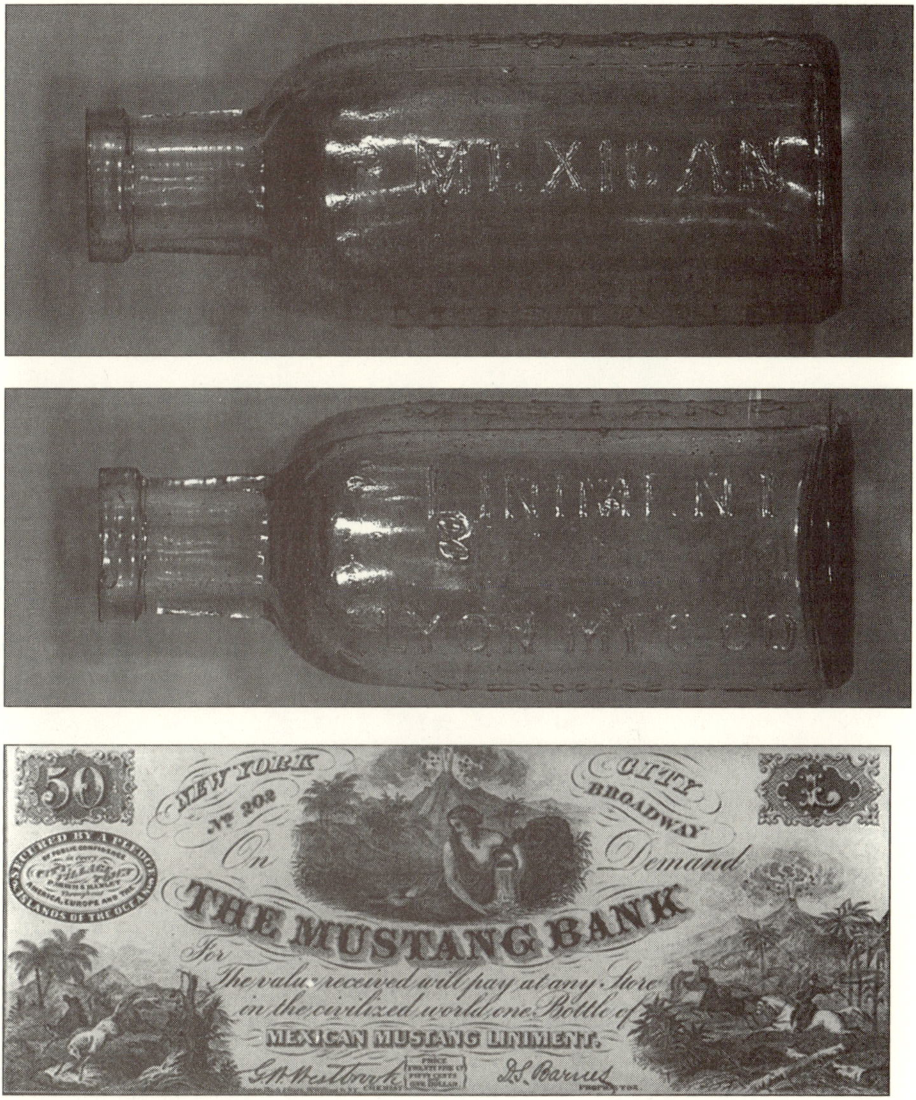

Figures 199a, b, c

G. W. Westbrook was another of Barnes' business partners. His claim to fame was his Mexican Mustang Liniment. Bottle, above. (Author's collection) Currency lookalike note. Imitation $50 The Mustang Bank, c. 1860. (Richard F. Riley photo)

reported. The following year, the take was over six million. By then his manufacturing facility had grown apace (cf. page 205). According to Drake, that year his employees then numbered more than 100, and he spent nearly $100,000 annually on periodical advertising.

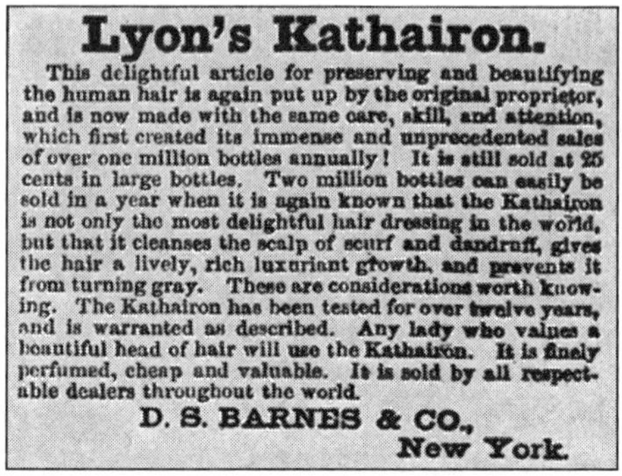

Lyon's Kathairon.

This delightful article for preserving and beautifying the human hair is again put up by the original proprietor, and is now made with the same care, skill, and attention, which first created its immense and unprecedented sales of over one million bottles annually! It is still sold at 25 cents in large bottles. Two million bottles can easily be sold in a year when it is again known that the Kathairon is not only the most delightful hair dressing in the world, but that it cleanses the scalp of scurf and dandruff, gives the hair a lively, rich luxuriant growth, and prevents it from turning gray. These are considerations worth knowing. The Kathairon has been tested for over twelve years, and is warranted as described. Any lady who values a beautiful head of hair will use the Kathairon. It is finely perfumed, cheap and valuable. It is sold by all respectable dealers throughout the world.

D. S. BARNES & CO.,
New York.

Figures 200a, b, c

E. Thomas Lyon was a third associate of Barnes. His principal contribution to the product mix was his Lyon's Kathairon, another hair preparation, above right. Ad, Harper's Weekly, *January 31, 1863, p. 80. (Oklahoma State University Library) Lyon's medicine stamp shows the association's building. Medicine stamp, Scott RS168-B. (Author's collection) The Park Row location to which Drake and associates moved from the Broadway building is shown at right. Woodcut. (Bowers and Merena)*

Drake's success attracted imitators. His distinctive bottle was largely copied by several competing potions. Likewise his trade style. Such imitation did not flatter the fiery Drake. "Sterling articles, in universal request, are always counterfeited," he wrote, "and the corsairs of trade, who pick up a living by depredating upon the rights of eminent firms, and cheating

Figures 201a, b

Currency lookalikes of several types are known to have been used to advertise Lyon's Kathairon. Notes have facsimile signatures of Lyon and Barnes, c. 1854. Top, imitation $20 The Kathairon Bank. (Coin World photo) Above, imitation $50 The Kathairon Bank. (Author's collection)

the public, have not overlooked the Plantation Bitters in their nefarious career," Drake charged. He continued:

> Both in the home and foreign markets they have contrived to introduce their villainous compounds, in some instances boldly affixing the name of the great cosmopolitan tonic to their philtres, and adopting slightly different names, in which, however, the word PLANTATION is conspicuous. Some of the parties to these atrocious deceptions have been prosecuted, and made to suffer the penalties which the law prescribes for counterfeiting trademarks; but in spite of the efforts of the proprietors to protect themselves and the community against fraud, considerable quantities of the noxious trash referred to, are sold. The public are therefore cautioned not to buy any article purporting to be PLANTATION BITTERS, which is not verified by the name, in full, on the bottle and label, and the same put up in bottles, a facsimile of the above. By exercising proper care in these particulars, the genuine preparation may always be obtained, and the tricks and dodges of the counterfeiters and imitators of the bitters will be effectually baffled.

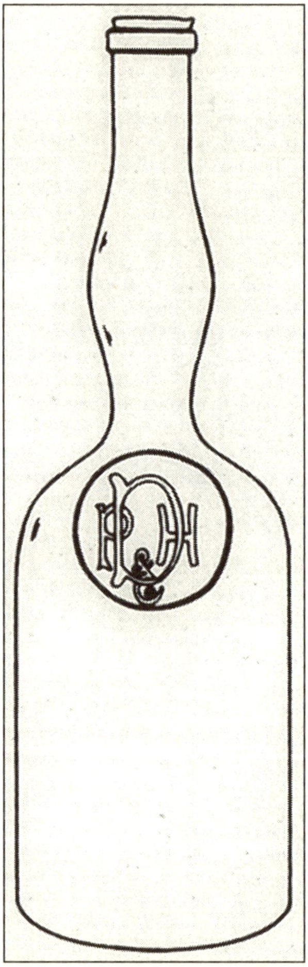

S. T.—1860—X.

Intelligent persons and physicians can judge of the efficacy of the Plantation Bitters from the following partial formula:

CASCARILLA BARK

Was known and used in Germany for Dyspepsia, Chronic Diarrhœa, Cholic, Dysentery, and Diseases of the Stomach and Bowels, as early as 1600.

DANDELION,

For Inflammations of the Loins, and Spleen in Dropsical Affections and Biliary Secretions, or obstructions of the Abdominal Viscera.

CALISAYA, OR KING'S BARK,

Was unknown to civilization until the middle of the 17th century. Humboldt makes favorable mention of the febrifuge qualities of this article as an

ANTIDOTE TO FEVER AND AGUE,

INTERMITTENT AND MALARIOUS FEVERS, in his extensive South American travels. The Countess, wife of the Viceroy of Peru, having experienced the beneficial effects of this Bark, sent it to Europe in 1640. It was sold by the Jesuits for the enormous sum of

ITS OWN WEIGHT IN SILVER,

And was thus called

JESUITS' POWDER.

In 1658, Sir John Talbot employed it with great effect in France in the treatment of Fever and Ague, Dyspepsia, Nervous Affections, Loss of Appetite, Weakness and Debility, Palpitation of the Heart, Diarrhœa, &c., under the name of

ENGLISH POWDERS,

And in 1679 he sold the secret of its origin to Louis XIV, by whom it was divulged. It is now a standard remedy in all Pharmacopœia, and is employed in preparing the

PLANTATION BITTERS.

CHAMOMILE FLOWERS,

For enfeebled digestion;

WINTERGREEN,

Valuable for Scrofula, Rheumatism, and Nefratic Affections;

LAVENDER FLOWERS,

Aromatic, stimulant, and tonic, highly invigorating in Nervous Debility;

ANISE,

An aromatic carminative, creating flesh, muscle and milk—much used in nursing.

S. T.—1860—X.

Figures 202a, b

Drake's log cabin bottle was not the only one in which his bitters were sold. His Sazerac Aromatic Bitters were put up in this simple, milk white bottle with his monogram on it. (Richard Watson illustration, courtesy Thomas Nelson & Sons) The wonders of his ingredients were part of its charm. Ad, Chicago Evening Journal, *October 15, 1862, p. 4. (Illinois State Library)*

The bitters success was not Drake's alone, of course. Partner Demas Barnes raked in the funds from the sale of the bitters, too. It was not as if he needed the money. Barnes was already the largest wholesaler of such medicines before Drake even graced New York. Also born in upstate New York, he also came to the metropolis to make his fortune. In 1849 he

Figures 203a-e

Prior to the war, Lyon advertised his exterminating products on brass store cards. His portrait piece depicts a nickel-sized facsimile of the American Institute medal design on its reverse (see below), Miller NY-511. His half dollar-sized Liberty Head / Eagle store card is a close copy of a $10 gold piece, Miller NY-508. Facsimile signature and store cards. (All, Author's collection) Left, Lyons product was a staple of mid-19th century pest control, earning the recommendation of – among others – the then current operator of the city's Irving House hotel. (Russ Rulau)

MAGNETIC POWDERS,

For Destroying Bedbugs, Cockroaches, Moths, Ants, Fleas, Flies, and Insects on Plants, and all other Insects.

Also PILLS for the instantaneous destruction of RATS and MICE and warranted *without poison* are sold by the inventor and proprietor. **EMANUEL LYON, 420 Broadway.** The following gentlemen have used them in their establishments, and have certified to their efficacy:

D. D. HOWARD, Esq., Irving House.
COLEMAN & STETSON, Astor House.
S. THAYER COZZENS, late of the American Hotel.
PRESTON H. HODGES. Esq., Carlton House.
J. L. ROOME, Esq., Superintendent of New York Hospital.

And many of the most eminent *Physicians* in the city, likewise the *first premium* of the American Institute.

arrived there, age 22, staying briefly before joining the exodus to the California gold fields. Unlike Gault and the other argonauts already described, Barnes chose the overland route. he traversed the stretch west of the railroads by wagon, horseback and foot before arriving in California. He returned to write widely of his experiences. His accounts were collected and published in New York in 1866 as *From the Atlantic to the Pacific, Overland.* Barnes was the consummate entrepreneur. From 1853 on, he collected successful remedies, promoted them and enjoyed their even greater success. He was a "promoter who bought and sold medicines as other men might buy and sell mills or railroads," a biographer records. Barnes was one of the first of the proprietary medicine purveyors to recognize the rewards of securing his own private die proprietary medicine stamps. He personally lobbied Congress to approve their issue. Then, certainly not lacking ego, he quickly did up multiple varieties with his own picture on them. They were approved by Commissioner Boutwell in late September 1862, but the backlog with the engraving and printing companies engaged to supply the stamps post-

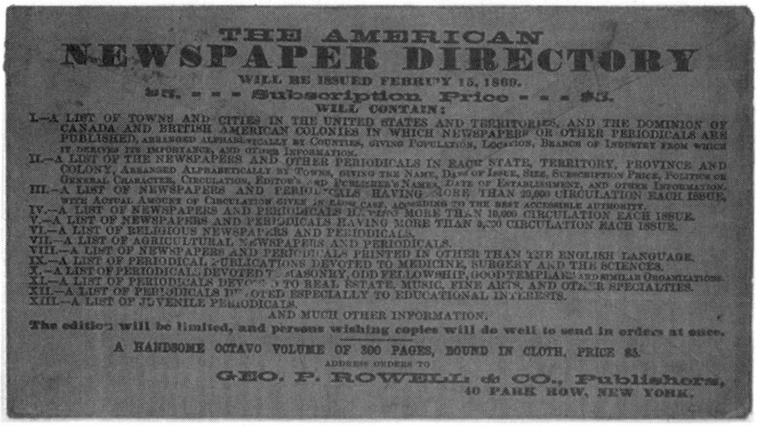

Figures 204a, b (above)

George P. Rowell's amazing advertising acumen wasted no opportunity. His ad cover reverse outlines in detail his publication The American Newspaper Directory. *At $5 a copy, it was pricey. It was easy for Rowell to manage the Drake account. They became neighbors on Park Row. Cover front and back. (Author's collection)*

Figure 205a (opposite)

Drake's post war "laboratory" on Park Row was a labyrinth of activity, compassing every facet of production, marketing, and distribution. Ad, Harper's Weekly, *June 29, 1867, p. 414. (Author's collection)*

poned their introduction until the following spring.

In addition to his affiliation with Drake, Barnes was also a partner of E. Thomas Lyon, John F. Henry, William P. Ward, and other owners of proprietary medicines. All this trade generated enormous funds for the Brooklyn Democrat. His annual sales from all sources for the last two years of the war averaged $44 million. After the war he turned his hand to politics, being elected to the U.S. House of Representatives. He served one term, but not finding the Radical Republican legislature to his liking, he did not stand for reelection. During

HARPER'S WEEKLY.

Laboratory of P. H. Drake & Co., New York.

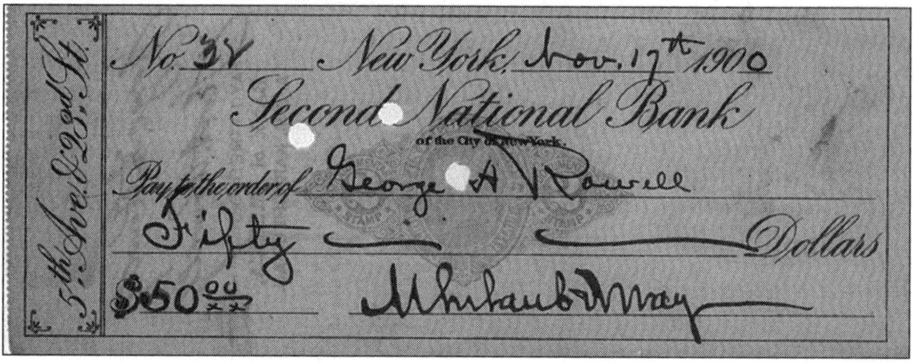

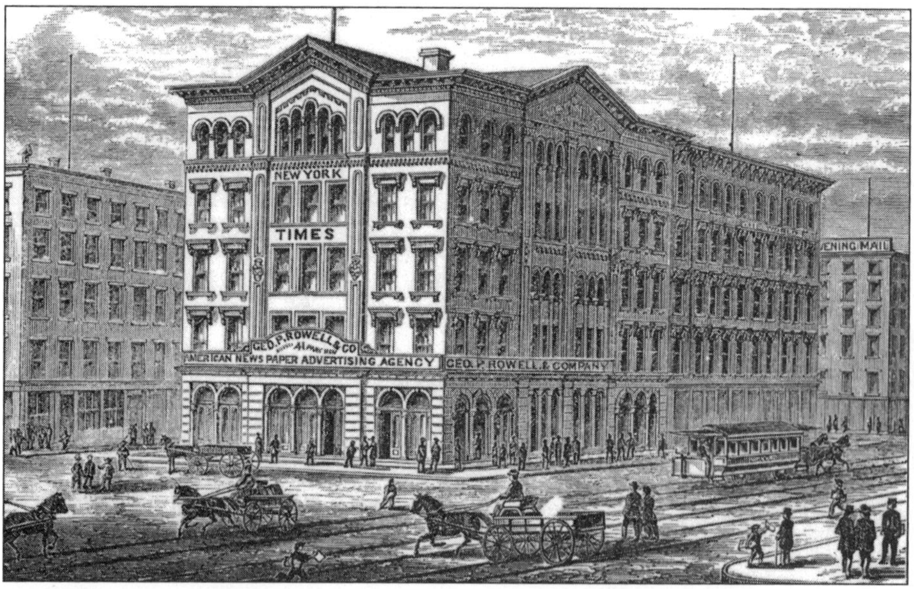

Figures 206a, b, c, d

Top, Rowell issued a copper nickel store card, Miller NY-736, for the U.S. Centennial, 1876. Middle, check payable to Rowell, November 17, 1900. Above, Rowell occupied the ground floor of the New York Times building in Publisher's Square. E. Sears Engraving, Lights and Shadows of New York Life, *1872, p. 32. (All, Author's collection)*

Figure 207a

Drake's patent bottle is a showcase item today, and several varieties have long decorated the author's offices. Fortunately, most varieties are not very expensive. (Boys' Town Museum photo)

his absence his business had declined. Barnes turned his attention to turning it back around, and in the next five years recorded record sales. About 1870 Barnes and Drake went their separate ways. Barnes retired from active participation in the drug trade, although he maintained ownership of the various brands. He turned day to day operations over to Henry. For his part, Barnes turned to watching his money grow. He went into banking and real estate, was a member of the board of education, and served as an original trustee of the Brooklyn Bridge. He also founded the Brooklyn *Argus* as a weekly democrat newspaper. In 1873 and for four years thereafter, he converted it to a daily newspaper, which he also edited. Thereafter it was united with another paper. Barnes died in New York City May 1, 1888.

Like Barnes, Drake became a millionaire several times over. In the 1870s he attempted

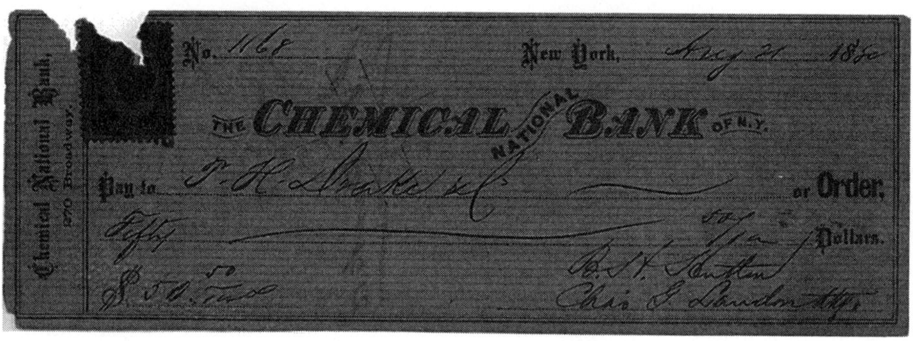

Figures 208a, b, c

Top, a satirical, advertising campaign piece Drake issued in 1880, DeWitt SJT 1876-9, relies on the popularity of his S. T. – 1860 – X slogan. Around the Democratic candidate's portrait is the cryptic prognosis of an unhappy (bitter) result to Samuel J. Tilden's electoral aspirations: 1880 – X – IT (EXIT). (Joe Levine photos) Above, check payable to P. H. Drake & Co., August 21, 1880, appropriately drawn at Chemical National Bank, Scott No. R152. (Author's collection)

to enter the cereal business, and during the decade shifted his premises several times. But by then his bitters were experiencing a sales decline. We may reliably calculate this fall based on the quantities of revenue stamps supplied Drake during the period in question. During the six years 1869 to 1875, Drake did slightly over $200 million worth of business. However, he averaged nearly three times as much annually during the early years as in the later years of that period. Drake died in 1883. The Plantation Bitters continued to be produced and sold into the 1890s, but, according to George P. Rowell, sales were minimal.

Auction Census Data Summary, 1891-1994

	1	2	3	5	10	12	24	30	90	Total	Pct
DR	151		158	70	55	21	10	12	13	490	
DR RB				4	7					11	
	151		**158**	**74**	**62**	**21**	**10**	**12**	**13**	**501**	**6%**

Lord & Taylor
Chapter XIV

It was a great surprise to the current management of this New York-based department store chain that this firm had issued its own brand of money during the Civil War. Although this long-lived company is extremely conscious of its expansive history, the thought of circulating approximately 15,000 pieces of inventor John Gault's New Metallic Currency in 1862 took them by surprise. It needn't have. They should have suspected it. Lord & Taylor's three- (Reed LT03), five- (Reed LT05) and ten-cent (Reed LT10) specimens are certainly among the most interesting pieces of the entire encased stamp series. As advertising store cards, they provide precise street locations of the firm's three outlets at the time, but this denominational preference reflects the company's greater interest was in providing change for its change-strapped customers. That kind of customer service orientation, which has characterized Lord & Taylor for nearly 170 years, is part and parcel of the longevity and success they have enjoyed. It also shouldn't have crept up on them: it has been suggested that a son of their founder was amply aware of the joys of the postage stamp. He has been put forward as the first philatelist, or stamp collector!

Just as a large, old oak may grow from an acorn if the conditions are right, a large enterprise may take birth from a small beginning if conditions are auspicious. The small beginning of pioneering fashion leader Lord & Taylor traces its roots to its namesakes, Samuel Lord and John Taylor at 49 Catherine Street in New York's Bowery. The time was April,

Figure 209a

Reed LT05 obverse, ex-James F. Ruddy specimen. (Bowers and Merena photo)

Figure 210a

Lord & Taylor's original store was on Catherine Street, shown here in an historic photo during its close out sale. Note employees in windows and doorways through the intentionally raised sun shade. Photo, c. 1868. King's Handbook of New York, *p. 848. (Dallas Public Library photo)*

1826, "when water was still being drawn from the public pump and pigs were the town's garbage collectors," according to one colorful account. The pair began by meeting the incoming vessels from Europe and reselling these imports on the streets and door to door. It was dealing with their customers on this intimate face-to-face basis that convinced Mr. Lord and Mr. Taylor to satisfy their desires at all costs. Soon their modest 20-by-50 foot Greenwich Village dry goods shop at Catherine Street Slip, close to both foreign sailing vessels and the Brooklyn horse ferry dock, became a beehive of activity. The Village was then the heart of the city's commercial life. Eager merchants crowded the narrow streets, Lord & Taylor among them, searching out merchandise. Catherine Street was "a lively, noisy, bustling market and the center of New York commerce." Although conditions were primitive, competition was keen.

"Mr. Lord visited auctions, selected goods and brought them back to the shop, where he measured them out for customers. Other fabrics were brought in by sailing vessel and stage coach," according to a company historian. Taylor's contribution to the firm's success lay in his financial expertise, and he devoted his attention to those aspects of the business. The arrangement "proved the ideal partnership." Company lore records the young entrepreneur's first customer: Her name was Anne Fernover Price. According to company tradition, she entered "the quaint little shop on Catherine Street because she was intrigued by the bolts of fabric she saw the two young men unloading from a wagon.", Another account suggests, she was attracted by the young men's activity "opening a case of dry goods in the basement." Perhaps, she was merely interested in the "young men." Whatever, she purchased a bolt of cloth.

Figures 211a, b *Samuel Lord and George Washington Taylor, left, took their brand of merchandising from Greenwich Village to Main Street U.S.A. (John C. Wood illustration, courtesy Lord & Taylor) Below, Lord & Taylor facsimile autographs represent the firm's trademarked slogan: "The Signature of American Style." Garment Tag. (Author's collection)*

From this beginning, the partners adopted a standing rule of customer service: Only items priced a dollar or more should be wrapped in "fancy" store paper, which could serve frugal housewives as shelf paper. Less expensive items were to be wrapped in "plain newspaper." This frugality is reckoned by several modern commentators to the founders' backgrounds. Samuel Lord was born in York, England, the youngest of a family of nine. Before his sixth birthday, Lord and his siblings were orphaned. From early childhood, it is recorded, the young man worked in an iron foundry apprenticed to an iron molder, spending "his childhood in poverty, misery, and hard work." Such a beginning might have capsized a weaker vessel. It made Lord strong. Eventually, he caught the owner's eye and became a master in the Marsden foundry. He also caught the owner's daughter's eye. At age twenty-one he married the foundry owner's daughter, Mary Taylor. Soon the young couple emigrated to the United States. At first Lord found employment as an iron molder in foundries in New Jersey and Pennsylvania.

Then with no previous retailing experience, he borrowed a thousand dollars from his wife's uncle, John Taylor, and went into the dry goods business. Taylor, interested in keeping close contact with his loan no doubt, joined the 23-year-old Samuel Lord in the enterprise to watch over the young man's financial dealings. Within a year, his wife's cousin, George Washington Taylor of New York, entered into the partnership. Reflecting on the early history of the firm, a commentator has suggested the loan terms may have stipulated that John Taylor's son be involved, but whatever the case the two young men became fast friends as

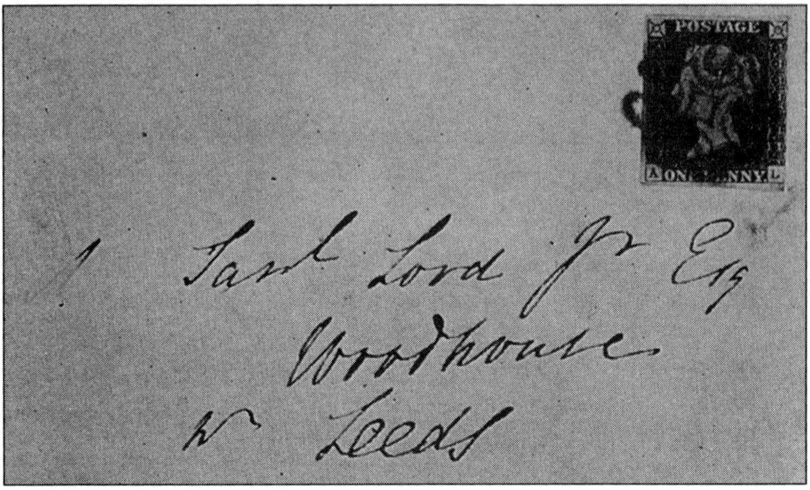

Figure 212a

According to a Canadian philatelist, Samuel Lord Jr. was the world's first stamp collector, beginning his boyhood collection in 1838. Cover, December 15, 1840. (Kasimir Bileski photo)

well as business associates. Lord named his first son John Taylor Lord after his mentor. He named his second son George Washington Taylor Lord after his partner. Finally, his third son was named Samuel Lord Jr.

It is said that in war the victor gets to write the history books. As much might be said about the wars of competing commercial enterprises. The winning survivors pen the tales. When Lord & Taylor launched their retail business, "their competitors were hiring young men to drag prospective customers in off the streets." These "pullers-in" as they were known were young street toughs who forcibly hustled pedestrians for their employers. Messrs. Lord and Taylor refused such practices. They preferred instead, company officials point out with pride, to let the quality of their merchandise and service speak for itself. Soon it became learned that pedestrians outside their Catherine Street store would not be jostled and hustled. "Perhaps as a gesture of gratitude, the customers flocked into the little shop," suggests a company historian. What is sure, though, is that the Lord & Taylor enterprise thrived. Within six years they had annexed an adjoining building. Within another six years, the enterprising young partners purchased a four-story building down the block, occupying the entire premises of 61-63 Catherine Street.

Prefacing the decades to come, the innovative partners challenged accepted horizons from the earliest years. During the 1840s, they opened an additional store in New Orleans. This was too remote "to be considered a branch," a modern writer has observed. He continued:

> [The partners] retired their profitable New Orleans store in the 1850s in order to have funds to move with New York's flow of business north to Grand and Chrystie Streets. . . . Most important, this move took them out of the south. Money and merchandise tied up and blockaded during the Civil War was a calamity for many merchants and one from which most of them didn't recover.

Figure 213a

Lord & Taylor's magnificent emporium 255-261 Grand Street at the corner of Chrystie. Engraved by W. Roberts, S. C., Goater Lithograph. City Directory, *1854, p. 101. (Dallas Public Library)*

The firm operated several additional New York locations briefly during this period, including one on Beaver Street (1852) and another on Maiden Lane (1850-54). These were merely temporary expedients.

In 1852, after 26 years in the partnership, George Washington Taylor retired and returned to Manchester, England. Samuel Lord remained, later admitting John S. Taylor into the firm. The surviving original partner remained dedicated to quality merchandise and innovative selling techniques. He launched a major expansion the following year. In 1853 he purchased a coal yard at the corner of Grand and Chrystie Streets and erected a luxurious second store at that location. Although historians of fashion merchandising have debated the issue of whether such enterprises were officially "department stores" at that time, Lord &

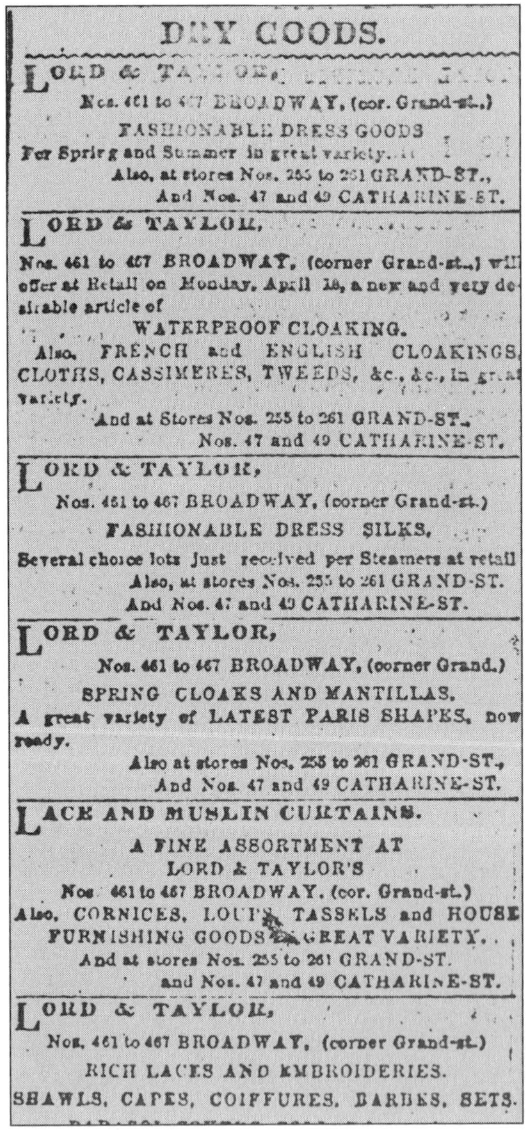

DRY GOODS.

LORD & TAYLOR,

Nos. 461 to 467 BROADWAY, (cor. Grand-st.)

FASHIONABLE DRESS GOODS

For Spring and Summer in great variety.

Also, at stores Nos. 255 to 261 GRAND-ST.,

And Nos. 47 and 49 CATHARINE-ST.

LORD & TAYLOR,

Nos. 461 to 467 BROADWAY, (corner Grand-st.,) will offer at Retail on Monday, April 18, a new and very desirable article of

WATERPROOF CLOAKING.

Also, FRENCH and ENGLISH CLOAKINGS, CLOTHS, CASSIMERES, TWEEDS, &c., &c., in great variety.

And at Stores Nos. 255 to 261 GRAND-ST.,

Nos. 47 and 49 CATHARINE-ST.

LORD & TAYLOR,

Nos. 461 to 467 BROADWAY, (corner Grand-st.)

FASHIONABLE DRESS SILKS,

Several choice lots just received per Steamers at retail

Also, at stores Nos. 255 to 261 GRAND-ST.

And Nos. 47 and 49 CATHARINE-ST.

LORD & TAYLOR,

Nos. 461 to 467 BROADWAY, (corner Grand.)

SPRING CLOAKS AND MANTILLAS.

A great variety of LATEST PARIS SHAPES, now ready.

Also at stores Nos. 255 to 261 GRAND-ST.,

And Nos. 47 and 49 CATHARINE-ST.

LACE AND MUSLIN CURTAINS.

A FINE ASSORTMENT AT

LORD & TAYLOR'S

Nos. 461 to 467 BROADWAY, (cor. Grand-st.)

Also, CORNICES, LOOPS, TASSELS and HOUSE FURNISHING GOODS IN GREAT VARIETY.

And at stores Nos. 255 to 261 GRAND-ST.

and Nos. 47 and 49 CATHARINE-ST.

LORD & TAYLOR,

Nos. 461 to 467 BROADWAY, (corner Grand-st.)

RICH LACES AND EMBROIDERIES.

SHAWLS, CAPES, COIFFURES, BARBES, SETS.

Figure 214a

The Broadway, Grand and Catherine Street stores were advertised on Gault's encased stamps. They offered a wide selection of dry goods, and advertised heavily in the local press. Right is a selection of "Sunday Best" apparel. Ads. New York Times, *Sunday, April 17, 1864, p. 6. (Illinois State Library)*

Taylor now unhesitatingly call this store "the forerunner of the modern shopping mall." Occupied in 1854, the building (depicted on page 213) was "among the most original and attractive of [its] day." It was among the first in the city to use a large glass-domed rotunda to light and ventilate its interior. "Shoppers could stroll and socialize [there] at their leisure. No longer was shopping an unpleasant chore: it had become a leisure activity," the company history affirms. During this antebellum period the range of goods offered in such a store is amazing. Rich American and imported items abounded, including fancy dry goods, silks,

Figure 215a

On the eve of the Civil War, Lord & Taylor's palatial store at 461-467 Broadway was a prime destination for the city's carriage trade. H. Lawrence Tinted Lithograph, 1860. Edward W. C. Arnold collection, Metropolitan Museum of Art. (Museum of the City of New York photo)

rich dress goods, shawls, mantillas, house furnishing articles, carpets, window shades, even gilt cornices.

Under Samuel Lord's guidance the firm continued to grow. A new third building pioneered retail trade on Broadway, locating on the northwest corner at Grand Street in August, 1859. This "stately manse" (above) designed by architect Henry Lawrence was termed "more like an Italian palace than a place for the sale of broadcloth," according to a notice in the New York *Times*. Its adornments included a $500 chandelier by Tiffany. Anywhere but New York, such luxury would be deemed extravagant, the newspaper said. It was this building that, eight days after the firing on Ft. Sumter, was festooned with red, white and blue flags and banners as part of the "greatest demonstration the world ever saw." A half million nationalistic New Yorkers "convulsed in a collective patriotism and marched down Broadway behind bands and flags." This was the same building, only two years later during the Draft Riots of 1863, that armed Lord & Taylor clerks were hard pressed to defend against the looting of "the mobs which raged up and down Broadway brandishing torches and weapons."

The Civil War was good for profits, but to assure profits a firm needed a steady supply of goods. "When the supply of cotton from the south was cut off, anyone with manufactured goods on hand could demand and get fabulous prices. The wartime profits made it possible for the Lords [sic] to retire when the conflict was over. Samuel Lord returned to . . . Chester, England, a wealthy man and lived out his days not far from Saddleworth, the scene of his childhood miseries." To assure business, a retailer also needed to be able to supply the wants

NOTICE OF LIMITED PARTNERSHIP -- Notice is hereby given that John Taylor Lord, John S. Lyle, and Samuel Lord, who respectively reside in the City, County, and State of New York, have formed a limited partnership, pursuant to the provisions of the Revised Statutes of the State of New York; that the name of the firm under which said partnership is to be conducted is LORD and TAYLOR; that the general nature of the business to be transacted is the buying and selling of dry goods, and such other articles as are usually dealt in by wholesale and retail dry goods dealers having business relations with foreign countries; that all the partners interested therein are the said John Taylor Lord and John S. Lyle, who are the general partners, and the said Samuel Lord, who is the special partner; that the amount of capital which the said Samuel Lord, as the special partner, has contributed to the common stock is two hundred thousand dollars in cash; and that the said partnership is to commence on the first day ofFebruary 2, 1864, and is to terminate on the 31st day of January, 1866.

Dated New York, January 31st, 1863,

JOHN TAYLOR LORD,
JOHN S. LYLE,
SAMUEL LORD.

Figures 216a-c

Co-partnership Notice, January 31, 1863, New York Journal of Commerce, *March 9, 1863. (Omaha Public Library) Right, an enigmatic Lord & Taylor encased stamp with Series 1851/57 one cent blue stamp, Scott 5 or 6. Reed LT01'51 obverse and reverse. (Dr. Robert D. Gardner collection, Dabney C. Jackson photos)*

of its customers in another way: it needed to make change on purchases. Although the episode involving Gault's encased stamps does not rank among the most memorable in the scope of this firm's long history, it's remarkable how quickly memory of its happening passed. In fact in 1928, within two generations of their use, a New York coin dealer found that the "present firm don't [sic] even remember them." Thirty years ago, a collector found that same collective amnesia still present. Their purchase of these store cards, however, is an important chapter in the success of John Gault's New Metallic Currency because potentially it represents his first sale of these pieces to a large retail *dry* goods (as distinguished from *wet* goods) merchant.

The pieces advertise the three locations of the early stages of what eventually became an interstate retailing conglomerate. The Broadway store was a virtual bazaar uptown, where fashionable shopping and the carriage trade became symbols of the firm. The Grand Street store, with its distinctive dome and accoutrement, marked the revolutionizing of fashion retailing on the populous East Side. The original Catherine Street store, still its "downtown" presence, continued to provide quality and service until liquidated in 1868. Following

Figure 217a
Delivery wagons on the Chrystie Street side of Lord & Taylor's store add authenticity to this classically posed store front exterior. Photograph, c. 1870. King's Handbook of New York, *p. 848. (Dallas Public Library photo)*

the hectic war years George Washington Taylor Lord and Samuel Lord Jr., the elder Samuel Lord's younger sons, were admitted into the firm. The new management was committed to the same successful operating principles as the original principals had been. Innovation in the post war years led to departmentalization. Lord & Taylor really became a collection of specialized stores housed under one roof. The firm also bucked the trend of discount merchandise, preferring instead to maintain its "quality label." This "recollection of value remains," John Taylor Lord was fond of saying, "long after price is forgotten."

The younger generation also shared the originators' vision of keeping up with the times and the flow of commerce northward on Manhattan. In 1869 Lord & Taylor broke ground for a magnificent five-story, cast-iron palace, at the southwest corner of Broadway and Twentieth Streets. The firm occupied this structure (see, over) at 895 Broadway in 1871. Such constant expansion brought a tremendous need for qualified clerks, accounting and sales personnel. In keeping with their times, Lord & Taylor actively recruited. For example, the company requested graduates of Harvey Gridley Eastman's National Business College "ten and twenty at a time" to fill newly created positions in their growing organization. Their new store was located on the "Ladies' Mile" as the city's fashion center rushed northward. The new building was described as a "French Second Empire extravaganza." Like its predecessors, the new edifice was considered an architectural masterpiece. It had a two-story entrance arch in the center of its Broadway facade. It was outfitted with technological marvels. A novelty, its Otis steam elevator or "vertical railroad," was said to have transported ten thousand shoppers during its first three days of operation. The contraption was hailed

Figure 218a

Lord & Taylor's Broadway store was a sight to behold, according to a post war tour guide. Engraving. Lights and Shadows of New York Life, *1872, p. 384. (Author's collection)*

by the farsighted as loosening the bonds on architecture of the future, wherein "altitude, rather than ground space" becomes the principal consideration. For those with less weighty matters on their minds, the conveyance was just plain fun, and the company accommodated the joy rider as well as the shopper. The contemporary accounts of the range of the goods are astounding. All five floors were joys to behold. In fact, a contemporary guide to New York City recommended a tour of the enormous emporium as a "must see" for a visitor to the big city. One needn't even venture inside to be impressed. "The show windows of this house are among the sights of Broadway," another contemporary observed.

A quaint description of customer service in that era cannot but help recall the proprietors disdain for "pullers-in" earlier in the century: Shoppers were met at the door by a small boy who opened the heavy plate glass affair for them. They were then escorted to the correct department for their needs by a "well-dressed gentleman of easy address," who turned them over to a sales clerk. Once the items were selected, the clerk wrote up the customer's order, accepted his payment and turned both over to a "cash boy" who brought the funds to the office and returned with any change due the customer. "The purchase is then delivered to the buyer, or sent to his residence. Thus the house is furnished with a check on all dishonest salesmen, and at the same time acquires accurate knowledge of their labors in their respective departments."

Although the new store held great promise for additional success, the first year of business at the new location was a bad one for the country generally. The Panic of 1873 profoundly affected all the merchants of the city. The Stock Exchange closed its doors. The

Figures 219a, b

The opening of the Brooklyn Bridge hailed it as the grandest suspension bridge of its day and one of the wonders of the new world. Lord & Taylor (note upper left obverse) issued a pressed wood commemorative plaque (medallion) to mark this event. The author's specimen was painted gold and mounted on velvet to a board, with gold rope borders. It is not known if this was the original method of issue or a later display. Wooden Plaque obverse and reverse, 1889. (Author's collection)

banking house of Jay Cooke failed, but Lord & Taylor managed to weather the storm. Hatches were battened down figuratively and literally. The first of the two Broadway stores

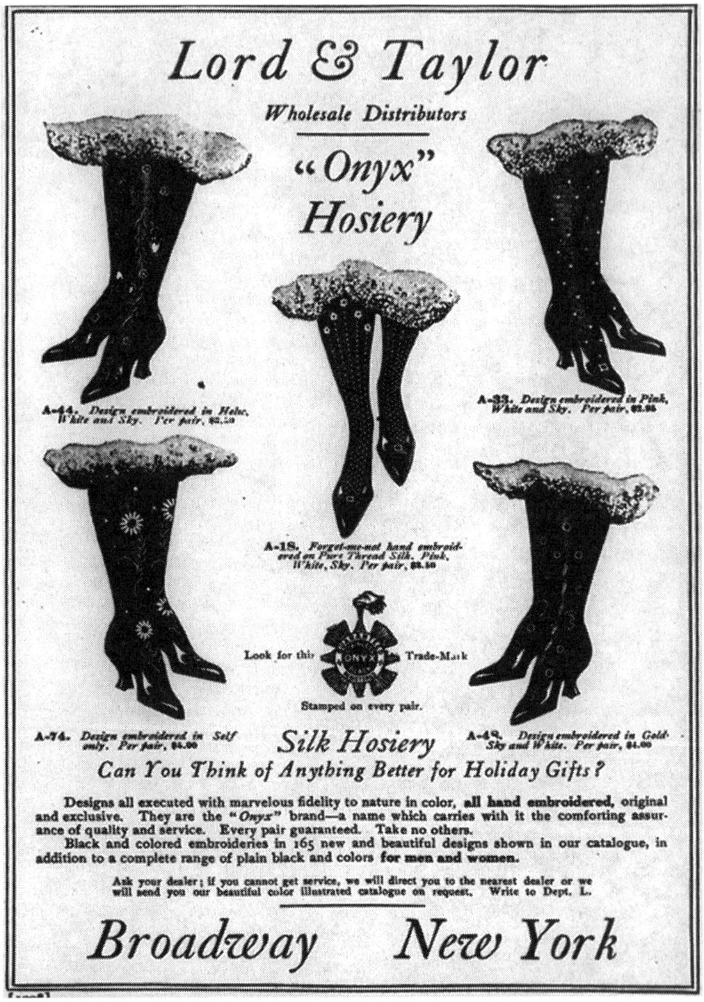

Figure 220a

In addition to its large retail trade, Lord & Taylor distributed clothing lines to department and furnishing goods stores across the country. This period piece prior to World War I pitches high fashion for its day. Ad, 1908. (Dallas Public Library)

closed its doors in 1874. A young "financial genius," Edward P. Hatch was brought in to solve the company's financial problems brought about by the crash. A successful New Jersey newspaper publisher and sewing machine promoter, Hatch bought out the interests of Samuel and John Taylor Lord. Later he purchased the portion owned by George Washington Taylor Lord. With the retirement of Samuel Lord Jr., Hatch became sole owner in 1895. The firm occupied the iron building at Broadway and Twentieth until 1902. Now substantially altered, the building is still standing.

Hatch shared the same breadth of vision of the original founders of the company. He incorporated the business as a stock company in 1904, becoming its president. Before his death in 1909, he had outlined an expansion of the store to the north and east.

Figure 221a *Following World War II, then Lord & Taylor president, Dorothy Shaver, selected the long stem, budding red rose as the company's corporate symbol, signifying beauty and quality. Today it graces everything from matches, to wrapping paper, to boxes and display items. Its designer, Paul Frame passed away November 8, 1994. Lord & Taylor Booklet Cover, c. 1976. (Author's collection)*

Consequently Lord & Taylor later led the fashion stores to New York's Fifth Avenue. It acquired a frontage on Fifth and Twentieth in 1902, and occupied its present 10-story granite and limestone building at the corner of Fifth and 39th Street in 1914. The firm lays claim to many merchandising innovations since, including the first electrical Christmas display, the first lunch counter for patrons, and the first departments catering to teens, short women and collegiate shoppers.

On September 22, 1976, in honor of its sesquicentennial of founding, Lord & Taylor staged a gala at its renovated New York "flagship store." More than 600 invited guests showed up for the occasion, including "celebrities, politicians, fashion designers and beautiful people." Of course, Lord & Taylor is still a "name" in fashion merchandising today. In a

Figure 222a
The flagship of Lord & Taylor's many stores across the country is a 10-story stylish emporium at 424 Fifth Avenue. (Photo courtesy of Lord & Taylor)

recent year nearly 40 locations were spread across the country with aggregate sales in the hundreds of millions of dollars. Not a bad success story. John Gault should be proud for his contribution to it.

Collectors should keep in mind that modern, counterfeit Lord & Taylor obverses exist, and that sets of fakes in a full range of denominations were produced. See chapter on "Collecting Encased Stamps" for details.

Auction Census Data Summary, 1891-1994

	1	2	3	5	10	12	24	30	90	Total	Pct
LT	27		50	41	53	30	24	14	9	248	
LT RB					0					0	
LT '51	1				1					2	
	28		**50**	**41**	**54**	**30**	**24**	**14**	**9**	**250**	**2.8%**

Mendum's Wine Emporium
Chapter XVIII

Another of the smaller businesses employing Gault's New Metallic Currency was the Family Wine Emporium of George E. Mendum who ordered upwards of 20,000 pieces from the patent small change inventor. Mendum was less interested in providing for the needs of commerce than in publicizing his wine mart and pub. Half his order was one-cent store cards (Reed ME01) which were very useful as an advertising vehicle. These Mendum encased stamps are a good opportunity for an intrepid researcher to show his or her mettle. Nothing had been previously published about this merchant before the present author contributed a short biography for the publication of the James F. Ruddy sale catalog. This dearth of information led one writer to wryly observe, "Apparently these people sold wine in a big way if they needed an emporium." Well, in fact, they did.

George E. Mendum opened originally as a wine merchant in 1854 on Wall Street near the terminus of Nassau Street. Almost from the first he also retailed such items as pickles, liquors and "segars." As a watering hole in the city's financial district, with high rents to pay, and higher rollers among the city's bankers and brokers for clients, Mendum was fast-tracking his business for success. Mendum must have been an astute merchant. His watering hole prospered at that location for five years, during which time he moved out of a boarding house and purchased a residence.

Toward the end of the decade, he relocated his business to 83 Cedar and in 1860 to the

Figure 223a

Reed ME10 obverse, ex-James F. Ruddy specimen. (Bowers and Merena photo)

90 Cedar Street location, at the corner of Broadway, advertised on his stamp cases. Mendum was a progressive merchant. In addition to his retail trade, in his new location – his "emporium" as touted on Gault's currency substitute – he sought out accounts in cities as far afield as St. Louis, Chicago, New Orleans, Charleston, Savannah, and Havana, Cuba. He offered his services to the trade in those cities as a wholesaler of wines and liquors. As shown in the detailed listing on the page opposite, Mendum really did operate an "emporium." It is interesting that among the diverse foreign and domestic porters and ales that he carried, Mendum did not stock William Sands' ales, brewed in nearby Troy, New York (cf. page 359). That Sands was the brother of another of Gault's clients, Josiah J. Sands.

It is instructive also to take note of the geography lesson the notice contained: Wheeling was indeed in Virginia in 1861. When the Richmond regime seceded from the Union, the northern counties of the Commonwealth of Virginia refused to sever ties with federal authorities in Washington, D.C. General McClellan, commander of federal forces in southern Ohio, came to the aid of these non-slaveholding, pro-Unionists. In June and July, 1861, he won three brief battles and subdued the Rebel contingent sent there by General Lee. This assured the continuing loyalty of the region and paved the way for the admittance of the new state of West Virginia into the Union in 1863.

According to the notice the selection contained many hard to get varietals. Since most of his business was wholesale bottling the success of his notices in the distant cities may have been outstanding. Orders were "constantly coming in from all parts," the article states. Mendum also dealt variously in a host of other edibles, including imported pickles, sauces, anchovies, caviar, cheese and "other luxuries of the table." His entire operation got the editor's highest personal recommendation: "Strangers visiting New York, appreciating a glass of good ale, or requiring any other of Mendum's edibles or bibibles, should stop in at the vaults . . . as they will be sure of finding the best there," they said.

The descriptions of the loosening of moral strictures during the Civil War are replete with many references to the increase in alcohol consumption during the period. Mendum was one of the recipients of this increased trade. His business boomed. Although it is coincidental to the period during which he was circulating his encased stamp store cards, it is probably due more to the nature of his product than to the direct influence of his one-cent store cards. Shortly after ordering the encased cards, however, Mendum opened two other locations for the sale of wines and spirits. These new emporia were to be found at 78 Franklin and uptown at Broadway and 18th Street. The following year's directory lists but a single location, but that probably is oversight. In 1865, four locations are given, and in 1866 an additional location. In the latter year, Mendum's prosperity permitted him to purchase a fine residence at 61 Amity, but shortly thereafter he died. His widow Ann continued to reside in New York for several years before she too disappears from the city's directories.

The die sinking on the Mendum piece is one of the poor quality products among Gault's series. It is one of several that hyphenate New York (i.e. N -- Y). This and its letter punch quality and atypical location of the patent information all suggest an early vintage for these pieces.

NOTICE

One of the oldest and largest of these is G. E. MENDUM's, at the corner of Cedar street and Broadway. His place during business hours is constantly crowded, and his men are kept busy drawing ales, of which he keeps the following home and foreign brands always on draught:

Allsopp's East India Tonic Pale Ale.
Bass's East India Tonic Pale Ale.
Younger's Scotch Ale.
Burton "On Trent," 1856.
Gaul's Philadelphia "Golden Ale."
Howard & Fuller's Delicious Spring Water ditto.
Jones's XXX Stock (Brewed from English Malt).
Smith's American Bitter Ale (Brewed in Wheeling, Va).
Smith's Champagne Ale (The finest ever offered in the U.S.).
Smith's Kennet Ale (Highly recommended to Dyspeptics and Consumptives).
Guinness's world-renowned Dublin Porter.
Murphy's celebrated Cork Porter.
Marr's Saratoga Cream Ale (From the celebrated Saratoga Springs).
Vassar's Imperial Ale, old and fresh.
Gray's Philadelphia XXXX Extra.

They are kept in cool cellars and drawn from the wood, thus preserving their pure flavor, and many of the ales, being rare productions, cannot be obtained elsewhere on draught. Such a reputation have they obtained for purity and flavor that his retail trade is comparatively small to his bottling business, orders constantly coming in from all parts for wines, liquors, ales, porters, &c., in quantities of a pint to a cask. Besides these he keeps on hand various foreign pickles, sauces, anchovies, caviare, cheese, and other luxuries for the table, and having the best facilities for obtaining them, he has always the choicest the various markets afford.

Figure 225a

A family business, Mendum's offered a wide assortment of "edibles" or "bibibles." Notice. The Union Sketch Book, *1861, pp 134-5. (The New-York Public Library)*

Auction Census Data Summary, 1891-1994

	1	2	3	5	10	12	24	30	90	Total	Pct
ME	105		11	52	25	17				210	
ME RB					9					9	
	105		**11**	**52**	**34**	**17**				**219**	**2.5%**

P.O. Box 118162 Carrollton, Texas 75011-8162

North America Life Insurance
Chapter XVI

A great deal of confusion and misinformation existed about North America Life Insurance Company prior to this author supplying details of its history for the 1984 sale of the James F. Ruddy collection. It's not obvious why an insurance company, which didn't need to make change for retail customers, would be interested in purchasing space on John Gault's New Metallic Currency. However, the company was newly founded in 1862, with an energetic and innovative chief executive eager to put his new company's name before prospects. His trade was life insurance – there was a war going on. What more need be said? So when John Gault showed up in New York City in the summer of 1862, North America's founder and president Nathan Denison Morgan was a relatively easy sell for the encased stamp store cards. Morgan purchased more than 20,000 pieces from Gault in total. From design characteristics it would appear that the so-called "curved" INSURANCE (Reed NA CU) were the first pieces delivered. If this is true, less than one-third of Morgan's initial order was filled with these pieces. What caused the creation of a second die and the production of the "straight" INSURANCE type (Reed NA ST) remains a mystery. Morgan was much more interested in the advertising potential of these pieces than in facilitating commerce. His order was overwhelmingly the low-valued one- and three-cent advertising store cards, especially so on the second (curved) series. This predominance of one-cent pieces

Figure 227a

Above left, Reed NA01CU obverse. (Dr. Wallace Lee photo) Right, Reed NA01ST obverse. ex-James F. Ruddy specimen. (Bowers and Merena photo)

Figure 228a
Nathan D. Morgan was an innovative executive. In 1854 he wrote the first group policy in the American insurance trade while working for the Manhattan Life Insurance Company. The policy insured the lives of "sundry Coolies" shipping aboard the vessel, Sea Witch. Illustration. The Old Reliable, *p. 17, 1950. (Illustration courtesy Manhattan Life Insurance Company)*

may be clearly observed in the auction census data at the end of this chapter. Nearly twice as many of these pieces of this denomination are recorded as compared to the next most plentiful, the three-centers.

In selecting his encased stamps, Morgan was very much in character. He was decisive. He also was innovative. Those personal characteristics were as much the cause of his successes as his failures in a checkered career marked with extremes of both kinds. From what can be pieced together concerning his life, he was born in Illinois about 1830. In his teens he came east, joining the Connecticut Mutual Life Insurance Company shortly after its founding in 1846. Although a youth, he quickly became the company's agent-in-charge at New York City. In this key role, he experienced early success. He was responsible for writing a large volume of insurance. However, he was also young and brash. He clashed with company officers about the scope and extent of his authority. The issue at stake was control of the purse strings for operating his office. He made an ill-advised attempt to bolster his position. Morgan felt he was given too little latitude in discharging his duties. Piqued by the attitude of the company executives, Morgan joined forces with the company's chief Boston agent and a minority of the stockholders in a battle to wrest control of the company. The showdown came in January, 1849, when Morgan was voted down and he resigned.

His reaction to his defeat was drastic. Morgan was among the first to leave the stable jobs of the East to seek personal fortunes in the unknown and unsettled gold regions of the American west. He was only 18 years old when he sailed aboard the *Pacific* on January 24, 1849, headed for California. Landing in California that summer, Morgan headed up the

Figure 229a
Morgan was Manhattan Life's first actuary and second president. Illustration, The Old Reliable, *p. 14, 1950. (Illustration courtesy Manhattan Life Insurance Company)*

American River northeast of Sacramento. In the pine timber country, at a town called Auburn, Sutter County, he threw in with three "older" adventurers, Isaac More, 25, from Massachusetts, Lyman Geer, 37, from Indiana, and Jesse Carson, 24, also from Illinois. The quartet rented a small hovel and pursued mining with negligible success for better than a year. None of the four claimed any value for their daily gold output to census enumerator T. C. Ripley on September 28, 1850. Morgan's stay in California was brief. He lasted out the winter, but still not finding much success, returned to the east.

Back in New York in 1851, he resumed a more familiar role by joining the newly organized Manhattan Life Insurance Company. This company, which had written its first policy August 1, 1850, while Morgan was panning the American River three thousand miles away, named him the company's first actuary in November, 1851. With his comparative wealth of insurance experience, Morgan's initial assignment was to analyze the business affairs of the 17-month-old company for its Directors, who were largely from other fields and had expressed "grave misgivings as to the stability and solvency of the company." Morgan's report to the board put their fears to rest. The company was "a sound concern with a bright future," he said. Business continued to bloom. Morgan industriously sought to expand that firm's market against the older established companies. This not only forced hard work but innovation. In early 1854, New York ship owners Howland and Aspinwall approached Manhattan Life with a novel offer. They sought insurance on a group of 700 Chinese Coolies who were bound on the clipper *Sea Witch* from Swatow, China, to Panama, Republic of New Granada, to construct the railway across the isthmus there. An American company had never written such a group insurance policy before. Morgan wrote the policy for $84,000 to insure the safe delivery of "Sundry Coolies". The ship reached Panama March

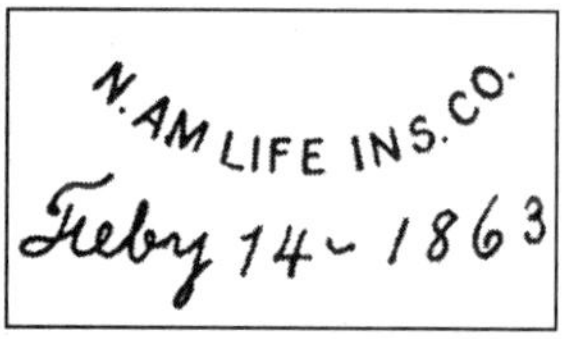

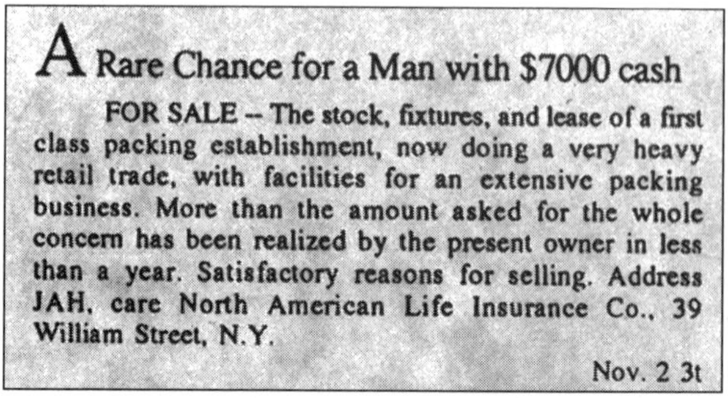

A Rare Chance for a Man with $7000 cash

FOR SALE – The stock, fixtures, and lease of a first class packing establishment, now doing a very heavy retail trade, with facilities for an extensive packing business. More than the amount asked for the whole concern has been realized by the present owner in less than a year. Satisfactory reasons for selling. Address JAH, care North American Life Insurance Co., 39 William Street, N.Y.

Nov. 2 3t

Figures 230a, b, c

Above, Revenue cancellation. (Jere. Hess Barr) Top, the company acted as agent for a blind sale. Note the misspelling of the name. Classified Ad, New York Journal of Commerce, *November 6, 1862. (Omaha Public Library) Right, North America's corporate symbol proclaims "The end crowns the work." Insurance Premium (detail), 1864. (Author's collection)*

31, 1854. The trip took 63 days. Although several of the Coolies died or jumped overboard, Morgan's company netted $432 on the contract. The Directors were well pleased with Morgan's services. With his field experience as an agent and his "fine actuarial ability," Morgan became that company's second president on April 21, 1854. The company history acknowledges his fine service through the rest of the decade. Grave dangers appeared on the horizon, however. On March 12, 1861, a month before the schism erupted in gunfire at Ft. Sumter, Morgan stepped down as president of Manhattan Life.

Morgan went on to found and become the first president of North America Life Insurance Company. When Gault's encased stamps appeared the firm was new and in need of recognition. The company flourished briefly, and was heavily represented in Chicago and elsewhere, but unfortunately for Morgan North America was a short-lived enterprise. In 1867 it relocated to the Astor House across from City Hall Park. Morgan remained there three years before moving to a Warren Street address. North America reported gross assets on January 1, 1871 of $770,000. But after 1871 North America Life disappears from the New York City directories, succumbing to what was known in the industry as "the Trying Seventies." During 1871 North America ceased to do business and entered into voluntary liquidation. Under Morgan the company reorganized and attempted a rebound in 1872. The firm was active in name at least as late as spring 1873, when about a dozen insurance companies came together to revive the defunct Chamber of Life Insurance, a trade association. The Chamber delegates elected North America's Nathan D. Morgan as vice president.

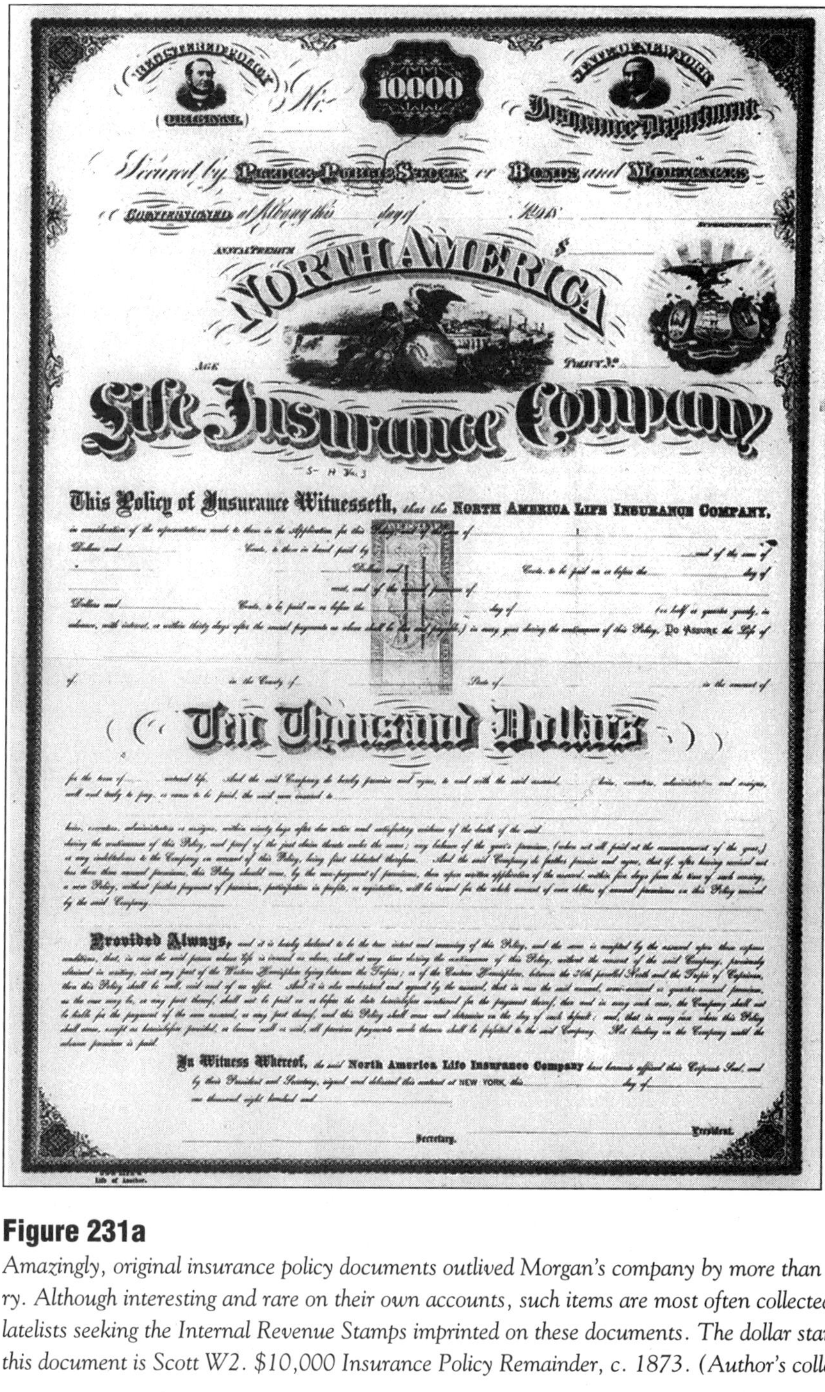

Registered Policy (Original.) No.

10,000

State of New York Insurance Department

Secured by Public Stocks or Bonds and Mortgages

Countersigned at Albany this day of 18

North America Life Insurance Company

This Policy of Insurance Witnesseth, that the North America Life Insurance Company,

Ten Thousand Dollars

Provided Always,

In Witness Whereof, the said North America Life Insurance Company

NEW YORK

Secretary. President.

Figure 231a

Amazingly, original insurance policy documents outlived Morgan's company by more than a century. Although interesting and rare on their own accounts, such items are most often collected by philatelists seeking the Internal Revenue Stamps imprinted on these documents. The dollar stamp on this document is Scott W2. $10,000 Insurance Policy Remainder, c. 1873. (Author's collection)

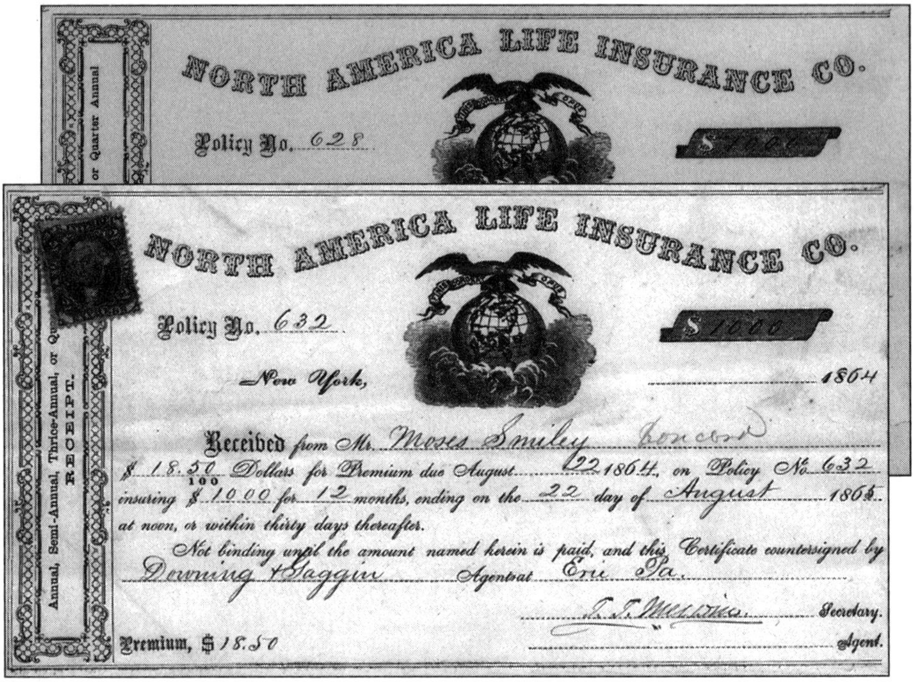
NORTH AMERICA LIFE INSURANCE CO.

Policy No. 628

NORTH AMERICA LIFE INSURANCE CO.

Annual, Semi-Annual, Thrice-Annual, or Quarter Annual RECEIPT.

Policy No. 632 $1000

New York, 1864

Received from Mr. Moses Smiley Concord
$18.50/100 Dollars for Premium due August 22 1864, on Policy No. 632
insuring $1000 for 12 months, ending on the 22 day of August 1865.
at noon, or within thirty days thereafter.
Not binding until the amount named herein is paid, and this Certificate countersigned by
Downing & Saggin Agent at Eri Pa.

Secretary.

Premium, $18.50 Agent.

Figures 232a, b

Receipts for $1,000 policies issued by North America Life Insurance Co. in 1864 bearing two-cent revenue stamps. Receipts for Policy No. 628 issued to Robert G. Dunn and Policy No. 632, Moses Smiley, August 22, 1864. Revenue Stamp Scott No. R9. (Both, Author's collection)

This association did not help North America's position much. The company was already in a weakened condition. Then when the general recession of 1873 hit in November 1873, the insurance industry was sent reeling. North America was the first large insurance company to go. Its unsound investment practices washed out the remainder of its foundation. Most of its funds were invested in city real estate "that proved highly speculative." When real estate values dropped sharply after 1873, these loans "were foreclosed at such a loss that the company became insolvent."

Auction Census Data Summary, 1891-1994

	1	2	3	5	10	12	24	30	90	Total	Pct
NA CU	66		15	0	10	2				93	
NA CU RB	1				8					9	
NA ST	103		77	13	26	7		1		227	
NA ST RB				2						2	
	170		**92**	**15**	**44**	**9**		**1**		**331**	**3.7%**

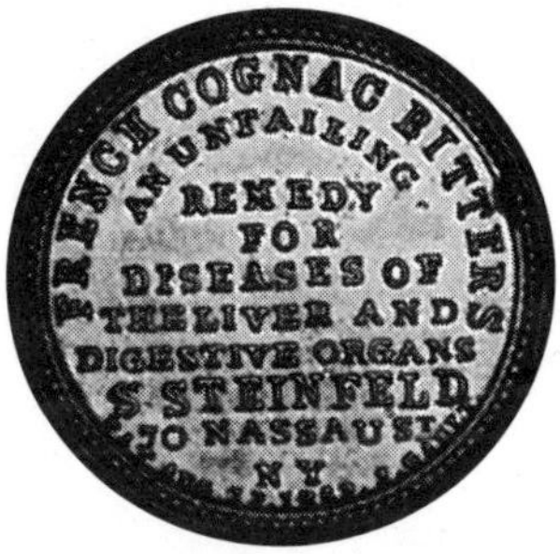

S. Steinfeld
Chapter XVII

Simon Steinfeld was a specialty retailer with a problem in fall 1862. He was a retail liquor dealer and saloon keeper and he couldn't make change for his customers. He was tired of getting beat on the tab, so he did what any reasonable merchant would do: he supplied himself with small change the best available way. At first he paid out postage stamps like the other merchants on Nassau Street, but of all the venues in which small gum backs would fail – a wet messy bar would be the worst. So when John Gault showed up with stamps encased in metal and mica, he bellied up and bought about 6,000 pieces of that New Metallic Currency from Gault. He was only interested in one-cent pieces (Reed ST01). Drinks were three cents apiece. A half dime would buy drinks and lunch. But of course there were no half dimes and the smallest denomination of Postage Currency was the replacement five-cent notes. So higher values of Gault's emergency medium were useless to his normal business trade. Besides, the outlay was only about $200 and he could tout his proprietorship as sole agent for the French Cognac Bitters. The piece was easy to design. Gault prepared it similar to Steinfeld's checkerboard ad in the early November New York *Times* that the New York City vendor shared with Stephen Ambler and other local merchants.

Simon Steinfeld appears first in the New York City directories c. 1849 producing cap fronts and trimmings at a Fulton Street address in partnership with a man named Florsheim. Florsheim quickly drops from sight, and Steinfeld continues in that trade for several more

Figure 233a

Reed ST01 obverse, ex-James F. Ruddy specimen. (Bowers and Merena photo)

Figure 234a

Simon Steinfeld was innovative in his approach to marketing. He participated in a co-op ad in the New York Times, *which incidentally also included Stephen Ambler's Aerated Bread. The checkerboard design prefigures his message on his encased stamps. Compare the language at right to the order he placed with Gault shortly thereafter. New York* Times, *November 1, 1862, p. 8. (Illinois State Library)*

years at several different locations. In 1855 he changed trades. He acquired the agency as sole importer of the French Cognac Bitters that he later advertised on his encased stamps. He also went into the confectionery business briefly with a relative, Frederick Steinfeld, at 70 Nassau, southeast corner at John Street. The location was only a block from the hatter, John Dougan, another of Gault's clients. Liquor won out quickly over sweets in that bustling downtown business district. Frederick departed. Simon hung out his liquor sign and refitted the premises as a saloon.

It was, of course, this line of endeavor that Steinfeld was pursuing during the change strapped early days of the Civil War. The French Cognac Bitters had been devised by a Monsieur Leroux as a remedy for cholera. As sole U.S. representative, Steinfeld touted this preparation far and wide. The remedy was "the greatest cure in the world for cholera, diarrhoea, bilious complaints and fevers" Steinfeld argued in city directories as far afield as New Orleans, Charleston, Savannah, St. Louis, Mobile, Chicago and Havana, Cuba. Such a descriptive notice appeared as a full page ad in the 1857 Mobile business directory. In addition to the usual promises made for such proprietary medicines, Steinfeld showed a remarkable social conscience, promising to attend "free of charge" those unable to pay, who would call at his premises in the afternoon from two to five o'clock. Of course that promise appeared in a directory published a thousand miles distant, with little chance of the readers taking him up on the offer. His pitch in the local New York City directory was much less generous: "All persons calling will be attended to with the utmost promptness," he said.

In typically flamboyant vocabulary, Steinfeld reveals his bitters to be "the wonder of the world." Steinfeld further claims that it relieved British troops in the Crimea "in five minutes." Typical for the highly alcoholic tonics, the product was purported to be an

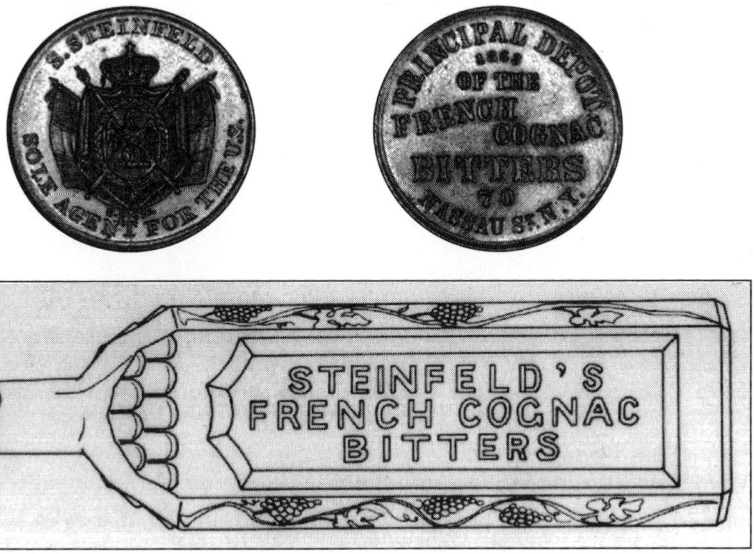

Figures 235a, b, c

Following his flirtation with Gault's encased stamps, Steinfeld turned to local die sinker Emil Sigel who produced the store card above, Fuld NY-630BU, in several varieties. This very common token indicates a very large issue in 1863. (Author's collection) Above, Steinfeld's stylish bottle depicted a grape arbor. (Richard Watson illustration, courtesy Thomas Nelson & Co.)

appetite stimulant and digestive aid, which it no doubt was. The New York directory editors Messrs. Wilson and Trow personally endorsed Steinfeld's product, adding that they always kept a bottle or two around the house.

In 1863 with the small change situation not all that much better, Steinfeld purchased another new metallic currency, but this time not John Gault's. He purchased and circulated several varieties of large cent-sized copper store cards, produced by New York die sinker Emil Sigel. These store cards are very common, indicating a very large issue. Such expedients helped publicize his saloon and product and of course aided him in making small change and keeping the product flowing. Steinfeld survived the Civil War in good style. He changed residences frequently, just about every other year. In fact during the period 1851 to 1872, he is recorded as having no fewer than 11 "home" addresses. During the war for instance he resided on East 16th or East 18th Streets. At the end of the period in question his residence was uptown at 210 West 46th Street.

The efficacy of the French Cognac Bitters may be questionable by today's standards, but the product really was internationally acclaimed. It won a first prize at the Paris Exposition of 1867. Although this author has never seen an example of a Steinfeld's French Cognac Bitters bottle, an illustration of one appeared in a book a number of years ago, reproduced here through the courtesy of the artist and the publisher. The artist based the

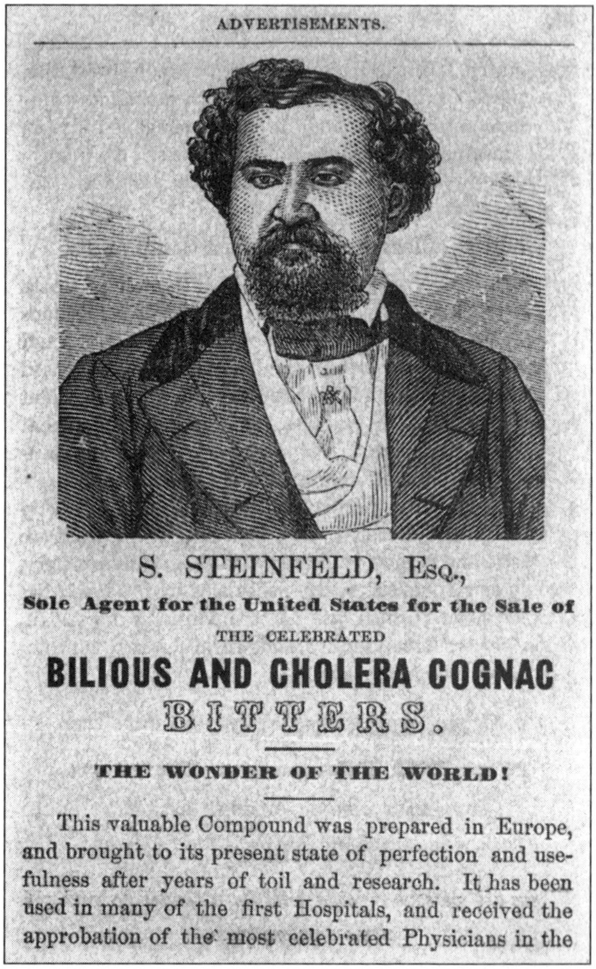

Figure 236a

Steinfeld looked the part to be the agent of a French remedy. He also looked the part of a saloon keeper, which he ultimately became. Woodcut. Wilson's New York City Business Directory, *1855, p. 105. (Special Collections, The Research Libraries, The New-York Public Library)*

drawing on a bottle in the collection of a Charles B. Gardner. As may be seen, it is a square bottle having a long-tapered collar with a ring beneath it. It has a smooth base, beveled corners with grapes and vine decor, a shingled room design on the bottle's shoulders, and the product's name in three lines on the recessed panel. What can't be seen in the drawing of this finely crafted bottle is that it was also a commemorative. According to the book's author, the panel on the bottle's reverse reads: "FIRST PRIZE // PARIS // (shield-like medallion) // 1867." The bottle is amber, 10 inches tall, and three inches wide. According to bottle experts consulted, such a bottle is of the highest rarity. Fewer than five specimens are believed extant, indicating a much, much, much smaller original sales than say Drake's bitters. It's rarity is attested by its high catalog value to collectors, estimated in the $700-$800 range.

Steinfeld remained in the saloon business at the Nassau Street address until 1869.

ADVERTISEMENTS.

old country. In the United States, particularly in this city, as well as in Europe, it has received the most unbounded approbation; and it has never failed in one single instance to produce a perfect cure. No family should be without it an hour, as many valuable lives may be saved by its use. For

Cholera, Diarrhœa, or Bilious Complaints,

it is without a rival in the history of Medicine. As a preventive or remedy for Cholera, Diarrhœa, Bilious Attacks, &c., it is pronounced without an equal; and among the Allied troops in the Crimea, it has been used with the most distinguished success, giving the patient perfect relief in FIVE MINUTES. It is also an excellent promotive of Digestion, restores the tone of a disorganized Stomach, and stimulates the Appetite. As a beverage it will take pre-eminent rank, being perfectly pure and unadulterated, and exceedingly pleasant to the taste, and it may be drank with the utmost safety, as only small quantities are necessary to produce the desired effect. Such we have invariably found it, whenever we have used it; and we are never without a bottle or two in our house.

MR. STEINFELD'S DEPOT IS

No. 70 Nassau Street,

SOUTHEAST CORNER OF JOHN STREET,

NEW YORK,

Where all persons calling will be attended to with the utmost promptness.

Figure 237a

A two-page ad in the city directory, as reproduced opposite and at left, shows Steinfeld's willingness to spend lavishly to promote his product. His use of the large portrait cut indicates a certain degree of vanity. Esquire, indeed! Ad. Wilson's New York City Business Directory, *1855, p. 106. (Special Collections, The Research Libraries, The New-York Public Library)*

Thereafter he continues to list his bitters for sale at several additional addresses through 1872.

Auction Census Data Summary, 1891-1994

	1	2	3	5	10	12	24	30	90	Total	Pct
ST	57		0	6	5	7				75	<1%
	57		**0**	**6**	**5**	**7**				**75**	**<1%**

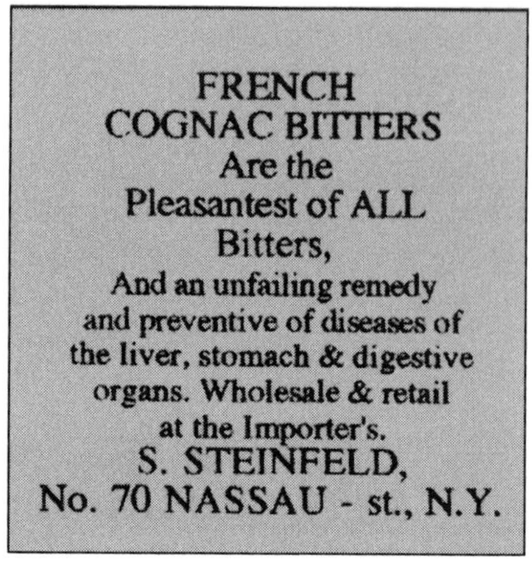

FRENCH
COGNAC BITTERS
Are the
Pleasantest of ALL
Bitters,
And an unfailing remedy
and preventive of diseases of
the liver, stomach & digestive
organs. Wholesale & retail
at the Importer's.
S. STEINFELD,
No. 70 NASSAU - st., N.Y.

Figure 238a

Steinfeld stuck to his guns with the image he wanted to create for his product in the public's mind: it worked every time. Ad. New York Times, *November 22, 1862, p. 8. (Illinois State Library)*

White the Hatter
Chapter XVIII

George W. White, Hatter, of Broadway was a long time veteran of the retailing wars by the time the smoke cleared on the first year of the Civil War and the incipient change shortage spread across the northern landscape. He had been plying his trade in New York City at least since 1849. His name was well known throughout the city as one of the premier hatters of his day – and the hat in that era was much more important as a fashion necessity than it is today. He had a premier location right on Broadway, near the Astor House, near St. Paul's Chapel, near Brady's Gallery, in P. T. Barnum's Museum building, across from City Hall Park. Broadway thronged with pedestrian traffic. He had a long established clientele. He wasn't "out back," so to speak, like John Dougan. So why would a businessman already established with scant necessity for much small change purchase upwards of 8,000 pieces of the New Metallic Currency from John Gault in the fall of 1862? He liked the publicity. He purchased mostly one-cent (Reed WH01) and three-cent pieces (Reed WH03) so he got a lot of pieces for his money. He liked seeing his name in the public arena. His competitors like Knox and James were already circulating the small postage stamp envelopes. He liked the idea of getting a leg up, either leg would do, on the other Broadway hatters like Knox two doors away and Genin across the street. It was typical showmanship that caused him to purchase and circulate the stamp currency substitutes. That's the way to play the game in New York's mid-19th century Hat Game. After all, he was located in Barnum's Museum.

Figure 239a

Reed WH01 obverse, ex-James F. Ruddy specimen. (Bowers and Merena photo)

Figures 240a, b, c

White was a tenant of the famous promoter P. T. Barnum, whose American Museum was located opposite the south end of City Hall Park, across Broadway from St. Paul's Church. It was from a Park Row balcony of Barnum's building that the photograph on this book's end papers was taken by Mathew Brady in 1862. Left, Lavinia Warren was one of Barnum's stars. Ad. Harper's Weekly, *January 17, 1863. (Oklahoma State University Library) The medal below left describes some of the other attractions, and also depicts White's shop. Miller NY59. (Bowers and Merena photos)*

Figure 241a (opposite)

White Hatter "under Barnum's Museum" did not lack for prospective customers in this period illustration. Look at all the hats! Harper's Weekly *Engraving (detail) c. 1860. (Author's collection)*

We don't know much about White personally, apart from his hat trade. He commenced business in Greenwich Village and lived there, too, before moving his residence to New Jersey in 1851. He first tried to crack the Broadway Hat Game in 1854 by renting space at 212 Broadway at the corner of Fulton Street. This is but two doors down from where he would be located when he circulated the encased stamps. The following year he tried 321

AMERICAN MUSEUM
WALLACE & REEVE'S
216 WHITE HATTER 216
BILLIARD ROOM

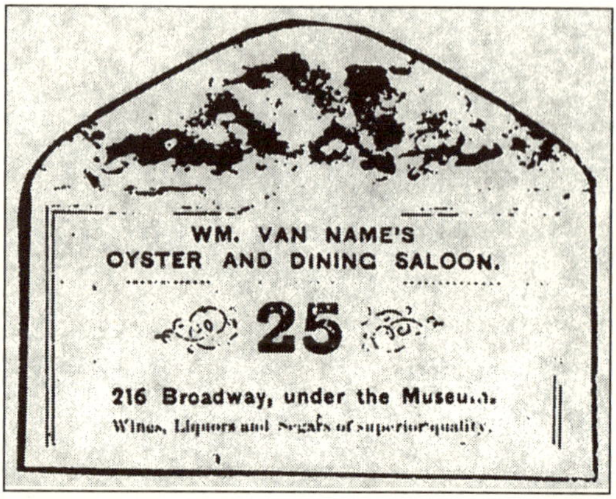

Figures 242a, b

Two of White's neighbors issued stamp envelopes. William Van Name's address is the same as White's, indicating that the rear portion of White's museum arcade location was one of the many small eating and drinking halls near the city's financial district in 1862. Postage Stamp Envelope. (Milton R. Friedberg) Captain Tom Reeves' billiard hall was next door to White as shown in the engraving on the previous page. Postage Stamp Envelope. (Kevin Foley photo)

Broadway, up the street across from the park, but competition was stiff and rents were high. He retreated to less expensive quarters at 148 Fulton Street for three years. Then in spring 1859, White made his move on the big hatters. He reopened his Greenwich Village hat shop and also moved in around the corner at the street level of Barnum's American Museum, the most popular attraction in the city. Business boomed in the new location. He didn't have the time to oversee both shops and there was enough business on Broadway anyway, so he closed the doors on the Greenwich location.

"Under Barnum's Museum" was all the direction he needed on his encased stamps because everyone was familiar with the great showman's location at the southeast corner of Broadway and Ann. Since everyone knew where the world's foremost showcase was, it was a simple matter to reach White. No. 216, White's address was immediately south of the entrance to the museum in a shop previously occupied by Edward Fox. Steinfeld's neighbors, Tom Reeves Billiard Saloon, and William Van Name's Oyster Saloon (there were a lot of saloons in New York) were already circulating the small stamp envelopes. His New Metallic Currency would go them one better, too.

The building was five stories. Barnum had been occupying it since 1841. He constantly

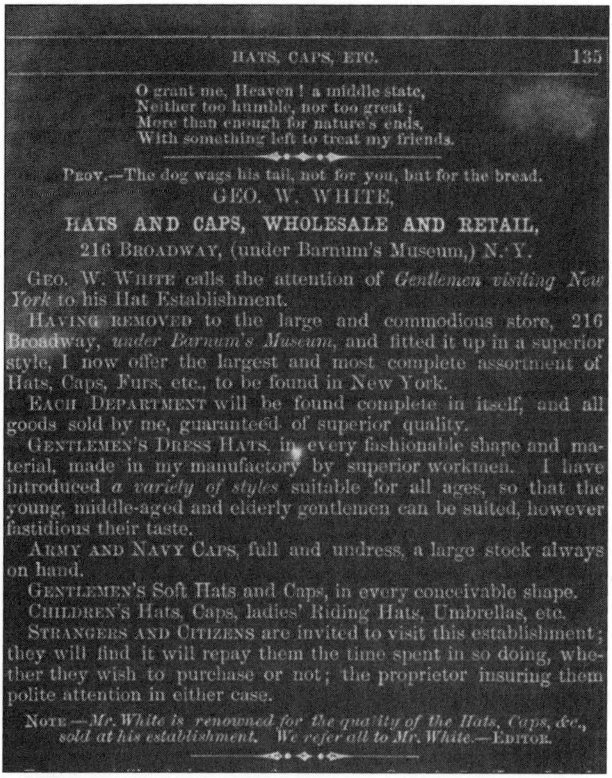

HATS, CAPS, ETC. 135

O grant me, Heaven ! a middle state,
Neither too humble, nor too great ;
More than enough for nature's ends,
With something left to treat my friends.

PROV.—The dog wags his tail, not for you, but for the bread.

GEO. W. WHITE,

HATS AND CAPS, WHOLESALE AND RETAIL,

216 BROADWAY, (under Barnum's Museum,) N. Y.

GEO. W. WHITE calls the attention of *Gentlemen visiting New York* to his Hat Establishment.

HAVING REMOVED to the large and commodious store, 216 Broadway, *under Barnum's Museum*, and fitted it up in a superior style, I now offer the largest and most complete assortment of Hats, Caps, Furs, etc., to be found in New York.

EACH DEPARTMENT will be found complete in itself, and all goods sold by me, guaranteed of superior quality.

GENTLEMEN'S DRESS HATS, in every fashionable shape and material, made in my manufactory by superior workmen. I have introduced *a variety of styles* suitable for all ages, so that the young, middle-aged and elderly gentlemen can be suited, however fastidious their taste.

ARMY AND NAVY CAPS, full and undress, a large stock always on hand.

GENTLEMEN'S Soft Hats and Caps, in every conceivable shape.

CHILDREN'S Hats, Caps, ladies' Riding Hats, Umbrellas, etc.

STRANGERS AND CITIZENS are invited to visit this establishment; they will find it will repay them the time spent in so doing, whether they wish to purchase or not; the proprietor insuring them polite attention in either case.

NOTE.—*Mr. White is renowned for the quality of the Hats, Caps, &c., sold at his establishment. We refer all to Mr. White.*—EDITOR.

Figures 243a, b, c

White won approval from Carroll's New York City Directory, *1860. (Research Libraries, The New-York Public Library) He issued a cent-sized store card in 1863, Fuld NY-630CG. (Author's collection)*

enlarged it as he added to his collection of curiosities. This made the museum popular and him prosper. Among the diverse exhibits in the museum were an animal menagerie, art works, wax figures and a varied troupe of anatomical and ethnic "originals." These included the famous and the merely pitiable, among whom General Tom Thumb and the original Chinese twins, Cheng and Eng, are perhaps the best remembered.

This was a very advantageous location. Broadway was the most famous street in the country. This was the very heart of the carriage trade. Only a block from the famous Astor House, street cars disgorged thousands of riders at White's doorstep daily. His neighbors included the finest stores and the most elegant hotels. The corner of Broadway and Fulton, right outside White's door, has been described as the Times Square of that day. Fulton was the grand highway to the Brooklyn ferries. Not only the locals, but every visitor to the great city sought out this part of town. What a fine location for a merchant who relied heavily on a walk-in trade. One can feel the excitement that the artist felt when he sketched and then engraved the scene shown on page 241. And there in the midst of it all: "WHITE HATTER."

This was the arena of the fashionable traffic, and the place to sell men's hats is where men pass. It was one of the most photographed and drawn sites in all of town. With its

Figures 244a, b

Right, a companion photograph to the one on this book's end papers looks back from the Astor House across Broadway toward Barnum's Museum where White was located. Photo. (Author's collection) Below, an illustration depicting the horrible fire which leveled the museum building and White's hat shop on July 13, 1865. Currier and Ives Lithograph. (Author's collection)

Figure 245a

Following the calamitous fire, White relocated in Brooklyn and several additional locations, where he advertised on the scorecard of the local professional base ball (sic) club, the Atlantics. Scorecard, June 14, 1870, Cincinnati Red Stockings vs. Brooklyn Atlantics, Baseball Hobby News, *December 1987, p. 26A. (Gordon Miller collection)*

potential for large patronage, especially among out-of-town visitors to whom there might never be another opportunity to make a sale, it was also the site of fierce competition among the various hatters. Competition was bitter. A hatter, such as White, might spend upwards of $12,000 a year for advertising, and frequently one hatter's "notices" would ridicule the competition. White specialized in placing small notices in the press. The public followed these notices. In those days, the newspaper was "news." Spring Hats at White's were news, too, and the public would be sure to pay him a visit. With a specimen of the New Metallic Currency in his pocket, or a bronze Indian Head store card, such as White circulated the following year, as a pocket piece, he just might return, too. During the war, White's notices increasingly mentioned other articles, too: ladies' furs, military goods . . . always at lowest prices . . . always at finest quality. It's hard to understand that in those days a gentleman visiting the city quite frequently stopped at the haberdasher first after securing his room. But he wasn't just there for a hat. He was there for a White hat, or a Genin hat, or a Knox hat, so that he might "be in the New York mode." Look at the engraving. Everyone is wearing a hat!

The war struck home Thanksgiving Day evening, 1864, when a Confederate plot to burn New York City to the ground succeeded in part. The plan was to torch hotels and other leading buildings as an act of terrorism. Barnum's Museum felt the torch. The smoke

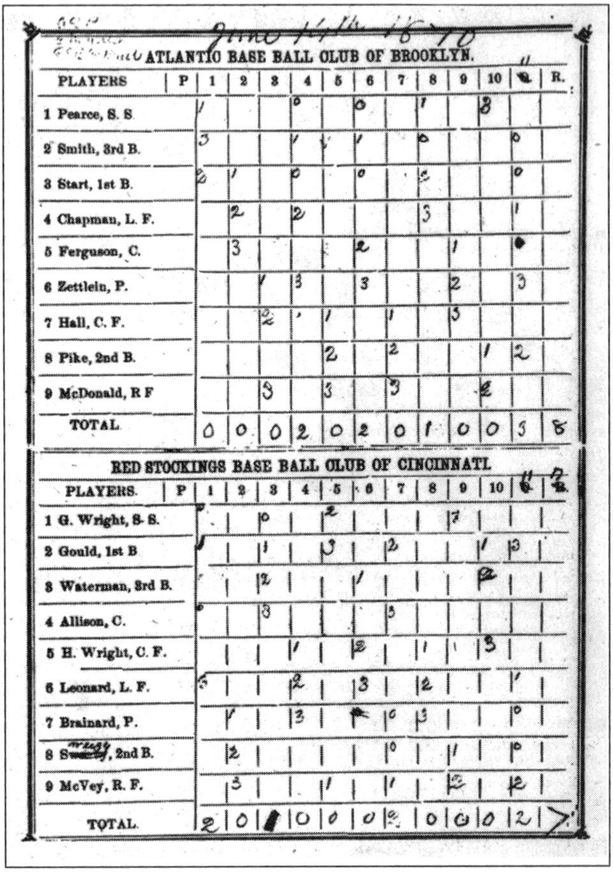

Figure 246a

The White scorecard records the progress of an historic game, the end of the Cincinnati Red Stocking's 130-game winning streak, 8-7 in 11 innings. Scorecard. (Gordon Miller collection)

emptied out the menagerie, but was brought under control. Eight months later, however, White was not so lucky. A raging inferno beginning in museum machinery leveled the whole block in a spectacular blaze. After six successful years in that location, White faced a serious problem, but like a phoenix he too arose from the ashes. He resumed business at 303 Canal Street. In the next few years White opened additional retail stores as well as a manufacturing facility at 293 Grand. There he manufactured his patent "detachable hat, which can be washed and ironed easily like any other article of clothing." He also operated a clothing store at 234 Broadway, two woolen goods shops, and a fancy goods store on Grand.

Auction Census Data Summary, 1891-1994

	1	2	3	5	10	12	24	30	90	Total	Pct
WH	48		25	12	12					97	1%
	48		**25**	**12**	**12**					**97**	**1%**

Weir & Larminie
Chapter XIX

The use of United States encased stamps in Montreal, Canada East in fall 1862 is one of the extreme oddities of this series, especially since Canada was not suffering under a similar small change shortage at the time. In fact, it was quite the opposite. United States silver coinage was so plentiful in Canada at the time that it went at a *discount* compared to Canadian paper currency. In fact, it was such an intractable problem for the Canadians that the senior member of the private banking and specie brokerage firm of Weir and Larminie, William Weir, made a political career in large part based on its resolution. It was, however, the junior member of the firm, G. H. Larminie who arranged for the manufacture of the New Metallic Currency with John Gault late in the year 1862. This merchant is one of those on whom we have good second hand information how their issue came to be. According to numismatist P. Napoleon Breton, who knew both Weir and Larminie personally, the issue was contracted for by "Mr. Larminie, on a visit to New York, [who] had a quantity made for his firm, although such change was not required in Canada." Since Weir was president of a local bank located in the same city in which Breton was writing in 1894, it seems safe to accept his explanation.

Much of this silver initially reached Canada in the purchase of supplies, however with the eastern banks suspended after December, 1861, Canadian banks took over movement of northwestern produce to markets greatly exaggerating the amount of U.S. silver in circula-

Figure 247a

Reed WL10 obverse, ex-James F. Ruddy specimen. (Bowers and Merena photo)

Figures 248a, b

Newspapers routinely reprinted articles to bring national and world news to their readers. The Detroit Advertiser *story, right, is typical of conditions in Eastern Canada during the war. U.S. silver coinage was so plentiful as to be a "glut," and thereby discounted. Thus, there was no practical necessity for the Weir and Larminie issue. They must have been thought of as a novelty by their issuers, and thus purchased for their advertising or prestige value.* Scientific American, *February 21, 1863, p. 118. (Dallas Public Library) Below, check drawn on Weir & Larminie, November 8, 1862. (Warren Baker collection)*

The Glut of Silver in Canada.

It is some gratification in these days of paper currency to know that there is coin still somewhere on the continent. If we have no specie the Canadians are surfeited with it, and are consequently in just about as bad a fix as we are. The following paragraph tells the whole story :—

"It would do a hard-money man good to go to Canada. The currency consists almost exclusively of American silver. Silver abounds everywhere. Everybody is loaded with it, and everybody tries to get rid of it, as people do of doubtful funds. The taxes are paid in silver, and the collectors take it by the bushel. The City Treasurer of Toronto has half a tun of it. The merchants have bags of it in their safes. The banks won't receive it. The Great Western Railway has issued printed notices that only five per cent of silver will be received for fare or freight. Only think of a country where you cannot pay your fare on the cars in silver coin! At Toronto, London and elsewhere, business men and firms have united in a general resolution to receive silver only at a discount of five per cent for Canada bank paper. This of course applies to American silver, as the Canadian and English coinage is a legal tender. Think again of a region, within one mile of Detroit, in which the 'dirty rags' issued by the bank are worth five cents on the dollar more than the shining coin!"—*Detroit Advertiser.*

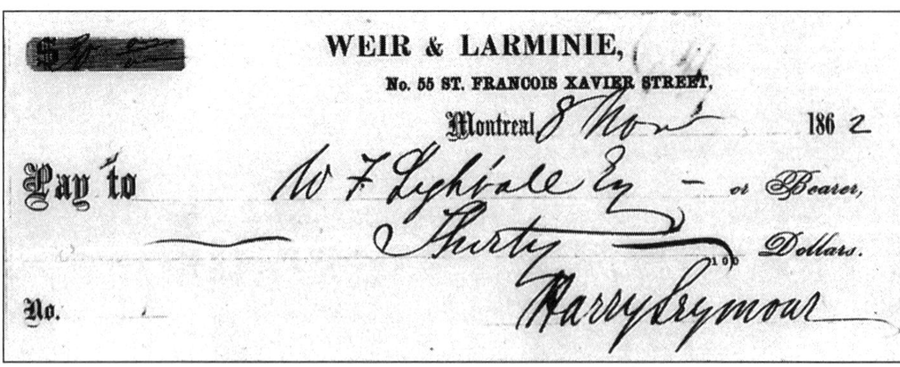

tion there. Brokers in Montreal and elsewhere quickly discounted the U.S. silver at 8-10 percent. It is quite probable the purpose of Larminie's trip to New York City was to sell this

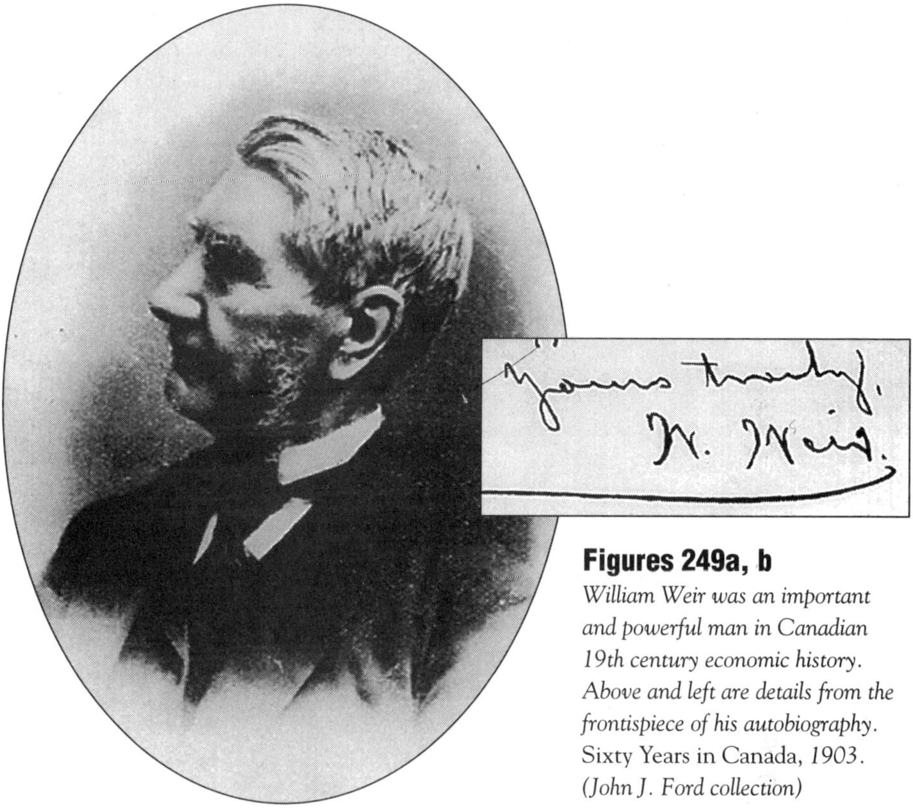

Figures 249a, b

William Weir was an important and powerful man in Canadian 19th century economic history. Above and left are details from the frontispiece of his autobiography. Sixty Years in Canada, *1903. (John J. Ford collection)*

silver to brokers in New York at the then current premium, approximately 20 percent. Such a transaction would have netted the partners a tidy sum. It's ironic Larminie chose to spend about $1,000 of those proceeds with John Gault to purchase about 9,000 encased stamps with a face value of about $800 to advertise their banking and brokerage firm.

William Weir and G. H. Larminie operated a private banking and specie brokerage business at 55 St. Francois Xavier in Montreal in 1862. The city was a thriving commercial metropolis of 130,000 population, located on the south side of the island of Montreal in the St. Lawrence River. The senior member of the firm, Weir, was born in Greenden, Scotland, October 28, 1823, where his boyhood was passed. Well educated in local parochial schools, he came to Canada in spring 1842. His initial employment was as a tutor, then as a public school teacher. He studied at the college and developed a life-long admiration for the French culture of the province. Following a brief stint in a retail store, Weir commenced the brokerage business in Montreal in 1847. Several years later, he took active part in a groundswell of interest among the business community in separation from Great Britain and annexation to the United States. Free trade with the large U.S. markets to bring about prosperity was the goal. "It was simply," Weir later contended, "a case of men holding loyalty to

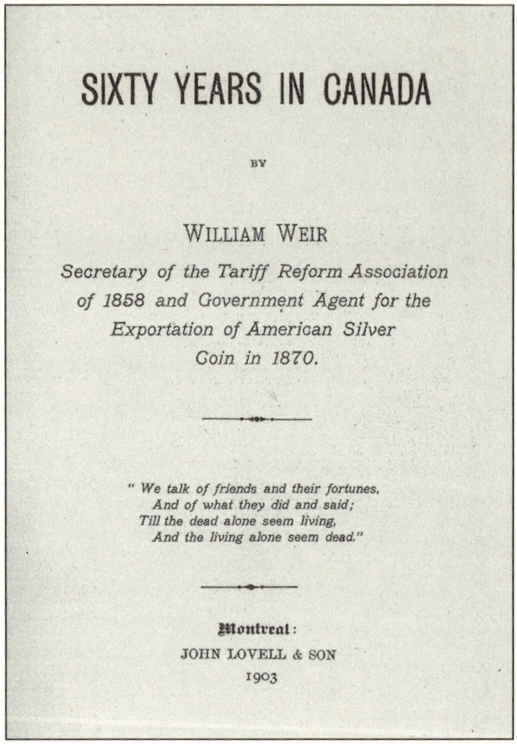

SIXTY YEARS IN CANADA

BY

WILLIAM WEIR

Secretary of the Tariff Reform Association of 1858 and Government Agent for the Exportation of American Silver Coin in 1870.

" We talk of friends and their fortunes,
And of what they did and said;
Till the dead alone seem living,
And the living alone seem dead."

Montreal:
JOHN LOVELL & SON
1903

Figure 250a
Weir's economic views became Canadian general government policy in the years following the U.S. Civil War. His autobiography is an interesting financial reflection of his times, although regrettably he fails to mention his own issuance of encased stamps. Interestingly the accumulation of American silver coinage in Canada proved such an intractable difficulty for the remainder of the decade that the national government hired Weir to export the coinage and relieve the problem. Title page. Sixty Years in Canada, *1903. (John J. Ford collection)*

families above loyalty to their Queen." Unfortunately, in Weir's view, the movement abated.

The problems, however, did not simply subside with the dissent. Weir and his family moved to Toronto in 1856, where in addition to his exchange business he established the *Canadian Merchant's Magazine*. In his roles, Weir took a leadership in the movement to secure protective tariff legislation to protect Canadian manufacturers. Such measures, which would improve domestic prosperity in Canada, would also increase immigration Weir contended. "Thousands of enterprising Americans would come to a country equal in every respect to their own with much more elbow room than they have at home," he wrote. Weir also played an active role in assisting Canadian Finance Minister Sir Francis Hincks in issuing its first decimal coinage in 1858.

The following year he moved back to Montreal where he associated with Larminie in the exchange business. It is perhaps one of the great ironies of history that a Canadian banker should be associated with a group of U.S. merchants and manufacturers caught up in the throes of a specie shortage in a book like this. It is no wonder George White couldn't pay out a silver half dime in New York or Bernard Schapker locate a silver quarter in Evansville; U.S. small coins had so inundated Canada that the government had to hire a banker – none other than Weir, himself – to dig Canadian commerce out from under the silver avalanche, which eventually reached gigantic proportions as U.S. banks and the Treasury Department remained suspended in the decade following the end of hostilities.

Figures 251a, b

La Banque Ville-Marie was the successor to the Weir and Larminie private bank. As bank president, Weir's autograph signature appears on the bank's very rare, bilingual notes at lower right. $5 (Cinq Piastres) and $10 (Dix Piastres), issued dated January 2, 1889. Bank of Canada, Canadian National Currency collection. (James Zagon photos)

Soon upon the release of the encased stamp, the partnership lapsed. In the years following, Weir devoted much of his energy to remedying this silver problem in his adopted land.

Weir devotes four chapters of his autobiography to this *silver nuisance*. He first arranged privately with principal merchants throughout Canada, and exported from $25,000 to $30,000 per week from cities and towns in Ontario and Quebec. He was so successful, that Finance Minister Hincks established Weir as the government agent to rid the country of the unwanted silver. Three and a half million dollars was exported to New York in 1870 and about half that much to England. Canada substituted small notes and a lesser quantity of its own silver coinage.

Such activities on his own and the government's behalf created a great capital reserve for Weir, who invested his profits in land. Within a year, his property tripled in value as a land boom hit. Eventually Weir sold his real estate for six times his initial cost. In 1876,

Figure 252a

William Weir's son, William Henry Weir was the senior member of W. H. Weir & Son, a brokerage firm established in 1876, and member of the Montreal Stock Exchange. Photo. Men of Canada, *1901, p. 49. (The Bank of Nova Scotia Archives)*

Weir established W. H. Weir & Son, members of the stock exchange. He also became vice president of the Jacques Cartier Bank. Six years later, he became president of La Bank Ville Marie. The bank had been on rocky footing and Weir and his sons sought to stabilize it. He also continued his active role in government financial matters of national and international scope. In March 1898, the discovery of a $58,000 theft by a teller precipitated a run on the bank and suspension of payments. The ensuing investigation uncovered a multiplicity of irregularities. Among them were the circulation of more notes than they were legally permitted to and filing fraudulent statements of circulation with the government. Bad debts, including $300,000 in promissory notes signed by Weir on behalf of bankrupt firms were also discovered. The inquiry revealed Weir was guilty of gross neglect and poor judgement. The Crown took a hard line. Warrants were issued for Weir's arrest, along with others implicated. Criminal prosecution followed and Weir was sentenced to jail for two years. The episode was trying for the 75-year-old man. He appealed and in 1901 was retried. The bank was liquidated. Depositors lost well over a million dollars. Interestingly enough, in his autobiography published only two years after these sad events, Weir makes no explicit mention at all of the episode, just a veiled disclaimer about the government "prosecuting the innocent with the guilty." Alas, he also makes no mention of his brief episode with encased stamps. He took his thoughts on both matters – grave and small – with him to the grave in 1905.

Auction Census Data Summary, 1891-1994

	1	2	3	5	10	12	24	30	90	Total	Pct
WL	21		9	3	79					112	1%
	21		**9**	**3**	**79**					**112**	**1%**

Bailey & Company
Chapter XX

Even Philadelphia, the home of the United States Mint, was not immune to the scarcity of small change in 1862. Because of the suspension of specie payments and consequent premium attached to all coinage, the Mint largely curtailed production of gold and silver, devoting almost its entire energies to producing the then current copper nickel cent which entered circulation rapidly. In the country's second city, with more than a half million residents, this large outpouring of "nickels" (as the white cents were colloquially termed, the five-cent coin of the time being the silver half dime) was insufficient to make up for the hoarded fractions of a dollar. As early as July 1862, the city's *North American* reported "so great is the temporary scarcity of small change that even nickel cents are at a premium." This brought well-worn Spanish fractional silver back into the marketplace temporarily, until these too passed for more than nominal value. "How long this state of things will last remains for time to determine," the newspaper speculated.

As elsewhere, Philadelphians were quick to resort to postage stamps as a remedy. By the third week of July, Philadelphia's harried postmaster telegraphed postal officials in Washington to remedy his plight. He needed a great many more stamps to meet the public's demand. "There is a great rush for them," he pleaded. By mid-October, with no relief in sight, the Philadelphia *Ledger* reported that the city's broker's were "ever vigilant" to acquire change. It's no wonder then that Philadelphia's estimable jeweler, Bailey & Company, 819

Figure 253a
Reed BC10 obverse, ex-James F. Ruddy specimen. (Bowers and Merena photo)

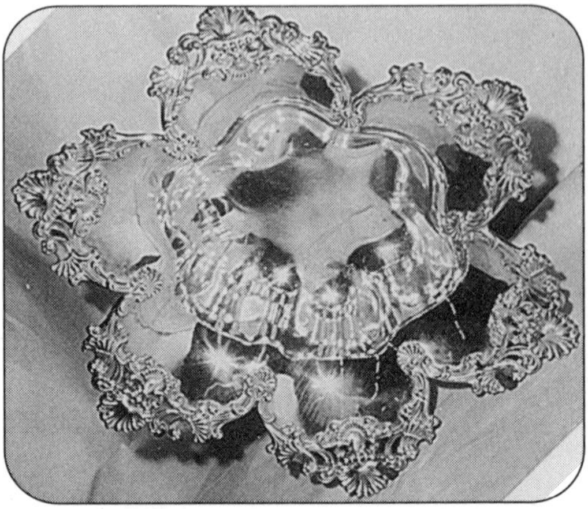

Figures 254a, b, c

Bailey & Co. produced some of the most striking of 19th century American silver service pieces. Clockwise from right, Scalloped sterling bowl, sterling pitcher, and sterling vase. (Herbert Wilson photos)

Chesnut Street, opted for the private currency which John Gault offered.

All the circumstantial evidence suggests that Bailey & Co. were Gault's first Philadelphia customer. The style of the merchant disk is very loose, all sans serif type. The display of the patent information in two lines in the lower field rather than along the bottom circumference is indicative of such early pieces. Additionally, however, punch links suggest a tie to the die sinking of Ambler's Aërated Bread issue. As in other issues, the pieces themselves exhibit die sinker difficulty handling his letter punches. He spelled the address Chesnut (sic), as did the die sinker of the Bailey & Co. store card issued the previous decade. The mathematical modeling suggests that the firm procured something on the order of 8,000 encased stamps from John Gault in fall 1862. Their order was in largely equal quantities of one-, three-, five- and ten-cent denominations (Reed BC01, BC03, BC05,

Figures 255a, b

Above, Bailey & Kitchen, Chestnut and Fifth, was established in 1832. Woodcut. (Bailey Banks & Biddle Company archives, courtesy, Mr. Paul Thurston) Left, Detail, Street Elevation. Baily (sic) & Kitchen, Rae's Philadelphia Pictorial Directory, *1851, plate 7. (Historical Society of Pennsylvania)*

BC10 respectively), as well as a much smaller number of twelve-cent pieces. The firm paid approximately $560 for $400 face value in this interesting change medium. Their expenditure thus represented an advertising premium of 40 percent. This was a pretty stiff premium for useful change, since fractional silver was available for about half that sum. It is obvious, Bailey & Company was much more interested in the encased stamps as an advertising medium.

This firm dates to September 20, 1832, when Joseph Trowbridge Bailey and Andrew B.

Figures 256a-e

Top, Neoclassical tea service, Bailey & Kitchen, 1832-46. (Christie's East photo) Above, Bailey & Co. store card, Miller PA-33, c. 1858. (Author's collection) Right, $10 Pike's Peak Gold, Clark Gruber & Co., dies reputedly by Bailey & Co., 1860. (Bowers and Merena photos)

Kitchen opened their doors as jewelers at 136 Chesnut, near the southeast corner above Fourth. The area was a substantial financial as well as mercantile center. Their original trade was the manufacture and sale of silverware. Shortly they added importation and manufacture of watches, and jewelry to their lines of business. From the first Bailey & Kitchen pioneered in the manufacturing arts. "With new and improved machinery, [they] created quite

Figures 257a, b, c
The visit of the Japanese ambassadors, left, marked the United States as an emergent world power. Photo. (Author's collection) On occasion of their grand tour, Bailey & Co. commissioned Robert Lovett Jr. for the presentation medal, above. Medal, 1860. (Author's collection, NASCA photos).

a revolution in the art of manufacturing silverware . . . [and] immediately took the lead in this department of [the] industry," according to a 19th century account. Among innovations claimed are the introduction of the British sterling standard to the American marketplace. Raising the fineness of the silver proportion in the pieces they produced from .900 fine to .925 fine effectively blocked importation of foreign silver and increased their trade. It also improved look by creating a whiter, brighter product.

Kitchen died in 1840 and Bailey became the sole proprietor. Through the next two decades various of his family members joined the enterprise restyled as Bailey & Co. as business in the antebellum period prospered. In 1858 the jewelers constructed a new store at 819 Chestnut, the location which they occupied during the Civil War when they circulated the New Metallic Currency. The new building was splendid. "Here we have a subject which dazzles us, when we inspect the marble palace of Bailey & Co. on Chestnut Street," a contemporary wrote. At this time the company was headed by Eli Westcott Bailey.

In addition to its fine silver pieces which command considerable attention in today's antique marketplace, as manufacturing silversmiths this firm and its successors have been involved in the production of numerous numismatic specimens through the years. Many are

Figures 258a-d

Die sinker Robert Lovett Jr. produced many store cards, including, right, Miller PA-355, and below, Miller PA-342, advertising his trade. (All, Author's collection, Coin World photos)

Figures 258e, f

On the eve of the war, Lovett also produced campaign medals, including the Lincoln piece, right. DeWitt AL 1860-51. (Author's collection)

illustrated in this chapter. The first apparently was the firm's store card issued for its silver anniversary and move to sumptuous new quarters in 1858. The date January 1, 1855 refers to its introduction of the sterling silver standard, not to the date of the piece's manufacture. This well-traveled commemorative was produced in silver and several additional metals by local die sinker Robert Lovett Jr. Several years later Bailey and Co. was commissioned by Milton Clark of the territorial banking firm of Clark Gruber & Co. to provide dies for its distinctive Colorado private gold pieces. Bailey & Co. again turned to Lovett, located around the corner from its shop, who provided the fictitious view for the Clark Gruber $10 and $20 gold coins struck in summer 1860. That summer, Bailey & Co. also tapped Lovett for dies for a presentation medal presented to the Japanese ambassadors in June on their grand tour of the United States. Again this excellent medal was struck in several metals.

Figures 259a, b, c
Top, Lovett's Phrygian Liberty Cap Bust Left design reappeared surreptitiously on a purported pattern for a Confederate Cent. (Steve Ivy photos) Bailey & Co. reputedly served as the liaison between the Confederate agents and Lovett on the aborted scheme, but that scenario has lately come under close scrutiny. The original Lovett dies passed through several collections before arriving in the hands of Robert Bashlow just in time to be used to create hubbed copy dies employed in restriking the pieces for the Civil War Centennial. These broken original dies (left) were later donated to the Smithsonian Institution. Photo, obverse and reverse original dies for Confederate Cent pattern. (Robert Bashlow photo)

In early 1861, however, Bailey & Co. became embroiled in a furtive plan to furnish a speculative cent coinage for the Confederate States of America. Allegedly agents of the Confederate government were dispatched northward to secure such a contract coinage. Bailey & Co. are believed to have arranged for their contract die sinker Lovett to produce essais for the cent. Prior to the Act of July 13, 1861, and the Presidential proclamation of August 16 pursuant to the act, designed to forbid conveyance of supplies or other commercial intercourse with persons in insurrection to the United States, such activities would not have been illegal nor even necessarily unpatriotic prior to the firing on Ft. Sumter. They would merely have been doing business where business was to be done. The specifics of this venture are subject of lively debate within the numismatic community. What is clear, though, is that the plan did not come to fruition. Reportedly, only a dozen copper nickel specimens were struck, and even these were not revealed until a dozen years later. Neither Bailey & Co. nor Lovett were manifestly southern sympathizers. During the war Bailey &

Figures 260a-e

Bailey Banks & Biddle (nee Bailey & Kitchen, Bailey & Co.) have long been active in the production of awards, decorations, commemorative and other medals. Top, Cincinnati Industrial Exposition Award Medal unissued, bronze, by Peter Krider and Biddle, c. 1880. (Author's collection) Above, Holland Society of New York Medal, bronze, January 1905, by Bailey Banks & Biddle. (Author's collection) Right, Title Page from the company's catalog of American orders and decorations, 1917. (Bailey Banks & Biddle Archives, Courtesy Mr. Paul Thurston)

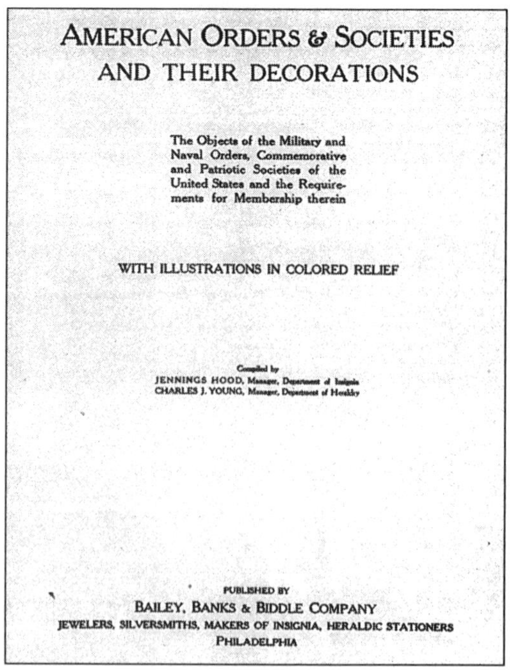

AMERICAN ORDERS & SOCIETIES
AND THEIR DECORATIONS

The Objects of the Military and Naval Orders, Commemorative and Patriotic Societies of the United States and the Requirements for Membership therein

WITH ILLUSTRATIONS IN COLORED RELIEF

Compiled by
JENNINGS HOOD, Manager, Department of Insignia
CHARLES J. YOUNG, Manager, Department of Heraldry

PUBLISHED BY
BAILEY, BANKS & BIDDLE COMPANY
JEWELERS, SILVERSMITHS, MAKERS OF INSIGNIA, HERALDIC STATIONERS
PHILADELPHIA

Figures 261a-e

In the company's long, distinguished history, Bailey & Co. and its successor have issued numerous heraldic and insignia devices for patriotic and similar societies. Left and below left is their member's badge for the Sons of the Revolution, 1882. Suspended medal with bezel by Bailey Banks and Biddle, awarded Carlton Annin Opel, March 28, 1932. (Author's Collection) Above, SoAR miniature badge. (Author's Collection) Below, Title Page from the company's definitive reference, Heraldry in America, 1909. *(Author's collection)*

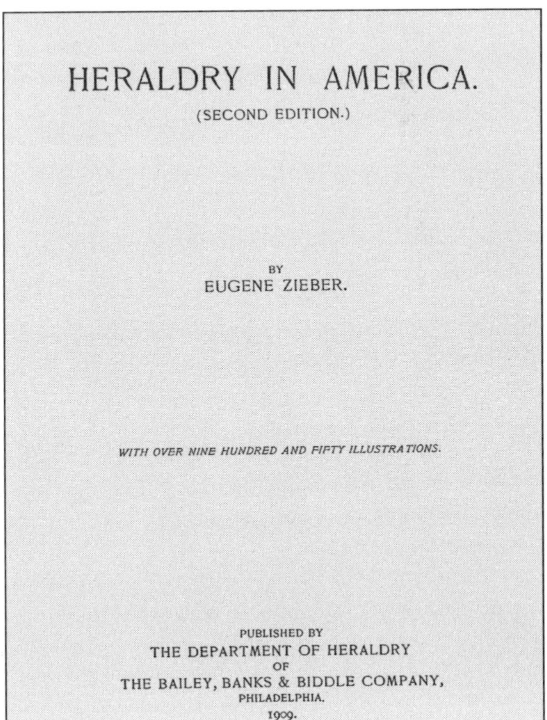

HERALDRY IN AMERICA.

(SECOND EDITION.)

BY
EUGENE ZIEBER.

WITH OVER NINE HUNDRED AND FIFTY ILLUSTRATIONS.

PUBLISHED BY
THE DEPARTMENT OF HERALDRY
OF
THE BAILEY, BANKS & BIDDLE COMPANY,
PHILADELPHIA.
1909.

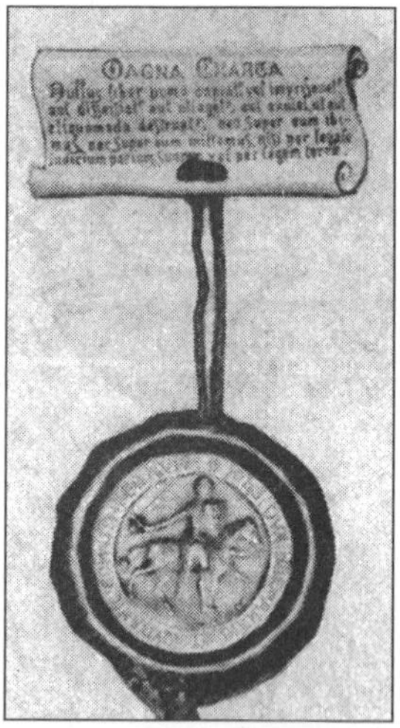

Figures 262a-e

The orders and decorations produced by Bailey, Banks & Biddle run the gamut of design. Clockwise from top left: Huguenot Society of America Badge, gold plated silver, 1883; Hereditary Order of Descendants of Colonial Governors Prior to 1750 Badge, 14K gold and enamel, 1896; Order of Runneymede Badge, gold plated silver and bronze; 1898; National Society of the Colonial Dames of America Badge and Lapel Pin, 14K gold, 1890. (Collectors' Auctions Limited photos) Below, the firm's fine and heraldic stationery department letterhead, c. 1890. (Author's collection)

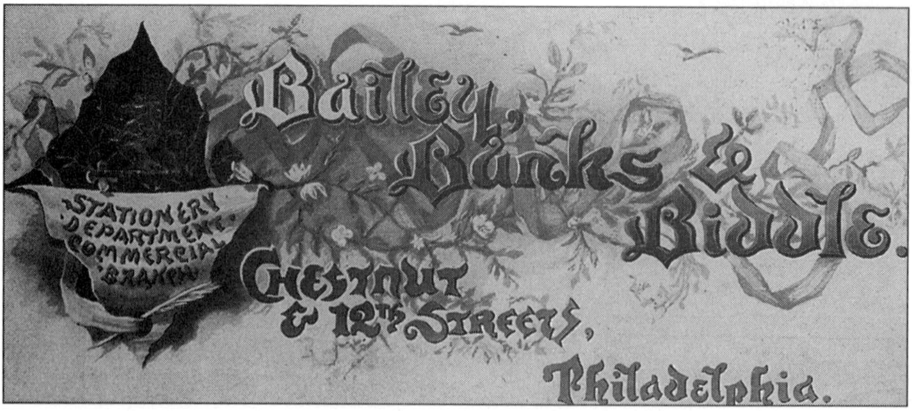

Figures 263a, b, c, d

Some of the company's finest pieces are the commemorative gold-plated medals it has issued this century. Two of these are the 1906 centennial medal for the Seventh Regiment New York National Guard and the official award medal of the U.S. Sesquicentennial Exposition held in Philadelphia in 1926. The latter piece was designed by Albert Laessle. Medals, gilt bronze. (Both, Author's collection)

Co. supplied the Union Army with sabers and swords. The company also was involved in the importation of British Enfield rifles for the U.S. Army in a minor way. Additionally Bailey & Co. were active during the war in assisting Philadelphia officials with recruiting efforts by furnishing funds for enlistment bounties. Lovett's sympathies were commercial not partisan, too. He was capable of concurrently producing trade pieces for all parties in a dispute. The prior year he had issued campaign medals for Lincoln and his opponents. And he would be actively involved shortly in producing store cards for merchants caught up in the

Figures 264a, b

More than a century and a half since opening its doors, Bailey Banks & Biddle, with its main location at Chestnut and 16th Streets, still offers a sparkling selection of merchandise. Right, Company Catalog, 1991. (Author's collection) Below, illustrated Trade Card. (Author's collection)

change crisis. During the war Bailey & Co. greatly curtailed its silver manufacturing operations. After the conflict, Bailey & Co. moved into new, even more elaborate premises, and developed a steady trade in producing patriotic and commemorative medals and decorations. The firm was reorganized as Bailey Banks and Biddle in 1878, its trade style even today. Its current flagship Philadelphia location at 16th Street and Chestnut was occupied in 1951. Active today as a leading fine jeweler and retailer, BBB has several suburban and national locations.

Auction Census Data Summary, 1891-1994

	1	2	3	5	10	12	24	30	90	Total	Pct
BC	32		39	37	35	5				148	1.7%
	32		**39**	**37**	**35**	**5**				**148**	**1.7%**

George G. Evans
Chapter XXI

The encased stamps issued by the extraordinary Philadelphia publisher and bookseller George G. Evans are the most misunderstood of all the species of New Metallic Currency. Both the issuer and his issue have long been clouded by inaccurate and misrepresentative assertions. Such enigmae would have confounded Evans, who was among the most accomplished mid-19th century entrepreneurs and self-promoters. He was widely known, extremely visible and left a plethora of published information about himself and his business ventures. Withal, he was a prolific advertiser and a robust drum-banger. His affinity for the possibilities of John Gault's New Metallic Currency were a natural opportunity to promote his wartime diversification into the wine business. His problems among numismatists and philatelists studying his encased stamps stem, of course, from the pieces themselves. First, the unfortunate use of sans serif letter punches for his name; second, the absence of the normal patent and patentee information; third, an illusory difference in the manufacturing

Figure 265a

Reed EV01 obverse. Collectors have been confused about the George G. Evans' encased stamp for generations. A decade ago the present author cleared up the misconceptions over his initials (rendered variously as C. C., C. G., or G. C) which are G. G. Confusion has persisted about the so-called "violation" of Gault's patent represented by this issue. The violation was a technical one. It was an error of omission, not an error of commission. Patent law required the patent date to appear on the article of manufacture. It was inexplicably omitted in this case. That was the violation. ex-James F. Ruddy specimen. (Bowers and Merena photo)

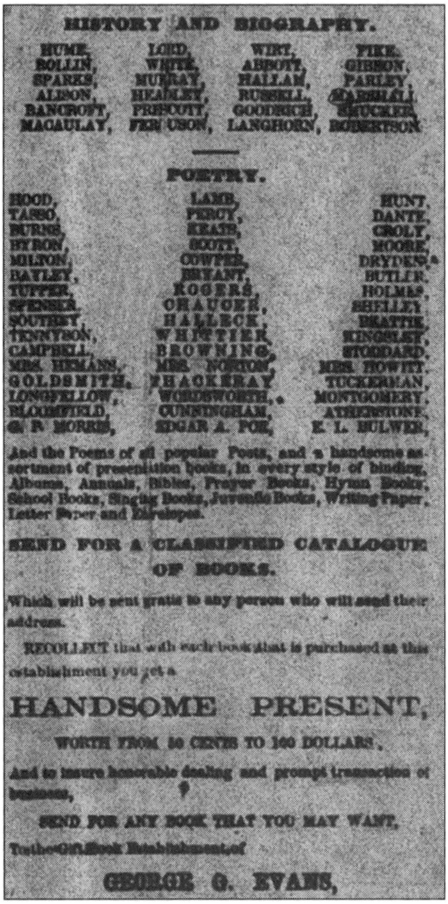

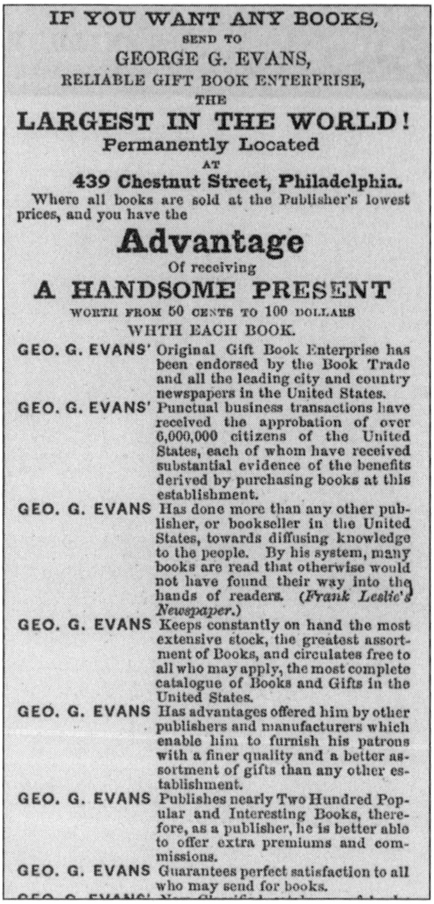

characteristics of his encased stamp cases; and finally, the stillborn nature of his wine trade. Many of these difficulties were addressed in an extended series on Evans published several years ago by the present author in *Coin World*. There's no reason that any such difficulties in these areas should persist past the publication of the present volume.

Fiery George G. Evans took to the New Metallic Currency the same way he did everything. He jumped in with both feet, ordering about 10,000 pieces from John Gault shortly after seeing the pieces circulated by his neighbors and friends at Bailey & Co. Evans obviously knew a good thing when he saw it. Already a widely heralded entrepreneur for his innovative publishing and book selling methods, he was in the process of establishing himself additionally as a leading eastern agent for the infant California wine industry. He understood the value of advertising and was eager to popularize his new trade in unadulterated western vintages. Thus his order was virtually all for one- and three-cent store cards (Reed EV01 and EV03 respectively) in approximately equal quantities so he could maximize his

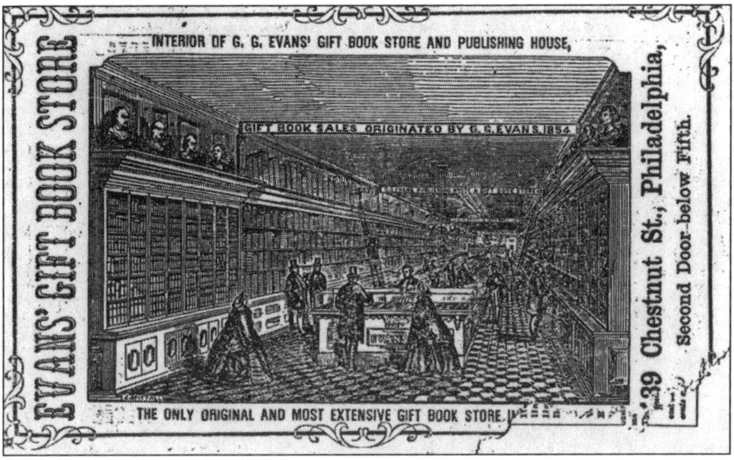

Figures 267a, b
Above, Woodcut by John Andrew, printed by J. Spittal. (Historical Society of Pennsylvania) Right, Fiery George G. Evans promoted literacy and enlightened self-interest capitalism in a big way. Original pen and ink drawing especially for this book by Sara Jenks Maneval. Copyright © 1994 Fred Reed. All Rights Reserved. (Author's collection)

Figures 266a, b (opposite)
Evans' back list included virtually any author and subject imaginable. Ad detail. (Bob Kincaid) His inventive merchandising techniques put more books in more hands than any like19th century publisher. Ad detail. Harper's Weekly, *August 25, 1860, p. 544, (Author's collection)*

exposure for his gross outlay. He was willing to pay Gault his commission and the 100+ percent advertising premium for the store cards because of their trade value in establishing his new franchise. Evans' cases are not clearly different from the other Gault issues, although

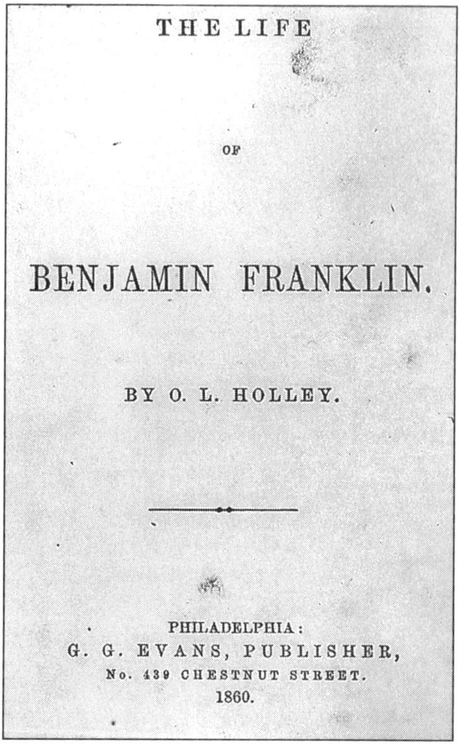

THE LIFE

OF

BENJAMIN FRANKLIN.

BY O. L. HOLLEY.

PHILADELPHIA:
G. G. EVANS, PUBLISHER,
No. 439 CHESTNUT STREET.
1860.

Figures 268a, b, c, d (above)

Left, if, as has been suggested, Evans' encased stamps were not made by Scovill, they may have been produced by a local Philadelphia or Baltimore company. Buttons by Jacob Reed's Sons, Philadelphia. (Author's collection) Right, Title Page, The Life of Benjamin Franklin *by O. L. Holley, published by G. G. Evans, 1860. (Author's collection)*

Figures 269a, b (opposite)

Exterior view and stockroom of Evans' Original Gift Book Store. Berghaus Engravings. Frank Leslie's Illustrated Newspaper, *December 31, 1859, p. 76. (Library of Congress photos)*

they needn't necessarily have been produced by Scovill in Connecticut. Evans was experienced in paying royalties for others' property rights, and surely the ebullient John Gault would have quashed the issue had they not been on the up and up, especially since Munn & Co. represented both Gault and Evans at various times! Furthermore, Evans personal character and business practices preclude stealing John Gault's idea. A much more plausible explanation is simple error of omission, certainly possible whether the pieces were manufactured in Connecticut or Philadelphia but much more understandable in the latter instance.

At the time Evans was contemplating entering the wine trade, domestic wines were looked down upon, especially California vintages which were notorious for being adulterated. By 1860, despite their mixed reviews, some six million vines were in production in California and a dozen varietals of white wine were in production. However, the product

was "offensively sour [with] a low percentage of alcohol," according to a contemporary account. The California vintners' solution was to adulterate their wines with "sugar cane and alcohol." This was unacceptable to the tastes and sensibilities of eastern gourmands. The California agricultural industry, however, was actively trying to turn the situation

A New Story by Arthur!

A New Serial, by T. S. ARTHUR, entitled, "OUT IN THE WORLD," is commenced in the January Number of ARTHUR'S HOME MAGAZINE. For sale by News Dealers. Yearly terms \$2. Four copies \$5. Published by T. S. ARTHUR & CO., 323 Walnut Street, Philadelphia.

BOOKS

PUBLISHED BY G. G. EVANS,

439 Chestnut St., Philadelphia.

T. S. ARTHUR'S WORKS.

The following Books are by T. S. ARTHUR, the well-known author, of whom it has been said, "that dying, he has not written a word he would wish to erase." They are worthy of a place in every household.

ARTHUR'S SKETCHES OF LIFE AND CHARACTER

An octavo volume of over 400 pages, beautifully Illustrated, and bound in the best English muslin, gilt. Price \$2.00.

LIGHTS AND SHADOWS OF REAL LIFE.

With an Autobiography and Portrait of the Author. Over 500 pages, octavo, with fine tinted Engravings. Price \$2.00.

TEN NIGHTS IN A BAR-ROOM, AND WHAT I SAW THERE.

This powerfully-written work, one of the BEST by its POPULAR AUTHOR, has met with an immense sale. It is a large 12mo., illustrated with a beautiful Mezzotint Engraving, by Sartain; printed on fine white paper, and bound in the best English muslin, gilt back. Price, \$1.00.

GOLDEN GRAINS FROM LIFE'S HARVEST-FIELD.

Bound in gilt back and sides, cloth, with a beautiful Mezzotint engraving. 12mo. Price \$1.00.

WHAT CAN WOMAN DO.

12mo., with Mezzotint engraving. Price \$1.00.

"Our purpose is to show, in a series of Life Pictures, what woman can do, as well for good as for evil."

ANGEL OF THE HOUSEHOLD, AND OTHER TALES.

Cloth, 12mo., with Mezzotint engraving. Price \$1.00.

Figures 270a, b

Above, Ad. Harper's Weekly. *(Oklahoma State University Library) Right, Evans was masterful in his book selection. He understood popular taste and built upon the public's natural inclinations. T. S. Arthur was the equivalent of a "best selling" writer of his era. His popular titles were a staple of Evans' trade. In 1859, alone, Evans paid Arthur \$6,250 in royalties on sales of 60,000 books. Broad sheet. (Author's collection)*

around. The leading wineries were engaging eastern agents to market their product, and in 1862 the California Wine Growers Association was formed. It sponsored a widely touted book by California's leading vintner. The group optimistically predicted 1862 product would reach five million gallons. The progress of the vintners was coming to be appreciated in the

Figures 271a

Above, Evans' store was both well appointed and a masterpiece in economy. Customers were well attended by a host of wait persons, often including the proprietor, himself, who may be seen in the left foreground attending to the needs of a female customer. Berghaus Engraving. Frank Leslie's Illustrated Newspaper, *December 31, 1859, p. 77. (Library of Congress photo)*

east. In fact, the Fruit Growers Society of Pennsylvania reported in November, 1862 that the "light wines of California have lately been much praised, but these wines have not yet been very commonly employed by the American people as a beverage." Evans was poised to ride the crest of this new market. He had a contract for "Absolutely Pure" California wines and with his New Metallic Currency he had a medium to capture the public's attention. Unfortunately Baccus and the other wine gods did not smile on him, nor the California wine industry. The 1862 grape crop failed. Very wet weather in May and June caused mildew and then grape rot. Not even warm, dry weather in the fall which raised the sugar content of the remaining grapes could save the vintage. Less than one-fourth the production expected was realized. With no product, Evans was out of the wine business before he could really even begin. His interest in the endeavor languished. He resumed the business he knew well, publishing and selling books, more books, lots of books.

George G. Evans was born c. 1828 in Maine although his family had early roots in Pennsylvania. Evans, himself, moved to Pennsylvania as a youth and was liberally educated in the classics. His early work experience was in the dry goods firm of an older brother, who

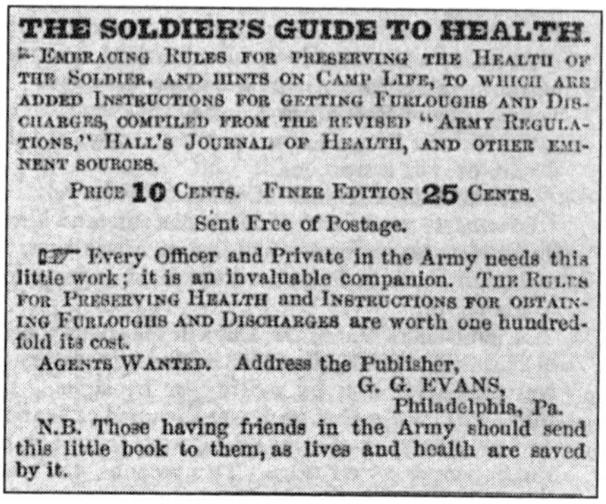

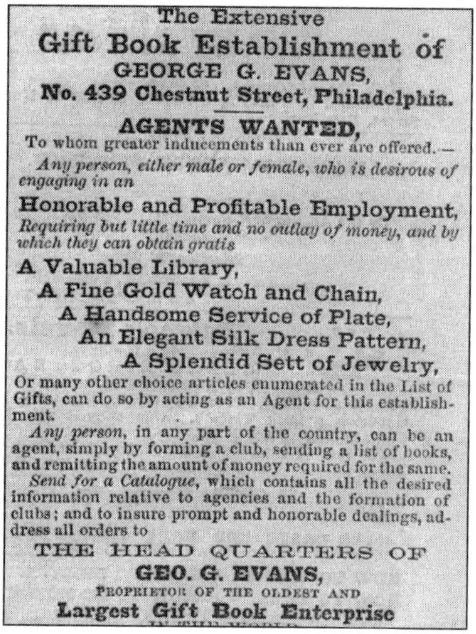

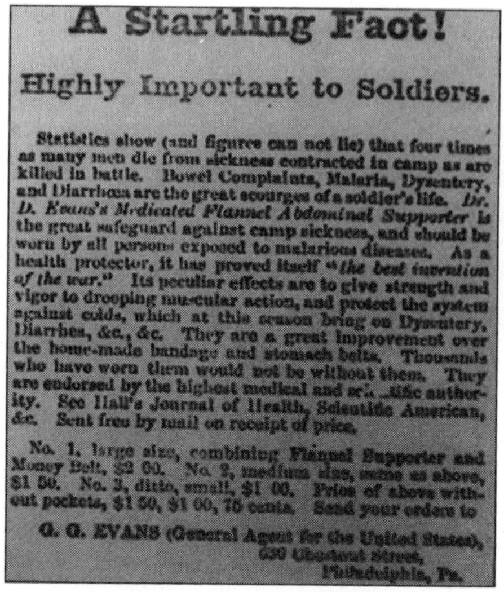

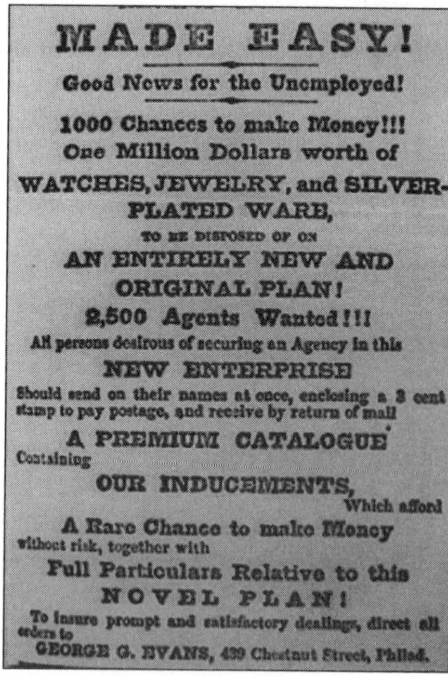

Figures 272a, b, c, d

Harper's Weekly *ads from top left: January 24, 1863, p. 64; September 24, 1864, p. 623; March 30, 1861, p. 207; August 25, 1860, p. 544 (a, d, Author's collection; b, c, Oklahoma State University Library)*

became immensely wealthy and for a time was the landlord for Bailey & Co. The 1850 census shows Evans living at a Philadelphia boarding house. He continued clerking for his brother until 1854 when he opened his Original Gift Book Store and Publishing House at 439 Chestnut Street, corner of Fifth. His location was in the city's most favorable shopping district, along bookseller's row and across the street from the then current location of Bailey

Figure 273a

George G. Evans attends to his thriving business from the catbird's seat in the gallery above his shipping room. Evans' titles reached thousands of hamlets across the nation. Berghaus Engraving. Frank Leslie's Illustrated Newspaper, *December 31, 1859, p. 77. (Library of Congress photo)*

& Co. Evans operated in a small way for the first two years while he perfected his marketing acumen. The copyright law was a much more informal code in his day. It was not international, so he could legally reprint foreign authors without paying royalties. Hence he could sell his imprints of their popular titles cheaply. On domestic titles, he purchased cheap reprint rights from the original publishers of the popular American authors. His basic marketing plan was to recruit groups to make book purchases *en masse*. He offered trinkets (hence "gift" in his trade style) as inducements and volume discounts. This was especially popular in rural areas with no ready access to traditional book stores. The individuals enjoyed the benefits of literature much more cheaply than from competing publishers and received the gifts as a bonus. Later he actively solicited individuals to place large orders for resale among their friends, a kind of precursor to the "Tupperware Party." Evans survived the Panic of 1857 and by 1858 was producing massive quantities of an extended back list of titles, both foreign and domestic.

He built this trade largely by his extensive advertising, which by decade's end encompassed more than 600 newspapers. By the time the 1860 census had rolled around, Evans was a grand success in his venture. He had achieved national publicity for his methods in the pages of *Frank Leslie's Illustrated Newspaper* and *Harper's Weekly*. He also had taken a wife, Nellie, sired a daughter, Florence, taken in a younger brother, Charles, and employed

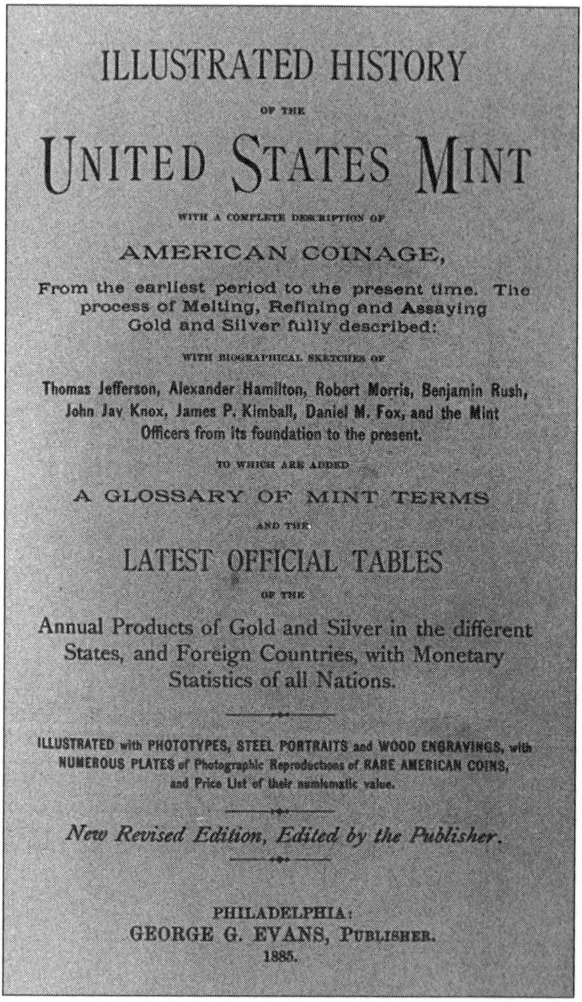
ILLUSTRATED HISTORY

OF THE

UNITED STATES MINT

WITH A COMPLETE DESCRIPTION OF

AMERICAN COINAGE,

From the earliest period to the present time. The process of Melting, Refining and Assaying Gold and Silver fully described:

WITH BIOGRAPHICAL SKETCHES OF

Thomas Jefferson, Alexander Hamilton, Robert Morris, Benjamin Rush, John Jay Knox, James P. Kimball, Daniel M. Fox, and the Mint Officers from its foundation to the present.

TO WHICH ARE ADDED

A GLOSSARY OF MINT TERMS

AND THE

LATEST OFFICIAL TABLES

OF THE

Annual Products of Gold and Silver in the different States, and Foreign Countries, with Monetary Statistics of all Nations.

ILLUSTRATED with PHOTOTYPES, STEEL PORTRAITS and WOOD ENGRAVINGS, with NUMEROUS PLATES of Photographic Reproductions of RARE AMERICAN COINS, and Price List of their numismatic value.

New Revised Edition, Edited by the Publisher.

PHILADELPHIA:
GEORGE G. EVANS, PUBLISHER.
1885.

Figure 274a

Evans' Illustrated History of the United States Mint *is a classic work in understanding the coinage of the country. Evans got a great deal of support from the mint establishment, and from various coin dealers in this venture. As the first numismatic best seller, the work went through numerous editions and reprints over two decades (and a reprint edition as late as 1977!). Expensive and inexpensive bindings made it perfect as a gift, and its practical eye witness approach to coinage and minting made it a useful guidebook to the mint, itself. More than 100,000 copies of this popular title were put into print. Title Page, 1885. (Author's collection, Coin World photo)*

two young Irish maids and a German butler. He had amassed a large personal fortune and had purchased a fabulous residence in German Town next door to his older brother. In addition his thriving emporium housed his own advertising agency, printer, and manufacturer of Morocco cases.

Evans' five-story iron building was impressive by any standards. *Leslie's* called the edifice "one of ornamental and architectural beauty." The Fifth Street trolley brought crowds right to Evans' doors. His delivery wagons trucked shipments of books to the express companies for forwarding to his book clubs. Business was enormous. Sales of 3,000 books daily were usual. Gold watches, bracelets and pens served as premiums to elicit larger orders. The books were inexpensive and readers could choose from more than 2,000 titles in his catalog. Many were potboilers. Evans specialized in popular fiction of the day, much of it moral in

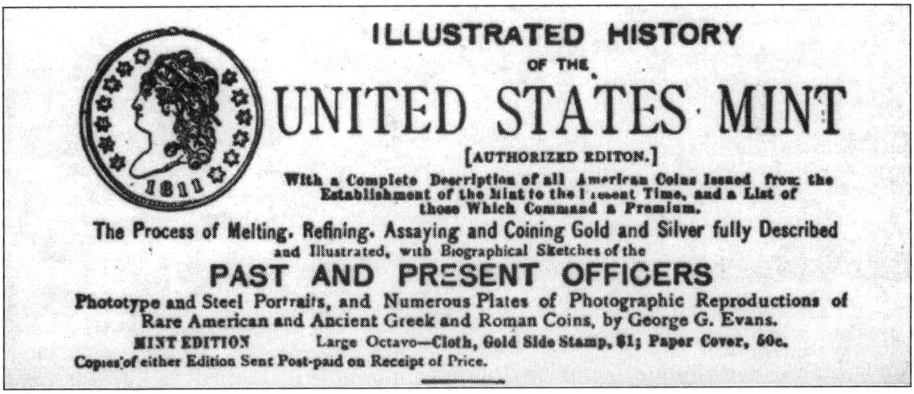

Figures 275a, b, c

Top, Evans sold copies of his mint guide inside the U.S. Mint building to tourists. Book purchasers received the 13-millimeter, miniature brass medalet with the nude bust of Washington and its minute engraved Lord's Prayer. Engraving the Lord's Prayer on successively smaller scales was a mark of accomplishment in 19th century die sinking. Gilt medalet (greatly enlarged). (Author's collection, Coin World photos) Above, Evans also sold his mint book direct to the numismatic trade. Ad published by Scott Stamp & Coin Co., c. 1890. (Author's collection)

tone. But he also offered romances, adventure tales, religious titles, biographies, health guides and historical narratives. He was very successful in identifying public taste. One of his popular sellers during the war was a self-help title, an instructional booklet detailing procedures for obtaining a discharge. There was hardly an aspect of human inquiry or need that Evans could not supply. He had all the popular authors. He also sold presentation editions, and a wide variety of stationery items. All told he was engaged in a lot of printing. He opened satellite emporia in Boston, Cincinnati, New York City and elsewhere. The New York shop was opened in fall 1862 two doors from George White the Broadway Hatter's location.

Like many of the merchants in this book, Evans thrived during the war. He was industrious, hard working, and superintended every detail of his enterprise personally. In 1863 he moved to a splendid residence on Sixth Street, within walking distance of his business.

LIST OF BOOKS PUBLISHED BY G. G. EVANS. 7

THE PRINCE

OF THE

HOUSE OF DAVID;

OR,

THREE YEARS IN THE HOLY CITY.

BEING

A SERIES OF THE LETTERS OF ADINA, A JEWESS OF ALEXANDRIA, SUPPOSED TO BE SOJOURNING IN JERUSALEM IN THE DAYS OF HEROD, ADDRESSED TO HER FATHER, A WEALTHY JEW IN EGYPT,

AND RELATING, AS IF BY AN EYE-WITNESS,

ALL THE SCENES AND WONDERFUL INCIDENTS

IN THE

LIFE OF JESUS OF NAZARETH,

FROM HIS

Baptism in Jordan to his Crucifixion on Calvary.

NEW EDITION, CAREFULLY REVISED AND CORRECTED BY THE AUTHOR,

REV. J. H. INGRAHAM, LL.D.

Rector of Christ Church, and of St. Thomas' Hall, Holly Springs, Miss.

WITH FIVE SPLENDID ILLUSTRATIONS.

ONE LARGE 12mo. VOLUME, CLOTH, $1.25.

THE SAME WORK IN GERMAN. One volume 12mo., cloth. PRICE $1.00

Figure 276a

Religious and moral issues were central to much of 19th century fiction and non-fiction alike. One of Evans' outstanding contributions to historical religious fiction was his support and publication of southerner J. H. Ingraham's The Prince of the House of David. *In this genre, Evans also published Ingraham's fictional biography of Moses,* The Pillar of Fire, *and* The Throne of David. *These books sold more than 500,000 copies! Broad sheet. (Author's collection)*

Eventually Evans advertised that he had 16,000 different titles at hand. Late in the war he was forced to move his business into larger quarters at 630 Chestnut. After the war Evans continued to prosper in the book trade for the rest of the century. Standard histories of book publishing largely credit Evans with pioneering legitimate reprint publishing in the United States. In later years his business address was on Filbert Street, adjacent to the presses of Dunlap Printing Co. which printed his books.

Auction Census Data Summary, 1891-1994

	1	2	3	5	10	12	24	30	90	Total	Pct
EV	53		48	8	4					113	1%
	53		**48**	**8**	**4**					**113**	**1%**

N. & G. Taylor
Chapter XXII

A third and final customer for John Gault's New Metallic Currency in the City of Brotherly Love was the venerable tin plate company of N. & G. Taylor. Founded in 1810, this family firm was very active during the war in producing advertising store cards. Its order from Gault was approximately 7,000 pieces, mostly divided between one-cent (Reed TA01) and three-cent (Reed TA03) denominations. Although slightly smaller, this issue parallels that of another Philadelphia client of Gault, George G. Evans. Clearly with such a distribution pattern the advertising value of the pieces was of paramount importance to this issuer. The company was primed to accept Gault's product. Earlier that year, it had circulated an extensive series of large cent sized brass and tin store cards. The following year, the Taylors ordered a large quantity of the cheaper, small cent sized copper store cards.

Commencing a half century before the Civil War, Taylor tin plate was already famous throughout the country for its durability and quality. The firm also produced sheet metal, wire, files and related items in vast quantities both here and abroad. Taylor's original tinning store was located on Philadelphia's Second Street by William Taylor who, with his brothers George and Tracy, then began the marketing of tin plate, tinware and kindred products. In 1830, according to the company historian, it sold the first terne plates ever made for roofing purposes. Terne was sheet iron coated with an alloy of approximately four parts lead to one part tin. Most readers today are unfamiliar with the importance of tin a century and a half

Figure 277a

Reed TA03 obverse, ex-James F. Ruddy specimen. (Bowers and Merena photo)

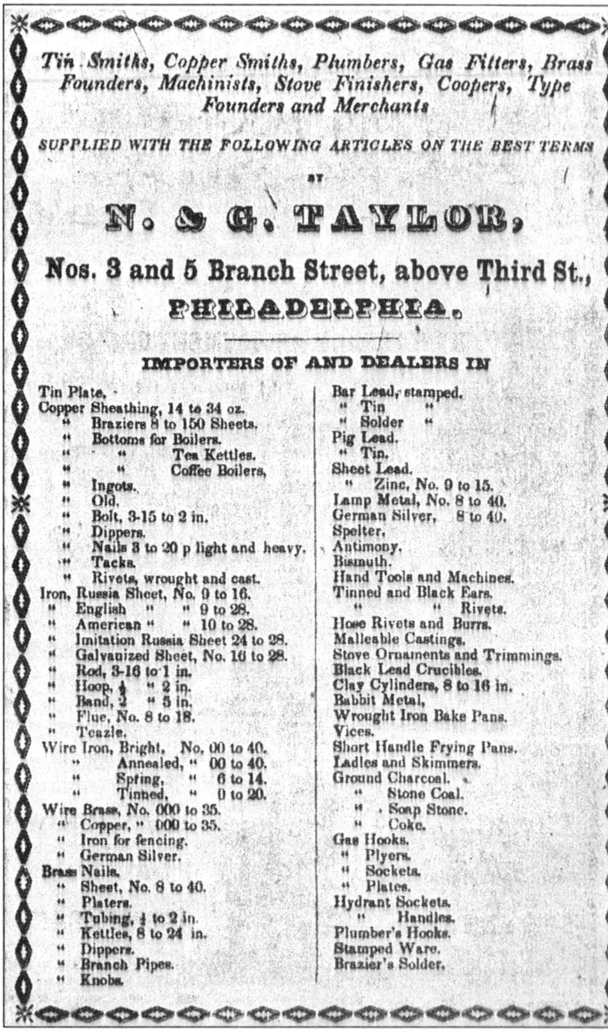

Figure 278a

Tin was a very useful metal to 19th century living. A measure of the breadth of the Taylors' wares during the antebellum period may be gleaned from their full page listing in the city directory. Ad. McElroy's Philadelphia Directory, *1853, unnumbered advertising page. (Dallas Public Library)*

ago. A soft, malleable metal that was alloyed with iron to improve its strength, tin was extremely useful in a variety of domestic and industrial ways. The local tinsmith was an important member of the community. On the eve of the Civil War, more than 150 Philadelphians made their living in that trade. Tinsmiths of that era were craftsmen as well as artisans. Tin was the common material for household goods in that era. The rich folks might have copper and brassware in their households; some poor folk might still be struggling with cumbersome iron pots, but most kitchens were equipped with decorated tinware, which was not only serviceable but sported bright designs calculated to please the housewife's aesthetic sense. Tinsmiths made their wares from tin plate, which was iron pressed thin at a rolling mill and then cleaned and dipped in molten tin at a plating works. A sheet

Figures 279a, b

Left, Nathan Taylor was a founder of the original N. & G. Taylor Co. He died in 1861. Photo. Philadelphia and Notable Philadelphians, *1901, p. 99. (The Research Libraries, The New-York Public Library) Below, Advertising cover reverse, showing the Taylor premises. Cover, May 13, [c. 1855], Scott U9. (Author's collection)*

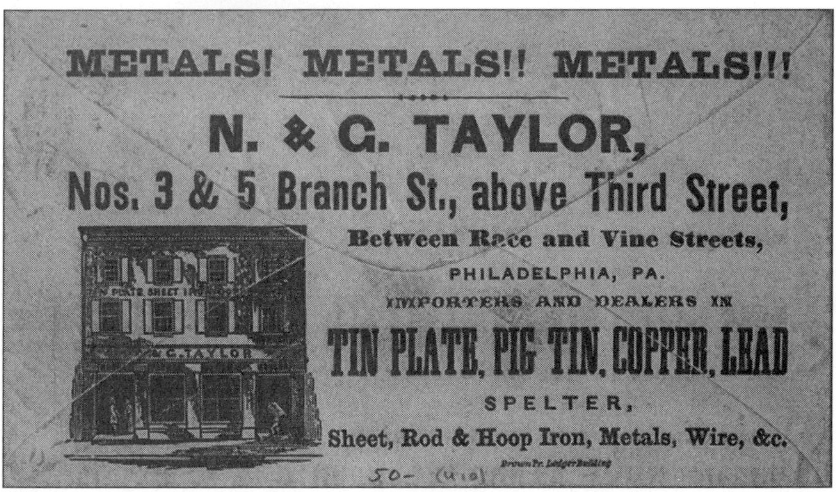

might be dipped several times depending on the desired thickness.

The process of making the tin sheets was laborious and thoroughly unglamorous. These were days long before child labor laws. Young children and women performed arduous tasks under difficult circumstances to fuel the industrial revolution. The Taylor firm left a prodigious quantity of sales catalogs and literature which amply illustrate the various phases of tin production. Several of these are reprinted in this book.

Figures 280a, b

Right, the Taylor firm was a major practitioner of advertising before embarking on the encased stamp chapter of its corporate history. Its brand name "Old Style" was meant to harken back to the quality standards of yesteryear. Ad. Philadelphia Advertising Broad sheet, c. 1874. (Author's collection) Below, the original Taylor premises, 1810. Taylor Advertising Materials, p. 16, c. 1874 (Historical Society of Pennsylvania)

The process of manufacturing tin plate is described in a history of that industry:

(1) The iron slabs are heated five times and rolled in five stages. Rolling sheet bar into a pack of thin sheets is a laborious task needing skilled workmen. Temperatures in the mill are high, and since the fires are always kept burning, men work in three eight-hour shifts.

(2) When rolled packs are cool, they pass to shearmen to be cut to desired size. Shears

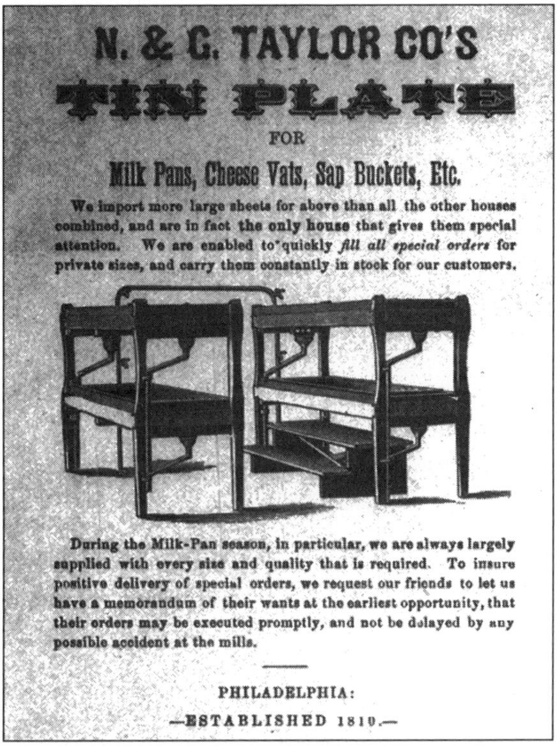

Figures 281a, b
Left, Ad. Guide Book to the Centennial City, *1876. p. 169. (New York Public Library) Below, Fine delivery wagons pull up to the Taylor Store House, one of the several buildings that the firm occupied by 1874. Taylor Advertising Materials, p. 12, c. 1874. (Historical Society of Pennsylvania)*

are driven by gears from the main shaft of the mill and are always in operation. Besides skilled workmen, a boy called a "behinder" works here bundling scrap.

(3) Sheets have become slightly welded, so they pass now to an opener's bench, where women tear the sheets apart with pieces of metal in the palms of their hands.

Figure 282a

Taylor issued a series of ad cover entires (advertising imprint over entire envelope surface) on government stamped envelope reverses during the Civil War, two of which complement one another on this and the facing page. Above, Cover, February 19, [c, 1865], Scott U59. (Author's collection)

(4) Girls pack sheets into cradles which are lowered into vats, one of sulphuric acid and one of water. The girls then unpack the vats. The pickling department is generally a dirty and unwholesome place. The workers are exposed to wet floors, acid fumes, and general humidity due to vapors from the pickling vats.

(5) At this stage sheets are brittle. They become tough and hardened through annealing. Sheets are rolled again with greater pressure to give a smoother surface. The sheets are fed and carried back and forth by little boys and girls.

(6) Sheets are next dipped into boiling palm oil, then into molten tin. They are usually dipped into the tin three times, then into a pot of grease.

(7) While still hot, the tin-plated sheets are polished by girls using sheepskins. Sheets are now ready to be sorted and packed.

Early sheets of tin were produced to a 10-inch by 14-inch standard. The Taylor family firm, however, was responsible for introducing increasingly larger sized tin plates into the trade, initially 28 X 20 and then 28 X 40. This was especially important, it may be allowed, since otherwise to make a large piece of tinware, a number of plates needed to be joined together. Even today the standard size is only 28 X 22. The Taylor's large plates gave them a competitive advantage. "Manufacturers especially, will find a great saving of time, labor and material in using this new size, which is adapted to a great variety of work. . . . It is a loss of time to inquire of other houses for our specialties," the firm claimed. "No other house has the variety we have, nor seeks to keep the trade constantly in all its wants. . . . We have done more than any other house to elevate the nature of the Tin Plate Trade, and give it

Figures 283a-d

With the U.S. Mint in town, the Taylors were change conscious. They issued several store cards during the Civil War. Top, Fuld PA-750V-5b obverse, was issued in brass and tin in 1862 prior to their encased stamps. (Civil War Token Society photo) Left, Fuld PA-750V-1a obverse and reverse was issued in 1863. (Author's collection) Below, Ad Cover Reverse, December 6, [c. 1864], Scott U59. (Author's collection)

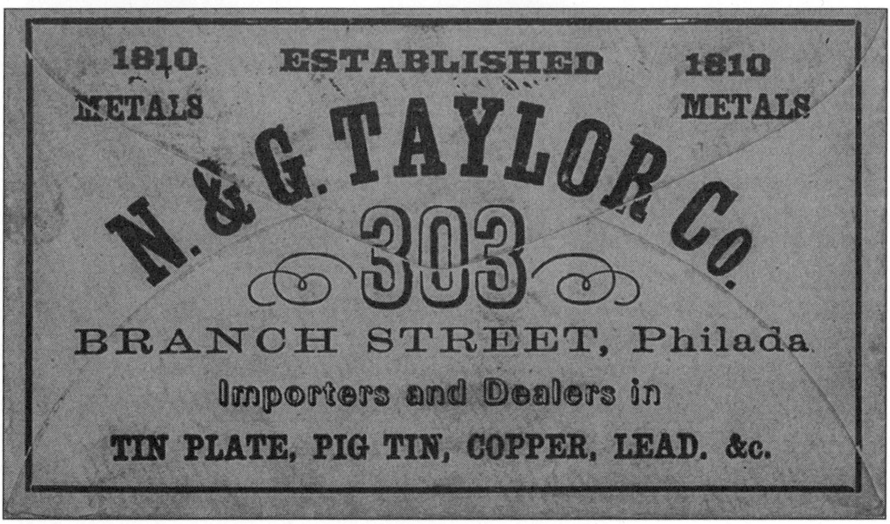

that prominence it so well deserves," according to a Taylor catalog.

The firm came to be called by a name familiar to collectors of encased stamps in 1845. In that year Nathan Taylor (a son of William Taylor) and his cousin, George E. Taylor (a son of the original George Taylor) were admitted to the firm. They introduced the "Target and Arrow Old Style" roofing tin which won a well-deserved reputation for its superior quality. The Taylors advocated the use of tin as a fireproof roofing material. As will be seen several times in the unfortunate circumstances experienced by various merchants in this book,

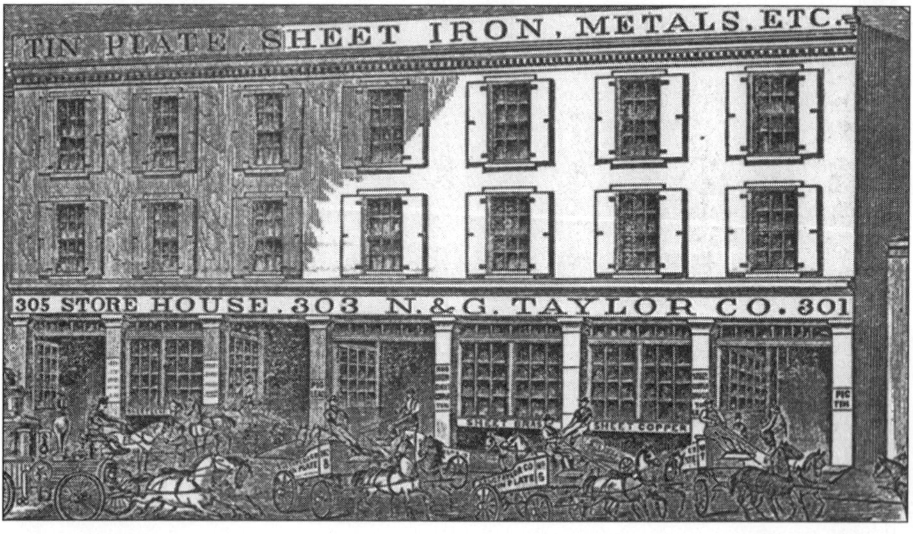

Figures 284a, b

Top, A female and male crew manufacture continuous roofing tin. Taylor Advertising Materials, 1873. (Historical Society of Pennsylvania) Above, the main building in the mid-1870s. The firm also dealt in articles of brass, copper, and iron. Taylor Advertising Materials, p. 28, c. 1874. (Historical Society of Pennsylvania)

fires were a clear and present danger even more last century than they are today. With much more of the construction being wood frame, with inadequate municipal water supplies and spotty – though often heroic – fire fighting companies, the threat of being burned out was always present. Many of the merchants in this book experienced the tragedy and the chal-

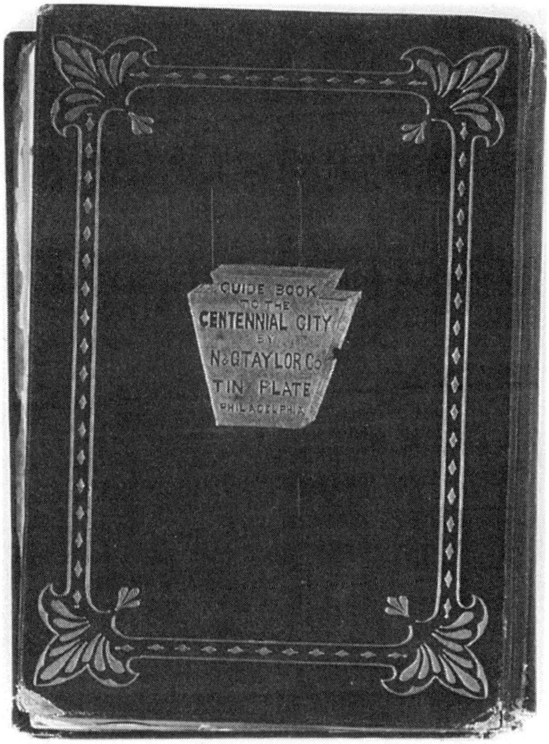

Figure 285a
The Taylor firm participated in the U.S. Centennial Exposition in Philadelphia. In addition to an elaborate display, it published this city guide for visitors to the Keystone State. Cover, Guide Book to the Centennial City, *1876. (New York Public Library)*

lenge of resuming business after losing their entire operations to the flame.

The cousins, Nathan Taylor and George E. Taylor, conducted their business as N. & G. Taylor at 303 Branch Street. In time they added copperplate as well as foreign and American iron and steel. In 1861 Nathan Taylor died and shortly thereafter two younger members of the family, George E. and William Y. Taylor, joined the firm, which was then restyled N. & G. Taylor & Company. It was this trade style which occasioned the issue of the large cent sized store cards in early 1862. This series of brass and tin store cards depict a nude bust of George Washington facing left on obverse, surrounded by the firm's name and address. Washington's bust was a favorite device for store card and medal designers of the period. Several varieties are known to collectors. At 38 millimeters in diameter, they are the largest Civil War store cards listed in the standard reference book on that series. These pieces were made by Philadelphian Peter H. Jacobus. The following year, the firm issued its small cent sized copper store card, with a right-facing bust of Washington. Although standard references list this piece as quite common, it may be substantially rarer.

The Taylors were heavy importers. This was natural since there was no domestic tin industry when the company had originally opened its doors in 1810. England was the center of the tin trade and English manufacturers jealously guarded their trade secrets. The Taylors were in the forefront of this import trade. According to the company's literature they

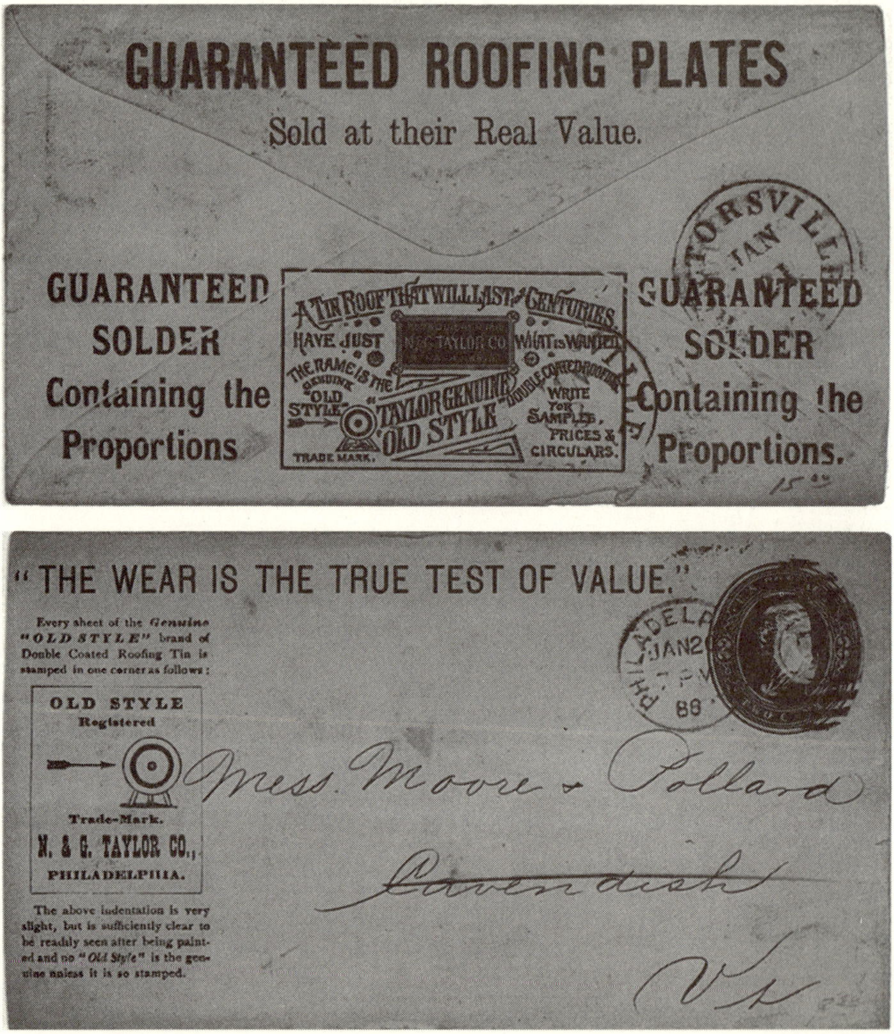

Figures 286a, b

A double entire advertising cover, reverse at top. Taylors' "Old Style" name was trademarked. As indicated on the cover, tin was stamped with the arrow and target logo. Cover, January 20, 1886, Scott U279 (Author's collection)

imported more sheets of tin plate "than all the other houses combined." The imports arrived direct from Liverpool at the nearby Philadelphia wharves. From there, the Taylors transshipped the product "direct from [the] wharf to all points north, south, east and west."

The Taylors were large advertisers in the Philadelphia directories of the 19th century.

Figure 287a

Taylor's manufactory following the Civil War was located in the block bounded by Tasker, Swanson and Meadow streets, served both by rail and the wharf. Lithograph. Philadelphia and Notable Philadelphians, *1901, p. 40c. (The Research Libraries, The New-York Public Library)*

Most years they took at least one page to list the variety of their wares in great detail. Although the tin roofing plate was the firm's strong suit, they also dealt in sheet iron, sheet brass, sheet zinc, sheet copper, sheet lead, and pig lead. Domestically produced wire, rivets, machines, tools and similar wares were also offered. The firm quoted "best terms" to tin and coppersmiths, plumbers, gas fitters, brass founders, machinists, stove fitters, coopers, type founders and merchants. "A variety of goods suitable for the professions [are] constantly on hand," an early ad states. Among the items they manufactured were tin cans, tin utensils, heater pipe, hot air flues, milk cans, cheese vats, milk pans, sap buckets, meters, gasometers, lining for stoves and range doors, and solder. The Taylor company pioneered the use of tin for lining heating flues. Air ducts were lined with very bright tin plate to reduce heat loss.

Following the war the Taylor catalogs began to mention the fact that the completion of the Atlantic Cable offered ready facilities for ordering supplies of tin plate from England. It also led to expansion of the Taylors' manufacturing plants in Wales and increased importation to meet the needs of their growing domestic trade. In Wales, they pioneered continuous roofing tin which they largely imported to the United States. As can be observed from illustrations reproduced in this book, their growing trade meant moving to increasingly larger quarters. Their main location in Philadelphia was a large three story building at 301-305 Branch Street. In addition they maintained several store houses around the city. The firm was justifiably proud of its accolades garnered at expositions in 1843, 1867, 1874 and the

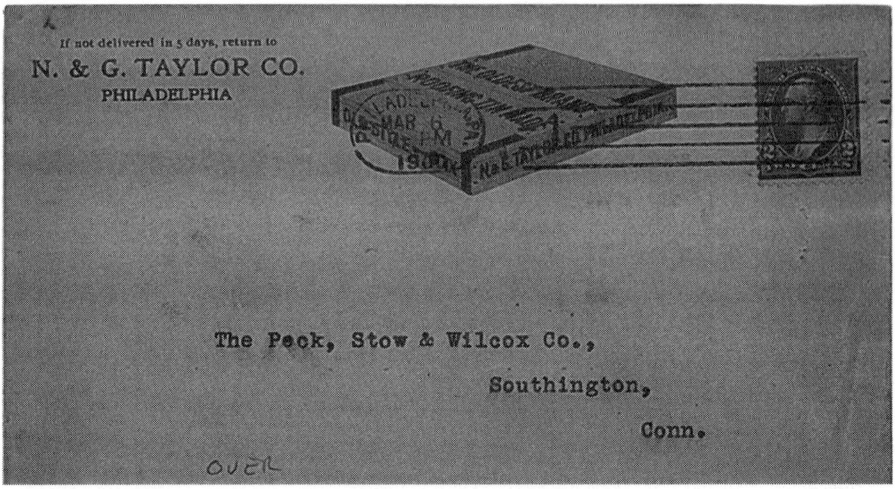

Figures 288a, b

Another interesting turn of the century advertising cover issued by N. & G. Taylor. The obverse shows a package of Taylor "Old Style" tin; its reverse reiterates the quality of the firm's product and its unconditional guarantee, fully three generations from the firm's founding. Advertising Cover, Scott No. 267, March 6, 1900, back stamped March 7, 1900. (Author's collection)

Centennial Exposition held in Philadelphia in 1876, at which they had a grand display.

For the U.S. Centennial, the company also issued an interesting "Guide Book to the Centennial City" for their customers. Among other things, the guide calls attention to the virtues of the host city as a manufacturing metropolis. In typical hyperbole, it states:

Figure 289a

Nathan A. Taylor. Photo. Philadelphia and Notable Philadelphians, *1901, p. 51. (The Research Libraries, The New-York Public Library)*

> For real centres (sic) of wealth, population and intelligence, we know of *but one* that possesses all the essential and most of the desirable advantages for manufacturing every variety of products, and which already contains many large and well managed manufacturing establishments. . . . The place to which we invite earnest and sagacious attention, as the best manufacturing centre in the United States, is PHILADELPHIA.

The firm itself mounted a notable display in four locations at the Centennial Fair, including two locations in the main United States building, one in the British building, and one in the Patent Office, U.S. Government Building. They described it in glowing terms in their city guide:

> Our display in the various departments of the Exhibition will be particularly fine, as much care and time has been devoted to its preparation. To those interested in this branch of trade it will undoubtably (sic) be of service. The display will show our Patent Tin Plate Patterns, secured by us under United State Patent and Royal Letters Patent in Great Britain and the Canadas.

The Taylor firm continued into this century, being operated by the grandsons of the original founder, William Taylor. As shown, their manufacturing facility had grown to immense proportions, and the family home shows the level of their prosperity. A contemporary account in an 1911 newspaper was glowing on the century-long reputation of the firm:

> The Taylor establishment has continued to maintain its individuality and independence under the personal management of the family, to which four generations have given their personal service. These men have always aimed to retain the old-time reputation for fair dealing and full value in the tin plate sold, and that they have been successful in doing so is known to many roofers, contractors, architects, and building owners, as well as to others interested in good tin plate for roofings.

Figure 290a

Nathan A. Taylor's residence, "Efnemheim," was a grand hilltop home overlooking Philadelphia. Photo. Philadelphia and Notable Philadelphians, *1901, p. 89. (The Research Libraries, The New-York Public Library)*

N. & G. Taylor & Co. was well known to the early writers on encased stamps, but little information regarding them was published besides a well-circulated centennial article reprinted in *The Numismatist* in 1911. One author, writing a year later, did say it continued to do an "immense business." The firm no longer exists.

Auction Census Data Summary, 1891-1994

	1	2	3	5	10	12	24	30	90	Total	Pct
TA	42		30	7	9	3				91	1%
	42		**30**	**7**	**9**	**3**				**91**	**1%**

Ellis McAlpin & Company
Chapter XXIII

Among Queen City residents, "McAlpin" and "Cincinnati" are virtually synonymous due to the successful department store chain based there. Among numismatists (many of whom have never set foot in the city itself) those names are still inextricably linked by the encased postage stamps the dry goods store paid out 130-plus years ago. It wasn't until recently, however, that research for this book revealed the key role EM encased stamps played in the acceptance of John Gault's emergency money in the West: These encasements are the direct historical link providing one bridge over which the New Metallic Currency spanned the metropolitan east into the country's hinterland. In addition to the named partners, a silent partner of the firm was also a business associate of John Gault, the inventor and purveyor of the encased stamps.

The McAlpin family began making its mark on the river city of Cincinnati long before issuing their New Metallic Currency. Its first member to attempt commercial success on the banks of the Ohio River was Andrew McAlpin, the father of the encased stamp issuer. An immigrant cabinet maker, the elder McAlpin came to the bustling river town from Glasgow, Scotland, as a 24-year-old in 1817. Both industrious and thrifty, he was one of the first Scots settlers in this area of the Midwest. McAlpin located his shop opposite the river front. He had a lot of competition. In 1831 more than 100 men were engaged in the trade of cabinet-making. McAlpin excelled in his work and he expanded his retail trade, opening his

Figure 291a

Reed EM12 obverse, ex-James F. Ruddy specimen. (Bowers and Merena photo)

Figure 292a
George McAlpin's father built an outstanding reputation as a tradesman. He schooled his son to meet customers' needs with quality and service. Such lessons served the younger man well. Ad. Williams' Cincinnati Directory, *1840, p. 27. (Dallas Public Library)*

"Furniture Ware Rooms" several years later. His family increasingly enjoyed the city's growing commercial prosperity. They moved into ever better residences as the city backed northward away from the river front. The younger McAlpin's patriotic given name (George Washington) arose from his birth on Independence Day, July 4, 1827. As the son of a thriving businessman, he "was given the best educational advantages the city afforded." In 1842, he went to work in the John Taylor wholesale dry goods store. John Washington Ellis, his longtime business associate, joined that firm as book keeper shortly thereafter.

Ellis was also a son of immigrant parents. Born in Williamsburg, Ohio, July 15, 1817, he was 10 years older than his protege, McAlpin. Ellis' parents immigrated from Sandwich, England, settling first in Massachusetts before coming to Cincinnati. Ellis was educated in Cincinnati, New York City, and at Kenyon College. At 17 he took up temporary residence in Cincinnati before venturing to New York for three years. He came back to Cincinnati in March, 1840. Although only a youth and newly returned to Cincinnati, Ellis was clear-headed and direct about his goals. He helped found the Young Men's Mercantile Library Association. At the outset, Ellis' business was a crude affair:

> [He] engaged in trade with the frontiersmen and once accompanied his merchandise as far north as Prairie-du-Chien. After disposing of his wares, he floated down the Mississippi with a cargo of lead from Galena, Ill., destined for New York by way of New Orleans. At New Orleans he visited the slave market and the scenes he witnessed there made him a strong anti-slavery man.

Eventually Ellis bought out Taylor. In 1851 McAlpin became a full partner in J. W. Ellis and Company. It is from 1852, however, that the current firm calculates its corporate anniversaries. John W. Ellis Co. removed from 23 Pearl to 77 Pearl Street in 1857. In addition to Ellis and McAlpin, the firm then included William V. Barkalow and James E. Polk, who acted as agents in New York City and elsewhere in the East. Polk had been a dry goods salesman in Cincinnati since about 1853. He joined Ellis' firm as a clerk in 1856 and became a partner two years later. Polk lived in a Cincinnati boarding house up until the war when he went East.

Figures 293a, b

Left, a fine steel plate engraving of George McAlpin by Western Biographical Publishing Co. captures the 19th Century merchant prince at the height of his powers. Above, facsimile autograph. Engraving and signature. Centennial History of Cincinnati and Representative Citizens, *1891. (Cincinnati Historical Society)*

Barkalow's association with John W. Ellis Co. dates from 1849. He became a partner in the Ellis company in 1851, but since his specialty was brokering, he increasingly became the itinerant "traveller" for the firm. He was absent from Cincinnati for long periods as he sought to expand the company's trade throughout the Midwest. For two years, 1855-56, Barkalow operated out of Philadelphia, although he failed to establish a permanent residence there. He returned to home base in the Queen city for the following two years, residing at the fashionable Burnet House. In 1859 he was dispatched to New York City, where he resided throughout the wartime period, except for at least one trip abroad. As wholesalers the senior partners, Ellis and McAlpin carried on the trade in Cincinnati, while Barkalow and later Polk acted both as purchasers and venders for the firm in the populous Eastern cities.

Numismatists are familiar with the trade style of the firm during the Civil War. Its name appears as "Ellis McAlpin & Co. Wholesale Dry Goods" on the encased stamps

Figure 294a

Right, Geo. W. McAlpin Co., successor to Ellis McAlpin & Co., has been a fixture in the Queen City since the horse and buggy era. Engraving. (Cincinnati Public Library)

ordered from John Gault late in 1862. This name change had occurred in 1860, according to city directory evidence. Shortly after changing its name, the firm relocated again since the encasement issued only two years later gives its address as 108 Pearl Street. Collectors had long speculated how John Gault sold merchants on purchasing his novel currency medium. Although it is now apparent that a variety of means were employed (including newspaper advertising), the EM issue can be directly accounted for: Barkalow was also a business associate of John Gault, himself! The present author first revealed this amazing fact a decade ago in the historical narratives he supplied for the sale of the James Ruddy EPS collection. An extended treatment of this subject was published in *Coin World* in 1988.

Briefly, McAlpin and Barkalow must have been very close, personal friends by 1862. They had worked together for at least 13 years, and McAlpin had named his first son William Barkalow McAlpin after his business associate. (Incidentally, McAlpin named his other sons and a daughter after their grandparents.) That alone suggests the mutual admiration that must have existed between the two men.

After Barkalow was dispatched to New York City in 1859, he first appeared in the New York City directories in 1860 listed as a dry goods merchant at 39 Park Place. By spring 1862

Figures 295a-e

Cincinnati was the dry goods capital of the west, so it's not surprising that Queen City yard goods merchants utilized both Gault's New Metallic Currency and the cheaper bronze store cards. These cent substitutes flourished in Cincinnati in 1862 which is the reason Gault's clients didn't need one-cent encased stamps. The competitive environment is reflected in newspaper advertising such as that shown for O'Reilly and Norris at Figure 316a. Like McAlpin's, Pogue's is still in business there. Top, Wright token, 1862, Fuld OH-165GS-3a. (Author's collection) Others from left: R. D. Norris, Fuld OH-165EF-4; O'Reilly Brothers, Fuld OH-165EH-1; and, Pogue and Jones, Fuld OH 165EN-3. (Civil War Token Society photos)

he styled himself as a commission merchant down the street at 1 Park Place, the very address from which Gault would peddle his stamp cases several months later. Also operating there at the time was Joseph Kirkpatrick who ran an express company. Kirkpatrick shipped dry goods for Barkalow. Gault had been in New York City for some time while his agents, the prominent New York patent firm Munn and Company, were assisting him in marketing his artillery shell designs. That summer, Barkalow had just returned from England. Flush with a ripe government contract to supply British Enfield rifles to the U.S. Army, he had money, expertise, and entrée to the Ordnance Bureau. Consequently Gault and Barkalow

John Stanton
Stamp and Brand Cutter
139 Fifth St.

Copper Cards

Sir:

Your attention is respectfully called to the **copper cards** that I am manufacturing for merchants and businessmen generally.

They are made of **pure copper**, the size of a cent, of nearly its intrinsic value, are beautifully finished — equalling coin in workmanship — and are the most attractive and durable cards that can be used.

Having made them during the past years in quantities amounting in the aggregate to millions, I can recommend them as a **very popular** advertising medium and a **profitable** one to those who used them.

The border of this circular is printed with dies that have been used for stamping the **copper cards**, and these specimens will give a perfect idea of the amount of lettering that can be used on them.

If you should think favorably of advertising your business in this way, I can furnish you these cards with **your business** on one side, and some neat design such as the Indian head on the other at —

Copper Cards

$10.00 for the first 1000 and
$8.00 for each additional 1000.

When lettering is wanted on both sides of a card or some design such as a hat, watch, boots, and shoes, boxes, barrels, etc., an additional charge of from $2.00 to $5.00 will be made for the extra side.

A specimen will be sent to any person wishing to see one before ordering.

John Stanton
Stamp and Brand Cutter
139 Fifth St.

Figures 296a, b

Local Cincinnati token manufacturers William K. Lanphear and John Stanton, among others, produced a prodigious volume of emergency coinage during the war. Their clientele was extensive as indicated by this facsimile of Stanton's handbill, which displays many of his customers' store cards. Much cheaper and easier to produce, this homegrown substitute small change appeared in 1862 and limited the use of Gault's one-cent substitutes in Cincinnati. Because of this large outpouring of cent substitutes, none of Gault's clients there ordered many one-cent pieces from him. This large outpouring of locally-produced store cards eventually hastened the demise of Gault's emergency medium in western commerce. Store card, Fuld OH-165CY, and Handbill. (Both, Author's collection)

struck a bargain by which Gault assigned his most recent artillery shell patent in part to Barkalow. It is interesting to note that Barkalow, himself, witnessed and signed Gault's latest patent papers as the original filing in the National Archives attests (see Figures 40a, c). Unfortunately, the claim printed for the Patent Office has an erroneous witness, F. F. Kirby, listed.

When Gault and Barkalow attempted to crack the Northern military-industrial complex with their exploding artillery shell, a multitude of manufacturers, merchants, and vendors of all kinds were gearing up to outfit the unprecedentedly large Army. There were big markups and large profits to be made across the board. The Army not only needed blankets, oil cloths, wool socks, undershirts and drawers (the kind of inventory Barkalow handled for

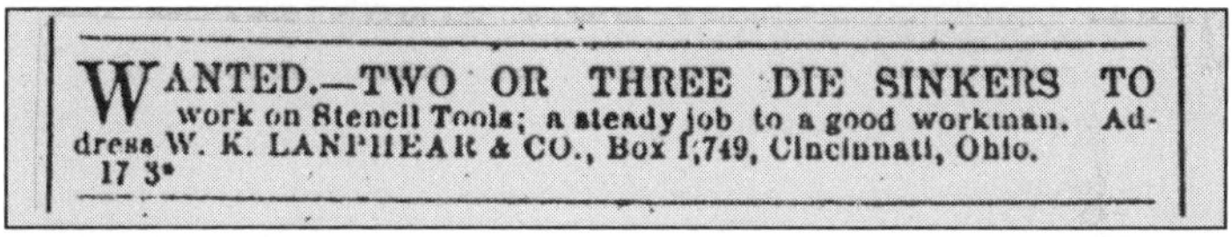

WANTED.—TWO OR THREE DIE SINKERS TO work on Stencil Tools; a steady job to a good workman. Address W. K. LANPHEAR & CO., Box 1,749, Cincinnati, Ohio. 17 3*

Figures 297a, b, c

Top, George McAlpen (sic) operated as a sutler for several Pennsylvania and New York units operating in the East. Tokens and paper scrip were issued. The rarer token and paper scrip spell his name correctly, McAlpin. Token, Schenkman PA-C25C. (David Schenkman photos) Above, the proliferation of store card issues in Cincinnati in 1862 led local die sinker William Lanphear to seek tradesmen in New York City and elsewhere to help him meet demands. He ran the ad for three weeks. Ad. Scientific American, *October 25, 1862, p. 271 (Dallas Public Library)*

Ellis McAlpin & Co.), but it also needed "more bang for its buck" if the Union would be saved and the insurrection suppressed.

Consequently as Barkalow continued to represent the Eastern interests of Ellis & McAlpin in New York City, additionally he engaged in these private munitions ventures. Then in the fall with the small change crisis worsening, it was natural for Barkalow to also approach his Western associates with his Eastern associate's novel remedy to their small change plight — U.S. government stamps in mineral and metal cases for circulation. By then the firm of Ellis & McAlpin was one of the leading mercantile houses in the Midwest. Barkalow's relationship probably also accounts for the issue of encased stamps by three other Queen City dry goods merchants during the war: (1) John Shillito; (2) Pearce, Tolle and Holton, and (3) Lewis C. Hopkins.

Ellis, McAlpin & Co. purchased about 8,000-9,000 encased stamps from Gault, principally of the 10-cent variety (Reed EM10) which accounted for about half the emission. In total, the order represented a face value of approximately $850. So Ellis McAlpin's total expenditure topped $1,000. The firm thus paid 15%-20% premium on its total order for the privilege of advertising on Gault's store cards. The denomination distribution of their order is interesting. Aside from the 10-cent pieces, the emission splits almost identically between the total of 3- and 5-cent pieces and that of the 12- and 24-cent pieces. Such a distribution pattern is unique among the 31 Encased Stamp merchant issuers. In fact, its closest parallel was the output of Gault himself prior to his association with Kirkpatrick.

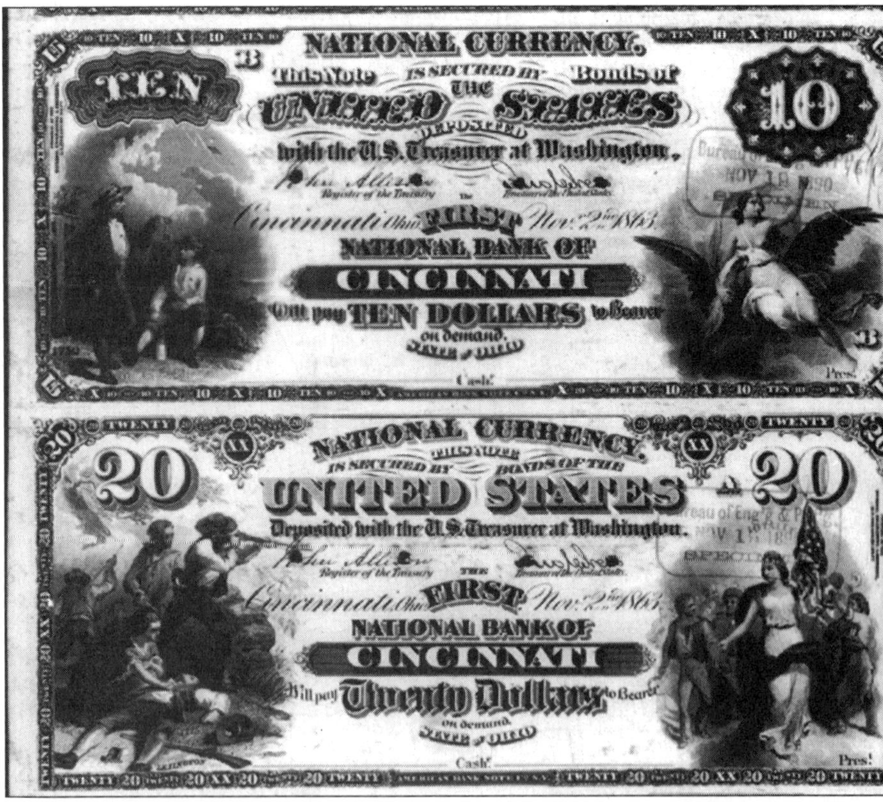

So Barkalow (and Polk, or other agent "travellers") obtained an excellent calling card. It was distinctive, au currént, and as high class as Broadway itself. This probably accounts for many of the lower denomination pieces ordered. The firm thus received a public relations boost among its Eastern suppliers and clients: Cincinnati merchants could be as

Figures 298a, b, c (opposite), 299a, b (above)

Few individuals served as presidents of large National Banks in two different cities, but John W. Ellis did. He was a major international financier following the Civil War. Before leaving Cincinnati for the broader vistas of New York City, he established the First National Bank of Cincinnati in which capacity he would have cosigned the bank's notes. Opposite and above, proof specimens of unsigned National Currency $5, $10, $20, $50, $100 denominations, November 2, 1863. (Smithsonian Institution photos)

"uptown" as their Eastern counterparts when it came to the affairs of the day! And throughout the change-starved Midwest and border regions where Ellis & McAlpin operated extensively, their star would be doubly ascendant! As a wholesaler, Ellis, McAlpin and Co. would not have needed excessive amounts of small change for petty transactions. But as a "cash only" operation (according to the legend on its EPS) some change would have been required. This again accounts for the relatively large quantities of higher value pieces given the relative scarcity of EM issues generally. So purchasing of the Gault small change medium was doubly good business for Ellis, McAlpin & Co. It also represented a slight net savings to the company, since the fractional silver premium at the time approximated 20%.

Figures 300a, b

Right and below, a Gay Nineties promotional brochure published by the McAlpin Company. Front and back covers, History of Feminine Costume, *1895. (Cincinnati Historical Society)*

Gault, Barkalow, Ellis and McAlpin all got a good deal in the bargain.

At war's end, Ellis left the firm to devote his full time efforts to banking. Ellis' early experiences at the New Orleans slave market were similar to those of a youthful Abraham Lincoln. For both, they were foundational to their identification with the Republican Party and its abolition principles. During the Civil War, Ellis was a loyal supporter of Lincoln's administration. An astute financier, he was also a long-time ally of fellow Cincinnatian, Treasury Secretary Salmon P. Chase, and an ardent advocate of the Secretary's national banking program to provide the nation with a uniform currency. Chase's program was implemented with the National Currency Act, passed by Congress February 20, 1863, and signed by Lincoln five days later. Ellis and his business associates saw the opportunities and seized them quickly. Within a week after the National Banking law was passed, he commenced organizing a bank. In May 1863, Ellis, McAlpin and other prominent businessmen in Cincinnati petitioned for a bank charter under the act. On July 13, 1863, Ellis' group was given Charter Number 24 for the First National Bank of Cincinnati. Ellis became president

Figures 301a, b

Ellis went on to great acclaim and importance in international financial circles in New York City. In his position as president of the Third National Bank of the City of New York, his autograph signature appeared on issued notes of that bank at lower right. The author would like to examine such notes for an updated edition of this volume. Proof specimens, $1 and $2 denominations National Currency, January 2, 1865. (Smithsonian Institution photos)

and McAlpin a director. With its capital of $1 million, the bank was the second largest in the country at the time. As FNB President, Ellis would customarily have signed the bank's Original Issue First Charter notes. It issued $1.7 million of these in denominations of $5, $10, $20, $50 and $100. Ellis remained president of the bank until 1869.

By then Ellis was ripe for new fields to conquer. He returned to New York where he experienced great success. For the next 14 years, he headed Winslow, Lanier and Co., an investment banking firm which principally financed the building and extension of the transcontinental railroad. Ellis was also instrumental in the purchase of the Panama Railroad for the Panama Canal Company. Few individuals have been privileged to serve as presidents of two different National Banks, but Ellis did. He succeeded his New York busi-

Figure 302a

Since installed by William McAlpin in 1901, the company's famous English street clock continues to mark the store's downtown location. (Author's photo)

ness partner James F. D. Lanier at Third National Bank of New York City in 1871. Thus his signature may appear on First and/or Second Charter notes of that bank too, although the author has not seen any such note at this writing. Ellis died December 28, 1910, in his 94th year at his residence near the south end of New York's Central Park. Private Episcopal services were held. With Ellis' departure, McAlpin became the driving force within the company. About 1880, it relocated to its present downtown site at 13 West Fourth Street. Ironically this location had been previously occupied by its competitor, Shillito's. In 1882, two decades after the Gault change medium had briefly flourished, the name was finally changed to George W. McAlpin and Company. McAlpin died April 20, 1890. He was buried in Spring Grove Cemetery, "upon which his splendid home looks down."

McAlpin's younger brother, William, reorganized the company in 1892 as a wholesale-retail operation. He increased its capital stock and constructed an elegant new store on the same location. In this century, the firm has gone through several reorganizations. Today the McAlpin Company at 13 West Fourth Street between Race and Vine is a huge retail store. Commencing in 1954, McAlpin's has opened numerous outlying locations, including several across the Ohio River in the blue grass country of Kentucky. In a recent year, sales of $85 million were registered.

Auction Census Data Summary, 1891-1994

	1	2	3	5	10	12	24	30	90	Total	Pct
EM	2		18	26	53	13	24			136	1%
	2		**18**	**26**	**53**	**13**	**24**			**136**	**1%**

Lewis C. Hopkins
Chapter XXIV

Many of those who issued New Metallic Currency did well for themselves. They prospered greatly and made great names for themselves. Some didn't. They remained obscure. Still others followed the fuller cycles of life to times of great accomplishment and times of great travail. One of these latter was Cincinnati dry goods merchant Lewis C. Hopkins. His encased stamp memorializes a fine man who went broke trying to benefit others, but eventually achieved great success and peace of mind. Collectors owning one of his encased stamps are very fortunate since Hopkins is the rarest of the Cincinnati issuers, and one of the most desirable of the entire series. It is highly suspected that he obtained his pieces through the efforts of William Barkalow, a commission merchant for the firm of Ellis, McAlpin and Co. and a business associate of the encased stamp's inventor, John Gault. Hopkins is certainly one of the most marginal of Gault's customers. His order was one of the smallest, estimated at about 3,500 pieces. These were principally three- (Reed HO03) and five-cent (Reed HO05) pieces. The former is believed to have accounted for about 60 percent of the order, while the latter denomination comprised much of the rest. Hopkins was most interested in the advertising aspects of Gault's small change medium. This is to be expected of a wholesale dry goods merchant. His outlay did very little to alleviate the change crunch, but his overhead (approximately $70 paid for the cases, discounting the face value of the stamps) purchased him a great measure of good will among those receiving his metal calling cards.

Figure 303a

Reed HO10 obverse, ex-James F. Ruddy specimen. (Bowers and Merena photo)

Hopkins led a roller coaster business life, but always showed great vision and willingness to take risks. He was descended from a family which had come to the New World in 1633, establishing a long line known for its "piety, patriotism, and good work." Born in Albion, N.Y., in 1828, he was 10 when his family came west to Ohio, settling in Cincinnati six years later. Initially, young Lewis was an errand boy for a dry goods firm at the princely salary of $2 per week. By sleeping on the store counter at night, he saved his money, and spent his long evening hours reading books. This industry was rewarded by being made a clerk. Shortly thereafter, however, his father's death placed support of his mother and sister on his young shoulders, a challenge he met squarely.

By 1851 he married the daughter of pioneer Cincinnati merchant John Whetstone. The couple moved in with Hopkins' in-laws for four years. Then about 1855 Hopkins made partner in the dry goods business, and he and his wife moved to a home of their own. Hopkins bought out his partner in 1861. A year later, George H. Warner and B. F. Turner joined Hopkins, and in the midst of a difficult financial crisis, Hopkins purchased his encased stamps. Hopkins' store was located on the first floor of a two story frame building. He rented out the upper floor as a public dance studio. By all accounts the war years were a time of plenty. In fall 1862 contemporaneously to advertising on John Gault's commercial change, Hopkins purchased the front cover space of the 1863 city business directory. The wartime economy was booming, and profiteering was the style of the day. Many companies supplied shoddy goods to the Union armies in search of exorbitant profits, but Hopkins repeatedly went out of his way to assure his orders were filled with the best merchandise available. His conscientiousness did not go unnoticed. Hopkins was rewarded with thriving sales. By 1863 L. C. Hopkins at the northeast corner of Fifth and Vine Streets "was one of the large wholesale and retail dry goods establishments in the middle west," a contemporary account said.

Hopkins' support of the war effort was both patriotic and good business practice. During the Civil War years Hopkins supplied clothing for the Union armies: "So satisfactory were his services for the Illinois troops that Governor Richard Yates of Illinois commissioned him a Colonel on his personal staff." As a Colonel of Volunteers, Hopkins outranks all the rest of Gault's patrons in terms of service to this country during its time of greatest need. Hopkins support of the Northern cause was principled. Substantial evidence exists that he truly did go to great lengths on behalf of his country. He became a leading member of the United States Sanitary Commission, formed to alleviate the sorry condition of the troops. The commission was a civilian auxiliary of the Army Medical Corps. It provided care for wounded and moral support. In many of its relief and humanitarian aspects, it was a forerunner of the Red Cross. Hopkins personally donated many thousands of dollars worth of goods to the infirm and needy troops. Through the Sanitary Commission, Hopkins was also active in organizing the Great Western Sanitary Fair. He was a member of the Sanitary Fair's executive committee. Such charitable and social events were instrumental in raising hundreds of thousands of dollars to support relief efforts.

With cessation of hostilities, the business climate changed drastically. The years following the Civil War were ones of great shaking out for merchants generally. This was espe-

Figure 305a

Left, Lewis Cheesman Hopkins. A visionary promoter of the arts and civic causes, Hopkins went through several fortunes backing unusual and unsuccessful ventures. Photo. Gift of Walnut Hills Congregational Church. (Cincinnati Historical Society)

cially true in the dry goods field, which had become over-saturated with competitors. Gone were the excess demands for war materiél. Gone were the large Quartermaster calls. Gone were the hundreds of thousands of young men who needed to be outfitted and equipped. In short, gone was the great booming demand of a wartime economy, where almost anyone with anything to sell could get rich on the inflated paper dollars flooding the country. The medicine for the economic high was doubly bitter for many: contraction of the currency to bring down inflation and reduction of the grand war debt cut into sales.

It is clear that Hopkins met these new challenges of a peacetime economy characteristically head on, but with indifferent success. He diversified his interests, exploring other avenues, but the succeeding six years proved to be ones of keen financial struggle. These struggles reveal yet another side of Hopkins' personality. As a prospering merchant, perhaps Hopkins greatest personal benefaction to his adopted city was his support of its fledgling cultural activities. For eight years he was president of the largest choral group, and with the destruction of Pike's Opera House, Hopkins built a modern concert hall, called Hopkins Hall, seating 700 and outfitted in style. When it opened January 29, 1867, it was furnished "with every modern convenience including a stage with depressed foot lights, dressing rooms, and a large and splendidly furnished reception room." Hopkins personally underwrote the costs of hiring a professional orchestra. These concerts were a grand success artistically, but patronage flagged and the venture proved a financial flop. Hopkins had "overextended himself financially, and after two seasons of musical as well as other business losses, he could no longer afford to underwrite the expenses of the orchestra." The community recognized that Hopkins was in severe financial straits. A testimonial event was held and organizers were able to tender him a substantial financial compliment, the Cincinnati *Commercial* reported. Down but not out, Hopkins traveled to Europe in the fall of that year. He spent heavily purchasing a collection of copies of the Old Masters and modern paintings from the French, German, and Italian schools, which he then imported to Cincinnati. In November 1868, he opened Hopkins' Gallery of Art to the public. Admission was free. Unfortunately, this venture failed, too.

Still Hopkins took the offensive. He sought to expand his business. In 1872 he opened a second dry goods store at the southwest corner of Fourth and Race Streets. There were fewer merchants in the field, but competition was keener for the remaining business than in the halcyon days of the early Sixties. According to a contemporary of Hopkins, "it was rumored at the time [that Hopkins' strategic move was] to fight John Shillito." Hopkins greatest assets continued to be his fine reputation for fairness and honesty in his dealings. His integrity, quality of his merchandise, and reputation were all unimpeachable. But head to head with the wily Shillito, "Hopkins was done for in two years time," while Shillito survived, grew, and remains a fixture in the Queen City today. The constant financial turmoil of the postwar years, his flops in the promotion of music and art, and finally his bankruptcy and public embarrassment might have done in a lesser man, but not Hopkins. He held out valiantly until spring 1874, when he could no longer sustain his business reverses. Shortly thereafter, he closed up shop, finally a victim of the severely depressed economic times.

A man of varied interests, he commenced his resurgence in the economic cycle in an entirely different field from that which had carried him to its pinnacle earlier. Instead of the broadcloth banner, this time Hopkins ran up a different pennant. He relocated to Indianapolis, opened a "one room" insurance office, and dealt in real estate. In 1881 Hopkins was called to New York, where he became "eminently successful" as president of an insurance company. For more than a decade he held a personal record for having written the single largest life insurance transaction. The premium for the annuity policies came to more than $500,000. Even 20 years after he had moved from Cincinnati, his accomplishments back East continued to be news to his many friends reading the papers in Cincinnati. Although his business success was not uninterrupted, Hopkins' record of service to his fellow man showed no lapses in civic-mindedness. He was also a leader in church, political and civic institutions and continued to be held in highest esteem by the civic and business communities. Admired for more than personal accomplishments, Hopkins was perceived to be a man of genuine, sterling character.

Auction Census Data Summary, 1891-1994

	1	2	3	5	10	12	24	30	90	Total	Pct
HO	6		34	17	11					68	<1%
	6		**34**	**17**	**11**					**68**	**<1%**

Pearce Tolle & Holton
Chapter XXV

The most obscure of the four Cincinnati dry goods merchants to employ John Gault's New Metallic Currency was the firm of Pearce, Tolle and Holton. Little has been written about this wholesaler because it was a short-lived with little direct impact on its local community. It was newly reorganized in 1862 when it issued its encased stamps, and became Tolle, Holton and Co. when Pearce left the firm after the war. The partners were William Pearce, W. B. Tolle, Alexander M. Holton, and later Thomas J. Porter Jr. Launched as a new enterprise in 1862, it is easy to understand the need for Gault's advertising medium. The size of Pearce, Tolle and Holton's encased stamp order is estimated at about 4,500 pieces, principally three- (Reed PE03) and five-cent (Reed PE05) values. About half the order consisted of three-centers, and most of the rest substitutes for the half dime. Given the nature of their business (wholesale, with very little retail trade requiring the frequent making of change), three- and five-cent pieces are the denominations we would expect them to order.

Pearce's family was active in Cincinnati since immigrating to the U.S. from Cornwall, England in 1831. They had been preceded to that frontier location 14 years earlier by William Pearce's uncles. The new locale was not a hospitable one to William Pearce's family. In 1832 both of his parents and five of his brothers and sisters died of cholera. He was shipped off to relatives in Maysville, Kentucky. He returned and was employed with his older brothers in the Pearce family's several interrelated firms, which date to 1817. Pearce's

Figure 307a

Reed PE05 obverse, ex-James F. Ruddy specimen. (Bowers and Merena photo)

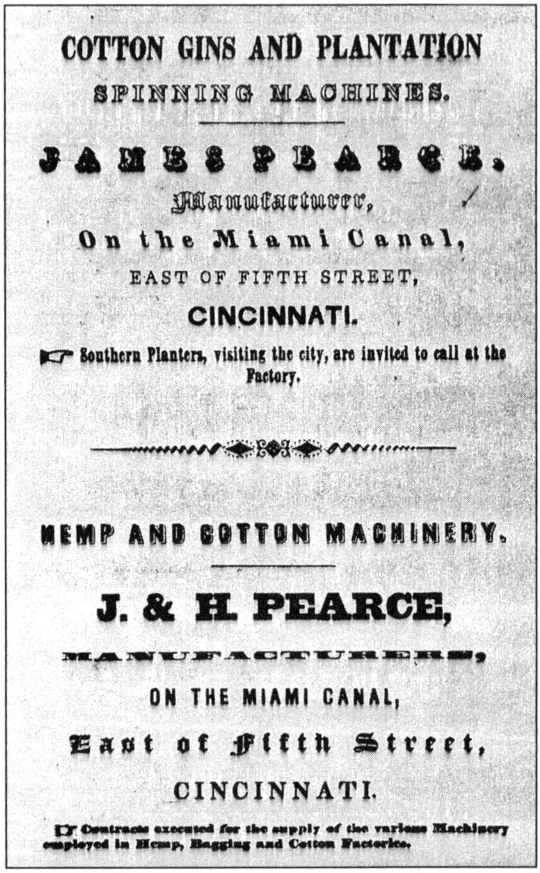

Figure 308a

The Pearce clan developed a thriving cotton goods trade during the generation preceding the Civil War. Ad, Cist Cincinnati Directory, *1842, [p. 466]. (Dallas Public Library)*

brothers James and Henry were machinists and patent cotton mill makers, who later expanded into the manufacture of cotton goods. A woodcut illustration in an early Cincinnati directory indicates the brothers had built an enormous factory by 1840 on a hillside at the east end of Fifth Street adjacent to the Miami Canal. The building housed a machine shop, a corn mill, and a hemp and cotton spinning manufacturing company.

By 1842 James Pearce was in control of the manufacturing and related ventures, which he consolidated under his own name. In addition to cotton fabrics, bags, carpet, and batting, James Pearce developed and marketed a much improved "Plantation Cotton-Spinning Machine." It enjoyed a great vogue in the South, and built up a steady trade for the company. A contemporary described Pearce's machine loquaciously in the accepted fashion of the times:

> The great peculiarity of this invention is, that, as it takes the cotton from the seed and puts it into yarn, without going through the usual detached processes, which always impair the beauty and strength of the cotton fibre, it furnishes the planter with an article altogether different from, and superior to, the cotton ginned and pressed into bales.

Simply put, yarn produced by the Pearce brothers' machine was stronger than that of their

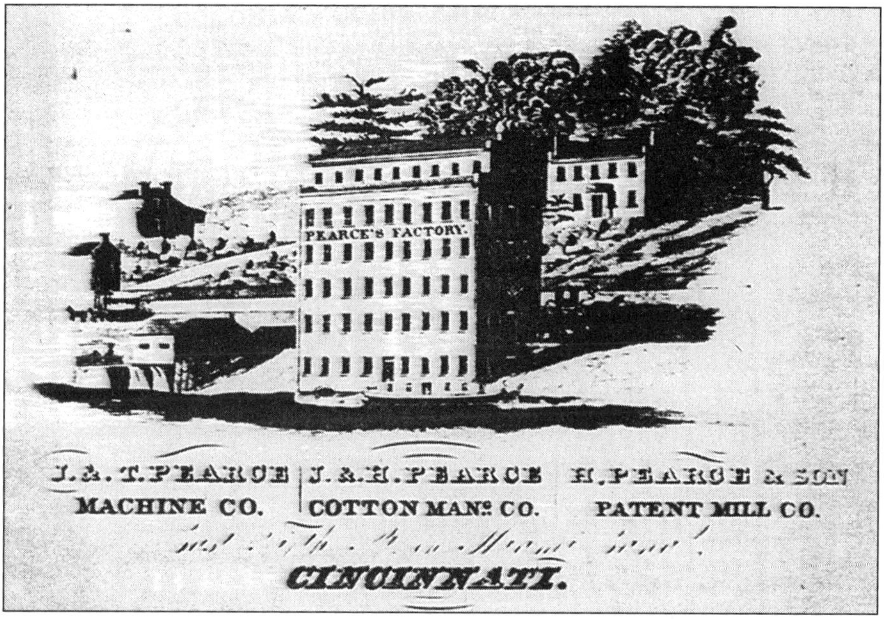

Figure 309a

The interrelated family businesses were conveniently located on a hillside above the Miami Canal. Above, Ad, Shaeffer's Cincinnati Directory, *1840, facing p. 313. (Dallas Public Library)*

competitors. In the mid-1840s, the factory's output accounted for about 150 machines annually. The family was eager for even more customers. To drum up this additional business, younger family members scoured the South in search of new opportunities. Four operatives combed the deep South canvassing planters, merchants, farmers, and capitalists for additional orders. William Pearce may have been one of the cousins who spent considerable time there representing his family's interests.

By 1846, the firm was restyled James Pearce and Brother. The brother was Henry Pearce, who eventually became a leading citizen in the community, and even served on the Cincinnati City Council on the eve of the Civil War. In the 1856 directory, William Pearce is listed as a "clerk" for the family's wholesale dry goods enterprise. At the time he was residing with his older brother James at 24 Lock Street. How William Pearce came to head the competing dry goods outlet of Tolle, Holton & Co. six years later has not been learned with precision. It appears as if PTH was set up to broaden merchandising of the Pearce products. Clearly William Pearce looked after his family's financial interests, and as PTH's senior partner served as its manager. Within the decade William Pearce left the firm which bore his name. His partners remained, and the company was restyled, Tolle, Holton & Co. again.

His associates each brought their own special expertise to the marriage. The middle man of the trio was W. B. Tolle. According to numismatist Arlie Slabaugh, writing many years ago, Tolle was the firm's New York City operative. As such he would have attended

Figure 310a

In addition to the three partners listed on Gault's encased stamp, the firm had a fourth principal, Thomas Porter, Jr. Ad. Williams' Cincinnati City Directory, *1865. (Dallas Public Library)*

auctions, and dealt with importers and manufacturers. Since PTH specialized in manufacturing yard goods, too, Tolle also would have repped the patent machines, and jobbed its cotton products. Perhaps, as Slabaugh speculates, "the encased stamps may have been obtained through him," although the present author favors the connection through Barkalow. A little more direct evidence exists regarding Alexander M. Holton, who managed the firm's financial affairs. Holton was born in Tennessee, but moved to Kentucky as a boy. He learned the dry goods business there and made the acquaintance of Pearce and Tolle. Holton came to Cincinnati about 1862, and eventually married his partner's sister, Susan P. Pearce. Holton was the firm's money man, whose "business post . . . was chiefly in the counting room." He managed the company's financial affairs until his retirement in 1878. According to a contemporary observer, THC continued to do "a very heavy wholesale business" especially in the south and west, but ceased on Holton's retirement. Holton died on a Sunday morning in August 1888 of "a very long and painful illness, commencing some years ago, and slowly but surely wearing him out." He was eulogized as:

> [A] man of rare qualities, [who] had hosts of friends all his life. He was very quiet and retiring in disposition, exceedingly amiable, and was devotedly fond of his family and his intimate friends — always on the side of justice and right, and a liberal supporter of measures for the public welfare.

The deceased also served as a director of a Cincinnati insurance company, and the Third National Bank. A regular member of St. Paul's Church, Holton was characterized as "a consistent Christian [whose] last days were those of peace."

Auction Census Data Summary, 1891-1994

	1	2	3	5	10	12	24	30	90	Total	Pct
PE	10	1	33	32	5	6	0			87	1%
	10	**1**	**33**	**32**	**5**	**6**	**0**			**87**	**1%**

John Shillito
Chapter XXVI

Synonymous with Cincinnati is the name Shillito, the city's "merchant prince" and one of four dry goods dealers who purchased advertising space on John Gault's New Metallic Currency in 1862. John Shillito is responsible for bringing the department store to the frontier a century and a half ago. In fact the "oldest [extant] store west of the Alleghenies," celebrated its sesquicentennial in 1980. This firm placed the largest order from Cincinnati with Gault, issuing upwards of 20,000 pieces. Half the emission were substitutes for the silver half dime (Reed SH05). About half of the rest were three-cent substitutes (Reed SH03). Remaining pieces were distributed among the one-, ten- and twelve-cent denominations. The modeling of his order indicates, Shillito was willing to pay an extremely high premium for his New Metallic Currency. He paid nearly $1,400 for about $1,000 in small change, an advertising premium of 40 percent – twice the premium that fractional silver coinage would have cost him for a like amount. This large emission and high premium shows he definitely was interested in the advertising value of these small change substitutes. If he just wanted to make change, he was simply a bad businessman, which we know was definitely not the case.

Shillito was born November 28, 1808, in Greensburgh, Pennsylvania, and came to Cincinnati at age nine. Incredibly, he found immediate employment as a clerk in a dry goods firm. At age 22, with 13 years experience, he "ceased to work for a salary and began to pay others to work for him." The Shillito firm traces its corporate history to January 2, 1830,

Figure 311a

Reed SH05 obverse, ex-James F. Ruddy specimen. (Bowers and Merena photo)

Figure 312a

William McLaughlin was mentor to young John Shillito. A hard task master, frugal merchant, and visionary entrepreneur, his young daughter was the key to Shillito's early success, when Shillito married into his company. Photo. (Cincinnati Historical Society)

when the partnership of William McLaughlin and John Shillito purchased the staple and fancy dry goods business and all the stock of J. W. and Oliver B. Blachly, in whose employ Shillito had learned the trade. McLaughlin had come to Cincinnati from Pennsylvania about 1825 and established a dry goods business. Their new partnership was not an auspicious choice. Cincinnati already had 128 dry goods merchants in a community of only 26,000 population! Those beginnings are quaintly described today, as being not much more "than a couple bolts of gingham and calico, a plain wooden counter and a heartful of hope," according to a company historian. At the time, however, Shillito and McLaughlin thought a lot better of their chances. When the new partners combined the stocks of the two firms, they offered the public "an assortment of goods not inferior to any in the market," according to a notice placed in the Cincinnati *Gazette* at the time.

The store was a success from the first, but the younger partner, Shillito, quickly became dissatisfied. He had bigger plans. He wanted to get more sales by adding more departments. McLaughlin demurred. Within two years, Shillito resigned, joining forces with Robert W. Burnet, son of the senator. Several years later, after two interim moves, John Shillito erected what at that time was "considered the most commodious dry goods store west of the Alleghenies." Requiring four clerks, one for each of its four floors, the store is shown at Figure 315a. Shillito was competing head to head with his former associates, since both

Figure 313a
John Shillito's legacy to American merchandising is the store which still bears his name in Cincinnati. Photo. (Courtesy John Shillito Company)

Blachly and McLaughlin were heading reorganized firms of their own. He bought out his partners in 1840 and launched John Shillito & Co. Innovation marked his success. He created his own retailing methods, including converting from candle light to gas lamp lighting throughout the store in December, 1842.

Business continued to boom at his East Fourth Street location. Shillito's success was phenomenal and in many ways mirrored the rapid growth of the river city itself. By the end of the decade, he found himself competing with 173 other dry goods and clothing merchants, but his success continued unabated. "Riverboats lined the city's public landing" bringing goods west along the Ohio River. Population doubled. By 1850 it topped 115,000 and during the decade, Cincinnati became the largest city west of Philadelphia. Shillito began importing large quantities of European goods and added carpeting to his trade. This surge of growth during two decades led to the inevitable: Shillito had to look for a still larger store. He secured a lot on the south side of Fourth Street between Race and Vine. His huge emporium was erected in 1856 and opened the following year. This is the building Shillito occupied when he paid out his encased stamps during the Civil War. It stood at 101-105 Fourth, two doors west of the U.S. Custom House. A contemporary view shows a patriotic flag flying four stories above the busy Fourth Street. It was termed a "princely business

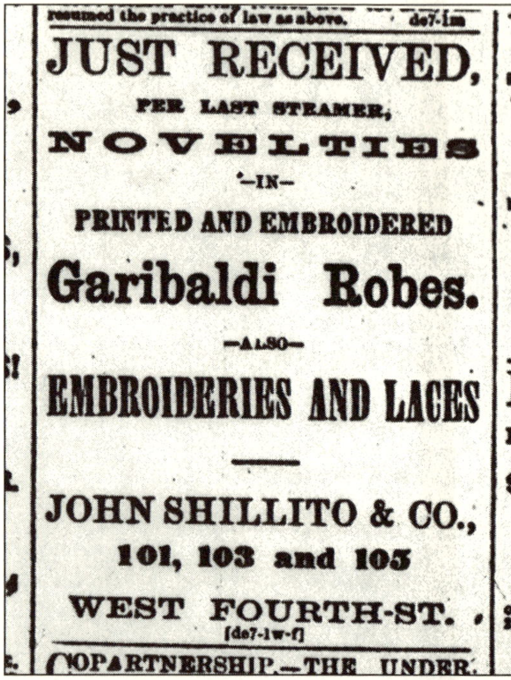

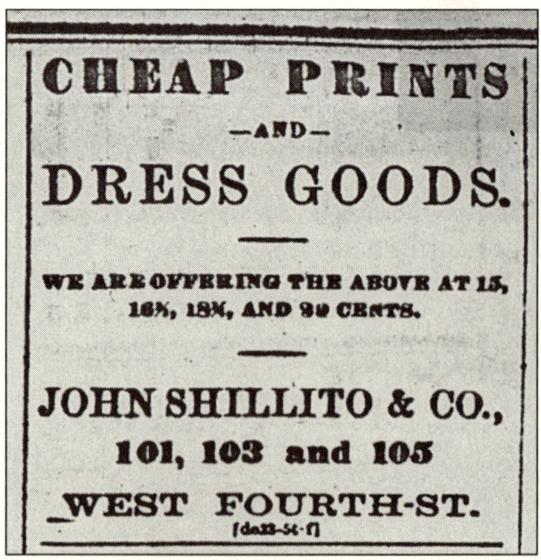

Figures 314a, b

In the heavily competitive Cincinnati marketplace Shillito took a back seat to no other merchant. A major advertiser, his ads indicate the range of his trade. Top, ad, Cincinnati Daily Enquirer, *December 10, 1862, p. 2. (Illinois State Library) Right, ad, Cincinnati* Daily Enquirer, *December 24, 1862, p. 2. (Illinois State Library)*

house," by a contemporary. His son Wallace joined the firm as a salesman in 1859, and another son John Jr. was added the following year. The business continued with uninterrupted success at its new location. "*It* (emphasis in the original) was the destination of many

Figure 315a

Prior to 1856 John Shillito & Co. occupied a four story building on old East Fourth Street, where the city's fashionable set was able to purchase the latest Paris fashions. Watercolor illustration. (Courtesy John Shillito Company)

riverboat travelers. *It* (again, emphasis in the original) grew with the city," the firm records with pride. Population continued to grow in the city known as Porkopolis because pigs roamed wild in its streets. By the end of the decade, an enterprising merchant calculated there were more than a million and a half people within 100 miles of Cincinnati. Shillito's was a major retailer by the Civil War. Its ads of the period demonstrate the range of its merchandise. Rich Paris dress silks, taffetas, *poult de soies* (satins) Garibaldi Robes, embroideries and laces, all arrived by the "latest steamer." Stylish ladies could choose from the latest designs and colors. Other departments in the store offered shawls, scarves, gloves, blankets, hosiery, corsets, cloaks, furs, merinoes, hats and caps, linen goods, skirts, handkerchiefs, suspenders, and "a wide variety of notions."

Business continued to boom through the war years. Eventually a third son, Gordon, also entered the company. By 1877, long after the change crunch of 1862 was forgotten, his increasing trade necessitated even larger quarters. For the fifth time in 46 years, Shillito's

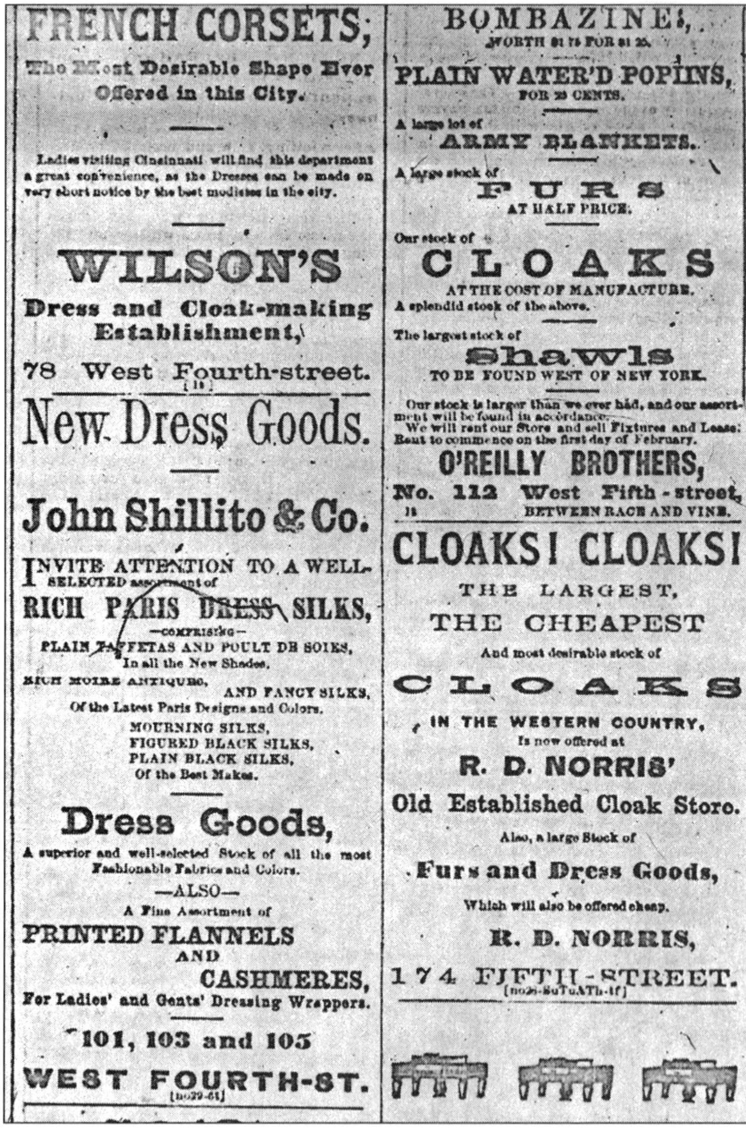

FRENCH CORSETS;
The Most Desirable Shape Ever Offered in this City.

Ladies visiting Cincinnati will find this department a great convenience, as the Dresses can be made on very short notice by the best modistes in the city.

WILSON'S
Dress and Cloak-making Establishment,
78 West Fourth-street.

New Dress Goods.

John Shillito & Co.
INVITE ATTENTION TO A WELL-SELECTED assortment of
RICH PARIS DRESS SILKS,
—COMPRISING—
PLAIN TAFFETAS AND POULT DE SOIES,
In all the New Shades.
RICH MOIRE ANTIQUES, AND FANCY SILKS,
Of the Latest Paris Designs and Colors.
MOURNING SILKS,
FIGURED BLACK SILKS,
PLAIN BLACK SILKS,
Of the Best Makes.

Dress Goods,
A superior and well-selected Stock of all the most Fashionable Fabrics and Colors.
—ALSO—
A Fine Assortment of
PRINTED FLANNELS
AND
CASHMERES,
For Ladies' and Gents' Dressing Wrappers.

101, 103 and 105
WEST FOURTH-ST.
[no29-6t]

BOMBAZINES,
WORTH $1 75 FOR $1 25.

PLAIN WATER'D POPLINS,
FOR 25 CENTS.

A large lot of
ARMY BLANKETS.

A large stock of
FURS
AT HALF PRICE.

Our stock of
CLOAKS
AT THE COST OF MANUFACTURE.
A splendid stock of the above.

The largest stock of
Shawls
TO BE FOUND WEST OF NEW YORK.

Our stock is larger than we ever had, and our assortment will be found in accordance.
We will rent our Store and sell Fixtures and Lease; Rent to commence on the first day of February.

O'REILLY BROTHERS,
No. 112 West Fifth-street,
BETWEEN RACE AND VINE.

CLOAKS! CLOAKS!
THE LARGEST,
THE CHEAPEST
And most desirable stock of
CLOAKS
IN THE WESTERN COUNTRY,
Is now offered at
R. D. NORRIS'
Old Established Cloak Store.
Also, a large Stock of
Furs and Dress Goods,
Which will also be offered cheap.
R. D. NORRIS,
174 FIFTH-STREET.
[no26-SuTuATh-tf]

Figure 316a

As noted earlier, Cincinnati was a fashion center in the mid-19th century and business was both brisk and bitter. Several of Shillito's competitors vied with him for attention and patronage in this advertising selection from the daily press. The competition was not limited to broadcloth alone. Both R. D. Norris and the O'Reilly Brothers issued store cards which competed with Shillito's encased stamps for public notice and use. Those store cards were made locally by John Stanton. See Figures 295d and 295c, respectively. Ads. Cincinnati Daily Enquirer, *1862. (Illinois State Library)*

Figure 317a

This is the building occupied by Shillito from 1856 to 1878, during the time he circulated the encased postage stamps. Old West Fourth Street was a wide thoroughfare. Shillito's neighbors were churches, splendid residences and other fine commercial structures. Wood cut engraving. (Courtesy John Shillito Company)

was on the move. This time Shillito took a page from the success book of his good friend, New York retailer A. T. Stewart, who had confounded critics earlier by moving uptown and constructing a costly store on Broadway far from New York City's commercial center of the day. "After a long canvass of the real estate market," Shillito came to the conclusion that the city's retail future would center to the north of Fourth Street, so with difficulty in spring 1877 he purchased a parcel of land bounded by Race, Seventh and George (now Shillito Place), the firm's present location. At the time this uptown area was far from the existing

Figure 318a

After the turn of the century, the rotunda of Shillito's palatial, new store was covered in the interest of increasing selling space. Woodcut. Reprinted in The Cincinnati Enquirer, *April 16, 1980. (Special Shillito's Anniversary Section, courtesy John Shillito Company)*

business district. "Other businessmen gave him funny looks because the neighborhood then was strictly residential and so far from the commercial action they predicted he would lose his shirt," a modern historian records. Other accounts call the area "completely devoted to fine residences," or an "idyllic residential and park area." Yet all these descriptions are merely euphemisms. In fact, narrow George Street was among the city's gamier red-light districts at the time. Prostitution and street walking were open and notorious. In purchasing the land and transforming its offerings from flesh pots to yard goods, Shillito came up against entrenched politicians and racketeers who were on the take from local madams. Shillito won out and renamed the disreputable George Street after himself.

An imposing six-story, red brick building was constructed to house the burgeoning business. Since he didn't feel physically equal to the ask himself, Shillito brought another son, Stewart, named in honor of his friend A. T. Stewart, home to superintend the task. Stewart was then in his last year at Yale, yet he managed the construction and removal. The firm officially threw open its doors in its new location on September 2, 1878. John Shillito proved his gainsayers wrong. At this new site, his company became the largest department store in the midwest, and was claimed to be unexcelled by any other in the country in its modern appointments and range of stock. This is the location of the flagship store today.

At the time it was termed "Shillito's Mammoth Dry Goods Store." In all respects the adjective "mammoth" was not misplaced. It had a frontage of 275 feet on Shillito Place, 176 feet on Race Street and 125 feet on Seventh Street. Nearly a thousand employees were occupied in the building's six above-ground floors and two basements. Its floor surface was seven acres. The highlight of the structure was the great rotunda, 60 feet in diameter, rising

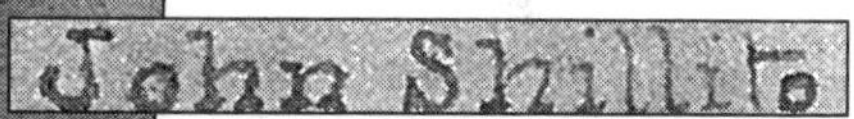

Figures 319a, b

The company John Shillito founded continues as a thriving adornment to the Ohio River city of its birth, as well as to suburbs on both sides of the Ohio River. Photo and signature. (Cincinnati Historical Society)

120 feet to a large glass dome which lit and ventilated its cavernous, balustraded expanse. From the first floor customers could see the other floors ringed with merchandise. It was an impressive sight. After the turn of the century the dome was covered in the interest of increased selling space. Getting to the store's other floors was easy on one of Shillito's five steam elevators. The store's effect was enormous. "The building is an ornament to the city," it was claimed. Not only resident Cincinnatians but shoppers from throughout the neighboring tri-state regions of Indiana, Kentucky and Ohio thronged to the store. Even visitors from the south and upper midwest treated it as a tourist attraction. Its success also changed the face of downtown Cincinnati, as other merchants followed Shillito northward, thus creating the modern downtown shopping district of today. As an anonymous newspaper writer mused, "John Shillito, Senior, was a progressive Cincinnatian. . . . Business always followed his lead. In every move he was a pioneer."

Personal prosperity went hand-in-hand with commercial success for the yard goods vendor. He married Mary Wallace of Kentucky, and the couple lived across the river in Covington and Longwood for a time. In addition to four sons, they had a daughter. Eventually, Shillito purchased the imposing Mount Auburn mansion constructed by the

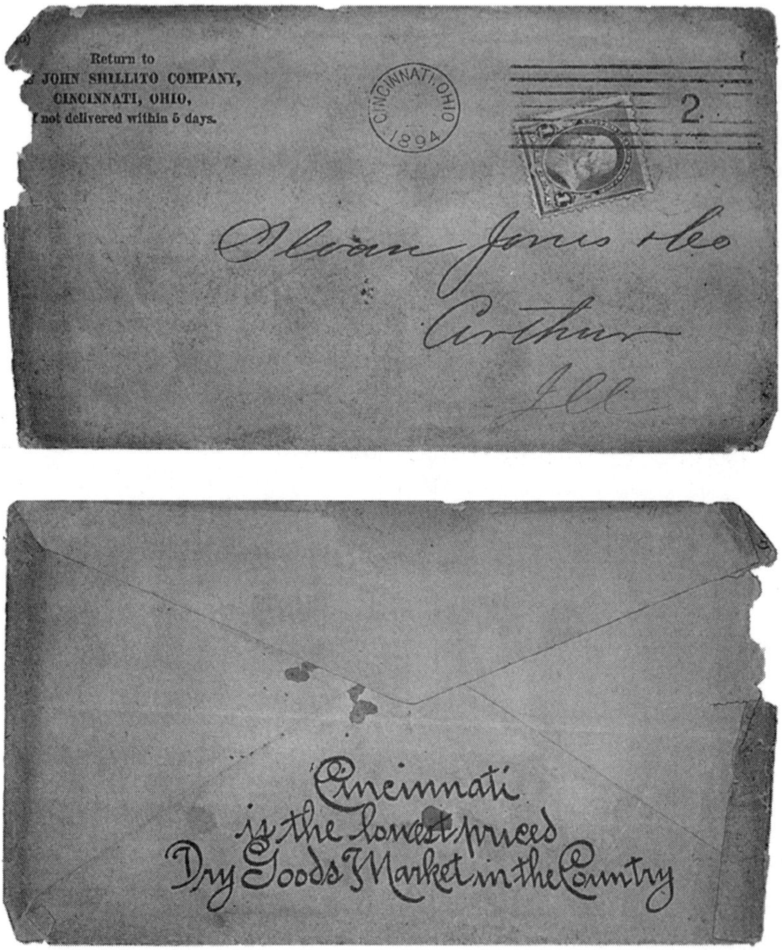

Figures 320a, b

John Shillito Company advertising cover, obverse and reverse, proclaims Cincinnati's preeminence in the dry goods trade a century ago. Ad cover, Scott No. 219, 1894. (Author's collection)

grandson of Chief Justice John Marshall, Truman B. Handy. This expansive, stone structure was located at Highland Avenue and Oak Street. The ornate three-story mansion was literally "the top of the heap" among residences of the city's commercial barons. It featured beautifully carved wooden interiors and allegorical scenes.

John Shillito was extremely active in community affairs and was eulogized as one of the city's best citizens. In the 1870s he was active in the Republican Party. He was a director of Spring Grove Cemetery, the Children's Home, and treasurer of his church. He had a special fondness for the arts and the groundswell of interest in making the city "the new Vienna."

Figure 321a

Like other prospering merchants of last century, Shillito lived in a palatial hilltop residence proclaiming his wealth and status in the community. The building was razed in the early 1960s. Illustration. (Cincinnati Historical Society)

He was an organizer of the city's music festival and instrumental in the erection of the Music Hall, personally underwriting much of the $30,000 cost of the organ. After his death, September 10, 1879, his mansion became the main building of the Cincinnati College Conservatory of Music. The Shillito sons, especially Stewart, continued to guide the company. Stewart was reportedly so straight-laced that he even disapproved Sunday "window shopping" so he ordered shades drawn to the bottom of show windows every Saturday night. In 1882 Shillito's became a stock company. Through the years the firm's retailing methods continued to be liberal. The entire building was electrified during the Gay Nineties. Its delivery wagons were pulled by palominos. Eventually they were replaced by a fleet of trucks. In 1913 the entire building was renovated, the rotunda closed and floored to provide more space for merchandise. The Twenties were a difficult time for the company. Fabric prices fell sharply and Shillito's was dangerously overstocked. It lost its first rank among city dry goods firms. "Many Cincinnatians were wondering if the John Shillito Company would ever realize its 100th birthday," a contemporary recorded. The simple fact was that Shillito's had fallen behind the times. Stewart Shillito died in 1925.

The firm was rejuvenated when purchased by F. & R. Lazarus & Company in 1928.

Figure 322a

Not many businesses have the longevity under a single trade style as Shillito's has, a Queen City fixture for generations. (Author's photo)

Headed by Fred Lazarus, Jr., a "driving, ambitious, little man," according to *Fortune* magazine, modernization followed. Customers returned, then they flocked in. The company upgraded merchandise and selection. Cincinnatians liked the new management and its liberal return policies. In the first year of Lazarus management, sales jumped 40 percent. Within a decade, the company was back in the driver's seat at the head of the Cincinnati pack. Fred Lazarus, however, was not content to be the largest merchant in Ohio. He added Filene's and Abraham & Strauss to the Lazarus and Shillito stores to form the vast Federated Department Stores. Bloomingdale's joined the group the following year. Business doubled and doubled again. By the mid-1950s Shillito's sales volume exceeded the combined sales of the city's next three leading department stores. The downtown store today employs 4,000. Nearly 30 years ago collector Arnold Perl scoured the company records attempting to glean insights on the firm's flirtation with encased stamps. He found none.

Auction Census Data Summary, 1891-1994

	1	2	3	5	10	12	24	30	90	Total	Pct
SH	19		60	116	36	8				239	2.7%
	19		**60**	**116**	**36**	**8**				**239**	**2.7%**

H. A. Cook
Chapter XXVII

The New Metallic Currency issues of Evansville, Indiana merchant Henry A. Cook provide key insights to the sales and circulation of John Gault's patent mineral and metal store card emergency money of 1862. This is one issuer of whom reliable second-hand evidence exists concerning their emission. Evansville was a town of only 15,000 during the Civil War. It was 337 miles down the Ohio River from Cincinnati by steamboat. In summer 1862, Henry A. Cook needed to make change at his grocery store, but was facing increasing difficulties in doing so. Stamps helped, but he found a better solution on his annual fall buying trip to New York. The trip was common practice for western merchants of his era. Cook received goods by both river boat and by railroad. Country merchants, like Cook, customarily thronged eastern markets twice annually to purchase wares of the day. These southern and western merchants normally made spring and fall buying trips. Cook arrived in early fall 1862 on one such trip. He was looking for new items to restock his shelves and build his trade. What he also found was a solution to his change-making dilemma: postage stamps put up in neat brass cases, which could survive in a venue of produce, fresh fish, poultry and meats, and other items hazardous to the sticky gumbacks. We can fix the timing of his discovery rather explicitly. It was most likely late September when he struck a deal with John Gault to supply his wants. Cook purchased about 6,000 of the five- and ten-cent change-making pieces that Gault was peddling. The kicker was he got his name and business

Figure 323a

Reed CO05 obverse, ex-James F. Ruddy specimen. (Bowers and Merena photo)

Figure 324a

Prior to the Civil War H. A. Cook built on the trade established by his father, soliciting the farm to market business as well as supplying ready-mades for both city and rural customers. Ad. Bennett's Evansville City Directory, *1863, p. 114. (Dallas Public Library)*

stamped on the cases in the bargain, thus creating Reed CO05 and CO10, respectively. These bear his name, his trade style "Eureka Bazaar" and his address, 73 Main Street. He received about $500 face value of these pieces, in a proportion roughly two of the tens to one of the lower value. Thus he was one of Gault's earlier customers, well before Gault began advertising in newspapers for additional clients. When Cook returned to Evansville and circulated his small change, not only his customers were delighted with the encased stamps. These pieces attracted the attention of another forward thinking, Main Street merchant, Schapker & Bussing, who followed through and purchased pieces from Gault, too.

The business style Cook chose to emblazon on his encased stamps, Eureka Bazaar, is interesting in itself. As a country style emporium, Cook handled a variety of merchandise in addition to foodstuffs. He styled and restyled various aspects of his trade under a variety of monikers as if seeking for the right name. "Eureka Bazaar" never appears in the Evansville directories of the period, either before, during, or after the period in question. Cook was a prolific advertiser in the pages of the local newspaper, even as the grocery ads are the stock in trade of small publications down to this day. For Cook such advertising was mandatory since much of his produce and other items were purchased fresh from the farm. If he didn't get the word out quickly when, say, fruit, vegetables or meats arrived they would be spoiled before he could unload these items. Operating on a small percentage, extensive losses from waste would have capsized his business. Other goods arrived almost daily by boat and train from distant markets. So Cook's notices of new arrivals appeared daily in the newspaper, but almost always under his own given name.

"Eureka Bazaar," on the other hand, from newspaper advertising evidence at hand apparently was a new feature of his business added late in 1862. One of the first indications

Figures 325a,b

Above, H. A. Cook's autograph appears on a scrip note. Jack Vorhies collection. (Society of Paper Money Collectors photo) Left, portrait. (Courtesy of a descendant)

of Cook's Eureka Bazaar was an advertisement he placed in late October, 1862, at which time he featured tapioca, wheat flour, split peas and lentils in an advertisement under that style. Somewhat later, under the heading "Good things for Christmas," Cook offered "200 large, fat, corn-fed turkeys, expressly for the Eureka Bazaar customers" at H. A. Cook. Additional classified ads styled under the Eureka Bazaar trade style offered other specialty items, such as codfish. Although how this department was different from his normal trade is somewhat problematical, apparently his view was that these were specialty items and the Eureka Bazaar designation was being employed to call special attention to them. Doubtless, he looked upon the encased stamp store cards, which he began paying out at the same time, as an additional attention getter for this line of business.

This hard working and creative grocer, Henry A. Cook was born September 10, 1835, at Blackstone, Massachusetts, one of four children of Zacharia Cook. He spent his boyhood at Ballston Spa, New York. Later the family moved to Cannelton, Indiana, and in 1852 to Evansville. Upon reaching Evansville, the elder Cook commenced the grocery business as a wholesale operation. The Cooks principally supplied hotels, restaurants, steamboats and boarding houses. Increasingly, however, Cook found a steady line of business catering to private families. The other merchants scoffed at the idea, but eventually his free delivery system commanded so much of the housewives' business that these other firms found it necessary to run delivery wagons to compete. Cook was first off the mark, though, and his busi-

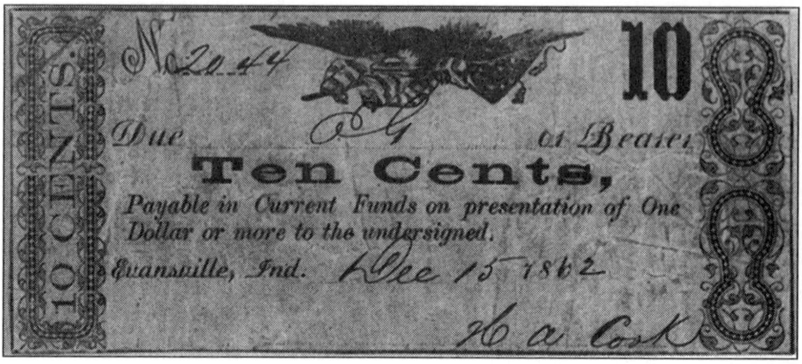

Figures 326a, b

Prior to Christmas, 1862, Cook issued an unknown amount of scrip. Ten cent note, No. 2044, December 15, 1862. Jack Vorhies collection. (Society of Paper Money Collectors photo) Ad. Williams' Evansville Directory, *1866, p. 60. (Evansville Public Library)*

ness thrived and grew. He guaranteed customer satisfaction, and his "genial attitude" won him a large following. His "dash and boldness" in business operations designated him as "a leader, not a follower" in the minds of his contemporaries.

His son, Henry, grew up in this business atmosphere and succeeded his father at the helm of the family grocery. A teenager when the store opened its doors, the younger Cook's energy and industry were said to be largely responsible for its success from its earliest years. His willingness to customize his business and flair for novelty – such as employing Gault's New Metallic Currency – were family character traits he inherited from his father. When the younger Cook took over the family business, for example, he picked up on his heritage and styled the enterprise as the city's "*original* family grocer."

His encasement says Cook offered "Choice Fancy and Staple Groceries." From the extensive advertising available, Cook's shelves were well stocked and his retail trade was varied. Among these items were New Orleans sugar, Rio and Java coffees. He dealt in English sauces in great variety, mentioning Wostersham, London Club, John Bull, Reading and Beef Steak brands. He imported mushroom catsup, French mustard, plain and mixed pickles, fresh pineapples, white onions, cauliflower, Turkish prunes, English walnuts, Brazil nuts, almonds and filberts. A housewife could purchase powdered, granulated or loaf sugar, Sugar House molasses, or Stewart's Excelsior or Baltimore Syrup. Fanciers of smoked and pickled herring, mackerel, pickled salmon could be accommodated, as could desires for Castile soap, or Colburn's, Tierman's and Durkee's bluing agents. The lists go on and on. Fruits aplenty, herbs and condiments, even London porter and Scotch ales could be found in the Eureka Bazaar or main grocery store. Of course, not all of this was always available.

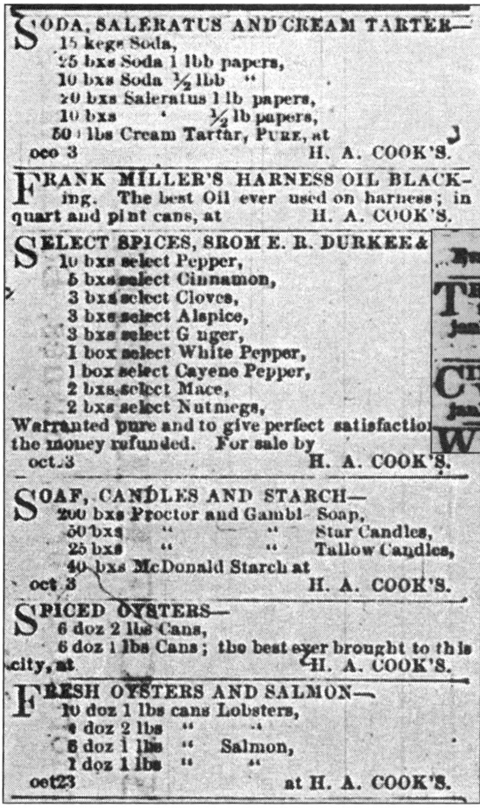

SODA, SALERATUS AND CREAM TARTER—
15 kegs Soda,
25 bxs Soda 1 lbb papers,
10 bxs Soda ½ lbb "
20 bxs Saleratus 1 lb papers,
10 bxs " ½ lb papers,
50 lbs Cream Tartar, PURE, at
oco 3 H. A. COOK'S.

FRANK MILLER'S HARNESS OIL BLACKing. The best Oil ever used on harness; in quart and pint cans, at H. A. COOK'S.

SELECT SPICES, SROM E. R. DURKEE &
10 bxs select Pepper,
5 bxs select Cinnamon,
3 bxs select Cloves,
3 bxs select Alspice,
3 bxs select G nger,
1 box select White Pepper,
1 box select Cayene Pepper,
2 bxs select Mace,
2 bxs select Nutmegs,
Warranted pure and to give perfect satisfactio[n or] the money refunded. For sale by
oct 3 H. A. COOK'S.

SOAF, CANDLES AND STARCH—
200 bxs Proctor and Gambl Soap,
50 bxs " " Star Candles,
25 bxs " " Tallow Candles,
40 bxs McDonald Starch at
oct 3 H. A. COOK'S.

SPICED OYSTERS—
6 doz 2 lbs Cans,
6 doz 1 lbs Cans; the best ever brought to this city, at H. A. COOK'S.

FRESH OYSTERS AND SALMON—
10 doz 1 lbs cans Lobsters,
4 doz 2 lbs " "
6 doz 1 lbs " Salmon,
1 doz 1 lbs " "
oct23 at H. A. COOK'S.

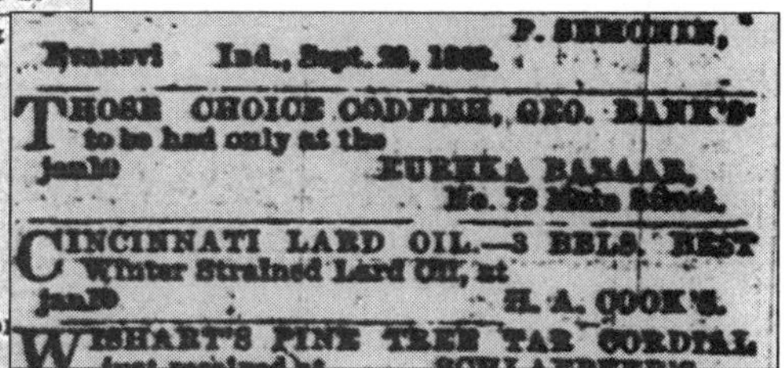

Evansvi Ind., Sept. 22, 1862. P. SHEOHIN,

THOSE CHOICE CODFISH, GEO. BANK'S to be had only at the
jan10 EUREKA BAZAAR, No. 73 Main Street.

CINCINNATI LARD OIL.—3 BBLS. BEST Winter Strained Lard Oil, at
jan10 H. A. COOK'S.

WISHART'S PINE TREE TAR CORDIAL

Figures 327a, b

Top, choice cod fish at the Eureka Bazaar, 73 Main Street, advertised on Cook's encased stamp, as well as a host of other goods were touted by the merchant during the winter of 1862-63. Ads, above, Evansville *Daily Journal, February 13, 1863. (Indiana State Library) Ads, left,* Evansville *Daily Journal, November 3, 1862. (Indiana State Library)*

Supplies were limited, hence the necessity of frequently updated advertising and the long paper trail of these ads in the columns of the local press. Staple items included canned goods, flavorings and spices, and the normal local produce available from farmers in the area. Cook's wholesale operations were also extensive during the period. One such ad offers 800 pounds of butter and 500 dozen (6,000!) eggs. Miscellaneous items included oil, stove polish, brooms, starch and the other necessities of life. Cook's policy was simple: Satisfaction guaranteed, or money refunded.

All indications are that Cook prospered greatly during the war. His encased stamps were a great success. He paid them all out in trade in less than two months (mid-October to mid-December). When supplies of his encased stamps ran short in December, he issued paper scrip to facilitate his trade. Evansville was a thriving and growing town. Cook helped create her success during this period. The war was not without its pain, though. Cook's brother, Norval, was drowned at St. Louis shortly after he entered the Union Army. Following the war, Cook took John H. Healy as a partner. After about a year, thirty-two year old Henry Cook returned to Ballston Spa to marry his childhood sweetheart. Returning to Evansville in 1870, he opened a new enterprise billed as his "Oriental Tea Store" in the city's new opera house. An admirer of extensive advertising, he purchased the tops of 240

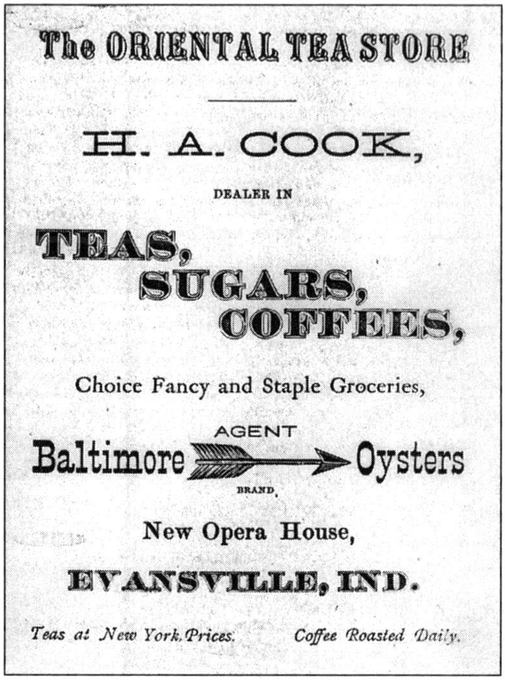

Figure 328a

Cook continued to thrive in Evansville following the war. Among his specialty teas were Imperial, Gunpowder, Young Hysop or Black brand teas, or Dandelion, Sano or Humel's coffee. Note, although opened in 1870, Cook linked the new enterprise to his family's grocery, which had been established in the community two decades before. Ad, Evansville, Her Commerce and Manufacturers, *1874, p. 211. (Evansville Public Library)*

consecutive pages in the city business directory to highlight the opening of his new business and his extensive lines of trade. Cook decorated his store with paintings, landscapes and florals. He dealt both wholesale and retail, stocked 26 varieties of teas, roasted and ground his own coffees. Specialty items included sauces and California wines "obtained direct from the wine sellers in San Francisco."

In 1882 H. A.'s father – affectionately known as Ziba – died, so Henry Cook took his own son Harry into the firm. Continuing the family heritage, the son was described as "the exact prototype of his father in commercial alertness, business comprehension, wide-awake industry, intelligent enterprise and social complaisance." Henry Cook lived to an advanced age, reportedly never missing a day's work even into his seventies. When he died on February 3, 1916, the world had changed considerably. He had not one of his encased stamps remaining, although a quantity had come into the hands of a local man who advertised the pieces in the numismatic press of the times. In later years, a Cook encasement was a highlight of the Evansville Museum's local history collection. Residents were able to see a small portion of their local history thereby until the museum's stamp collection was sold in 1979 by a New York auction house.

Auction Census Data Summary, 1891-1994

	1	2	3	5	10	12	24	30	90	Total	Pct
CO				29	44					73	<1%
				29	**44**					**73**	**<1%**

Schapker & Bussing
Chapter XXVIII

Evansville, Indiana was a small western community during the Civil War. Located down river from Cincinnati, it was an unlikely place for John Gault to find a customer – let alone two – for his New Metallic Currency. The firm of Bernard S. Schapker (called Ben) and John W. Bussing were one of the two firms which employed John Gault's advertising store cards. Their issue was approximately 15,000 pieces, the larger of the two orders Gault filled for Evansville merchants. Most of the order divided among three-, five- and ten-cent denominations (Reed SB03, SB05, SB10 respectively). As with the Cincinnati dry goods stores, advertising was the principal reason for their purchase. Schapker & Bussing were active and accomplished advertisers. They used the media available to them extensively. Gault's new medium, his New Metallic Currency, was an apt device to employ. The hard circulation of extant encased stamps from this merchant indicate that Gault's pieces served their purposes well: They circulated extensively for a lengthy period. The pieces call attention to the partner's stone front store located at 49 (later 47 and 49) Main Street, a location very near the waterfront, where they were serviced by the steamboats that plied the Ohio River and by rail. Both partners had been clerks in the dry goods firm of Samuel Embich & Co., whom they succeeded with their new business venture.

Schapker was born in Germany c. 1834. He came to America with his parents when he was nine. The family resided in Cincinnati for several years before settling in Indiana, where

Figure 329a

Reed SB10 obverse, ex-James F. Ruddy specimen. (Bowers and Merena photo)

Figure 330a

During the time the encased stamps circulated, Schapker & Bussing was still advertising itself as a new establishment, although both partners had learned the business in the employ of S. Embich & Co. Ad, Williams' Evansville Directory, *1863, p. 34. (Evansville Public Library)*

his father engaged in farming. In 1850, the 16-year-old left the farm for Evansville, and a life clerking in a dry goods store. Eight years later he was made a partner in the firm. In 1860, the owner died, and shortly thereafter John W. Bussing joined with Schapker in the dry goods trade. The new partnership was launched in 1861. The partner's millinery department was an especially active part of its trade. It featured bonnets, hats, ribbons, flowers, plumes, and rushes. They offered a fine selection of cloaks and shawls, mantillas, and Balmoral skirts.

The following year their business faced the small change crunch that was rampant throughout the country. As change making difficulties grew onerous, Schapker and Bussing turned to advertising for stamps to fill the want of change. Beginning October 18, they placed notices in the newspaper that they needed stamps. In the meantime, the Evansville City Council agreed to issue $2,000 in 25- and 50-cent notes "for accommodation of the public, in consequence of the scarcity of silver change" but to no avail. The situation worsened. Schapker and Bussing persisted. In the November 3rd issue of the *Journal*, under the heading "Postage Stamps Wanted," they posted the following notice:

> "We will give bankable money for postage stamps,
> when brought in sums of one dollar or more."

By then their notice had been running for more than two weeks. Obviously it was to their distinct advantage to receive large quantities of stamps. By the end of the month, the notice "N.B. – Postage stamps redeemed in money" appeared at the bottom of nearly all the firm's advertisements. There's little doubt, that this merchant came to issue encased stamps after seeing the local issues of H. A. Cook in fall 1862. That these notices continued to be published throughout the winter, even after federal officials started to redeem the stinking gum backs, tends to indicate that the small change crisis in Evansville persisted months after it was somewhat abated in the larger, eastern cities. For example on January 12, 1863, the firm

Figure 331a

German immigrant, John W. Bussing was called "wooden shoe Dutchman" by schoolmates. So incensed was he, he "took a hatchet to his shoes and chopped them up," according to a descendant. Portrait. (Courtesy Marilyn Bussing Oldenburg)

offered dozens of childs', misses' and ladies' hoods; it also asked for stamps. A month later, on February 13, the story was the same. It has been suggested that the firm was still soliciting stamps for use in their stamp cases, but more likely their supply of New Metallic Currency had been already paid out; Postage Currency was in short supply, and the firm still needed to make change.

That the small change crisis might still have been acute in a western community like Evansville well into 1863 is plausible if not down right likely. Local brokers at the time were paying much higher premiums for specie and Demand Notes than eastern brokers. Copeland's Savings Bank, for example, offered 30-35 percent on silver and 45-50 percent for gold. Demand Notes fetched 40-45 percent. Even Kentucky and Indiana state bank notes were rated above par. Schapker & Bussing persisted advertising for postage stamps until mid-March, although no other local merchant did so.

Schapker & Bussing were noted for their frugality. In fact their economy and business sense were something of a local legend. A contemporary, writing in the Evansville *Daily Journal*, March 12, 1863, had this to say about them:

> SCHAPKER & BUSSING advertise this morning a fresh arrival of choice Linen and Cotton Sheetings, Brown and Bleached Sheetings, as well as a large assortment of the latest Spring styles of dress goods. We need hardly say to our readers, that this enterprising firm are always wide awake to procure the most fashionable patterns, as well as the best quality of goods. They do business on the principle that is best calculated to retain all their customers, by selling them no goods that

Figures 332a, b, c
Schapker and Bussing were very much aware of the circulation of stamps as small change during the period of intense change shortfall. Top, in mid-October they actively solicited stamps for outright purchase. Ad. Evansville Daily Journal, *November 3, 1862. (Omaha Public Library) Six weeks later they were still looking for additional quantities for small change. Ads, right and below, Evansville* Daily Journal, *November 25, 1862. (Indiana State Library)*

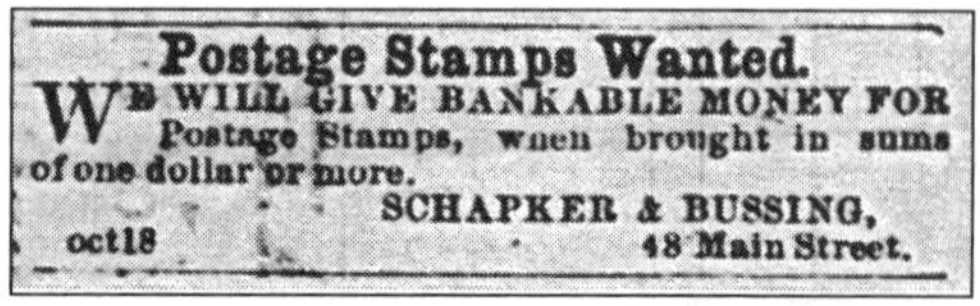

Postage Stamps Wanted.

WE WILL GIVE BANKABLE MONEY FOR Postage Stamps, when brought in sums of one dollar or more.

SCHAPKER & BUSSING,
oct18 48 Main Street.

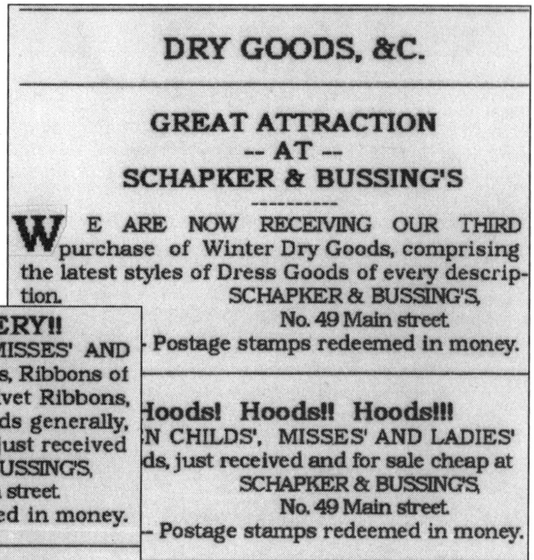

DRY GOODS, &C.

GREAT ATTRACTION -- AT -- SCHAPKER & BUSSING'S

WE ARE NOW RECEIVING OUR THIRD purchase of Winter Dry Goods, comprising the latest styles of Dress Goods of every description.
SCHAPKER & BUSSING'S,
No. 49 Main street.
Postage stamps redeemed in money.

Hoods! Hoods!! Hoods!!!
N CHILDS', MISSES' AND LADIES' ds, just received and for sale cheap at
SCHAPKER & BUSSING'S,
No. 49 Main street.
- Postage stamps redeemed in money.

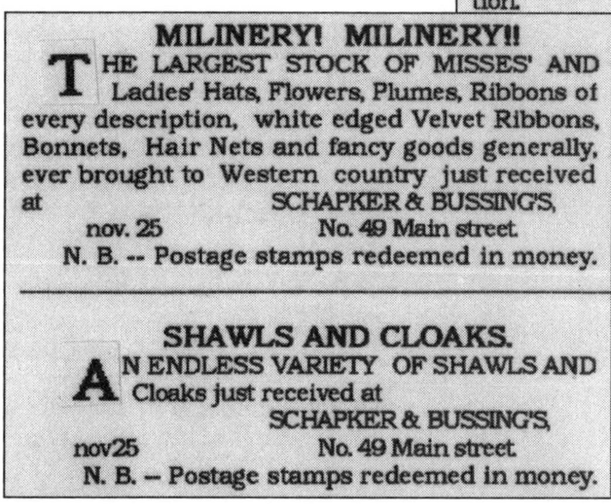

MILINERY! MILINERY!!

THE LARGEST STOCK OF MISSES' AND Ladies' Hats, Flowers, Plumes, Ribbons of every description, white edged Velvet Ribbons, Bonnets, Hair Nets and fancy goods generally, ever brought to Western country just received at
SCHAPKER & BUSSING'S,
nov. 25 No. 49 Main street.
N. B. -- Postage stamps redeemed in money.

SHAWLS AND CLOAKS.

AN ENDLESS VARIETY OF SHAWLS AND Cloaks just received at
SCHAPKER & BUSSING'S,
nov25 No. 49 Main street.
N. B. – Postage stamps redeemed in money.

> will not prove to be just what they are represented. Another motto adopted and acted upon by this establishment is, 'quick sales and small profits.' knowing that the dollar, like the snow ball increases fastest by constant rolling.

Following the war, the partners took Joseph Goelzhauser into the firm, and the name was changed to Schapker, Bussing & Co. They continued to prosper. Schapker, especially was known in the community as "a man of great resources and splendid business ability." He appeared to enjoy the confidence of the entire business community and the esteem of a loyal clientele. However, the picture changed dramatically with the financial disarray known as the Panic of 1873. The Depression following the inflation brought on by the Civil War wrecked many businesses. Like many of their contemporaries, Schapker & Bussing was forced to close its doors.

The partners went their separate ways. Schapker, who continued in the millinery line, occupied the second floor of a Main Street building. Bussing became a clerk in another local firm. "Nothing daunted by reverses, Ben Schapker at once set about to establish himself in a new line of business and in this venture he was successful," according to a contemporary. He

Figure 333a

Wilhelmina Bussing was born in Holland. Her family came first to Cincinnati, then to Evansville. Photo. (Courtesy of Marilyn Bussing Oldenburg)

went into the manufacture of mattresses and mosquito net frames. He obtained patents on mosquito bar frames and the renovating of feather mattresses. The reader will remember that a century ago before the days of central air conditioning and public sanitation, summer ventilation by open windows was something of a necessity, but mosquitoes presented an ever constant hazard. Mosquito netting, in the words of the day, "provided the only sure and practical protection." A light, durable mosquito bar frame and fine mesh netting was a practical necessity for comfort as well as health. Schapker pushed this line "with an energy born of an indomitable will and a determination to win in the struggle for a large family dependent on his exertions." He died February 28, 1889.

His partner in the issue of New Metallic Currency, John Wenceslas Bussing, was born March 16, 1832 in Westphalia (Germany). He landed at New York in 1844, and his citizenship papers were issued July 4th, 1848. His eldest son, Bernard, was named for his friend and partner Ben Schapker. Like many of his contemporaries, Bussing purchased a substitute to fight in his stead during the war. According to a descendant, this was a matter of no small embarrassment to him in later years. Able-bodied men between 20-45 were subject to mili-

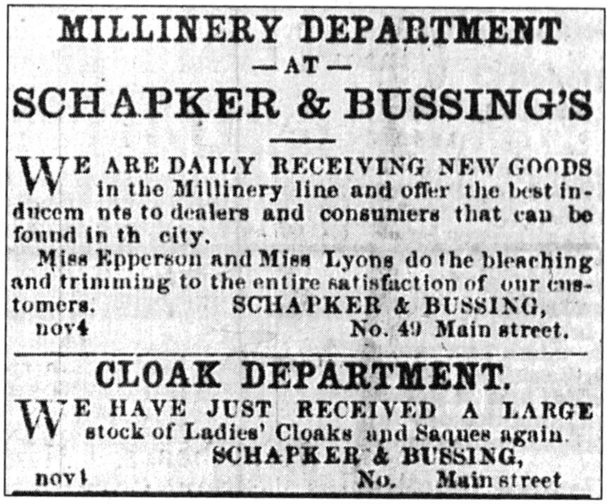

MILLINERY DEPARTMENT
— AT —
SCHAPKER & BUSSING'S

WE ARE DAILY RECEIVING NEW GOODS in the Millinery line and offer the best inducem nts to dealers and consumers that can be found in th city.

Miss Epperson and Miss Lyons do the bleaching and trimming to the entire satisfaction of our customers. SCHAPKER & BUSSING,
nov4 No. 49 Main street.

CLOAK DEPARTMENT.

WE HAVE JUST RECEIVED A LARGE stock of Ladies' Cloaks and Saques again.
SCHAPKER & BUSSING,
nov1 No. Main street

Figure 334a

Ad. Evansville Daily Journal, *November 4, 1862, p. 2. (Omaha* Public Library*)*

tary obligation. Men liable for the draft could hire the services of a substitute who would serve in their place by furnishing his commutation money, typically $300 but in Indiana only $200. This was severely criticized in some quarters as a "rich man's loophole" which shifted the burden and the sacrifice of fighting the war to the poor. Nevertheless it was legal and many men were willing to serve for the financial inducement. In old age, Bussing was particularly chagrined about the topic, it was said, because he had paid his way out of the army by supplying the bounty money to purchase (in his case) the wartime services of a Black man. Neither event was exceptional. Nearly 118,000 substitutes were hired in this manner during the war, and approximately 180,000 colored troops served in the Union Army. Following the demise of the Schapker & Bussing firm, Bussing owned several small department stores in southern Indiana. In addition to his own firm in Evansville, one was in New Harmony and a third, at Vincennes. Bussing outlived his former partner by many years, dying May 26, 1912 from "infirmities of old age." A devout Catholic, he was buried at Saint Joseph Cemetery.

Pieces of this issue were handed down within the families of the principals as heirlooms. Faran Zerbe recorded that he made the acquaintance of a Bussing descendant who had a number of pieces. According to family members, these pieces are now well dispersed. We also know that in later years a quantity of Schapker & Bussing pieces came into the hands of a local resident, W. E. Deeds. Unfortunately, we don't know the extent of the hoard this Evansville man obtained. Pieces that do show up are generally well circulated, indicating that they served their purposes in commerce and were ultimately redeemed by the firm although there was no obligation to do so.

Auction Census Data Summary, 1891-1994

	1	2	3	5	10	12	24	30	90	Total	Pct
SB	13		57	47	76	5				198	2%
	13		**57**	**47**	**76**	**5**				**198**	**2%**

Fred Buhl
Chapter XXIX

On the eve of the Civil War Detroit was not the major metropolis we know today, but it was a growing, thriving city only a generation removed from the frontier. In 1830, the town had only about 2,000 residents. Thirty years later, the population was pegged at nearly 90,000, the 18th in size among U.S. cities. John Gault only enticed a single merchant there to advertise on his New Metallic Currency, a hatter named Frederick Buhl. Buhl has long been an enigmatic figure in the encased stamp story, but he needn't have been so. The sole Detroit merchant to purchase encasements from Gault, Buhl is also the only mayor among the select group of Gault's customers. By personal habits of temperance, frugality, and industry, Fred Buhl created a major enterprise and prospered accordingly. Along the way, he purchased about 10,000 encased stamps from Gault in 1862: roughly equal quantities of one-cent (Reed BU01) as well as five- and ten-cent pieces (Reed BU05 and BU10 respectively).

One to witness Detroit's dynamic growth during that three decade period, Fred Buhl's beginnings were humble. Born November 27, 1806, in Zelienople, Pennsylvania, he was the second son of 11 children born to German immigrant parents. The Horatio Alger-type story of Squire Christian Buhl, Fred Buhl's father, and his family's rise is one of the more outstanding of the many success stories which characterize those who can to be associated with Gault's patent currency. It is only possible to present a brief resume of that story here, but a

Figure 335a

Reed BU10 obverse, ex-James F. Ruddy specimen. (Bowers and Merena photo)

Figures 336a, b

Buhl built up an extensive trade in western and Canadian furs. Right, Ad. Johnston's Detroit Directory and Business Advertiser, *1853, p. 43. (Dallas Public Library) Below, the original store of F. and C. H. Buhl, northwest corner of Jefferson and Griswold, c. 1849. Woodcut reproduction. Ad, Detroit* News, *March 14, 1921. (Buhl File, Detroit Public Library)*

fuller presentation of its details is available through the local historical society, which looks upon the Buhl family as a major source of local pride.

The elder Buhl came to the U.S. from Bavaria in 1802, as a journeyman hatter and furrier. He quickly showed his industry in the manufacture of wools hats and built a thriving trade with Pittsburgh, 25 miles away. It was a family enterprise. Mother and children worked, too, and the family built a three and one half story house which is still standing. "Owing to the exigencies of time and place, the educational facilities afforded Frederick Buhl were meagre," according to a biographer. The young Buhl overcame these circumstances, however, by virtue of "his strong mentality and determination to win his way in the world."

Fred Buhl left home in 1823 at age 16. He went to Pittsburgh initially to learn a trade other than his father's. His father suggested he learn watch repair, so he took up the jeweler's

Figure 337a
Fred Buhl's industry and thrift led to a specular rise on the western frontier. It was a family characteristic. His brother Christian thrived on the opportunities avaiable there, too. Photo. (Buhl file, Detroit Public Library)

arts. Much later in his life Fred Buhl recounted for his own son that momentous decision:

> When I was 16, Father asked me what trade I would like to learn. As I had no genius more than other boys, I had no choice. He then thought it would be a nice thing for me to learn the watch-making business, or rather repairing. . . .So it was decided I should learn that business. He took me with him to Pittsburgh to see if he could get a place for me. I thought it was a great thing to go to so large a city so far from home. He finally bound me to Mr. Thompson for five years to learn the art and mystery of the business. The terms of the indenture were that Father was to find me in clothing and pay for going to night school, and I was to have one week's vacation in the summer and one in the winter to go home on a visit.

Buhl engaged in this pursuit for two years. When Thompson sold out and went into the business of building steam engines, he took Buhl with him into that line, also. Buhl continued in that trade building steam engines and his nest egg. When the indenture was up, he took up river boating, endeavoring to "engineer" vessels down the Ohio River. These travels took him from Pittsburgh as far as New Orleans. Eventually he was given an engineer's job on a steamer that plied the Mississippi between St. Louis and New Orleans. Despite the opportunity to travel and see the frontier, Buhl did not like the occupation. "Steamboat men are generally immoral and rough people, but I followed it because I could make some

Figure 338a

By the time the Civil War erupted, Buhl's trade had expanded far beyond furs to other leather and straw goods and apparel. The firm's merchandise and business practices merited the approving pen of the local guide book editor. Ad, Umberhine's Detroit City Business Directory and Advertiser, 1862. *(Detroit Public Library)*

money," Buhl wrote. Buhl bided his time. He continued to live frugally, banking at least half his salary and waiting for a better opportunity to present itself. It did. His younger brother Christian Henry Buhl wrote him from Detroit that a local hatter's estate was badly in debt and the business was to be sold. The brother advised Fred Buhl "that it would be a good thing to buy and [he] and I carry on the business," Buhl later recalled.

Frederick Buhl succumbed to his brother's urging. On July 28, 1833, he arrived in Detroit, then a busy lake port and fur trading center in Michigan Territory, with $2,000 in savings in his pocket. The brothers purchased the hat business and three days later threw open the door to their new enterprise. The brothers initially set up shop in a "modest frame building on the northwest corner of Jefferson and Griswold Streets." The building had been a private residence. They manufactured their hats in the rear of the building. A glass

Figures 339a, b

Left, for three decades, 1852-1882, Buhl occupied a four- (later five-) story building at 146-148 Jefferson Avenue. Engraving. History of Detroit and Wayne County, *1883, p. 783. (Detroit Public Library photo) Below, a late spring ad for Buhl's family hat trade. Ad, Detroit* Free Press, *May 16, 1862. (Omaha Public Library)*

STRAW GOODS

MEN'S, BOYS' & CHILDREN'S

HATS,

Of all the the most desirable styles, received this day, by F. BUHL & CO.

MISSES' HATS,

Of all the newest styles, at low prices, received this day, by F. BUHL & CO.

MAY 15TH my 16

window separated the work area from the showroom. They could work in the rear and still attend to business in the storefront. Both were still single, lived frugally and slept in the store. C. H. Buhl became purchasing agent, buying pelts from Indians and trappers on trips

COMMON COUNCIL.

DETROIT, Tuesday, Oct. 22. 1862.

In the absence of the President, the Council was called to order by the Clerk.

Present—Ald. Bond, Ford, Frost, Gallagher, Gies, Godfrey. Hoek, LeFavour. LeRoy, Lingeman, Miller, Purcell, Shearer, Williams, 4th,—14.

On motion of Ald. Gallagher, Ald. Godfrey was called to the chair.

The proceedings of the last Council were approved as printed

The President, Hon. F. B. Phelps, came in and took the chair.

Petitions Presented.

By Ald. Godfrey;

Of F. Buhl & Co., and 38 others, asking the Common Council to take some immediate action, whereby the business men and citizens generally, may be relieved from the inconvenience attending the great scarcity of small change.

On motion of Ald Godfrey, referred to a special committee and the City Attorney.

The Chair appointed Ald Godfrey, Williams, 4th, and Miller as such Committee.

On further motion of Ald. Godfrey, the City Treasurer and Controller were added to said Committee.

By Ald. Frost,

Of Wm. A. Butler and 5 others. asking the Common Council to take some measures to prevent cattle and pigs from running at large.

Ald. Frost moved to refer it to the Mayor.

Ald. Williams, 4th, moved to amend by substituting the Controller and two Aldermen.

Lost as follows:

Yeas—Ald. Ford, Frost, Hoek, LeFavour, LeRoy, Shearer, Williams 4th,—7.

Nays—Ald. Bond, Gallagher, Godfrey, Lingeman, Miller, Purcell, President.—7.

The question then recurring on the original mo-

Figure 340a

New business at the Detroit city council meeting October 22, 1862, was propelled by a delegation of 39 businessmen headed by Fred Buhl seeking relief for the city's change shortage. Minutes of the Common Council, October 22, 1862, p. 133. (Detroit Public Library)

to the north country, while Frederick made the hats. Working hard and implementing their father's business philosophy: "Sell the best goods obtainable, deal fairly – and hustle!" the business prospered.

The pair advertised for furs and deer skins and added buffalo robes prominently to their line of hats. Eventually they expanded their purchases to muskrat, beaver, and other furs throughout Canada and the Great Lakes' region. In time, Fred Buhl became "one of the largest shippers of furs in the country, as well as an importer and manufacturer of everything pertaining to furs." To seek out customers for their growing trade, C. H. Buhl ranged as far afield in the east as New York City and west to St. Louis.

With the Buhls' commercial success came the opportunity for public service. Their fine hats were awarded to the local councilmen as tokens of esteem. In 1845 and 1846, the hat was on the other head, so to speak. Fred Buhl represented the First Ward as an alderman. He was one of the original directors of the Detroit Merchants Exchange and City Board of Trade. In 1848, his neighbors elected Fred Buhl mayor of Detroit, although he did not seek the post. He was one of the one-term businessmen mayors who contributed to Detroit's early

Figure 341a

Fred Buhl's son left the University of Michigan to volunteer for the Union Army. He was wounded in furious action at the Battle of Gettysburg. Union forces were commanded by General George Meade, shown above. Young Buhl recovered, transferred to the cavalry, was again wounded and died. Photo, Mathew Brady collection, National Archives. (U.S. Army Signal Corps photo)

growth.

The brothers' trade continued to grow. By 1850 they were one of the four largest manufacturing hatters and fur dealers in town. They added fur mittens and buckskin gloves, and continued to ship large quantities of fur and deer skins back to the east. In 1852, they constructed a four-story "skyscraper" to house their growing business. The building was located at 146-148 Jefferson. The following year C. H. Buhl withdrew and entered the wholesale hardware business. In 1854 Fred Buhl extended his fur trade to Russia.

Buhl's business thrived during the war, but like every merchant caught up in the exigencies of the times, he needed some way to make change for his customers. Detroit was no different from other communities in that regard. Like other cities, residents there circulated thousands of dollars worth of postage stamps. "So great was the demand for these sticky substitutes that enough could not be procured," a contemporary wrote. Private scrip was dumped into the void, but business conditions remained deranged.

Figure 342a
Ad. Umberhine's Detroit City Business Directory and Advertiser, 1860, p. 152. (Dallas Public Library)

As a community leader and as one of the city's most influential and active businessmen, Fred Buhl felt a pressing need to open up the dammed-up channels of commerce. The city was coming to a standstill for want of small change. On October 22, 1862, Buhl appeared at a meeting of the city's Common Council. He presented a petition, introduced by Alderman Godfrey, on his behalf and that of 38 other businessmen requesting "the Common Council to take some immediate action, whereby the business men and citizens generally, may be relieved from the inconvenience attending the scarcity of small change." The council referred the matter to a committee for study, and then proceeded to the important business of how to prevent cattle and pigs from running at large in the streets of Detroit.

Meanwhile the federal Postage Currency was not forthcoming. It wasn't until a week later, October 30, that the first shipment of that precious commodity arrived in Detroit. The situation which transpired mirrors that recounted for other communities across the land:

> At the hour designated for the distribution the office of the depository was literally besieged. The office, hall, doorway, and even the walk in front, were densely packed with business men, merchants and clerks, each man wildly brandishing fifteen dollars in treasury notes, that being the largest amount that one person was allowed to obtain. It was almost at the risk of life that the happy spot where change was dispensed was reached. The doors were closed and guarded by police.

As a thriving young merchant, Fred Buhl was a good prospect. He married the young daughter of a U.S. congressman. Their first son died in infancy. The second son, Frederick Augustus Buhl, was the apple of his parents' eyes. As the son of a thriving merchant and a well-to-do and politically connected mother, the younger Buhl was granted all the opportunities for education and social graces that the rich typically shower on their young. F. A. or "Gus" was sent to the University of Michigan, intent on pursuing a course of study and life to which his upbringing had called him.

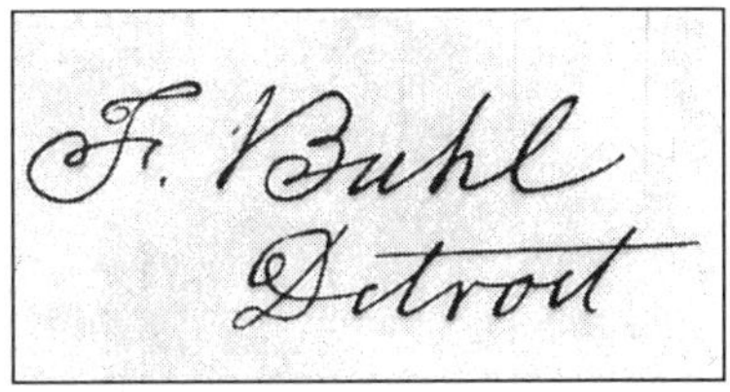

Figures 343a, b

Fred Buhl, left, was an imposing figure in his old age. Copy photo of unpublished Cabinet Card by Tomkins & Co., Detroit. (Detroit Historical Museum) Above, autograph. Burton Historical collection. (Detroit Public Library)

As black clouds rolled northward during the war, Fred Buhl came forth as a leading supporter of the northern cause, outfitting 11 Michigan volunteer infantry regiments. Buhl did more than donate caps and swords, though. In 1862 when President Lincoln issued a call for 300,000 more men to reinforce the Union Army after its heavy losses, one of the regiments raised was the 24th Infantry in Detroit. Fred Buhl was elected as vice president of a grand Union Meeting held in the city July 22nd to stir up the patriotism of the people and encourage enlistments. One of those stirred up was his teenaged son, Gus, who dropped out of college and enlisted as a Second Lieutenant. Fred Buhl presented his son's regiment its regimental colors before it departed for combat. The unit fought with distinction at Fredericksburg, Chancellorsville and Gettysburg, where Gus Buhl was wounded. He wasn't the only one. The 24th Michigan of the famed Iron Brigade suffered a staggering 80 percent casualties at McPherson's Woods.

Recovering from his thigh wound, Gus Buhl transferred to the First Michigan Cavalry as a Captain, serving under General George Armstrong Custer. Young Buhl left a lucid account of his military career. His diary reflects a conscientious young man eager for action and glory, full of a sense of duty and honor. His entry recorded on his 21st birthday bears repeating. His words reveal a young man with a real sense of purpose, a mature head on his youthful shoulders. He was both self-reliant and humble. These character traits reflect the values imbued in him by his father and mother. This was a young man "to the manner born." He was definitely his father's son. On August 23, Gus wrote:

> Today I arrived at man's estate. I cannot see that I feel any very unusual sensation. My boyhood and youth have been for the most part very pleasantly – and I hope not unprofitably – spent. I now enter upon the most active period of life. My determination is strong to conduct myself as a man should, and I pray God to sustain me in this resolve.

The war clouds closed in, however, on the Buhl family two days later. Gus was severely

Figure 344a

Business was good during the Civil War. Fred Buhl erected this imposing residence in 1864 on the south side of Fort Street near 24th Street. He and his wife pose in the circular drive. Engraving, Moss Engraving Co., N.Y. Burton Historical collection. (Detroit Public Library photo)

wounded at Shepardstown, Virginia. Moved to a succession of Army hospitals, he died September 15. The young life never bore the fruit of maturity. The promise remained unfulfilled. The door closed silently. Gus Buhl was laid to rest at Annapolis, Maryland. Fred Buhl had lost a second son.

Fred Buhl threw himself into his business. He constructed a palatial mansion. He continued to thrive. In 1868, Buhl reported the highest personal income in all of Detroit and Wayne County, according to filings under the wartime income tax law. In fact, his $40,816 was not merely the highest, it was twice that of anybody countywide. Fred Buhl continued running his business until 1877. A decade later, he sold it to his third and oldest surviving son, Walter. A daughter married a son of Henry Ford, indicating how far the family had come in one generation. Fred Buhl died May 12, 1890, "at the close of a useful and clean life," according to a biographer. His younger brother, C. H. prospered in his own fashion, too. Among his other ventures he became the president of the Second National Bank of Detroit, and sat on the boards of several trusts and railroads. His son married the daughter of Canadian whiskey magnate Hiram Walker. When C. H. Buhl died in 1893, he left an estate valued at $6 million. In 1925, a 27-story building, the Buhl Building in Detroit's financial district, was erected on the site of the original 1833 hatter's shop to house the growing Buhl commercial empire.

Auction Census Data Summary, 1891-1994

	1	2	3	5	10	12	24	30	90	Total	Pct
BU	38		4	39	36	5	7			129	1%
	38		**4**	**39**	**36**	**5**	**7**			**129**	**1%**

John W. Norris
Chapter XXX

In 1862 the "Windy City," although much smaller than today, was already a cross roads of business and finance, served by a dozen busy railroads and the lake steamers. It had been the site of Lincoln's launching onto the national political scene. But in the summer of that year, its 100,000-plus residents were increasingly focusing their attention on the lack of small change in their pockets. By mid-July, this "scarcity of small change [was] becoming 'no better very fast,'" the press reported. As we have seen in other cities, a plethora of scrip and other makeshift notes were employed as remedies, as were government stamps: $2,000 in postage stamps were being paid out at the post office daily for use as currency by late July.

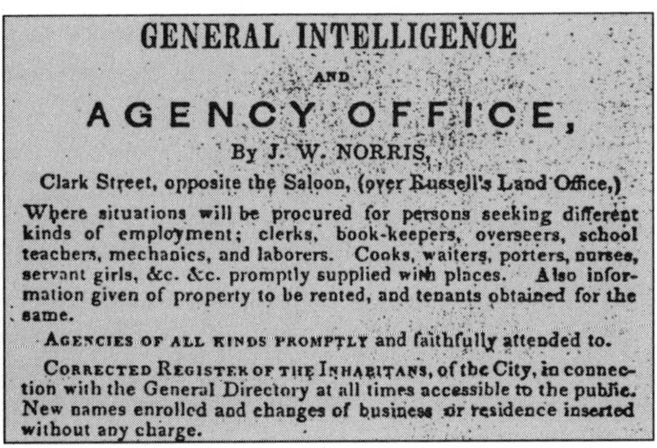

GENERAL INTELLIGENCE
AND
AGENCY OFFICE,
By J. W. NORRIS,
Clark Street, opposite the Saloon, (over Russell's Land Office,)

Where situations will be procured for persons seeking different kinds of employment; clerks, book-keepers, overseers, school teachers, mechanics, and laborers. Cooks, waiters, porters, nurses, servant girls, &c. &c. promptly supplied with places. Also information given of property to be rented, and tenants obtained for the same.

AGENCIES OF ALL KINDS PROMPTLY and faithfully attended to.

CORRECTED REGISTER OF THE INHABITANTS, of the City, in connection with the General Directory at all times accessible to the public. New names enrolled and changes of business or residence inserted without any charge.

Figures 345a, b

Above, Reed NO05 obverse, ex-James F. Ruddy specimen. (Bowers and Merena photo)

Left, the first J. W. Norris on the Chicago scene was a lawyer and publisher, who also operated an early 19th century employment agency. Norris' Chicago Business Directory, 1844. *(Chicago Historical Society)*

Figures 346a, b

Top, Ad. Smith & DuMoulin City Directory, *1859, p. 295. (Dallas Public Library). John W. Norris found employment in the building at right. Engraving. (Private collection)*

Relief finally seemed forthcoming in October when the Chicago *Evening Journal* enthusiastically reported on its front page "A NEW CURRENCY . . . is being carried out by parties in Connecticut," (c.f. Figure 67a) That new currency, of course, was John Gault's New

Figure 347a

Unpublished photograph of John W. Norris, c. 1875. After the war Norris became better known as a manufacturer of safes than his antebellum and wartime occupation as a periodical and book seller. Cabinet Card, albumin silver print. (Chicago Historical Society photo, ICHi-18867)

Metallic Currency. Within a month *that* new currency would be circulating in Chicago, too, brought out by news dealer John W. Norris. Norris' pieces are historically important as a bridge to the then ninth largest city in the nation. Once again we know the specifics of how Norris came to place his order with Gault. He was on his fall periodical purchasing trip to New York when he made arrangements with Gault to supply him with about 6,000 pieces of encased stamps, roughly one-third of them one-cent pieces (Reed NO01), one-third ten-cent pieces (Reed NO10) and the remaining third divided between three- and five-cent issues (Reed NO03 and NO05 respectively). He began paying the pieces out in change in mid-November. One of the pieces showed up in a church collection plate at Thanksgiving.

John Norris followed in the footsteps of his uncle James Wellington Norris, a pioneer Chicago publisher and news agent, who was also co-founder and founding editor of the Chicago *Daily Journal*. The younger Norris was a native of Boston, born there March 14,

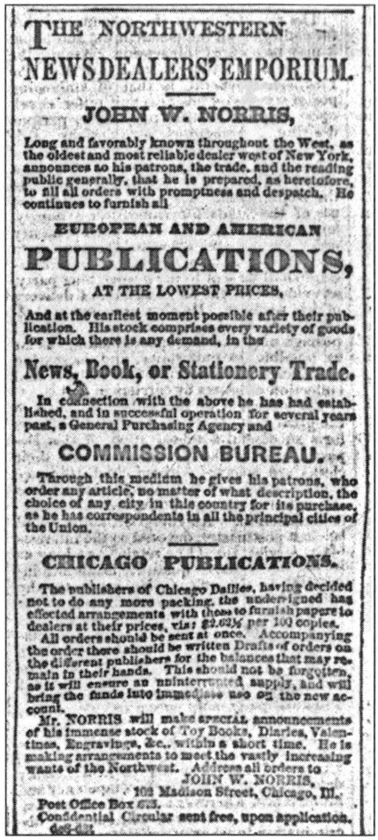

THE NORTHWESTERN NEWSDEALERS' EMPORIUM.

JOHN W. NORRIS,

Long and favorably known throughout the West, as the oldest and most reliable dealer west of New York, announces to his patrons, the trade, and the reading public generally, that he is prepared, as heretofore, to fill all orders with promptness and despatch. He continues to furnish all

EUROPEAN AND AMERICAN

PUBLICATIONS,

AT THE LOWEST PRICES,

And at the earliest moment possible after their publication. His stock comprises every variety of goods for which there is any demand, in the

News, Book, or Stationery Trade.

In connection with the above he has had established, and in successful operation for several years past, a General Purchasing Agency and

COMMISSION BUREAU.

Through this medium he gives his patrons, who order any article, no matter of what description, the choice of any city in this country for its purchase, as he has correspondents in all the principal cities of the Union.

CHICAGO PUBLICATIONS.

The publishers of Chicago Dailies, having decided not to do any more packing, the undersigned has effected arrangements with them to furnish papers to dealers at their prices, viz: \$2.62½ per 100 copies.

All orders should be sent at once. Accompanying the order there should be written Drafts or orders on the different publishers for the balances that may remain in their hands. This should not be forgotten, as it will ensure an uninterrupted supply, and will bring the funds into immediate use on the new account.

Mr. NORRIS will make SPECIAL announcements of his immense stock of Toy Books, Diaries, Valentines, Engravings, &c., within a short time. He is making arrangements to meet the vastly increasing wants of the Northwest. Address all orders to

JOHN W. NORRIS,
102 Madison Street, Chicago, Ill.

Post Office Box 613.

Confidential Circular sent free, upon application.

Figure 348a

Norris' Northwestern News Dealers' Emporium was a key client for Gault since he operated as the news agent for the Chicago daily press. Ad. Chicago Evening Journal, *December 8, 1862, p. 1. (Illinois State Library)*

1836. His father was a Methodist minister and prominent journalist, himself, who for many years edited *The Olive Branch.* This was a weekly literary newspaper, and one of the leading periodicals in Boston in its day. As a young boy, John W. Norris was sent to New York to be educated. In 1856, at age 20, he came to Chicago to seek his fortune. Through the intercession of his uncle, young Norris found employment in John McNally's news and periodical business on Randolph Street. Shortly thereafter Norris took over management of McNally's business. By December, 1858, Norris had joined with Amos M. Hyde in his own newsstand styled the "Great Western Book and News Agency" at 100 Dearborn, corner of Washington Street. Their "little frame building" was one of about two dozen newsstands in the city at that time, a contemporary noted. Norris was set up in the venture by his uncle as an outlet to distribute the *Journal* throughout Illinois and the surrounding region. In addition to local and out-of-town periodicals, they sold books, stationery, and the like. Their corner was a good location, and their cheap prices built a thriving trade. In 1860 the enterprising partners opened a second newsstand, this one at the 102 Madison Street location shown on the encased stamps. Norris' store front on Madison was narrow, but the building itself was deep giving him a cavernous expanse for his high volume wholesale periodical business. The fol-

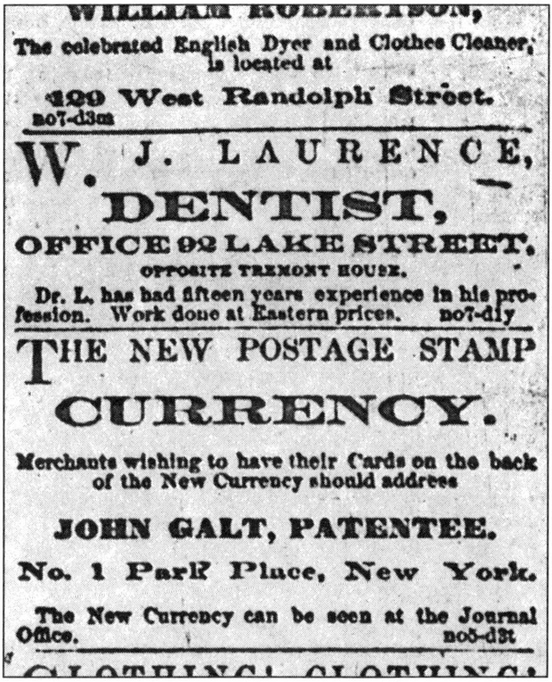

WILLIAM ROBERTSON,
The celebrated English Dyer and Clothes Cleaner, is located at
129 West Randolph Street.
no7-d3m

W. J. LAURENCE,
DENTIST,
OFFICE 92 LAKE STREET,
OPPOSITE TREMONT HOUSE.
Dr. L. has had fifteen years experience in his profession. Work done at Eastern prices. no7-d1y

THE NEW POSTAGE STAMP
CURRENCY.
Merchants wishing to have their Cards on the back of the New Currency should address
JOHN GALT, PATENTEE.
No. 1 Park Place, New York.
The New Currency can be seen at the Journal Office. no5-d3t

Figure 349a

In fall 1862, John Gault (Galt, sic) advertised "The New Postage Stamp Currency" in newspapers throughout the northeast and midwestern U.S. Samples were supplied with the ad so that merchants desiring to view the product close-up would have the opportunity to do so. Gault's notice at left ran three days only – November 5-7 – in Chicago. Ad. Chicago Evening Journal, *November 7, 1862, p. 1. (Illinois State Library)*

lowing year, they added patriotic envelopes to their lines of trade. In 1862, Hyde dropped out of the partnership, likely to go into the Army. Norris closed the original newsstand.

The change crisis hit Chicago hard. "Probably at no time in our history has there been such a scarcity of silver," the local press cried. For a small merchant selling inexpensive goods like periodicals, small change was anything but small change. His competitors at McNally's, which he had managed only a couple years before, attempted to solve their problems making change by printing postage stamp envelopes (c.f. Figure 48b). When Norris commenced his fall business trip to the eastern publishing houses, he needed an edge on the competition. He already had the "lowest prices," "fastest delivery," and "widest selection" in town. Luckily he found just the thing while in New York.

"That new currency manufactured in New York for Mr. Norris, the news-dealer, and brought out by him . . . meets universal approbation," the *Evening Journal* reported. "It is regular government money and is better in every respect than the new paper currency." Besides reporting how satisfactory the encased stamps were, the significant message in the story to reading public and Norris alike was the fact that "Mr. Norris uses it as change at his news-rooms." It was a sure fire way to attract business. It was also a strange admission by the newspaper editor. At that very time the *Evening Journal* was soliciting merchants to print private scrip for them. Of course, the publication was Norris' uncle's. In addition to dispensing his new, clean and neat small change, Norris was also in the process of refurbishing his store. Repainting and restocking were well under way, the editor noted. "This will make it one of the most attractive stores in town," the editor affirmed. Norris' business relied heavily

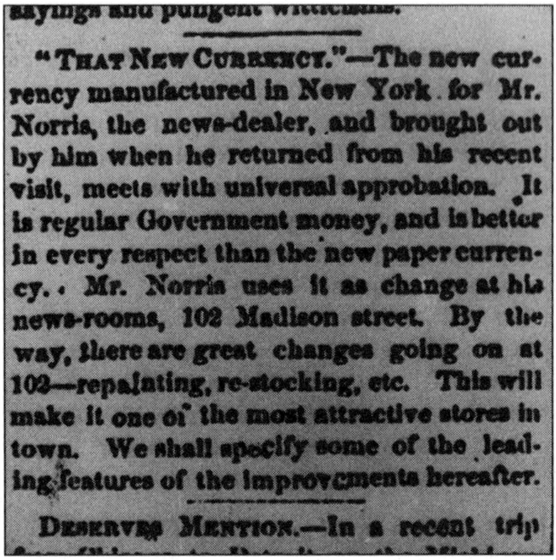
sayings and pungent witticisms.

"THAT NEW CURRENCY."—The new currency manufactured in New York for Mr. Norris, the news-dealer, and brought out by him when he returned from his recent visit, meets with universal approbation. It is regular Government money, and is better in every respect than the new paper currency. Mr. Norris uses it as change at his news-rooms, 102 Madison street. By the way, there are great changes going on at 102—repainting, re-stocking, etc. This will make it one of the most attractive stores in town. We shall specify some of the leading features of the improvements hereafter.

DESERVED MENTION.—In a recent trip

Figure 350a

Self-explanatory, and a key notice of Gault's encased stamps by the press, the article at right leaves little doubt how Norris came to issue his encased stamps. "That New Currency," Chicago Evening Journal, *November 21, 1862, p. 4. (Illinois State Library) In recent years, Norris' Civil War address at Madison and Clark Streets is the location of Maxim's, a cafe frequented by the author on business trips to the Windy City.*

on his wholesale distribution to outlying areas. As a distributor between the publisher and the public, Norris handled thousands of newspapers daily, which he dispatched by rail throughout the region. The product, news, was an extremely perishable one. Time was of the essence and profit margins were small, but constant. By his effective management of this distribution pattern, Norris took the lead in the extensive western trade. Hours counted. We must remember that in those days without the ready access we have today to the electronic media, the *news*paper really was *news*. To a public hungry for tales of the exciting events of the day, Norris' jobbing activities were both necessary and vital, as well as being a public service. In 1863 with the opening of the southern Mississippi River, Norris headed for New Orleans to establish "himself in business on his own account." It is not clear what that might have been, but apparently he stayed there eight years.

In 1871, he joined the Diebold Safe and Lock Company, which had been established in Cincinnati just prior to the outbreak of the Civil War. When the company moved to Canton, Ohio in 1872 so did Norris. Diebold was one of the principal safe manufacturers in this country. By 1875, Norris was vice president of the company. In that year he returned to Chicago to take over the branch there. Norris' sales territory was the western United States. "Under his management, the house has prospered greatly, doing now a business amounting to over $500,000 per annum," a Chicago historian recorded a decade later. Successful and rich, Norris married the daughter of a former U.S. Senator.

Auction Census Data Summary, 1891-1994

	1	2	3	5	10	12	24	30	90	Total	Pct
NO	26		11	16	23					76	<1%
	26		**11**	**16**	**23**					**76**	**<1%**

Sands' Ale
Chapter XXXI

Another enterprising Chicagoan who quickly saw the virtues of advertising his product on the backs of Gault's encasements was brewer Josiah J. Sands, whose pieces boldly proclaim "DRINK SANDS' ALE." Because these pieces do not bear a precise location, they have often been misidentified in the past. The record was set straight a decade ago when the present author supplied biographical and historical information for the cataloging of the Ruddy collection. Further details were related by this author in a major front page story in *Coin World* two years later. That article, the lead feature story slanted toward coverage supporting 1986's American Numismatic Association convention in Milwaukee, has been since mistakenly represented to mean that the Sands' Ale pieces exclusively represent Milwaukee in a handful of derivative, published accounts by several authors. Although such accounts have sparked the interest of Wisconsin collectors, at the time Josiah Sands' ordered 3,000 pieces of John Gault's New Metallic Currency, he was a Chicagoan who also had business interests in Milwaukee. As this author wrote in *Coin World*: "It was in the last two locations [Chicago and Milwaukee] that Josiah J. Sands issued his encased stamps of Civil War fame." His reason for not putting an address on the piece in the first place was simply that he sold a nationally distributed product and had agencies in virtually all the major cities. Thus, alas, Sands' Ale pieces are probably the closest to a national issue of New Metallic Currency that

Figure 351a

Reed SA05 obverse. John Wilson collection, ex-James F. Ruddy specimen. (Bowers and Merena photo)

Figure 352a

Looking out at the Chicago Water Tower, center, and Water Works, left, from adjacent to the Sands' Brewery. Unpublished Albumin Silver Print, one half of a stereo view by Lovejoy & Foster, 1871. (Author's collection)

John Gault ever got, excepting the Ayer's issue.

Virtually all of the pieces Josiah Sands ordered were five-cent pieces (Reed SA05). Thus Sands received but $150 face value of these unique store cards. The advertising premium he paid was stiff: 40 percent. Sands was willing to pay this high advertising markup for two reasons. He didn't need small change for customers like the retail merchants who ordered Gault's New Metallic Currency. Besides if this had been his desire, half dimes at the time were selling at about 20 percent premium, or about six cents each compared to the seven cents Gault was charging him. But Sands was strictly interested in the pieces' advertising value, even though this was an expensive price to pay compared to other advertising media available to him. But five cents was the retail price of a beer at the time. What better tout for one's product. Think what a national burger franchise would pay today to overprint a $2 bill with "EAT A BIG BURGER" or some similar message. Gault's currency substitute was a natural for a vendor such as Sands, who was interested in building the value of his franchise. He didn't need to put an address on his pieces. All that was necessary was the slogan: "DRINK SANDS' ALE." The small initial order and wide circulation make this issue one of the three great merchant rarities of this series for the collector today.

At the time brewer Josiah J. Sands purchased his New Metallic Currency he was "well known throughout the West as an energetic and thorough business man." He was born to the trade. His family was an enterprising, upstate New York brewing dynasty who apparently took up the brewers arts in the 1840s. Within a generation members of the Sands family employed their talents in at least six locations in four states. The patriarch of the clan was William Sands of Troy, New York, whose brewery there dates to the 1840s. He had at least

Figure 353a

A large crowd assembled for the laying of the cornerstone for the Chicago Water Tower, March 25, 1867. The large building in the background is Josiah Sands' Columbian Brewery and Malt House built in 1855. Perhaps Sands himself is one of the crowd assembled on the building's roof for a better view of the ceremony. Copy photo of a Copelin and Melander stereoscopic view, 1867. (Chicago Historical Society photo)

four sons who followed him in his business. John G. Sands (born c. 1827) was engaged in brewing in Albany, New York by 1849. William J. Sands joined his father's business in Troy about 1858.

Meanwhile the elder William Sands came west to scout out a location there. He arrived in Chicago in 1853. The city's location was ideal with its proximity to Wisconsin hops and Illinois grains. William Sands must have liked what he saw because his third son, Josiah J. Sands, came west to Chicago in 1854. Josiah found immediate employment at the William Lill and Michael Diversey Brewery on Chicago Avenue. The following year the Sands family constructed their own brewery two blocks to the north. After tearing down a

Figures 354a, b

Right, detail, Wm. J. Sands five-cent scrip, November 1, 1862. (Author's collection) Below, Sands Pale Cream Ale headlined Frank Munroe's Green Room next to McVicker's Theatre. Jeune and Almini lithograph, 1866. (Chicago Historical Society photo, ICHi-06872)

number of small frame buildings, north of Pearson, on the Johnston Roberts and Storr's addition only a block from the then lake front, Josiah Sands constructed the enormous Columbian Brewery and Malt House.

In the new Chicago location, Sands was not only competing with his former employers but a half dozen other established brewers. By the early years of the Civil War, however, Sands' ales were rapidly superceding all the other popular beverages, "a fact," a newspaper account said, "attributable quite as much to their excellency as to any exertion of his [Josiah's]." For those unfamiliar with malt liquors, the grain was steeped in water and then hops were added. Sugar formed in the malt berry during malting. Pale ale, like Sands' product, was made from a high quality light malt to which large amounts of hops were added. Porter was made from a dark, roasted malt. From the first Josiah Sands supplied Milwaukee with the fruits of his Columbian Brewery. His Milwaukee agent was the largest dealer in gro-

Figure 355a

Sands' Ale appealed across social and economic lines: Whether the carriage trade (opposite) or the working class from Charles Tobey's furniture company across the street from this corner pub (note sign above entrance in the lower left), at the corner of State and Randolph Streets. Copy photograph of a daguerreotype, c. 1859. (Chicago Historical Society)

ceries and wines in that city. In Cincinnati, his agent was located across from that city's famous hotel, the Gibson House. Other agents were located as far away as New Orleans. Newspapers of the day claimed Sands' Ale enjoyed a nationwide reputation. This was possible because Sands' ales were not affected by the lack of refrigeration like lager beers were. Consequently Sands could ship his beverages across the union. His "ale is now in every family," a contemporary observed.

Four years after coming to Chicago, Josiah decided he had whet Wisconsin's appetite for his ales. Determined to expand his booming trade, he dispatched his brother Henry 95 miles north to Milwaukee in 1859 to purchase the Eagle Brewery there. The deal was consummated December 8th. This was another bold move. Milwaukee already had two dozen brewers. Even at that early day, the foundations of the city's brewing dynasties were being laid. Sands' purchase made front page news in the Milwaukee press. According to a newspaper account, the building was "the largest establishment of the kind in the city, and probably in the west." It was renamed Sands' Spring Brewery and outfitted in the finest style for the

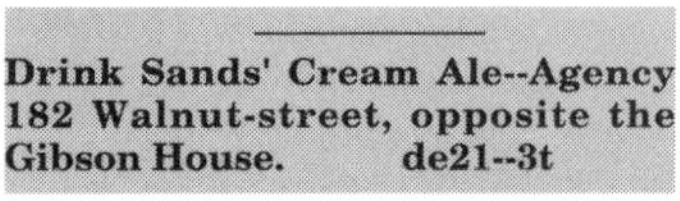

Drink Sands' Cream Ale--Agency 182 Walnut-street, opposite the Gibson House. de21--3t

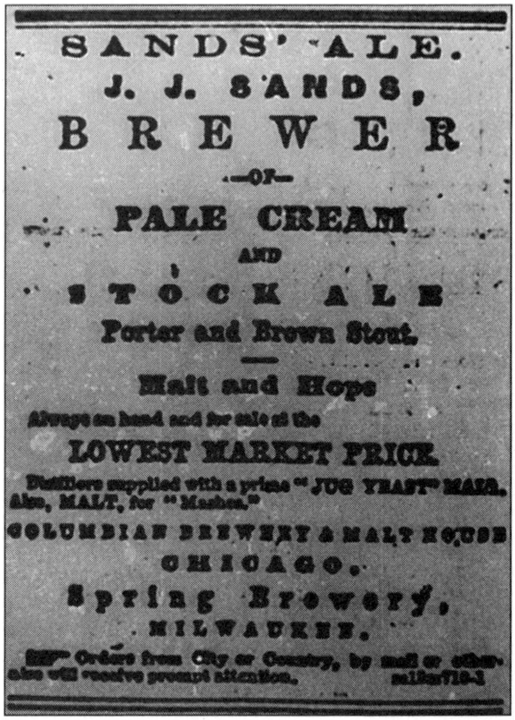

SANDS' ALE.
J. J. SANDS,
BREWER
—OF—
PALE CREAM
AND
STOCK ALE
Porter and Brown Stout.
Malt and Hops
LOWEST MARKET PRICE.
COLUMBIAN BREWERY & MALT HOUSE
CHICAGO.
Spring Brewery,
MILWAUKEE.

Figures 356a, b

Right, Josiah J. Sands, proprietor of breweries in Chicago and Milwaukee, issued the DRINK SANDS' ALE encased stamps. These issues were not, as has been stated, Wisconsin products per se. Sands' Chicago enterprise was the profit center. The Milwaukee branch was a satellite operation. Ad. Chicago Evening Journal, *January 3, 1862, p. 3. (Illinois State Library) Above, Sands' agents were located throughout the major cities, wholesaling his product to local retailers. Ad. Cincinnati* Daily Enquirer, *December 21, 1862, p. 2. (Illinois State Library)*

production of ale. Initially the Spring Brewery was operated by this fourth brother, Henry. He was joined by John G. Sands in 1860. Shortly thereafter Henry moved on to Lansingburg, N.Y., where he operated another brewery briefly before returning to Milwaukee to deal in real estate and lumber. Additionally in the early 1860s William J. Sands operated a sixth brewery in Hartford, Connecticut.

It is clear from a close study of the business arrangements between the two western enterprises that Josiah J. Sands considered the Milwaukee branch to be a satellite of his venture in Chicago. He maintained the strong hand in the family's western brewing ventures. Josiah publicly solicited orders in Milwaukee in his own name. These were forwarded to him in Chicago via a Milwaukee post office box, and then returned to Milwaukee to be filled by his brothers. The large brewery quickly rose to the front rank of producers in that city. Josiah Sands purchased a summer home nearby to enjoy the scenery. After 1864 only malting was done in Milwaukee. Brother John managed the Milwaukee brewery until 1867, when it was sold. Incidentally, Sands' Pale Cream Ale is credited with giving Milwaukee the nickname of the "Cream City." That appellation came to be applied to the Wisconsin city "when Sands' Cream Ale began to be known abroad," according to a Milwaukee newspaper account in 1862.

A frequent advertiser in the press of their day, the Sands' family ales came to enjoy considerable favorable publicity from the newspapers. Sands courted such favorable publici-

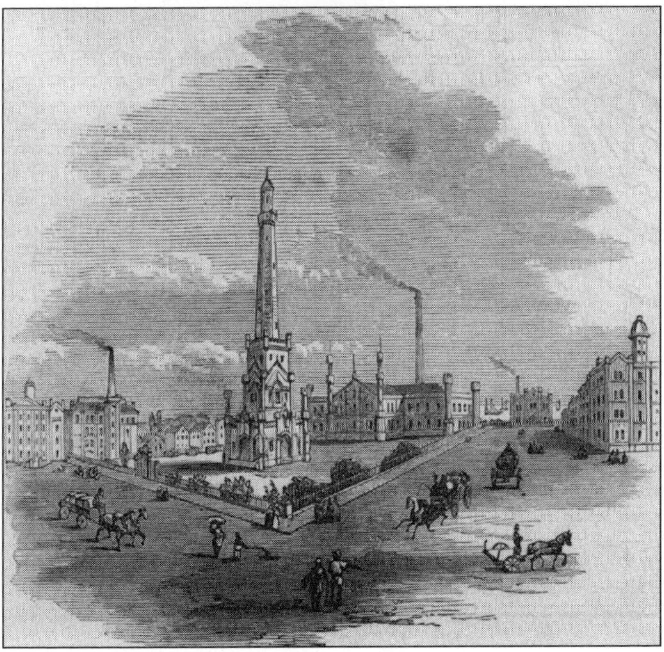

Figures 357a, b
The plaza surrounding the showpiece Chicago Water Tower was an artist's dream. These two remarkably similar renditions are shown for comparative purposes. Both depict Sands' Brewery on the north (left) side of the Water Tower. Top, Lithograph. (Chicago Historical Society, ICHi-17885) Left, engraving. The Illustrated London News, *October 21, 1871, p. 381. (Author's collection)*

ty. A front page account in one of the Milwaukee journals noted:

> The Messrs. Sands of Chicago, have been eminently successful in manufacturing a beverage containing all the wholesome qualities of English porter, without any of its deleterious characteristics. They have produced an article of ale, which has become a staple of commerce all over the Union, and is universally acknowledged by good judges to be a healthier and better drink than the imported bottled beers.

Figure 358a

Sands' Spring Brewery, Milwaukee, Wisconsin. Lithograph, Milwaukee City Directory, *1863. (Wayne L. Kroll collection)*

The newspaper account touted "its palatable taste," calling it slightly aromatic and unintoxicating "even for women and children." Our saloons and citizens would do well to patronize this product, the editor said.

According to ancient legends, ale was the gift of the gods to those "unfortunate ancients whose land was too poor to raise grapes." Both Aristotle and Herodotus speak of 'barley wine, " but even old "Baccus himself would say could he get astride of one of Sands' casks: 'I believe you my boy, here is the best brewer after all,'" a contemporary tout-master opined. Sands advertised his ale for its healthfulness. "Ale is probably one of the most healthful beverages known, and is made with a view to please the palate as well as to conduce [sic] to the benefit of the physical system," he wrote. Elsewhere, he touted his "pure and palatable, popular potation" as "liquid bread."

Nowhere was Sands' Ale appreciated more than in its hometowns. Besides glowing contemporary reviews in the press, contemporary illustrations showing local saloons prove conclusively two things: (1) Josiah Sands was astute about building the franchise for his ales, and (2) saloon owners were well aware of the marquee value and drawing power of Sands' Ale. Saloons emblazoned with such signs catered to all classes of trade. One such is shown in Figure 354b. Frank Munroe's Green Room, located adjacent to McVicker's Playhouse, features Sands' Pale Cream Ale. Since McVicker's was the most costly and impressive theater in the West at that time, and a showcase for impressive drama, it drew notable crowds

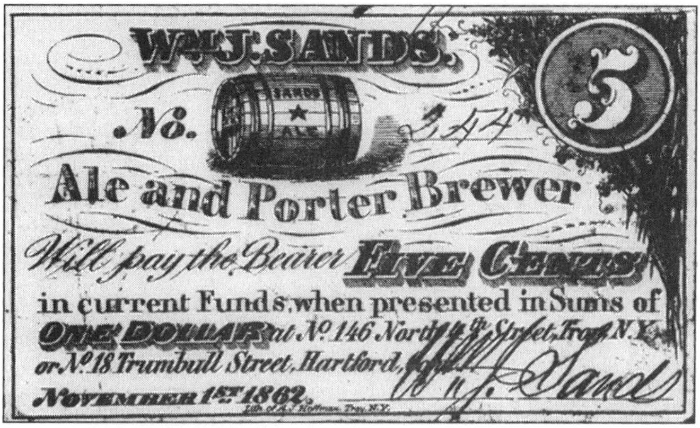

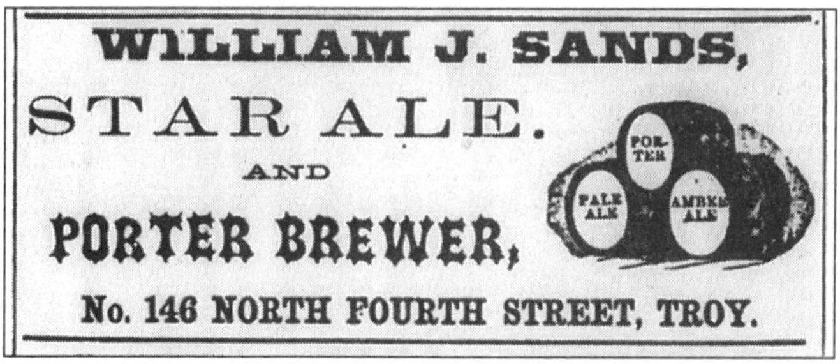

Figures 359a, b

An earlier writer identified William J. Sands, principally of Troy, N.Y., as the issuer of the Sands' Ale encased stamps. Although he apparently had nothing to do with Gault, he was related to the Chicago Sands. He also suffered from the same chronic change shortage. His solution was to issue emergency scrip November 1, 1862. Five-cent note. (Gordon Harris collection) Ad. Troy City *Directory, 1868, p. 302. (Troy Public Library)*

who could be expected to patronize Munroe's pub. As much could be said, though, for the working class poor. Sands' Ale transcended social lines. A contemporary photograph of a small saloon also clearly shows a Sands' Ale sign at Figure 355a. This saloon is located directly across from a large furniture warehouse, where the price of a five-cent drink likely included a sausage and bread lunch for good measure.

In Chicago, Josiah Sands establishment was going gangbusters. His ale was displacing imported English ales. He had a splendid house at the northwest corner of Superior and Rush Streets. With the opening of the Lower Mississippi River, he resumed his ale shipments to New Orleans. In 1863 he restyled his company Sands' Ale Brewing Company, and took Henry M. Fuller, the son of a prominent family, into this company as bookkeeper. In 1866 Richard McClevey became secretary of the company. In the post-war years, Sands' brewery was one of the great dozen of the Chicago companies engaged in the brewing arts. In spring 1867, the workers at the brewery had front row perches to witness the historic laying of the corner stone for the city's water tower. The brewery is shown clearly in a stereoscopic view taken at the time. A number of men are on the roof of the four-story brick brewery viewing the ceremonies nearby. Perhaps Josiah Sands was one of them. In 1869 he hired John F. Stafford to run the company as president and installed a cadre of supporting managers.

Josiah Sands' fortunes were about to change. Sands' brewery was one of five located in

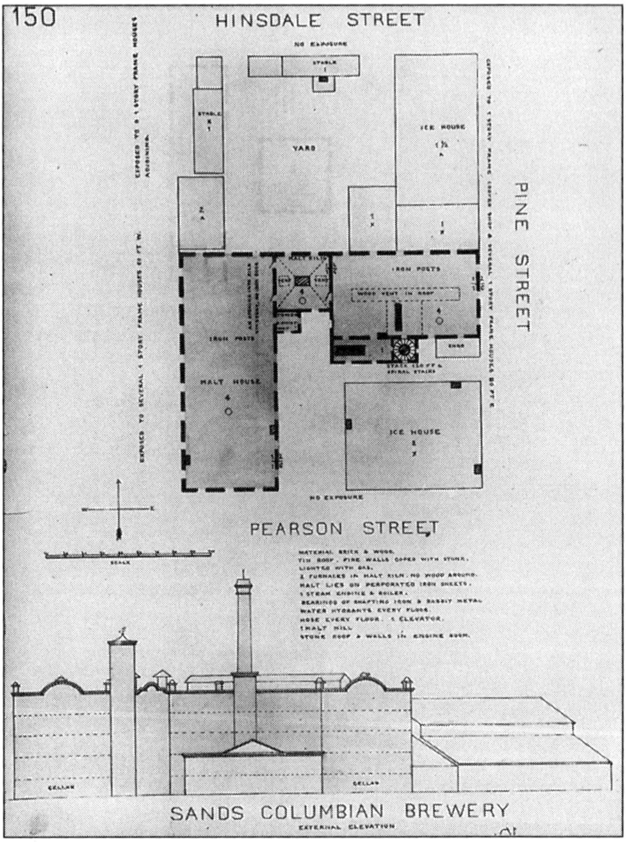

Figure 360a

Interestingly, the street elevation and floor plan from the fire insurance papers on Sands' Brewery survived the Great Chicago Fire. Although the brewery was well equipped with hydrants and hoses, and the municipal water system was right outside its front door, the buildings were exposed on east and west to frame structures which spread the blaze to Sands' Brewery. Illustration. (Chicago Historical Society)

the city's North Division which were destroyed by the Great Chicago Fire of 1871. At the time of the blaze, the superintendent of the brewery was T. D. Stuver, a Dutch immigrant who had previously been a Sands' sales agent. The raging inferno reached Sands' brewery about 3:30-4:00 a.m. and ravaged the building for two hours. A survivor recalled witnessing "very many trying scenes among the wounded, crippled and dying" near Sands' burning brewery. A sad vignette of the overwhelming terror which was brought on by the fire has been preserved by another eyewitness:

> Alderman Bateham reported that night having seen twenty-seven dead bodies during the day, some so mutilated as to be beyond recognition. One of the horrible sights seen . . . was near Sands' Brewery, and which manifested a mother's love. The spectacle presented was that of a dead woman, who had first dug a hole in the sand, and therein placed her child, and while bending over it, to protect it from the fire, both had perished in the flames.

According to the records, Sands' business loss was estimated at $335,000, the third largest loss among the city's brewers. He also lost his house in the blaze. For most, the fire was a financial as well as a personal tragedy. There was little or no insurance on most such buildings. But at least the fire was not a complete loss for Josiah Sands. In an era when fire was a primary terror, Sands fortunately carried fire insurance on his Columbian Brewery.

Figures 361a, b

Above, the devastation to Sands' Brewery in the wake of the October 9, 1871, blaze is clearly shown in the above engraving. Illustration, History of the Great Conflagration, *1871, p. 395. (Author's collection) This devastation is confirmed by the photograph at left. Unpublished Albumin Silver Print, one half of a stereo view by Lovejoy and Foster, 1871. (Author's collection)*

While researching this book, the present author discovered a detailed rendering of Sands' brewery among the fire insurance maps of the city. From information available, Sands' insurance agent was the firm of B. W. Phillips and Co. As can be seen in an engraving of the brewery's gutted remains, there was little left of this once thriving commercial enterprise in the fire's wake.

The passing of Sands' brewery was not lamented by everyone. At least one of the local religious newspapers applauded the progress of the fire which "also fortunately destroyed a large number of [Chicago's] breweries and saloons." Sands' brewery was not rebuilt after the fire. He sold his real estate through Hiram Wheeler to Charles B. Farwell and John V.

Figure 362a

Right, Sands' brewery's location was a prime one. It still is. The former location of Sands' Brewery is now the site of I. Magnin department store, shown at right with the familiar Water Tower in the foreground. To its right are Water Tower Place shopping mall and the John Hancock Building farther up Michigan Avenue. Photo (Author's collection)

Farwell. They built palatial homes there overlooking the nearby lakefront. Josiah Sands engaged in the lumber business briefly, but left the city in 1874. Today, of course, that portion of Chicago – just south of its "Miracle Mile" – is among the most precious real estate parcels in the country. Located across from Chicago's famous international trade center, Water Tower Place, the site is presently occupied by the fashionable retailer I. Magnin and the Blackhawk commercial and residential building.

At the peak of its production, Sands' breweries turned out about 100 barrels of ale a day. Each barrel held 30 gallons. Some 5,000 gallons of stock ale were on hand in the brewery's vaults at any one time. Since most of the ale was shipped in casks of varying sizes to distant locations, bottling was not a primary activity. Despite its large output, according to an expert in the field of collecting breweriana, no Sands' Ale bottles are known.

Auction Census Data Summary, 1891-1994

	1	2	3	5	10	12	24	30	90	Total	Pct
SA				41	10	2	0	5		58	<1%
				41	**10**	**2**	**0**	**5**		**58**	**<1%**

Tremont House
Chapter XXXII

The largest customer John Gault had west of the Hudson River was the proprietorship of Chicago's Tremont House hotel, who in 1862 were brothers George W. and David A. Gage and John B. Drake. This trio purchased more than 25,000 pieces of Gault's New Metallic Currency in fall 1862. Eighty percent of this order was for five-cent (Reed TH05) and ten-cent (Reed TH10) pieces. Remaining pieces were approximately evenly divided among one-, three- and twelve-cent denominations. Face value of the purchase came to about $1,750. The purchase totalled about $2,300. The premium over face was thirty percent, a high price for small change. This enormous quantity of store cards is highly indicative of both the hotel's stature as a public house and of its proprietors' business acumen. All three of the proprietors had diverse and lucrative business interests. Their hotel was at the forefront of the carriage trade. And each of the individuals fancied himself as a business and civic leader and man about town. In fact, of all the clients John Gault served with his emergency currency, Drake and the Gages are probably the most interesting characters of the lot. Each deserves his own chapter, but alas not in the present work.

The name "Tremont House" in Chicago is almost as old as the city itself, and the saga of the successive hotels which have borne that name there are illustrative of the entire canvass of that great city's remarkable history during the past century and a half. In fact the first such structure there was built in 1832, the same year that Chicago received its town charter.

Figure 363a

Reed TH05 obverse, ex-James F. Ruddy specimen. (Bowers and Merena photo)

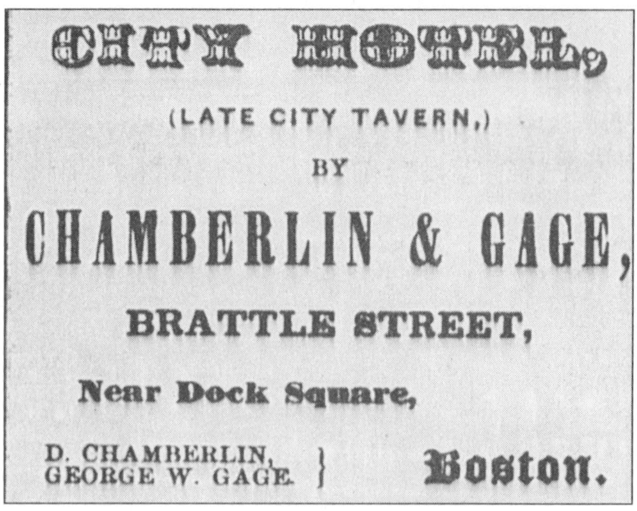

Figures 364a, b

George W. Gage learned the inn-keeping business from Daniel Chamberlin at Boston's City Hotel, a converted public house. Above, reversed copy photo of Southworth and Hawes daguerreotype, Brattle Street, c. 1855. (Author's collection) Right, Ad. Adams' Boston City Directory, 1846, p. 15. (Dallas Public Library)

Figure 365a

An unpublished cabinet photo of George W. Gage by Copelin and Son. (Chicago Historical Society photo, ICHi-10358)

Built by Alanson Sweet, the name was borrowed from the famous Boston hotel of that name, which had opened its doors five years earlier and launched luxury hotels across the country. Unlike its namesake, however, this Tremont at the northwest corner of Lake and Dearborn Streets was a crude three story frame building, with boarding rooms over a saloon. Several years later easterners James and Ira Couch leased the building, outfitted it in style and conducted a successful business there until fire levelled the building in 1839. The Couches were not quitters. They leased property katycorner to the burned out hulk a month later, and constructed a 100 room hotel there. This was the first of several successive structures of the same name which would occupy that same lot for most of the next century. A success for a decade, this second Tremont succumbed to the same fate as its predecessor. In 1849, it too burned to the ground. Still determined, the Couches purchased additional adjacent land, and vowed the next Tremont House would be fire proof. A new five-story Tremont literally arose from its own ashes as the city's largest hotel. Dubbed "Couch's Folly," it contained 260 rooms and cost an unprecedented $75,000 to erect. Its furnishings cost

Figures 366a,b

Chicago's first Tremont House was the building on the corner in this watercolor by N. Roswell Gifford, probably painted c. 1900. It clearly shows Dearborn and Lake Streets prior to the fire of 1839. Photo. (Chicago Historical Society photo, ICHi-04304). The "Brother" in Gage Brother and Drake was David A. Gage, right. Photo. (Chicago Historical Society photo, ICHi-10356)

another $30,000. The hotel was the tallest brick building in the city when it opened to the public September 29, 1850. "No hotel in the Union [is] superior to it in any respect," a contemporary observed.

This is the elegant Tremont House of encased stamp fame a dozen years later, at that time still one of the finest accommodations in the country. The Couches managed the property until 1853 when they decided to shop its lease around. In Boston, a young hotel manag-

Figures 367a, b

The last member of the triumvirate which issued the encased stamps was John B. Drake, left. Copy photo (reversed) from a daguerreotype, c. 1850-55. Gift of Miss Helen Drake. (Chicago Historical Society photo ICHi-16347) Contrary to published views elsewhere, the trade style of the partnership is correctly rendered on the encased stamp, to wit: GAGE BROTHER *(sic) &* DRAKE. *Witness the ad, below.* Hall's Chicago City Directory, *1855, p. 64. (Dallas Public Library) Also, see advertising cover at Figure 372a.*

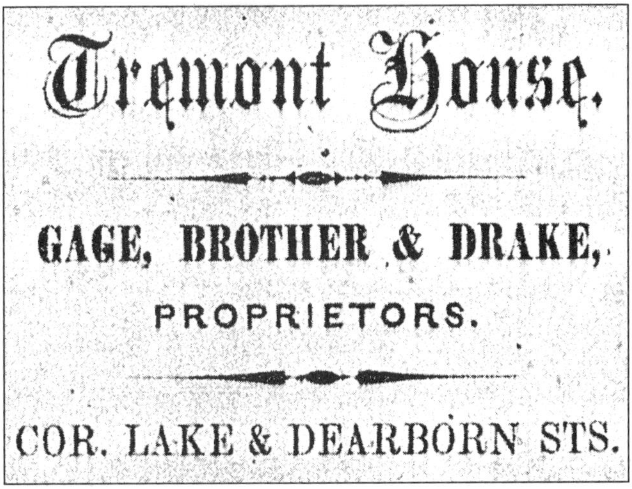

Tremont House.

GAGE, BROTHER & DRAKE,

PROPRIETORS.

COR. LAKE & DEARBORN STS.

er with capital and vision was interested in just such an opportunity. He was George W. Gage, then co-proprietor of Boston's City Hotel. Gage had been born March 9, 1812, the sixth of 15 children. An ancestor had been an officer in the French & Indian War and Revolutionary War. Reared on a New Hampshire farm, he began working in a tavern at age 14. He saved $14 from his wages for a winter's work. He moved on to a job as a room clerk

Figures 368a, b, c

Both Abraham Lincoln and Stephen A. Douglas frequented Tremont House. Engravings. (Author's collection) Each addressed large crowds from the hotel's balcony, below, to kick off their famous series of debates. Photo, one half of a stereo view by J. Carbutt. (Chicago Historical Society photo, ICHi-00771)

Figures 369a, b

The Chicago Philatelic Society has commemorated the Tremont's central role in the Lincoln-Douglas Congressional campaign drama several times. Left, detail from CPS cover, Scott 1115 Lincoln Douglas Debates commemorative stamp cover, 1958. Below, CPS cover, Scott 1116 Daniel Chester French Statue of Lincoln commemorative stamp cover, 1959. (Both, Author's collection)

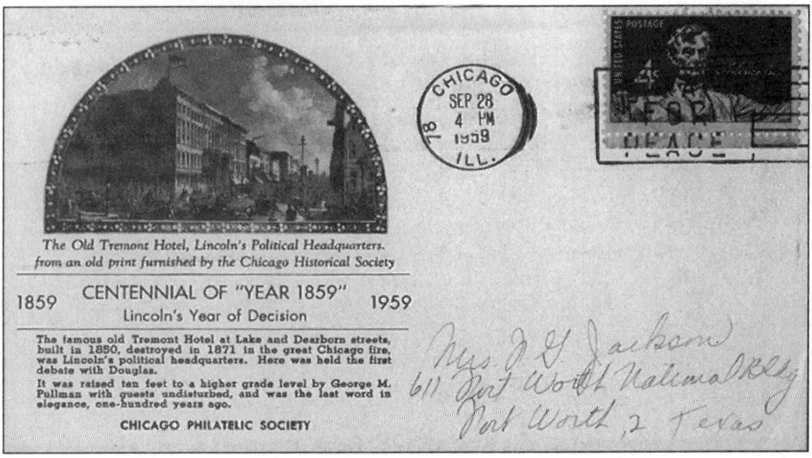

at a Lowell, Massachusetts hotel and saved up a thousand dollars. About 1840, he came to the City Hotel in Boston, first becoming a clerk and then five years later partner. After seven years, he amassed $17,000. Then hearing of the opportunity in Chicago, he dispatched his younger brother David A. Gage to Chicago to investigate its prospects. Dave, as he was called, "reported Chicago [as] a big mud hole, but from the location justified to be a big city." George came west, leased the Tremont and purchased its furnishings for $3,000 from the Couch brothers. He left the City Hotel in the care of his brother-in-law William F. Tucker. In 1853, the Tremont's new management was styled Gage & Brother. Dave had been born June 30, 1822. His early occupation was as a train conductor on the Keene, N.H., Railroad, but in 1852 he became a steward in his brother's hotel. Under the Gages, the

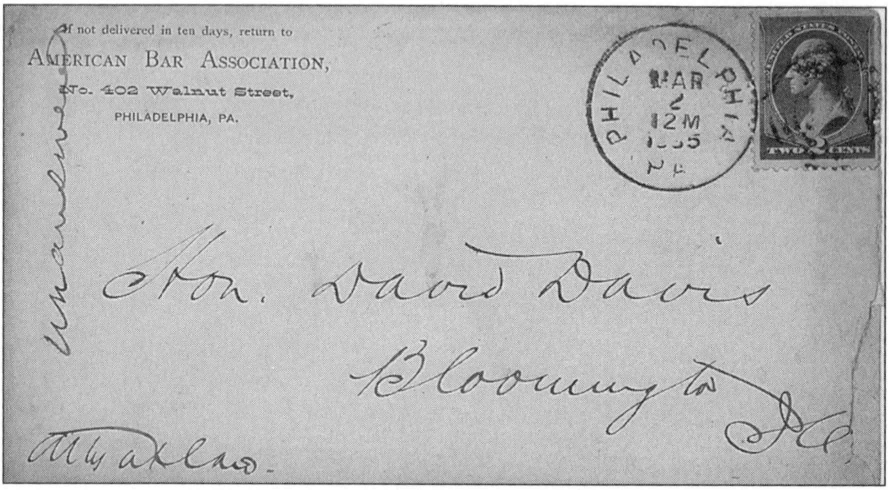

Figures 370a, b

In 1860 the Tremont was Lincoln's campaign headquarters for the Republican Nominating Convention. Lincoln's chief strategist, 350-pound David Davis, top, roamed its halls muscling delegates in a masterful display of political maneuvering. Lincoln rewarded the hulking politico with a seat on the U.S. Supreme Court. Cover from American Bar Association to Justice Davis, Scott No. 210, March 2, 1885. (Author's collection) Above, eccentric author and presidential candidate George Francis Train (first row, third from left) also posed on a Tremont balcony with his party in 1865. Carte de Visite. (Chicago Historical Society photo, ICHi-14249)

Tremont prospered. The Couches sued for higher rent, but the Gages won.

In 1855, John B. Drake, born January 17, 1826 in Lebanon, Ohio, purchased one-fourth interest in the Tremont from the Gages. Forced at age 11 by the death of his father to

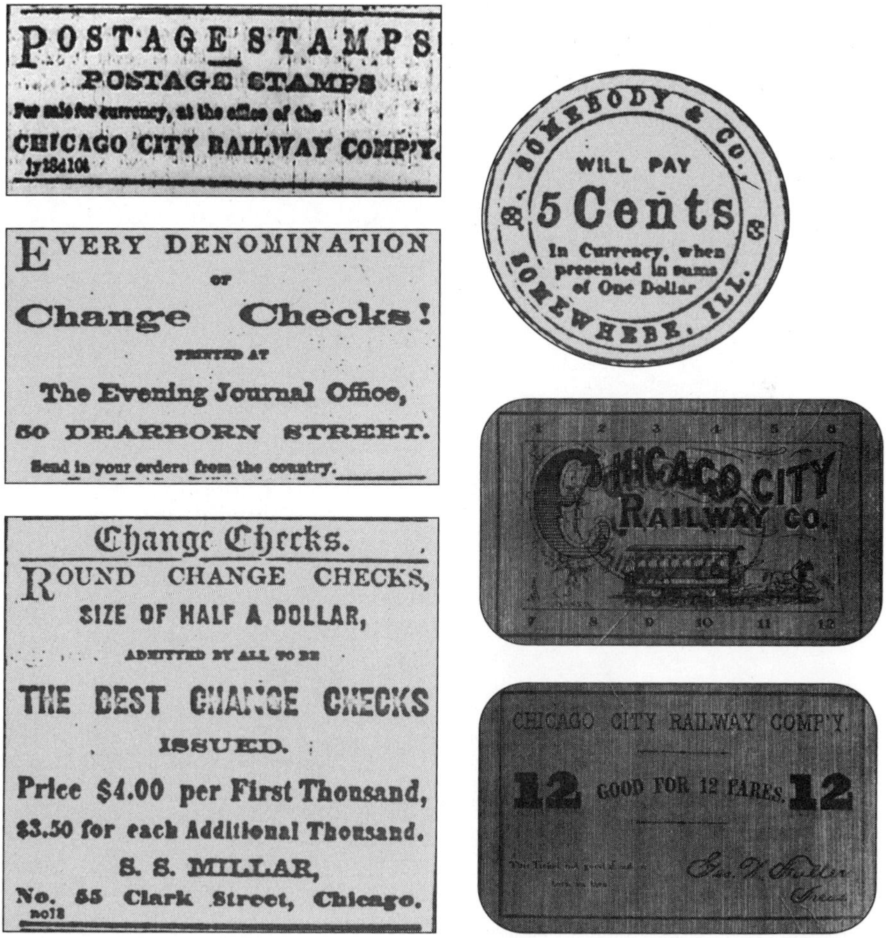

Figures 371a-f

David A. Gage was a principal in the Chicago City Railway, which cornered the market offering postage stamps for sale as currency for 10 days in the later half of July, 1862. Ad, top left, Chicago Evening Journal, *July 28, 1862, p. 1. (Illinois State Library). When stamp supplies ran short, the company's tickets, above right, circulated as small change. Woodcuts.* History of Chicago, *Vol. 2, 1886, p. 120. (Dallas Public Library) Change checks, round cardboard discs, printer's sample top right, proliferated in Chicago. Even the newspaper offered to print them for interested parties. Ads, left, Chicago* Evening Journal, *November 5 and 13, 1862. (Illinois State Library)*

seek employment, he clerked in a local general store for several years. He then clerked in a road house, before arriving in Cincinnati in 1845, where he obtained a position at the Pearl Street House and eventually as steward of the newly-completed Burnet House. In 1854 he moved to Chicago and sold insurance briefly before joining the Gage brothers as their stew-

Figures 372a, b

Advertising covers trace the lineage of the Tremont House ownership. Top, yellow Illustrated Cover reverse, Gage, Brother & Drake, Proprietors, November 12, 1857. (Dennis Forgue collection) Bottom, yellow Illustrated Cover reverse, Gage & Drake, Proprietors, September 18, 1867, received (Chicago) September 20, 1867. (Dennis Forgue collection)

ard. Thereafter the trade style of the hotel became Gage, Brother & Drake, just as it is on the encased stamps. The Gages were quick movers. In 1857 they built the five story Massasoit House, which they leased to other operators.

Under its new management, the Tremont developed an illustrious style hosting sporting, civic and society functions. It also developed an illustrious clientele. Abraham Lincoln became a frequent visitor and close friend of the proprietors. George W. Gage, especially, became an intimate of the prairie lawyer. A New England abolitionist, the elder Gage

Figures 373a, b, c

David A. Gage came into his own with his move to the newly erected Sherman House hotel in 1863 shortly after circulating the New Metallic Currency. Briefly, out from under the wing of his older brother and no longer the least member of an odd menage a trois management team at the Tremont House, he cut a dashing swath across Chicago civic and social life. Dave Gage's meteoric career crashed a decade later. Left, Advertising Handbill. (Chicago Historical Society) Below, elder brother George, at attention in his Chicago Light Guard regalia (detail, inset), and other dignitaries who included John B. Drake receive Lincoln's hearse and funeral procession in Chicago en route to burial in Springfield, Illinois. Photo. (Library of Congress)

Figures 374a, b

Left, John B. Drake, Watercolor Portrait. (Chicago Historical Society) Below, Illustrated Cover reverse, John B. Drake Proprietor, Scott No. 147, September 15, 1870. (Author's collection)

Figures 375a, b

Opposite, David A. Gage was Treasurer of Chicago's White Stockings in 1870. Carte de Visite. (Walter Handelman collection) The club played both amateur and professional clubs, compiling an enviable record. (Original Compilation by the Author)

Kearl, Sub. Duffy, S.S. Tracy, L.F. Hodes, Sub. Flynn, R.F. Cuthbert, C.F. Meyerle, 3dB. Pinkham, P. Wood, 2dB. McAtee, 1stB. King, C.

1870 Chicago White Stockings Season Record

1870 Date	Versus	W-L	Score	Pro Record	Overall Record
5/8	@ New Orleans Lone Stars	W*	18-10		1-0
6/20	@ Cleveland Forest Citys	W	24-8	1-0	2-0
6/27	@ Troy Haymakers	W	25-21	2-0	3-0
6/30	@ Harvard	W*	33-7		4-0
7/4	@ Brooklyn Atlantics	L	20-30	2-1	4-1
7/6	@ New York Mutuals	L	4-13	2-2	4-2
7/8	@ Morrisania Union	W	28-12	3-2	5-2
7/9	@ Brklyn vs NJ Waverly Stars	W*	9-6		6-2
7/11	@ Philadelphia Athletics	L	12-17	3-3	6-3
7/16	@ Washington Olympics	W	27-9	4-3	7-3
7/23	@ New York Mutuals	L	6-9	4-4	7-4
7/26	@ Harvard	L*	6-11		7-5
7/30	Brooklyn Atlantics	W	12-4	5-4	8-5
8/1	Philadelphia Athletics	L	11-18	5-5	8-6
8/4	New Orleans Lone Stars	W*	42-8		9-6
8/5	Troy Haymakers	L	11-16	5-6	9-7
8/10	Washington Olympics	W	16-15	6-6	10-7
8/17	Chicago Aetna	W*	43-8		11-7
8/23	Brooklyn Eckfords	W	22-6	7-6	12-7
9/7	Cincinnati Red Stockings	W	10-6	8-6	13-7
9/17	Cleveland Forest Citys	W	9-8	9-6	14-7
9/26	Philadelphia Athletics	W	12-11	10-6	15-7
9/26	Brooklyn Atlantics	W	9-4	11-6	16-7
9/27	New York Mutuals	W	22-11	12-6	17-7
10/1	Chicago Aetna	W*	37-9		18-7
10/13	Cincinnati Red Stockings	W	16-13	13-6	19-7
11/1	New York Mutuals	W	7-5	14-6	20-7

* = amateur team

quickly identified with the Republican party and became active in its circles. His hotel became Lincoln's Chicago home when he was in town to attend to the District Court. It

Figures 376a, b

In 1871 the White Stockings, right, were members of the first professional baseball league, the National Association. Carte de Visite by Lovejoy and Foster, 1871. (Transcendental Graphics photo) The ball club played its games in a lakefront park constructed on public lands near the Illinois Central railroad yards, secured by Dave Gage and his cronies. This site lay opposite Michigan Avenue south of the river, shown at number 3 below. Bird's-eye Engraving (detail), Harper's Weekly, *October 21, 1871. (Author's collection)*

Figure 377a

Another view of the 1871 White Stockings. Carte de Visite composite photo by O. F. Weaver, 1871. This club had the best talent money could buy. Pitcher George Zeitlein, known as "the Snake" or "the Charmer" for his inviting but unhitable pitching arsenal, had learned the game while serving in the Union Army. Batsman James Wood, one of the feared hitters in the league, played second sacker and most other positions as well. As may be imagined from the composite photo, the club's young, good-looking cast played as hard as they worked at the game. Gage and its other owners saw to it that a good time was had by all. The club's owners were innovative. They pioneered Spring Training by taking their crew to New Orleans and barnstorming north prior to the season's opening. Not nearly so famous as the Cincinnati Red Stockings, this club is the direct ancestor of Chicago's Cubs, not its White Sox. Copeland collection. (Sotheby's photo)

also increasingly became a political rallying point for Lincoln's successive campaigns. Lincoln addressed a large crowd there during his 1858 congressional campaign. During the 1860 Republic convention, the Tremont was Lincoln's campaign headquarters. Judge David Davis and Lincoln's other "handlers" roamed its halls wrestling the nomination from the grasps of the other Republican contenders. Following Lincoln's nomination, a cannon atop the hotel was fired "one hundred times, while Chicago [turned] itself upside down with rapture." After his election, Lincoln and his family lived at the hotel for a week before going on to Washington for the inauguration.

With the coming of the war, George Gage, who had been active as an officer in the Chicago Light Guard turned his attention to fund raising to equip Illinois units forming for military service. A genuine patriot, after all his given name was George Washington Gage, he raised tens of thousands of dollars in this patriotic cause. He also purchased the services of two representative recruits. These enlistees were different from substitutes. Recruited at the expense of private individuals, the recruit represented the individual who recruited him. These recruiters were men of means who were not obligated to military service. Gage was also active in supporting the relief corps, and in assisting prisoners at Camp Douglas. During the war he was elected to the city council and to the state legislature. Following Lincoln's assassination, Gage and Drake were among principals who received Lincoln's remains *en*

1871 Chicago White Stockings

Date	Opponent	W-L	Score	Pro Record	Overall Record
3/26	@ New Orleans Lone Stars+	W?*	6-?		(1-0)
4/16	@ New Orleans Lone Stars+	W?*	7-?		(2-0)
4/23	@ St. Louis Empire	W*	34-8		3-0
5/8	Cleveland Forest Citys	W	12-14	1-0	4-0
5/11	@ Cleveland Forest Citys	W	18-10	2-0	5-0
5/13	Fort Wayne Kekiongas	W	14-5	3-0	6-0
5/16	Washington Olympics	W	14-4	4-0	7-0
5/19	Washington Olympics	W	9-7	5-0	8-0
5/22	Rockford Forest Citys	W	15-6	6-0	9-0
5/30	@ Brooklyn Stars	W*	1-?		10-0
6/2	@ Boston Red Stockings	W	16-14	7-0	11-0
6/5	@ Brooklyn Mutuals	W	8-5	8-0	12-0
6/7	@ Elizabeth (NJ) Resolutes	W*	17-4		13-0
6/8	@ Philadelphia Athletics	L	11-15	8-1	13-1
6/9	@ Philadelphia Olympics	W*	17-2		14-1
6/10	@ Philadelphia Experts	W*	24-2		15-1
6/10	@ Washington Olympics	L	3-12	8-2	15-2
6/21	Chicago Aetna	W*	12-3		16-2
6/22	Chicago Aetna	L*	8-16		16-3
6/26	Rockford Forest Citys	W	18-8	9-2	17-3
---	Washington Olympics	L	8-13	9-3	17-4
7/4	Rockford Forest Citys	W	17-12	10-3	18-4
7/7	Boston Red Stockings	W	7-1	11-3	19-4
7/14	Philadelphia Athletics	W	11-9	12-3	20-4
7/22	New Orleans Lone Stars	W*	15-3		21-4
7/28	Brooklyn Mutuals	W	17-6	13-3	22-4
8/1	Brooklyn Mutuals	W	15-4	14-3	23-4
8/5	Fort Wayne Kekiongas	W	13-10	15-3	24-4
8/10	Cleveland Forest Citys	L	10-12	15-4	24-5
8/12	Chicago Aetna	W*	27-2		25-5
8/16	Washington Olympics	W	12-11	16-4	26-5
8/23	Brooklyn Stars	W*	2-?		27-5
8/28	@ Brooklyn Mutuals	W	6-4	17-4	28-5
8/30	@ Philadelphia Athletics	W	6-3	18-4	29-5
9/4	@ New York Fire Flies	W*	14-8		30-5
9/5	@ Boston Red Stockings	L	3-6	18-5	30-6
9/18	Philadelphia Athletics	L	6-11	18-6	30-7
---	Boston Red Stockings	W	10-8	19-6	31-7
10/2	Chicago Aetna	W*	26-4		32-7
10/8	GREAT CHICAGO FIRE				
	Cleveland Forest Citys	DNP			
10/21	@ Troy Haymakers	W	11-5	20-6	33-7
10/23	@ Troy Haymakers	L	12-19	20-7	33-8
10/30	Phil. Athletics @ Brooklyn	L	1-4	20-8	33-9
11/1	Troy Haymakers @ Brooklyn	L	9-13	20-9	33-10
---	Troy Haymakers	DNP			
---	Fort Wayne Kekiongas	W#	Forfeit	21-9	34-10

+ 1871 Southern Champions

* = amateur team

sources conflict re. game's status in standings

Figure 378a (opposite), Figure 379a (above)

The 1871 White Stockings were a powerhouse, mowing down opposition in baseball's first professional season. Well on its way to a pennant as the first champion of the National Association, disaster struck on October 8 as shown on the reconstructed game summary, opposite. (Original Compilation by the Author) This disaster, of course, shown above in a powerful engraving of the conflagration torching the Tremont House, was felt in more severe ways than an interruption to the baseball season. However, its stadium gone, the team finished its season on the road losing its championship, too. When the team was revived two years later George Gage became its president. Engraving. Frank Leslie's Illustrated Newspaper, *October 28, 1871. (Author's collection)*

route to burial in Springfield. He narrowly lost election as Chicago's mayor, but became a park commissioner.

His younger brother, who had been left a widower with a young daughter by the death of his first wife in 1850, married a vivacious beauty who became a social charmer in Chicago society. She was also a charming hostess for affairs at the hotel. David, himself, "was a handsome man with a fascinating personality," according to an admiring female. He worked hard. He played harder. He was very prominent in the fast crowd of rich, young men out to create a social swirl in the community. He was active in betting circles. He became a prime mover in sports regattas, horse racing, and eventually in the formation of Chicago's first professional baseball club, the White Stockings. He was one of the original subscribers to its incorpo-

Figure 380a

The blazing inferno that raced across Chicago leveled the city and many of its most elegant buildings, including the Tremont House. The destruction of the famous Chicago landmark was total. Inexplicably the back bar bottle at right survived the holocaust. Only two such bottles are known. This pint bottle bears the legend JOHN B. DRAKE / TREMONT HOUSE / CHICAGO / ILLS. (Electronic imaging by Omar Mediano, Author's collection)

ration in 1869, and served as its president and treasurer. Dave Gage was active in securing a public park near the lake front for construction of its ball park. The club enjoyed great success in 1870. The following season, it was on the brink of capturing the first professional championship when the holocaust burned its park, its equipment, and sent the team on the road only to collapse at season's end.

David Gage also was active in local politics. As a measure of his independence, he was originally a Douglas-Democrat, and the great orator had also been a frequent visitor to the hotel. Douglas had kicked off his successful 1858 Senatorial campaign there, and in fact died while in residence at the hotel in summer 1861. Finally succumbing to the tenor of his time, on the local scene, David Gage became a Republican and was elected city treasurer. During and following the war, Gage and his cronies played fast and loose with the city's finances. They succeeded in securing a favorable treatment for their plan for constructing a street railway. During the change shortage, the railway cornered the market on postage stamps, which it sold at a profit to the public. This was done despite the law of March 1855 which made it illegal to sell stamps above face value. Thereafter, the railway furnished $150,000 of its tickets to the public on the same basis, becoming – practically speaking – a bank of issue.

Figures 381a, b

Art imitates life in the total devastation of the Tremont House. Above, an historic reproduction from a glass slide. Three men pose amidst the ruins. The man in bowler at center is believed to be John B. Drake. Photo. (Chicago Historical Society photo, ICHi-02848) Left, A dozen survivors pick through the hotel's rubble. Engraving. The Illustrated London News, *November 18, 1871, p. 472. (Author's collection)*

Figure 382a

John B. Drake was not the only inn keeper to suffer the cruel results of the inferno. David A. Gage's Sherman House was similarly leveled. It's not hard to imagine that the two gentlemen in the lower right, above, are the former business partners – turned friendly competitors – commiserating upon their losses. Engraving. The Illustrated London News, *November 11, 1871, p. 448. (Author's collection)*

The third party to the issue of the encased stamps, John B. Drake, was also a bon vivant and raconteur. "A political, business and social gadfly of the era, . . . [Drake] was probably the most distinctive of the hotel's operators," according to a local historian. He was famous for the elaborate cuisine he prepared, especially at Thanksgiving time. Menus included such exotica as antelope, buffalo hump, mountain sheep or blackbirds, in addition to traditional fare. Social balls and debutante fetes were a specialty, as was a gentlemen's club organized at the hotel. Originally a Breckinridge-Democrat, Drake readily embraced republicanism and became a willing host to a succession of political and military guests at elaborate festivities at his hotel. At the time they issued their encased stamps, the Tremont was a beehive of activity. The year before the hotel had been raised eight feet by George Pullman, 1,200 workers and 5,000 jackscrews. When it had reached the appropriate height, a solid foundation was fitted underneath the hotel. The entire structure was then lowered 22 inches, coming to rest six feet and two inches above its original level. This miracle, to raise the hotel out of the muck and mire, was completed in seven weeks. Business proceeded as usual, and "not a mortared joint cracked." The streets were then raised to a similar grade level. At that time, the hotel itself underwent extensive renovations, making it practically new. The Michigan Central Railroad ticket office was located on its first floor. Other merchants along its arcade were a jeweller, a clothier, a hatter, a furniture store, a tailor, a drug-

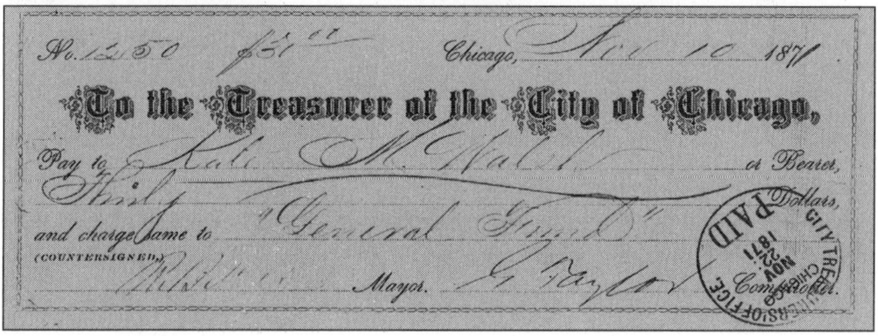

Figures 383a, b

The Gages' frustration must have been great when their newly erected Pacific Hotel suffered the same fate as their Sherman House. Top, Engraving. The Illustrated London News, *November 11, 1871, p. 448. (Author's collection) As city treasurer, Dave Gage was responsible for expending city relief funds in the tumultuous days following the fire. Above, draft from the mayor and comptroller to Gage, paid by him November 22, 1871. (Dennis Forgue collection)*

gist and a tobacconist. All created a lot of traffic for the proprietors' New Metallic Currency. The *Evening Journal*, with its presses printing change checks, was just across the street.

Wartime business boomed, but Dave Gage was growing restive. As Drake came on in the partnership, he felt increasingly odd-man-out. Further, he was tired of being second fiddle to his older brother. He was looking for a chance to make his own mark. This falling out found its opportunity for action shortly after circulating the New Metallic Currency. In 1863, David Gage withdrew from the Tremont's management, sold his share, and became a partner in the rival Sherman House two blocks west. The Sherman was newly built, having opened in July 1861. It too was large, and splendid. Overlooking the Public Square at the corner of Clark and Randolph, it was valued at more than a half million dollars. The Tremont's management was restyled Gage & Drake. By 1868 Drake became sole owner of the Tremont. Eventually, family differences repaired, George Gage joined his younger brother in the management of the Sherman House. By decade's end, the Gages were also erecting

Figure 384a

Drake did not own the hotel, only the Tremont's lease, when it was levelled in the massive Chicago blaze. The hotel of encased stamp fame was still owned by James Couch, right, who made a career and became a legend in Chicago by resurrecting his Tremont House from its own ashes. Couch built and rebuilt successively more splendid edifices at the southeast corner of Lake and Dearborn Streets following the devasting fires of 1839, 1849, and 1871. His rebuilt Tremont House reappeared in even grander style following the Great Chicago Fire. Cabinet Card Photo by Brisbois. (Chicago Historical Society photo, ICHi-16344)

an even more splendid palace, the Grand Pacific Hotel.

Although all three men were actively involved in a plethora of business deals during this time, most of which were farsighted and successful, Dave Gage especially was on a bewildering roller coaster ride of speculative ventures involving him with a fast crowd of tough businessmen. These were the same individuals with whom he was associated in the sporting and gaming ventures. The schemes were overlapping and interlocking, as the city's merchant capitalists attempted to outdo one another in a very real game of one upmanship. Often they merely "borrowed" Gage's good name for a minor piece of the action, putting him on the top of their letterhead as superintendent, president, treasurer and the like. It must have been a heady experience for the dashing, debonair, mutton-chopped Gage.

Drake played the grand host in style in the years following the war. He relished the opportunities to mingle with the rich, the powerful, the talented and good looking. He fancied himself a dandy. One of Drake's most controversial guests was eccentric world traveler George Francis Train. Train addressed a packed audience on Saturday night October 7, 1871. He drew his talk to a close and brought the crowd to its feet with his final remark: "This is the last public address that will be delivered within these walls! A terrible calamity is impending over the city of Chicago! More I cannot say; more I dare not utter." He might just as well have cried the proverbial "Fire." The hotel was dead in the path of the calamity which shortly befell the city and claimed nearly 18,000 of its buildings. The hotel's tin roof caught fire about 3 a.m. Monday morning October 9th. As vividly shown by the illustrations in this chapter, this once magnificent structure was reduced to a pile of rubble by the flames and attendant explosions. Nothing escaped from the once proud hotel except a proverbial single Bible page from an Old Testament prophesy about judgement, and a few phantoms such as the bar bottle shown in this chapter. The first hand accounts of the survivors, including George Gage's daughter, are poignant. But the decisive Drake snatched deliver-

Figures 385a, b
Left, 19th century Chicago without its Tremont House at the southeast corner of Lake and Dearborn Streets would have been unthinkable. Couch's splendid phoenix restoration of the historic hostelry, left, truly represented the city's remarkable resurgence from its holocaust. Copelin Photo, c. 1878-79. (Chicago Historical Society photo, ICHi-00774) Below, in keeping with the manner reborn, Couch's lovely advertising cover was splendidly engraved with pennants and flags unfurled by Western Bank Note Co. Cover, probably Scott No.158, June 24, c. 1874. (Dennis Forgue collection)

ance from the ovens of Hell. Even while the Tremont was aflame, Drake purchased the Michigan Hotel in a bizarre fire sale. He paid out $1,000 in the street for the hotel's lease-

Figures 386a, b

Far from being personally wiped out, Drake emerged from the fire's aftermath to the most successful chapters of his life. Fabulously rich, with a Midas touch, the raconteur added to his personal legend in his new digs at the Grand Pacific Hotel. Right, Engraving. Chicago and Its Makers, *p. 646. Genealogy collection, Dallas Public Library. (James Chefchis photo) Below, he numbered among his successful real estate ventures the rebuilt Drake Block on Wabash Avenue at Washington Street. Stereo view by Copelin and Melander, c. 1874. (Author's collection)*

hold. Drake's gamble paid off. The Michigan Hotel ultimately escaped the blaze. Drake renamed the building the Tremont. As the only public house still standing in the area, the purchase was a bonanza. It was filled to capacity for the next two years while the city cleared its rubble and restored its infrastructure. The Sherman House suffered the same ignoble fate as the Tremont House. But Drake's former partners, the Gage brothers, also turned their loss to gain by purchasing the newly built but not yet occupied Gault House on the city's west

Grand Pacific Hotel

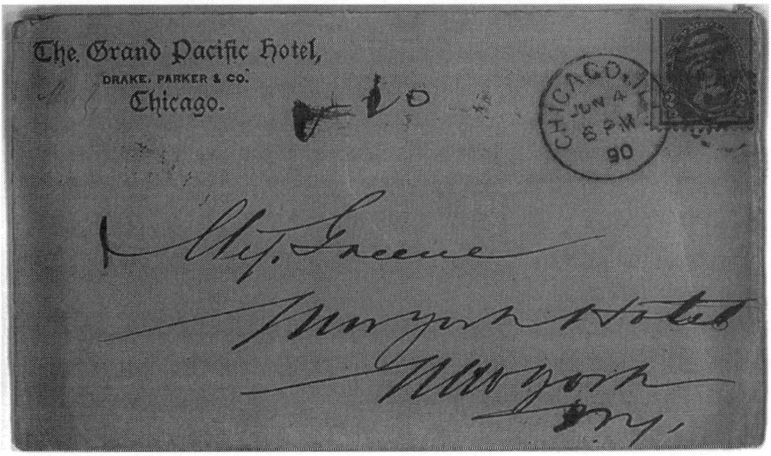

Figures 387a, b

As seen at top, Drake's reborn Grand Pacific, was truly grand indeed. Engraving. (Author's collection) Ironically, his vastly understated Advertising Cover carries only the hotel's name, location and that of the proprietors, Drake, Parker & Co. Advertising Cover, Scott No. 220, June 4, 1890, cancelled the day after the stamp's release. (Author's collection)

side the following day. As the only large hotel still standing in that vicinity, it too was filled for months with displaced persons needing lodging. The Gages continued to operate this "Little Sherman" for two years while rebuilding the burnt out Grand Pacific Hotel at the northwest corner of Clark and Jackson. They made money "from day one" at the Grand Pacific until the depression of 1873 sapped George W. Gage's finances. He was over-invested in real estate, and saw his "money little by little transferred into the hands of others,"

PHOTOGRAPHERS' ASSOCIATION OF AMERICA.

FIRST ANNUAL CONVENTION HELD IN CHICAGO, ILL., AUGUST 23D, 24TH, 25TH, 26TH, AND 27TH, 1880.

AGREEABLY to the call made repeatedly in these pages, a large body of the photographers of the United States and Canada assembled at the above time and place, in convention, for the permanent organization of a new national association, and for mutual improvement and good.

A great number had arrived in the city by Monday, the 23d inst., and of these some were busily engaged all day placing their specimens of work in the exhibition rooms.

As arranged, the entire exhibition and all the meetings were held in the apartments of the Grand Pacific Hotel (Messrs. John B. Drake & Co., proprietors), whose magnificent dining-hall was given free for feature in these convocations. Each member of the Photographic Association of America was provided with a beautiful ticket of admission, in the form of a palette, handsomely decorated and printed, a reduced photo-engraving of which we give.

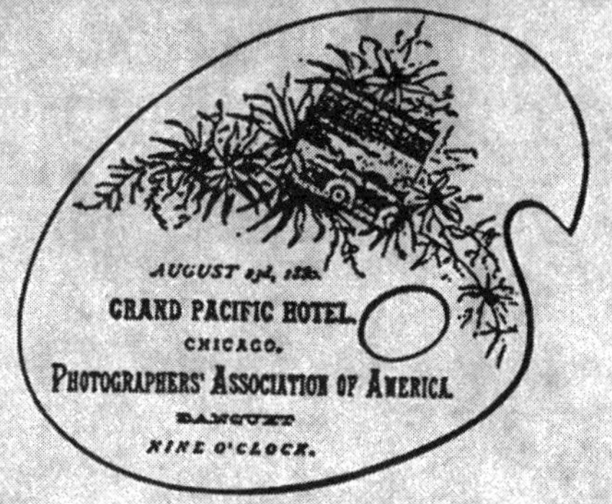

It was artistically and tastefully gotten up, and reflected great credit upon the Committee, as did everything pertaining to the whole grand affair.

Figure 388a

Drake treated PAA royally. Philadelphia Photographer, *Sept. 1880, p. 18. (Author's collection)*

including the infamous Hetty Green.

Coupled with this were the misfortunes of his younger brother, David. Although obscured by the jaundiced biases of the local press, city finances had fallen to disarray. Gage and his crowd publically represented themselves as "reformers." As treasurer, Gage was responsible for investing the city's funds. Unfortunately these "investments" proved unsatisfactory and he was short a great deal in his public accounts. Older brother George worried the public would think the missing funds had financed the magnificent Grand Pacific. While it was never proved that the Gage crowd had absconded with the money, at issue was more than a half million dollars of city funds. Much of it was relief funds Gage was responsible to hold in trust following the Chicago fire. Gage's default eventually became public knowledge although his party successfully covered it up for many months. Gage and his cronies were voted out of office. The city brought suit against Gage for the discrepancy. He was tried and found guilty, but won an appeal. The appeal was overturned by the Supreme Court and David Gage was forced to surrender a great deal of property to satisfy the default.

Thus, the Gages lost their lease to John B. Drake. He purchased the lease and furniture for just under a million dollars, taking formal possession of the hotel on January 1, 1875. The Grand Pacific thrived under Drake's direction. Its salons became the toast of the town. Drake entertained royalty and merchant princes. "It was the kind of place, where wealthy western cattlemen and distinguished eastern statesmen could rub elbows," a local historian

Figures 389a, b

John B. Drake's legacy of being "host with the most" in the Windy City continued through his sons, who erected several hotels including their namesake "The Drake" at the enviable location of Lake Shore Drive and Michigan Avenue. Left, the tradition of hosting galas extended to the NAC in 1941. Cinderella Stamp Label. (Author's collection) Below, soon after its 1921 opening The Drake, top right, witnessed massed bathers and gawkers to the city's Oak Street Beach front during Chicago's Roaring Twenties. Photo by Kaufmann and Fabry. (Courtesy, Joanne Bongiorno, The Drake)

notes. He brought his famous Thanksgiving bashes to the hotel. He entertained conventioneers. He formed his famous Duck and Drake Club, an obvious pun on his last name, "his famous game dinners that contributed so much to the social life of the city."

Drake survived both his unfortunate former partners. George W. Gage died in 1875. David A. Gage died in 1889. Drake succumbed November 12, 1895, but his memory remains in the form of the 20th century landmark constructed by his sons, John B. Drake II and Tracy Corey Drake. Educated in the finest schools and growing rich in their own rights,

Figure 390a

Times have certainly changed along Chicago's "Miracle Mile." The Drake no longer dominates the city's skyline, but still anchors the city's reputation with travelers and conventioneers. Most recently 1992's Columbia Pictures' release, "Hero" featured Dustin Hoffman and Andy Garcia struggling upon the hotel's window ledges. Photo, c. 1980. (Courtesy Joanne Bongiorno, The Drake)

Drake's sons built Chicago's Drake hotel on land reclaimed from Lake Michigan with rubble cleared from the great fire. Overlooking Oak Street beach, now Lake Shore Drive and North Michigan Avenue, they named the hotel in their illustrious father's memory. From the first, the 13-story Drake became a hotel of choice among the well-heeled and socially prominent. Even today, at the head of Chicago's "Miracle Mile" and part of the Hilton chain, the hotel's red carpet is always out as one of the city's classiest hotels.

Auction Census Data Summary, 1891-1994

	1	2	3	5	10	12	24	30	90	Total	Pct
TH	25		18	129	126	15				313	
TH RB					3					3	
	25		**18**	**129**	**129**	**15**				**316**	**3.7%**

B. F. Miles
Chapter XXXIII

Peoria, Illinois, was a small western city of 36,000 at the outbreak of the Civil War, and a long way from both the military struggles and the great financial turmoil that followed in its wake. Yet both hit even the hamlets, too. Benjamin Fullerton Miles' response was to purchase a small quantity of John Gault's New Metallic Currency for use at his drug store. His order probably amounted to about 2,000 five-cent encased stamps (Reed MI05) and an even smaller quantity of the one-cent denomination (Reed MI01). For many years Miles' pieces were considered the rarest in the entire series. This was the only merchant lacking in the great William F. Dunham collection. Another prominent collector could only acquire a single, damaged specimen in 10 years of searching. Some collectors still feel Miles is the rarest, while others accord that distinction to the Claflin issue. A dealer intimately familiar with the series said it best, though: "either of the two denominations . . . [of Miles' encased stamps] can be considered as rare as any encased stamp."

Benjamin Fullerton Miles was born September 5, 1825, at Glen Connell, Huntington County, Pennsylvania. His father, John George Miles, was a noted lawyer and his mother, Juliana McConnell Miles, a writer of repute. Forebears on both sides had played important roles during the American Revolution. Miles was probably the best educated of any of John Gault's customers. He attended Dartmouth College and later Marshall College, from which he was graduated in 1847 at the head of his class. He subsequently studied medicine at the

Figure 391a
Reed MI05 obverse, ex-James F. Ruddy specimen. (Bowers and Merena photo)

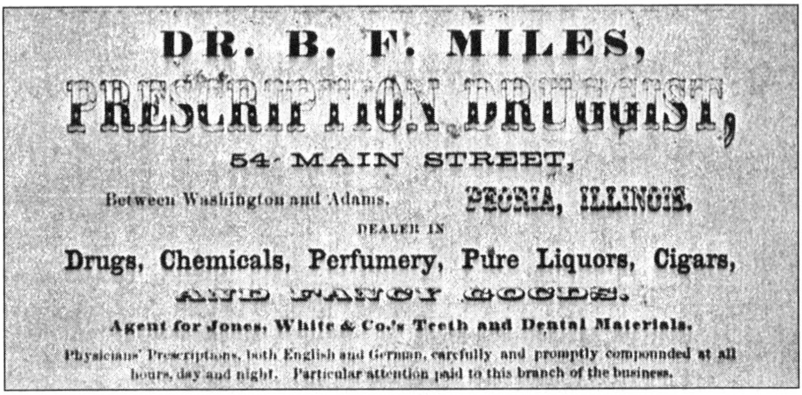

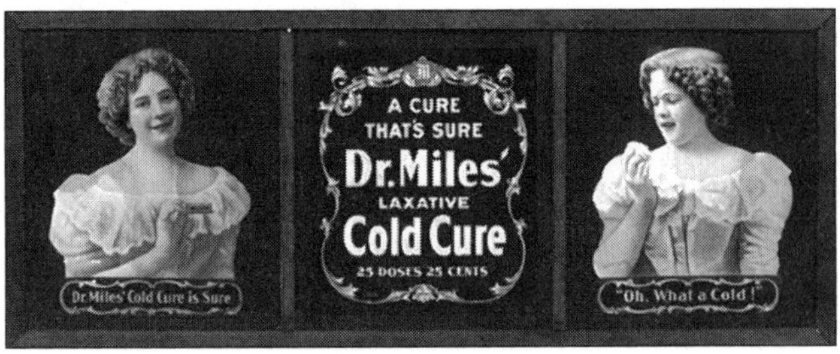

Figures 392a, b

Dr. B. F. Miles was a Philadelphia physician. Ad. Peoria City Directory, *1857, p. 39. (Dallas Public Library) Right, Dr. Franklin Miles trade sign. (Gene Harris photo)*

Jefferson School of Medicine of Pennsylvania Medical College, Philadelphia. A man of many skills, Miles served for a time as a civil engineer surveying the Pennsylvania Railway route through the Allegheny Mountains. His father was attorney for the railroad. Thereafter Miles sailed to England, serving as ship's doctor. On his return to America he opened a medical practice in Camden, New Jersey.

Miles came to Peoria, Illinois, about 1853, by way of Chicago and LaSalle. He became partners with Col. William A. Thrush in a drug firm. In addition to drugs, his encasements advertise paints, oils and glass. It was common practice in that day for druggists to stock a variety of products, including dye-stuffs, paints, oils, varnishes, petroleum and similar products. Miles, no doubt, stocked them all and more. The firm was celebrated as a gathering place for the local celebrities of the day. Afterwards he continued in the same trade with Dr. A. W. H. Reen. Still later, he conducted his business alone. In the process, he became one of Peoria's most prominent businessmen. Dr. Miles was one of 13 pharmacists advertising in the 1856 Peoria city directory. He was distinctive, though, in that he solicited the trade of both English and German physicians. Not only was Miles bilingual, but he would arise in the middle of the night to fill an emergency prescription, he advertised. Not many pharmacists today would do the same! Miles was also agent for Jones, White and Company's false teeth and dental materials. In 1859 and thereafter, he also advertised "pure liquors." Somewhat later, a separate firm Erskine H. Miles and Co. advertised itself as dealers in preserves and liquors. Erskine Miles lived at Dr. Miles' residence on South Jefferson Street.

A number of products from the 19th century bear the style of a Dr. Miles, including Dr.

Figures 393a, b

Left-handed, B. F. Miles was an easterner who made a name for himself in the west during the mid-19th century. Copy photograph and autograph. Historical Encyclopedia of Illinois: History of Peoria County, *1902, facing p. 400. (Lee Roten photo)*

Miles' Wine of Sarsaparilla, Dr. Miles' Anti-Pain Pills, Dr. Miles' Liver Pills, and Dr. Miles' Restorative Tonic. A long-lasting remedy which may well be familiar to many readers still bears this name – Miles' Nervine. As originally introduced, Miles' Restorative Nervine was recommended for "epilepsy, hysteria and St. Vitus' Dance, nervousness, sleeplessness, neuralgia, nervous dyspepsia and nervous prostration." A truly wondrous product, it would also cure "tobacco and alcoholic excess and the opium and morphine habits," according to sales' literature. These products were compounded by Dr. Franklin L. Miles, another midwestern physician, but based in Elkhart, Indiana. Apparently, these products have nothing directly to do with Dr. Benjamin Fullerton Miles of Peoria. They are mentioned only to save the reader the confusion possible in attempting to link the two.

Dr. Benjamin Fullerton Miles did create his own products, too, however. Miles' "Premium Baking Power" was well known, having received an award at the 1870 St. Louis Fair. "Actual tests were made on the ground[s] by baking bread mixed from each kind of baking powder there exhibited, and the result was the awarding of the highest premium to B. F. Miles' Celebrated Baking Powder," according to a notice in an historical publication. The product then took premiums at two other state fairs, and was the "best and the cheapest on the market," according to its manufacturer. The wholesale department of Miles' firm occupied the first floor and basement of a building 25 feet by 130 feet at South Adams and Fulton Streets. Its retail drug department was described in 1873 as "one of the finest,

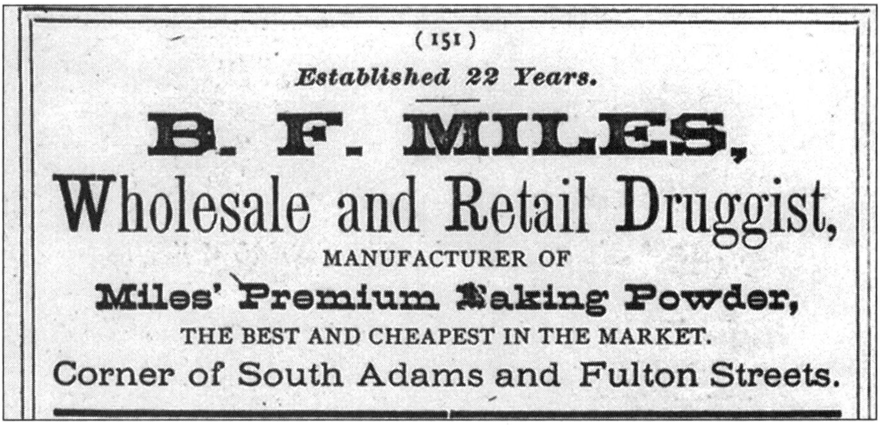

Figure 394a

Ad. Edwards' Peoria Census Report *[City Directory], 1876, p. 151. (Peoria City Library)*

superbly fitted throughout with heavy black walnut. It is a beauty, everything is nicely arranged, and the order and system of this establishment give to all who enter therein a feeling of pleasure," according to a local commentator. His employees were described as extremely courteous and polite, "and all can rely on being promptly served with the purest drugs in Peoria," he continued. Three years later the local directory editor challenged any city to provide "a finer or more elegantly fitted store for the drug business in the West." His wholesale trade was described as extensive, but several years later he left the drug trade. By 1880 Miles was a grain commission merchant, located at the Peoria Chamber of Commerce Building. During the last few years of his life, he also dealt in insurance. A gentle man, Dr. Miles moved to Chicago in his last years. He died of Bright's Disease on April 22, 1889. This was the same affliction which would ultimately bring the demise of both John Gault and his spouse. Miles was remembered as a wide-ranging reader who "possessed a large fund of valuable information on general topics." His cultivated literary tastes made him a very entertaining conversationalist, and his drug store was a social center of the town.

It is believed that Miles purchased his encased stamps through the operation of Carlos A. Cook, a cousin of J. C. Ayer, who traveled extensively in that region prior to the war on behalf of Ayer's remedies. For a salesman, peddling drugs and health aids, Miles' drug store would have been one of his normal stops. Leaving Ayer's employ, Cook first opened a drug store of his own in Rock Island, Illinois. In 1862 he moved to Peoria, where he ran a brewery, before later moving on to Chicago as a drug wholesaler and advertising agent.

Auction Census Data Summary, 1891-1994

	1	2	3	5	10	12	24	30	90	Total	Pct
MI	8			36						44	<1%
	8			**36**						**44**	**<1%**

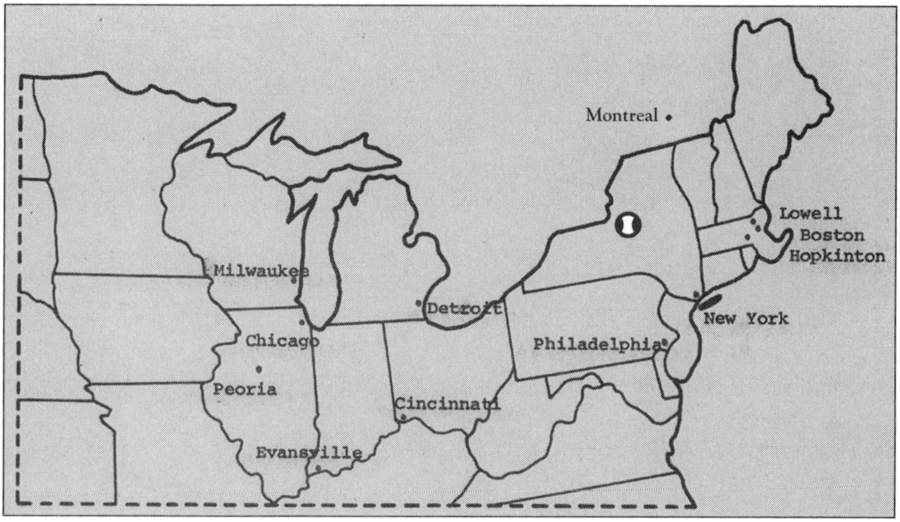

Gault After Encased Stamps
Chapter XXXIV

Spurned by the Federal authorities, John Gault never-the-less made a grand splash if somewhat limited financial success of his encased stamp scheme. In the first week of November, 1862, Gault placed ads in the leading publications. One of the first of these notices to appear ran in the New York *Herald* on Thursday, November 5th. The notice ran in the newspaper's miscellaneous classified section for four days, and read: "THE NEW METALLIC CURRENCY. – APPLICATIONS for stamping business cards on the new metallic currency, to be made to J. GAULT, patentee, No. 1 Park place, New York." His ad in the Chicago *Evening Journal* ran for three days, also commencing Nov. 5. Similar advertisements appeared in the New York *Tribune*, and a newspaper in Providence, Rhode Island,

Auction Census Data Summary, 1891-1994

	1	2	3	5	10	12	24	30	90	Total	Pct
Totals	1918	26	2151	1791	1813	458	278	211	104	8750	
	22%		**24%**	**20%**	**21%**	**5.2%**	**2.3%**	**2.4%**	**1.2%**		

Figures 395a, b

Gault's encased stamp production can be presented in a variety of ways. By denomination, above, there is a remarkable consistency although pieces were created for merchants across the sweep of northern states and Canada.

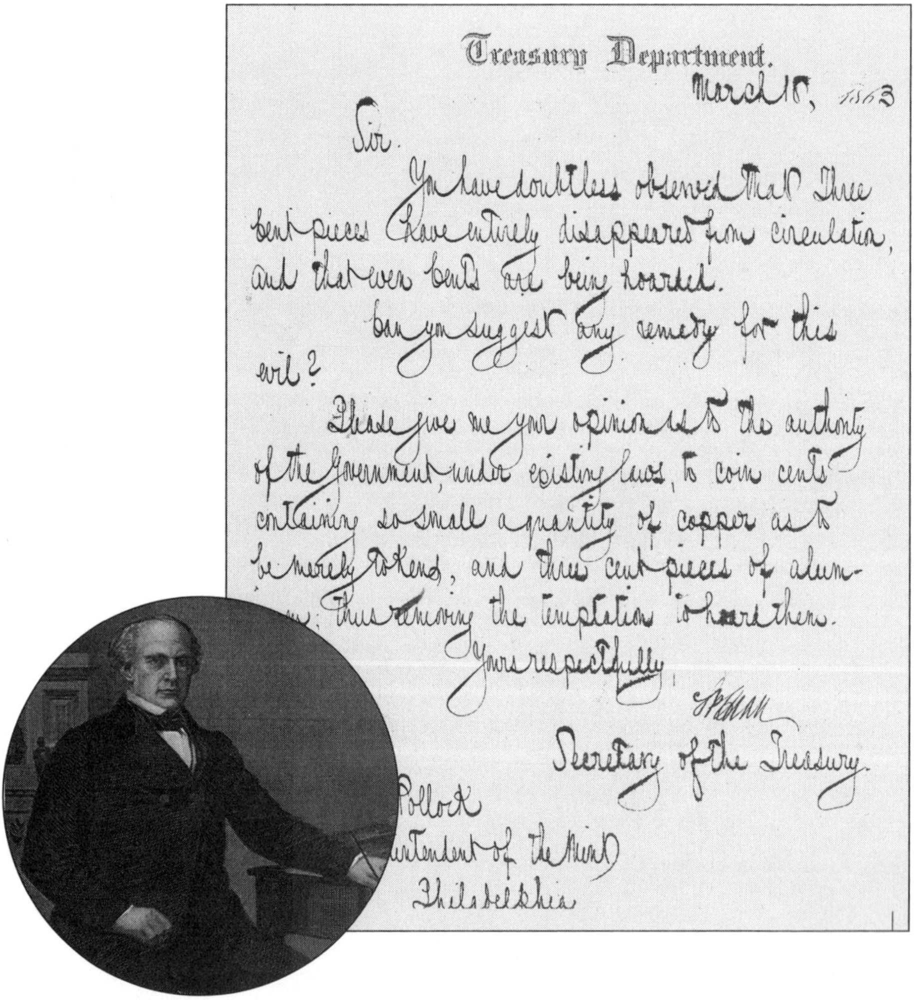

Treasury Department.
March 18, 1863

Sir.

You have doubtless observed that Three cent pieces have entirely disappeared from circulation, and that even cents are being hoarded.

Can you suggest any remedy for this evil?

Please give me your opinion as to the authority of the Government, under existing laws, to coin cents containing so small a quantity of copper as to be merely tokens, and three cent pieces of alum- ...; thus removing the temptation to hoard them.

Yours respectfully,
S P Chase
Secretary of the Treasury.

Pollock
...intendent of the Mint
Philadelphia

Figures 396a, b

By spring 1863, Postage Currency was beginning to fill the public's needs for the absent silver fractional coinage, but Secretary of the Treasury Salmon P. Chase (above) was still searching for a remedy for the shortage of the smallest denominations. Letter, S. P. Chase to James Pollock, March 18, 1863. (Coin World photo) Steel Plate Engraving (detail) by Johnson, Fry & Co. after a painting by Alonso Chappel, 1863. (Author's collection)

beginning November 6th. The *Tribune* ad cost Gault eight-bits, $1.00, per insertion. If the pieces were inappropriate as a federal circulating medium, they were still highly effective as a commercial advertising store card at a time when almost anything of seeming commercial

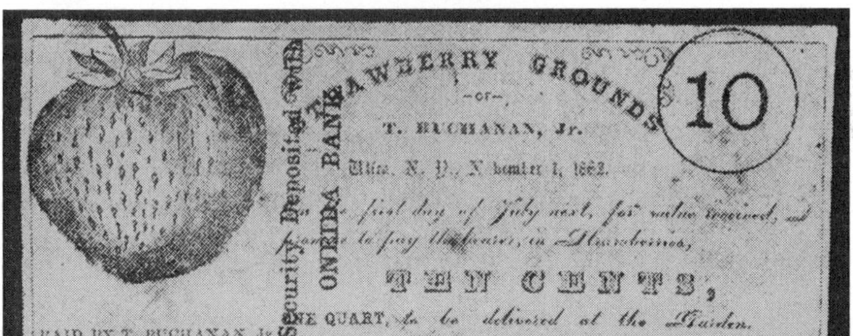

Figures 397a,b,c,d

Top, "This is all the change I could get – I had to take these or nothing!" the husband reported to his wife on returning from a shopping trip contemporaneous to the Chase letter, opposite. Cartoon. Frank Leslie's Illustrated Newspaper, *March 21, 1863. (Coin World archives) Below, the essentially barter aspect of the cartoon was funny, of course, because it bore a semblance of reality. Proof of this is the scrip I.O.U. issued by T. Buchanan Jr. promising to pay the bearer in strawberries July 1, 1863. (Herb Melnick, NASCA photo) In the meantime, tokens proliferated like the unique die variety at left, Fuld 226A/322A, discovered by the author nearly 30 years ago. (Author's collection)*

Figure 398a-f

Chase's inquiry ultimately led to legislation providing for the coinage of bronze cents, bronze two-cent pieces and copper nickel three-cent pieces, the intrinsic (metal) value of each of which was insufficient to induce hoarding. In other words the devalued coinage copied the private tokens then in circulation. Above from left, pattern two-cent pieces of the adopted (Shield, Judd 316) and rejected (Washington bust, Judd 305) designs, and adopted (Judd 410) three-cent design. (Bowers and Merena photos)

value was being employed as a medium of exchange. In four instances the details of the purchase transaction are known (Ellis McAlpin of Cincinnati, Norris of Chicago, Cook of Evansville, and Weir & Larminie of Montreal). In all other cases we may reliably infer that Gault sold the pieces personally (i.e. in Massachusetts, New York and probably Philadelphia) or merchants were attracted by specimens observed or such advertising. In the East these ads did not even mention stamps. In November 1862 *stamps* were a dirty word. By this time, merchants, public, and government officials alike already had their fills of the circulation of postage stamps. The worst fears of those farsighted enough to reject the circulation of the small, messy gumbacks in July had long since come to pass by November. And public opinion of the fragile and scarce federal fractional notes was not much higher.

Gault's small change, on the other hand, proved highly popular. It was paid out in change and circulated immediately. Both Cook and Claflin paid out virtually every piece they ordered, they later recalled. Several pieces bearing dated inscriptions have appeared in the marketplace over the years, and there is a newspaper report of pieces showing up in a Thanksgiving collection plate. Gault's cumulative output for himself, his clients, and the thousands of additional pieces he sold in small quantities for public accommodation and to small merchants generally, reliably totalled upwards of three-quarters of a million pieces. Although a large issue, the face value represented was probably not much over $50,000, hardly enough to be a serious solution to the small change crisis in a national sense. Clearly if the federal government had adopted the measure the output would have necessarily been much, much larger.

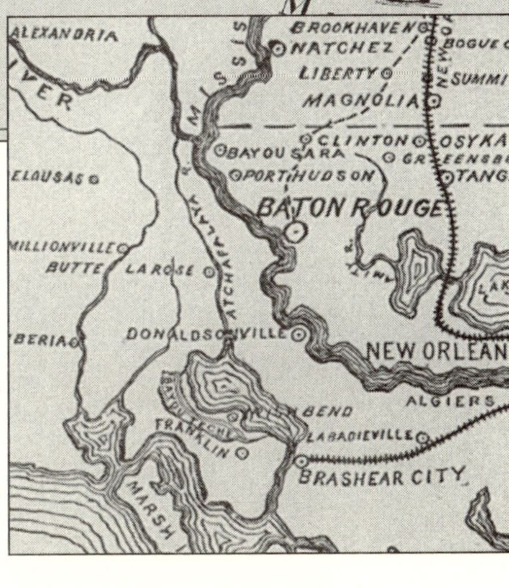

Figures 399a, b

Captain Samuel Gault's military career and life was cut short in the bayous of southern Louisiana. Map and inset detail by Walter A. Lane, The Soldier in Our Civil War, *c. 1870, p. 82. (Author's collection)*

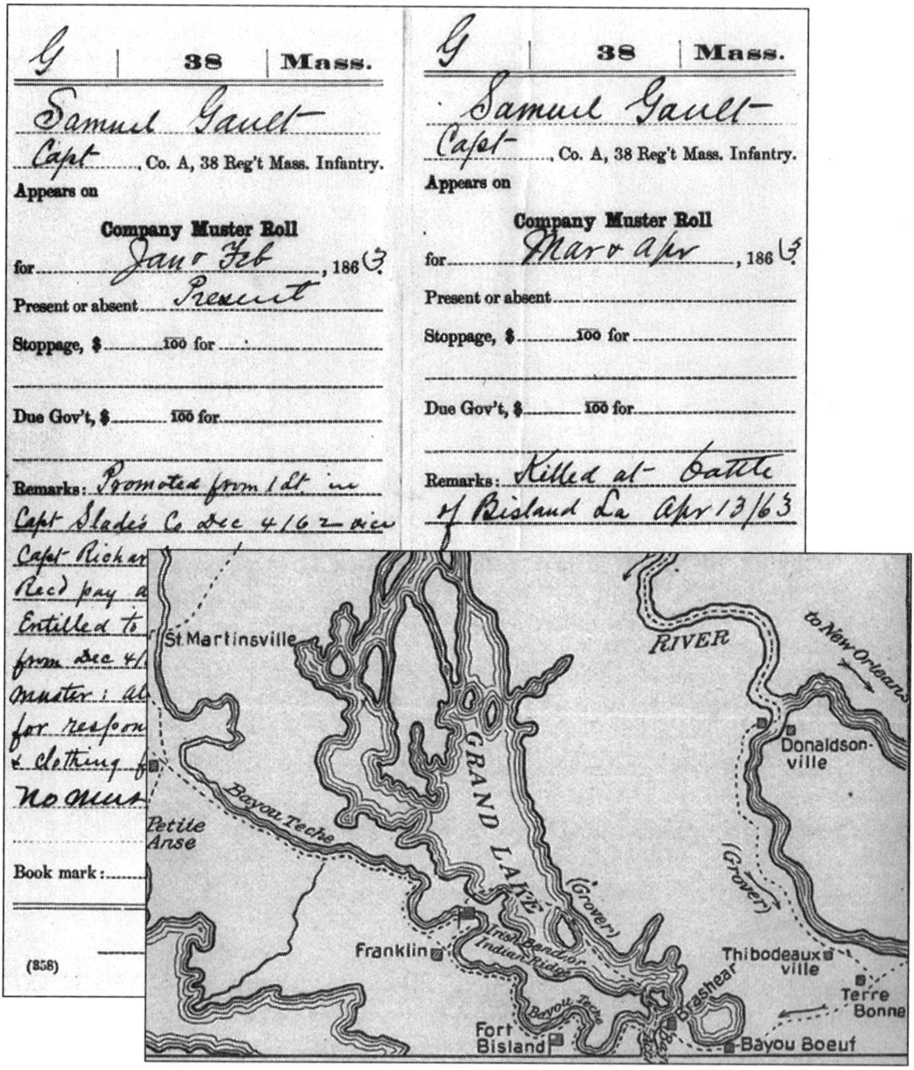

G | 38 | Mass.

Samuel Gault
Capt, Co. A, 38 Reg't Mass. Infantry.
Appears on
Company Muster Roll
for Jan & Feb, 1863
Present or absent Present
Stoppage, $ ... 100 for ...
Due Gov't, $ ... 100 for ...
Remarks: Promoted from 1 Lt in Capt Slade's Co. Dec 4/62 vice Capt Richar...
Rec'd pay a...
Entitled to ...
from Dec 4/...
muster: al...
for respon...
& clothing f...
No mus...
Book mark: ...
(358)

G | 38 | Mass.

Samuel Gault
Capt, Co. A, 38 Reg't Mass. Infantry.
Appears on
Company Muster Roll
for Mar & Apr, 1863
Present or absent ...
Stoppage, $ ... 100 for ...
Due Gov't, $ ... 100 for ...
Remarks: Killed at Battle of Bisland La Apr 13/63

Figures 400a, b

The official military record of John Gault's younger brother and a detail map of operations around Franklin, La., in April 1863 leading up to Sam Gault's untimely death, April 13, 1863. The pay record shows the government was in arrears at the time. Muster Roll, Co. G, 38th Massachusetts Volunteers. (Adjutant General's Office, AG1501295, National Archives) Map. History of the Fifty-second Regiment Massachusetts Volunteers, *1893, p. 110. (Author's collection)*

Figures 401a, b, c

The government introduced the two-cent Jackson postage stamp July 1, 1863, somewhat late for an issue of Gault's emergency encased stamps, but leading to an enigmatic and small issue never-the-less. Top, two-cent black postage stamp, Scott 73. (Author's collection, Clifford Cole photo) Above, Reed JG02, ex-Arnold Perl, ex-Donald H. Kagin collections. (Len Glazer photos)

One cannot help but wonder how financially successful the encased stamp venture was to its originator. Although admittedly a guess, it needn't be an imprudent one. Calculations performed in several ways based on the mathematical model of encased stamp production created especially for this book – the results of which appear in the respective chapters on Gault's customers – indicate that something like $1,600 could have been gleaned by Gault from this enterprise. That was a considerable sum in 1862-63. It's no wonder, then, that he moaned in later years that "he could have made a million dollars in a year if the Post Office Department had not shut down on him." This assertion has been repeatedly stressed by every commentator on the series since the days of J.Walter Scott and Ben Green. And some

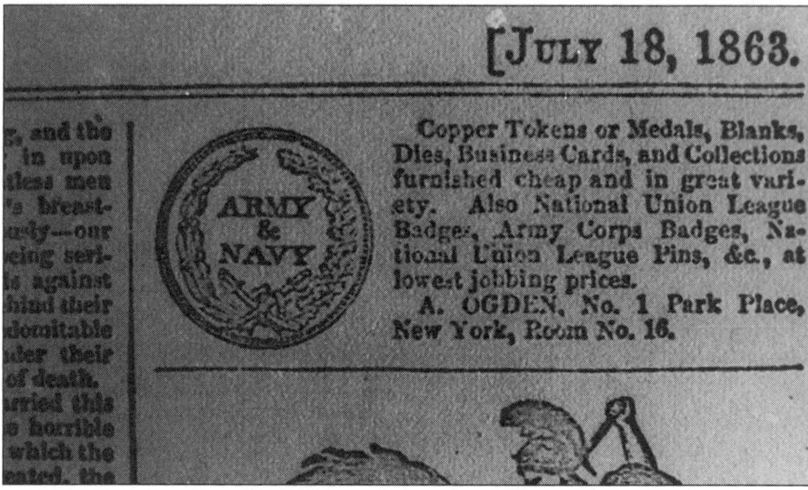

[JULY 18, 1863.

ARMY & NAVY

Copper Tokens or Medals, Blanks, Dies, Business Cards, and Collections furnished cheap and in great variety. Also National Union League Badges, Army Corps Badges, National Union League Pins, &c., at lowest jobbing prices.

A. OGDEN, No. 1 Park Place, New York, Room No. 16.

Figure 402a

By Summer 1863 the issue of private bronze tokens in New York and elsewhere was in full swing. A. Ogden had an office in the same building as John Gault, No. 1 Park Place. Judging from his ad he was a jobber for a variety of small, struck metal pins, badges and other devices, too. Ad. Harper's Weekly, *July 18, 1863, p. 462. (Oklahoma State University Library)*

have gone so far as to indicate that the Post Office refused him available stamp supplies. Although attributed to Gault, himself, it somewhat misses the point. Gault wasn't PO'ed out of large funds. He couldn't have achieved such liberal success after early November even if stamp supplies had been unlimited (which they weren't). Indications are that Gault was already finding supplies of stamps difficult to locate by mid-November. Schapker and Bussing may have supplied Gault with the stamps he encased for them. In December postal officials would commit to a policy of redeeming the outstanding stamps by substitution for currency. So in reality, Gault's road to riches was blocked by Boutwell's decision in early November. Gault was probably out of the small change business not long after the first of the year. He was K0'ed by the IRS. So what else is new?

By spring, 1863, the premium on silver being quoted by brokers was upwards of 35-40 percent. Postage Currency was more plentiful, although in some instances it too was being quoted at a premium. Large masses of stamps had been coaxed from circulation. Cent-sized tokens and store cards had proliferated. Private scrip was still being issued. A perplexed Treasury Secretary was still searching for remedies to the small change vexation. Stamps themselves continued to serve as small change in a pinch. Persons accustomed to using the gumbacks in lieu of coins pressed them for such. "Stamps" had become synonymous with "money." Gault's encased stamps would have continued to circulate so long as they were deemed a necessary change expedient. Random strays turned up in circulation as late as the 1870s. The silvering wore off easily. The mica cracked. The brass frames became mottled,

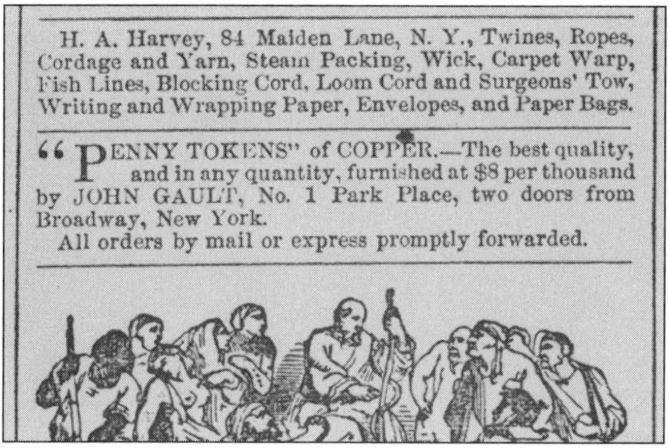

H. A. Harvey, 84 Maiden Lane, N. Y., Twines, Ropes, Cordage and Yarn, Steam Packing, Wick, Carpet Warp, Fish Lines, Blocking Cord, Loom Cord and Surgeons' Tow, Writing and Wrapping Paper, Envelopes, and Paper Bags.

"PENNY TOKENS" of COPPER.—The best quality, and in any quantity, furnished at $8 per thousand by JOHN GAULT, No. 1 Park Place, two doors from Broadway, New York.
All orders by mail or express promptly forwarded.

Figure 403a
John Gault knew a thing or two about selling small change for a profit. He hopped on the bandwagon, quickly offering his own selection of copper cent-sized tokens. Ad. Harper's Weekly, *August 29, 1863, p. 559. (Author's collection)*

tarnished and bent. Eventually the stamps inside became soiled or with considerable time faded. The public may have put back a few pieces as souvenirs. Quantities are known to have accumulated in old retail stores, especially in New England. Eventually *most* of Gault's ingenious frames were plundered of the only thing of value they contained. The last person to receive them plucked out and used the stamp to post a letter or package. The greater the value of the stamp, the greater the temptation to redeem it. This more than anything accounts for the great scarcity of specimens today. Some pieces survived circulation and the onslaughts of stamp-hungry postal patrons, only to fall prey in later years to stamp collectors. Colonial coin specialists talk in terms of 2-3 percent survival rates. Civil War token specialists estimate a general survival rate of four percent for that series. For Gault's fragile mineral and metal stamp money, the number of pieces suriving is something like .005 to .01 of the original issue. The current population is reliably estimated at 3,500 to 7,000 pieces of all types.

During the war John Gault was not a permanent resident of New York. From the onset of hostilities, he split his time between his business activities there and his family responsibilities in Boston. He also traveled some, and frequently borrowed small amounts from his brothers. According to a writer with access to some of the family correspondence, he was often late in making payments. He wasn't necessarily short of funds, nor was he a welsher. He was busy, and distracted. On top of all the other irons he had in the fire, his family situation worsened. As written in earlier chapters, it will be remembered that up until that time, the bachelor Gault had maintained a home in Boston and was pursuing a career as a machinist. He prospered some and had maintained a house and home for his widowed mother, Mary Ann, and his younger bachelor brother, Sam, since he had returned from the California gold fields.

In 1861, Sam married. That winter Sam and his wife Ellen welcomed a daughter, Addie Florence. The Gault family house was getting crowded. By the end of June, 1862 John Gault's artillery shell enterprise was heating up. He had achieved some recognition for his unique designs, had the backing of Munn & Co., had signed contracts with a foundry to

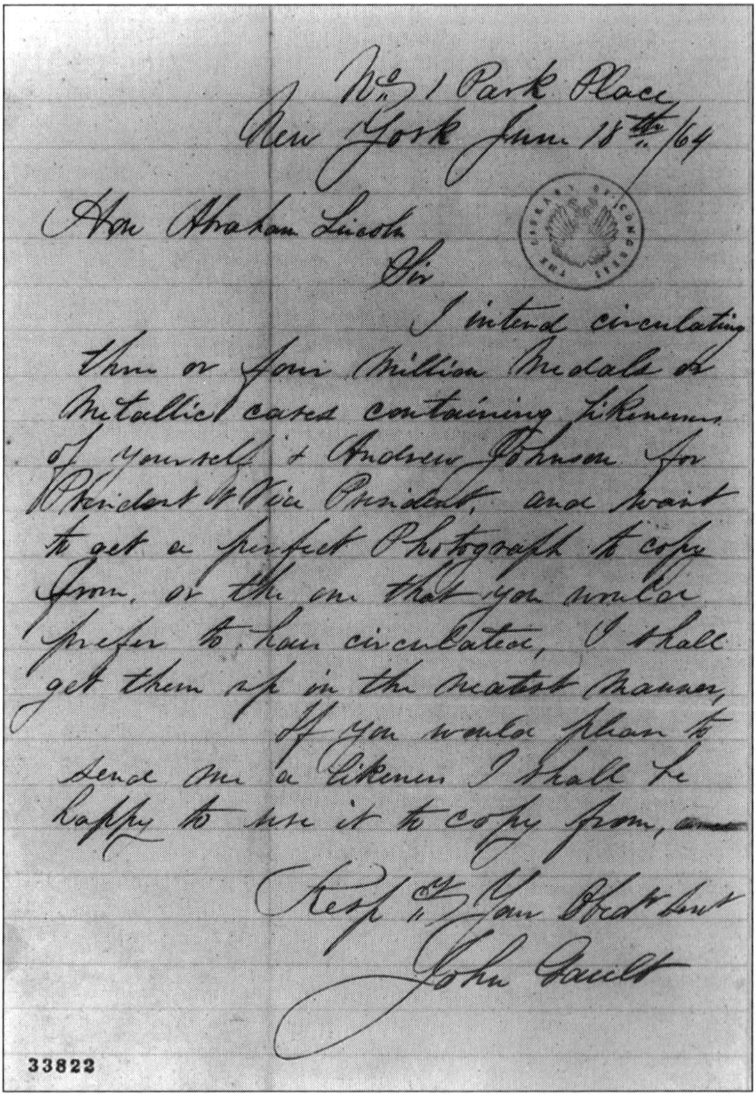

No. 1 Park Place
New York June 18th/64

Hon Abraham Lincoln

Sir

I intend circulating three or four Million Medals or Metallic cases containing likeness of yourself & Andrew Johnson for President & Vice President, and wait to get a perfect Photograph to copy from, or the one that you would prefer to have circulated, I shall get them up in the neatest manner,

If you would please to send me a likeness I shall be happy to use it to copy from,

Resp'y Your Obdt Servt
John Gault

33822

Figure 404a

Gault wrote to candidate Abraham Lincoln in late Spring 1864 seeking a photo from which he could duplicate ferrotype campaign buttons. Letter, John Gault to Abraham Lincoln, June 18, 1864. (Library of Congress photo, No. 33822)

license production of his shells, and most auspiciously of all had made a business acquaintance and partnership with an influential and successful international arms broker, William V. Barkalow. Additionally, he had found time to conceive his encased stamp remedy, and

Figure 405a

Although there is no record of Lincoln answering Gault, the latter did obtain a copy of the above photograph taken by Mathew Brady, Friday, January 8, 1864. Photo reproduced from a collodion glass plate, Ostendorf 86. (National Archives) Inset, Gault duplicated and reversed the image for his ferrotype campaign tokens. Tintype brass medal, DeWitt AL 1864-94. (Joe Levine photo)

filed several other commercial patents which needed developing. We remember that he wrote his brother that he could not return to Boston for the Fourth of July celebration with his family. Never-the-less he soon must have traveled back to Boston because John I. Brown became his second commercial customer for his venture in mid-August. That time period

Figures 406a, b, c, d

Gault returned to Scovill Manufacturing Co. to produce his brass, photographic campaign medals. Scovill was a natural. In addition to its extensive lines of brass items, the company was intimately involved in the burgeoning photographic trade of its day, manufacturing photographic plates and other supplies in immense quantities. Top, Scovill Store Card, Miller NY-805, c. 1850. (Author's collection) Above, Scovill Store Card, Miller NY-802, c. 1855. (Author's collection)

was critical to the Gault family. It was August 16th that the war really reached where they lived. On that day Sam, then a 23-year-old bookkeeper, enlisted at Springfield for three years in Slade's Company (Co. K) of the 38th Regiment Massachusetts Volunteers. A week later the company was activated and shipped off for Baltimore. By Christmas, when brother John was wrapping up his encased stamp enterprise, Sam's unit had reached Louisiana. A month later, a son, named little Sam, was born to John Gault's sister-in-law. After three months of skirmishing, Sam Gault's unit was ordered to participate in operations in western Louisiana. The first of these was the Teche Campaign to capture Fort Bisland. They departed Berwick City April 11. In the morning of April 13, 1863, Sam – now a captain of Company A – led his men across a pontoon bridge under enemy fire. That afternoon they were ordered to advance against Fort Bisland on Bayou Teche. They skirmished through the sugar cane until about 2:30, when they ran out of ammunition. They advanced with fixed

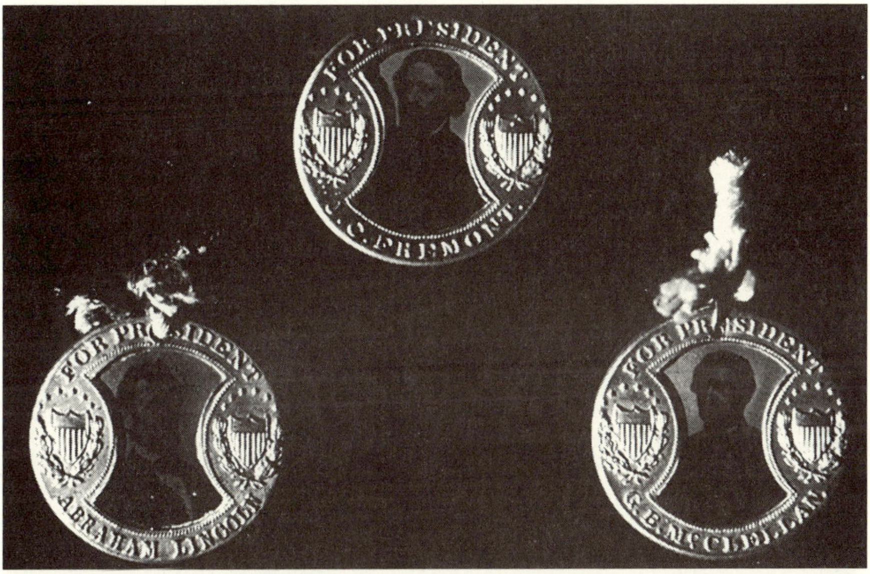

Figures 407a-f

In 1864 Gault issued campaign medals for three tickets, obverses top and reverses above. Tintypes replaced stamps and mica was unnecessary. Their design was similar to the encased stamps, but the brass frames, holed for suspension, were more elaborate with thicker rims and tabs. Campaign Medals, DeWitt AL 1864-94, JF 1864-7, GMcC 1864-49. (Edmund B. Sullivan photos)

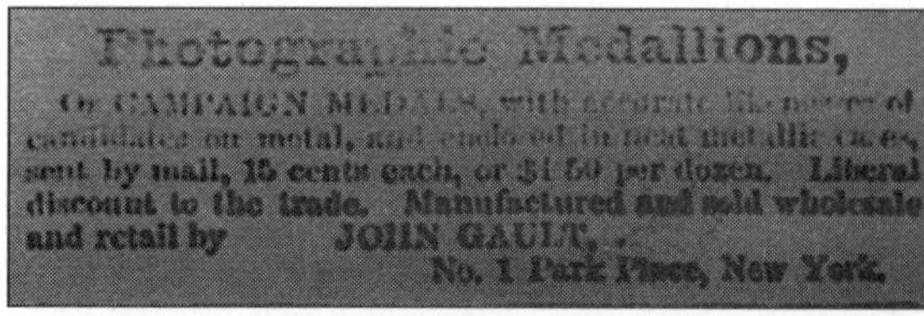

Photographic Medallions,

Or CAMPAIGN MEDALS, with accurate likenesses of candidates on metal, and enclosed in neat metallic cases, sent by mail, 15 cents each, or $1 50 per dozen. Liberal discount to the trade. Manufactured and sold wholesale and retail by JOHN GAULT, No. 1 Park Place, New York.

ADVERTISEMENTS.

PHOTOGRAPHIC MEDALLIONS.
CAMPAIGN MEDALS,
BEST STYLE FOR 1864.
For sale by
JOHN GAULT, No. 1 Park Place, New York.

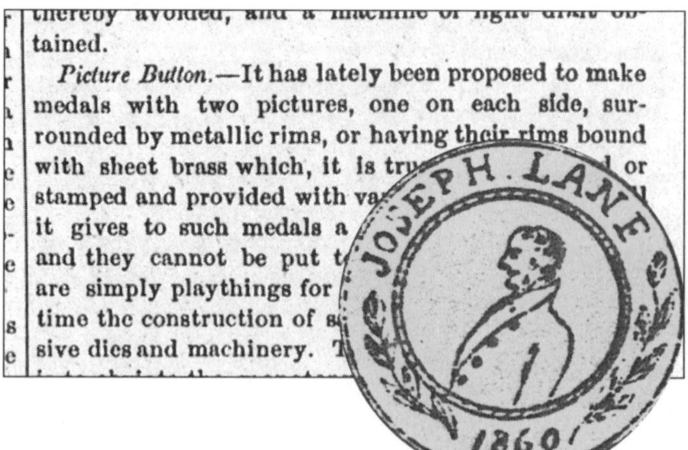

tained.

Picture Button.—It has lately been proposed to make medals with two pictures, one on each side, surrounded by metallic rims, or having their rims bound with sheet brass which, it is tr... or stamped and provided with va... it gives to such medals a ... and they cannot be put t... are simply playthings for ... time the construction of s... sive dies and machinery. T...

Figures 408a, b, c, d

Gault rushed into production with his pieces. It was less than a month after he wrote the president that he first advertised his campaign medals. He advertised widely. He had to because the competition was tough. Ads from top. Harper's Weekly, *July 9, 1864, p. 447. (Oklahoma State University Library).* Harper's Weekly *September 24, 1864, p. 623. (Oklahoma State University Library) Detail Photo of Lincoln/Johnson medal showing the Gault Encased Stamp Design Patent date, AUG. 12. 1862. (Joe Levine photo) Notice, "Picture Button,"* Scientific American, *August 31, 1861, p. 141. (Dallas Public Library) Also right, contemporary patent application drawing by one of Gault's competitors. (U.S. Patent Office)*

bayonets under "furious fire of artillery and musketry." Sam's side of the line (the left) came under withering fire from heavy Rebel artillery. Several hundred yards short of the enemy's earthworks, the advance halted with a price. According to the regiment's commander, Sam Gault's leg was completely shot off by an artillery shell, and "he died on his way to the hos-

THE REASON WHY.

CUSTOMER. "Your PAPA says he hain't no Pennies to make change with. You seem to have lots of 'em."

GROCER'S SON. "Guess I have; and POP's got *six barrels* full down cellar. He's waitin' for 'em to rise."——(*You should have seen the* EXPRESSION *of* POP'S FACE.)

Figure 409a

The U.S. Mint switched to bronze cents in mid-1864. It had to. Even copper nickel cents were hoarded at the time. Cartoon. Harper's Weekly, *August 6, 1864, p. 512. (Author's collection)*

pital." Sam was gallant and accomplished, beloved by his men . . . and dead. By daybreak, the rebels had beat a retreat, and the national colors were raised. It took 17 days for notice to reach Boston. By then Sam had been quickly buried near where he had fallen. John's brother left a 25-year-old widow with a year-old daughter and two-and-a-half month-old

MAGIC POCKET BOOKS, with elastic band, for the new Postage Currency, made and sold wholesale and retail by SNOW & HAPGOOD, Pathfinder Office, 22 Court Street, Boston, Mass. Agents wanted. Sample sent, post-paid, for 15 cents.

TO CONSUMPTIVES.—You will get the Recipe

Improved Currency-holder.

The substitution of the postal currency for the sticky stamps, as a means of giving fractional parts of a dollar in business transactions, is a desirable improvement. Riches take wings, it is said, and the proverb is literally true in handling the present "change;" it is inconvenient, not to say mortifying, to see it scattered in the air like snow-flakes when one is engaged in distributing it. To prevent any such disaster and expedite settlements of the kind in question, the currency-holder, herewith illustrated, has been specially designed. It is merely a box, A, made of tin, having partitions corresponding in number to the different denominations of the bills, these boxes have a wire, *a*, extending through them on which tin cylinders, B, are suspended. The money

Figures 410a, b, c, d

John Gault was not the only entrepreneurial soul to sense opportunity in the commercial dislocations of the day. The Boston firm of Snow & Hapgood was intimately acquainted with the small change crisis and its remedies, too. Top, the firm sold the postage stamp envelopes. Later, it offered both a commercial cash box and personal wallet for the diminutive Postage Currency. Twenty-five cent Postage Stamp Envelope. (Milt Friedberg illustration) Ad, Magic Pocket Book. Harper's Weekly, *1862. (Oklahoma State University Library) Improved Currency Holder illustration and article.* Scientific American, *February 28, 1863, p. 136. (Dallas Public Library) This firm also patented stamp cancelling devices.*

SNOW'S PATENT CURRENCY-HOLDER.

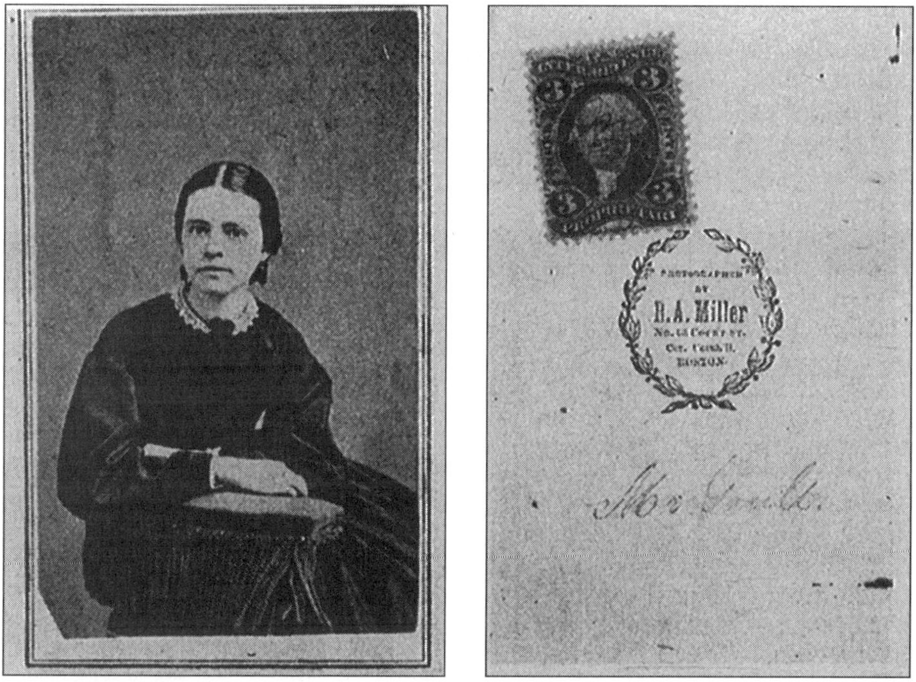

Figures 411a, b

Millie Gault, thought by an earlier writer to be John's wife, is actually his niece Amelia, the daughter of his brother Henry. Card de Visite, front and back, with three-cent Internal Revenue Stamp, Scott R18. (Coin World photos)

son. The news was devastating for Sam's and John's infirm mother. It must have had a peculiar effect on brother John, too. He and his brother Henry now had full responsibility for their younger brother's wife and small children. In addition their aging mother was dealt a severe blow. The theoretical killing radius, timed-fuse, and chain length equations of artillery shell manufacture were theoretical no more. Sam's remains were returned to Boston for reburial 13 months later, at which time John Gault Sr., their father, was also reburied in the family plot that John had purchased in 1850 with his gold strike earnings.

The summer of 1863 was an eventful one. July opened with the high tide of the Confederacy breaking on the parallel ridges of southern Pennsylvania at Gettysburg. In four days there and at Vicksburg in the west, not only the course of the war but the nation's history was inalterably changed. "We're living in a glorious hour," *Harper's Weekly* told its readers. However, the commercial disarray was still manifest. The specie premium was still soaring, and although the Fractional Currency authorized in March had appreciably relieved the fractional silver shortage, nothing had been done to effectively remedy the cent shortage. These copper-nickel, white cents too were being hoarded and replacing them was vital.

Figures 412a, b

Following the war, Gault removed from No. 1 Park Place, at which he dealt in encased stamps, copper tokens and political medals. Other businessmen, however, continued active trade from its precincts. From right, Private Express Stamp. Boyd's Dispatch, No. 1 Park Place, Scott 20L45, 1879. (Author's collection) Proprietary Match Stamp, New York Match Company, No. 1 Park Place, Scott R138B, c. 1870s. (Author's collection) In recent years a fast food establishment has been operated at that location.

	Hot spiced rums.	Hot whiskeys.	Whiskeys straight.	Brandies.	Wines.	Mixed liquors.	Ale, beer, etc.	Bottles Champagne.
L. Dardy..........	56	59	62	15	23	30	105	6
Mike's............	65	110	70	20	28	23	90	10
V. B. Carpenter....	43	62	112	30	35	27	110	5
Young............	35	40	52	10	12	15	65	2
P. Murphy........	34	49	63	12	15	25	45	2
Schedler..........	51	48	112	35	52	45	315	18
Delmonico.........	213	205	315	90	135	180	210	35
Riley	105	123	180	25	30	62	80	6
Sammis & Sharp..	23	31	30	8	10	15	35	1
Van Riper........	27	22	19	10	13	18	40	1
Ed. Schultze.......	18	29	38	12	15	20	60	2
Delatour's.........	15	20	45	27	30	12	25	2
Gault's	28	32	125	23	35	28	85	5
Total...........	713	830	1223	317	433	500	1265	94

Figure 412c

For his part Gault went into a more lucrative business. He opened up a saloon and prospered, being numbered among the most frequented watering holes in the city's financial district, according to a moralist of the day who was decrying alcohol consumption in New York City. Chart. Lights and Shadows of New York Life, *1872, p. 707. (Author's collection)*

New York City's die sinkers were relieving the cent shortage with large outpourings of copper tokens, both cheap cent imitations and store card advertising tokens. Several of Gault's customers purchased such pieces, including N. & G. Taylor, George White the

Figures 413a,b

Top, one of Gault's principal competitors, and the largest purveyor of distilled and other spirits on the chart opposite was Charles Delmonico, whose restaurant is still a prominent fixture of lower Manhattan night life. Fifteen-cent scrip, 1862. (Author's collection) Another competitor on the chart, Edward Schulze (Schultze, sic) issued an enormous quantity of tokens in 1863. Token obverse, Fuld NY-630BO obverse. (Civil War Token Society photo) Gault's bar did not last. He only pursued that career for a quarter of a century. Late in his career, he came out of retirement to take a final fling at something he thought he knew, a profession he may well have been born for: advertising. He located in the Tribune Building. Cover, January 3, 1903, Scott 279B. (Author's collection)

hatter, and Simon Steinfeld. In the weeks immediately following Gettysburg, a jobber named A. Ogden advertised to supply the trade with these lightweight coppers. The wholesale firm of Hill and Ogden had been in business in New York for many years. Ogden's location was the same as Gault's, No. 1 Park Place. Ogden rented room 16. The curtain goes up

Figure 414a
The final years of John Gault's life were passed in the ease and comfort afforded by the Murray Hill Hotel, 112 Park Avenue. Gault's retirement home was a splendid 19th century residential hotel in the bustling midtown district. (Note: Chrysler Building and clouds in the background) Photo by Berenice Abbott, November 19, 1935. Museum of Modern Art collection, Abbott 40. (Museum of the City of New York photo)

on John Gault again six weeks after Ogden's ad. Now he is no longer selling *his* new metallic currency, but he is selling metallic currency never-the-less. In the August 29, 1863 issue of *Harper's Weekly*, the national, illustrated tabloid of the day, Gault advertised: " 'PENNY TOKENS' of COPPER. – The best quality, and in any quantity, furnished at $8 per thousand by JOHN GAULT, No. 1 Park Place, two doors from Broadway, New York. All orders by mail or express promptly forwarded." It is apparent that Gault was now thinking like the commission merchants he'd been officing with and doing business with for years. Since Gault had not chosen to advertise his encased stamps in *Harper's Weekly*, his choice this time around is interesting. Harper's Weekly "was the leading newspaper in the country from an advertiser's standpoint," according to one who should have known, George P. Rowell. It was a favorite of Rowell's for his clients. Gault's ad cost him only about $8, or one sale, and its potential returns could have been enormous. They either were . . . or they weren't. Gault advertised only the one time.

Gault was not done with commission sales, nor *Harper's Weekly*, though. Continuing to

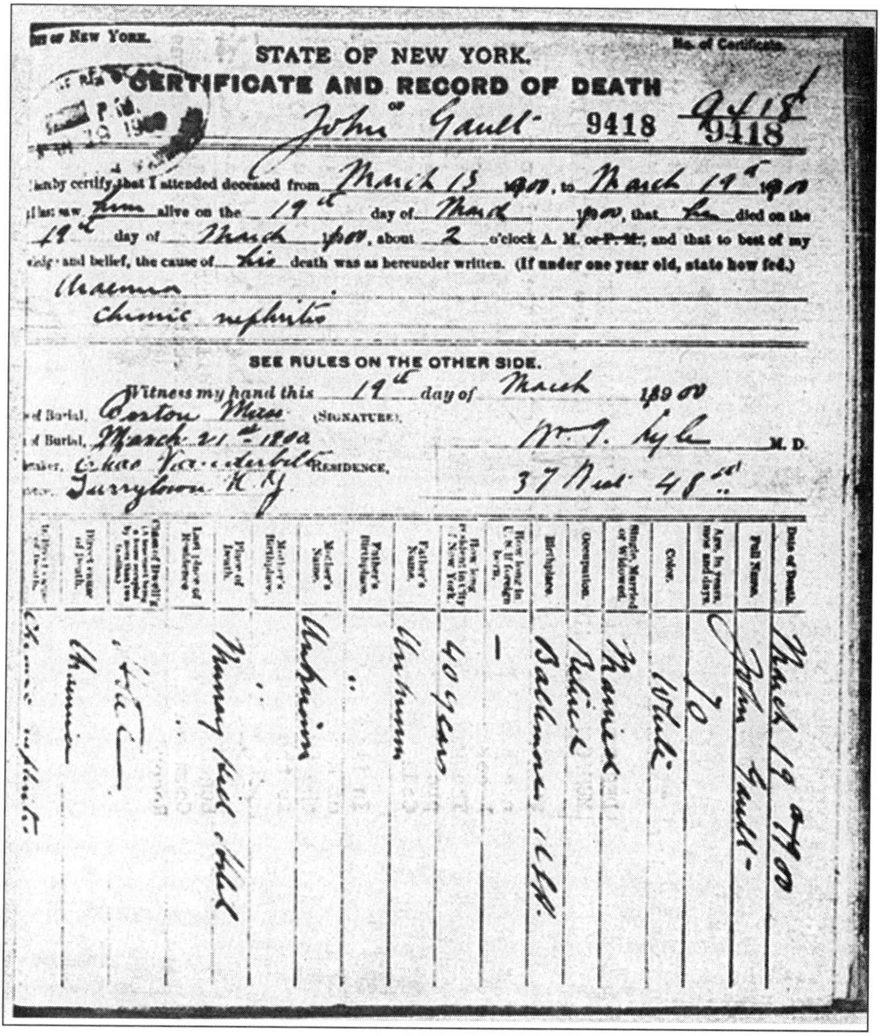

STATE OF NEW YORK.

CERTIFICATE AND RECORD OF DEATH

of John Gault 9418 9418 9418

I hereby certify that I attended deceased from March 13 1900, to March 19 1900

that I last saw him alive on the 19 day of March 1900, that he died on the 19 day of March 1900, about 2 o'clock A. M., and that to the best of my knowledge and belief, the cause of his death was as hereunder written. (If under one year old, state how fed.)

Uraemia

chronic nephritis

SEE RULES ON THE OTHER SIDE.

Witness my hand this 19 day of March 1900

Place of Burial, Boston Mass (SIGNATURE), W. T. Lyle M. D.

Date of Burial, March 21 1900

Undertaker, Chas Vanderbilt RESIDENCE, 37 West 48

Residence, Tarrytown N. Y.

Date of Death.	Full Name.	Age, in years, months and days.	Color.	Single, Married or Widowed.	Occupation.	Birthplace.	How long in U.S. if foreign born.	How long resident in City of New York.	Father's Name.	Father's Birthplace.	Mother's Name.	Mother's Birthplace.	Place of Death.	Last place of Residence.	Place of Dwelling, if tenement	Direct cause of Death.	Indirect cause of Death.
March 19 1900	John Gault	70	White	Married	Retired	Baltimore Md.	–	40 years	Unknown	"	Unknown	"	Murray Hill Hotel	"	Hotel	Uraemia	Chronic nephritis

Figure 415a

John Gault's Death Certificate sketches the official details of his life. He died during the night, March 19, 1900, barely into the present century from kidney failure. Certificate and Record of Death. (Bureau of Vital Statistics, New York City)

split his time commuting between New York and Boston 200 miles to the northeast, John Gault cast around for another line of business. He was living in the Brandreth Hotel in New York while continuing to maintain his Boston residence, but his mother's health was deteriorating. His young sister-in-law had remarried. Eighteen hundred sixty-four was another election year. The long drawn out war and squabbling in the Republican Party made it look

JOHN GAULT.

John Gault died early yesterday morning at the Murray Hill Hotel from Bright's disease. He was seventy years of age. Mr. Gault had been ill for six months and confined to his room since February.

Mr. Gault was born in Boston. At the time of the discovery of gold in California in 1849 he embarked in a sailing vessel bound round the Horn. After a six months' voyage, in the course of which he visited several South American countries, he arrived in California. He remained there five years, meeting with some success. Upon leaving California he came to New-York City, which from that time was his home, although he spent much time elsewhere. Many of his winters were passed in Florida and Virginia.

Mr. Gault was possessed of some inventive genius. He patented a number of inventions, some of which found their way into everyday use.

Mr. Gault married Miss Amelia Patten, of Connecticut, in New-York, thirty years ago. She survives him. He left no children. The funeral services will be held at the Murray Hill Hotel this afternoon at 4 o'clock. Burial will be at Mount Auburn Cemetery, Boston.

of the Incarnation, Gates-ave., near Classon.
Interment private.

GAULT—On Monday, March 19, 1900, John Gault, aged 70 years.
Funeral services Tuesday, March 20, at 4 p. m., at Murray Hill Hotel.
Boston papers please copy.

HARRIS—At White Plains, N. Y., on March 19, Richard Harris, M. D., in his 73d year.
Funeral services Wednesday, March 21, at 3 o'clock.
Carriages will be in waiting at White Plains on the arrival of the 2:05 p. m. train from Grand Central

Figures 416a, b

John Gault's Obituary, right, and Death Notice, below. Although valuable for documentation, the obituary is inaccurate in some of its details. Its length may be attributed to the fact that Gault had worked in the building and may have been known to the anonymous obituary writer. New York Daily Tribune, *March 20, 1900. (New York City Public Library)*

like a toss up. The war had dragged on interminably. Thousands of young boys like John's brother Sam had failed to come home alive. There was real resistance to the Lincoln administration and a bevy of candidates were seeking their own political day in the sun. After the conventions, it boiled down to a two-way race: Lincoln and a new running mate, Andrew Johnson, for the Republicans; and George McClellan and George Pendleton for the Democrats. Additionally John C. Fremont and John Cochrane attempted a run, but withdrew before the election. Never at a loss for drumming up something else on the side, Gault dusted off his old encased stamp patent. On June 18, 1864, he inquired of the incumbent for the nation's highest office. Sitting in his room at No. 1 Park Place, John Gault wrote a letter to the Honorable Abraham Lincoln. Anything remotely associated with Lincoln is a cherished item. Fortunately Gault's letter to Lincoln has been preserved among the Lincoln papers. Gault's request was direct and to the point:

> Hon. Abraham Lincoln
> Sir
> I intend circulating three or four million medals in metallic cases containing likenesses of Yourself & Andrew Johnson for President and Vice President and want to get a perfect Photograph to copy from, or the one, that you would prefer to have circulated. I shall get them up in the neatest manner. If you would please to send me a Likeness I shall be happy to use it to copy from.
> Resp[y] Your Obed[t] Serv[t] John Gault

Ever the entrepreneur, the fearless Gault had high hopes. Millions, and millions and millions of photo campaign buttons were his goal. Conceivably Lincoln, who largely credited photographs for his election victory four years earlier, would have found such prospects auspicious. There is no record that Lincoln answered Gault. Presumably Gault wrote the

Figures 417a, b

Following the death of her husband, John Gault's widow Pamelia removed to the classier, uptown Plaza Hotel and took up residence there. The Plaza, shown at top right, overlooked Central Park at 59th Street and Fifth Avenue, site of the heroic statue of General William Tecumseh Sherman by Augustus St. Gaudens, above. Post Cards, c.1938, 1917. (Author's collection)

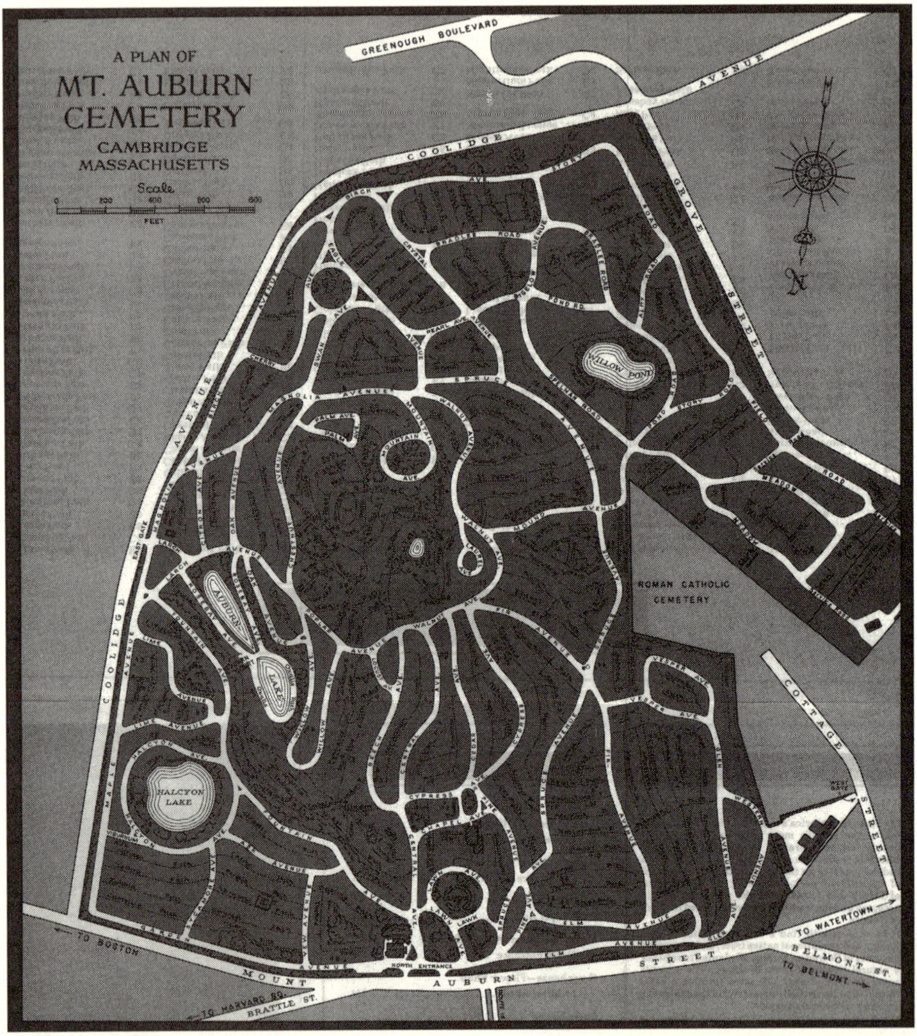

Figure 418a

Mount Auburn Cemetery in Cambridge raised internment to an art form. Its grounds, sculpture and other monuments, landscaping and design created an environment of memorial and tribute as a fitting final resting place to many of New England's best and brightest. These included Henry W. Longfellow, Oliver W..Holmes, Francis Parkman, Charles Sumner, Edward Everett, Winslow Homer, Edwin Booth, Mary Baker Eddy, and John Gault. Cemetery map. (Courtesy Mount Auburn Cemetery)

other candidates too. But likenesses of all the tickets were available locally, and he quickly rushed the pieces into production. Gault returned to Scovill Manufacturing Co. to manufac-

Figures 419a, b

Two of the many memorials at Mount Auburn Cemetery depict the range of commemoration. Top, John W. Damon Memorial in front of the Memorial Fountain, c. 1880. Stereo view. (Author's collection) Above, John Gault's Tombstone. (John and Susan Montague photo)

ture the pieces, and we know he must have paid all his bills on the earlier venture because Scovill responded quickly with a lovely case based on Gault's August 12, 1862 design. Three

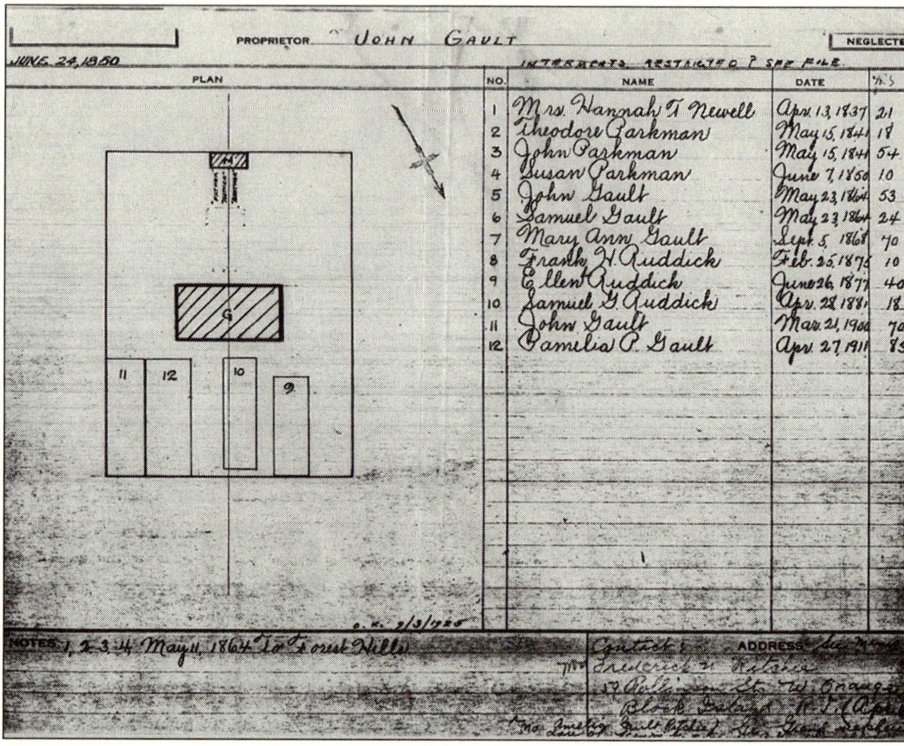

PROPRIETOR JOHN GAULT — NEGLECTED
JUNE 24, 1950

NO.	NAME	DATE	
1	Mrs. Hannah T. Newell	Apr. 13, 1837	21
2	Theodore Parkman	May 15, 1841	18
3	John Parkman	May 15, 1841	54
4	Susan Parkman	June 7, 1850	10
5	John Gault	May 23, 1864	53
6	Samuel Gault	May 23, 1864	24
7	Mary Ann Gault	Sept. 5, 1868	70
8	Frank H. Ruddick	Feb. 25, 1875	10
9	Ellen Ruddick	June 26, 1877	40
10	Samuel G. Ruddick	Apr. 28, 1881	18
11	John Gault	Mar. 21, 1900	70
12	Pamelia P. Gault	Apr. 27, 1911	83

NOTES: 1, 2, 3, 4 May 11, 1864 To Forest Hills

ADDRESS

Figure 420a

Reburial was a common practice. While he was in California, John Gault purchased a plot at Mount Auburn Cemetery, which had previously belonged to the Parkman family. Following the death of his younger brother, Sam, he caused reburial there of the remains of his father and younger brother. Later his mother and other family members were also interred. Ultimately, John and his wife were buried there, too. Plot Map and Cemetery Record of John Gault. (Mount Auburn Cemetery)

weeks after he wrote Lincoln, Gault's ad appeared in the pages of *Harper's Weekly*. He called his pieces "photographic medallions, or campaign medals." They were accurate likenesses enclosed in neat metallic cases, according to Gault. The pieces are among the best of a proliferation of such items issued for the campaign. They are the same size as the encased stamps, and wonderfully made. Prices were 15 cents each, $1.50 per dozen and "liberal discount to the trade." Two months later, Gault was still peddling his campaign medals. He took out another ad in the September 24th issue of *Harper's Weekly*. Although these medals really were an artistic success for Gault, his sales must have disappointed him. Judging by the frequency with which Gault's political medals are encountered today in the marketplace, his sales were not nearly so brisk as that of his larger competitors, B. T. Hayward, E. N. Foote, or John W. Everett.

I, JOHN GAULT, of the City, County and State of New York, do hereby make, publish and declare the following as and for my last Will and Testament:

First: I give, devise and bequeath unto my executors hereinafter named all the real estate owned by me at the corner of Columbus Avenue and West Ninety-third Street, New York City, and commonly known as Number 72 West 93rd Street, in trust, however, to receive the rents and profits, to pay all taxes, insurance and other charges thereupon and to pay over the net income thereof at stated periods to my wife, Pamelia P. Gault, during her life; and upon her death, I give the said premises to my brother, Henry Gault, and my sister, Ann Jane Rutledge, both of Boston, Massachusetts, in equal shares. And I give my said executors and trustees full power to sell the said premises in their discretion at any time during the term of the said trust, and also in their discretion to mortgage said premises, in case in their judgment a necessity therefor should arise; and in case said premises should be destroyed or injured by fire, I authorize my said executors and trustees to expend any moneys received for insurance in rebuilding or restoring said premises. And in case of sale, I direct my said executors and trustees to hold the proceeds upon the trust above declared.

Second: I give to my brother, Henry Gault, Ten thousand dollars.

Third: I give to my brother Henry's son, John A. Gault, the sum of Ten thousand dollars; but if at the time of my death, he shall not have reached majority, then I desire my executors to retain the amount of said legacy and to pay over the income thereof to his guardian for his

Figure 421a

Gault's estate was fairly simple. Although he owned a house west of Central Park, he and his wife had enjoyed the relative luxury and ease of life at a residential hotel. He left the house to his wife Pamelia. He left considerable sums of money to his brother Henry, and his nephew and namesake, John A. Gault. Certified Copy of John Gault's Will, page 1 [57], dated March 2, 1897. (Surrogate's Court, New York)

Lincoln won the election, of course. The nature of Gault's business dealings immediately following the war are problematical. Gault continued to split time between the two eastern cities. He lived at the Brandreth Hotel and maintained an office at No. 1 Park Place. The directories record two brief career changes. First he's listed as an agent, but for whom or what is a mystery. Likely this was a time when he was "between jobs" dealing as a commission broker like his pals down the hall. Then he's listed as being in the "oil" business briefly. Although, petroleum was coming to the fore, this may have been an offshoot from

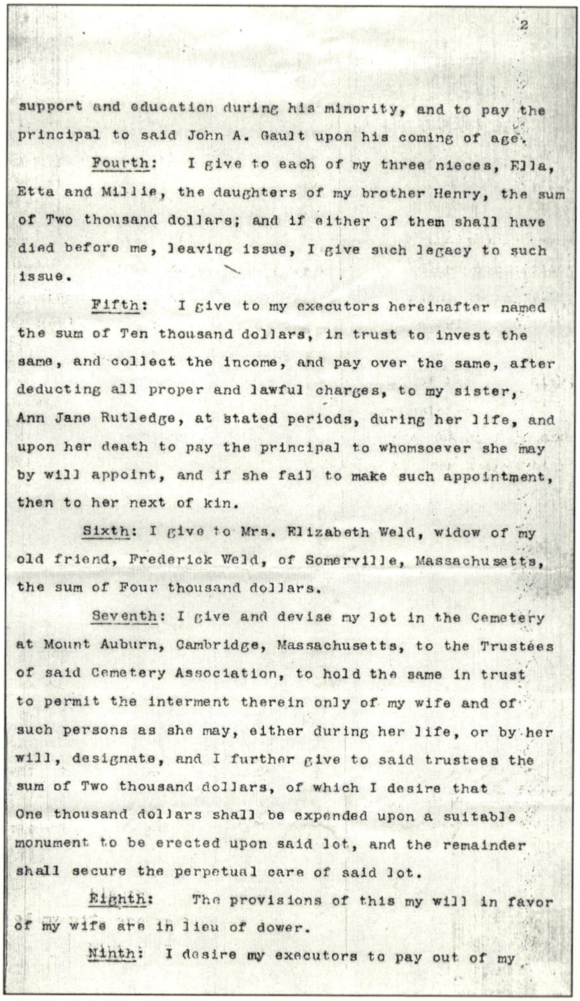

2

support and education during his minority, and to pay the principal to said John A. Gault upon his coming of age.

Fourth: I give to each of my three nieces, Ella, Etta and Millie, the daughters of my brother Henry, the sum of Two thousand dollars; and if either of them shall have died before me, leaving issue, I give such legacy to such issue.

Fifth: I give to my executors hereinafter named the sum of Ten thousand dollars, in trust to invest the same, and collect the income, and pay over the same, after deducting all proper and lawful charges, to my sister, Ann Jane Rutledge, at stated periods, during her life, and upon her death to pay the principal to whomsoever she may by will appoint, and if she fail to make such appointment, then to her next of kin.

Sixth: I give to Mrs. Elizabeth Weld, widow of my old friend, Frederick Weld, of Somerville, Massachusetts, the sum of Four thousand dollars.

Seventh: I give and devise my lot in the Cemetery at Mount Auburn, Cambridge, Massachusetts, to the Trustees of said Cemetery Association, to hold the same in trust to permit the interment therein only of my wife and of such persons as she may, either during her life, or by her will, designate, and I further give to said trustees the sum of Two thousand dollars, of which I desire that One thousand dollars shall be expended upon a suitable monument to be erected upon said lot, and the remainder shall secure the perpetual care of said lot.

Eighth: The provisions of this my will in favor of my wife are in lieu of dower.

Ninth: I desire my executors to pay out of my

Figure 422a

He left smaller sums to Henry's three daughters, Ella, Etta and Millie. Millie is the young girl shown at Figure 411a. Other sums of money were bequeathed to his sister, Ann Jane, and the wife of a friend. Money was also left to purchase and erect the tombstone shown at Figure 419b, and to care for the lot in perpetuity. Certified Copy of John Gault's Will, page 2 [58], dated March 2, 1897. (Surrogate's Court, New York)

his earlier association with the coal industry, since coal oil was a commonly used commodity. Unsettled, he returned to Boston for nearly a year and resumed his career there as a machinist. By spring 1867, however, he had determined a major career move. The war had contributed to a general social decline in New York City. He had found his calling. He opened up a liquor store at 71 Broadway in the vicinity of Wall Street, and took up residence on Staten Island, a short ferry ride away. He couldn't have embarked on a tougher trade. There were 9,000 watering holes in the thirsty city. But business boomed. After nearly a decade of living in hotel rooms in New York, he purchased a home on West 12th Street, the first that he had owned in the city. "Very few liquor sellers fail in this city," a reporter wrote. "The majority grow rich, and their children not infrequently take their places in the fashionable society of the city," he added. Predictably, he was right on the mark.

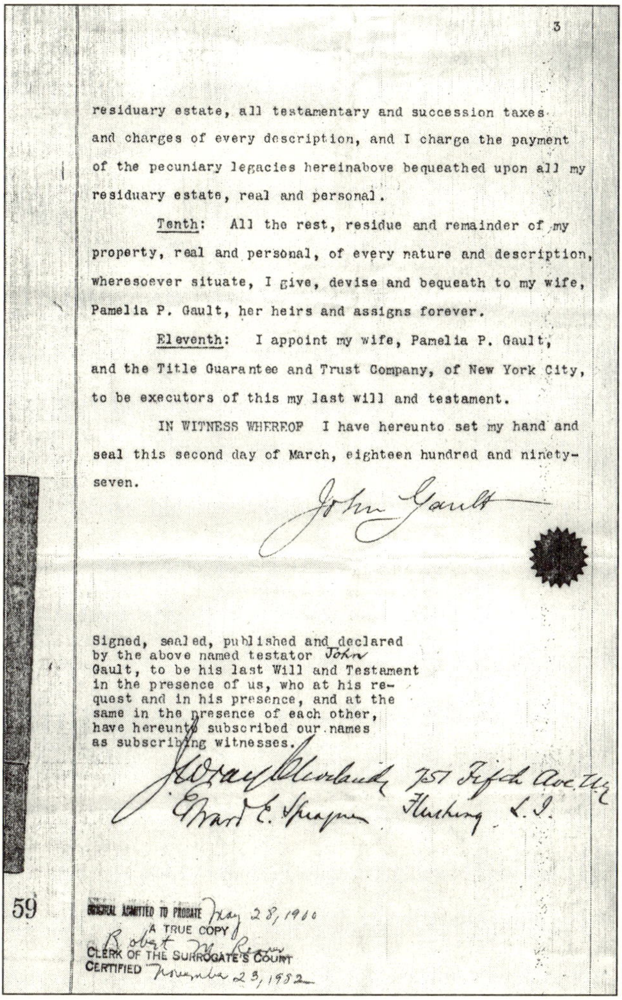

3

residuary estate, all testamentary and succession taxes and charges of every description, and I charge the payment of the pecuniary legacies hereinabove bequeathed upon all my residuary estate, real and personal.

<u>Tenth</u>: All the rest, residue and remainder of my property, real and personal, of every nature and description, wheresoever situate, I give, devise and bequeath to my wife, Pamelia P. Gault, her heirs and assigns forever.

<u>Eleventh</u>: I appoint my wife, Pamelia P. Gault, and the Title Guarantee and Trust Company, of New York City, to be executors of this my last will and testament.

IN WITNESS WHEREOF I have hereunto set my hand and seal this second day of March, eighteen hundred and ninety-seven.

John Gault

Signed, sealed, published and declared by the above named testator John Gault, to be his last Will and Testament in the presence of us, who at his request and in his presence, and at the same in the presence of each other, have hereunto subscribed our names as subscribing witnesses.

J. Wray Cleveland 751 Fifth Ave. N.Y.
Edward E. Sprague Flushing L.I.

59

ORIGINAL ADMITTED TO PROBATE May 28, 1910
A TRUE COPY
Robert McKeon
CLERK OF THE SURROGATE'S COURT
CERTIFIED November 23, 1982

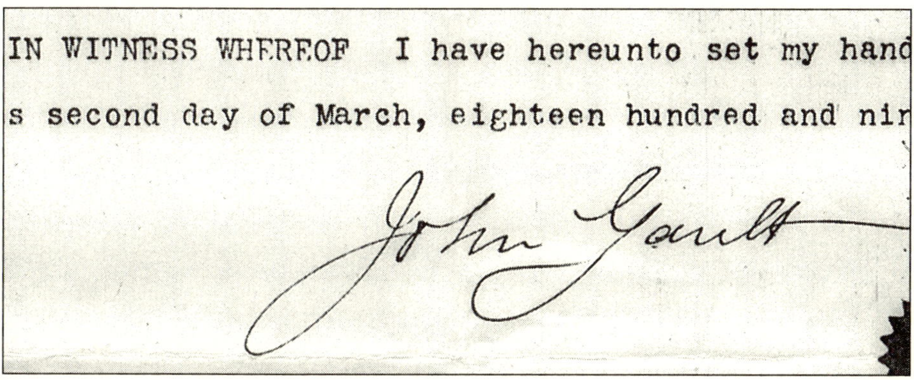

IN WITNESS WHEREOF I have hereunto set my hand
s second day of March, eighteen hundred and nin
John Gault

Figure 423a, b

Left, Gault further directed that whatever was left after paying taxes would accrue to his wife, Pamelia. Below, detail showing Gault's autograph. Certified Copy of John Gault's Will, page 3 [59], dated March 2, 1897. (Surrogate's Court, New York)

Figure 424a

John Gault's surviving brother, Henry, died about a year after John's demise. Henry's widow Lucinda purchased a separate lot at Mount Auburn Cemetery, where she was buried beside her husband in 1905. Lucinda Alden Gault's Tombstone. (John and Susan Montague photo)

Gault's new business enterprise revolutionized his life. He returned to Boston briefly in 1868 to bury his mother, who passed away in September, and to sell his home there. These changes effectively ended his split lifestyle. He was nearing 40, and tiring of chasing the proverbial rainbow for the pot of gold that had always eluded his outstretched fingertips. He was settling into middle age. The confirmed bachelor married Pamelia Patten Pryor of Connecticut about 1870. Pam was a widow, several years older than he was, with two boys by her previous marriage. John Gault's younger stepson, Frank, died in February, 1875, at age 10. The other stepson, Samuel, died in April 1881, age 18.

Gault's saloon trade prospered during the 1870s as shown by the chart which ranks his business in the upper echelons for the city (cf. Figure 412c). Years ago, this author owned a check Gault wrote out for a payment in 1872. For a short while he opened a second saloon across from the Irving House, his former encased stamp client. Eventually he and his wife moved briefly to Long Island. Gault remained in the saloon business for 25 years until he retired. The following year he took one last fling, he went to work briefly as an advertising agent for George P. Rowell in the *Tribune* Building. During the later years, although he owned several properties in the city, John and Pam preferred to live in hotels. They travelled extensively. They spent their winters in Florida and Virginia. His last years were spent residing in the Murray Hill Hotel, a fine midtown hotel near the present location of Grand Central Station and the Empire State Building. Located between 40th and 41st Streets, the seven-story building with two pointed corner towers had more than 500 rooms. It featured

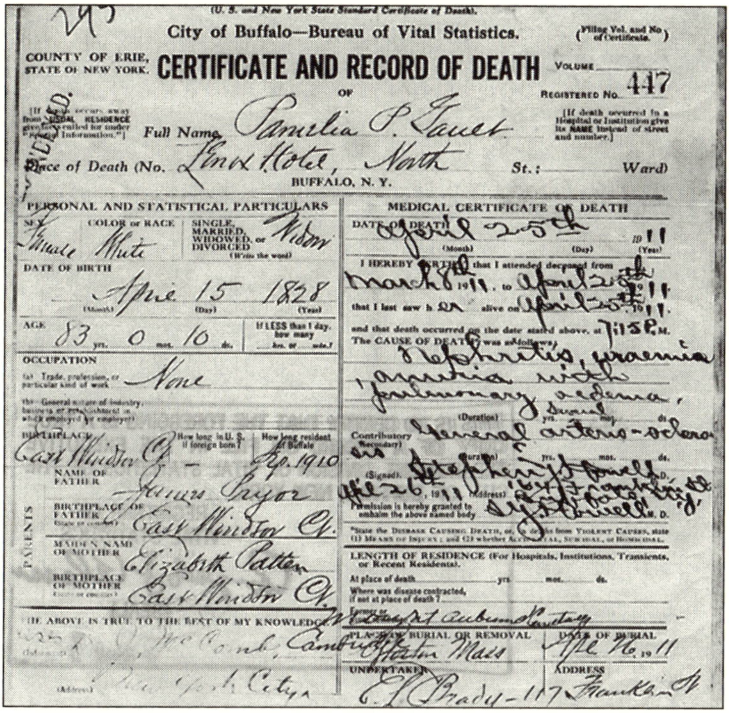
(U. S. and New York State Standard Certificate of Death.)

City of Buffalo—Bureau of Vital Statistics.

COUNTY OF ERIE, STATE OF NEW YORK.

CERTIFICATE AND RECORD OF DEATH OF

Volume 447

Full Name Pamelia P. Gault

Place of Death (No. Lenox Hotel, North St.: Ward) BUFFALO, N. Y.

PERSONAL AND STATISTICAL PARTICULARS

Sex Female. Color or Race White. Single, Married, Widowed, or Divorced Widow

Date of Birth Apr. 15 1828

Age 83 yrs. 0 mos. 10 ds.

Occupation None

Birthplace East Windsor Ct.

Name of Father James Pryor

Birthplace of Father East Windsor Ct.

Maiden Name of Mother Elizabeth Patten

Birthplace of Mother East Windsor Ct.

MEDICAL CERTIFICATE OF DEATH

Date of Death April 25th 1911

I hereby certify that I attended deceased from March 8th 1911, to April 25th 1911, that I last saw her alive on April 25th 1911, and that death occurred on the date stated above, at 7:15 P.M. The cause of death was as follows: Nephritis, uraemia, angina with pulmonary oedema.

Contributory (Secondary) General arterio-sclerosis

Place of Burial or Removal Cambridge Mass

Date of Burial Apr. 26, 1911

Undertaker C. J. Brady - 117 Franklin St.

Figure 425a

Six months after moving to upstate New York, John Gault's widow celebrated her 80th birthday, and shortly thereafter succumbed to a long standing illness. Certificate and Record of Death. (Bureau of Vital Statistics, Buffalo, N.Y.)

both American and European Plans, an elegant establishment of the highest class, according to a contemporary description. Mr. and Mrs. John Gault had achieved a level of affluence and leisure. Within one generation from his parents struggles in their new homeland, their industrious, green-eyed son had arrived.

John Gault, very much a man of his – the 19th – century and its exciting tumult, lived to witness the dawning of the new age – barely. Death came about 2 a.m., Monday morning, March 19, 1900, in his suite at the Murray Hill Hotel on Park Avenue. He died of chronic nephritis or Bright's disease. Simply put, his years as a saloon keeper had caught up with him. His kidneys failed. He had been ill for six months and confined to his room in the hotel for 30 days prior to his death. Gault's funeral services were at four p.m. the following day at the hotel. His body was then transported one final time back to his native Massachusetts. There he was lain to rest in the family plot he had purchased a half century earlier while still a bright-eyed youth in the California gold fields. John Gault's passing did not go unnoticed, although the *Tribune* writer who paid him his final respects got some of

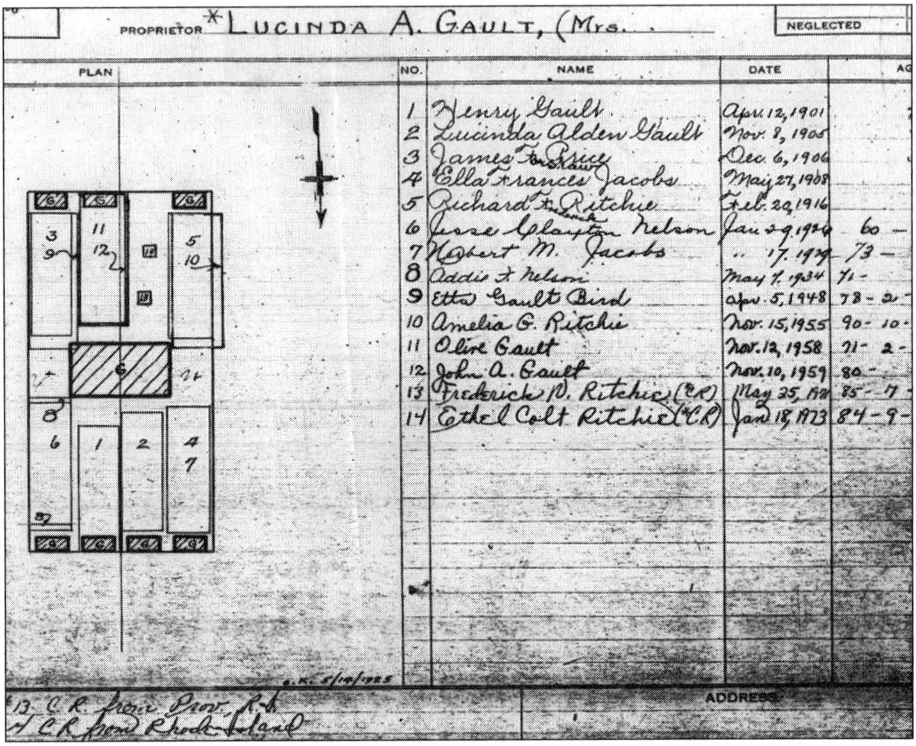

PROPRIETOR *LUCINDA A. GAULT, (Mrs.

NEGLECTED

NO.	NAME	DATE	AGE
1	Henry Gault	Apr. 12, 1901	
2	Lucinda Alden Gault	Nov. 8, 1905	
3	James Erskine Price	Dec. 6, 1906	
4	Ella Frances Jacobs	May 27, 1908	
5	Richard Ritchie	Feb. 20, 1916	
6	Jesse Clayton Nelson	Jan 29, 1924	60 —
7	Robert M. Jacobs	" 17, 1929	73 —
8	Addie F. Nelson	May 7, 1934	71 -
9	Etta Gault Bird	Apr. 5, 1948	78 - 2 -
10	Amelia G. Ritchie	Nov. 15, 1955	90 - 10 -
11	Olive Gault	Nov. 12, 1958	71 - 2 -
12	John A. Gault	Nov. 10, 1959	80 -
13	Frederick D. Ritchie (CR)	May 25, 1971	85 - 7 -
14	Ethel Colt Ritchie (CR)	Jan 18, 1973	84 - 9 -

13 C.R. from Prov. R.I.
14 C.R. from Rhode Island

ADDRESS

Figure 425a

The family plot of Henry and Lucinda Gault became the final resting place for their children, too, the nieces and nephews mentioned in John Gault's will. Plot Map and Cemetery Record of Lucinda A. [Mrs. Henry] Gault. (Mount Auburn Cemetery)

the details confused. The anonymous scribe did pay him a suitable tribute: "Mr. Gault was possessed of some inventive genius. He patented a number of inventions, some of which found their way into everyday use." Gault's last will and testament shows that he left a fine estate and was very generous toward his surviving kin. Shortly after returning to New York from the funeral, Gault's widow Pam moved from the Murray Hill to New York's Plaza Hotel. In September, 1910, she moved to Buffalo and died there seven months later, from causes similar to her husband's.

Conclusion
Chapter XXXV

John Gault's basic idea was to encase five- and ten-cent stamps for sale to merchants as small change. It *was* an ingenious idea. The merchant was allowed to make change for his customers, a basic retail necessity then as now. The customers were likewise facilitated. It was indeed "a happy solution to our common plight," as noted in the press of that day. If it had gone no farther than that, Gault's effort would have been but a footnote to the Civil War change crisis. But genius and circumstances converged and Gault's New Metallic Currency swept to horizons undreamt of on the hot, humid July days when Gault was conceiving and perfecting his idea. Volume wholesalers were given a new advertising medium to launch new projects into the public's awareness, or build further on established franchises. New enterprises were given public visibility on virtual coin of the realm. Even the United States government, stymied in resolving the small change difficulties, studiously pondered whether it too would employ Gault's medium as a remedy.

Was John Gault merely a dreamer? Was his success merely fortuitous?

Who was *this* John Gault, anyway?

Fortunately we have ample testimony by his own hand to enter into the courtroom of History. Several caches of Gault family papers have trickled down to the present. In addition, Gault left a trail of public records which record snapshots at various stages of his lifetime. Such of these items as have been made available for study have been scrutinized according to the tenets of graphology, the study of handwriting for the purpose of character analysis. While such an unorthodox methodology may be hokum to some readers, four sepa-

Summary of Auction Census Data, 1891-1994											
	1	2	3	5	10	12	24	30	90	Total	Pct
Totals	1918	26	2151	1791	1813	458	278	211	104	8750	
Percentage	22%		24%	20%	21%	5.2%	3.2%	2.4%	1.2%		
JG/KG Total	84	19	92	419	400	137	152	132	64	1499	17%
Percentage	5.6%	1.2%	6.1%	28%	27%	9.1%	10%	8.8%	4.2%		
Minus JG/KG	1834	7	2059	1372	1413	321	126	79	40	7251	
Percentage	25%		28%	19%	19%	4.4%	1.7%	1%	<1%		

Figure 428a

John Gault's emphasis on issuing five- and ten-cent encased postage stamps demonstrates that he considered the medium a change-making convenience primarily, and an advertising medium secondarily – even though he had the most to gain in terms of exposure by shifting to lower denomination pieces.

rate and careful analyses according to three systems of graphology show marked similarities in their conclusions and striking insights corroborated by other sources of information about John Gault.

Finding Number 1

John Gault was ambitious.

John Gault was animated, emotional, enthusiastic.

John Gault could be irritable and mildly passionate.

John Gault was sincere, frank, honest and dependable.

John Gault was imaginative and intuitive.

John Gault's writing was hasty.

John Gault's most dominant characteristics were his energy and his initiative.

Finding Number 2

John Gault was a "quick trigger" mentally and physically.

John Gault was a good salesman, generous, with an affectionate and warm nature.

John Gault was demonstrative, with an ability to express himself.

John Gault had a well-balanced mind.

"He does things and gets things done, . . . never lets the grass grow under his feet. He is the type of person who is always thinking up schemes and seeing them through. [He] nearly always takes a chance on a new venture."

John Gault had an insistent nature, [a] distinctive personality.

John Gault was creative, made decisions quickly, instinctively.

John Gault [had] plenty of imagination, generally known as an idea man.

John Gault was inventive, imaginative, witty.

"He is quick on the trigger, sizes up [a] situation almost instantly. [His] likes, dislikes [are] formed on first impression."

John Gault was an original thinker, a person with imagination.

Finding Number 3

John Gault "yields to strong appetites or desires."

"If he is attracted to people, they can take advantage of him."

John Gault was inclined to show off, present himself in the best possible light.

John Gault was very honest.

John Gault had a strong desire to be active [and] enterprising.

"He conceals his tendency to dominate behind apparent kindness and humility."

Finding Number 4

John Gault had a longing for greatness.

"He has an emphasis on [the] material, [a] faculty for organization, [a] dependence on subconscious instincts."

John Gault had many ideas, intuitions, observations.

John Gault was an extrovert, [a] fondness for the company of others.

John Gault had a sharp, critical mind, a lack of sensuality.

John Gault had aristocratic feeling, pride, arrogance.

It would be wrong to put too much emphasis on such insights. But, in fact, John Gault really was all these things and more. He was a hard worker from his boyhood days. He was a risk taker, and adventurer. He was considerate of his family, provided for his mother, his siblings, his heirs. He was a tinkerer. He had a creative and fertile imagination. He had a desire to succeed, a drive to accomplish something and make a difference. He was an excellent salesman. He was very much an idea man, but often left the details of follow through to others because he was already off in another direction. He could be fanciful. He often was not very good with money. He was very human. He could be a braggart. He could be sensitive. He evidently lost his heart to create munitions when his younger brother was killed by an artillery barrage. He liked to travel and see new vistas, a pattern he followed throughout his life. He liked people. He associated with a diverse cross section of them. He enjoyed living well, and by all available accounts did so.

Who is John Gault, indeed?

"But a character on life's stage,
He played out his allotted part
And went to face his maker."

Leaving behind scant testimony, it might be added, except a few cursory government records, some brief public acknowledgements and the concrete evidence of his New Metallic Currency.

Many years and pages ago, my colleagues, readers and I entered upon the stream of History wanting to know more about John Gault, his associates and their times. This book then is a good body of evidence to the wisdom of the American Numismatic Society motto: *Parva Ne Pereant* ("Let not the little things perish"). For it is from that small acorn of encased stamps that this rather large oak in the reader's hands has grown.

Yet perhaps the most pointed questions for some inquirers have only been addressed in cursory fashion. Eighty years ago Edgar Adams, a prolific and serious student of such things, lamented that "there is no known record in existence to show how many specimens [of encased stamps] were put into circulation." No writer has dared to venture an opinion on this matter, although Arnold Perl eloquently raised the Issue: "If Gault operated as long as he seems to have (about eight months is my [Perl's] opinion), what happened to all the postage he encased. Where, in short are the snows of yesteryear?" Slabaugh at least attempted to answer this question. He has gone as far as any, when he suggests that for "the smaller users" the number originally made was likely 500-2000. "Larger users such as Ayer's . . . were probably made in a good many thousands." Rather than throw our hands up in the air, as other writers have done, it is now possible to provide a framework for the answer to Adams' question. Even if it is not possible to give scientific precision to such an answer, yet we find we can know something about what such an answer would be.

After much investigation and debate, we now have a good handle on rarities of merchants and varieties. We have the testimony of approximate orders for two merchants (Cook and Claflin). Veteran dealer-collector Ben Green is the source. He recounted at the 1912 American Numismatic Association Convention, that H. A. Cook of Evansville, Indiana, recounted to him that he had ordered $500 worth of five- and ten-cent pieces in 1862 while on a business trip to New York City. From the same source, Arthur M. Claflin, of Hopkinton, Massachusetts, was said to have purchased "several hundred dollars worth" of Gault's patent money. If our understanding of current rarities bears semblance to original emissions we can derive a ballpark answer to Adams' question with regard to these two merchants. We can then use that standard in a normative way with the issues of the other merchants.

Such methodology is admittedly imprecise, but it is precedented. Walter Breen and others have used similar methods to good advantage with other undocumented series in the past. It relies, of course, on assumptions: (1) that rarity ratings are accurate; and, (2) that the survivors are random samples, no denominations nor merchants having been too heavily favored from destruction by the ravages of time. So in constructing a mathematical model of original issue estimates, a certain detachment is advisable. There are caveats which the modeling has attempted to account for, i.e. the greater inducement to liberate high-valued stamps from their cases *vis-a-vis* low valued stamps; the seemingly greater reason to save high-valued encased stamps in the first place; the absence or presence of modifying other media (for example, cent substitutes were more necessary in Chicago and Cincinnati than in the eastern cities because they were less favored by Mint distribution of small cents, yet they were also more quickly served by cheaper cent imitations), and other factors. The needs of the merchant were also a factor leavening the raising up of such a model. These cases were expensive. For example, at two cents each, the cost of manufacture was twice the nominal value of a one-cent encased stamp, a markup of 200 percent. At the other end of the spectrum, the manufacture only represented a two percent markup of a ninety-cent encased stamp. The lower the value of the stamp, the higher the advertising premium was. Other factors needed to be considered too. Was the customer a retailer actually needing small change? Was the customer launching a new enterprise in need of publicity? Was the customer also active in issuing postage stamp envelopes, store cards, or scrip?

These considerations and others were then used as rules to apply to the 8,750 speci-

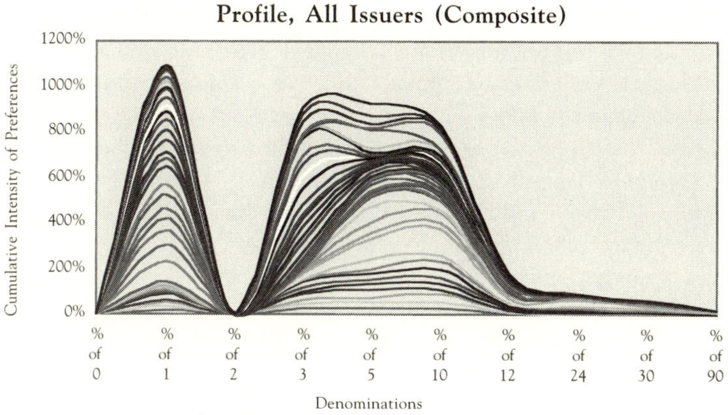

Figure 431 a

An understanding of the purposes to which the various merchants assigned their orders for Gault's New Metallic Currency is revealed by plotting their preferences for certain denominations. Depicted are trend lines of these cumulative preferences for (successively left-to-right) one-cent (peak); two-cent (valley); three-, five-, and ten-cent (plateau); 12-, 24-, 30-, and 90-cent (decline) encased stamps. This is different from plotting numbers. This is a measure of intensity. A composite cumulative profile reveals the duality of preference among Gault's clients (taken as a whole): one- and three-cent preference on one hand, five- and ten-cent preference on the other.

mens that the auction, retail, impounded large collection database had surveyed, covering specific pieces over a time frame of more than a century, 1891-1994. This is by far the largest survey of encased stamp appearances ever analyzed. The components to this database appear in an annotated fashion in the bibliography. Several definite trends emerged. These are summarized on pages 74-75, and printouts are contained in the Appendices. The results of this activity, these "ballpark estimates," have been incorporated into the main text of this book.

What this methodology suggests strongly is that Gault sold upwards of three-quarters of a million pieces of his New Metallic Currency to his several dozen customers. The largest users among his customers were the proprietary medicine vendors: (1) J. C. Ayer; (2) Joseph Burnett; and (3) Patrick Drake. Secondary large users were the insurance company and the hotels: (4) North America Life; (5) Irving House; and (6) Tremont House. Retailers trailed. But even among issuers with approximately the same gross numbers, preferences for certain denominations emerged. These are observable in the models, listed in the summary, and explained in the individual merchant chapters, themselves. Obviously one may play this speculative game with many different scenarios. However, there are limits as to what is reasonable and we should keep these in mind. Silver change was available – for a price, commonly 20-30 percent during the time period in question. If all that was necessary was a medium of exchange, how much would a merchant pay above the going price for fractional silver coinage? Evidence suggests that John Gault was on target with his plan to sell merchants and public five- and ten-cent pieces, where the premium was 40 percent and 20 percent respectively, for change-making purposes. A merchant purchasing such pieces was paying about what the specie would have cost him, and he was getting a commercial plug in the transaction for good measure.

On the other hand, the large advertisers really were willing to pay for the advertising value of this novel invention. By and large they were the largest advertisers in all media available to them. More pieces were available in the lower denominations for a given outlay. More pieces = more exposure, more advertising value. Comparing a merchant's use of the lowest denominations where the advertising premium was highest, i.e. one- and three-cent pieces, to that merchant's use of the change-making pieces, i.e. five- and ten-cent pieces, shows the purpose or psychology of the issuer in placing his order. Several examples will quickly suffice. Ayer, the largest issuer of all, was a wholesaler with an expansive trade worldwide. Seventy-four percent of his issue was one- or three-cent pieces, predominantly advertising values. Only twenty percent of his issue was five- and ten-cent denominations. Drake was another wholesaler with enormous distribution. Sixty percent of his output was the one- and three-cent pieces. Only twenty-eight percent was fives and tens. North America sold insurance, which may be equated with wholesaling. The firm did little or no walk in commerce for modest sums requiring small change. Fully eighty percent of its pieces were ones and threes. Only eighteen percent were fives and tens.

Likewise, we can examine the similarities in the orders of the two hotels, the Irving House in New York City and the Tremont House in Chicago. Both hotels were run by enterprising young men. Both featured fine cuisine and splendid accommodations. Both hotels were run by partnerships, dividing the duties of innkeeper and caterer. Circumstances in both cities were similar, and both groups had similar expectations from Gault's New Metallic Currency. Strikingly, both the quantities of encased stamps and the pattern of distribution among their denominations are remarkably similar. Only fifteen percent of Tremont House encased stamps were one- and three-cent values. Seventy-nine percent were five- and ten-cent denominations. A similar pattern is shown for the New York hotel. About ten percent of the Irving House's order was the two lowest denominations. Fully seventy percent was fives and tens.

The circulation of these pieces, if the quantities are established, presents something of a paradox itself. If Gault's small change substitutes were really so preferable to the other make shifts in circulation, i.e. stamps, scrip, etc., a fact which is universally acknowledged, due to their uniform size and weight, their accepted intrinsic (or stamp) face value, their cleanliness and durability, etc., Gresham's law would assure that they *would not* circulate. As the most precious or dear medium available, the New Metallic Currency would be among the last spent by the public, in fact probably the last medium to be placed into circulation. Those items with least perceived value (i.e. the questionable paper "trash" and miscellaneous items of questionable value) would be spent first and would be paid back first. Dirty stamps would be passed second. Scarce Postage Currency and the New Metallic Currency would be spent third. Ultimately the hoarded subsidiary silver change would be the coin of last resort.

That the New Metallic Currency did circulate is sure. Many pieces, especially the proprietary medicine issues and those from the midwest typically show heavy circulation. Accounts in the press attest to their circulation. Brief anecdotal references to their circulation exist. Such instances occur for upwards of a decade following the introduction of these pieces. The fact that any still exist for collectors today indicates that eventually the pieces were saved up as curiosities, or merely fell through the cracks of commerce and accumulated in purses, drawers or other forgotten places.

Finally, how much was Gault's novel invention worth to him? What about Green's recollection of Gault's assertion that he (Gault) could have made a million dollars had the Post Office not shut him down? This has always been interpreted in the past to mean that the Post Office would not furnish Gault quantities of stamps sufficient to his purposes for producing his New Metallic Currency. It was Post Office policy to discourage large purchases for currency purposes. Supplies of stamps were limited, and the Post Master General was not much pleased at the prospects of redeeming wads of circulated stamps. But clearly if the model is anywhere in the ballpark of possibility, Gault did acquire large quantities of stamps over a period of months.

But his assertion of riches denied seems patently absurd. Gault sold his own pieces for a five percent advance, according to published records in the press. This was a worthwhile markup in his estimation for the pieces he made up for himself and his partnership with Kirkpatrick. We may reliably infer that Gault's profit on these pieces was the five percent plus the difference between his cost and the nominal value of the encasements. If Gault was selling the cases for $20 per thousand as was also published in the press at the time, and if his costs of manufacture were between 1.2 cents and 1.5 cents per piece, his gross profit on the total output was several thousand dollars. For several months work, he wouldn't have fared badly at that rate. Eight hundred dollars a year was considered good wages for a working man in that era. But at that rate, he would have had to sell orders totalling *hundreds* of times the orders he did sell. Even if the stamps had been made available to him, who would have purchased such enormous quantities? There were surely other large advertisers around, but clearly lack of stamps would not have been the limiting factor here. Rather lack of demand would have curtailed his orders much below such an inflated figure.

It is clear that he was a long way from becoming rich on his patent money selling it to merchants after the manner that he eventually adopted. Perhaps what Gault really meant was this: If the government had purchased his remedy and paid him royalties, the idea was a million dollar idea. The only way he could have gained anything approximating the million dollar figure, Green reports he claimed, would have been if Boutwell had sanctioned use of his New Metallic Currency as the government's solution to "our common plight." Of course this did not happen, although as related in earlier chapters it was actively considered to some extent. In such a case, Gault's five percent premium for use of his patent on a $20 million issue would have been precisely $1 million. It is interesting that within 12 months from the monetization of stamps in summer 1862, $20 million worth of Postage Currency is precisely what the federal government had in circulation.

Of course the decision not to use his patent metal and mica emergency stamp money was not a Post Office decision at all. It was, as it should have been, a Treasury Department decision. In fact, we know precisely who made that decision. George Boutwell, the Commissioner of Internal Revenue and the man tasked by Treasury Secretary Salmon P. Chase to solve the small change problem, "shut" John Gault down.

That Gault did as well with his invention as he did is a tribute to his initiative, hard work, shrewdness, inventiveness, salesmanship *and* the circumstances of the times. Opportunity knocked. John Gault was imaginative, creative, adaptable, aggressive, intuitive, impulsive, enthusiastic, energetic, possessing a quick, active mind. He had business acumen, self-confidence, and the ability to act on hunches. He possessed a keen if somewhat fanciful mind. In short, by whatever measure, John Gault is no longer the foreigner, the stranger, the enigma. He seized the initiative. He solved others' problems, and profited thereby. He acted, and in so doing left behind his New Metallic Currency as his testament.

Who is John Gault then?

When all is said and done, John Gault is green-eyed, with thinning, russet hair, and crystal-clear gaze, afterall.

Collecting Encased Stamps
Chapter XXXVI

Encased stamps have been collected actively for a century now, yet due to the extensive number of varieties and the general rarity of the series it has been difficult until recently for any but the most advanced collector to do so in an informed way. Cataloging of the series has languished despite the best attempts of a dozen or so sources. Accurate historical information has only been forthcoming in the last decade, largely at the impetus of the pre-

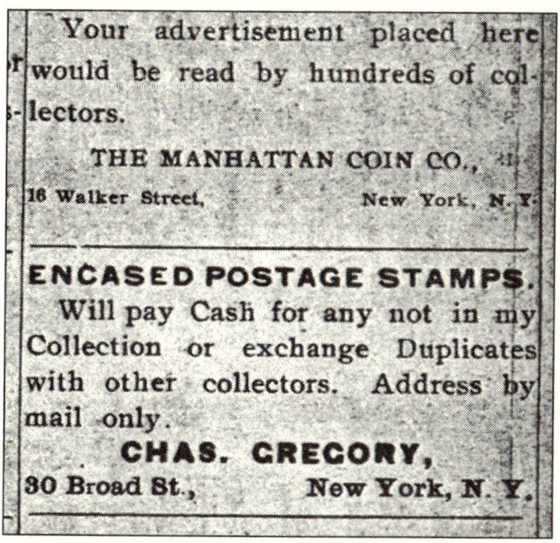
Your advertisement placed here would be read by hundreds of collectors.

THE MANHATTAN COIN CO.,
16 Walker Street, New York, N. Y.

ENCASED POSTAGE STAMPS.
Will pay Cash for any not in my Collection or exchange Duplicates with other collectors. Address by mail only.
CHAS. GREGORY,
30 Broad St., New York, N. Y.

Figures 435a,b

Charles Gregory, left, was among the earliest collectors of encased postage stamps of record. Not only did he advertise to buy them, but in 1889 he published the first catalog listing the pieces by type and variety. Ad. Manhattan Coin Co. 2nd Auction Sale Catalog, C. S. *Stiles collection, October 18, 1902. (Wineburgh Philatelic Library, University of Texas at Dallas)*

Figures 436a, b

Charles Gregory knew John Gault and purchased Gault's remaining pieces in 1889 shortly after penning the article at right. Philatelic Journal of America, *1889. (Wineburgh Philatelic Library) A stamp collector, Gregory called that side its obverse. W. Elliot Woodward entered the coin trade prior to the Civil War. No stranger to the change crisis, his notes were redeemable at his pharmacy or at the bookstore two doors from Joseph L. Bates' store. Scrip, January 1, 1863. (Author's collection) Coin dealers cataloged the encased stamps as merchant store cards.*

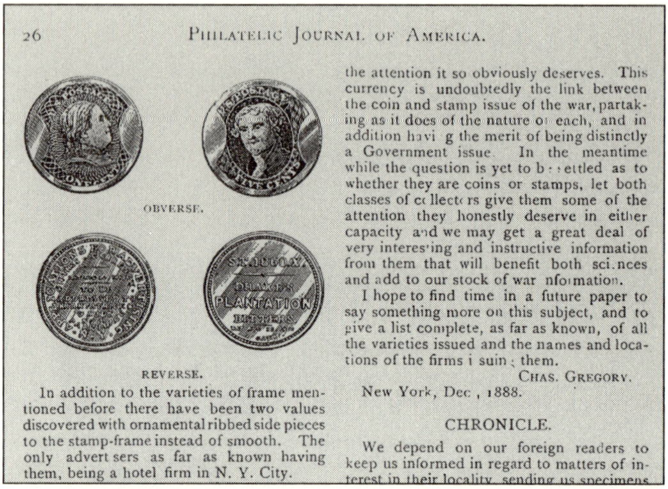

26 PHILATELIC JOURNAL OF AMERICA.

OBVERSE.

REVERSE.

In addition to the varieties of frame mentioned before there have been two values discovered with ornamental ribbed side pieces to the stamp-frame instead of smooth. The only advert sers as far as known having them, being a hotel firm in N. Y. City.

the attention it so obviously deserves. This currency is undoubtedly the link between the coin and stamp issue of the war, partaking as it does of the nature of each, and in addition having the merit of being distinctly a Government issue. In the meantime while the question is yet to be settled as to whether they are coins or stamps, let both classes of collectors give them some of the attention they honestly deserve in either capacity and we may get a great deal of very interesting and instructive information from them that will benefit both sciences and add to our stock of war information.

I hope to find time in a future paper to say something more on this subject, and to give a list complete, as far as known, of all the varieties issued and the names and locations of the firms issuing them.

CHAS. GREGORY.

New York, Dec , 1888.

CHRONICLE.

We depend on our foreign readers to keep us informed in regard to matters of interest in their locality, sending us specimens

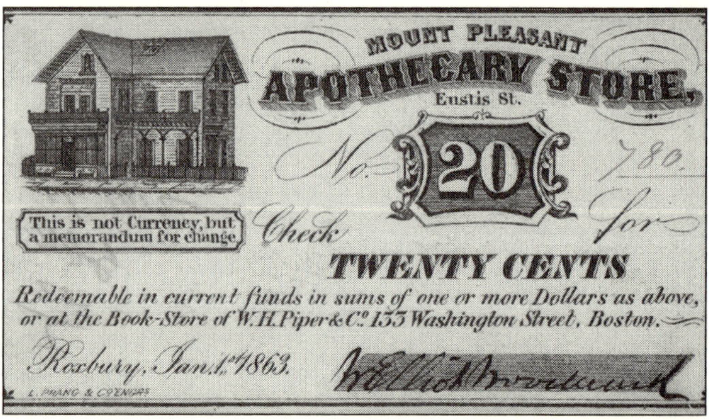

sent writer and a small handful of other interested parties.

Cataloging of the series has proceeded by fits and starts. The first collector of note was Charles Gregory who compiled the first catalog of record in the *Philatelic Journal of America* in 1889. Gregory, a Brooklyn, New York, collector took up the series in earnest about 1887. He advertised extensively in *The American Philatelist*, the *Philatelic Gazette* and elsewhere. He presented his catalog to the local Brooklyn Philatelic Club at Christmas time in 1888, and published his findings several months later. The following year Lyman Low contributed a revision of Gregory's list in the Scott's *Copper Coin Catalogue*. The next significant catalog was prepared by Ben Green in 1902 (revised in 1905), his *Numismatist's Reference and Check List*, followed shortly thereafter by the Springfield, Massachusetts Stamp Club listing. Edgar Adams, a noted collector and cataloger of exonumia, published a listing in Mehl's *Numismatic Monthly* in 1909. Eighty years ago in 1914, the American Numismatic Society staged a monumental collaborative display of encased stamps from January 17 to February 18. Howland Wood prepared a catalog of that exhibition, which was based on the combined

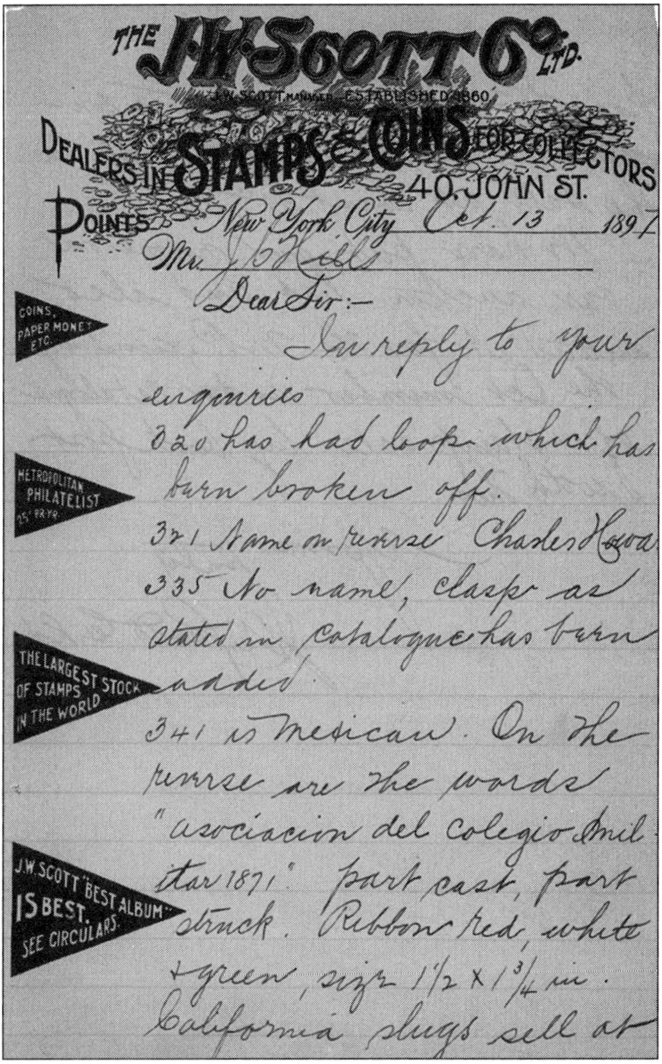

THE J.W. SCOTT Co. LTD.
J.W. SCOTT, MANAGER. ESTABLISHED 1860
DEALERS IN STAMPS & COINS FOR COLLECTORS
40, JOHN ST.
POINTS
COINS, PAPER MONEY ETC.
METROPOLITAN PHILATELIST 25¢ PR YR.
THE LARGEST STOCK OF STAMPS IN THE WORLD
J.W. SCOTT'S BEST ALBUM IS BEST. SEE CIRCULARS.

New York City Oct. 13 1897
Mr. J B Hills
Dear Sir:—
In reply to your enquiries
320 has had loop which has been broken off.
321 Name on reverse Charles Howa
335 No name, clasp as stated in catalogue has been added.
341 is Mexican. On the reverse are the words "asociacion del colegio mil itar 1871" part cast, part struck. Ribbon red, white + green, size 1 1/2 x 1 3/4 in.
California slugs sell at

Figure 437a
John Walter Scott is known as the "Father of American Philately," and justifiably so. He inaugurated the first stamp auctions in this country, produced its first journal, and his name continues down to the present as a division of Amos Press, publisher of stamp and coin periodicals and books. Lyman Low's catalog of encased stamps in his copper coin catalog of 1890 was the first numismatic catalog of this series. But his lasting impact has been on stamp collectors. "Scott" numbers are the system by which encased stamps have been traditionally collected by philatelists and others since 1937. Letter, October 13, 1897. (Author's collection)

collections of Charles Gregory and Ben Green. This catalog became a mainstay for subsequent generations.

Julius Guttag chronicled the series in 1927. Collector W. F. Dunham contributed his *Easy Finding List* in 1929 (updating his 1915 auction price checklist). C. E. Green took up the task in 1936 in his *Mint Record and Type Table [of] U.S. Coins*. Scott's *U.S. Postage Stamp Catalog* commenced listing the series on an annual basis in 1937. John F. Jones published his seminal study in *The Numismatist* in September, 1939. Wayte Raymond took up the task in 1940 in his *Standard Catalog of United States Coins*. The Friedbergs have listed the series since 1953 in their *Paper Money of the United States*. Robertson came on line in 1959.

Figure 438a

Hiram Deats, of Flemington, N. J., amassed the first great collection of encased stamps sold at auction. A president of the American Philatelic Society (originally American Philatelic Association), his 163 pieces were offered by Ben Green in 1906. The comprehensiveness of the selection he put together was amazing given the low level of appreciation for this series in his day. Photo. (American Philatelic Research Library)

Slabaugh published his pamphlet in 1967. Gene Hessler's *Comprehensive Catalog of U.S. Paper Money* has listed the series since 1977. Krause-Lemke joined the field in 1981. And Hodder-Bowers produced their listing, *Standard Catalogue of Encased Postage Stamps*, in 1989.

With all this cataloging going on – why another list?

The answer is simple. John Gault's New Metallic Currency deserved an accurate and simple catalog which brought together a comprehensive understanding of the series without the hangovers of the past. One that published reasonable values and accurate rarities based on objective facts and not subjective nor self-serving wishes. First, it was determined that the earliest catalogers were a whole lot smarter than the standard numismatic and syngraphic references of the present day on this matter. Cataloging organization should be by merchant not stamp denomination for several reasons: (1) A respective merchant purchased products and emitted encased stamps, not vice versa; (2) Such a grouping made possible longitudinal studies of emission and mathematical modeling; (3) The rarity of merchants became quickly apparent; and lastly, (4) as merchant store cards of several denominations this is a sensible way to list the pieces.

Once this was determined it was necessary to devise a scheme that was easy to update. Sequential number series have drawbacks. What is a number 116? What is a number 33? What about new varieties? Is a number 73a part of the series or not? What ever happened to number so-and-so. A cataloging system ought to provide a shorthand shortcut to identifying the pieces cataloged. Every number system requires not only the sequential number but a description of the piece to describe the piece. For example, this piece is a Merchant Name, Denomination, and then its sequential number. What good then is the sequential number?

Figure 439a

The Hiram Deats collection of encased postage stamps was one of the featured consignments to Ben G. Green's 27th Auction, November 30, 1906. This was truly a landmark offering in the history of this series. Its 163 pieces fetched nearly $2,000. Cover. (Bob Kincaid collection)

It is really redundant. What was necessary was a good shorthand description that was the catalog number, too. Hence the Reed Numbering System used in this book.

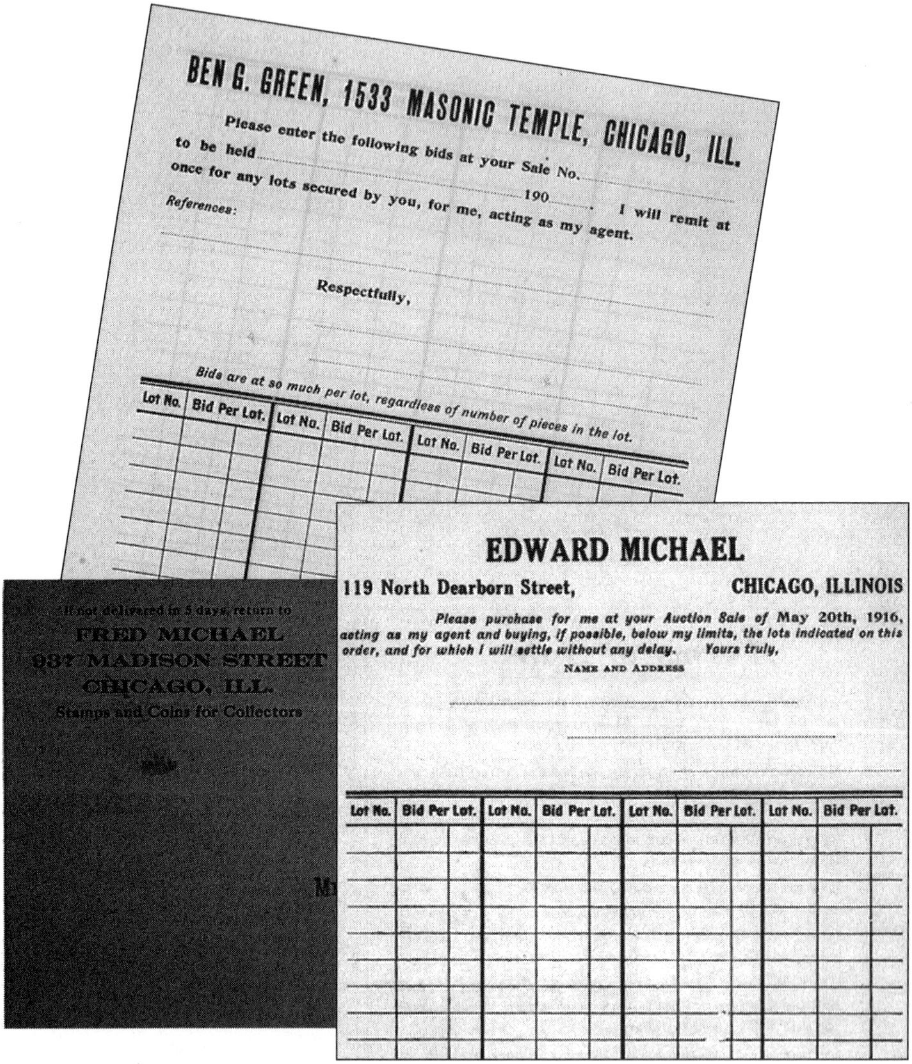
BEN G. GREEN, 1533 MASONIC TEMPLE, CHICAGO, ILL.

Please enter the following bids at your Sale No. .... to be held .... 190..... I will remit at once for any lots secured by you, for me, acting as my agent.

References:

Respectfully,

Bids are at so much per lot, regardless of number of pieces in the lot.

Lot No.	Bid Per Lot.	Lot No.	Bid Per Lot.	Lot No.	Bid Per Lot.	Lot No.	Bid Per Lot.

If not delivered in 5 days, return to
FRED MICHAEL
937 MADISON STREET
CHICAGO, ILL.
Stamps and Coins for Collectors

EDWARD MICHAEL

119 North Dearborn Street, CHICAGO, ILLINOIS

Please purchase for me at your Auction Sale of May 20th, 1916, *acting as my agent and buying, if possible, below my limits, the lots indicated on this order, and for which I will settle without any delay. Yours truly,*

NAME AND ADDRESS

Lot No.	Bid Per Lot.	Lot No.	Bid Per Lot.	Lot No.	Bid Per Lot.	Lot No.	Bid Per Lot.

Figures 440a, b, c

Collectors desiring to understand the evolving cataloging and collecting of the encased stamp series would do well to concentrate on the offerings of Chicagoans Ben G. Green and Ed and Fred Michael early in this century. Many of the enigmatic and obscure pieces passed through their hands. Green also amassed an amazing collection of encased stamp rarities. He died while they were on display at the ANS in 1914. Shortly thereafter Ed Michael offered the 133 pieces for sale. They were purchased en masse by Chicagoan William F. Dunham for $1,035. Fred Michael was among the first dealers to offer encased stamps at fixed prices in the pages of The Numismatist. *Unused Bid Sheets and Advertising Cover, Scott 406, January 3, 1914. (All, Author's collection)*

Figure 441a

Right, William F. Dunham issued his Check List and Auction Record Prices of Encased Postage Stamps *on March 17, 1915. Four years later he gave a talk at the Chicago Coin Club expressing the view that "encased stamps were not proper numismatic material." He went on to amass a legendary collection of same. (Western Pennsylvania Numismatic Society archives)*

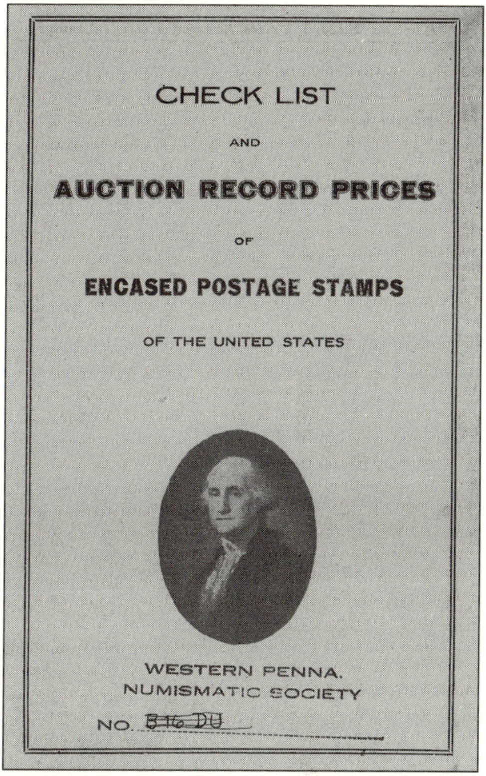
CHECK LIST

AND

AUCTION RECORD PRICES

OF

ENCASED POSTAGE STAMPS

OF THE UNITED STATES

WESTERN PENNA.
NUMISMATIC SOCIETY

NO.

Figure 441b

Left, mega-collector Josiah K. Lilly's encased stamps were a landmark when offered by Robert Siegel in 1967. Son of the founder of pharmaceutical giant Eli Lilly & Co., the 176 pieces realized $30,425.90. Photo. (Eli Lilly & Co. Archives)

This system is based on a simple premise: Use what active collectors of this series are already calling their pieces. Build around their familiarity with this series. When conflicts arise, resolve them sensibly. The system that emerged after some trial and error is painless. This system really is simple. Anybody can get the hang of it in a short period of time.

Every piece is listed first by the merchant who issued it or the product advertised, next by the denomination of the stamp encased, and then by any additional variety information necessary. Simple naming conventions were employed:

(1) Use the first two letters of the prominent name: That convention works well for nearly half the pieces. But some difficulties present themselves. So a second convention was utilized;

(2) Use the first letter of consecutive prominent names: This worked well for most of

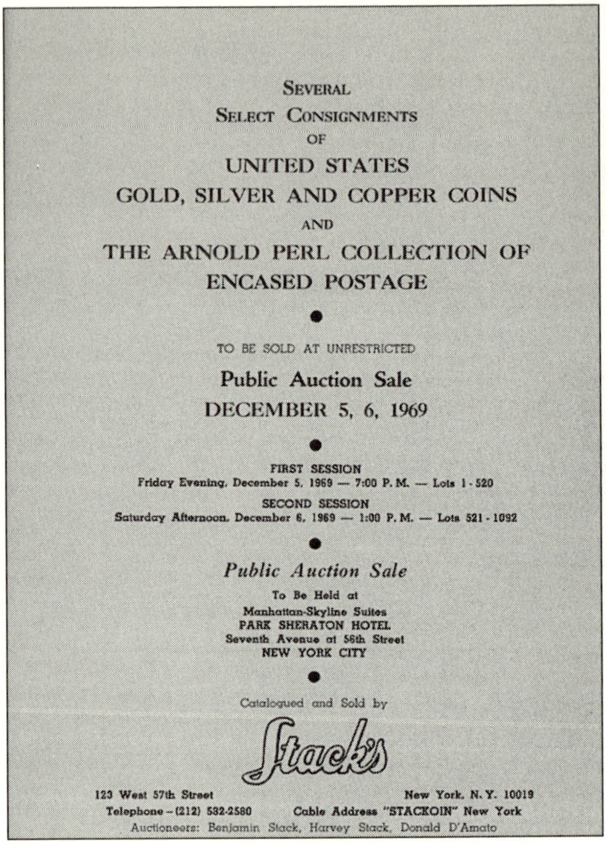

SEVERAL
SELECT CONSIGNMENTS
OF
UNITED STATES
GOLD, SILVER AND COPPER COINS
AND
THE ARNOLD PERL COLLECTION OF
ENCASED POSTAGE

TO BE SOLD AT UNRESTRICTED
Public Auction Sale
DECEMBER 5, 6, 1969

FIRST SESSION
Friday Evening, December 5, 1969 — 7:00 P.M. — Lots 1-520
SECOND SESSION
Saturday Afternoon, December 6, 1969 — 1:00 P.M. — Lots 521-1092

Public Auction Sale
To Be Held at
Manhattan-Skyline Suites
PARK SHERATON HOTEL
Seventh Avenue at 56th Street
NEW YORK CITY

Catalogued and Sold by
Stack's
123 West 57th Street New York, N.Y. 10019
Telephone – (212) 582-2580 Cable Address "STACKOIN" New York
Auctioneers: Benjamin Stack, Harvey Stack, Donald D'Amato

Figure 442a
Arnold Perl's excitement about his encased stamp collection was evident in the essay, "On the Joys of Specialized Collecting," which Stack's published in the catalog offering his pieces in 1969. The basic collection contained 132 pieces as well as collateral material. Four years earlier the same firm had offered 37 duplicate pieces from Perl's collection. Catalog Title Page. (Author's collection)

the rest of the pieces; and

(3) Use the prominent first two letters of the specific product advertised: This is especially helpful in those instances where a merchant advertises several different products on different varieties. Thus the series is cataloged and described simply as:

AB = Aerated Bread
AC = Ayer's Cathartic
AP = Ayer's Pills
AS = Ayer's Sarsaparilla
BA = BAtes
BC = Bailey & Company
BE = Burnett's Extracts
BK = Burnett's Kalliston
BT = Brown's Troches
BU = BUhl
CL = CLaflin
CO = COok
DO = DOugan
DR = DRake
EM = Ellis McAlpin
EV = EVans
HO = HOpkins
IH = Irving House
JG = John Gault
KG = Kirkpatrick & Gault
LT = Lord & Taylor
ME = MEndum's
MI = MIles
NA = North America
NO = NOrris
PE = PEarce
SA = Sands' Ale
SB = Schapker & Bussing
SH = SHillito
ST = STeinfeld
TA = TAylor
TH = Tremont House
WH = White Hatter
WL = Weir & Larminie

Figure 443a

Exceptional encased stamp collections have been put together by auction bidders John J. Ford (left foreground), and Dr. Donald H. Kagin (center). Ken Bressett (right) was instrumental in the awarding of an American Numismatic Association research grant for this book. (Author's photo)

So, the first two characters of every catalog listing indicate the merchant or specific product(s) advertised. Second, the next two characters list the stamp denomination:

01 = one-cent	05 = five-cent	24 = twenty-four-cent
02 = two-cent	10 = ten-cent	30 = thirty-cent
03 = three-cent	12 = twelve-cent	90 = ninety-cent

Thus *only* four characters describe – as well as catalog – more than 60 percent of all the varieties known. It's simple to describe nearly 170 different varieties and catalog them at the same time. Examples:

AB01 = Aerated Bread one-cent	BT10 = Brown's Troches ten-cent
CL05 = Claflin five-cent	JG03 = John Gault three-cent
MI01 = Miles one-cent	WL10 = Weir & Larminie ten-cent

Only one or two additional characters take care of most of the rest. These may distinguish die varieties:

SA = Short Arrows	FG = FANCYGOODS	SM = Small AYER'S
LA = Long Arrows	F/G = FANCY GOODS	MD = Medium AYER'S
RB = Ribbed	CU = Curved Insurance	LG = Large AYER'S
	ST = Straight Insurance	

Or they may distinguish stamp varieties:

'51 = 1851 Series Stamp	RS = Revenue Stamp	Y = Yellow five-cent
'57 = 1857 Series Stamp	ES = Envelope Stamp	G = Gray 24-cent

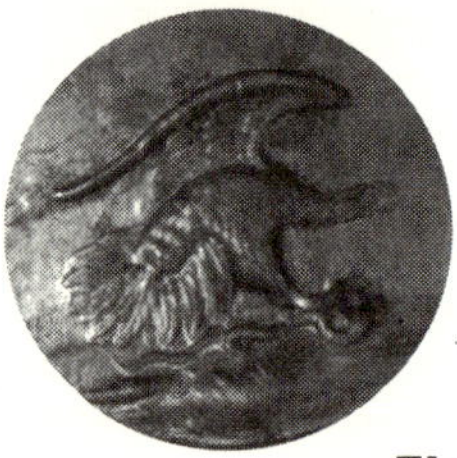

Figures 444a-f

Above right, although not one of Gault's encased stamps, collectors often acquire the so-called "Feuchtwanger" strip as an ancillary item. Reed FE09 Feuchtwanger nine-cent strip, ex-James F. Ruddy specimen. (Bowers and Merena photos) Right, c. 1859 National Medallion plaque (Feuchwanger device above, detail from plaque's top left) presumably by S. H. Black. Could Black have produced the strip after the war, too? Plaque. (Author's collection, electronic imaging by Omar Mediano) Above, comparison of (from top) Feuchtwanger cent (Author's collection, Coin World photo), strip detail and plaque detail.

Auction Census Data Summary, 1891-1994

	4	9	20	27	Total	Pct
FE	1	139	1	5	146	
	1	**139**	**1**	**5**	**146**	

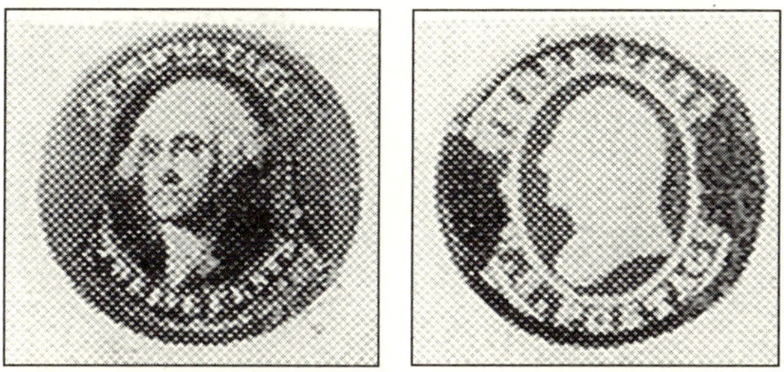

Figures 445a-k

An enigmatic selection of 11 pieces has defied explanation for decades. Purportedly given by a former Scovill employee to that company in 1884, these pieces were presented to the Mattatuck Historical Society four decades later. They were subsequently dispersed. These pieces bear either Gault or Irving House obverses and non-standard stamps. The stamps comprising that lot are depicted here. (Coin World archives)

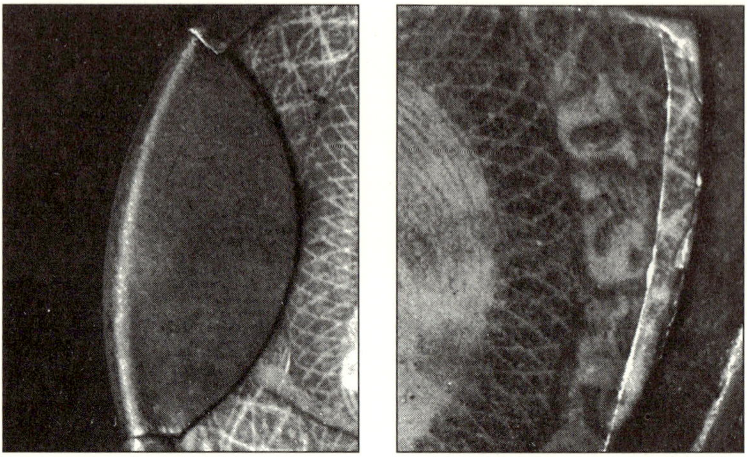

Figures 446a, b

Fantasy pieces and fake rarities created by substituting stamps have plagued this series for more than a century. Impairments caused by such doctoring are not often found on the encased stamp reverses (stamp sides), but some do occur. Some of the fakes are crudely made like the piece above left. The frame tabs were pulled back ripping the fragile brass wrap-around. (INSAB photo) Sometimes, improving the appearance of the encased stamp seems to have been the goal as above right. Wrap around lip was pried up evidently to replace defective mica insert. (INSAB photo)

Of course cataloging the series is only one challenge, no matter which system is used. Collecting the pieces is the basic desire for most people. Collecting all 275 (or so) recognized varieties that actually exist is out of the question for all but the richest, the luckiest, the most patient. Even then it would be impossible. Very large collections have half that many varieties. So most collectors try to assemble type sets. These sets typically involve one for each issuer (31 pieces), or one for each product (34 pieces). A denominational type set requires eight pieces. Other possibilities exist.

Let's examine a denominational type set. What would the commonest variety of each of the denominations reasonably cost in collectable condition? Remember these are just suggested price estimates. Many factors can influence prices drastically:

Denomination	Base Value	Example	Denomination	Base Value	Example
1-cent	$100-$200	AS01MD	12-cent	$450-$800	JG12
3-cent	$100-$200	AS03MD	24-cent	$650-$900	JG24
5-cent	$125-$225	JG05	30-cent	$1250-$1700	JG30
10-cent	$125-$225	JG10	90-cent	$3000+	JG90

How about a merchant/product type set. What would an average specimen of the commonest variety of each merchant reasonably cost, if one had the requisite money, luck and patience? Remember, these are just suggested prices. Nicer condition specimens will cost more. Rarer varieties will cost more. The amount a dealer or collector paid for a piece will affect the asking price. The method of sale does too, and so forth:

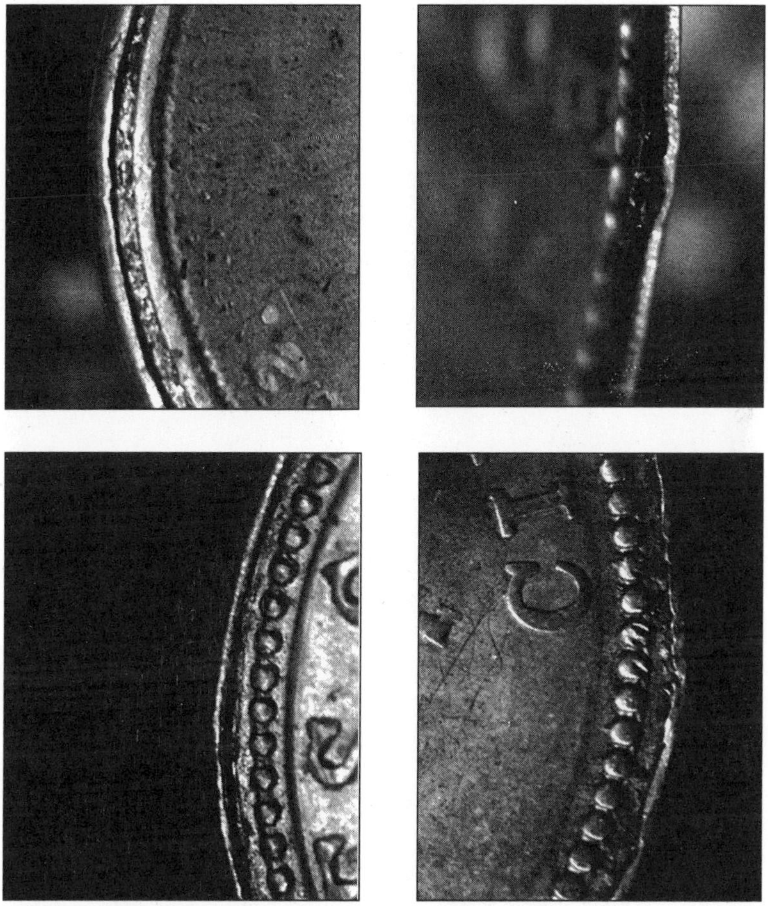

Figures 447a, b, c, d

More frequently encountered, however, are impairments left on encased stamp obverses (merchant sides) by prying tools. Four examples are shown above. These range from subtle indentations in the lips of the rim to gross deformations of the rim itself caused by the prying tools. (INSAB photos)

Merchant	Common	Type	Merchant	Common	Type	Merchant	Common	Type
AB01	$1,000-	$1,600	CO10	$1,000-	$1,400	NA01ST	$300-	$400
AC03LA	125-	250	DO01	750-	1,000	NO01	1,200-	1,500
AP03	125-	250	DR03	125-	225	PE03	1,250-	1,750
AS01MD	100-	200	EM10	650-	900	SA05	1,650-	2,750+
BA01F/G	300-	500	EV01	700-	1,000	SB10	350-	550
BC03	800-	1,000	HO03	1,000-	1,500	SH05	300-	500
BE05	250-	400	IH05RB	350-	500	ST01	1,000-	1,500
BK10	275-	475	JG10	125-	225	TA01	750-	1,250
BT05	250-	450	KG05	200-	350	TH05	150-	250
BU05	850-	1,200	LT10	400-	600	WH01	1,000-	1,500
CL01	6,000+	up*	ME01	300-	400	WL10	650-	850
+ higher values likely			MI05	5,000+	up*	* denotes speculative values		

Figures 448a, b, c

Other telltale signs of such activity include, above, scratching on outer case from attempting to reclose the case; above right, failure to fully reclose the rim revealing a separation of the wrap around rim from the merchant insert disc (INSAB photos); and right, irregularly shaped (out of round) cases caused by uneven pressure when reclosing cases. (Bob Kincaid photo)

Collectors should be aware that numerous spurious pieces are available in the marketplace. These spurious pieces are of several types. Over the years many encased postage stamp cases have been pried open for a variety of reasons, i.e. to improve the grade of the stamp, change out the stamp denomination, improve the mica, create new varieties, etc. Although collectors are often advised that these substitutions are easy to detect, this is not always the case. Inexperienced collectors do not know what to look for. Often even experienced collectors are gullible, i.e. they want the piece to be "good" so they overlook obvious telltale signs. But as recent history attests, sophisticated prying, substitution and reclosing procedures are

Figures 449a, b, c, d

More deceptive are the spurious pieces created in the mid-1960s and marketed at that time. These pieces styled generically as "Romains" are known to advanced collectors by their "fingerprints" (telltale imperfections), but easily fool the novice. Four pieces are illustrated here. Above left, look for the depression between the G of GAULT and the PA of PARK PLACE on the Kirkpatrick and Gault issue. Left middle, look for the depression between the N and G in ADVERTISING on the KG issue. Lower left, look for the tooling marks above 461 on the purported Lord & Taylor issue. Above, look for the pimple above the right serif of R in AYER'S and the depression midway between the R in AYER'S and the R in SARSAPARILLA on the ASMD issue. (INSAB photos)

often very difficult to discern, and even then experienced eyes may have differing opinions about specific pieces. Collectors are encouraged to examine the enlarged photographs in this section and familiarize themselves with the techniques employed. Prying tools will leave telltale marks. Burnishing tools will leave telltale marks. Be skeptical of rare varieties. Before you spend your money, be satisfied of the genuineness of a particular piece. This author has examined hundreds of pieces in major collections, and *in his opinion* even long-time collectors, emotionally attached to their pieces, see what they want to see on this

Figure 450a

Another telltale "Romain" fingerprint occurs on the spurious AP obverse. Look for the granular surface and the depression in the center of the serif on the mid bar of the E in AYER'S. (INSAB photo)

matter. This advice applies also to purported grooved (ribbed frame) specimens. As explained in the text, only the first issues of John Gault and Irving House customarily come with these grooved wrap-around frames. Any other merchant should be checked twice.

Much less well publicized are the fake encased stamps created in the late 1960s and marketed to the numismatic community then. These pieces are known in the trade as "Romains." They are out and out frauds created to deceive collectors. They include modern-made merchant inserts and have a plastic material instead of mica over the stamps. They were suppressed due to the vigilance of a leading coin dealer in concert with a leading numismatic periodical, in whose pages these pieces were being advertised. However, they were good enough to fool collectors before the perpetrator was shut down. Surviving pieces still do. Recently (summer 1994) I examined a lot of 15 encased stamps offered by an antique dealer at an antique show in Dallas, Texas. The dealer was from the midwest. His small "collection," as he called it, included the following pieces: AP01, AP03 (2), AP05, AP10, AP24, AS30MD, BC03, BU10, JG05, JG24, KG03 (3) and SB10. They were distinctively packaged in neat little holders and the holders themselves were in a neat presentation album. They all bore Scott catalog pricing. The suggested catalog value of the "collection" was $7,975, but of course he said he would bargain.

During the course of the three-day show, I visited with this dealer each day. Little by little he explained how he had come by this small "collection." He was very nice. He may even have been honest. The trouble was 10 of the pieces were these "Romains." Of the four "Romain" fake merchant inserts (see photos on pages 449-450), three were represented in this little grouping. Several of the other pieces looked curious, too. They looked to have been tampered with. Be that as it may, there was no question about the two-thirds of the pieces which were made in the 1960s and not in the 1860s. The six TAKE AYER'S PILLS (see telltale diagnostics, above) pieces were all fakes. The three KIRKPATRICK & GAULT pieces (see telltale diagnostics, page 449) were all fakes, as was the AYER'S SARSAPARILLA piece (see telltale diagnostics, page 449).

Five months later I saw this same collection on a numismatic dealer's table at a currency show in St. Louis. He was a very knowledgeable currency dealer. Unfortunately, he paid the bargain price of $4,000 for the bogus pieces the month before at an antique show in Atlanta, Georgia. He bought the pieces from the midwestern antique dealer for 50 percent

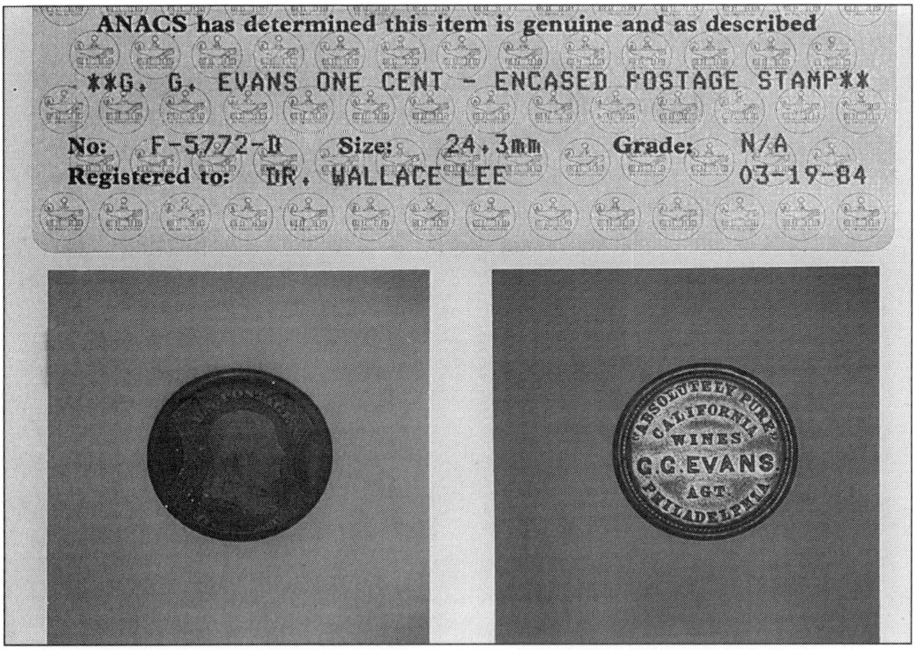

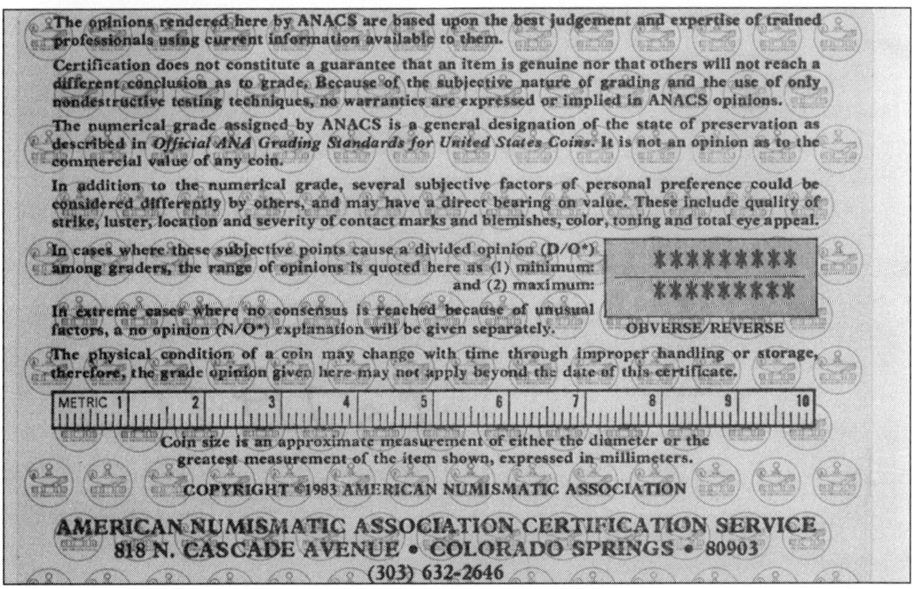

The opinions rendered here by ANACS are based upon the best judgement and expertise of trained professionals using current information available to them.

Certification does not constitute a guarantee that an item is genuine nor that others will not reach a different conclusion as to grade. Because of the subjective nature of grading and the use of only nondestructive testing techniques, no warranties are expressed or implied in ANACS opinions.

The numerical grade assigned by ANACS is a general designation of the state of preservation as described in *Official ANA Grading Standards for United States Coins.* It is not an opinion as to the commercial value of any coin.

In addition to the numerical grade, several subjective factors of personal preference could be considered differently by others, and may have a direct bearing on value. These include quality of strike, luster, location and severity of contact marks and blemishes, color, toning and total eye appeal.

In cases where these subjective points cause a divided opinion (D/O*) among graders, the range of opinions is quoted here as (1) minimum: and (2) maximum:

****
****

In extreme cases where no consensus is reached because of unusual factors, a no opinion (N/O*) explanation will be given separately.

OBVERSE/REVERSE

The physical condition of a coin may change with time through improper handling or storage, therefore, the grade opinion given here may not apply beyond the date of this certificate.

METRIC 1 2 3 4 5 6 7 8 9 10

Coin size is an approximate measurement of either the diameter or the greatest measurement of the item shown, expressed in millimeters.

COPYRIGHT ©1983 AMERICAN NUMISMATIC ASSOCIATION

AMERICAN NUMISMATIC ASSOCIATION CERTIFICATION SERVICE
818 N. CASCADE AVENUE • COLORADO SPRINGS • 80903
(303) 632-2646

Figures 451a, b

Certification by one of the services which render informed opinion is helpful, but no guarantee. Such opinion is only as good as its source. ANACS No. F-5772-D. (Dr. Wallace Lee collection)

Figures 452a-e

Impairments can reduce eye appeal and value of legitimate pieces. Clockwise from above, a piercing hole for suspension, crazed mica, broken mica, case ding, and flaking mica. Mica impairments. (Bob Kincaid and Kagin Numismatic Auctions photos)

off. Four weeks later, he examined the photos on galleys of pages from this book and compared them to his pieces to his growing chagrin. Apprised of the details of his unfortunate purchase, the purchaser offered to buy a dozen copies of this book when it came out. He also said he hoped he could recoup his money from the antique dealer. This is a sad story. Unfortunately, it is also a true story. This can happen to anybody, so beware.

Knowledgeable dealers do exist. Several independent certifying or authenticating bureaus will give informed opinions about suspect pieces. Unfortunately, I've seen authenticated fakes, too. Any opinion is only as good as the person making the judgement. A highly publicized and arbitrated case shows that even very knowledgeable and competent professional numismatists may disagree over certain pieces. Any purchaser would do well to satisfy himself on any piece. Again, I've examined pieces in institutional collections, formed years ago by famous collectors, studded with fabrications.

Grading is another thorny issue in collecting circles. Sophisticated grading schemes have been worked out for many numismatic items, but encased stamps are complex pieces. Simple grading schemes are not possible. Soft brass cases lose silvering, or silvering is replaced. Brass tarnishes and deforms rather easily. Many of the stamps were not in great shape 133 years ago when then were encased. In the scores of years since, they are subject to fading. Mica is a mineral. It flakes. It breaks. Many pieces have been holed to wear suspended from ribbons. All impairments should reduce a particular piece's value. Consequently absence of such impairments should make a piece more valuable. Catalogs which price encased stamp varieties in all grades are wish lists. Very few of the 275 or so varieties are ever available in the marketplace with sufficient frequency and in a variety of grades to jus-

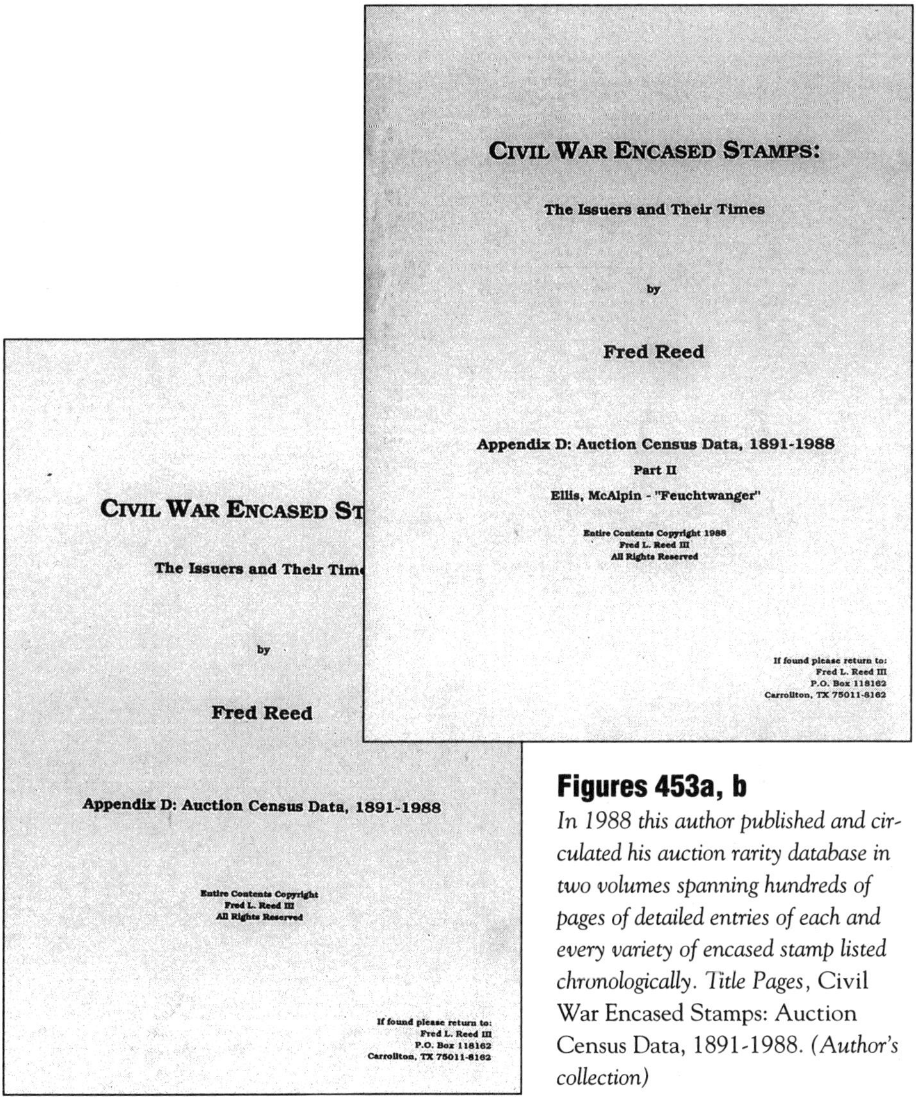

CIVIL WAR ENCASED STAMPS:

The Issuers and Their Times

by

Fred Reed

Appendix D: Auction Census Data, 1891-1988

Part II

Ellis, McAlpin - "Feuchtwanger"

Entire Contents Copyright 1988
Fred L. Reed III
All Rights Reserved

If found please return to:
Fred L. Reed III
P.O. Box 118162
Carrollton, TX 75011-8162

CIVIL WAR ENCASED ST

The Issuers and Their Tim

by

Fred Reed

Appendix D: Auction Census Data, 1891-1988

Entire Contents Copyright
Fred L. Reed III
All Rights Reserved

If found please return to:
Fred L. Reed III
P.O. Box 118162
Carrollton, TX 75011-8162

Figures 453a, b
In 1988 this author published and circulated his auction rarity database in two volumes spanning hundreds of pages of detailed entries of each and every variety of encased stamp listed chronologically. Title Pages, Civil War Encased Stamps: Auction Census Data, 1891-1988. *(Author's collection)*

tify such lists. Catalogers do well to describe all the impairments of a piece when justifying suggested prices.

The availability of the different merchant specimens, denominations and varieties is also important. The Auction Census Database summarized on pages 454-456 demonstrates availability by variety over a period of a century in the auctions, price lists, institutional and other major "impounded" collections consulted. These sources are listed in the annotated bibliography. These tables do not necessarily indicate rarity, *per se*, but rather availability in those sources over that time period.

	1	**2**	**3**	**5**	**10**	**12**	**24**	**30**	**90**	**Total**	**Pct**
AB	56			4						60	<1%

	1	**2**	**3**	**5**	**10**	**12**	**24**	**30**	**90**	**Total**	**Pct**
AC SA	107		133	31	53	9	9	5		347	
AC LA	7		187	19	18	11	3	1		246	
AP	96		229	38	48	22		3	6	442	
AP RB	1	1	7							9	
AP '51		1								1	
AP RS		1								1	
AS SM	75		102	4	24	3				208	
AS MD	257	2	267	59	62	22	14	11	6	700	
AS MD RB			7		6					13	
AS MD CD	1		1							2	
AS MD '57	1									1	
AS LG	11		139	12	11	3	1			177	
AS LG RB										0	
AS '51	1									1	
	557	4	1066	170	222	70	27	20	12	2148	24%

	1	**2**	**3**	**5**	**10**	**12**	**24**	**30**	**90**	**Total**	**Pct**
BA FG	68		2	5	11	0				86	
BA FG RB	1			5	3					9	
BA F/G	103		16	13	23	16	2			173	
	172		18	23	37	16	2			268	3%

	1	**2**	**3**	**5**	**10**	**12**	**24**	**30**	**90**	**Total**	**Pct**
BC	32		39	37	35	5				148	1.7%

	1	**2**	**3**	**5**	**10**	**12**	**24**	**30**	**90**	**Total**	**Pct**
BE	54		78	99	97	22	7	8	3	368	
BE RB					10					10	
BK	50	1	56	70	101	16	5	7	3	309	
	104	1	134	169	208	38	12	15	6	687	8%

	1	**2**	**3**	**5**	**10**	**12**	**24**	**30**	**90**	**Total**	**Pct**
BT	16		70	80	63	18	3	3		253	3%

	1	**2**	**3**	**5**	**10**	**12**	**24**	**30**	**90**	**Total**	**Pct**
BU	38		4	39	36	5	7			129	1%

	1	**2**	**3**	**5**	**10**	**12**	**24**	**30**	**90**	**Total**	**Pct**
CL	22		3	12	3	5				45	<1%

	1	**2**	**3**	**5**	**10**	**12**	**24**	**30**	**90**	**Total**	**Pct**
CO				29	44					73	<1%

	1	**2**	**3**	**5**	**10**	**12**	**24**	**30**	**90**	**Total**	**Pct**
DO	40		40	21	11					112	1%

	1	**2**	**3**	**5**	**10**	**12**	**24**	**30**	**90**	**Total**	**Pct**
DR	151		158	70	55	21	10	12	13	490	
DR RB				4	7					11	
	151		158	74	62	21	10	12	13	501	6%

	1	2	3	5	10	12	24	30	90	Total	Pct
EM	2		18	26	53	13	24			136	1%

	1	2	3	5	10	12	24	30	90	Total	Pct
EV	53		48	8	4					113	1%

	1	2	3	5	10	12	24	30	90	Total	Pct
HO	6		34	17	11					68	<1%

	1	2	3	5	10	12	24	30	90	Total	Pct
IH	9		20	37	33	22	12	9		142	
IH RB	3		5	80	73	5	5			171	
IH '51	1									1	
IH '51 RB						1				1	
IH '61 ES					2					2	
	13		25	117	108	28	17	9		317	3%

	1	2	3	5	10	12	24	30	90	Total	Pct
JG	45	18	44	185	259	93	92	63	43	842	
JG RB	11		13	110	71	12	11	9	1	238	
JG '57					1					1	
Blank	3		2	1						6	
	59	18	59	296	331	105	103	72	44	1087	12.1%

	1	2	3	5	10	12	24	30	90	Total	Pct
KG	25	1	33	123	69	32	49	60	20	412	
KG RB					0	0				0	
	25	1	33	123	69	32	49	60	20	412	4.7%

	1	2	3	5	10	12	24	30	90	Total	Pct
LT	27		50	41	53	30	24	14	9	248	
LT RB					0					0	
LT '51	1									1	
LT '51 ES					1					1	
	28		50	41	54	30	24	14	9	250	2.8%

Notes to Charts on these pages and following page:

The charts on pages 454, 455 and 456 summarize the data contained in the 1988 publication by the present author, Civil War Encased Stamps: Auction Census Data, 1891-1988, as supplemented through 1993. The tables record 8,750 specific appearances of encased stamps in the 364 entries cited in the Annotated Bibliography: Auction Catalogs, Fixed Price Lists, Institutional and Private Collections. This is by far the largest database of information on encased stamps ever assembled. The summary, together with the 1988 detailed listing, provides an excellent means to track pedigrees and develop an appreciation for the relative availability of each encased stamp variety. It also provides one kind of data on which to model the estimated production numbers, economic impact, and psychological profiles of the merchants appearing in the text of the present work. **Please Note**: *this is not a rarity table, per se. Although dealers and collectors may be tempted to use it that way: as a shorthand method for determining rarities (an abusively prevalent practice in catalogs today where "rarity" guesstimates are a primary marketing tool); it is not intended nor suitable for that use.*

	1	2	3	5	10	12	24	30	90	Total	Pct
ME	105		11	52	25	17				210	
ME RB					9					9	
	105		11	52	34	17				219	2.5%

	1	2	3	5	10	12	24	30	90	Total	Pct
MI	8			36						44	<1%

	1	2	3	5	10	12	24	30	90	Total	Pct
NA CU	66		15	0	10	2				93	
NA CU RB	1				8					9	
NA ST	103		77	13	26	7		1		227	
NA ST RB				2						2	
	170		92	15	44	9		1		331	3.7%

	1	2	3	5	10	12	24	30	90	Total	Pct
NO	26		11	16	23					76	<1%

	1	2	3	5	10	12	24	30	90	Total	Pct
PE	10	1	33	32	5	6	0			87	1%

	1	2	3	5	10	12	24	30	90	Total	Pct
SA				41	10	2	0	5		58	<1%

	1	2	3	5	10	12	24	30	90	Total	Pct
SB	13		57	47	76	5				198	2%

	1	2	3	5	10	12	24	30	90	Total	Pct
SH	19		60	116	36	8				239	2.7%

	1	2	3	5	10	12	24	30	90	Total	Pct
ST	57		0	6	5	7				75	<1%

	1	2	3	5	10	12	24	30	90	Total	Pct
TA	42		30	7	9	3				91	1%

	1	2	3	5	10	12	24	30	90	Total	Pct
TH	25		18	129	126	15				313	
TH RB					3					3	
	25		18	129	129	15				316	3.7%

	1	2	3	5	10	12	24	30	90	Total	Pct
WH	48		25	12	12					97	1%

	1	2	3	5	10	12	24	30	90	Total	Pct
WL	21		9	3	79					112	1%

	1	2	3	5	10	12	24	30	90	Total	Pct
TOTALS	**1918**	**26**	**2151**	**1791**	**1813**	**458**	**278**	**211**	**104**	**8750**	
PERCENT	**22%**		**24%**	**20%**	**21%**	**5.2%**	**3.2%**	**2.4%**	**1.2%**		

Tables on pages 454-456 summarize an update of the 1988 published data

About the Author

Daniel Potter, Picture Past Photography

Fred L. Reed III

Figure 457a (over) Fred L. Reed, III

The author of this book has been active in collector circles since 1955. His first published articles on Civil War numismatics ran in 1961. While still a teenager he was named the Numismatic Editor for the Journal of the Blue and the Grey, *the publication of the Civil War Philatelic Society which was active in celebrating the Civil War Centennial. Nearly 30 years ago, he published his first article on encased stamps and fractional currency in* Linn's Weekly Stamp News. *A decade later he joined the staff of* Coin World, *where in six years he published a great many news and research articles on various aspects of Civil War numismatics.*

The author has been a member of many collector organizations since his teen years. He is a charter member of the Civil War Token Society, has had articles published in its Journal, and served six years as an associate editor of the Patriotic Civil War Token Catalog *revision team. He joined the American Numismatic Association in 1964, and the American Numismatic Society in 1975. The author is also a member of the Numismatic Literary Guild, the American Philatelic Society, the Society of Paper Money Collectors, the Token and Medal Society, the Fractional Currency Collectors Board, American Medallic Sculpture Association, and a lifetime honorary member of the Oklahoma State University Civil War Roundtable.*

A lifetime professional journalist, the author is currently Vice President, Publishing of Beckett Publications, the world's largest producer of hobby price guides. That firm currently produces nine magazines on monthly, bimonthly or quarterly bases and several books annually. During his 25-year career in journalism the author has worked on daily, weekly and monthly publications and contributed freelance articles to several dozen periodicals. For three years he was an U.S. Army newspaper editor. While in the service, the author won the Department of Defense Information School Distinguished Honors Graduate award, the Army Times *award, and an Army Commendation Medal for his journalism. His publications have consistently won awards at every level. His displays of Civil War numismatics have garnered a half dozen "Best of Show" prizes.*

As a former Advertising Director, advertising memorabilia interests the author. In addition to encased stamps, he also collects items depicting Abraham Lincoln, business college currency from Eastman National Business Colleges, medals and art of James Earle Fraser and Laura Gardin Fraser, medals and tokens of Joseph Merriam, and sports memorabilia of Hall of Fame catcher Yogi Berra, Hall of Fame running back Jim Brown, Hall of Fame basketball forward Dolph Schayes, 19th century photography of Yosemite National Park, and Civil War tokens and scrip.

He has written and published extensively in many of the areas of his collecting interests. Civil War Encased Stamps: the Issuers and Their Times *is the first volume of a planned seven-volume series entitled "A Numismatist's Perspective of the Civil War." Thirteen articles based on this present work have been previously published in* Coin World. *The author is also co-author of books on error currency, basic coin collecting and editor of books on Civil War tokens, U.S. silver dollars and commemorative coinage. His novel,* The Apple and the Coke, *was published in 1975.*

The author is a member of several professional organizations, including the American Management Association, American Society of Magazine Editors, the Society for American Baseball Research, and the Dallas Press Club. He is listed in American Numismatic Biographies, *and has been invited to appear in* Who's Who, Who's Who in the West and Southwest, *and the* International Who's Who of Professionals.

Married for 25 years to the former Patricia DeVaney, the couple has two children, Rebecca Anne Reed Cornelius and Fred L. Reed IV.

Figure 459a

Right, Bob Kincaid contributed to various aspects of this work. His principal contributions included genealogical input on the Gault family, major additions to the Auction Census Data, and assistance in popularizing the study of encased stamps. However, he also contributed in smaller ways to many other aspects of this book. He was very generous in sharing his information. He suggested an early version of the mnemonic EPS alpha-numeric, variety numbering system used in this book. He provided photos of his pieces and later the pieces for further study. He engaged competent genealogical researchers in various cities. He searched a variety of sources not readily available to the author, and also correctly placed Hopkinton for the first time in modern EPS research.

Figure 459b

Left, Wayne Homren also contributed in major ways to the success of this study. Wayne spent long hours researching New York City reference repositories for research leads on merchants John Gault and Joseph Kirkpatrick. He compiled extensive listings from city directories, and secured valuable photographic resources. Wayne helped popularize collection and study of these items through his speaking engagements and writing. He loaned the author association items such as trade cards and almanacs for study. He contributed to the Auction Census, and critiqued and proofread book galleys. Additionally he and Bob located Gault's grave in Cambridge, and Wayne located Gault's letter to Lincoln. He now resides in Pittsburgh and is very active in various numismatic groups.

Figure 459c

Right, George Cuhaj played a key role in a variety of tasks associated with this study. Located in the New York City area, he like Wayne made full use of its resources. George furnished the author information on the encased stamps at the American Numismatic Society. He researched its extensive library, including auction catalogs which added to the Auction Census Data. In more recent years he proved a key contact at Stack's in following up on leads. Recently employed by Krause Publications, George is very active in medallic circles, and has published extensively on such diverse areas as the numismatics associated with scouting, Catholicism, and transportation. George has exhibited his medallic sculptures internationally.

Figure 460a

Right, Dr. Wallace Lee, a practicing dentist, has been a numismatist for more than 30 years. Wally made major contributions to our understanding of Detroit issuer Fred Buhl, coming up with biographical and illustrative material. He also uncovered Buhl's 1864 income tax records! He unselfishly provided photographs of the pieces in his collection for study. He also provided the American Numismatic Association Certification Service Certificate illustrated in the chapter on "Collecting Encased Stamps." In addition to encased stamps, he specializes in Michigan bank notes and obsolete currency. A longtime collector with special interests in the Civil War, Wally is also Treasurer of the Fractional Currency Collectors Board.

Figure 460b

Left, Bill Gibbs made major contributions to the research of the Cincinnati merchants. A veteran of nearly two decades at Coin World, *Bill spent a portion of a vacation chasing down leads in Cincinnati historical archives for the author. His discoveries included key photographs which found their way into this book. Bill also contributed to the Auction Census Data, supervised photography, and helped provide key information from* Coin World *sources. Last, but certainly not least, Bill edited and oversaw production of 13 encased stamp articles, and many other historical pieces that this author has had published in* Coin World *in recent years. Thanks for your professionalism, Bill.*

Figure 460c

Right, Dr. Robert D. Gardner made outstanding contributions to a variety of lines of inquiry associated with this book. Possessing an extensive collection, he graciously invited the author to examine its contents piece by piece on a halcyon visit to his Virginia office. Like many others, he also shared auction data from his extensive holdings, provided pedigree information on a great number of pieces, and permitted the photography of several significant encased stamps in his collection. Furthermore, he had the Gault receipt photographed for this book, critiqued the author's views on a variety of topics, and permitted the author to examine and have photographed some ancillary items depicted in this book.

Appendix A: Rarity and Values

John Gault's basic idea was to encase five- and ten-cent stamps for sale to merchants as small change. It was an ingenious idea. If it had gone no farther than that, Gault's effort would have been but a footnote to the Civil War change crisis. But genius and circumstances converged and Gault's New Metallic Currency swept to horizons undreamt of on the hot, humid July days when Gault was conceiving and perfecting his idea. Consequently, he created many varieties, and encased many denominations for several dozen clients. These varieties are cataloged in this appendix. Questions exist about some pieces, indicated by "?"

The tables in the chapter, "Collecting Encased Stamps" indicate availability. The tables in this catalog appendix indicate rarity and values. There is a difference. Very often pieces offered at auction do not sell. They are bought back in because they fail to meet a reserve minimum. Pieces often trade back and forth between dealers, for whatever reason. Often prices reported from auctions are not truthful. Some houses report sales when there are none. Very often dealers or advanced collectors agree beforehand to carve up certain collections by agreeing not to bid competitively against one another for certain pieces suppressing prices. This is probably not more true with encased stamps than in other fields. The prices listed are suggestions. Pieces can be purchased at these levels. But, **willing buyers and willing sellers make the marketplace. They determine prices**. Three columns are given: VG-F and VF-EF and AU/Comments. Unpriced varieties are speculative due to extreme rarity. *Prices suggest ranges and presume the piece is genuine as made*. They give the average reader, who may be more interested in the Civil War in general than collecting a set of encased stamps, a good handle on relative values. Pieces may sell above or below these prices in the marketplace and both buyer and seller may be happy with the transaction.

Key to Rarity Guide

R-10	Unique	R-5	21-30
R-9	2-4	R-4	31-40
R-8	5-10	R-3	41-50
R-7	11-15	R-2	51-100
R-6	16-20	R-1	101+

Merchant	*First*	*Scott*	*F'berg*	*Rarity*	*VG-F*	*VF-EF*	*AU/Com'nts*
Aërated Bread							
AB01	1889	S 1	EP 1	R- 7	1000	1600	-----
AB05	1906			R-10?	-----	-----	? - unique
James C. Ayer							
AC01SA	1889	S 2	EP 2	R- 3	175	375	500
AC03SA	1889	S 3	EP 32	R- 2	125	350	450
AC05SA	1904	S 4	EP 60	R- 7	350	700	-----
AC10SA	1889	S 5	EP 96	R- 7	300	600	-----
AC12SA	1905	S 6	EP135	R- 8+	600	1000	-----
AC24SA	1906	S 7	EP159b	R-10?	-----	-----	?
AC30SA	1920		EP172b	R-10?	-----	-----	? - unique
AC90SA	1920			-----	-----	-----	Fake
AC01LA	1906			R-10?	-----	-----	? - unique
AC03LA	1889	S 3	EP 32a	R- 1	125	250	350
AC05LA	1906	S 4	EP 60a	R- 8+	600	800	?
AC10LA	1889	S 5	EP 96a	R- 9	600	1000	?
AC12LA	1908	S 6		R- 9	-----	-----	2 known
AC24LA	1914			R-10?	-----	-----	? - unique
AC30LA				R-10	-----	-----	-----
AP01	1889	S 8	EP 3	R- 3	175	350	500
AP01RB	1929			-----	-----	-----	Doesn't exist
AP02'51				-----	-----	-----	?
AP02RS	1988			-----	-----	-----	Unique
AP03	1889	S 9	EP 33	R- 1	125	250	350
AP03RB	1908			-----	-----	-----	Doesn't exist
AP05	1905	S 10	EP 61	R- 8	350	700	-----
AP05RB	1906	S 10a	EP 62	R-10	-----	-----	-----
AP10	1905	S 11	EP 97	R- 6	300	500	700
AP10RB				-----	-----	-----	?
AP12	1905	S 12	EP136	R- 8	400	800	-----
AP24				R-10?	-----	-----	?
AP30	1981			R-10	-----	-----	Unique
AP90	1920		EP183a	R- 9?	-----	-----	? - 2 known
AS01SM	1901	S13a	EP 4	R- 4	175	350	450
AS02SM	1920			-----	-----	-----	Fake
AS03SM	1889	S15	EP 34	R- 2	125	275	375
AS05SM	1905			-----	-----	-----	?
AS10SM	1905	S17b	EP 98	R- 8+	600	800	-----
AS12SM	1920	S18a	EP137a	R-10	-----	-----	-----

Merchant	*First*	*Scott*	*F'berg*	*Rarity*	*VG-F*	*VF-EF*	*AU/Com'nts*
James C. Ayer							
AS01MD	1889	S 13	EP 4a	R- 1	100	200	275
AS01MD'51	1988			-----	-----	-----	?
AS01CD	1908			-----	-----	-----	?
AS02MD	1929	S 14		-----	-----	-----	Fake
AS03MD	1889	S 15a	EP 34a	R- 1	100	200	275
AS03MDRB	1944	S 15c	EP 35	R-10	-----	-----	?
AS03MDCD	1908			-----	-----	-----	?
AS05MD	1889	S 16	EP 63	R- 6	300	600	750
AS10MD	1889	S 17	EP 98a	R- 6	300	600	750
AS10MDRB	1906	S 17a	EP 99	R-10?	-----	-----	? - 1 known
AS12MD	1905	S 18	EP137	R- 8	400	750	1000
AS24MD	1906	S 19	EP160	R- 9	-----	-----	-----
AS30MD	1906	S 20	EP173	R- 9	-----	-----	2-4 known
AS90MD	1915		EP183b	R- 9?	-----	-----	? - 3 known
AS01LG	1889			-----	-----	-----	?
AS01'51				-----	-----	-----	
AS03LG	1889	S 15b	EP 34b	R- 3	200	300	400
AS05LG	1906	S 16a	EP 63a	R- 9	-----	-----	-----
AS10LG	1906	S 17c	EP 98b	R- 9+	-----	-----	-----
AS12LG	1905			?	-----	-----	?
AS24LG	1914			-----	-----	-----	Doesn't exist
Joseph L. Bates							
BA01FG	1889	S 26	EP 6a	R- 6	750	1000	-----
BA01FGRB				-----	-----	-----	-----
BA03FG	1938	S 27	EP 37a	-----	-----	-----	Doesn't exist
BA05FG	1889	S 28	EP 66a	R- 9	-----	-----	2 known
BA05FGRB	1912	S 28b	EP 66	R- 9	-----	-----	2 known
BA10FG	1889	S 29	EP102a	R- 9	-----	-----	2-3 known
BA10FGRB	1908	S 29b	EP102	R-10	-----	-----	unique
BA12FG	1967			?	-----	-----	?
BA01F/G	1889	S 26a	EP 6	R-4	300	500	600
BA03F/G	1905	S 27a	EP 37	R-8+?	500	700	?
BA05F/G	1901	S 28a	EP 65	R-9	-----	-----	-----
BA10F/G	1905	S 29a	EP101	R-8	500	700	-----
BA12F/G	1905	S 30	EP139	R-9	-----	-----	-----
BA24F/G	1982			R-9	-----	-----	? - 2 known
BA90F/G	1988			?	-----	-----	?

Bailey & Co.	*First*	*Scott*	*F'Berg*	*Rarity*	*VG-F*	*VF-EF*	*AU/Com'nts*
BC01	1889	S 21	EP 5	R- 8	800	1000	-----
BC03	1889	S 22	EP 36	R- 8	800	1000	-----
BC05	1889	S 23	EP 64	R- 8	800	1000	-----
BC10	1889	S 24	EP100	R- 8	800	1000	-----
BC12	1912	S 25	EP138	R- 9	-----	-----	2 known
BC24				-----	-----	-----	?
Joseph Burnett							
BE01	1889	S 52	EP 10	R- 6	350	600	750
BE03	1889	S 53	EP 40	R- 6	350	600	750
BE05	1889	S 54	EP 70	R- 4	250	400	500
BE10	1889	S 55	EP106	R- 4	250	400	500
BE10RB	1906		EP107	R- 9	-----	-----	-----
BE12	1905	S 56	EP143	R- 8	600	800	-----
BE24	1905	S 57	EP164	R- 9	-----	-----	2-3 known
BE30	1905	S 58	EP176	R- 9	-----	-----	2-3 known
BE90	1981		EP184a	R-10?	-----	-----	? - unique
BK01	1889	S 44	EP 9	R- 6	350	600	750
BK02				R-10?	-----	-----	?
BK03	1889	S 45	EP 39	R- 6	350	600	750
BK05	1889	S 46	EP 69	R- 6	350	600	750
BK10	1889	S 47	EP105	R- 4	275	475	575
BK12	1905	S 48	EP142	R- 8	600	800	-----
BK24	1914	S 49	EP163	R- 9	-----	-----	2 known
BK30	1914	S 50	EP175	R- 9	-----	-----	2-3 known
BK90	1902	S 51	EP184	R-10?	-----	-----	? - unique
John I. Brown							
BT01	1889	S 31	EP 7	R- 8+	700	1000	-----
BT03	1889	S 32	EP 38	R- 6	350	600	750
BT05	1889	S 33	EP67	R- 4	250	450	550
BT10	1889	S 34	EP103	R- 6	350	600	750
BT12	1905	S 35	EP140	R- 9	-----	-----	-----
BT24	1929	S 36	EP161	?	-----	-----	?
BT30	1929	S 37	EP174	?	-----	-----	?

Key to Rarity Guide

R-10	Unique	R-5	21-30
R- 9	2-4	R-4	31-40
R- 8	5-10	R-3	41-50
R- 7	11-15	R-2	51-100
R- 6	16-20	R-1	101+

Fred Buhl	*First*	*Scott*	*F'Berg*	*Rarity*	*VG-F*	*VF-EF*	*AU/Com'nts*
BU01	1889	S 38	EP 8	R- 8	850	1200	-----
BU03	1905	S 39	EP 38a	R-10?	-----	-----	?
BU05	1905	S 40	EP 68	R- 8	850	1200	-----
BU10	1905	S 41	EP104	R- 8	850	1200	-----
BU12	1906	S 42	EP141	?	-----	-----	?
BU24	1944	S 43	EP162	?	-----	-----	?
Arthur M. Claflin							
CL01	1889	S 59	EP 11	R- 8	6000	8000	12,000
CL03	1905	S 60	EP 40a	R- 9	-----	-----	2 known
CL05	1905	S 61	EP 71	R- 9	8500	13,500	4 known
CL10	1908	S 62	EP108a	R- 9	-----	-----	2 known
CL12	1914	S 63	EP144	R- 9	-----	-----	2 known
H. A. Cook							
CO05	1889	S 64	EP72	R- 8	1100	1600	-----
CO10	1889	S 65	EP108	R- 7	1000	1400	-----
Dougan the Hatter							
DO01	1889	S 66	EP 12	R- 7	750	1000	-----
DO03	1889	S 67	EP 41	R- 7	750	1000	-----
DO05	1889	S 68	EP 73	R- 8+	1100	1400	-----
DO10	1908	S 69	EP109	R- 9	-----	-----	2-3 known
P. H. Drake							
DR01	1889	S 70	EP 13	R- 2	125	275	350
DR03	1889	S 71	EP 42	R- 2	125	275	350
DR05	1889	S 72	EP 74	R- 5	250	400	500
DR05RB	1936	S 72a	EP 75	R- 9	-----	-----	2 known
DR10	1889	S 73	EP110	R- 5	350	500	600
DR10RB	1936	S 73a	EP111	R- 9	-----	-----	2-3 known
DR12	1905	S 74	EP145	R- 8	800	1200	-----
DR24	1905	S 75	EP165	R- 9	-----	-----	2-3 known
DR30	1905	S 76	EP177	R- 9	-----	-----	2-3 known
DR90	1905	S 77	EP185	R- 8+	4000	7500	2-5 known

Key to Rarity Guide

R-10	Unique	R-5	21-30
R- 9	2-4	R-4	31-40
R- 8	5-10	R-3	41-50
R- 7	11-15	R-2	51-100
R- 6	16-20	R-1	101+

Ellis McAlpin	*First*	*Scott*	*F'Berg*	*Rarity*	*VG-F*	*VF-EF*	*AU/Com'nts*
EM01	1936	S 78	EP 13a	R-10?	-----	-----	?
EM03	1889	S 79	EP 43	R- 9	-----	-----	-----
EM05	1890	S 80	EP 76	R- 8	800	1200	-----
EM10	1889	S 81	EP112	R- 5	650	900	1200
EM12	1908	S 82	EP146	R- 9	-----	-----	-----
EM24	1890	S 83	EP166	R- 8	1500	2500	-----
George G. Evans							
EV01	1889	S 84	EP 14	R- 7	700	1000	-----
EV03	1889	S 85	EP 44	R- 7	700	1000	-----
EV05	1889	S 86	EP76a	R- 9	-----	-----	2-3 known
EV10	1914	S 87	EP113	R- 9	-----	-----	2 known
L. C. Hopkins							
HO01	1889	S102	EP 17a	R- 9?	-----	-----	? - 2 known
HO03	1889	S103	EP 48	R- 8	1000	1500	-----
HO05	1889	S104	EP 80	R- 8+	1250	1750	-----
HO10	1959	S105	EP117a	R- 9	-----	-----	2-3 known
Irving House							
IH01	1889	S106	EP 18	R-10?	-----	-----	-----
IH01'51	1884			R-10	-----	-----	Unique
IH01RB	1902			?	-----	-----	? - unique
IH01ES	1914				-----	-----	-----
IH03	1906	S107	EP 49	R- 8+	700	1000	-----
IH03RB	1936	S107a	EP 49a	R- 9	-----	-----	2 known
IH05	1889	S108	EP 81	R- 8	500	800	1000
IH05RB	1889	S108a	EP 82	R- 4	350	500	700
IH10	1889	S109	EP118	R- 8+	600	800	-----
IH10RB	1889	S109a	EP119	R- 5	450	600	800
IH10ES	1965			R-10	-----	-----	? - unique
IH12	1889	S110	EP150	R- 8	600	800	1100
IH12RB	1936	S110a	EP151	R- 9?	-----	-----	? - 2 known
IH12RB'51	1988			R-10?	-----	-----	? - unique
IH24	1906	S111	EP169	R- 9	-----	-----	-----
IH24RB	1944	S111a	EP170	R- 9?	-----	-----	? - 2 known
IH30	1914	S112	EP180	R-10	-----	-----	Unique

? indicates unresolved issues regarding the piece in question

John Gault	*First*	*Scott*	*F'berg*	*Rarity*	*VG-F*	*VF-EF*	*AU/Com'nts*
JG01	1889	S 93	EP 16	R- 7	500	800	950
JG01RB	1905	S 93a	EP 17	R- 9	-----	-----	-----
JG02	1886	S 94	EP 31	R- 8+	8500	-----	Fakes exist
JG03	1889	S 95	EP 46	R- 7	500	800	950
JG03RB	1905	S 95a	EP 47	R- 8+	-----	-----	-----
JG05	1889	S 96	EP 78	R- 1	125	225	325
JG05RB	1889	S 96a	EP 79	R- 4	300	500	600
JG05Y	1889			-----	-----	-----	? - Yellow
JG10	1889	S 97	EP116	R- 1	125	225	325
JG10RB	1889	S 97a	EP117	R- 6	450	600	700
JG10'57	1988			-----	-----	-----	?
JG12	1889	S 98	EP148	R- 4	450	800	1000
JG12RB	1906	S 98a	EP149	R- 9	-----	-----	2-4 known
JG24	1889	S 99	EP167	R- 4	650	900	-----
JG24RB	1905	S 99a	EP168	R- 9	-----	-----	2 known
JG24G	1914			-----	-----	-----	Gray
JG30	1889	S100	EP178	R- 6	1250	1700	-----
JG30RB	1905	S100a	EP179	R- 9	-----	-----	2 known
JG90	1889	S101	EP186	R- 8	3000	5000	Fakes exist
JG90RB				R-10?	-----	-----	? - unique
Kirkpatrick & Gault							
KG01	1889	S113	EP 19	R- 8+	750	900	-----
KG02				-----	-----	-----	? - unique
KG03	1889	S114	EP 50	R- 8	550	750	-----
KG05	1889	S115	EP 83	R- 3	200	350	450
KG10	1889	S116	EP120	R- 5	250	400	500
KG10RB	1936			-----	-----	-----	Doesn't exist
KG12	1889	S117	EP152	R- 8	550	800	-----
KG12RB	1936			-----	-----	-----	Doesn't exist
KG24	1889	S118	EP171	R- 6	750	1000	-----
KG24G	1914			-----	-----	-----	Gray
KG30	1889	S119	EP181	R- 6	1350	1750	-----
KG90	1905	S120	EP187	R- 8	4000	6000	-----

Key to Rarity Guide

R-10	Unique	R-5	21-30
R- 9	2-4	R-4	31-40
R- 8	5-10	R-3	41-50
R- 7	11-15	R-2	51-100
R- 6	16-20	R-1	101+

Lord & Taylor	*First*	*Scott*	*F'Berg*	*Rarity*	*VG-F*	*VF-EF*	*AU/Com'nts*
LT01	1889	S121	EP 20	R- 8+	650	850	950
LT01'51	1884			R-10	-----	-----	Unique
LT03	1889	S122	EP 51	R- 6	400	600	700
LT05	1889	S123	EP 84	R- 7	450	750	850
LT10	1889	S124	EP121	R- 6	400	600	750
LT10RB				-----	-----	-----	Doesn't exist
LT10ES				R-10	-----	-----	Unique
LT12	1889	S125	EP153	R- 8	850	1100	-----
LT24	1889	S126	EP172	R- 8	-----	-----	-----
LT30	1889	S127	EP182	R- 9	-----	-----	-----
LT90	1914	S128	EP188	R- 9	-----	-----	-----
Mendum Wine Emporium							
ME01	1889	S129	EP 21	R- 4	300	400	550
ME03	1889	S130	EP 52	R-10?	-----	-----	?
ME05	1889	S131	EP 85	R- 6	400	600	750
ME05Y	1908			-----	-----	-----	? - Yellow
ME10	1905	S132	EP122	R- 8	750	1000	-----
ME10RB	1914	S132a	EP123	R- 9?	-----	-----	?
ME12	1905	S133	EP154	R- 8	850	1100	-----
B. F. Miles							
MI01	1889	S134	EP 22	R- 9	-----	-----	2 known
MI05	1905	S135	EP 86	R- 8	5000	7500	10,000
North America Life Insurance							
NA01CU	1889	S140	EP 24a	R- 6	650	850	-----
NA01CURB	1929			?	-----	-----	?
NA03CU	1889	S141	EP 53a	R- 9	-----	-----	-----
NA05CU				-----	-----	-----	Doesn't exist
NA10CU	1905	S143a	EP125a	R- 9	-----	-----	-----
NA10CURB	1912	S143b	EP126	R- 9	-----	-----	-----
NA12CU				?	-----	-----	?
NA01ST	1889	S140a	EP 24	R- 4	300	400	500
NA03ST	1889	S141a	EP 53	R- 5	400	600	750
NA05ST	1889	S142	EP 88	R- 9	-----	-----	-----
NA05STRB	1963	S142a	EP88a	R-10	-----	-----	Unique
NA10ST	1905	S143	EP125	R- 8	750	1000	-----
NA12ST	1914	S144	EP155	R- 9	-----	-----	2 known
NA30ST				R-10?	-----	-----	? - unique

John W. Norris	***First***	***Scott***	***F'Berg***	***Rarity***	***VG-F***	***VF-EF***	***AU/Com'nts***
NO01	1889	S136	EP 23	R- 8	1200	1500	-----
NO03	1905	S137	EP 52a	R- 9	-----	-----	-----
NO05	1905	S138	EP 87	R- 9	-----	-----	-----
NO10	1907	S139	EP124	R- 8+	1250	1750	-----
Pearce Tolle Holton							
PE01	1908	S145	EP 24b	R-10	-----	-----	Unique
PE02	1915			?	-----	-----	?
PE03	1889	S146	EP 54	R- 8	1250	1750	-----
PE05	1889	S147	EP 89	R- 8	1250	1750	-----
PE10	1914	S148	EP127	R- 9	-----	-----	2 known
PE12	1906	S149	EP156	R-10	-----	-----	Unique
PE24	1939	S150	EP172a	-----	-----	-----	Doesn't exist
Sands' Ale							
SA05	1889	S151	EP 90	R- 8	1650	2750	5000
SA10	1889	S152	EP128	R- 9	-----	-----	2-3 known
SA12	1939	S153	EP156a	?	-----	-----	?
SA24	1967			-----	-----	-----	Doesn't exist
SA30	1939	S154	EP183	R-10?	-----	-----	? - unique
Schapker & Bussing							
SB01	1908	S155	EP 25	R- 9	-----	-----	-----
SB03	1889	S156	EP 55	R- 6	400	600	700
SB05	1889	S157	EP 91	R- 7	500	750	875
SB10	1889	S158	EP129	R- 5	350	550	650
SB12	1914	S159	EP157	R- 9	-----	-----	2 known
John Shillito							
SH01	1889	S160	EP 26	R- 8+	800	1100	-----
SH03	1889	S161	EP 56	R- 6	400	600	750
SH05	1889	S162	EP 92	R- 4	300	500	600
SH10	1889	S163	EP130	R- 8	950	1400	-----
SH12	1906	S164	EP158	R- 9	-----	-----	2 known
S. Steinfeld							
ST01	1889	S165	EP 27	R- 7	1000	1500	-----
ST03	1967			-----	-----	-----	Doesn't exist
ST05	1906	S166	EP 93	R- 9?	-----	-----	?
ST10	1914	S167	EP131	R- 9?	-----	-----	?
ST12	1936	S168	EP159	R- 9	-----	-----	?

N. & G. Taylor	*First*	*Scott*	*F'Berg*	*Rarity*	*VG-F*	*VF-EF*	*AU/Com'nts*
TA01	1889	S169	EP 28	R- 7	750	1250	1500
TA03	1889	S170	EP 57	R- 8	900	1400	-----
TA05	1889	S171	EP 93a	R- 9	-----	-----	3 known
TA10	1889	S172	EP132	R- 9?	-----	-----	? - 2 known
TA12	1939	S173	EP159a	R-10	-----	-----	Unique
Tremont House							
TH01	1889	S 88	EP 15	R- 8	600	800	-----
TH03	1889	S 89	EP 45	R- 8	650	900	-----
TH05	1889	S 90	EP 77	R- 2	150	250	350
TH10	1889	S 91	EP114	R- 2	150	250	350
TH10RB	1944	S 91a	EP115	R- 9?	-----	-----	? - 2 known
TH12	1905	S 92	EP147	R- 9	-----	-----	-----
White the Hatter							
WH01	1889	S178	EP 30	R- 7	1000	1500	1750
WH03	1889	S179	EP 59	R- 8	1100	1600	1850
WH05	1889	S180	EP 95	R- 9	-----	-----	2-4 known
WH10	1889	S181	EP134	R- 9	-----	-----	2-3 known
Weir & Larminie							
WL01	1889	S174	EP 29	R- 8+	1100	1500	1750
WL03	1908	S175	EP 58	R- 9	-----	-----	2 known
WL05	1890	S176	EP 94	R-10	-----	-----	Unique
WL10	1889	S177	EP133	R- 5	650	850	1000

Figure 470a

Dealer Tom Denly (left) and the author discuss encased stamps while Denly examines an advance copy of Civil War Encased Stamps, the Issuers and Their Times *at the Chicago Paper Money Exposition, February 1995. (Krause Publications photo)*

Appendix B: Suggested Emission Models

Emission modelling is a new subject to most students of encased stamps. While several writers in the past and collectors generally have often wondered how many pieces were produced, no prior author has attempted an unified nor coherent answer to these concerns. The extended series on encased stamps published by the present writer in *Coin World* in the 1980s plowed this fertile ground for the first time. While it is plain that encased stamps served *both as* a medium of exchange and as an advertising vehicle, differing merchants generally favored one or the other benefits to a greater extent. Their desire expressed itself in their orders from John Gault. Their particular concerns have been addressed in each of the separate merchant chronicles (chapters) in the present work. As has been mentioned, considerations in placing orders with Gault included: (1) publicity value for a new enterprise, new product or service; (2) necessity for small change in a retail setting, or lack of such necessity in a wholesale setting; (3) other small change substitutes readily available; (4) funds available for encased stamp purchase; (5) the specie premium then current for fractional silver; and, so forth. Such considerations were taken into account when modelling individual merchant orders.

As has been repeatedly mentioned in the course of the present work, John Gault, himself, was intent on manufacturing and selling five-cent and ten-cent pieces to the public and general merchants at a markup near the prevailing specie premium (20%). This is identical to the 12-cent sales price for 10-cent encased stamps (i.e. cost of stamp plus encasement). Gault's fives and tens were change-making pieces, superior to the other small change expedients in circulation and were best sellers. But in fact, John Gault favored 10-cent pieces over five-cent pieces. Both his first issue of grooved frame pieces and his second issue of plain frame pieces (characterized as the August and September releases of encased stamps, bearing only his identity and patent information) show this marketing preference decidedly. When he issued new pieces for his partnership with Joseph Kirkpatrick in October, he again favored the five- and ten-cent denominations, but his preference shifted noticeably toward the lower, five-cent value. Gault's reason was his *increased interest* in the *advertising value* of his New Metallic Currency. Simply put, he could get more pieces, hence greater saturation, for a given expenditure, by circulating a greater preponderance of the smaller denomination.

Similar analysis of each of the other 29 merchants and their 32 different product issues appears in the merchant chronicle chapters. When these individual models are compared, distinct groupings appear. The trend line charts in this appendix are the result. They group the "cumulative intensity of preferences" for certain denominations for the *merchant class* charted. Strictly speaking, these preferences should be shown on bar graphs (i.e. cumulative preferences for merchants (a) + (b) + (c) for 1-cent encasements; (a) + (b) + (c) for 3-cent encasements, etc.) and not continuous line graphs, but since there is no easy way to show various small increments for individual values on bar graphs, continuous graphs were selected as a compromise. **Remember,** individual lines reflect the *increment of preference* for the merchant charted over and *above the level of the accumulated preferences* for that denomination for merchants charted below him, and not that merchant's preference for that denomination *per se*. **Hint,** think of the "thickness" of the strata at a given denomination and not the height of the strata itself. For example, this preference for Tremont House (Figure 475a) is 40% for both five- and ten-cent values and not 250% for these pieces.

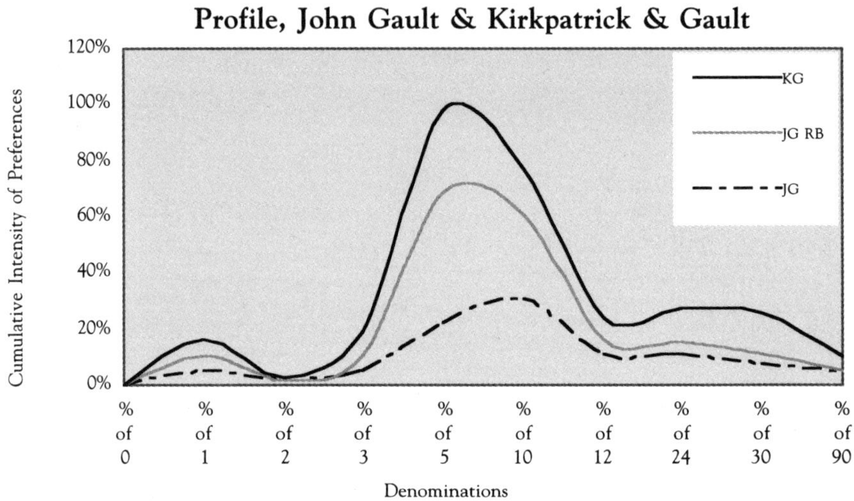

Figure 472a

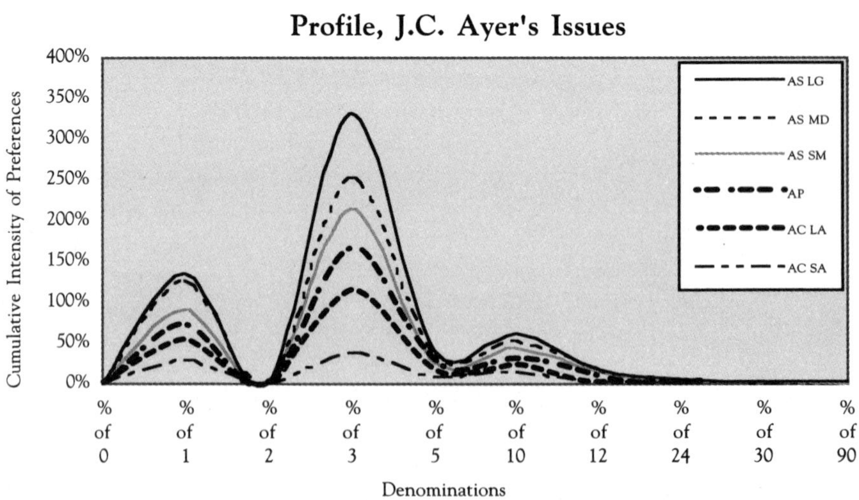

Figure 472b

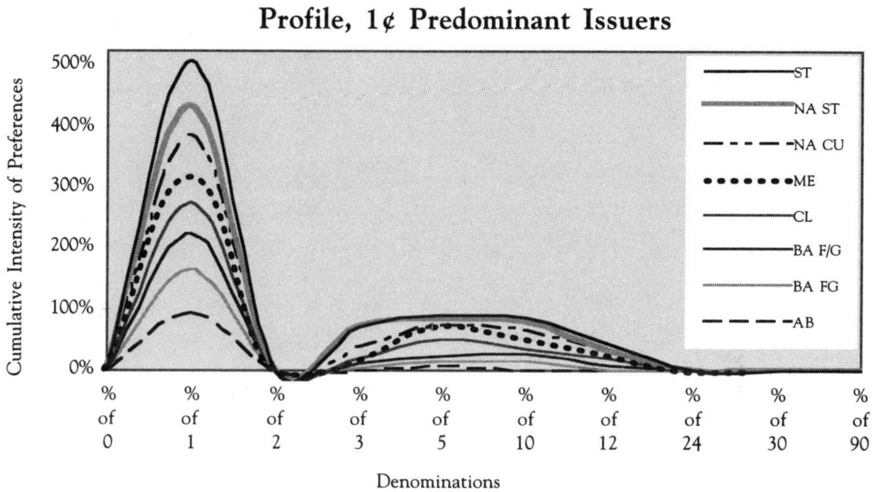

Figure 473a

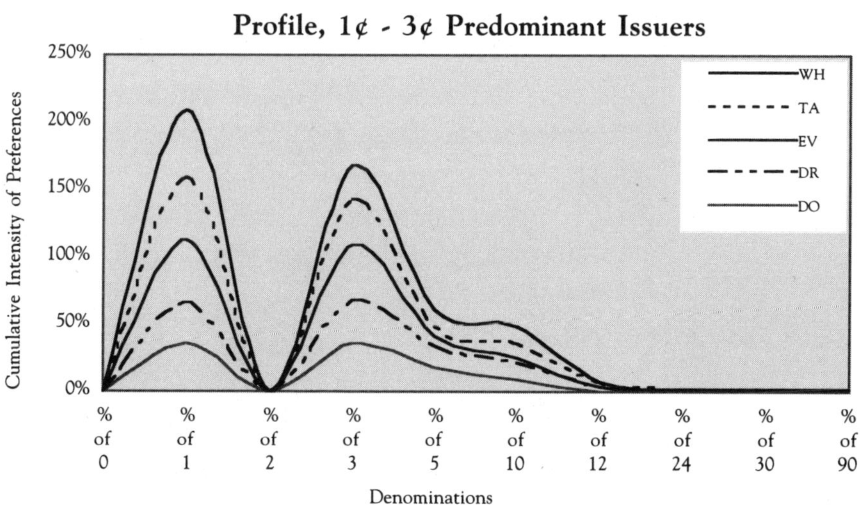

Figure 473b

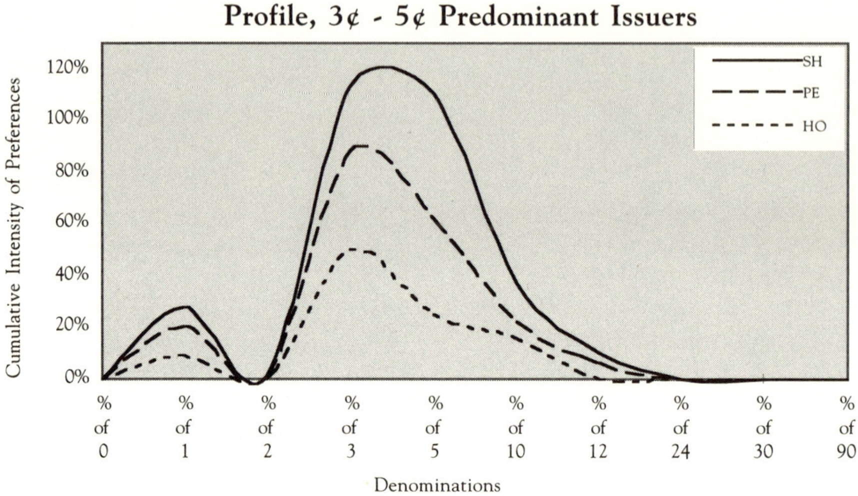

Figure 474a

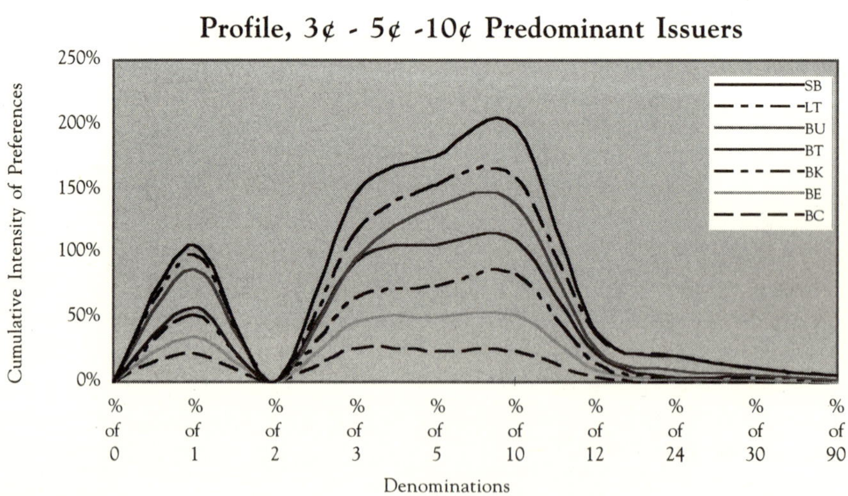

Figure 474b

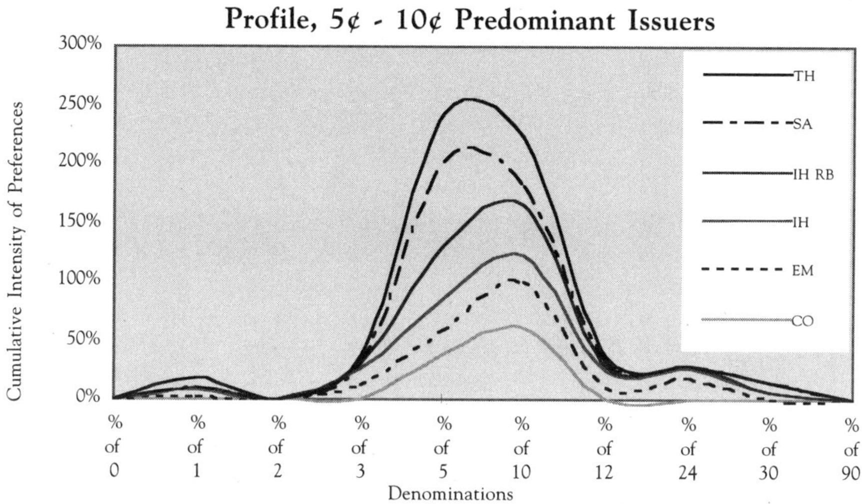

Figure 475a

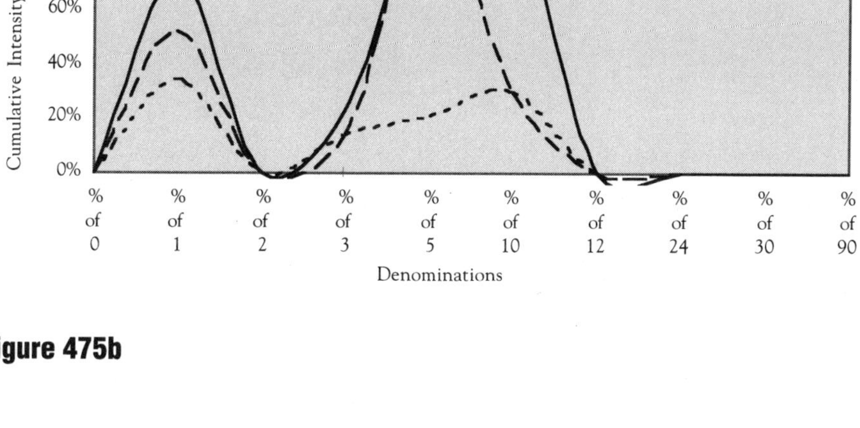

Figure 475b

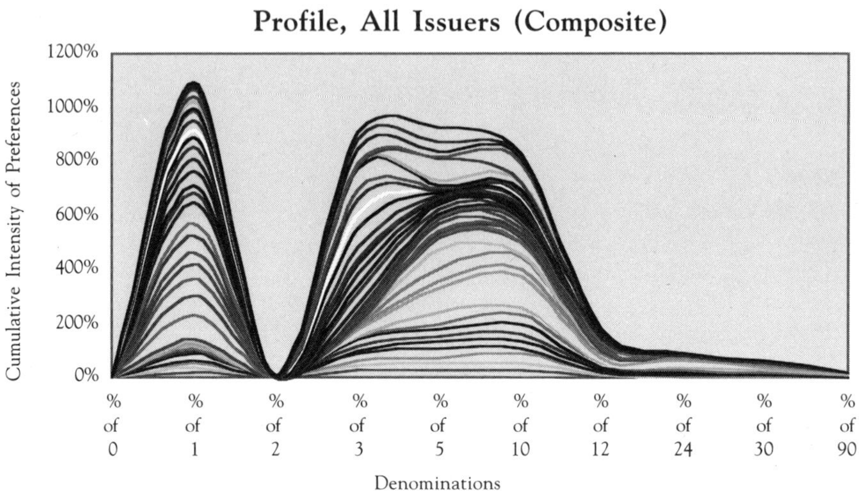

Figure 476a

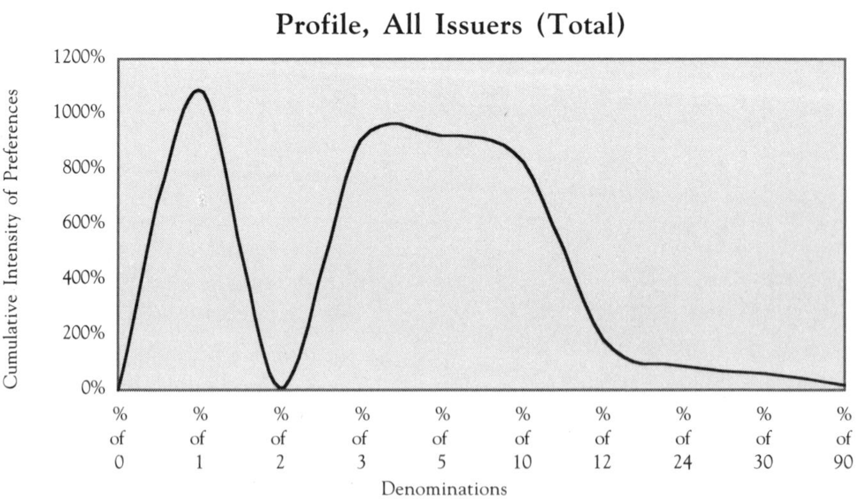

Figure 476b

Appendix C: Major Institutional Collections

The superiority of the descriptive cataloging system outlined in the present work may be easily demonstrated by comparison to the old-style systems, which number varieties in consecutive fashion. Those systems, whether they organize encased stamps by issuer (clearly the preferable way) or denomination (oddly, the most prevalent way), suffer two common stumbling blocks: (1) users are locked into inflexible grids of arbitrary designations when subsequent discoveries occur; (2) users must remember the hundreds of numbers or have conversion charts readily at hand; and (3) users must describe pieces *in addition to* using the arbitrary catalog numbers. The present system readily solves all these dilemmas. New varieties are easily cataloged. The descriptive catalog "number" (actually an alpha-numeric designator) **is a shorthand notation which *both* describes *and* catalogs a piece**. After a little practice, no conversion chart is necessary: AB01 is Aerated Bread one-cent, not number X, number Y, nor number Z *plus* a description of the piece. AP12 is Ayer's Pills twelve-cents. BA05F/G is Bates five-cent FANCY GOODS (2 words), and so forth.

Regardless of biases, readers may prove this for themselves by examining the following listings of several major institutional collections included in the Auction Collection Database developed for this book. Cover up the first column. Columns two and three describe the present state of cataloging (no matter which alternative system is used). Now, cover columns two and three. Voila, in simple shorthand one knows precisely what he would expect to find should he gain access to the holdings of these institutions. The description is unnecessary. Additional catalog numbers are irrelevant. Which system is simpler?

American Numismatic Society (22 pieces)

The American Numismatic Society, located in New York City, holds major collections of many types of coin, currency, medallic and emergency currency pieces. Its encased stamp holdings were examined by major contributor George Cuhaj, who supplied the present listing. Apparently these pieces were acquired prior to 1939, since John Jones refered to the "22 encased postage stamps in their large collections."

AB01	Aërated Bread .01	EP1
AC03LA	Ayer's Cathartic .03 Long Arrows	EP32A
AP01	Ayer's Pills .01	EP3
AP03	Ayer's Pills .03	EP33
AS01MD	Ayer's Sarsaparilla .01 Medium AYER'S	EP4A
AS03MD	Ayer's Sarsaparilla .03 Medium AYER'S	EP34A
BA01F/G	Bates .01 FANCY GOODS (2 words)	EP6
BE05	Burnett's Extracts .05	EP70
BE10	Burnett's Extracts .10	EP106
BK10	Burnett's Kalliston .10	EP105
DR03	Drake's .03	EP42
DR05	Drake's .05	EP74

EM10	Ellis McAlpin .10	EP112
IH12	Irving House .12	EP150
JG01	John Gault .01	EP16
JG05	John Gault .05	EP78
JG10	John Gault .10	EP116
KG05	Kirkpatrick & Gault .05	EP83
ME01	Mendum's .01	EP21
SH05	Shillito's .05	EP92
SH10	Shillito's .10	EP130
TH05	Tremont House .05	EP77

Buffalo Historical Society (36 pieces)

The Buffalo Historical Society has owned the encased stamp collection of Lancaster, N.Y., physician Dr. James since 1893. It was called "the finest collection of these encased stamps seen" by John Jones in 1939. At that time Jones reported the collection contained 92 pieces, including three 90-cent pieces. More recently an inventory of the collection was obtained by major contributor Robert Kincaid comprising the following 36 pieces.

AC03SA	Ayer's Cathartic .03 Short Arrows	EP32
AP03	Ayer's Pills .03	EP33
AS01SM	Ayer's Sarsaparilla .01 Small AYER'S	EP4
AS03SM	Ayer's Sarsaparilla .03 Small AYER'S	EP34
AS03SM	Ayer's Sarsaparilla .03 Small AYER'S	EP34
AS03SM	Ayer's Sarsaparilla .03 Small AYER'S	EP34
AS10SM	Ayer's Sarsaparilla .10 Small AYER'S	EP98
AS90MD	Ayer's Sarsaparilla .90 Medium AYER'S	EP183B
BA01F/G	Bates .01 FANCY GOODS (2 words)	EP6
BE05	Burnett's Extracts .05	EP70
BE10	Burnett's Extracts .10	EP106
BK03	Burnett's Kalliston .03	EP39
BK05	Burnett's Kalliston .05	EP69
BT03	Brown's Troches .03	EP38
DO03	Dougan .03	EP41
DR03	Drake's 03	EP42
DR05	Drake's 05	EP74
EM10	Ellis McAlpin .10	EP112
EV01	Evans .01	EP14
HO03	Hopkins .03	EP48
IH05	Irving House .05	EP81
IH10	Irving House .10	EP118
JG01	John Gault .01	EP16
JG10	John Gault .10	EP116
JG12	John Gault .12	EP148
KG30	Kirkpatrick & Gault .30	EP181
NA01ST	North America .01 Straight INSURANCE	EP24
PE03	Pearce .03	EP54
PE05	Pearce .05	EP89
SB03	Schapker & Bussing .03	EP55
SB10	Schapker & Bussing .10	EP129
SH03	Shillito's .03	EP56
TA05	Taylor .05	EP93A
TH03	Tremont House .03	EP45
TH10	Tremont House .10	EP114
WH01	White Hatter .01	EP30

Smithsonian Institution (33 pieces)

The National Numismatic Collection at the Smithsonian Institution in Washington, D.C. is incomparable in many ways. Its representation of encased stamps was derived from two donations, those of the late collector H. K. Crofoot (denoted HKC below) and the pieces belonging to the Chase Manhattan Bank (CMB) when that institution's money museum was closed in New York City. The inventory which follows was of 33 pieces cataloged by the author at the Smithsonian on August 25, 1986.

AC01SA	Ayer's Cathartic .01 Short Arrows	EP2	HKC
AC03LA	Ayer's Cathartic .03 Long Arrows	EP32A	HKC
AC03LA	Ayer's Cathartic .03 Long Arrows	EP32A	HKC
AP01	Ayer's Pills .01	EP3	HKC
AP03	Ayer's Pills .03	EP33	HKC
AS01MD	Ayer's Sarsaparilla .01 Medium AYER'S	EP4A	HKC
AS03MD	Ayer's Sarsaparilla .03 Medium AYER'S	EP34A	CMB
AS03MD	Ayer's Sarsaparilla .03 Medium AYER'S	EP34A	CMB
AS03MD	Ayer's Sarsaparilla .03 Medium AYER'S	EP34A	CMB
AS03MD	Ayer's Sarsaparilla .03 Medium AYER'S	EP34A	HKC
AS03MD	Ayer's Sarsaparilla .03 Medium AYER'S	EP34A	HKC
AS05MD	Ayer's Sarsaparilla .05 Medium AYER'S	EP63	HKC
BE01	Burnett's Extracts .01	EP10	HKC
BE03	Burnett's Extracts .03	EP40	HKC
CO05	Cook .05	EP72	CMB
DR01	Drake .01	EP13	CMB
DR03	Drake's .03	EP42	CMB
JG05	John Gault .05	EP78	CMB
JG05	John Gault .05	EP78	CMB
JG05	John Gault .05	EP78	HKC
JG10	John Gault .10	EP116	HKC
KG05	Kirkpatrick & Gault .05	EP83	HKC
KG10	Kirkpatrick & Gault .10	EP120	CMB
KG10	Kirkpatrick & Gault .10	EP120	CMB
MI05	Miles .05	EP86	CMB
NA01ST	North America .01 Straight INSURANCE	EP24	HKC
SB03	Schapker & Bussing .03	EP55	CMB
SB10	Schapker & Bussing .10	EP129	CMB
SB10	Schapker & Bussing .10	EP129	HKC
TH05	Tremont House .05	EP77	CMB
TH10	Tremont House .10	EP114	HKC
FE09	"Feuchtwanger" .09	EP95A	CMB
FE09	"Feuchtwanger" .09	EP95A	HKC

Western Reserve Historical Society (115 pieces)

By far the largest institutional collection available for study is that owned by the Western Reserve Historical Society in Cleveland. These were in the possession of the society by 1922, ex-Cathcart, at which time they were displayed in mahogany and glass frames for members of the Western Reserve Numismatic Club to see. The exhibit was described as being more than 100 pieces, including two 90-cent varieties. This inventory of 115 pieces was supplied by museum director Kermit Pike.

AB01	Aërated Bread .01	EP1
AC01SA	Ayer's Cathartic .01 Short Arrows	EP2
AC03SA	Ayer's Cathartic .03 Short Arrows	EP32
AC05SA	Ayer's Cathartic .05 Short Arrows	EP60
AC10SA	Ayer's Cathartic .10 Short Arrows	EP96
AC03LA	Ayer's Cathartic .03 Long Arrows	EP32A
AC05LA	Ayer's Cathartic .05 Long Arrows	EP60A
AP01	Ayer's Pills .01	EP3
AP03	Ayer's Pills .03	EP33
AP05	Ayer's Pills .05	EP61
AP10	Ayer's Pills .10	EP97
AP12	Ayer's Pills .12	EP136
AS01SM	Ayer's Sarsaparilla .01 Small AYER'S	EP4
AS03SM	Ayer's Sarsaparilla .03 Small AYER'S	EP34
AS10SM	Ayer's Sarsaparills .10 Small AYER'S	EP98
AS12SM	Ayer's Sarsaparilla .12 Small AYER'S	EP137A
AS01MD	Ayer's Sarsaparilla .01 Medium AYER'S	EP4A
AS03MD	Ayer's Sarsaparilla .03 Medium AYER'S	EP34A
AS05MD	Ayer's Sarsaparilla .05 Medium AYER'S	EP63
AS10MD	Ayer's Sarsaparilla .10 Medium AYER'S	EP98A
AS03LG	Ayer's Sarsaparilla .03 Large AYER'S	EP34B
AS05LG	Ayer's Sarsaparilla .05 Large AYER'S	EP63A
BA01FG	Bates .01 FANCYGOODS (1 word)	EP6A
BA05FG	Bates .05 FANCYGOODS (1 word)	EP66A
BA10FG	Bates .10 FANCYGOODS (1 word)	EP102A
BA01F/G	Bates .01 FANCY GOODS (2 words)	EP6
BA05F/G	Bates .05 FANCY GOODS (2 words)	EP65
BA12F/G	Bates .12 FANCY GOODS (2 words)	EP139
BC01	Bailey & Co. .01	EP5
BC03	Bailey & Co. .03	EP36
BC10	Bailey & Co. .10	EP100
BE01	Burnett's Extracts .01	EP10
BE05	Burnett's Extracts .05	EP70
BE10	Burnett's Extracts .10	EP106
BK01	Burnett's Kalliston .01	EP9
BK03	Burnett's Kalliston .03	EP39
BK05	Burnett's Kalliston .05	EP69
BK10	Burnett's Kalliston .10	EP105
BT01	Brown's Troches .01	EP7
BT03	Brown's Troches .03	EP38
BT05	Brown's Troches .05	EP67
BT10	Brown's Troches .10	EP103
BU01	Buhl .01	EP8
BU05	Buhl .05	EP68
BU10	Buhl .10	EP104
CL01	Claflin .01	EP11
CL05	Claflin .05	EP71
CL10	Claflin .10	EP108A
CO05	Cook .05	EP72
CO10	Cook .10	EP108
DO01	Dougan .01	EP12
DO03	Dougan .03	EP41
DR01	Drake's .01	EP13
DR03	Drake's .03	EP42
DR05	Drake's .05	EP74
DR10	Drake's .10	EP110
DR12	Drake's .12	EP145
DR90	Drake's .90	EP185

EM05	Ellis McAlpin .05	EP76
EM10	Ellis McAlpin .10	EP112
EV01	Evans .01	EP14
EV03	Evans .03	EP44
HO03	Hopkins .03	EP48
IH05RB	Irving House .05 Ribbed Frame	EP82
IH10RB	Irving House .10 Ribbed Frame	EP119
IH10	Irving House .10	EP118
IH12	Irving House .12	EP150
JG05RB	John Gault .05 Ribbed Frame	EP79
JG10RB	John Gault .10 Ribbed Frame	EP117
JG01	John Gault .01	EP16
JG03	John Gault .03	EP46
JG05	John Gault .05	EP78
JG10	John Gault .10	EP116
JG12	John Gault .12	EP148
JG24	John Gault .24	EP167
JG30	John Gault .30	EP178
KG01	Kirkpatrick & Gault .01	EP19
KG03	Kirkpatrick & Gault .03	EP50
KG05	Kirkpatrick & Gault .05	EP83
KG12	Kirkpatrick & Gault .12	EP152
KG24	Kirkpatrick & Gault .24	EP171
KG30	Kirkpatrick & Gault .30	EP181
KG90	Kirkpatrick & Gault .90	EP187
LT03	Lord & Taylor .03	EP51
LT10	Lord & Taylor .10	EP121
LT12	Lord & Taylor .12	EP153
NA01CU	North America .01 Curved INSURANCE	EP24A
NA03CU	North America .03 Curved INSURANCE	EP53A
NA01ST	North America .01 Straight INSURANCE	EP24
NA03ST	North America .03 Straight INSURANCE	EP53
NA05ST	North America .05 Straight INSURANCE	EP88
NA10ST	North America .10 Straight INSURANCE	EP125
PE03	Pearce .03	EP54
SA05	Sands' Ale .05	EP90
SA10	Sands' Ale .10	EP128
SB03	Schapker & Bussing .03	EP55
SB05	Schapker & Bussing .05	EP91
SB10	Schapker & Bussing .10	EP129
SH01	Shillito's .01	EP26
SH03	Shillito's .03	EP56
SH05	Shillito's .05	EP92
SH10	Shillito's .10	EP130
ST01	Steinfeld .01	EP27
TA01	Taylor .01	EP28
TA05	Taylor .05	EP93A
TH01	Tremont House .01	EP15
TH03	Tremont House .03	EP45
TH05	Tremont House .05	EP77
TH10	Tremont House .10	EP114
WH03	White Hatter .03	EP59
WH05	White Hatter .05	EP95
WL01	Weir & Larminie .01	EP29
WL10	Weir & Larminie .10	EP133
WH01	White Hatter .01	EP30
FE09	"Feuchtwanger" .09	EP95A

Appendix D: Catalog of Ancillary Items

Frontispiece, & Figure 41a, Civil War era print, *Punch*	$25-30
Figure 6b, stamp company label	$1-2
Figure 16a, Lincoln contemporary print, *Harper's Weekly*	$65-100
Figure 18a, mid-19th century Boston map	$25-35
Figures 30a, b, Munn & Co. 1868 embossed brass store card	$40-50
Figure 30c, Munn & Co. advertising trade card (postal card)	$3-5
Figure 30d, check payable to Munn & Co. with internal revenue stamp	$3-5
Figure 32a, Civil War era steel engraving, George E. Perine	$20-25
Figure 37a, Civil War era *Scientific American*	$25-30
Figure 37d, Munn & Co. advertising cover	$3-5
Figures 42b, c, 1862 U.S. quarter dollar, uncirculated	$350-625
Figures 42d, e, 1862 U.S. silver dollar, uncirculated	$3,000-7,150
Figure 43a, [1861] unused S. P. Upham patriotic envelope	$ 20-25
Figure 44a, 1861 U.S. 1-cent stamp, Scott 63 type, mint	$ 50-60
Figure 44b, 1861 U.S. 3-cent stamp, Scott 65 type, mint	$ 25-30
Figure 44c, 1861 U.S. 5-cent stamp, Scott 75 type, mint	$500-600
Figure 44d, 1861 U.S. 10-cent stamp, Scott 68 type, mint	$ 90-100
Figure 45a, 1861 U.S. 12-cent stamp, Scott 69 type, mint	$200-300
Figure 45b, 1861 U.S. 24-cent stamp, Scott 70 type, mint	$200-300
Figure 45c, 1861 U.S. 30-cent stamp, Scott 71 type, mint	$250-300
Figure 45d, 1861 U.S. 90-cent stamp, Scott 72 type, mint	$500-700
Figure 46a, [1862] unused W. H. Murphy patriotic envelope	$10-15
Figure 46b, [1862] W. H. Murphy 50-cent stamp envelope	$250-275
Figure 47a, [1862] J. Leach 50-cent stamp envelope	$200-225
Figure 47b, [1862] Arthur, Gregory & Co. 50-cent stamp envelope	$350-400
Figure 47c, [1862] Jno. C. Force 50-cent stamp envelope	$350-400
Figure 48a, [1862] Wm. Robins 25-cent stamp envelope	$250-275
Figure 49a, [1862] Metropolitan Hotel 10-cent stamp envelope	$450-500
Figure 49b, [1862] Lansignh's 50-cent stamp envelope	$350-400
Figures 49c, d, [1862] Long's Varieties 1-cent stamp on cardboard (unique, valued by owner @ $3,000)	$ ----
Figure 49e, [1862] William Newton & Co. 5-cent stamp scrip (valued by R. M. Smythe @ $5,000)	$ ----
Figure 50b, 1862 5-cent Postage Currency, uncirculated	$135-180
Figure 50c, 1862 10-cent Postage Currency, uncirculated	$135-180
Figure 51a, 1862 25-cent Postage Currency, uncirculated	$225-300
Figures 51b, c, 1862 50-cent Postage Currency, uncirculated	$250-400
Figures 52a, b, 1862 M. L. Marshall Civil War store card (Fuld NY 695A)	$45-60
Figure 53b, Hatch & Co.currency lookalike advertising note	$75-100
Figure 54c, Ferd Mayer The Shinplaster Bank currency lookalike advertising note	$150-250
Figure 55a, 1862 Chas. P. Poinier 5-cent merchant scrip	$15-20
Figure 55b, 1862 Rushton's Drugs 3-cent merchant scrip	$30-40
Figure 55c, 1862 City of Troy, N.Y. 10-cent municipal scrip	$20-25
Figure 55d, 1862 Harris & Chapman 25-cent merchant scrip	$20-25
Figure 55e, 1862 R. Walton 1-cent cardboard merchant scrip	$50-75
Figure 55f, 1862 Mathews & Bro. 2-cent cardboard merchant scrip	$30-50
Figure 55g, 1862 C. Dautremont 50-cent merchant scrip	$125-200
Figures 56d, e, 1862 Morris & Messinger Civil War brass store card (Fuld MI 770B-2b, R-8)	$75-100
Figure 60a, Civil War era *Boston Almanac*	$40-50
Figure 69a, [1862] Scovill military button, brass common type	$15-20
Figure 69a, [1862] Scovill military button, silvered common type	$45-60
Figure 69a, [1862] Scovill military button, gilt common type	$75-100
Figure 69a, [1862] Scovill state regimental, common type	$25-35
Figure 69a, [1862] Scovill naval button, gilt common type	$100-125
Figure 70a, 1883 Scovill check, with revenue imprint	$35-50
Figure 84a, Irving House 10-cent stamp envelope	$500-600
Figure 88c & 95b, Brown's Troches pill box	$ 20-30
Figure 90b, Brown's Bronchial Troches pill box	$ 35-50
Figure 91a, Brown's Vermifuge Comfits 1-cent proprietary revenue stamp	$ 30-40
Figure 91b, Brown's Bronchial Troches 1-cent proprietary revenue stamp	$ 40-50
Figure 91c, Brown's Bronchial Troches 2-cent proprietary revenue stamp	$40-50
Figure 92a, Brown's Dentifrice trade card, common type	$10-12
Figure 93a, 1872 Mrs. *Winslow's Domestic Receipt Book*	$20-25
Figure 94a, Mrs. Winslow's Soothing Syrup 2-cent proprietary revenue stamp	$15-25
Figure 94b, Mrs. Winslow's Soothing Syrup trade card, type	$15-20
Figure 94c, 1913 Mrs. Winslow's advertising cover	$5-7

Figure 100a, Ayer's Cherry Pectoral trade card, common type	$5-15
Figure 100b, Ayer's Cherry Pectoral bottle, type	$15-25
Figure 102a, Civil War era *Ayer's American Almanac*	$25-30
Figure 108a, 1858 Ayer's draft	$50-75
Figure 110a & 111a Ayer's Pills trade card, common type	$5-15
Figure 111b, 1867 check payable to J.C. Ayer & Co., with revenue stamp	$35-50
Figure 112a, Ayer's Pills original package	$25-30
Figure 112b & 113a, Ayer's Pills trade card, common type	$5-10
Figure 112c, Ayer's 1-cent proprietary revenue stamp, type	$55-65
Figure 114b, Ayer's Cathartic Pills trade card, type	$20-25
Figure 115a, Ayer's Hair Vigor bottle, full labeling (extremely rare, thus)	$250-300
Figure 115b, Ayer's Hair Vigor trade card, common type	$8-12
Figure 117a, Ayer's 4-cent star burst proprietary revenue stamp	$60-75
Figures 117b-d, Ayer's Sarsaparilla bottle, type	$10-12
Figure 118a, Theatrical advertising card, with Ayer's ad	$50-75
Figure 119a, Ayer's Sarsaparilla trade card, over-sized (reprints exist)	$50-75
Figure 121a, 1878 Ayer's check, with revenue imprint	$75-100
Figure 121b, 1879 check payable to J. C. Ayer Co. with revenue imprint	$20-25
Figure 122a, 1890 Ayer's advertising cover	$90-125
Figure 124b, Ayer's Sarsaparilla trade card, common type	$5-10
Figure 126a, Ayer's Sarsaparilla trade card, large size common type (reprints exist)	$25-35
Figure 133a, [1866] Joseph L. Bates stereo trade card	$200-250
Figure 135a, [1862] Ticknor & Fields 50-cent stamp envelope	$450-500
Figure 137b, [1870] Joseph L. Bates stereo card, type	$20-30
Figure 139b, [1865] Joseph Ward, Lincoln and Tad carte de visite	$50-60
Figure 140a, [1870] Bates stereo viewer	$150-200
Figures 153a, b, Burnett's Standard Extract bottles, type	$5-10
Figure 154b, Burnett's 4-cent proprietary revenue stamp	$40-60
Figure 154c, 1876 check payable to Joseph Burnett & Co. with revenue imprint	$10-12
Figures 156a, b, Burnett's trade card, over-sized	$15-20
Figure 158b, *Burnett's Floral Hand Book*	$10-15
Figure 162a, 1869 Claflin, Saville & Co. invoice with revenue stamp	$15-25
Figure 163b, 1862 Arthur M. Claflin 25-cent merchant scrip	$100-150
Figures 176a, b, Kirkpatrick & Gault encased stamp advertising insert	$35-50
Figure 185a, J. A. Dougan Hatter trade card, die cut	$45-55
Figure 185b & 186a, John A.Dougan Hatter trade card, type	$25-30
Figures 191a & 207a, Drake's Plantation Bitters bottle, common type	$85-125
Figure 192b, 1868 Geo. P. Rowell currency lookalike coupon	$30-40
Figure 197a, Demas Barnes 4-cent proprietary revenue stamp, type	$20-30
Figure 197b, Demas Barnes & Co. 2-cent proprietary revenue stamp, type	$10-15
Figure 198b, The Plantation Bank $100 currency lookalike	$50-65
Figures 199a, b, Mexican Mustang Liniment bottles, type	$8-10
Figure 199c, The Mustang Bank $50 currency lookalike	$35-50
Figure 200b, Lyon Manufacturing Co. 2-cent proprietary revenue stamp, type	$10-12
Figures 201a, The Kathairon Bank $20 currency lookalike	$45-55
Figure 201b, The Kathairon Bank $50 currency lookalike	$50-60
Figures 203a, b, 1850s E. Lyon brass store card (Miller NY-511)	$12-15
Figures 203d, e, 1850s E. Lyon brass store card (Miller NY-508)	$15-20
Figures 204a, b, Geo. P. Rowell advertising cover	$25-35
Figures 206a, b, [1876] Geo. P. Rowell & Co. U.S. Centennial store card, type	$30-35
Figure 206c, check payable to George P. Rowell with revenue imprint	$10-15
Figures 208a, b, 1880 Drake's Plantation Bitters political store card (DeWitt SJT 1876-9)	$150-200
Figure 208c, 1880s check payable to P. H. Drake & Co. with revenue stamp	$10-15
Figure 212a, envelope addressed to Samuel Lord Jr.	$50-75
Figures 219a, b, 1889 Lord & Taylor wooden plaque commemorating Brooklyn Bridge	$125-150
Figure 231a, North America Life Insurance Co. $10,000 insurance policy with revenue imprint	$300-500
Figures 232a, b North America Life Insurance Co. receipts with revenue stamp	$50-60
Figures 235a, b, 1863 S. Steinfeld Civil War store card, type copper (Fuld NY-630BU)	$8-10
Figures 235a, b, 1863 S. Steinfeld Civil War store card (Fuld NY-630BU-2m), unlisted variety (ckashed dies), tin	$----
Figures 240c, d, Barnum's American Museum medal (Miller NY59)	$85-100
Figure 242a, Wm. Van Name's 25-cent postage stamp envelope	$300-350
Figure 242b, Capt. Tom Reeves 25-cent postage stamp envelope	$400-450
Figures 243b, c, 1863 White Hatter Civil War store card (Fuld NY-630CG)	$7-10
Figures 245a & 246a, 1870 White Hatter baseball scorecard	$850-950
Figure 248b, 1862 Weir & Larminie check	$100-125
Figure 251a, 1889 $5 Banque Ville-Marie bank note	$1,000-1,500
Figure 251b, 1889 $10 Banque Ville-Marie bank note	$1,800-2,000
Figures 256b, c, [1858] Bailey & Co. store card (Miller PA-33)	$60-75
Figures 256d, e, 1860 Clark Gruber & Co. Pikes Peak territorial $10 gold coin	$8,000-10,000
Figures 257a, b, 1860 Bailey & Co. Japanese Embassy medal (bronze)	$100-150
Figures 258a, b, 1860 Robert Lovett Jr. store card (Miller PA-355), type	$40-50
Figures 258c, d, [1860] Robert Lovett Jr. store card (Miller PA-342)	$60-75

Figures 258e, f, 1860 Lincoln campaign medal (DeWitt AL 1860-51)	$50-60
Figures 259a, b, [1861] Confederate Cent, copper nickel original	$5,000-8,000
Figures 260a, b, [1880] Cincinnati Industrial Exposition award medal	$35-45
Figures 260c, d, 1905 Holland Society of America medal	$25-30
Figures 261a, b, Sons of the American Revolution badge	$125-150
Figures 261c, d, Sons of the American Revolution badge, miniature	$75-85
Figures 263a, b, 1906 Seventh Regiment New York National Guard medal	$85-100
Figures 263c, d, 1926 U.S. Sesquicentennial award medal	$150-175
Figures 268a-c, Civil War era miliary buttons, Jacob Reed's Sons, type	$15-20
Figure 274a, Evans' *Illustrated History of the United States Mint*, type	$75-100
Figures 275a, b, [1885] Lord's Prayer medalet (holed, as made)	$10-15
Figure 279b, 1855 N. & G. Taylor advertising cover	$50-75
Figures 282a & 283d, Civil War era N. & G. Taylor advertising cover	$35-40
Figure 283a, 1862 N. & G. Taylor Co. Civil War store card (Fuld PA-750V-5b)	$75-85
Figures 283c, d, 1863 N. & G. Taylor Co. Civil War store card (Fuld PA-750V-1a)	$35-40
Figures 286a, b, 1880s N. & G. Taylor Co. advertising cover	$50-60
Figures 288a, b, 20th century N. & G. Taylor Co. advertising cover	$40-50
Figures 295a, b, Robert Wright Civil War store card (Fuld OH-165GS), type	$8-10
Figure 295c, R. D. Norris Civil War store card (Fuld OH-165EF), type	$12-15
Figure 295d, O'Reilly Bros. Civil War store card (Fuld OH-165EH), type	$30-40
Figure 295e, Pogue & Jones Civil War store card (Fuld OH-165EN), type	$15-20
Figure 296a, W. K. Lanphear Civil War store card (Fuld OH-165CY), type	$20-25
Figures 297a, b, Geo. McAlpen Civil War sutler token (Schenkman PA-C25C)	$175-250
Figures 320a, b, late 19th century John Shillito Company advertising cover	$5-10
Figure 326a, 1862 H. A. Cook 10-cent merchant scrip	$60-75
Figure 352a, 1871 Chicago stereo view, type	$10-15
Figure 359a, 1862 Wm. J. Sands five-cent merchant scrip	$35-45
Figure 361b, 1871 Chicago post-fire stereo view, type	$35-50
Figures 369a, b, Chicago Philatelic Society commemorative covers	$3-5
Figure 370a, cover addressed to Supreme Court justice Hon. David Davis	$50-60
Figure 371d, [1862] Chicago circular cardboard 5-cent merchant change check	$200-225
Figures 371e, f, [1862] Chicago City Railway fare tickets	$25-30
Figure 372a, 1850s Tremont House, Gage Brother & Drake advertising cover	$35-40
Figure 372b, 1860s Tremont House, Gage & Drake advertising cover	$30-35
Figure 374b, 1870s Tremont House, John B. Drake advertising cover	$30-35
Figure 375a, 1870 Chicago White Stocking baseball club carte de visite	$3,000-5,000
Figures 376a & 377a, 1871 Chicago White Stocking baseball club carte de visite	$2,000-3,000
Figure 380a, [1871] Tremont House, John B. Drake back bar bottle (one of two known)	$1,000-1,500
Figure 385b, post-fire Tremont House, James & Ira Couch advertising cover	$75-85
Figure 387b, 1890s The Grand Pacific Hotel, Drake, Parker & Co. advertising cover	$15-20
Figure 389a, 1940s Drake Hotel label	$2-3
Figure 396b, Civil War era Salmon P. Chase steel plate engraving, Johnson, Fry & Co.	$25-30
Figure 397b, 1862 T. Buchanan 10-cent Strawberry Currency merchant I. O. U.	$400-500
Figures 397c, d, [1863] patriotic Civil War token (Fuld 226A/322A, R-10, valued by owner @ $2,500)	$----
Figures 398a, b, 1863 U.S. two-cent coin pattern (Judd 316)	$5,000-6,000
Figures 398c, d, 1863 U.S. two-cent coin pattern (Judd 305)	$2,000-2,500
Figures 398e, f, 1865 U.S. three-cent coin pattern (Judd 410)	$800-1,000
Figure 401a, 1863 U.S. 2-cent stamp, Scott 73 type, mint	$100-125
Figures 406a, b, [1850] Scovill's Daguerreotype Materials store card (Miller NY-805)	$50-60
Figures 406c, d, [1855] Scovill's Daguerreotype Materials store card (Miller NY-802)	$75-85
Figures 407a, d, 1864 Lincoln/Johnson campaign ferrotype (DeWitt AL 1864-94)	$1,500-1,800
Figures 407b, e, 1864 Fremont/Cochrane campaign ferrotype (DeWitt JF 1864-7)	$700-800
Figures 407c, f, 1864 McClellan/Pendleton campaign ferrotype (DeWitt GMcC 1864-49)	$800-1,000
Figure 412a, Boyd's Dispatch private express stamp (Scott 20L), type	$3-5
Figure 412b, New York Match Company 1-cent proprietary match stamp (Scott 138B)	$3-5
Figure 413a, [1862] C. Delmonico 15-cent merchant scrip	$80-100
Figure 413b, Edw. Schulze's Restaurant Civil War store card (Fuld NY-630BU), type	$8-10
Figure 413c, 20th century New York *Tribune* advertising cover	$5-7
Figure 414a, 1935 Berenice Abbott photograph	$1,500-2,000
Figures 417a, b, New York City chromolithograph postcards	$2-3
Figure 436b, 1862 W. Elliot Woodward Mount Pleasant Apothecary Store 20-cent merchant scrip	$15-20
Figure 440b, 1914 Fred Michael advertising cover	$2-3
Figure 444a, 1837 Feuchtwanger cent, type	$100-125
Figure 444f, [1859] S. H. Black National Medallion plaque	$550-600

Annotated Bibliography: Auction Catalogs, Fixed Price Lists, Institutional Collections

More than 360 sales and inventories of institutional and leading private, "strongly held" collections have been studied in the preparation of the book. From these sources 8,750 specific appearances of encased stamps have been verified over a period of more than a century. This is the largest database of information about John Gault's New Metallic Currency ever compiled. These sources are useful in tracing pedigrees and determining rarities for the approximately 275 varieties of encased stamps. This information was published in two volumes by the present author in 1988 under the title *Civil War Encased Stamps: Auction Census Data.* Summary tables based on this information were also furnished leading collectors and dealers over the years. An update of the summary tables appears in the chapter on "Collecting Encased Stamps" in the present volume.

Sales and collections consulted in the preparation of this book appear below:

Geoffrey Adams. Auction Sale. April 16, 1904.
Geoffrey Adams. Joseph Armstrong Temple Collection Sale. April 29, 1905. (31 pcs)
Geoffrey Adams. Auction Sale. September 27, 1905. (5 pcs)
American Numismatic Association. Collection. (1 pc)
American Numismatic Society. Exhibition. 1914. (179 pcs)
American Numismatic Society. Collection. (22 pcs)
Anonymous. Miscellaneous Private Treaty Sales to Fred C. C. Boyd. c. 1942-1949. (20 pcs)
Earl P. L. Apfelbaum. Auction Sale 283. January 6, 1973. (3 pcs)
Martin A. Armstrong. Fixed Price Sale. December 18, 1978. (3 pcs)
George Bauer. Private Treaty Sales to Fred C. C. Boyd. c. 1942-1949. (3 pcs)
Barney Bluestone. Sale No. 35. October 16, 1937. (54 pcs)
Barney Bluestone. Sale No. 91. February 15-16, 1946. (23 pcs)
M. H. Bolender. Sale No. 115, David A. Woods Collection (ex-Virgil Brand). April 2, 1938. (38 pcs)
M. H. Bolender. Private Treaty Sales to Fred C. C. Boyd. c. 1942-1949. (3 pcs)
Bowers and Ruddy Galleries. Armand Champa Collection Sale. May 19, 1972. (1 pc)
Bowers and Ruddy Galleries. Stanislaw Herstal Collection Sale. February 7, 1974. (1 pc)
Bowers and Ruddy Galleries. The Newport Collection Sale. January 30-February 1, 1975. (54 pcs)
Bowers and Ruddy Galleries. Rare Coin Review No. 22. Spring, 1975. (7 pcs)
Bowers and Ruddy Galleries. Rare Coin Review No. 23. Summer, 1975. (35 pcs)
Bowers and Ruddy Galleries. Auction Sale. December 12, 1975.
Bowers and Ruddy Galleries. Rare Coin Review No. 25. Spring, 1976. (38 pcs)
Bowers and Ruddy Galleries. Montgomery Collection Sale. February 20, 1976.
Bowers and Ruddy Galleries. Rare Coin Review No. 26. Summer, 1976. (23 pcs)
Bowers and Ruddy Galleries. River Oaks-Krugjohann Collections Sale. November 11, 1976. (7 pcs)
Bowers and Ruddy Galleries. Blauvelt & Treasure Fleet Collections Sale. February 17, 1977. (2 pcs)
Bowers and Ruddy Galleries. Doolittle-Russell Collections Sale. February 17, 1977. (2 pcs)
Bowers and Ruddy Galleries. Fairfield Collection Sale. October 6, 1977. (1 pc)
Bowers and Ruddy Galleries. Auction Sale. April, 1978. (3 pcs)

Bowers and Ruddy Galleries. Robert E. Branigan Estate Sale. August 21, 1978. (6 pcs)
Bowers and Ruddy Galleries. Robert C. Hall Estate Sale. October 26, 1978. (5 pcs)
Bowers and Ruddy Galleries. Wilfred Helwig Collection Sale. February 5, 1979. (1 pc)
Bowers and Ruddy Galleries. University of Rochester Collection Sale Part 3. June 10, 1980. (1 pc)
Bowers and Ruddy Galleries. The Garrett Collection Sale No. 4. March 26, 1981. (3 pcs)
Bowers and Ruddy Galleries. Roy Harte Collection Sale. March 27, 1981. (3 pcs)
Bowers and Ruddy Galleries. William R. Sieck Collection (ANA Convention Sale). July 28-August 1, 1981. (30 pcs)
Bowers and Ruddy Galleries. Rare Coin Review No. 40. September, 1981. (2 pcs)
Bowers and Ruddy Galleries. Springfield Collection Sale. September 22, 1981. (4 pcs)
Bowers and Ruddy Galleries. New York Public Library Collection Sale. October 30, 1982. (2 pcs)
Bowers and Ruddy Galleries. Rare Coin Review No. 46. December, 1982. (1 pc)
Bowers and Merena Galleries. Connecticut Historical Society-Sheldon Collections Sale. April 8, 1983. (17 pcs)
Bowers and Merena Galleries. George Hatie Collection Sale. August 3-5, 1983. (11 pcs)
Bowers and Merena Galleries. Rare Coin Review No. 40. (James F. Ruddy Collection). January, 1984. (41 pcs and 5 additional pcs)
Bowers and Merena Galleries. Rudy Sieck-Roy Harte Collections Sale. March 26, 1984. (6 pcs)
Bowers and Merena Galleries. Dodson-Collier Collections Sale. (James F. Ruddy Collection). June 20, 1984. (41 pcs)
Bowers and Merena Galleries. Arnold-Romisa Collections Sale. September 17-19, 1984. (20 pcs)
Bowers and Merena Galleries. Milton Cohen Collection Sale. January 24, 1985. (1 pc)
Bowers and Merena Galleries. Russell Patterson Collection Sale. March 25, 1985. (1 pc)
Bowers and Merena Galleries. Hoke Green Collection Sale. June 10, 1985. (3 pcs)
Bowers and Merena Galleries. Four Memorable Collections Sale. September 9, 1985. (24 pcs)
Bowers and Merena Galleries. Abe Kosoff Estate Sale. November 4, 1985. (11 pcs)
Bowers and Merena Galleries. Ezra Cole Collection Sale. January 23, 1986. (30 pcs)
Bowers and Merena Galleries. Stuart Levine Collection Sale. April 10, 1986. (2 pcs)
Bowers and Merena Galleries. Harry Einstein Collection Sale. June 23, 1986. (17 pcs)
Bowers and Merena Galleries. Princeton-Ingle Collections Sale. September 8, 1986. (7 pcs)
Bowers and Merena Galleries. Von Stetten-Smith Collections Sale. November 10, 1986. (28 pcs)
Bowers and Merena Galleries. Saunders Collection Sale. November 9-11, 1987. (99 pcs)
Bowers and Merena Galleries. Everson and Faught Collections Sale. June 13-15, 1988. (138 pcs)
Bowers and Merena Galleries. Fixed Price Sale. July 27, 1988. (34 pcs)
Bowers and Merena Galleries. Byron F. Johnson Collection Sale. January 26-28, 1989. (2 pcs)
Bowers and Merena Galleries. Four Landmark Sales. March 27-31, 1989. (3 pcs)
Bowers and Merena Galleries. Auction Sale. September 11-13, 1989. (3 pcs)
Bowers and Merena Galleries. Saccone Collection Sale. November 6-8, 1989. (22 pcs)
Bowers and Merena Galleries. Chris Schenkel Collection Sale. November 12-14, 1990. (15 pcs)
Bowers and Merena Galleries. Robert W. Miller Collection Sale. November 20-21, 1992. (2 pcs)
Briggs. Auction Sale. June, 1982. (7 pcs)
Buffalo Historical Society. Collection. (36 pcs)
S. H. and H. Chapman. S. Emlen Meigs-P. Napoleon Breton Sale. May 4, 1901. (5 pcs)
S. H. and H. Chapman. Dr. Ellwood Hopkins Sale. July 22, 1901. (4 pcs)
S. H. and H. Chapman. C. S. Wilcox Collection Sale. November 6-7, 1901. (88 pcs)
S. H. and H. Chapman. J. O. Stevens Sale. January 31, 1902. (11 pcs)
S. H. and H. Chapman. Auction Sale. February 1, 1904. (12 pcs)
Coins & Currency Inc. Auction Sale. November 19, 1971. (2 pcs)
Tom Denly. Fixed Price Sale. October, 1993. (55 pcs)
William F. Dunham. Listing. 1929. (171 pcs)
William F. Dunham-Fred C. C. Boyd Collection. Private Inventory. (257 pcs)
Dutch County Auction Sale. February 28, 1971.
Eastern Collection. (158 pcs)
Thomas Elder. Auction Sale. September 30, 1905.
Thomas Elder. Auction Sale. November 23, 1905.
Thomas Elder. Auction Sale. December 7, 1905.
Thomas Elder. Auction Sale. December 17, 1907. (5 pcs)
Thomas Elder. Auction Sale. April 23, 1910.
Thomas Elder. Auction Sale. June 8, 1912.
Thomas Elder. Auction Sale. April 2, 1928. (14 pcs)
Thomas Elder. Guttag Brothers Collection Sale. November 7, 1929. (49 pcs)

Thomas Elder. Guttag Brothers Collection Sale. December 13, 1929. (63 pcs)
Thomas Elder. William P. Brown Collection Sale. June 24-27, 1930. (16 pcs)
Federal Coin Exchange. Auction Sale. October 13, 1956.
Ed. Frossard. Andrew C. Zabriskie Collection Sale (EPS property "of a well known Brooklyn collector"). January 9-10, 1891. (71 pcs)
Ed. Frossard. Auction Sale. January 25, 1901. (2 pcs)
Ed. Frossard. Auction Sale. March 18, 1901. (5 pcs)
Ed. Frossard. Auction Sale. May 17, 1901. (1 pc)
Ed. Frossard. Auction Sale. June 11, 1901. (1 pc)
Ed. Frossard. Auction Sale. July 19, 1901. (4 pcs)
Ed. Frossard. Moritz Collection Sale. September 16, 1901. (58 pcs)
Len and Jean Glazer (Fractional Currency Inc.) Mail Bid Sale No. 1. June 26, 1979. (49 pcs)
Len and Jean Glazer (Fractional Currency Inc.) Auction Sale No. 2. June 17-18, 1980. (42 pcs)
Len and Jean Glazer (Fractional Currency Inc.) Fixed Price Catalog. August 20, 1980. (189 pcs)
Gold Medal. Mail Bid Sale. September 17, 1974. (2 pcs)
Gold Medal. Mail Bid Sale. December 23, 1983. (1 pc)
Charles Gregory. Listing. 1889. (121 pcs)
Ben Green. Auction Sale. May 29, 1902. (6 pcs)
Ben Green. Listing. 1902-1905. (165 pcs)
Ben Green. Auction Sale. February 18, 1905. (14 pcs)
Ben Green. Auction Sale. June 17, 1905. (33 pcs)
Ben Green. Auction Sale (Property of Robert Young and others). September 16, 1905. (49 pcs)
Ben Green. Auction Sale. November 11, 1905. (18 pcs)
Ben Green. Auction Sale (Property of A. P. Button). January 12, 1906. (27 pcs)
Ben Green. Auction Sale. March 9, 1906. (8 pcs)
Ben Green. A. L. Schuyler Collection Sale. May 25, 1906. (28 pcs)
Ben Green. Auction Sale. June 29, 1906. (2 pcs)
Ben Green. Auction Sale. July 12, 1906.
Ben Green. Auction Sale. September 28, 1906. (1 pc)
Ben Green. Hiram E. Deats Collection Sale. November 30, 1906. (163 pcs)
Ben Green. Auction Sale. March 29, 1907. (5 pcs)
Ben Green. Auction Sale. April 19, 1907. (20 pcs)
Ben Green. Auction Sale. May 31, 1907. (13 pcs)
Ben Green. Auction Sale. September 3, 1907. (22 pcs)
Ben Green. Auction Sale. October 18, 1907. (1 pc)
Ben Green. Auction Sale. November 8, 1907. (8 pcs)
Ben Green. Auction Sale. January 31, 1908. (6 pcs)
Ben Green. Auction Sale. February 28, 1908. (5 pcs)
Ben Green. Auction Sale. May 22, 1908. (1 pc)
Ben Green. Auction Sale. June 19, 1908. (2 pcs)
Ben Green. Auction Sale. April 8, 1910. (13 pcs)
Ben Green. Auction Sale. June 10, 1910. (2 pcs)
Ben Green. Auction Sale. September 23, 1910. (13 pcs)
Ben Green. Auction Sale. February 24, 1911. (1 pc)
Ben Green. Auction Sale. May 12, 1911. (6 pcs)
Ben Green. Auction Sale. August 30, 1911. (9 pcs)
Ben Green. Auction Sale. October 13, 1911. (18 pcs)
Ben Green. Auction Sale. December 8, 1911. (2 pcs)
Ben Green. Auction Sale. February 16, 1912. (7 pcs)
Ben Green. Auction Sale. March 29, 1912. (1 pc)
Ben Green. Auction Sale. May 4, 1912. (3 pcs)
Ben Green. Auction Sale. June 1, 1912. (7 pcs)
Ben Green. Auction Sale. July 26, 1912. (13 pcs)
Ben Green. Auction Sale. October 25, 1912. (1 pc)
Ben Green. Auction Sale. December 13, 1912. (3 pcs)
Ben Green. Auction Sale. April 25, 1913. (8 pcs)
Ben Green. Auction Sale. July 18, 1913. (5 pcs)
Ben Green. Chas. Morris Collection Sale. October 10, 1913. (4 pcs)

Ben Green. Auction Sale. November 7, 1913. (1 pc)
Ben Green. Auction Sale. January 23, 1914. (7 pcs)
Julius Guttag. Listing. 1927. (117 pcs)
H. R. Harmer. Franklin D. Roosevelt Collection Sale Part I. February 4-5, 1946. (1 pc)
H. R. Harmer.Auction Sale. April 28, 1970. (5 pcs)
Harmer's of New York. Sale No. 2465. July 18-20, 1978. (32 pcs)
Harmer, Rooke Numismatics. Million Dollar Sale. February 4-5, 1970. (33 pcs)
Harmer, Rooke Numismatics. Absentee Auction Sale No. 32. April 12, 1989. (1 pc)
Rich Hartzog (World Exonumia). Mail Bid Sale. December 1, 1980. (6 pcs)
Rich Hartzog (World Exonumia). Auction Sale. August 14, 1982. (9 pcs)
J. M. Henderson. Private Treaty Sales to Fred C. C. Boyd. c. 1942-1949. (6 pcs)
Herman Herst. Auction Sale No. 169. December 3, 1968. With annotations by John J. Ford. (42 pcs)
Herman Herst. Auction Sale No. 169. December 3, 1968. With annotations by Herman Herst. (included above)
Herman Herst. Auction Sale. March 25, 1970. (19 pcs)
Herman Herst. Auction Sale. July 8, 1970. (22 pcs)
Herman Herst. Auction Sale. May 12, 1971. (20 pcs)
Herman Herst. Auction Sale. December 6, 1972. (41 pcs)
Hickman and Oakes. Memphis International Paper Money Show Auction Sale. June 16, 1979. (8 pcs)
Hollinbeck, Kagin Coin Co. 262nd. Mail Bid Sale. January 27, 1966. (12 pcs)
Kagin's. American Numismatic Association Convention Auction Sale. August 26, 1977. (6 pcs)
Kagin's. Metropolitan Washington Auction Sale. July, 1979. (1 pc)
Kagin's. Numismatic Association of Southern California Auction Sale. January, 1981. (1 pc)
Kagin's. Memphis International Paper Money Show Auction Sale No. 324. June 19-21, 1981. (24 pcs)
Kagin's Numismatic Investment Corp. Inventory Price List. August 31, 1981. (223 pcs)
Kagin's. Great Eastern Numismatic Association Auction Sale No. 325. September 25, 1981. (22 pcs)
Kagin's. Numismatic Association of Southern California Auction Sale. January, 1983. (4 pcs)
Kagin's. American Numismatic Association Convention Auction Sale. August 16-20, 1983. (26 pcs)
Kagin's. Long Beach Auction Sale. February 2, 1984. (7 pcs)
Kagin's. Memphis International Paper Money Show Auction Sale. June 15-16, 1984. (13 pcs)
Kagin's. Western Reserve Historical Society Collection Sale. March 29-30, 1985. (2 pcs)
Kagin's. Long Beach Auction Sale (Kagin Collection). February 4, 1988. (159 pcs)
Kagin's. Auction Sale. May 6, 1988. (3 pcs)
Frank Katen. Auction Sale. June 19, 1948. (15 pcs)
Peter Kenedi (Eastland Stamp Auctions). Auction Sale. September 11, 1970. (2 pcs)
Peter Kenedi (Eastland Stamp Auctions). Auction Sale. April 1, 1971. (3 pcs)
Charles Kirtley. Mail Bid Sale. January 19, 1993. (1 pc)
Michael Kolman (Federal Brand Enterprises). American Numismatic Association Convention Auction Sale. August 19, 1964. (34 pcs)
Michael Kolman (Federal Brand Enterprises). Auction Sale. August 6, 1965. (20 pcs)
A. Kosoff. Prann Collection Sale. c. 1949. (43 pcs)
A. Kosoff. American Numismatic Association Convention Auction Sale. August 19, 1966. (1 pc – HO05)
A. Kosoff. Auction Sale. February 19, 1970. (8 pcs)
Abner Kreisberg. Mail Bid Sale. June 28, 1965. (7 pcs)
Abner Kreisberg, Hans M. F. Schulman, and Jerry Cohen. Auction Sale. April 6-8, 1967. (9 pcs)
Abner Kreisberg. Mail Bid Sale. September 25, 1967. (5 pcs)
Abner Kreisberg and Jerry Cohen (Quality Sales Corp.). Auction Sale. November 18, 1968 (29 pcs)
Abner Kreisberg and Jerry Cohen (Quality Sales Corp.). Mail Bid Sale. January 19, 1970. (4 pcs)
Abner Kreisberg and Jerry Cohen (Quality Sales Corp.) Mail Bid Sale. June 29, 1970. (1 pc)
Abner Kreisberg and Jerry Cohen (Quality Sales Corp.) John A. Beck Collection Sale Part II. February 12, 1976. (2 pcs)
Kurt Krueger. Auction Sale. January 30, 1981. (1 pc)
Kurt Krueger. Auction Sale. June 11, 1981. (1 pc)
Joseph Lepczyk. Michigan State Numismatic Society Sale. May 4-5, 1984. (1 pc)
Joseph Lepczyk. Auction Sale. November 23, 1984. (10 pcs)
Joseph Lepczyk. Auction Sale. March 13, 1985. (4 pcs)
H. Joseph Levine (Presidential Coin and Antique Co.). Auction Sale. December 5, 1992. (3 pcs)
Dana Linett (Early American Numismatics). Mail Bid Sale. February 27, 1984. (28 pcs)
Dana Linett (San Diego Coin Show, Inc.). Auction Sale. September 18, 1987. (54 pcs)

Dana Linett (San Diego Coin Show, Inc.). Auction Sale. January 22, 1988. (77 pcs)
Dana Linett (Early American Numismatics). Fixed Price Sale. May, 1988. (161 pcs)
Dana Linett (Newport Beach Coin Show, Inc.). Auction Sale. October 14-15, 1988. (31 pcs)
Dana Linett (Newport Beach Coin Show, Inc.). Auction Sale. June 23-24, 1989. (37 pcs)
Dana Linett (Early American Numismatics). Auction Sale. May 24, 1991. (49 pcs)
Dana Linett (Early American Numismatics). Auction Sale. March 21, 1992. (45 pcs)
Dana Linett (Early American Numismatics). Auction Sale. August 29, 1992. (80 pcs)
Dana Linett (Early American Numismatics). June 26, 1993. (59 pcs)
Lyman Low. Desy Collection Sale. July 26, 1899. (1 pc)
Lyman Low. Gasten Collection Sale. December 29, 1900. (1 pc)
Lyman Low. Price Collection Sale. February 25, 1901. (1 pc)
Lyman Low. Boucher Collection Sale. May 10, 1901. (4 pcs)
Lyman Low. Auction Sale. January 17, 1902. (1 pc)
Lyman Low. Lussier Collection Sale. February 27, 1902. (6 pcs)
Lyman Low. C. S. Stiles Collection Sale. October 18, 1902. (4 pcs)
Lyman Low. Altmeyer Collection Sale. March 20, 1905. (3 pcs)
Lyman Low. Flanders Collection Sale. April 18, 1917. (9 pcs)
George Masamore. Auction Sale. October 17, 1902. (4 pcs)
J. L. McGuire. Mail Bid Sale. March 25, 1983. (14 pcs)
J. L. McGuire. Mail Bid Sale. June 25, 1983. (2 pcs)
J. L. McGuire. Mail Bid Sale. December 16, 1983. (1 pc)
B. Max Mehl. "Encased Postage Stamps For Sale At Fair Prices," The Numismatist (August 1908), p. 291. (13 pcs)
B. Max Mehl. Auction Sale. July 17, 1918. (14 pcs)
B. Max Mehl. Excell, Trowbridge and McQuestern Collections Sale. April 12, 1927. (18 pcs)
B. Max Mehl. D. Thomas Rees Collection Sale. March 27, 1928. (8 pcs)
B. Max Mehl. Listing. 1932. (81 pcs)
B. Max Mehl. Auction Sale. April 12, 1927. (18 pcs)
B. Max Mehl. Auction Sale. June 23, 1936. (22 pcs)
B. Max Mehl. William F. Dunham Collection Sale. June 3, 1941. (166 pcs)
B. Max Mehl. Auction Sale. June 23, 1942. (14 pcs)
B. Max Mehl. Lyman Low Collection Sale. February 8, 1944. (16 pcs)
B. Max Mehl. King Farouk Collection Sale. March 23, 1948. (24 pcs)
B. Max Mehl. Private Treaty Sales to Fred C. C. Boyd. c. 1942-1949. (26 pcs)
Herbert I. Melnick. Auction Sale. February 17, 1984. (1 pc)
Kennedi Numismatic Auctions. Auction Sale. January 16, 1986. (34 pcs)
Lester Merkin. Auction Sale. November 20, 1968. (9 pcs)
Lester Merkin. Auction Sale. April 17, 1970. (38 pcs)
Lester Merkin. Auction Sale. September 25, 1970. (19 pcs)
Lester Merkin. Auction Sale. October 16, 1972.
Edward Michael. Ben G. Green Collection Sale. May 9, 1914. (133 pcs and 23 duplicates)
Edward Michael. Ben G. Green Stock Sale. June 27, 1914. (23 pcs)
Edward Michael. Sale No. 11, Ben G. Green Stock Sale. September 26, 1914. (25pcs)
Edward Michael. Sale No. 13. November 28, 1914. (10 pcs)
Edward Michael. Sale No. 15. March 6, 1915. (76 pcs)
Edward Michael. Sale No. 16. April 24, 1915. (5 pcs)
Edward Michael. Sale No. 17, E. P. Douglas Collection Sale. July 10, 1915. (51 pcs)
Edward Michael. Sale No. 23, E. H. Owen Collection Sale. May 20, 1916. (6 pcs)
Fred Michael. Auction Sale. October 18, 1911. (3 pcs)
Fred Michael. Auction Sale. March 20, 1912. (8 pcs)
Fred Michael. "U. S. Price List No. 1," The Numismatist (August, 1913), p. 445. (9 pcs)
Fred Michael. "U. S. Price List No. 2," The Numismatist (February, 1914), p. 103. (8 pcs)
Fred Michael. Auction Sale. September 15, 1915.
Fred Michael and Bro. Frederick L. Fake Collection Sale. September 27-28, [c. 1916]. (2 pcs)
Vahan Mozian. Auction Sale. November 13, 1969. (1 pc)
Vahan Mozian. Auction Sale. January 29, 1970. (2 pcs)
Vahan Mozian. Auction Sale. May 5, 1971. (39 pcs)
NASCA. T. James Clarke Collection Sale. June 29, 1978. (10 pcs)
NASCA. Memphis '80 Collection Sale. June 7, 1980. (3 pcs)

NASCA. New York '80 Collection Sale. (80 pcs)
NASCA. Dr. Joseph Vacca Collection Sale. April 27, 1981. (9 pcs)
NASCA. Auction Sale. September 12, 1981. (19 pcs)
NASCA. Auction Sale. April 19, 1982. (8 pcs)
NASCA. Charles J. Affleck Collection Sale. January 10, 1983. (13 pcs)
NASCA. Abner Reed Collection Sale. October 31, 1983. (3 pcs)
NERCA. Auction Sale. November, 1978. (2 pcs)
NERCA. Auction Sale. October, 1981. (2 pcs)
NERCA. Auction Sale. January 7, 1982. (9 pcs)
Pacific Coast Auction Galleries. Auction Sale. May 31-June 2, 1989. (3 pcs)
Pacific Stamp and Coin Sales. Fixed Price List. October, 1981. (8 pcs)
Paramount. The Century Sale. May 1, 1965. (2 pcs)
Paramount. American Numismatic Association Convention Auction Sale. August 8, 1967. (77 pcs)
Paramount. Auction Sale. October 31, 1969. (10 pcs)
Paramount. Auction Sale. February 20, 1970. (5 pcs)
Jess Peters. American Numismatic Association Convention Auction Sale. August 23, 1973. (3 pcs)
RARCOA. Auction '83 Sale. July 29, 1983. (20 pcs)
James V. Rasdale. Auction Sale. December 4, 1970. (5 pcs)
James V. Rasdale. Auction Sale. January 27, 1971. (10 pcs)
Rasdale Stamp Co. Auction Sale. February 7, 1972. (30 pcs)
Wayte Raymond. Auction Sale. December 8, 1910. (18 pcs)
Wayte Raymond (United States Coin Co.) Auction Sale. May 10, 1916. (37 pcs)
Wayte Raymond and James G. McAllister (J. C. Morgenthau & Co.). Jascha Heifetz Collection Sale. December 22, 1937. (35 pcs)
Sol Salkind. Auction Sale. June 12, 1971. (1 pc)
Jacques Schiff. Auction Sale. June 24, 1970. (2 pcs)
Hans M. F. Schulman. Burdette G. Johnson Sale. April 26-28, 1951. (2 pcs)
Schulman Coin & Mint. Herdegen Collection Sale. December 10-12, 1973. (63 pcs)
J. W. Scott Co. F. S. Winston Collection Sale. October 21, 1897. (14 pcs)
Elmer S. Sears. "Catalog of a Valuable Collection . . . offered for sale at fixed prices." Swansea: MA, n. d. [c. July 10, 1914]. (33 pcs)
Robert A. Siegel. Josiah Lilly Collection Sale. September 13, 1967. (176 pcs)
Robert A. Siegel. Makepeace Collection Sale. September 10, 1968. (3 pcs)
Robert A. Siegel. Auction Sale. January 12, 1971. (10 pcs)
Robert A. Siegel. 444th. Auction Sale. January 30, 1974. (2 pcs)
Robert A. Siegel. 506th Auction Sale. February 14, 1977. (6 pcs)
Robert A. Siegel. 597th Auction Sale. May 12, 1982. (45 pcs)
Robert A. Siegel. Auction Sale. October 23, 1986. (27 pcs)
Robert A. Siegel. 676th Auction Sale. February 25, 1987. (138 pcs)
Robert A. Siegel. 684th Auction Sale. September 16, 1987. (6 pcs)
Smithsonian Institution. National Numismatic Collection. (33 pcs)
Sotheby, Parke Bernet. Auction Sale S-4. October 17, 1977. (1 pc)
Sotheby, Parke Bernet. The Comprehensive Collection Sale S-23. October 3, 1978. (30 pcs)
Sotheby, Parke Bernet. Evansville Museum of Arts and Sciences Sale S-29. February 6, 1979. (4 pcs)
Sotheby, Parke Bernet. John W. Sandlewick Collection Sale S-31. April 9, 1979. (66 pcs)
Sotheby, Parke Bernet. Auction Sale S-42. March 18, 1980. (6 pcs)
Sotheby, Parke Bernet. "United States Postage Stamps and Postal History" Auction Sale. June 24-26, 1980.
Southern Collection. (158 pcs)
Spink Coin Auctions. Auction Sale. March 6, 1985. (12 pcs)
Springfield Stamp Club. Listing. 1908. (185 pcs)
Stack's. Auction Sale. November 30, 1956.
Stack's. Auction Sale (Consignment ARPE, Arnold Perl duplicates). September 17-18, 1965. (37 pcs)
Stack's. Auction Sale. January 31-February 1, 1969. (45 pcs)
Stack's. Arnold Perl Collection Sale. December 5-6, 1969. (132 pcs)
Stack's. Auction Sale. April 2, 1971. (7 pcs)
Stack's. Massachusetts Historical Society Collection Sale. May 6-8, 1971. (33 pcs, c. 1915-1920)
Stack's. Shapiro Collection Sale. October 22, 1971. (24 pcs)
Stack's. Auction Sale (Consignment Z.Z., Robert D. Gardner duplicates). December 3, 1971. (28 pcs)

Stack's. Turrini Collection Sale. February 4, 1972. (1 pc)
Stack's. Nate Smith Collection Sale. March 2, 1973. (49 pcs)
Stack's. Auction Sale. April 3, 1975. (7 pcs)
Stack's. Auction Sale. September 11, 1975. (5 pcs)
Stack's. Auction Sale. May 4, 1979. (6 pcs)
Stack's. Auction Sale. March 10, 1981. (13 pcs)
Stack's. Auction Sale. October 20-22, 1982. (3 pcs)
Stack's. Auction Sale. December, 1982. (5 pcs)
Stack's. John L. Roper Collection Sale. March 20, 1984. (6 pcs)
Stack's. Generales, Trackman, Starr-II Collections Sale. December 4, 1984. (2 pcs)
Stack's. Auction Sale. June 18, 1986. (1 pc)
Stack's. Auction Sale. June 16, 1987. (31 pcs)
Stack's. Auction Sale. September 9, 1987. (30 pcs)
Stack's. Auction Sale. January 18-19, 1989. (4 pcs)
Stack's. Auction Sale. November 7, 1990. (1 pc)
Stack's (Coin Galleries). Auction Sale. April 14, 1993. (1 pc)
Stack's. Auction Sale. May 5-6, 1993. (1 pc)
Stack's (Coin Galleries). Auction Sale. November 10, 1993. (36 pcs)
Stampazine. Auction Sale. October 25, 1969. (8 pcs)
Stampazine. Auction Sale. June 10, 1972. (3 pcs)
Rex Stark. Fixed Price List. December, 1992. (3 pcs)
Charles Steigerwalt. "Cheap Price List," Supplement to Numismatic News (May, 1895). (16 pcs)
Superior Galleries. Jerry Buss Collection Sale. January 1, 1985. (16 pcs)
Western Collection. (217 pcs)
Western Reserve Historical Society Collection. (115 pcs)
Whittier Philatelic Services. Net Price List No. 1. July, 1984. (2 pcs)
Richard Wolffers. Auction Sale. February 1, 1974. (5 pcs)
Richard Wolffers. Auction Sale. December 7, 1974. (2 pcs)
Richard Wolffers. Auction Sale. April 23, 1986. (83 pcs)
W. Elliott Woodward. Auction Sale. March 9, 1880. (10 pcs)
W. Elliott Woodward. Auction Sale. October 28, 1886.
Charles M. Wormser and John J. Ford (New Netherlands Coin Co.). Sale No. 45 (Various owners incl. large collection of E.P.S. consigned by C. J. H., Chautauqua County, N. Y.). April 22, 1955. (150 pcs)
Charles M. Wormser and John J. Ford (New Netherlands Coin Co.). Sale No. 51. June 19-20, 1958. (1 pc)
Charles M. Wormser and John J. Ford (New Netherlands Coin Co.). Sale No. 56. June 27-28, 1962. (6 pcs)
Charles M. Wormser and John J. Ford (New Netherlands Coin Co.). Sale No. 60. December 3-4, 1968. (2 pcs)
Charles M. Wormser and John J. Ford (New Netherlands Coin Co.). Auction Sale. October 12, 1971. (4 pcs)

Annotated Bibliography: Additional Resources and Literature

Reference collections held by a great many institutions and individuals have been consulted in the preparation of this work. An exhaustive listing of all such resources is beyond the scope of this work or the patience of most readers. Acknowledgement citations to a great many individuals representing these institutions and assisting in the research or preparation of this text are found earlier in this work, but various anonymous contributors have aided the author or his collaborators through the years. Institutions, organizations, or private collections consulted include: American Numismatic Association Collections, Library and Certification Service, American Numismatic Society Collections and Library, American Philatelic Society Research Library, Bailey Banks & Biddle (Philadelphia), Bank of Canada National Currency Collection, Bank of Nova Scotia, Barton County [KS] Historical Society, Baylor University Library, Boston Athenaeum Library, Boston Museum of Fine Arts, Boston Public Library, Bostonian Society (Old State House), Buffalo and Erie County Public Library, Buffalo [NY] Historical Society, Le Chateau Ramezay Musée Ethnographique (Montreal), Chicago Historical Society, Chicago Museum of Science and Industry, Christ Church (Boston), Cincinnati Historical Society, Cincinnati Mercantile Library, Cincinnati Public Library, Civil War Token Society, Connecticut State Historical Society (J. Doyle DeWitt Collection), *Coin World* Library and Archives, Dallas Genealogical Society, Dallas Public Library and Genealogical Collections (the library is a repository of a collection of 1,800 city directories from various locations on microfiche, supposedly copies of all known municipal directories through 1860-1861), Detroit Public Library and Burton Historical Collection, Detroit Historical Museum, Drake Hotel (Chicago), East Texas State University, Elmwood Cemetery (Detroit), Federal Archives and Records Center (Denver), Free Library of Philadelphia, Florida State University (Robert Manning Strozier Collection, Tallahassee), John J. Ford Jr. Collection, Dr. Robert D. Gardner Collection, Genealogical Society of Pennsylvania, General Services Administration National Archives and Records Service (n.b., for brevity's sake in numerous citations abbreviated NARS) and National Archives Microfilm Publications (rendered as NAMP), Great Bend [KS] Public Library, Hingham [MA] Public Library, Historical Society of Pennsylvania, Wayne Homren Collection, Hopkinton [MA] Public Library, Illinois State Historical Library (rendered as Illinois State Library), Illinois State Historical Society, Independent Township Library (Claflin, KS), Indiana State Library, International Museum of Photography (George Eastman House), International Numismatic Society Authentication Bureau (rendered as INSAB in citations), Irving [TX] Public Library, Lyndon B. Johnson Presidential Library (Austin, TX), Donald B. Kagin Collection, Robert Kincaid Collection, James Krejci Collection, Philip B. Kunhardt Jr. Collection, Dr. Wallace Lee Collection, Library of Congress (including Rare Books, Prints and Graphics collections), Lord & Taylor (New York), Louisiana State University Library, Manhattan Life Insurance Co. (New York), Massachusetts Historical Society, Mattatuck [CT] Historical Society, McAlpin's (Cincinnati), Metropolitan Museum of Art (New York), Milwaukee [WI] County Historical Society, Milwaukee Public Library, Mount Auburn Cemetery (Cambridge, MA), Museum of the City of New York, National Baseball Library, Hall of Fame and Museum, National Numismatic Collection and National Portrait Gallery of the Smithsonian Institution, New England Historic Genealogical Society, Newport News (Virginia) Mariners Museum, New York [County of] Clerk's Office, New-York Historical Society Collections (including Library, Prints and Graphics, and Bella C. Landauer Collection of Business and Advertising Art), New-York Public Library, Astor, Lexox and Tilden Foundations (various collections), New-York Public Library Rare-Book Collection, Nicholson Memorial Library (Garland, TX), Ohio State University Library, Oklahoma State University Library, Graduate Library and Rare Books Collection, Peabody Essex Museum Stephen Phillips Library; Peoria Public Library, H. S. Pogue Co. (Cincinnati), Samuel S. Pollard Memorial Library (Lowell, MA), Princeton University Firestone Library and Microforms Division, Providence [RI] Public Library, Fred L. Reed III Collection, Rensselaer [NY] County Historical Society, James F. Ruddy Collection, Rutgers University Library, Salina [KS] Public Library, Scovill Manufacturing Company (Waterbury, CT), Shillito's (Cincinnati), Society of Paper Money Collectors, Southwestern Texas University Cody Memorial Library (San Marcos, TX), Southern Methodist University Bridwell, DeGolyer and Fondren Libraries, Springdale Cemetery (Peoria), Texas A&M University Library, Texas Christian University Mary Couts Burnett Library, Texas State Library (Austin), Token and Medal Society, Tremont Hotel (Chicago), Troy [NY] Public Library, University of Arkansas Library, University of Dallas Library, University of Evansville (IN] Library and Archives, University of Houston Library, University of Lowell [MA] Library, University of Jacksonville [FL] Carl S. Swisher Library, University of Michigan Library, University of Oklahoma Library and Bass Collection of Business History, University of Texas at Dallas Eugene McDermott Library and Wineburgh Philatelic Research Library, University of Texas Health Science Center Southwestern Medical School Library, University of Pittsburgh Library, Louis A. Warren Lincoln Library and Museum, Western Pennsylvania Numismatic Society, Western Reserve Historical Society, Willard Library (Evansville, IN), Wisconsin State Historical Society, Zelienople [PA] Historical Society, United States Department of Commerce, Patent and Trademark Office, United States Treasury Department Bureau of the Mint and Internal Revenue Service.

Unpublished Material

Adams, Larry. Correspondence with the author.

Alexander, David T. Interviews, photocopies and tapes, also correspondence with the author.

American Numismatic Association. "Agreement For Research Grant" between the ANA and the author providing research grant funding for the present work, June, 1985. Typescript and handwritten, 4 pages.

American Numismatic Association Certification Service. Correspondence from Kenneth E. Bressett, director, with the author.

——. Additional correspondence re. Item Nos. JTZ099-JTZ108, dated June 21, 1988, July 8, 1988, August 5, 1988 and August 16, 1988. Typescript, 7 pages.

——. Opinion No. F-5772-D, dated March 19, 1984. Typescript, 2 pages with illustrations.

American Numismatic Society. Encased stamp collection inventory. Handwritten, 1 page.

Ayer family genealogy. Handwritten, 1 page.

Ayer, J. C. & Co. 19th century checks, business correspondence, invoices, etc., various sources.

Bailey Banks & Biddle. Archival material. Also, interviews and correspondence with Paul Thurston, vice president Insignia Department.

Baker, Warren. Correspondence.

Barton County [KS] Historical Society. Local history scrapbooks.

Bauer, George. Private treaty encased stamp sales to Fred C. C. Boyd.

"Bernard Joseph Bussing," biographical data, handwritten and typescript, 3 pages from family sources.

Bishop, James. Correspondence with the author, advertising items, photographs and miscellaneous family papers relating to the Burnetts.

———. Handwritten family and corporate history, 11 pages.

Bolender. M. H. Private treaty encased stamp sales to Fred C. C. Boyd.

Boston Ship Registers, 1841-1850 volume. From U.S. Customs sources, Hugh Jameson, deputy surveyor. Vol. 48, p. 298. "Edward Fletcher," page 253. Typescript. Peabody Essex Museum.

Bowers, Q[uentin] David. Interviews and correspondence with the author, including letter of February 10, 1984, soliciting merchant chronicles for inclusion in the auction sale catalog of the James F. Ruddy collection.

Boyd, Fred C. C. Encased stamp collection inventory and pedigree lists. Handwritten, 11 pages.

Branan, Bob. Interview with the author.

Bressett, Ken. Interview and correspondence with the author, including a letter to the author June 24, 1992.

Buffalo Historical Society. Encased stamp collection inventory. Ex-Dr. James, Lancaster [PA], collection.

Buhl, Christian Frederick and Matilda Beatty family genealogical record, compiled by Trudy [Gertrude Mohlin] Ziegler, May 1981. Typescript, 1 page.

Burnett Genealogy. Compiled by a family member. Southborough [MA] Library.

Burnett, Joseph & Co. Checks, invoices, etc., various sources.

Burnett, Robert M. Family photographs, and correspondence with the author.

Bussing, Lois A. Correspondence.

Carter, Amon Jr. Interviews with the author.

Chase Manhattan Bank. Encased stamp collection, personal inspection and inventory. Smithsonian Institution.

Chicago, City of. Warrants directing City Treasurer David A. Gage to expend city funds immediately following the Great Chicago Fire. Private collection.

Chicago Historical Society. Reading Room Subject File. Various entries re. David A. Gage, Mrs. E. M. W. Gage, and George W. Gage.

Chicago Historical Society. "Reference Report - Tremont House," dated July 2, 1974, typescript, 6 pages with bibliography.

Christ Church, Boston. "The Clark's (sic) Register of Christ Church, Boston," Records of Baptisms, 1830s.

"Claflin," early history of Claflin, Kansas. Independent Township Library. Typescript, 1 page.

Coin World. Archival material. Documents, photographs, correspondence.

Conlon, James A., director, Bureau of Engraving and Printing. Correspondence with the author.

Cook, Michael Lewis. Genealogical correspondence.

Crofoot, H. K. Collection of Postage Currency samples and encased stamps, personal inspection and inventory. Smithsonian Institution.

Crowther, Mary. Interview with the author.

Cuhaj, George. Correspondence with the author.

DeLorey, Tom. Correspondence with the author and written critique of *Civil War Encased Stamps* galley proofs.

Denly, Tom. Interview.

Drake Hotel. Archival material. Also, interviews and correspondence with JoAnn K. Bongiorno, director of public relations.

Drake, John B. Biography. Genealogical resources, Chicago Historical Society. Handwritten, 2 pages.

Drake, John B. Letter to A. V. Konsberg.

Drake, Tracy C. "Financial Report to Present and Prospective Stockholders of the Whitestone Company," 1923.

———. "Prospectus of the Drake, Chicago," 1919.

Early American Numismatics (also San Diego Coin Show, Inc., and Newport Beach Coin Show, Inc., i.e. Dana Linett) correspondence with Robert Welch, including "Special Encased Postage Stamp Price List," January 17, 1989.

Edward Fletcher (Bark) *Journal*, Aaron Holbrook, master. September 15, 1848 to February 2, 1849. Photocopied selections, 8 pages. The Mariners Museum Library.

Elmwood Cemetery, Detroit. Death record of Christian Frederick Buhl.

Encased stamp collections. Confidential inventories, pedigrees, and price information. Various private collections. Many verified by personal inspection. Typescripts and handwritten.

"Family History of W. C. Bussing Sr.," biographical data from family sources. Typescript and handwritten, 2 pages.

Fitch, William H. "United States Private Stamps," philatelic exhibition, open competition. Frames 318-327, American Philatelic Society STaMps SHOW '84, August 23-26, 1984.

Ford, John J. Jr. Auction catalog notes, correspondence, inventory and miscellaneous papers, Typescript and handwritten, 45 pages.

———. Manuscript providing an overview of encased stamps and details of fraudulent specimen detection, with illustrations. Typescript, 25 pages.

———. A hypothetical flow chart diagram of encased stamp manufacture, illustrated with annotations. 1 page.

"Frederick Buhl to one of his sons." Typescript, 6 pages.

Fuld, Dr. George. Interviews and correspondence with

the author.

Fuld, Melvin. Correspondence with the author.

Gage, Captain Amos. Family line and descendents. Genealogy resources, Chicago Historical Society. Handwritten, 3 pages.

Ganz, David L. Correspondence with the author.

Gardner, Dr. Robert D. Interviews, papers, photographs and correspondence with the author. Inventories and personal inspection of the Gardner encased stamp collection. Notes relating to same. Handwritten, 16 pages.

Gault, John. "Last Will and Testament," dated March 2, 1897. True copy by Robert M. Reaves, Clerk of the Surrogates Court, County of New York, dated November 23, 1982. Typescript, 3 pages.

———. Letter to Abraham Lincoln, dated June 18, 1864, with handwritten notations by Presidential secretary, in Firestone Library, Princeton University, "Lincoln Papers," Reel 76, no. 33823. [Note: this letter was recently published in Harold Holzer's *Dear Mr. Lincoln, Letters to the President* (1993)]

[John] Gault family miscellaneous papers, various sources.

General Services Administration, National Archives and Records Service, Washington, D. C. Correspondence from William F. Sherman, Judicial, Fiscal and Social Branch, Civil Archives Division.

George, Gerald. "Town Founding on the Central Kansas Frontier," Kansas Collection, Salina Public Library. Typescript, 51 pages.

Gibbs, William. Correspondence with the author.

Gladfelter, David D. Correspondence with the author.

Glazer, Len. Interviews, papers, photographs and correspondence with the author. Personal inspection of various encased stamp holdings, including the "Merchant Set" collection offered in 1980, and the "Romain Reference Set Collection" maintained by this dealer. Notes relating to same. Handwritten, 4 pages.

———. Encased stamp variety rarity charts. Typescript and handwritten, 2 pages.

Gould, Maurice. Reminiscences.

Hammaker, Phil W. Letter to "Coin World's Collector's Clearinghouse," dated February 21, 1969.

Hatie, George. American Numismatic Association general counsel. Correspondence with the author.

Henderson, J. M. Private treaty encased stamp sales to Fred C. C. Boyd.

Herst, Herman. Auction catalog notes, interviews and correspondence with the author.

Hetrich, Dr. George. Manuscript, "The Shortage of Small Change During the Civil War and How the Merchants of Bucks County Met It."

Homren, Wayne. Interviews and correspondence with the author, including notes, photo copies, advertising trade cards and almanacs, and miscellaneous items, and written critique of *Civil War Encased Stamps* galley proofs.

———. Manuscript of address to Western Pennsylvania Numismatic Society, March 1, 1994 on collecting encased stamps. Typescript, 12 pages.

———. Manuscript of address to American Numismatic Society "Coinage of the America's Conference," November 5, 1994 on John Gault and J. C. Ayer. Typescript, 11 pages.

———. Encased stamp variety rarity charts. Typescript, 2 pages.

Hopkinton [MA] Public Library. Hopkinton vital records microfilm.

Hotel Irving Tenants Association correspondence.

Huff, Wayne. Interview with the author, personal papers and records.

International Numismatic Society Authentication Bureau. Photographs and correspondence with the author.

Irving House papers, New-York Historical Society.

Jendrzejewski, John P. "Materials Evaluation Laboratory Incorporated Project No. 2621-E," cover sheet dated October 27, 1981, typescript, 1 page.

Joseph Burnett Co. Biographical Review, Worcester County. Typescript, 1 page.

[Joseph Burnett Co.]. "The Firm." Typescript, 2 pages.

Kagin's Numismatic Investment Corporation. "Encased Postage Inventory Appraisal List," August 31, 1981. Computer print out, 14 pages. Interviews with Art Kagin, Donald H. Kagin, George Fuld and interviews and correspondence with David T. Alexander regarding same.

———. Correspondence and inventory relating to the sale of the Donald H. Kagin encased stamp collection. Typescript, 21 pages. Also, appraisal for same by Fractional Currency, Inc. [Len and Jean Glazer] dated January 19, 1981. Typescript, 2 pages. Letter from Donald H. Kagin to author regarding selling same as a whole, dated September 15, 1987. Typescript, 1 page. Notes of interviews with Donald Kagin regarding prospective sale of collection as a whole. Handwritten, 3 pages.

———. Photographs, negatives and personal inspection of the entire Kagin encased stamp collection. Auction Lot preview notes of the "Abbey Collection Sale" [Kagin encased stamp collection], handwritten, 21 pages. Hand-priced catalog, 16 pages. Auction Notes. Hand written, 4 pages.

Kincaid, Bob. Interviews and correspondence with the author. Photographs and personal inspection of the Kincaid encased stamp collection. Notes relating to same. Handwritten, 2 pages.

———. Encased stamp variety auction census data charts, listing 2,078 auction appearances in 40 major sales, 1891-1981, compiled July 1982. Posterboard, 24X36 inches, handwritten, 10 sheets. [Much of this information duplicated a similar list prepared by the author and dealer Len Glazer in 1980-1981.]

———. Encased stamp variety rarity charts. Typescript and handwritten, 8 pages.

———. Text of "Little Theater Educational Forum Speech," American Numismatic Association Annual Convention held in Boston, August 17, 1982. Handwritten, 4 pages.

Kinney, Joe. Society of Paper Money Collectors archivist, correspondence with the author.

Kolbe, George Frederick. Correspondence with the author regarding various editions of George G. Evans' U.S. Mint history.

Koref, Mathias. "United States Medicine Company Trade Cards," philatelic exhibition, "National Class (U.S.A.)." Frames 888-890, Interphil '76, 7th U.S.A. International Philatelic Exhibition, May 29-June 6, 1976.

Krejci, Jim. Interviews, papers, photographs and correspondence with the author. Inventories and personal inspection of the Krejci encased stamp collection. Notes relating to same. Handwritten, 4 pages.

Krueger, Kurt R. Correspondence with the author.

Lainhart, Ann S. Genealogical correspondence.

LaTuchie, Herbert. "The United States Private Die Proprietary Medicine Stamps," philatelic exhibition, "World Series of Philately." Frames 176-184, STaMps SHOW '84, August 23-26, 1984.

Lee, Dr. Wallace. Correspondence with the author. Photographs of the Lee encased stamp collection.

Leuver, Robert. American Numismatic Association. executive director. Correspondence with the author.

Linett, Dana. Interviews, photographs and correspondence with the author. Personal examination of various encased stamp offerings by this dealer. Post-sale interview following January 22, 1988 sale of "The Celebrity Collection," a complete merchant set of encased stamps. Handwritten, 2 pages.

Lochner, Edwin F. Genealogical correspondence.

Lord & Taylor. Archival material.

"Marriage Records, Saline County, Kansas," First Marriage Book, 1860-1866. Copied by Edith Scott, typed and indexed by Ovie E. Sypher.

Marston, Mary Barker Gage. "The Life Story of George W. Gage." Typescript, 9 pages. Chicago Historical Society. [She was his daughter.]

Martin, David Allan. "The Evolution of a National Composite Legal Tender Coinage in the United States, 1792-1860." Unpublished Doctoral Dissertation, Syracuse University, 1964.

Materials Evaluation Laboratory, Inc., Baton Rouge, Louisiana. Various findings.

Mayes, Catharine Gardner. "Glamor Gramps," a remembrance of Joseph Burnett by his then oldest living grandchild, age 98 in March 1984. Typescript, 11 pages.

McAlpin's. Archival material.

McNamara, Louise. Correspondence.

Medlar, Bob. Interviews with the author.

Mehl, B. Max. Private treaty encased stamp sales to Fred C. C. Boyd.

Morgan, James Frederick. "Confederate Monetary Policy." Unpublished Doctoral Dissertation, Oklahoma State University, 1977. [Subsequently published as *Graybacks and Gold: Confederate Monetary Policy*. Vol. II, "Southern History and Genealogy Series." Pensacola [FL]: The Perdido Bay Press, 1985.]

Mount Auburn Cemetery. Plot records relating to Lot 1745, Hawthorne Lane, proprietor John Gault, and Lot 6064 Althaea Path, proprietor Lucinda A. Gault. Miscellaneous papers, including letter from Duncan W. Munro, superintendent, to Mrs. A. W. Skinner, August 31, 1983.

National Numismatic Collection, Smithsonian Institution. Inventory, pedigrees, and personal inspection of encased stamp collection. Ex-H. K. Crofoot and ex-Chase Manhattan Bank collections. August 25, 1986. Notes relating to same. Handwritten, 2 pages.

———. "History of Money," permanent exhibition, observed September 24, 1986.

———. Interview with Dr. Richard Doty, assistant curator.

New England Historic Genealogical Society. Death records of Joseph L. Bates and John I. Brown.

Newman, Eric P. Interview and correspondence with the author.

Numismatic Antiquarian Service Corporation of America. Interviews, photographs and correspondence with Herbert I. Melnick, Douglas B. Ball and Martin Gengerke. Personal examination of New York '80 encased stamp collection. Notes relating to same. Handwritten, 4 pages. Hand-priced catalog relating to same.

Oldenburg, Marilyn Bussing. Correspondence, photographs, family history, relating to the Bussing family, including the citizenship papers issued to J. W. Bussing July 4, 1848. Typescript and handwritten, 10 pages.

Ostendorf, Lloyd. Correspondence with the author.

Paley, Irv. Director, Chicago Museum of Science and Industry. Interview with the author.

Pipher, Gary. Correspondence with the author.

Pogue, H. S. Co. Archival material.

Reed, Fred L. "Address to the ANA Board, February 20, 1985 in support of research grant request." Typescript, 11 pages. Board meeting contemporaneous notes. Handwritten, 1 page.

______. Emission model of encased stamp output. Handwritten, 1 page.

———. "An Historical Summary of the Civil War Token Phenomenon," a paper presented before the Educational Forum of the Metropolitan Washington Numismatic Association 11th Annual Convention, July 10, 1976. Typescript with handwritten notations, 20 pages. Charts relating to same, 4 pages.

———. "Proposal for a Research Grant from the American Numismatic Association," dated 6 July 1984. Typescript, 1 page. [Similar proposals were submitted to the Civil War Token Society, Society of Paper Money Collectors, and Token and Medal Society.]

______. "Prospectus – That New Metallic Currency: CIVIL WAR ENCASED STAMPS, the Issuers and their Times." Typescript, 1 page.

———. Unpublished manuscript on Civil War die sinking, store card and token ascription, 88 pages.

———. Unpublished manuscript on encased stamps. Typescript, 1180 pages, including 840 pages of text and 340 pages of auction census data with 4,200 listings. [n.b. This is the manuscript examined by American Numismatic Association Board of Governors, Executive and Professional Staff in awarding the author a research grant at the 1985 ANA Mid-Winter Convention in San Antonio, Texas.]

———, and Glazer, Len. Encased stamp auction census data charts. Approximately 2,000 auction sale entries compiled by the author and dealer Glazer in 1980-1981. Approximately 40 pages, typescript and handwritten.

Reminiscences of Frederick Ayer. Handwritten, 11 pages. New York Public Library.

Rikhoff, Francis J. Correspondence. [a Schapker descendant]

Robb, David D. Interview. [legatee of the Claflin family]

Rochette, Edward C., executive vice president, American Numismatic Association. Correspondence with the author, including, "Agenda: Board of Governors' Meeting, Wednesday, February 20, 1985, 9:00 a.m. Menger Hotel, San Antonio,Texas." Typescript, 3 pages.

Rothert, Matt. Interviews, photocopies and correspondence with the author.

Russell, Margo [Mrs. Marion]. Personal papers and correspondence.

Rutledge, Ann Jane. "Last Will and Testament," dated June 10, 1912. Handwritten, 2 pages. [John Gault's sister]

Salina [KS] Public Library. Local history map and photograph collections.

Schapker, Henry A. and J. G. Correspondence.

Schenkman, David. Correspondence with the author.

Schwan, Carlton F. Interviews and correspondence with the author.

Scovill Manufacturing Co., Waterbury, Conn. Various checks, stocks and miscellaneous papers. Also, E. H. Davis, company historian, correspondence with the author dated February 15, 1973.

Shafer, Neil. Correspondence with the author.

Shapiro, Sy. The Great North Coast Tea Company. Interviews, 1994. Personal examination of encased stamp collection. Notes relating to same. Handwritten, 1 page.

Shillito's. Archival material.

Shillito's scrapbook, gift of Mrs. Helena Adams, August 14, 1968, and archival material, including "Lease between the Fourth and Central Trust Co., trustee, and John Shillito Co.," dated May 1, 1924, and trust agreements between the parties securing Shillito land trust certificates. Cincinnati Historical Society.

Simons, John. "A History of Early Day Barton County, Kansas." Unpublished Master's Thesis, Kansas State Teachers College of Emporia, August 1971.

Slabaugh, Arlie. Correspondence with the author.

Slaten, James W. Correspondence with the author.

Springdale Cemetery, Peoria. Miles' family death and burial records. Handwritten and typescript, 3 pages, and diagram of lot 182 Bluff Division North, gravesite of B. F. Miles, No. 4630.

St. Paul's Episcopal Church history, Evansville. Typescript, 2 pages.

Sturdevant, Pvt. Samuel W. Co. I, 6th Regt., New York State Volunteer Cavalry. Diary, January 1, 1864 to December 31, 1864. Typescript copy, courtesy of Lynda Sturdevant.

Totten, Ruth Ellen Patton [Mrs. James W.] Correspondence with the author, and unpublished family photograph of Frederick Ayer. [She is General George Patton's daughter, and granddaughter of Frederick Ayer.]

U.S. Department of Commerce, Patent and Trademark Office. Correspondence with the author.

Walter, John F. Research Report, "Capsule History of the Thirty-Eighth Massachusetts Infantry," dated February 14, 1986. Typescript, 5 pages.

Wenzel, J. Arthur. Correspondence with the author.

Western Reserve Historical Society. Encased stamp inventory, also interview and correspondence from Kermit Pike, museum director.

White, Martha E. D. "Southborough, St. Mark's School." re. the contributions of Joseph Burnett. Written in 1902. Typescript, 6 pages.

Wilson, John. Correspondence with the author.

Government Documents

Ambler, Stephen F. "Improvement in the Manufacture of Aerated Bread," Letters Patent No. 36,134, dated August 12, 1862. U.S. Patent Office, 1 page.

Annual Report of the Secretary of the Treasury on the State of the Finances for the year 1881. Washington: Government Printing Office, 1881.

Ayer, James C. "Improvement in Pill Machines," Patent No. 17,865, dated July 28, 1857. U.S. Patent Office, 2 pages.

———. "Improved Process for Desulphurizing and disintegrating Ores," Patent No. 46,619, dated March 7, 1865, antedated January 24, 1865. U.S. Patent Office, 1 page.

———. "Improved Process for Desulphurizing and Disintegrating Ores," Patent No. 46,620, dated March 7, 1865, antedated January 24, 1865. U.S. Patent Office, 1 page.

———. "Improved Process for Disintegrating, Desulphurizing, and Oxidizing Ores," Patent No.

46,621, dated March 7, 1865, antedated January 24, 1865. U.S. Patent Office, 1 page.

______ and Haeffely, Edward. "Composition for Coloring Hair," Patent No. 73,865, dated January 28, 1868. U.S. Patent Office, 1 page.

[Bailey, Eli Wescott.] Administration of the will of Eli Westcott Bailey, April 6, 1899, Register of Wills, Philadelphia.

[Balding, James R.] Administration of the will of James R. Balding, March 2, 1872, Register of Wills, Philadelphia.

"Barnes, Demas." *Biographical Directory of the American Congress, 1774-1971*, Senate Document No. 928, p. 554. 92nd Congress, 1st Session. Washington: Government Printing Office, 1971.

[Bates, Joseph L.] Administration of the estate of Joseph L. Bates, April 5, 1886, Probate Court, Suffolk County, Massachusetts. No. 75350, Vol. 581, page 482.

[Bates, Joseph L.] "Petition of Hilman B. Sampson to be appointed administrator of the estate of Joseph L. Bates," April 1, 1886. Allowed April 5, 1886, Probate Court, Suffolk County, Massachusetts.

[Bates, Joseph L.] "Appointment of appraisers in re. Joseph L. Bates, June 22, 1886, Probate Court, Suffolk County, Massachusetts.

[Bates, Joseph L.] "Schedule of Personal Estate, of."

[Bates, Joseph L.]. "Report of the administrator to the Probate Court, in re. estate of Joseph L. Bates," March 18, 1887.

[Bates, Joseph L.] "Appointment of commissioners to receive and examine claims against the estate of," March 21, 1887, Probate Court, Suffolk County, Massachusetts.

[Bates, Joseph L.] "List of claims allowed by commissioners against the estate of."

Beede, Annie A. and Conant, Elva B. "Petition to the probate Court of Suffolk County, Massachusetts, to vacate decree (dated September 23, 1915) proving will of Ann J. Rutledge," dated February 29, 1915. [March 18, 1916] Typescript, 1 page.

[Bishop, William D.] *Report of the Commissioner of Patents for the Year 1859, Arts and Manufactures*, January 26, 1860. 2 vols. Senate Executive Document No. 12. 36th Congress, 1st Session.

Blair, Montgomery. *Annual Report of the Post Master General, Conditions for Fiscal Year Ended June 30, 1862*, December 1, 1862. House Executive Document No. 1. Serial No. 1159. 37th Congress, 3rd Session. Washington: Government Printing Office, 1862.

———. *Annual Report of the Post Master General for the Year Ending June 30, 1863*, October 31, 1863. House Executive Document No. 1. Serial No. 1184. 38th Congress, 1st Session. Washington: Government Printing Office, 1864.

Boston, City of. Marriage Records, 1800-1849, Vol. 1, p. 34.

Boston, City of, Registry Division. "Certified Copy of Record of Death of Henry Gault," No. 3315, dated April 10, 1901. True copy No. 42605, dated October 25, 1982, by Joanne A. Prevost, City Registrar.

Boston, City of, Registry Division. "Certified Copy of Record of Death of Mary Ann Gault (mn McGee), No. 3816, dated September 3, 1868. True copy No. 42606, dated October 25, 1982, by Joanne A. Prevost, City Registrar.

Boutwell, George S., Commissioner of Internal Revenue. Letter to A. Hollingsworth, chairman Finance Committee, Wilmington, Del., dated August 9, 1862, [re. the legality of corporation currency] in Cincinnati *Daily Enquirer*, November 26, 1862, p. 2.

———. *Report of the Commissioner of Internal Revenue*, January 13, 1863. Senate Executive Document No. 20. Serial No. 1149. 37th Congress, 3rd Session.

———. *Report from the Commissioner of Internal Revenue for 1863*. Senate Executive Document No. 50. 38th Congress, 1st Session.

"Boutwell, George Sewel (sic)," *Biographical Directory of the American Congress, 1774-1971*, Senate Document No. 928, pgs. 616-617. 92nd Congress, 1st Session. Washington: Government Printing Office, 1971.

Bowlsby, George W. "Improvement in Stamp Cancellation," Patent No. 51,782, dated December 26, 1865.

Breckenridge, Roeliff Morton and National Monetary Commission. *The History of Banking in Canada*. Senate Document No. 332. 61st Congress, 2nd Session. Washington: Government Printing Office, 1910.

Buffalo, New York, City of. Bureau of Vital Statistics. "Certificate and Record of Death of Pamelia P. Gault," dated April 25, 1911.

[California, State of]. *California Census of 1852*. Vol. II, County of Eldorado. No. 25087. Published by the Genealogical Records Committee, Daughters of the American Revolution [State] of California. n.p.: 1934.

Carson, Enoch T., U. S. Depositary. Letter to Messrs. Gould, Pearce & Co., dated November 8, 1862, in Cincinnati *Daily Enquirer*, November 9, 1862, p. 3. [This letter regarding the tardy issuance of Postage Currency was addressed to the older brothers of the encased stamp issuer.]

———. "Postage Currency. Notice," in Cincinnati *Daily Enquirer*, November 7, 1862, p. 2.

———. "Rules for the Redemption of Postage Stamps. Notice," in Cincinnati *Daily Enquirer*, December 28, 1862, p. 2.

Chase, Salmon P. *Letter from the Secretary of the Treasury, in Relation to the Issue of an Additional Amount of United States Treasury Notes*. House Miscellaneous Document No. 81. Serial 1141. 37th Congress, 2nd Session. Washington: Government Printing Office.

———. *Letter from the Secretary of the Treasury, in Relation to the Printing and Issuing of Fractional*

Currency, June 3, 1864. House Report No. 140. 38th Congress, 1st Session.

———. Letter to James A. Pollock, March 18, 1863. Records of the U. S. Mint at Philadelphia. Vol. 3, October 11-1860 to September 16, 1870. U. S. National Archives (Record Group 104).

———. *Report of the Secretary of the Treasury for the Fiscal Year Ending June 30, 1861*, December 9, 1861. Senate Executive Document No. 2. 37th Congress, 2nd Session. Washington: Government Printing Office, 1862.

———. *Report of the Secretary of the Treasury on the Finances for the Fiscal Year Ending June 30, 1862*, December 4, 1862. Senate Executive Document I No. 1. 37th Congress, 3rd Session. Washington: Government Printing Office, 1863.

———. *Report of the Secretary of the Treasury on the Finances for the Fiscal Year Ending June 30, 1863*, December 10, 1863. House Executive Document VI No. 3. 38th Congress, 1st Session. Washington: Government Printing Office, 1864.

———. *Report of the Secretary of the Treasury on the State of the Finances for the Year Ending June 30, 1863*. Senate Executive Document. 38th Congress, 1st Session. Washington: Government Printing Office, 1863.

Chicago Board of Public Works. *Plat Showing the Burnt District of Chicago, 1871*. A map. Eleventh Annual Report, Year Ending March 31, 1872. n.p. [Chicago]: n.d. [1872]

Chilson, Gardner. "Furnace-Baker," Letters Patent No. 1,627, dated June 10, 1840. United States Patent Office, 3 pages.

Chittenden, Lucius, Register of the Treasury. Statement No. 3, dated November 29, 1862.

———. Statement No. 4. Dated November 27, 1863.

Cobb, Howell. *Report of the Secretary of the Treasury for the Year Ending June 30, 1860*, November 3, 1860. Senate Executive Document No. 9. 36th Congress, 2nd Session. Washington: Thomas H. Ford, printer, 1860.

Conant, Elva B. "Motion to amend petition to vacate decree in the matter of the will of Ann J. Rutledge," Probate Court of Suffolk County, Massachusetts, undated. Typescript, 2 pages.

Copeley, Humphrey E. "Photographic Medal," Letters Patent No. 31,871, dated April 2, 1861.

Detroit, City of. Proceedings of the Common Council, October 22, 1862.

Drake, P. H. "Design for a Bottle," Patent No. 1,538, dated February 18, 1862. U.S. Patent Office, 2 pages.

Duncan, Wm. C., Mayor of Detroit. "To the Public," a mayoral proclamation, in Detroit *Free Press*, January 7, 1863.

Evans, George G. "Design for Shoulder Strap Case," Patent No. 37,143, dated December 9, 1862. Serial No. 1166, p. 696 and Serial No. 1167, p. 427. Washington: Government Printing Office, 1863.

Failor, Kenneth M. and Hayden, Eleonora. *Medals of the United States Mint*. Washington: Government Printing Office, 1969.

Fessenden, W. P. *Report of the Secretary of the Treasury on the Finances for the Year 1864*, December 6, 1864. House Executive Document VII No. 3. 38th Congress, 2nd Session. Washington: Government Printing Office, 1864.

Feuchtwanter, Lewis. "Substitute for Copper." Memorial of [Dr.] Lewis Feuchtwanter, September 13, 1837. House Document No. 7. 25th Congress, 1st Session.

Fisher, Samuel S. *Annual Report of the Commissioner of Patents for the Year 1869*, January 27, 1870. 4 vols. House Executive Document No. 102. 41st Congress, 2nd Session. Washington: Government Printing Office, 1870.

Foote, Elisha. *Report of the Commissioner of Patents for the Year 1868*, January 20, 1869. 4 vols. House Executive Document No. 52. 40th Congress, 3rd Session. Washington: Government Printing Office, 1869.

Frisbie, James W. "Proclamation No. 2," in Detroit *Free Press*, November 22, 1862.

[Gault, Henry]. "Certified Copy of Record of Death." Registry Division, City of Boston. No. 3315, dated April 10, 1901. Certificate No. 42605, by Joanne A. Prevost, city registrar, dated October 25, 1982.

[Gault, John]. Certificate of and Record of Death. City of New York Bureau of Vital Statistics. No. 9418, dated March 19, 1900. True copy, Department of Records and Information Services, Municipal Archives, by Idilio Gracia-Pena, director, dated 1983.

Gault, John assignor to Moore, Wm. H. "Coal-Hole Cover," Letters Patent No. 32,865 (Design Patent No. 1,861), dated July 23, 1861. U.S. Patent Office, 2 pages.

———. "Combination of Eraser and Eraser-Sharpener," Letters Patent No. 33,304 (Design Patent No. 2,300), dated September 17, 1861. U. S. Patent Office, 2 pages.

———. "Design for Postage Stamp Case," National Archives RG 165 "Designs, Stationery," U. S. Patent Office. Received and filed July 24, 1862, Southern District of New York. Patent No. 1,627, dated August 12, 1862. 1 page, "No Printed Specifications Available." U. S. Patent Office, 1 page.

______. "Design for Encasing Government Stamps," Claim [for]. Design Patent No. 1,627 dated August 12, 1862. In *Annual Report of the Commissioner of Patents for the Year 1862, Arts and Manufactures*, Vol. I. U. S. House Executive Document No. 52, Serial 1166, pg. 747. Printed by order of the House of Representatives, 37th Congress, 3rd Session. Washington: Government Printing Office.

———. Assignor to Gault, John and W. V. Barkalow. "Improvement in Chain-Shot," Letters Patent No. 35,734, dated June 24, 1862. U.S. Patent Office, 2 pages.

———. "Improvement in Chain-Shot for Ordnance,"

Letters patent No. 34,628, dated March 11, 1862. U.S. Patent Office, 2 pages.

———. "Improvement in Projectiles for Ordnance," Letters Patent No. 32,689 (Design Patent No. 1,685), dated July 2, 1861. U. S. Patent Office, 4 pages.

———. "Improvement in Setting Vault-Lights," Letters Patent No. 33,480 (Design Patent No. 2,476), dated October 15, 1861. U. S. Patent Office, 2 pages.

[Gault, John Alden]. Certificate of Death. State of Rhode Island and Providence Plantations Department of Health, Division of Vital Statistics. No. 2856-7352, dated November 7, 1959. True copy by Richard Boly, State Registrar, dated May 27, 1983.

Gault, John H. "Design for a Bottle," Patent No. 535,151, filed January 16, 1895. U. S. Patent Office, 2 pages.

———. and Schrader, Charles F. assignors to Rowley, Dalmon B. "Valve-Stopper for Bottles," Patent 508,300, filed April 20, 1894. U. S. Patent Office, 2 pages.

[Gault, John W.] Muster Roll, Co. C., 1st Massachusetts Cavalry. September 7, 1861 to October 3, 1864. Adjutant General's Office, AG14621406, n.d. National Archives.

[Gault, Mary Ann]. "Certified Copy of Record of Death." Registry Division, City of Boston. No. 3816, dated September 3, 1868. Certificate No. 42606, by Joanne A. Prevost, city registrar, dated October 25, 1982.

[Gault, Olive Constance]. Certificate of Death. State of New Hampshire, No. 58-5481, dated November 12, 1958. True copy by Charles E. Sire, State Registrar, dated April 28, 1983.

[Gault, Pamelia P.]. Certificate and Record of Death. City of Buffalo [NY] Bureau of Vital Statistics. No. 447, dated April 25, 1911. True copy by Angelo J. Alessi, n. d.

[Gault, Samuel]. Muster Roll, Cos. K and A, 38th Massachusetts Volunteers. August 16, 1862 to June 30, 1865. Adjutant General's Office, AG1501295, dated March 19, 1909. National Archives.

Graham, Gladys M. and Colleran, Mary A. "Petition to Probate Court, Suffolk County, Massachusetts, to be appointed guardians of Laura R. Rutledge," dated March 29, 1954. Typescript, 1 page.

Grant, Judge Robert. "Summons to appear at Suffolk County Probate Court," re. estate of Ann J. Rutledge, dated March 18, 1916. Handwritten, 1 page.

———. "Decree dismissing petition of Annie A. Beede and Elva B. Conant to vacate decree admitting the will of Ann Jane Rutledge," dated July 8, 1916. Handwritten, 1 page.

Gray, Joshua assignor to Gray, Joshua and Gault, John. "Improvement in Sewing Machines." Letters Patent No. 16,566, dated February 3, 1857. U. S. Patent Office, 3 pages.

Hall, Alfred S. "Affidavit in support of petition to file a bill of review on the ground of newly discovered evidence in the matter of the allowance of the will of Ann J. Rutledge," Suffolk County, Massachusetts, Probate Court, undated. Typescript, 3 pages.

Hamilton, O. P. Letters to Governor Anthony from Buffalo, Kansas, October 2-3, 1878, regarding Indian uprising and massacre south of Fort Dodge, Kansas, in "Marking an Epoch – the Last Indian Raid and Massacre," *Eighteenth Biennial Report of the Board of Directors of the Kansas State High Schools for the Biennial Period July 1, 1910 to June 30, 1912*. Topeka: State Printing Office, 1913. [He was Claflin's brother-in-law, and named Claflin, Kansas, after his wife, Claflin's sister Delia.]

Hanna, John, U.S. District Attorney. "Small Note Currency," in Evansville *Daily Journal*, November 3, 1862.

Hay, John. Letter to Mr. Herndon, Legation of the U.S. at Paris, September 5, 1866.

Herron, James P. "Device for Preserving Postage Stamps," Patent No. 39,147, dated July 7, 1863.

Hitchcock, R. E. "Picture-Button," Letters Patent No. 33,038, dated August 13, 1861. U. S. Patent Office, 2 pages.

Holloway, D. P. *Report of the Commissioner of Patents for the Year 1861, Arts and Manufactures*, January 31, 1862. 3 vols. House Executive Document No. 53. Serial Nos. 1131-1133. 37th Congress, 2nd Session.

———. *Report of the Commissioner of Patents for the Year 1862, Arts and Manufactures*, January 30, 1863. 2 vols. House Executive Document No. 52. 37th Congress, 3rd Session.

———. *Report of the Commissioner of Patents for the Year 1863, Arts and Manufactures*, January 30, 1864. 2 vols. House Executive Document No. 60. 38th Congress, 1st Session.

Holt, J. *Report of the Commissioner of Patents for the Year 1857, Arts and Manufactures*, January 20, 1858. 3 vols. House Executive Document No. 32. 35th Congress, 1st Session.

———. *Report of the Commissioner of Patents for the Year 1858, Arts and Manufactures*, January 31, 1859. 3 vols. House Executive Document No. 47. 35th Congress, 2nd Session.

Hopkinton, Massachusetts, City of. Vital records microfilm. Hopkinton, Massachusetts, Public Library.

Illinois, State of. Appellate Court of Illinois, First District, October Term. "David A. Gage, et al. vs. the City of Chicago." Reply of Plaintiffs in Error to Argument for Defendant in Error. Wirt Dexter, Lawrence, Campbell & Lawrence, John N. Jewett for Plaintiffs in Error. 1878. Typescript, 91 pages.

Illinois, State of. Criminal Court of Cook County, January Term. "Points and Authorities . . . on Motion to Quash Indictment, in case of People vs. David A. Gage." Brief. Walker, Dexter & Smith, attorneys for the defendant. 1874. Typescript, 31 pages.

Illinois, State of. Supreme Court of Illinois, Third Grand Division, September Term. "Franklin Parmelee and David A. Gage, Appellants, vs. Daniel Lawrence,

Appellee." Brief for Appellants. Beckwith & Ayer, B. F. Ayer Counsel for Appellants. Typescript, 27 pages.

Indiana, State of, Adjutant General's Office. *Indiana in the War of the Rebellion*. "Indiana Historical Collections," Vol. XLI. [Reprint of Vol. 1 of 8, prepared by W. H. H. Terrell, 1869.] n.p.: Indiana Historical Society, 1960.

Isham, George B. "Bill and Currency Holder," Patent No. 39,148, dated July 7, 1863.

Kansas, State of. *Eighth Biennial Report of the Auditor of the State and Register of State Land Office*, for the fiscal years ending June 30, 1892. Topeka: Hamilton Printing Co., Edwin H. Snow, State Printer, 1892.

———. *Eighth Biennial Report* [of the] *Department of Public Instruction*, for the years ending June 30, 1891 and June 30, 1892. George W. Winans, state superintendent, "Abstract IV, Private Institutions of Learning and County High Schools." Topeka: Edwin H. Snow, State Printer, 1892.

———. *Transactions of the Kansas State Historical Society*, edited by F. G. Adams, secretary. "Governor [Gen. James W.] Denver's Administration," V (1889-1896), p. 478. Topeka: Press of the Kansas State Printing Co., J. K. Hudson, State Printer, 1896.

———. *The University Geological Survey of Kansas*. Vol. V. Grimsley, G. P. and Bailey, E. H. S., "Special Report on Gypsum and Gypsum Cement Plasters," pgs. 63-170. Topeka: J. S. Parks, State Printer, 1899.

Landis, John H. and Comparette, T. L. *Catalogue of Coins, Tokens and Medals in the Numismatic Collection of the Mint of the United States at Philadelphia, Pa.* Treasury Department Document No. 2612. Washington: Government Printing Office, 1912, 1914.

Lee, Wm. H., Canada East Consul. Letter to His Excellency the Governor General, October 31, 1862. re. the depreciation and consequences of depreciated U.S. currency in commerce. Published in *Annual Report on Foreign Commerce, British Dominions*, p. 48. U.S. House Executive Document 63, "Commercial Relations, 1862." 37th Congress, 3rd Session.

"Letters from George S. Denison to [Salmon P.] Chase, 1862-1865," *Annual Report of the American Historical Association*, 1903. Vol. II. Washington: Government Printing Office, 1903.

Lewis, Joseph J. *Report of the Commissioner of Internal Revenue on the Operation of the Internal Revenue System for the Year Ending June 30, 1863*, December 21, 1863. Washington: Government Printing Office, 1864.

———. *Report of the Commissioner of Internal Revenue*, December 1, 1864. Washington: Government Printing Office, 1865.

"List of Persons Who Put in Representative Recruits, and Names of Recruits." *Official Records*, Series 3, Vol. 5, p. 929. [See U. S. Department of War]

Mason, Charles. *Report of the Commissioner of Patents for the Year 1855, Arts and Manufactures*, January 31, 1856. 2 vols. House Executive Document No. 12. 34th Congress, 1st Session.

———. *Report of the Commissioner of Patents for the Year 1856, Arts and Manufactures*, January 31, 1857. 3 vols. House Executive Document No. 65. 34th Congress, 3rd Session.

Massachusetts, Commonwealth of. *Historical Data Relating to Counties, Cities and Towns in Massachusetts*. Frederic W. Cook, secretary. No. 24590, June 9, 1948.

———. *Massachusetts in the Army and Navy During the War of 1861-65*. Compiled by Higginson, Thomas Wentworth. 2 vols. Boston: Wright & Potter Printing Co., State Printers, 1895.

Massachusetts, Commonwealth of, State Adjutant General's Office. "Gault, Samuel," *Massachusetts Soldiers, Sailors, and Marines in the Civil War*. Vol. IV, p. 42. "Gault, John W." Vol. VI, p. 150. [Compiled and Published by The Adjutant General in accordance with Chapter 475, Acts of 1899 and Chapter 64, Resolves of 1930.] Norwood [MA]: The Norwood Press, 1933.

Massachusetts, Commonwealth of, State Department of Public Health Registry of Vital Records and Statistics. "Copy of Record of Death of (newborn with no first name) Gault," date of death March 10, 1867. Vol. 202, page 136, No. 17. True copy No. 93597, dated January 21, 1983, by Elaine B. Trudeau, Acting Registrar.

———. "Copy of Record of Death of Mary Ann Gault," date of death September 2, 1868. Vol. 213, page 155, No. 16. True copy No. 93911, dated April 4, 1983 by Elaine B. Trudeau, Acting Registrar.

———. in re. George E. Rutledge (38:268), Ann J. Rutledge (1:930), Elva B. Conant (2:149), John H. Rutledge (30:372), Annie A. Beede (73:88), and Laura Rutledge (30:504).

McCulloch, Hugh. "Report of the Comptroller of the Currency, November 28, 1863." Statement A in *Finance Report, 1863*, pages 49-61. Senate Executive Document. 38th Congress, 1st Session. Washington: Government Printing Office, 1863.

———. *Report of the Secretary of the Treasury on the State of the Finances for the Year 1865*, December 4, 1865. Washington: Government Printing Office, 1865.

McNeely, James H., U.S. Postmaster. "Plenty of Postage Currency," in Evansville *Daily Journal*, February 10, 1863.

______. "Postage Currency," in Evansville *Daily Journal*, January 8, 1863.

Michigan, State of. *Alphabetical General Index to the Public Library Sets of 85,271 Names of Michigan Soldiers & Sailors Individual Records*. [Published under authority of Act 147, Public Acts of 1903 and Supplemental Act 165, Public Acts of 1913.] Lansing [MI]: Wynkoop Hallenbeck Crawford Co., State Printers, 1915. Reprinted by Detroit Press Books, n.d.

Moroney, Rita Lloyd. *Montgomery Blair, Postmaster General*. Washington: Government Printing Office,

1963.

Morrow, Col. Henry A., Twenty-Fourth Michigan Infantry, First Brigade. "Report on the Battle of Gettysburg," February 22, 1864. *Official Records*, Series 1, Volume 27, Part 1, pgs. 267-273.

Pollock, James. *Report of the Director of the Mint*, October 10, 1861. Senate Executive Document IV Nos. 2-9. 37th Congress, 2nd Session. [He was the recipient of the letter at Figure 396a.]

———. *Report of the Director of the Mint*, October 27, 1862. Senate Executive Document I Nos. 1-5. 37th Congress, 3rd Session.

———. *Report of the Director of the Mint*, October 21, 1863. House Executive Document VI Nos. 3-S. 38th Congress, 1st Session.

———. *Report of the Director of the Mint*, October 3, 1864. House Executive Document VII Nos. 3-U. 38th Congress, 2nd Session.

———. *Report of the Director of the Mint*, September 29, 1865. House Executive Document VI No. 3. 39th Congress, 1st Session.

———. *Report of the Director of the Mint*, September 18, 1866. House Executive Document V No. 4. 39th Congress, 2nd Session.

Prifti, George N. (for the petitioners Gladys M. Graham and Mary A. Colleran). "Guardianship of Insane (Laura R. Rutledge)," Probate Court, Suffolk County, Massachusetts. File No. 374728, schedule of real and personal estate, dated February 24, 1954. Typescript, 2 pages.

Quarterly Abstracts of Passenger Lists of Vessels Arriving at Baltimore, 1820-1869. National Archives Microfilm Publications, Microcopy No. 596. Roll 1, January 1, 1820 to December 31, 1829. Washington: NARS, GSA, 1969.

Queens County [NY] Supreme Court, Special Term, Part 1, before Justice Leviss. Confirmation of arbitration award in re. Glazer v. Ford. *New York Law Journal*, August 13, 1983, p. 13.

Report of the Commissioner of Patents for the Year 1864 Arts and Manufactures, n. d. Vol. II, "Illustrations." House Executive Document No. 51. 38th Congress, 2nd Session.

Richardson, William A. *Report of the Secretary of the Treasury on the State of the Finances for 1873*, December 1, 1873. 43rd Congress, 1st Session. Washington: Government Printing Office, 1873.

Rodman, Lt. Col. William L. "Report of . . . Thirty-eighth Massachusetts Infantry, of engagement at Fort Bisland," dated April 18, 1863. *Official Records*. Series I, Vol. 15, Chapt. 27 "Operations in West Louisiana," No. 21, pages 350-353.

"Rules for the Redemption of Postage Stamps," in Cincinnati *Daily Enquirer*, December 28, 1862, p. 2.

Rutledge, Laura. "Petition to Probate Court, Suffolk County, Massachusetts, to be named executrix of the estate of Ann Jane Rutledge," dated June 21, 1915. Handwritten, 1 page.

———. "Petition to Probate Court, Suffolk County, Massachusetts, to be named administratrix of the estate of Elva B. Conant," dated October 29, 1929. File No. 243435. Handwritten, 2 pages.

[Rutledge, Laura.] "Schedule of Personal and Real Estate in Detail," dated February 24, 1954. Typescript, 2 pages.

Salina [KS] Federal Land Office. Map No. 27 in *Historical Atlas of Kansas* by Homer E. Socolofsky and Huber Self. [Land Office est. May 1, 1871, removed to Topeka December 21, 1893.]

Shepley, et al. for National Park Service. *Lowell National Historical Park and Preservation District Cultural Resources Inventory*. 1980. "Research Report, 28 Jackson Street (re. first James C. Ayer building)." Lowell City Library. Typescript, 4 pages.

———. "Research Report, 165 Market Street (re. Dr. J. C. Ayer & Co. building)." Lowell City Library. Typescript, 5 pages.

———. "Research Report, 176-190 Middle Street (re. J. C. Ayer Co. building)." Lowell City Library. Typescript, 4 pages.

———. "Research Report, 267 Pawtucket Street (re. Stone House, also the Ayer Home)." Lowell City Library. Typescript, 5 pages.

Shugert, S. T. [acting commissioner]. *Report of the Commissioner of Patents for the Year 1860, Arts and Manufactures*, January 29, 1861. 2 vols. Senate Executive Document No. 7. 36th Congress, 2nd Session.

Snowden, James Ross. *Report of the Director of the Mint*, November 3, 1860.

Spaulding, E. G. speech of, on *National Finances, National Bank, State Banks, Taxation, Legal Tender Notes*, in House of Representatives, January 12, 1863. Printed copy, 8 pages.

Spinner, F. E., Treasurer of the United States. Letter dated October 4, 1862, reprinted in Chicago *Evening Journal*, October 8, 1862, p. 4.

———. *Report of the Treasurer*, October 25, 1865. House Executive Document VI No. 3. 39th Congress, 1st Session.

———. *Report of the Treasurer*, October 27, 1868.

———. "Rules for Redemption of Mutilated Postage Currency," April 1, 1863, in Cincinnati *Daily Enquirer*, April 11, 1863, p. 3.

Stein, Max Henry. "Improved Press for Forming Dies," Letters Patent No. 38,767, dated June 2, 1863, ante-dated April 9, 1863. U. S. Patent Office, 3 pages.

Theaker, T. C. *Annual Report of the Commissioner of Patents for the Year 1865*, January 31, 1866. 3 vols. House Executive Document No. 52. 39th Congress, 1st Session.

———. *Annual Report of the Commissioner of Patents for the Year 1866*, January 30, 1867. 3 vols. House Executive Document No. 109. 39th Congress, 2nd Session.

———. *Annual Report of the Commissioner of Patents for*

the Year 1867, January 14, 1868. 4 vols. House Executive Document No. 96. 40th Congress, 2nd Session.

Title Guarantee and Trust Co. "Petition to Surrogate Court, County of New York, to be named executors of the estate of John Gault," dated April 11, 1900. Handwritten, 2 pages.

Tower, Levi L. "Currency and Stamp Box," Patent No. 39,184, dated July 7, 1863.

U.S. Bankruptcy Court. District of Massachusetts. Case No. 87-10219-BKC–HAL, in re. Standard Financial Management Corporation, d/b/a New England Rare Coin Galleries. "Notice of Meeting Date of Creditors, and Filing Date for Complaints," February 17, 1987. Typescript and handwritten, 2 pages.

U.S. Congress, House. *Annual Report of the American Historical Association for the Year 1902*. 2 vols. "Sixth Report of Historical Manuscripts Commission: With Diary and Correspondence of Salmon P. Chase." Vol. II. Document No. 461, Pt. 2. U.S. House of Representatives, 57th Congress 2nd Session. Washington: Government Printing Office, 1903.

———. *Annual Report of the Commissioner of Patents for 1862 - Arts and Manufactures*. House Executive Document No. 52. Vol. 1. 37th Congress, 3rd Session. Washington: Government Printing Office, 1864.

------. *Ceremonies and Re-Enactment of the One Hundredth Anniversary of the First Inauguration of Abraham Lincoln, 1861-1961*. On the East Front of the Capitol of the United States, March 4, 1961. House Document No. 523. 87th Congress, 2nd Session. Washington: Government Printing Office, 1962.

------. *Letter from the Secretary of the Treasury Transmitting Estimates of Appropriations Required for the Fiscal Year Ending June 30, 1876*. House Executive Document No. 5. 43rd Congress, 2nd Session. Washington: Government Printing Office, 1874.

------. *Patent Office Report for the Year 1861 - Mechanical*. House Executive Document No. 53. Vol. V, Parts 1-2. 37th Congress, 2nd Session. Washington: Government Printing Office, 1862.

U.S. Department of Commerce, U.S. Bureau of the Census. *Historical Statistics of the United States, Colonial Times to 1970*. Bicentennial edition. 2 vols. Washington: Government Printing Office, 1975.

U.S. Department of the Interior, Census Office. National Archives Record Group No. 29. *Population Schedules of the Fifth Census of the United States, 1830*. Massachusetts, Roll 67. National Archives Microfilm Publications, Microcopy M-19. Washington: National Archives, 1947.

———. *Population Schedules of the Sixth Census of the United States, 1840*. Maryland, Vol. 9, Roll 172; Massachusetts, Rolls 187, 198. National Archives Microfilm Publications, Microcopy No. 704. Washington: NARS, General Services Administration, 1967.

———. *Population Schedules of the Seventh Census of the United States, 1850*. California, Rolls 34, 36; Illinois, Rolls 98, 117; Massachusetts, Rolls 326, 334, 335; New York, Rolls 472, 571; Pennsylvania, Roll 815. NAMP Microcopy No. 432. Washington: NARS, GSA, 1963-1964.

———. *Population Schedules of the Eighth Census of the United States, 1860*. Ohio, Vol. VI, Rolls 939, 970. NAMP Microcopy No. 653. Washington: NARS, GSA, 1967.

———. *Population of the United States Compiled from the Original Returns of the Eighth Census, 1860*. Washington: Government Printing Office, 1864.

———. *The Statistics of the Population of the United States Compiled from the Original Returns of the Ninth Census, 1870*. Washington: Government Printing Office, 1872.

———. *Statistics of the Population of the United States at the Tenth Census, 1880*. Washington: Government Printing Office, 1883.

[U.S. Department of State.] *Passengers Who Arrived in the United States September 1821 to December 1823*, from transcripts made by the U.S. State Department. Baltimore: Magna Carta Book Co., 1969.

U.S. Department of War. *The War of the Rebellion: A Compilation of the Official Records of the Union and Confederate Armies*. 4 Series. Series 1, Vol. 9, p. 337; Series 1, Vol. 15, pgs. 319, 346-353; Series 1, Vol. 20, Pt. 2, p. 289; Series 1, Vol. 27, Pt. 1, pgs. 267-273; Series 2, Vol. 1, p. 130; Series 2, Vol. 2, pgs. 57-58; Series 3, Vol. 2, p. 314; Series 3, Vol. 5, pgs. 649-650, 929. Washington: Government Printing Office, 1880-1901.

U.S. Department of War, Adjutant General's Office. *Official Army Register for 1863*. Washington: Government Printing Office, 1863.

U..S. Patent Office. *Official Gazette*. V (1874). Specification 280, drawing No. 86, p. 676.

U.S. Post Office Department. Third Assistant Postmaster General, Division of Stamps. *A Description of United States Postage Stamps*. Washington: Government Printing Office, 1937.

U.S. *Statutes at Large*. "An Act to Authorize Payments in Stamps and to Prohibit Circulation of Notes of Less Denomination than One Dollar," dated July 17, 1862. Vol. XII, p. 592.

U.S. Treasury Department. *Fines and Imprisonments in Counterfeiting Cases*. Washington: Government Printing Office, 1935.

———. *History of the Bureau of Engraving and Printing, 1862-1962*. Washington: Government Printing Office, n.d. [1964].

[U.S. Treasury Department.] *Passenger Arrivals at the Port of Baltimore, 1820-1834*, from Customs passenger lists. Edited by Michael Tepper. Baltimore: Genealogical Publishing Co., 1982.

U.S. Treasury Department. Postage Currency permits.

New York, November 13, 1862, $30 on Monday and Thursday, No. 972; and November 13, 1862, $30 on Tuesday and Friday, No. 1331. Issued by John J. Cisco, assistant Treasurer of the U.S.

------. *The United States Treasury*. Washington: Government Printing Office, 1966.

———. *The United States Treasury Register, Containing a List of Persons Employed in the Treasury Department*. Treasury Document No. 470. Washington: Government Printing Office, 1883.

Works Progress Administration, Cincinnati Federal Writers' Project. *They Built a City: 150 Years of Industrial Cincinnati*. Cincinnati: The Cincinnati Post, 1938.

———, Illinois Federal Writers' Project. *Baseball in Old Chicago*. Chicago: A. C. McClurg & Co., 1939.

------, New York City Federal Writers' Project. *Changing New York*. New York: E. P. Dutton, 1939.

Printed Company Literature

Anderson, Mary. *Drake-A-Day*. Nos. 1-51 (November 26, 1921 to November 11, 1922).

Anglo-American Drug Co. Advertising cover.

Associated Dry Goods. *Annual Report*, 1980.

Ayer, Dr. J. C. & Co. *Ayer's American Almanac*. Various editions including 1863, 1867, 1868, 1877, 1878, 1884, 1886, 1889 and an 1859 German language edition. Lowell: Dr. J. C. Ayer & Co., various years.

———. *Ayer's Preserve Book*, n.d.

[Ayer, Dr. J. C. & Co.]. *A Night wtih Rameses II*. Illustrated booklet, n. d., 16 pages.

Ayer, J. C. & Co. Various advertising covers and proprietary medicine stamps.

Ayer's Ague Cure. Various lithographed trade cards.

Ayer's Cherry Pectoral. Various lithographed trade cards and large lithographed poster.

Ayer's (Cathartic) Pills. Various lithographed trade cards.

Ayer's Sarsaparilla. Various lithographed trade cards, flyer, and lithographed posters.

Bailey Banks & Biddle. Catalog and trade card, 1991.

Barnes, D. S. "The Kathairon Bank," advertising handbills resembling $20 and $50 bank notes.

Barnes, Demas & Co. Various proprietary medicine stamps.

"Books Published by G. G. Evans, 439 Chestnut St., Philadelphia," in Holley, O. L. *The Life of Benjamin Franklin*. Following page 468, 12 pages. Philadelphia: G. G. Evans, Publisher, 1860.

Brown, John I. and Curtis, Jeremiah. *Mrs. Winslow's Domestic Receipt Book for 1873*. Boston: John I. Brown Co., 1872.

Brown, John I. & Son. Various proprietary medicine stamps.

Brown's Bronchial Troches. Various lithographed trade cards and lithographed flyer.

Brown's Vermifuge Comfits and Camphorated Saponaceous Dentifrice. Various lithographed trade cards.

Burnett, Joseph & Co. Company invoices and a "National Advertising" instructional sheet for salesmen, courtesy of a family descendant, 3 pages.

-------. *Burnett's Floral Hand Book*. 1872, 1877 and 1882 editions. Boston: Joseph Burnett & Co., various years.

———. *Burnett's Floral Hand Book* trade card.

———. *The Story of Vanilla*. Boston, Providence and New York: Livermore & Knight Co., 1926, 30 pages.

———. A printed history of the company, c. 1947, 3 pages photocopied. Original source unknown, from family sources.

———. Various proprietary medicine stamps.

Curtis & Brown. Various proprietary medicine stamps.

Dougan, John A., Hatter. Various lithographed trade cards. New-York Historical Society.

"The Drake," promotional package including brochures, news releases and historical information.

The Drake. *Family Album*, hotel employees' publication, XLI (January to April 1985).

Drake, P. H. & Co. *Morning, Noon and Night*, 1871.

Drake, P. H. & Co. Various proprietary medicine stamps.

Drake's Plantation Bitters. "The Plantation Bank," advertising handbill resembling $100 bank note.

Evans, G. G. "The National Gallery of Eminent Americans," published by G. G. Evans and H. E. Hoyt, Philadelphia and Baltimore, 1860. Library of Congress, Rare Books and Prints Division.

-------. Advertising envelope, "G. G. Evans' Great Original Gift Book Store and Publishing House." Richard Wolffers Inc. Stamp Auctions, August 10-13, 1983, lot 2831.

———. G. G. *Evans Great Gift Book Store*. A catalog, 1854.

Evans, George G. *Illustrated History of the United States Mint*. New Revised Edition. Philadelphia: George G. Evans, Publisher, 1885 and 1886 editions. [According to best evidence, this volume went through five printings during 1885-86; thereafter it underwent an *additional* 16 printings, totalling 100,000 copies in print!]

Evans, George G. *Tour Guide to Washington, D. C.* Philadelphia: George G. Evans, n.d.

Hatch & Co. "Small Currency" advertising note, 1862.

Hood, Jennings and Young, Charles J. *American Orders & Societies and Their Decorations*. Philadelphia: Bailey, Banks & Biddle Co., 1917.

Lord & Taylor. *The History of Lord & Taylor, Founded 1826*. New York: By the Company, 1929.

———. "The Lord and Taylor Touch," a pamphlet history of the firm, 16 pages.

Lyon, E. Thomas. "The Mustang Bank," advertising handbill resembling $50 bank note.

Lyon Manufacturing Co. Various proprietary medicine stamps.

Mayer, Ferd. "Shinplaster Bank," advertising note, 1862.

McAlpin, Geo. W. Co. *History of Feminine Custume*. n.p:

Rand, McNally & Co., 1895.

Munn & Co. Divers papers, notifications, postcards, advertising covers.

Rowell, Geo. P. *American Newspaper Directory*. New York: Geo. P. Rowell, various editions. [Ironically, a copy of this annual directory was also observed at the Dwight D. Eisenhower Birthplace Memorial library.]

———. Printed advertising handbill resembling a banknote. Coupon, $1, May 1868.

———. Various advertising covers.

Scovill and Adams Co. "Our Founder Gone," *The Photographic Times*, Vol. XXVIII No. 2 (February 1896), pgs. 65-66, 105.

Scovill Manufacturing Co. *Brass Roots*. Privately Printed, 1952.

Sherman House. Lettersheet.

Shillito, John & Co. Advertising cover.

------. *Catalogue of Goods Specially Adapted to the Holiday Trade and Where to Find Them*, Christmas, 1878.

------. Special Advertising Supplement to the Cincinnati *Enquirer*, April 16, 1980.

Stanton, John. Handbill, c. 1862.

Steinfeld S. Advertising handbills for French Cognac Bitters, 1855, 1857.

Taylor, N. & G. Various advertising covers, and handbills.

------. Catalog, 1873, and catalog, n.d. Ref. Tq/40/TAY and Wf/996/Vol. 10 at Historical Society of Pennsylvania.

------. *A Guide Book to the Centennial City*. Philadelphia, 1876.

"The Tremont," promotional package including brochures, news releases, reprints of magazine articles re. The Tremont Hotel, 100 East Chestnut St., Chicago.

Tremont House. Business correspondence, advertising covers, miscellaneous papers.

Updegraff, Robert R. *The Story of Two Famous Hatters*. New York: Privately Printed, Knox Hat Co., 1926.

White (George W.) Hatter. Scorecard, June 14, 1870.

Zieber, Eugene. *Heraldry in America*. Second Edition. Philadelphia: The Department of Heraldry of The Bailey, Banks & Biddle Co., 1909.

Civil War Periodicals and Other Primary Sources

Adams, George. *Adams's (sic) Boston Directory, 1847-1848*. Boston: James French and Charles Stimpson, 1847.

"Aërated Bread in California," *Scientific American*, September 20, 1862, p. 186.

Agur, Lemuel. "My Operation in Gold," *Harper's New Monthly Magazine*, XXVII (September, 1863), pgs. 527-570.

Albany [NY] City Directories, 1849-1855, various printers.

"Ale, Historically, Chemically and Locally Considered," Milwaukee *Sentinel*, June 17, 1861, p. 1.

"Alexander M. Holton," in Smithsonian E. Wright "Scrapbook of Obituaries of Cincinnatians," Cincinnati Historical Society.

"All That It Claims To Be," Cincinnati *Daily Enquirer*, December 7, 1862, p. 2.

Ambrose, letter to "Father." HQs 14th Wisconsin Volunteer Infantry, in camp near Vicksburg, Mississippi, February 17, 1865.

The American Life Assurance Magazine, 1862-1873.

"An Amusing Quarrel Concerning Paper Change," New York *Times*, October 30, 1862. p. 2.

Andreas, Alfred Theodore. *Atlas Map of Peoria County, Illinois*. Chicago: By the Author, 1873.

"Another Help," New York *Times*, October 2, 1862, p. 2.

"Arthur M. Claflin Dead," Salina *Daily*, November 7, 1904.

Atlantic Monthly. Vol. 5. Boston: Ticknor and Fields, 1860.

"The Atlantic Monthly for December, 1862," Chicago *Evening Journal*, November 24, 1862, p. 1.

"At Peace. Death of Bernard Schapker Yesterday Afternoon." Evansville newspaper, March 1, 1899.

Ayer, Fred Jr. *Before the Colors Fade: Portrait of a Soldier, George S. Patton Jr.* Dunwoody, GA: Norman S. Berg, Publisher, 1971. [The author was the grandson of Frederick Ayer and nephew of General Patton.]

"Ayer, Frederick Jr." obituary notice, New York *Times*, January 5, 1974.

Ayer, I. Winslow. *The Great Northwestern Conspiracy in All Its Details*. Chicago: Rounds and James, 1865.

"Ayer's Cherry Pectoral," Detroit City Directory, 1853-54, p. 239.

"Ayer's Cherry Pectoral," *Harper's Weekly*, June 6, 1863, p. 366.

"Ayer's Cherry Pectoral," Hurt's Cincinnati Directory, 1856-57, p. 104.

"Ayer's Cherry Pectoral," Richmond [VA] *Enquirer*, March 14, 1862, p. 3.

"Ayer's Pills," New York *Times*, October 21, 1862, p. 5.

"Ayer's Sarsaparilla," New Orleans *Bee*, December 15, 1862, p. 2.

"Bailey, Eli Westoctt," obituary, Philadelphia *Inquirer*, March 30, 1899, p. 12.

Ballou's Pictorial, 1857.

Baltimore City Directories, 1824-1860, various printers.

"The Banishment of Shinplasters," Springfield *Daily Republican*, January 29, 1863.

Banker's Magazine. *The Merchant's and Banker's Register for 1859*. New York: J. Smith Homans, Jr. 1859.

Barnes, Demas. *From the Atlantic to the Pacific, Overland*. New York: 1866.

"Barnum's American Museum," New York *Times*, November 20, 1862, p. 7.

Bennett, E. or H. Thornton. Evansville City Directories, 1863-1912, various printers.

"Bernard Bussing, Retired Druggist, Dies Here at 96," newspaper unknown, n.d.

Bestor, Geo. C, postmaster. "Redemption of Soiled Postage Stamps," Peoria *Star Journal*, December 23, 1862.

Bigelow, M. B. and Hardy, Anson. "J. Burnett & Co.," Boston *Daily Advertiser*, December 30, 1862.

Binghamton [NY] City Directories, 1857-1861, various printers.

"Bogus Silver Coin and Shinplasters," Cincinnati *Daily Enquirer*, November 13, 1862, p. 2.

Boston Annual Advertiser. Boston: Hunt and Stimpson, 1828.

Boston City Directories, 1823-1900, various printers.

Boston *Commercial Advertiser*, 1862.

Boston *Daily Evening Transcript*, 1853.

Boston *Post*, 1863.

Boutwell, George S. *Reminiscences of Sixty Years in Public Affairs*. 2 volumes. New York: McClure Phillips & Co., 1902.

———. *Speeches and Papers Relating to the Rebellion and the Overthrow of Slavery*. Boston: Little Brown & Co., 1867.

———. *The Tax Payer's Manual: Containing the Entire Internal Revenue Laws, with the Decisions and Rulings of the Commissioner, etc.*, Boston: Litrtle Brown & Co. 1865.

"Brady's Gallery," *Harper's Weekly*, November 14, 1863, p. 722.

Brigham, Alasco D. *Brigham's Binghamton and Broome County Directory and Business Advertiser, 1861-62*. 1861.

Brooklyn [NY] City Directories, 1855-1875, various printers.

"Brown's Bronchial Troches," New York *Times*, April 18, 1864, p. 5.

Buell, Wm. "View of Park Place, New York, from Broadway to Church Street, North Side." Lithograph, No. 1855. New York: W. Stephenson & Co., 1855. [The New-York Historical Society Collection, No. 49904]

Buhl, Frederick A. "Civil War Diary of Captain Frederick Augustus Buhl, May 4, 1864 to August 25, 1864." Transcribed by Barbara King Snair and Gertrude Mohlin Ziegler. Zelienople, PA: Zelienople Historical Society, 1981. Typescript, 24 pages.

"Burnett's Extracts," Cincinnati *Daily Enquirer*, October 26, 1863, p. 3.

"Burnett, Joseph," in "Necrology of Historic Genealogical Society, 1895." *Proceedings of New England Historic Genealogical Society*. Vol. IL (1895), pgs. 79, 85.

"A Bushel of Soiled Stamps in One Package," New York *Herald*, c. February 12, 1863.

Carpenter, F. B. *Six Months at the White House with Abraham Lincoln*. New York: Hurd and Houghton, 1867.

Carroll, G. Danielson. *New York Directory to the Hotels, etc.* New York: Carroll & Co., 1859.

"Causes of Bank Failures," *Journal of the Canadian Bankers' Association*, XVII (1909-1910), pgs. 48-49.

"Caution to Correspondents," Cincinnati *Daily Enquirer*, October 9, 1862, p. 1.

Chadwick, Henry. *Beadle's Dime Base-Ball Player*. 10th annual edition. New York: Beadle & Co., 1871.

———. *Beadle's Dime Base-Ball Player*. 11th annual edition. New York: Beadle & Co., 1872.

"Change, Change," Detroit *Free Press*, October 22, 1862.

"Change, Change," Peoria *Star Journal*, October 23, 1862.

Charlestown [MA} City Directories, 1838-1848, various printers.

Chicago City Directories, 1851-1878, various printers.

Chicago City Railway Company. "Postage Stamps," Chicago *Evening Journal*, July 28, 1862, p. 1.

Chicago *Daily Tribune*, 1895.

"A Chicago Directory," Chicago *Evening Journal*, October 10, 1871.

Chicago *Evening Journal*, 1861-1862, 1871. [n.b. the daily financial column in the newspaper was headed "Finance"]

Chittenden, Lucius E. *Recollections of President Lincoln and His Administration*. New York: Harper and Brothers, 1891. [He was Register of the Treasury during the Civil War.]

Cincinnati City Directories, 1825-1866. Various printers.

Cincinnati *Commercial*, 1868.

Cincinnati *Commercial Tribune*, 1904, 1906.

Cincinnati *Daily Enquirer*, 1852, 1862-1864. [n.b. the daily financial column in the newspaper was headed "Commercial Intelligence"]

Cincinnati *Gazette*, 1889.

Cist, Charles. *The Cincinnati Miscellany*. 2 vols. (October 1, 1844-April 1, 1846). Cincinnati: Caleb Clark, Robinson and Jones, 1845-46.

"The City," Milwaukee *Sentinel*, January 13, 1860, p. 1.

The City Government," New York *Times*, November 11, 1862, p. 2.

"City Passenger Railway Tickets," Philadelphia *Enquirer*, October 30, 1862.

Clarke, Herman. Letter to Silas Clarke, dated Nobember 9, 1862, in *Back Home in Oneida: Herman Clarke and His Letters*. ed. by Harry F. Jackson and Thomas F. O'Donnell. Syracuse: Syracuse University Press, 1965.

"The Coming Currency," New York *Times*, August 12, 1862, p. 6.

"Commerce and Currency of the United States," *The North American Review*, XC (January, 1860), pgs. 39-57.

Cook, Frederic. *Fire Insurance Maps of the City of Chicago, Illinois*. Lithographed by Ed Mendel. Chicago: B. W. Phillips & Co., Insurance Agents, 1865.

Coolidge, George. *The Boston Almanac For the Year 1862*. No. XXVII. Boston: J. E. Tilton & Co., 1861. Also 1857 and 1869.

"Corporation Currency," Cincinnati *Daily Enquirer*,

November 26, 1862, p. 2.

"Council Chamber," Evansville *Daily Journal*, October 22, 1862.

"Counterfeit Shinplasters – A Question to be Settled," Chicago *Evening Journal*, November 29, 1862, p. 2.

"Counterfeit Shinplasters – A Question to be Settled," Detroit *Free Press*, December 2, 1862.

Cowell's New York Business Directory, 1861.

[Cowley, Charles.] "Frederick Ayer," in Hurd, D. Hamilton, *History of Middlesex County, Massachusetts*, vol. 2, p. 105. Philadelphia: J. W. Lewis & Co., 1890.

Cowley, Charles. "Frederick Fanning Ayer," in Hurd, D. Hamilton, *History of Middlesex County, Massachusetts*, vol. 2, pgs. 105-107. Philadelphia: J. W. Lewis & Co., 1890.

———. *A Hand Book of Business in Lowell with a History of the City*. Lowell [MA]: E. D. Green, 1856.

———. *Illustrated History of Lowell*. Revised edition. Boston: Lee & Shepard, 1868.

———. "James Cook Ayer," in Hurd, D. Hamilton, *History of Middlesex County, Massachusetts*, vol. 2, pgs. 101-105. Philadelphia: J. W. Lewis & Co., 1890.

———. *Reminiscences of James C. Ayer and the Town of Ayer*. Third Edition. Lowell [MA]: Penhallow Printing Co., n. d. (c. 1879).

"Cream City," Milwaukee *Sentinel*, March 31, 1862, p. 1.

The Currency Question," New Orleans *Bee*, August 6, 1862, p. 1.

"David A. Gage's Widow is Dead," Chicago *Tribune*, November 30, 1894.

"Death of Dr. J. C. Ayer," Lowell *Courier*, July 8, 1878.

"Death of Dr. Miles," Peoria *Herald*, April 24, 1899, p. 5.

"Death of Ex.-Ald. Sands," [re. William J. Sands], Troy *Daily Times*, June 15, 1872.

"Debasing the Coin," Cincinnati *Daily Enquirer*, March 28, 1864, p. 1.

"Decision in Relation to the Legality of Shinplasters," Cincinnati *Daily Enquirer*, November 25, 1862, p. 2.

"Defaced Postage Stamps," Chicago *Evening Journal*, October 16, 1862, p. 1.

"The Delay in the Issue of the Stamp Currency," New York *Times*, October 9, 1862, p. 5.

DeRosier, Arthur H. Jr. (ed.). *Through the South With a Union Soldier*. Johnson City, TN: Research and Planning Center East Tennessee State University, 1969.

Detroit *Advertiser and Tribune*, 1862.

Detroit City Directories, 1837-1862, various printers.

Detroit *Free Press*, 1862-1863. [n.b. the daily financial column was headed "Financial Matters"]

Detroit *Weekly Advertiser*, 1862.

"Disappearance of Silver Coin," Springfield [MA] *Daily Republican*, July 15, 1862.

"Distributing Change," Cincinnati *Daily Enquirer*, December 3, 1862, p. 3.

"Distribution of Postage Currency," Pittsburgh *Post*, December 12, 1862.

"Dr. Ayer's Funeral," Lowell *Courier*, July 8, 1878.

"Drake, John B." obituary, Chicago *Daily Tribune*, November 13, 1895.

Drake, P. H. & Co. Letter to Geo. P. Rowell & Co., September 18, 1868. In Rowell, George P., *The Men Who Advertise*, p. 40. New York: Nelson Chesmen, 1870.

"Drake's Plantation Bitters," Chicago *Evening Journal*, October 16, 1862, p. 4.

"Drink Sands' Cream Ale," Cincinnati *Daily Enquirer*, December 21, 1862, p. 2.

Edwards, John P. *Edward's Atlas of Saline County, Kansas*. Philadelphia: A. H. Mueller, 1884.

Ellis, John Washington. *Six Letters on the Necessity and Practicability of a National Currency*. Privately Printed, c. 1865.

"Ellis, John Washington, Obituary Notes," New York *Times*, December 30, 1910, p. 11.

"Ellis, Mrs. John W., Obituary Notes," New York *Times*, September 4, 1943, p. 13.

"Envelopes For Postage Stamps," Chicago *Evening Journal*, August 1, 1862, p. 4.

"Establishment of Geo. G. Evans, of Philadelphia, Penn.," *Frank Leslie's Illustrated Newspaper*, December 31, 1859.

Evansville City Directories, 1858-1912, various printers.

Evansville *Daily Journal*, 1862-1863.

"Every Denomination of Change Checks," Chicago *Evening Journal*, November 21, 1862, p. 1.

Ferd. Mayer & Co. "Small Currency Bills," New York *Times*, November 19, 1862, p. 3.

"The Final Summons. Death Yesterday Afternoon of Mr. B. Schapker." Evansville *Journal*, March 1, 1899.

"First Delivery of Stamp Currency," New York *Times*, August 20, 1862, p. 5.

"First Issue of the New Government Small Notes," New York *Herald*, August 20, 1862.

"The Flood of Shinplasters," Chicago *Evening Journal*, November 19, 1862, p. 1.

"Folly of Hoarding Small Coin," Cincinnati *Daily Enquirer*, April 7, 1863, p. 3.

"Forgery of 'Trade Marks,'" Cincinnati *Daily Enquirer*, April 8, 1864, p. 1.

"Fourth and Main," newspaper clipping, source and date unknown, Cincinnati Historical Society.

Frank Leslie's Illustrated Newspaper, 1859, 1862-1863, 1871

"Frederick Buhl and Christian H. Buhl," Detroit *Free Press*, December 16, 1877.

"Funeral of John I. Brown," Boston *Daily Advertiser*, November 25, 1882, p. 8.

"Funeral This Afternoon" [obituary of Arthur M. Claflin], Salina *Evening Journal*, November 9, 1904.

"The Gage Defalcation. Inaccurate Statements Regarding the Deficit Corrected," Chicago Daily Tribune, April 13, 1889, p. 9.

Galt (sic), John. "The New Postage Stamp Currency." Chicago *Evening Journal*, November 7, 1862, p. 1.

"Gault, [John, death notice]," New York *Daily Tribune*,

March 20, 1900.
Gault, John. "The New Metallic Currency," New York *Daily Tribune*, November 6, 1862, p. 3.
———. "The New Metallic Currency," New York *Herald*, November 5-8, 1862.
"Gault, John [obituary]," New York *Daily Tribune*, March 20, 1900.
Gault, John. "'Penny Tokens of Copper," *Harper's Weekly*, August 29, 1863, p. 559.
———. "Photographic Medallions," *Harper's Weekly*, July 9, 1864, p. 447.
———. "Photographic Medallions," *Harper's Weekly*, September 24, 1864, p. 623.
"Gault [John A.] death notice, Providence *Journal* and *Evening Bulletin*, c. November 10, 1959.
"Gault, John A." [obituary], Conway [NH] *Reporter Press*, November 12, 1959.
"Gault, Mrs. Olive C." [obituary], Conway [NH] *Reporter Press*, November 13, 1958.
"Gault [Pamelia P. obituary], Buffalo *Evening News*, April 26, 1911, p. 1.
"George W. Gage. A Dangerous Attack of Illness – No Hope of His Recovery. A Brief Sketch of His Life," Chicago *Tribune*, September 23, 1875, p. 3.
Gleason's Pictorial Drawing-Room Companion, 1854, 1857
"The Glut of Silver in Canada" *Scientific American*, February 21, 1863, p. 118.
"The Glut of Silver in Canada," Detroit *Advertiser*, in Springfield *Republican*, February 23, 1863.
Gobright and Dawes. *The Union Sketch Book*. New York: Rudd and Carleton, 1861.
"Government Stamped Envelopes," New York *Journal of Commerce*, November 8, 1862.
H. J. "The Mysteries of New York," Cincinnati *Daily Enquirer*, December 16, 1862, p. 3.
Hamilton, Mrs. R. L. "Memories of Early Claflin," Claflin *Clarion*, October 26, 1933, p. 2. [She was a relative of the Claflin family.]
"A Happy Riddance," New York *Times*, November 15, 1862, p. 4.
Harper's Weekly, 1859-1870.
Hart, Henry. *City of Chicago, Cook County, Illinois*. A map, surveyed by Henry Hart and lithographed by Sarony & Co., New York. Chicago: Published by Henry Hart, 1853.
Hartford [CT] City Directories, 1852-1858, various printers.
Hawes, George W. (comp.) *Illinois State Gazetteer (sic) and Business Directory for 1858 and 1859*. Chicago: Scripps, Bross & Spears, n. d. [1858].
"A Heavy Transaction," Cincinnati *Daily Enquirer*, October 23, 1862, p. 3.
Hellier's & Co. "Commercial Register of the Business Men of New York for 1860," *Hellier's & Co.'s Chicago Business Directory*. New York: Hellier's & Co., 1859.
"Henry A. Cook is Claimed By Death," Evansville *Courier*, February 4, 1916.
Hodgskin, J. B. "Financial Condition of the United States," *The North American Review*, CVIII (April, 1869), pgs. 517-541.
———. " Our Currency, Past and Future," *The North American Review*, CXI (July, 1870), pgs. 78-101.
"A Home Brood of Shinplasters," Cincinnati *Daily Enquirer*, December 28, 1862, p. 3.
"Home Interests," Evansville *Daily Journal*, March 12, 1863. [re. Schapker and Bussing]
Horse Railway Monopoly. *Report of Committee with Accompanying Documents*. Proceedings of public meeting of citizens, February 9, 1865. Chicago: Tribune Book & Job Office, 1865.
"Humors of the Day," *Harper's Weekly*, November 15, 1862, p. 723.
Hunt, G. W., Obituary Notes," New York *Times*, August 1, 1877, p. 1.
Hunter, Herman. "John Stanton, Stamp and Brand Cutter," *Journal of the Civil War Token Society*, II (Spring 1968), p. 9.
Illustrated London News, 1871
"Immediate Use of Postage Stamps as Currency," New York *Tribune*, July 28, 1862.
"Important Rules for Redemption of Postage Currency," Cincinnati *Daily Enquirer*, April 11, 1863, p. 3.
"Improved Expanding Projectile," *Scientific American*, September 14, 1861, p. 168.
"In Memoriam, George Washington McAlpin," Cincinnati *Commercial Gazette*, April 21, 1890.
"Index of War and Naval Inventions, *Scientific American*, November 30, 1861, p. 347.
Insurance Monitor, 1862-1873.
The [New York] *Insurance Times*, 1862.
"Internal Revenue Stamps," Boston *Daily Advertiser*, January 10, 1863, p. 1.
"The Issue of Postal Currency," Detroit *Free Press*, November 4, 1862.
"The Issue of Shinplasters," Springfield [MA] *Daily Republican*, July 23, 1862.
"Items of Importance to Inventors and Patentees," *Scientific American*, October 4, 1862, p. 219.
"It Won't Do," New York *Times*, August 17, 1862, p. 6.
"J. W. Bussing Dead," Evansville *Journal-News*, May 27, 1912, p. 3.
Jackson, Isaac. Letter to Ethan A. Jackson, dated November 6, 1862, in *The Civil War Letters of Isaac Jackson, 1862-1865*. ed. by Joseph Orville Jackson. Carbondale [IL]: Southern Illinois University Press, 1960.
"Job Printing at the Enquirer Office," Cincinnati *Daily Enquirer*, October 9, 1862, p. 4. [soliciting, among other things, printing of merchant scrip]
"John H. Rutledge" obituary. Hingham, Massachusetts, newspaper clipping, n.d. [c. August 1, 1928]
"John L. Tucker, Esq." *Gleason's Pictorial Drawing Room Companion*, Vol. I, No. 4 (1851), p. 72.
"John W. Bussing, Aged Merchant, Dead," Evansville *Courier*, May 27, 1912.
"Joseph Burnett, Apothecary," *Boston Almanac*, 1850,

unnumbered advertising page.
"Killed at the Battle of the Teche, La.," Boston *Post*, April 30, 1863.
"Laboratory of P. H. Drake & Co., New York," *Harper's Weekly*, June 29, 1867, p. 414.
Lain's Brooklyn New York Directory, 1859-1875.
"The Law of Kentucky in Regard to Shinplasters," Cincinnati *Daily Enquirer*, November 15, 1862, p. 3.
"Leeds and Franklin Envelope," *Scientific American*, July 12, 1862, p. 32.
"Leeds & Franklin's Patent Stamp-Sealing and Post-Mark-Preserving Envelopes," New York *Times*, November 19, 1862, p. 8.
"Lewis C. Hopkins," Cincinnati *Gazette*, January 31, 1889, p. 12.
Life magazine, 1889-1890
Lodge, John C. and Quaife, M. M. *I Remember Detroit*. Detroit: Wayne University Press, 1949.
Longworth's American Almanac . . . for the Sixty-Second Year of American Independence. New York: Thomas Longworth, 1837.
"Look Out for Bogus Postage Currency," Pittsburgh *Post*, December 12, 1862.
"Look Out for Shinplasters," New York *Times*, November 21, 1862, p. 3.
"Lord, J. T., Obituary Notes," New York *Times*, January 5, 1903, p. 9.
Lowell City Directories, 1833-1880, various printers.
Lowell of Today. Lowell: Lowell Daily Citizen, 1873.
"Making Money at the Philadelphia Mint," *Harper's New Monthly Magazine*, 1861, pgs. 3-15.
McCulloch, Hugh. *Men and Measures of Half a Century*. New York: Charles Scribner's Sons, 1888.
McNally and Co., "Envelopes for Postage Stamps," Chicago *Evening Journal*, August 1, 1862, p. 4.
"Mexican Mustang Liniment," *Scientific American*, September 20, 1862, p. 179.
Midgley, R. L. *Sights in Boston and Suburbs, or Guide to the Stranger*. Boston: John P. Jewett & Co., 1856.
Millar, S. S. "Circular Change Checks," Chicago *Evening Journal*, July 12, 1862, p. 1.
------. "New Ads," Chicago *Evening Journal*, November 19, 1862, p. 1.
———. "New Style of Round Change Checks," Chicago *Evening Journal*, December 26, 1862.
———. "Round Change Checks," Chicago *Evening Journal*, November 13, 1862, p. 1.
———. "Style of Change Checks," Chicago *Evening Journal*, November 19, 1862, p. 1.
——— "Style of Round Change Checks," Chicago *Evening Journal*, November 10, 1862, p. 1.
Milwaukee City Directories, 1857-1861, various printers.
Milwaukee *Sentinel*, *1857*-1862.
"The Mint at Philadelphia," *Scientific American*, March 7, 1863, p. 151.
"Money and Credit," *The North American Review*, XC (April, 1860), pgs. 322-345.
Montreal City Directories, 1858-1914, various printers.
"More Complaints of the Scarcity of Small Change," Cincinnati *Daily Enquirer*, October 19, 1862, p. 3.
Morris, Thomas F. "The History of the Bureau of Engraving and Printing," *The Stamp Specialist*. Gray Book, pgs. 92-101. New York: H. L. Lindquist, 1943.
Mount Auburn Cemetery. "A Plan of Mt. Auburn Cemetery, Cambridge, Massachusetts." A pamphlet.
Munn & Co. "Patents for New Inventions," *Harper's Weekly*, September 28, 1861, p. 624.
Murphy's. "Postage Stamp Envelopes," New York *Times*, August 3, 1862.
———. "Postage Stamps Envelopes," New York *Tribune*, August 3, 1862.
"The Mysteries of New York," Cincinnati *Daily Enquirer*, December 16, 1862, p. 3.
"The Mysteries of New York," New York *Daily Tribune*, November 17, 1862, p. 5.
"A National Currency," *The North American Review*, IC (July, 1864), pgs. 204-245.
"The National Resources, and Their Relation to Foreign Commerce and the Price of Gold," *The North American Review*, C (January, 1865), pgs. 126-160.
"Neat and Handy. General City News," New York *Times*, October 8, 1862, p. 2.
Nevins, Allan (ed.). *The Diary of Philip Hone*, 1828-1851. 2 vols in one. New York: Arno Press & The New York Times, 1970.
"A New Brewery," Milwaukee *Sentinel*, September 30, 1857, p. 1.
"A New Currency," Chicago *Evening Journal*, October 18, 1862, p. 4.
"That New Currency," Chicago *Evening Journal*, November 21, 1862, p. 4.
The New-England Historical and Genealogical Register, re. James Cook Ayer, XXIII (July 1869), p. 362, XXXIV (January 1880), p. 112; re. Frederick Ayer, XXVIII (July 1874), p. 285; re. Frederick Fanning Ayer, XXXIII (December 1879), p. 62; re. Joseph Burnett, XLV (April 1891), p. 58, XLIX (January 1895), pgs. 79, 85. Boston: New-England Historic Genealogical Society.
"The New Issue of Postage Stamps," *Harper's Weekly*, October 19, 1861, p. 671.
New Orleans *Bee [L'Abeille de la Nouvelle Orleans]*, 1862.
"The New Patent Law," *Scientific American*, April 6, 1861, p. 217.
"New Postage Currency," Chicago *Evening Journal*, October 13, 1862, p. 4.
"The New Postage Currency – Difficulties in the Distribution," New York *Herald*, October 4, 1862.
"The New Postage Stamp Currency," Chicago *Evening Journal*, July 23, 1862, p. 1.
"The New Postage Stamp Currency," Chicago *Evening Journal*, November 7, 1862, p. 1.
"The New Postage Stamp Currency," New York *Times*, July 20, 1862, p. 4.
"The New Stamp Currency," New York *Times*, August 16, 1862, p. 4.

"The New Stamp Currency," New York *Tribune*, July 28, 1862.
New York City Directories, 1834-1900, various printers.
New York *Herald*, 1862.
New York *Journal of Commerce*, 1862-1863.
New York *Times*, 1861-1864.
New York *Daily Tribune*, 1862.
"Nickel Cents," *Scientific American*, July 19, 1862, p. 36.
"Nickel Cents," *Scientific American*, March 21, 1863, p. 187.
Norris, J. W. *General Directory and Business Advertiser of the City of Chicago for the Year 1844*. Chicago: Ellis & Fergus Printers, 1844.
"The Northwestern Newsdealers' Emporium," Chicago *Evening Journal*, December 8, 1862, p. 1.
"A Novel Envelope," *Scientific American*, December 13, 1862, p. 371.
"A Nuisance," New York *Times*, November 7, 1862, p. 3.
"Obituary. Dr. James C. Ayer," Boston *Daily Advertiser*, July 7, 1878.
"Obituary Notes [re. John I. Brown]," Boston *Daily Advertiser*, November 23, 1882.
Ogden, A. "Copper Tokens or Medals," *Harper's Weekly*, July 18, 1863, p. 462.
"On Change," New York *Times*, July 15, 1862, p. 7.
"Our Financial Future," *The North American Review*, CII (January 1866), pgs. 100-135.
"Our New Small Note Currency," New York *Times*, August 29, 1862, p. 3.
"The Patent Office," Detroit *Free Press*, undated newspaper clipping c. December 9, 1862.
Patton, Beatrice Ayer. *Reminiscences of Frederick Ayer*. Boston: Privately Printed, 1923.
"Pennies," *Scientific American*, March 7, 1863, p. 154.
Peoria City Directories, 1856-1876, various printers.
Peoria *Star Journal*, 1862.
Philadelphia City Directories, 1835-1872, various printers.
Philadelphia *Enquirer*, 1862.
"Philadelphia Mint," Cincinnati *Daily Enquirer*, December 6, 1862, p. 4.
"The Philadelphia Mint," *Scientific American*, August 16, 1862, p. 98.
"The Philosophy of Projectiles," *Scientific American*, May 3, 1862, p. 278.
"Picture Button," *Scientific American*, August 31, 1861, p. 141.
Plat [Map] *of Smoky Hill Township* [KS] 14 South, Range 3 West. Salina [KS] Public Library Collections.
"Pleasant" cartoon. *Harper's Weekly*, August 9, 1862, p. 512.
"Plenty of United States Treasury Small Notes to be Issued," Cincinnati *Daily Enquirer*, November 10, 1862, p. 3.
"The Postage Currency," *Harper's Weekly*, November 1, 1862, p. 691.
"The Postage Currency," New York *Herald*, September 21, 1862, in New Orleans *Bee*, October 3, 1862, p. 1.
"Postage Currency Wanted," Detroit *Free Press*, October 23, 1862.
"The Postage Stamp Currency," Cincinnati *Daily Enquirer*, October 7, 1862, p. 3.
"The Postage Stamp Currency," New York *Times*, July 24, 1862, p. 3.
"The Postage Stamp Currency," New York *Times*, October 11, 1862, p. 8.
"The Postage Stamp Currency," Pittsburgh *Gazette*, July 22, 1862.
"Postage Stamp Currency," Springfield [MA] *Daily Republican*, July 22, 1862.
"The Postage Stamp Currency," Springfield [MA] *Daily Republican*, July 23, 1862.
"The Postage Stamp Difficulty," New York *Evening Post*, in Chicago *Evening Journal*, October 13, 1862, p. 3.
"The Postage Stamp Nuisance," *Harper's Weekly*, October 18, 1862, p. 659.
"Postage Stamps," Chicago *Evening Journal*, July 18, 1862, p. 1.
"Postage Stamps," Chicago *Evening Journal*, October 3, 1862, p. 4.
"Postage Stamps," New York *Times*, July 23, 1862, p. 1.
"Postage Stamps," *Scientific American*, August 9, 1862, p. 85.
"Postage Stamps, A Nice Little Government Speculation," Chicago *Evening Journal*, October 3, 1862, p. 4.
"Postage Stamps as a Currency," Chicago *Evening Journal*, July 22, 1862, p. 1.
"Postage Stamps – Postage Currency – City Currency," New York *Times*, October 11, 1862, p. 4.
"Postage Stamps to be Redeemed," Chicago *Evening Journal*, November 21, 1862, p. 2.
"Postal Currency," Chicago *Evening Journal*, December 20, 1862.
"Postal Currency," Detroit *Free Press*, December 9, 1862.
"Postal Currency," Pittsburgh *Post*, December 9, 1862.
"The Postal Currency," Cincinnati *Daily Enquirer*, November 2, 1862, p. 3.
"Postal Currency Books," Detroit *Free Press*, November 22, 1863.
"The Postmaster General & Commissioner of Internal Revenue To-day Approved Specimens of Postage Stamp Currency," Chicago *Evening Journal*, July 31, 1862, p. 1.
"The Postmaster General's Report," Detroit *Free Press*, December 4, 1862.
Prang, L. & Co. "Small Currency," Boston *Daily Advertiser*, December 30, 1862.
"Proposed New Postal Currency," *Scientific American*, October 25, 1862.
"The Proposed Stamp and Mica Currency. News From Washington," New York *Times*, October 18, 1862, p. 4.
Punch, or the London Charivari, 1862
"The Question of Small Change," New York *Times*, October 6, 1862, p. 4.

Rae. "Chestnut Street Panorama," between Fourth and Fifth Streets, Plate 7, *Rae's Philadelphia Pictorial Directory*. Philadelphia: By the author, 1851.

"Real Estate Sale," Milwaukee *Sentinel*, December 10, 1859, p. 1.

"The Reason Why," *Harper's Weekly*, August 6, 1864, p. 512.

"Receipts from the Internal Revenue," New York *Times*, May 2, 1863, p. 4.

"Recent American Inventions," *Scientific American*, July 27, 1861, p. 55.

"Recent Deaths, Dr. Joseph Burnett." Boston *Transcript*, August 13, 1894.

"Redeeming Postage Stamps," Cincinnati *Daily Enquirer*, December 23, 1862, p. 3.

"Redemption of Old Postage Stamps," Cincinnati *Daily Enquirer*, December 14, 1862, p. 1.

"Redemption of Postage Stamps," Chicago *Evening Journal*, November 17, 1862, p. 1.

"Redemption of Postage Stamps," New York *Times*, December 30, 1862.

"The Redemption of Postage Stamps," New York *Times*, December 15, 1862, p. 4.

"The Redemption of Soiled Postage Stamps," New York *Times*, December 17, 1862, p. 2.

"Redemption of Soiled Postage Stamps," Peoria *Star Journal*, December 31, 1862.

"Redemption of Soiled Stamps," New York *Times*, November 16, 1862, p. 5.

"Redemption of the Soiled Stamps," *Scientific American*, February 21, 1863, p. 115.

"Redemption of Stamps," New York *Times*, December 14, 1862, p. 8.

Register of First Class Business Houses in San Francisco, California. San Francisco: F. A. Bonnard, 1852.

"Regular Session of the City Council – Reports on the Small Change Question," Cincinnati *Daily Enquirer*, November 8, 1862, p. 3.

"Remains of Late Citizen Reaches the City," Evansville *Journal*, February 4, 1916, p. 3. [re. H. A. Cook]

"Report of the Commissioner of Patents," New York *Times*, April 26, 1864, p. 8.

"Repudiation of Postage Stamps," New York *Times*, November 14, 1862, p. 3.

"Revenue Stamps," Detroit *Free Press*, October 19, 1862.

"Revenue Stamps Ready for Delivery," New York *Tribune*, November 6, 1862.

Richmond *Enquirer*, 1861-1864.

Riddle, Albert Gallatin. *Recollections of War Times: Reminiscences of Men and Events in Washington, 1860-1865*. New York: G. P. Putnam's Sons, 1895.

Robert, Charles E. *Evansville: Her Commerce and Manufacturers; A Descriptive Work on the Business Metropolis of Indiana*. Evansville: Courier Co., 1874.

Rowell, George Presbury. *Forty Years An Advertising Agent, 1865-1905*. New York: Franklin Publishing Co., 1926.

------. *The Men Who Advertise: An Account of Successful Advertisers, Together With Hints on the Method of Advertising*. New York: Nelson Chesmen, 1870.

"The Rush for Postage Currency," Pittsburgh *Post*, December 17, 1862.

"The Rush for Postage Stamps," Chicago *Evening Journal*, July 22, 1862, p. 1.

"The Rush for Postal Currency," Cincinnati *Daily Enquirer*, October 8, 1862, p. 3.

"Rutledge, John H. [obituary]," photocopy, n. p., n. d.

Salina City and Saline County [KS] Directories, 1879-1907, various printers.

San Francisco *Alta California*, 1862.

San Francisco *Daily Herald*, 1855.

"Sands [William J.]" obituary, Troy *Daily Times*, June 15, 1872.

"Sands' Ale," Chicago *Evening Journal*, January 3, 1862, p. 3.

"Sands' Ale," Milwaukee *Sentinel*, June 17, 1861, p. 1.

"Sands' Cream Ale," Milwaukee *Sentinel*, December 30, 1859, p. 1.

"Scarcity of Change," Chicago *Evening Journal*, July 15, 1862, p. 3.

"Scarcity of Change in Boston," Boston *Transcript*, October 22, 1862, in New Orleans *Bee*, November 14, 1862, p. 1.

"Scarcity of Change – Proposed Remedy," Chicago *Evening Journal*, July 15, 1862, p. 4.

"The Scarcity of Change – A Senseless Panic," New York *Times*, July 12, 1862, p. 3.

"The Scarcity of Change – The Market Flooded with Shinplasters," Detroit *Free Press*, October 30, 1862.

"The Scarcity of Coin – A Question By Far the Most Important of the Day," New York *Times*, July 11, 1862, p. 2.

"Scarcity of Currency," Philadelphia *Ledger* in Chicago *Evening Journal*, Octoger 18, 1862, p. 1.

"The Scarcity of Silver Change," Chicago *Evening Journal*, July 11, 1862, p. 1.

"The Scarcity of Small Change," New York *Times*, July 11, 1862, p. 2.

"The Scarcity of Small Change – The 'Check' System," Chicago *Evening Journal*, July 7, 1862, p. 4.

"Scarcity of Small Silver Change," Philadelphia *North America* in Chicago *Evening Journal*, July 5, 1862, p. 1.

Schapker & Bussing. "Postage Stamps Wanted," Evansville *Daily Journal*, November 3, 1862.

Scientific American, 1861-1865.

"The 'Sensation' Struggle in America," *Punch, Or the London Charivari*, June 7, 1862.

"Sentence of a Trade Mark Counterfeiter," Cincinnati *Daily Enquirer*, April 13, 1864, p. 1.

"[Shillito, John]," Cincinnati *Daily Enquirer*, October 15 1852, p. 3. [clipping at Cincinnati Historical Society]

"The Shinplaster Currency," Detroit *Free Press*, November 1, 1862.

"The Shinplaster Party," New York *World* in Detroit *Free*

Press, November 5, 1862.
"Shinplasters," Chicago *Evening Journal*, December 2, 1862.
"Shinplasters," anonymous letter to the Editor, New York *Times*, November 24, 1862, p. 3.
"Shinplasters," New York *Times*, January 10, 1863.
"Shinplasters," New York *Times*, January 12, 1863.
"Shinplasters Supplanted," New Orleans *Bee*, August 2, 1862, p. 1.
"Shinplasters to be Suppressed," New York *Times*, November 21, 1862, p. 2.
"Shinplasters Versus Silver Coin," Springfield [MA] *Daily Republican*, July 2, 1862.
"Silver in Canada," Cincinnati *Daily Enquirer*, December 24, 1862, p. 3.
"Silver in Canada," from Montreal *Advertiser*, November 22, 1862, in New York *Times*, November 30, 1862, p. 5.
Sketches and Business Directory of Boston, Massachusetts, 1860-1861.
"Small Change," Chicago *Evening Journal*, July 14, 1862, p. 1.
"The Small Change," Chicago *Evening Journal*, October 8, 1862, p. 1.
"Small Change," St. Louis *Daily Missouri Republican*, July 11, 1862.
"Small Change," St. Louis *Daily Missouri Republican*, July 17, 1862.
"Small Change – A New Legal Tender – Plenty of Currency," New York *Times*, July 18, 1862, p. 4.
"Small Change – A Suggestion," Detroit *Weekly Advertiser*, October 18, 1862.
"Small Change at the Mint," Philadelphia *Enquirer*, July 19, 1862, in St. Louis *Daily Missouri Republican*, July 23, 1862.
"Small Change at the Mint," Philadelphia *Enquirer*, October 1, 1862.
"The Small Change Ordinance – The City Solicitor's Opinion," Cincinnati *Daily Enquirer*, November 22, 1862, p. 3.
"The Small Change Panic in Cincinnati," Cincinnati *Daily Enquirer*, November 5, 1862, p. 3.
"The Small Change Question Before the City Fathers," Detroit *Free Press*, October 23, 1862.
"The Small Currency Bother," New York *Times*, July 15, 1862, p. 4.
"Small Note Currency," Evansville *Daily Journal*, November 3, 1862.
"Small Postage Stamps – Is Their Circulation Prohibited?" Cincinnati *Daily Enquirer*, October 21, 1862, p. 3.
"Snow's Patent Currency Holder," *Scientific American*, February 28, 1863.
"Soiled and Defaced Postage Stamps," Chicago *Evening Journal*, October 14, 1862, p. 1.
"Soldier Health," *Scientific American*, October 4, 1862, p. 215.
"A Solution for the Small Change Problem," New York *Times*, July 12, 1862, p. 4.
"Spiritual Shinplasters," *Scientific American*, February 7, 1863, p. 91.
Springfield [Massachusetts} *Daily Republican*, 1862.
"S–T–1860–X," Chicago *Evening Journal*, July 9, 1862, p. 1.
"S–T–1860–X, The Mystery is Solved," Chicago *Evening Journal*, July 9, 1862, p. 4.
"Stamp and Mica Currency," Chicago *Evening Journal*, October 31, 1862, p. 2.
"Stamping Patented Articles," *Scientific American*, October 4, 1862, p. 219.
"Stamps and How They Go," New York *Times*, July 23, 1862, p. 5.
"Stimson's Advertising Chess and Checker Board," New York *Times*, November 1, 1862, p. 8.
Strong, George Templeton. *The Diary of George Templeton Strong*. 4 vols. Ed. by Allan Nevins and Milton Halsey Thomas. New York: Octagon Books/Farrar, Straus and Giroux, 1974.
"Subjects for Invention," *Scientific American*, November 30, 1861, p. 346.
"Suspension of Specie Payments," *Harper's Weekly*, January 11, 1862, p. 18.
"Suspension of Specie Payments by Eastern Banks," Chicago *Evening Journal*, December 30, 1862, p. 1.
"Take Warning;" Chicago *Evening Journal*, November 21, 1862, p. 4.
"Tax Stamps," Detroit *Free Press*, October 23, 1862.
"That New Currency," Chicago *Evening Journal*, November 21, 1862, p. 4.
"To an Old Postage Stamp," Springfield *Daily Republican*, January 16, 1862.
Tomlinson, Helyn W. [ed.]. *"Dear Friends:" The Civil War Letters and Diary of Charles Edwin Cort*. n.p.: By the compiler, 1962.
"To Silver Brass," *Scientific American*, September 27, 1862, p. 202.
"Treasury Notes and Postage Stamps," Chicago *Evening Journal*, July 22, 1862, p. 1.
"The Trouble in Canada about the American Currency," Cincinnati *Daily Enquirer*, November 11, 1862, p. 2.
Trow, John F. New York City Directories, 1852-1872.
Troy [New York] Directories, 1851-1876, various printers.
"The True Remedy for the Scarcity of Change," *Scientific American*, July 26, 1862, p. 57.
Twitt & Company's New York Business Directory, n.d.
"Unfermented Bread," *Scientific American*, August 3, 1861, p. 71.
The Union Sketch Book, 1861.
"United States Revenue Stamps," New York *Times*, January 15, 1863.
"United States Silver in Canada," Toronto *Leader* in Cincinnati *Daily Enquirer*, December 16, 1862, p. 1.
U.S. Sanitary Commission, Cincinnati Branch. "Head-Quarters Great Western Sanitary Fair" advertising cover. Robert A. Siegel Auction Galleries, 426th

Sale, February 14-16, 1973, lot No. 1840.

"U.S. Silver in Canada," *Scientific American*, December 13, 1862, p. 379.

"The Voice," Chicago *Evening Journal*, January 25, 1862, p. 4.

Weir, William. *Sixty Years in Canada*. Montreal: John Lovell & Son, 1903.

"What Becomes of the Silver?" Cincinnati *Daily Enquirer*, December 31, 1862, p. 1.

"Whispered About," Cincinnati *Daily Enquirer*, January 15, 1863, p. 3.

Whitefield, Edwin. *Map of the Business Portion of Chicago*. Chicago: Press of Rufus Blanchards, 1862.

Williams, C. S. *Williams' Cincinnati Directory and Business Advertiser*, 1850-1866.

Williams and Co. *Williams' Evansville Directory, 1863-1878*. Evansville: various printers.

Wilson's Binghamton Directory. New York: John F. Trow, 1857.

Wilson's Business Directory of New York City. New York: John F. Trow, 1855.

Wilson's Co-Partnership Directory for 1860-61. New York: John F. Trow, 1860.

[Wilson, John L., ed.] editorial "The Scarcity of Change – Proposed Remedy," Chicago *Evening Journal*, July 15, 1862, p. 4.

[Wilson, John L., ed.] editorial "Scarcity of Small Change – The 'Check' System," Chicago *Evening Journal*, July 7, 1862, p. 4.

[Wilson, John L., ed.] editorial "Suspension of Specie Payments by Eastern Banks," Chicago *Evening Journal*, December 31, 1861, p. 1.

[Wilson, John L., ed.] editorial "Worth of Money," Chicago *Evening Journal*, November 29, 1862, p. 2.

[Wilson, John L. ed.] editorial "The Flood of Shinplasters A Word in Time," Chicago *Evening Journal*, November 19, 1862, p. 1.

"Wines of California," *Scientific American*, November 29, 1862, p. 343.

"Worthless Banks," Cincinnati *Daily Enquirer*, January 3, 1863, p. 4.

Wright, Smithsonian E. "Scrapbook of Obituaries of Cincinnatians." Cincinnati Historial Society.

Articles and Periodicals (Secondary Sources)

Adams, Edgar H. "Dr. Lewis Feuchtwanger," *The Numismatist*, XXVI (June 1913), pgs. 297-302.

———. "Encased Postage Stamps," *Mehl's Numismatic Monthly*, Vol. II No. 2 (February, 1909), pgs. 17-20.

———. "Exhibits at the Convention," *The Numismatist*, Vol. XXIV (September, 1911), p. 325-326.

———. [ed.] letter to Charles Gregory, *The Numismatist*, Vol. XXVII (May 1914), p. 255.

———. "Live American Numismatic Items," *The Numismatist*, Vol. XXIV (March 1911), p. 105.

———. "Live American Numismatic Items," *The Numismatist*, Vol. XXIV (June 1911), p. 226.

Adams, Eva. "Numismatography – 1888 to 1977," Foreword to the reprint edition of Evans' Mint history. New York: Sanford J. Durst Numismatic Publications, 1977.

Adams, Samuel Hopkins. "The Nostrum Evil: Peruna and the Bracers," *Collier's Weekly*, October 28, 1905.

———. "The Patent Medicine Conspiracy Against the Freedom of the Press," *Collier's Weekly*, November 4, 1905.

American Numismatic Association. *The Numismatist*. [The official journal of the American Numismatic Association has recorded a wealth of information about encased stamps. Miscellaneous and unsigned reports, exclusive of foreign encased stamps, include:]. December 1895, inside back cover; June 1902, p. 172; June 1903, p. 186; November 1903, p. 356; January 1905, p. 35; May 1906, p. 157; June 1906, p. 217; August 1906, pgs. 290, 291; November 1906, p. 380; December 1906, p. 408; October-November 1907, p. 287; December 1907, p. 341; September-October 1909, p. 263; December 1909, pgs. 351-352; August-September 1910, p. 202, 341; March 1911, p. 105; June 1911, pgs. 213, 226; August 1911, p. 283; September 1911, p. 326; December 1911, p. 432; March 1912, p. 92; May 1912, p. 172; July 1912, p. 250; September 1912, pgs. 320, 337; December 1912, p. 479; March 1913, p. 159; July 1913, pgs. 350-351; August 1913, p. 445; September 1913, p. 468; October 1913, p. 504; November 1913, p. 601, February 1914, pgs. 83, 95, 103; April 1914, pgs. 172, 186, 197, 234; May 1914, pgs. 255, 280; June 1914, p. 308; January 1915, p. 32; February 1915, pgs. 60-61, 84; May 1915, p. 174; October 1916, pgs. 432-433, 451-452; April 1917, pgs. 185, 186; May 1917, p. 212; June 1917, p. 265; August 1917, p. 320; September 1917, p. 388; December 1917, p. 498; June 1918, p. 268; January 1919, p. 32; February 1919, p. 98; January 1920, p. 34; May 1920, pgs. 181-187, 203; September 1920, p. 404; June 1921, p. 249; October 1921, p. 460; February 1922, p. 96; March 1922, p. 143; June 1922, p. 296; July 1922, p. 336; August 1922, p. 381; October 1922, pgs. 475-476, 491, 494, 495; July 1923, p. 309; June 1924, p. 286; November 1924, p. 508; December 1924, p. 585; January 1926, pgs. 10-11; February 1926, p. 88; April 1926, p. 185; May 1927, p. 275; June 1927, p. 365; August 1927, p. 481; February 1928, p. 110; April 1928, p. 249; June 1928, p. 364; October 1928, p. 624; December 1928, p. 745; March 1929, pgs. 185, 187; June 1929, p. 388; August 1929, pgs. 592, 593; October 1929, p. 701; June 1930, p. 405; November 1930, p. 767; January 1931, p. 48; February 1931, p. 136; May 1931, p. 351; March 1932, p. 196; July 1932, pgs. 463-464, 471, 472; December 1932, p. 785; January 1933, pgs. 51, 52; February 1933, pgs. 125, 126; March 1933, p. 202; May 1933, p. 381; October 1933, p. 709; February 1934, pgs. 131-132; March 1934, p. 199; December 1934, p. 827; February 1935, p. 108; October 1935, pgs. 744, 746; November 1935, p. 802; April 1936, p. 301; May 1936, p. 409; June 1936, pgs. 456, 466, July 1936, pgs. 576, 589; September 1936, p. 779; November 1936, p. 927; December 1936, pgs. 984, 1019; February 1937, p. 132; May 1937, pgs. 435-436; June 1937, pgs. 535-536, 549; July 1937, pgs. 623, 649; December 1937, pgs. 1126, 1174; May 1938, p. 468; June 1938, p. 558; November 1939, p. 916; May 1953, p. 472.

"The American Numismatic Society," *The Numismatist*, XXVIII (February 1915), p. 60-61.

American Philatelic Association. *The American Philatelist*. II (October 1887-September 1888). Philadelphia: The Literary Board of the American Philatelic Association, 1888.

———. "Annual Convention," *The Western Philatelist*, I (September 1887), pgs. 162-187.

Ames, F. H. Jr. "Classifying Encased Postage Stamps," *S.P.A. Journal*, XV (June 1953), p. 501.

———. "Encased Postage Stamps," *S.P.A. Journal*, XV (March 1953), pgs. 329-331,

———. "A New Encased Stamp," *The Numismatist*, LXVI (May 1953), p. 472.

"ANA Votes Grant for Numismatic Book Series," *Coin World*, March 13, 1985, p. 3.

"Another Major Encased Stamp Collection Sold," *Bank Note Reporter*, July 1988, p. 6.

"Answers to Correspondents," *The Coin Collector's Journal*, I (May 1876), p. 96.

Anthon, Charles E. "Salutatory," *American Journal of Numismatics*, II (May 1867), p. 2.

"Arbitration – Confirmation of Award – Intervention," *New York Law Journal*, August 12, 1983, p. 1.

"Arbitration. Confirmation of Award." *New York Law Journal*. August 12, 1983, pgs. 1, 13.

Aston, Joe. "Special Receptions . . . Will Mark Centennial," Cincinnati newspaper clipping, n. d. Cincinnati Historical Society.

Ashbrook, Stanley. "The 'Premiere Gravures' of 1861," *American Philatelic Miscellany*: Selections from *The Stamp Specialist*, pgs. 129-130. Arr. by Susan M. McDonald. Lawrence [MA]: Quarterman Publications, 1976.

"Auction Report of R. R. Bogert & Co.," *Philatelic Journal of America*, V (July 1889), p. 211.

Aue, Gustav [ed.]. "New York Notes," *The Collector's Ledger*, Vol. VI No. 10, Whole No. 38 (January 1889).

"Ayer, Frederick," *Who Was Who in America*, Vol. 1 (1897-1942), p. 39. Chicago: Marquis Who's Who Inc., 1943, 1968.

"Ayer, Frederick Fanning," *Who Was Who in America*, Vol. 1 (1897-1942), p. 39. Chicago: Marquis Who's Who Inc., 1943, 1968.

"Ayer, Frederick Jr.," *Contemporary Authors*. Vol. 73-76. Detroit: Gale Research Co., 1976.

"Ayer, James Cook," *Appleton's Cyclopedia of American Biography*. Vol. I, p. 123. New York: Appleton Co., 1891.

"Ayer, James Cook," *Dictionary of American Biography*. Vol. I, p. 450-451. New York: Scribner's, 1944.

"Ayer, James Cook," *Who Was Who in America*. Historical Volume (1607-1896), p. 101. Chicago: Marquis Who's Who Inc., 1963, 1967.

[Balbaton, Richard J.] "New Variety of Encased Postage Stamp Found," *The Essay-Proof Journal*, No. 155 (Summer 1982), p. 127.

[Balbaton, Richard J.] "New Variety of Encased Postage Stamp Found," *Paper Money*, XXI (September-October, 1982), p. 236.

Barnard, B. W. "Use of Private Tokens for Money in the United States," *Quarterly Journal of Economics*, XXXI (August 1917), pgs. 600-634.

"Barnes, Demas." *Who Was Who in America*. Historical Volume (1607-1896), p. 41. Chicago: Marquis Who's Who Inc., 1963, 1967.

Barr, Jere. Hess. "Insurance Cancellations on Civil War Revenues, 1862-1871," *The Stamp Specialist*. Black Book, pgs. 69-93. New York: H. L. Lindquist, 1945.

"A Bit of History Indicative of the Growth of Cincinnati," Cincinnati *Enquirer*, December 2, 1921.

Bond, Beverley W. "Jacob Burnet," *Dictionary of American Biography*. Ed. by Allen Johnson. Vol. III. New York: Charles Scribner's Sons, 1929.

"Bookmarks," *The Numismatist*, CVIII (March 1995), p. 349. [brief announcement and review of the present work]

"Boston Civil War Substitute Currency," *The Numismatist*, XXIX (April 1916), p. 183.

"Boutwell, George Sewall," *Dictionary of American Biography*. Edited by Allen Johnson. Vol. I, pgs. 489-490. New York: Charles Scribner's Sons, 1927, 1936.

"Boutwell, George Sewall," *Who Was Who in America*. Vol. I (1897-1942), p. 120: Chicago: Marquis Who's Who Inc., 1963, 1967.

Bowers, Q. David. "Adjunctives Appealing," *Coin World*, April 25, 1979, p. 70.

———. "I Don't Touch the Hard Stuff – I Only Drink Drake's Plantation Bitters," Bowers and Merena Galleries. *Rare Coin Review*, No. 50 (January 1984), pgs. 71-77. [This article was reprinted in *Coins*, XXXI (August 1984), pgs. 62-67.]

[Bowers, Q. David]. "Encased Postage Stamps," Bowers and Merena Galleries. *George Hatie Collection*, August 3-5, 1983, pgs. 168-169.

[Bowers, Q. David]. "The James F. Ruddy Collection of Encased Postage Stamps," Bowers and Merena Galleries. *Rare Coin Review*, No. 50 (January 1984), pgs. 78-80.

Bowers, Q. David. "Musings About an Encased Postage Stamp," *The Numismatist*, XCVI (October 1983), pgs. 2070-2073.

———. "Numismatic Americana," *The History of U.S. Coinage as Illustrated by the Garrett Collection*. Wolfeboro [NH]: Bowers and Merena Galleries, 1979.

[Bowers, Q. David]. "Some Casual Reading About Encased Postage Stamps," *Rare Coin Review*, No. 63 (Winter 1986), pgs. 78-80.

Bowers and Merena Galleries. "A Complete Collection of Encased Postage Stamps," *Special Coin Letter No. 1065*, July 27, 1988, pgs. 2, 3, 5.

———. "A Remarkable Offering of Encased Postage Stamps," *Linn's Stamp News*, August 29, 1988, p. 33.

Boyer, Aden Scott. "A Little News From . . .," *The Numismatist*, Vol. XXXV (June 1922), p. 296.

———. "A Little News From . . .," *The Numismatist*, Vol. XXXV (August 1922), p. 381.

[Bradfield, Elston, ed.]. "Nine Cent Strip of Dubious Origin," *The Numismatist*, LX (July 1947), p. 519.

Brand, H. A. "Card Money," *Cincinnati Numismatically*. Cincinnati: Cincinnati Numismatic Association, 1931.

Bush, Conrad. "Civil War Postal Currency Envelopes," *American Philatelist*, CIV (August 1990), pgs. 714-715.

Bushnell, George D. "Chicago's Leading Men's Clubs," *Chicago History*, XI (Summer 1982), pgs. 78-88.

———. "Chicago's Miraculous Patent Medicines," *Chicago History*, III (Fall 1974), pgs. 78-87.

Carroll, Bob. "For the Hall of Fame, Twelve Good Men," *The National Pastime*, IV (Winter 1985), pgs. 14-27.

Carson, Gerald. "Hair Today, Gone Tomorrow," *American Heritage*, XVII (February 1966), pgs. 42-47.

———. "Sweet Extract of Hokum," *American Heritage*, XXII (June 1971), pgs. 18-27.

Casterline, Gail Farr. "A Preview of Chicago History Galleries," *Chicago History*, VII (Winter 1978-79), pgs. 250ff.

"Causes of Bank Failures," *Journal of the Canadian Bankers' Association*, XVII (October 1909 to July 1910), pgs. 48-49. Montreal: Gazette Printing Co., 1910.

Chase, Carroll. "The 1861 Issue," in *Classic U.S. Stamps*, pgs. 23-29. Shrub Oak [NY]: Herman Herst Jr., 1962.

Chase, Pliny E. "Trade Currency Illicitly Circulating During the War, Catalog of," *Proceedings of the American Philosophical Society*, IX (September 18, 1863), pgs. 241-258.

"Christian Henry Buhl," *America's Successful Men of Affairs*. Edited by Henry Hall. Vol. 2, pgs. 127-128. New York: The New York Tribune, 1896.

"City is Given Lease on Oakdale Park," Salina [KS] *Evening Journal*, April 8, 1922.

"Civil War Stamp Volume Soon to be Released," *Numismatic News*, June 6, 1995, xerox clipping. [a brief notice of the imminent release of the present volume]

"Claflin," *Biographical History of Barton County, Kansas*, p. 312. Great Bend [KS]: Great Bend Tribune, 1912.

"Claim $100,000 Value for 1921 Canada Half, *World Coin News*, June 10, 1975, p. 25. [re. Weir & Larminie encased stamps]

Coatsworth, A. Earl. "United States Encased Postage Stamps – With Descriptive Checklist of All Varieties Known to Date," *Numisma*, II (June and October 1961), pgs. 27-31 and 41-46.

Coburn, Frederick W. "James Cook Ayer," *Dictionary of American Biography*. Vol. I, p. 450-451. New York: Charles Scribner's Sons, 1944.

Coffing, Courtney. "Gault Patent: Encasements Fit in Numismatic, Philatelic, Paper Money Areas," *Numismatic Scrapbook Magazine*, XXXIV (September 1968), pgs. 1438-1441, (October 1968), pgs. 1584-1587.

Cooper, Tom E. "Early Day Barton County," *Barton County* [KS] *Historical Society Collections*, I (Spring 1970), pgs. 165-166.

Copple, O. A. "History of Claflin," *The Claflin* [KS] *Clarion*, June 19, 26; July 3, 10, 17; August 7, 14, 1947), p. 1.

Criswell, Grover. "Collecting Trends in Obsolete Currency," in *America's Currency, 1789-1866*, pgs. 51-56. Published proceedings of the Second "Coinage of the America's Conference" at the American Numismatic Society, October 31-November 2, 1985. New York: American Numismatic Society, 1985.

Cummings, Ken. "The Cigarette Makers: How They Get Away With Murder . . . With the Press as an Accessory," *The Washington Monthly*, XVI (April 1984), pgs. 14-24.

Curto, James J., Fuld, Dr. George, and Hoch, Alfred D. "Sutler Tokens Rarities and Valuations," *TAMS Journal*, IV (July-August 1964), pgs. 143-145, 154.

Davidson, Robert L. D. "APS: The First Century," "*American Philatelist*, C (January 1986), pgs. 29-35, and (April 1986), pgs. 321-324.

Davis R. Edward. "Meetings of Numismatic Societies and Clubs," *The Numismatist*, XXXII (January 1919), p. 32.

———. "The Circulating Medium of the Civil War Period," *The Numismatist*, LIII (July 1940), pgs. 477-481.

Davis, Stephen M. "Of the Class Denominated Princely: The Tremont House Hotel," *Chicago History*, (Spring 1982), pgs. 26-36.

Davison, Peter. "The Hub of the Solar System," *American Heritage*, XL (April 1989), pgs. 54-65.

Deeds, W. E. "To Exchange," *The Numismatist*, XIX (November 1906), p. 380.

Deisher, Beth. "Opening Numismatic Doors" [an editorial commending the ANA board's approval of a research grant for the present work], *Coin World*, March 13, 1985, p. 4.

Denly's of Boston. "Encased Postage," *Bank Note Reporter*, May 1993, p. 7.

———. "Encased Postage," *Bank Note Reporter*, October 1993, p. 24.

———. "Encased Postage Listing," Fax transmission November 22, 1994. Typescript, 13 pages.

"Drake, John Burroughs," *Who Was Who in America*. Historical Volume (1607-1896), p. 225. Chicago: A.

N. Marquis Co., 1967.

"Dr. James Cook Ayer," *America's Successful Men*. pgs. 38-40.

"Drowne, Henry Russell. "U.S. Postage Stamps as Necessity War Money," *American Journal of Numismatics*, LII (1918).

———. "U.S. Postage Stamps as Necessity War Money," *Mekeel's Weekly Stamp News*, XXXIV (August 14, 1920), pgs. 435-436.

———. "U.S. Postage Stamps as Necessity War Money," *The Numismatist*, XXXIII (May 1920), pgs. 181-187.

[Drowne, Henry Russell]. "Very Rare Private Paper Necessity Money." *The Numismatist*, XXVI (July 1913), pgs. 350-351.

Duffield, Frank G. [ed.]. "Mr. Drowne's Paper on Necessity War Money, *The Numismatist*, XXXIII (May 1920), p. 203.

Early American Numismatics [Dana Linnett]. "The Largest Specialized Offering of Rare Encased Postage Stamps," *Coin World* April 6, 1988, p. 38 and April 13, 1988, p. 24.

"Ellis, John Washington." *Who Was Who in America*. Vol. IV, pg. 285. Chicago: Marquis Who's Who Inc., 1968.

"Encased Frenzy Continues," *Bank Note Reporter*, July 1988, p. 1.

"Encased Postage Active," *Coin World*, December 12, 1984, p. 42.

"Encased Postage Featured in Bowers & Ruddy ANA Paper Section," *Bank Note Reporter*, August, 1981, p. 14.

"Encased Postage In Sale," *Coin World*, April 18, 1984, p. 75.

"Encased Postage Stamp Forgery Donated to ANACS Reference Collection," *The Numismatist*, XCVII (November 1984), pages 2332-2333.

"Encased Postage Stamps," *Coin Prices*, (July 1985), pgs. 75-78.

"Encased Postage Stamps a Buyer's Market," *Bank Note Reporter*, January 1988, p. 8.

"Encased Postage Stamps Flooding Market," *Bank Note Reporter*, January 1988, p. 1.

"Encased Stamps Subject of Coming Bowers-Merena Book," *Bank Note Reporter*, August 1988, p. 6.

"EPS Research Collection Offered in Fixed Price List," *Bank Note Reporter*, July 1988, p. 6.

Evans, Meryle R. "Knickerbocker Hotels and Restaurants," *New-York Historical Society Quarterly*, XXXVI (October 1952), pgs. 376-409.

Falkner, R. P. "Private Issue of Token Coins," *Political Science Quarterly*, XVI (June 1901), pgs. 303-327.

Ferguson, J. Douglas. "Weir & Larminie Encased Stamp," *The Coin Collector's Journal*, New Series, VII (September 1940), p. 264, and (December 1940), p. 331.

"Feuchtwanger, Lewis," *Appleton's Cyclopedia of American Biography*. Edited by James Grant Wilson and John Fiske, Vol. II, pgs. 445-446. New York: D. Appleton & Co. 1888.

"Firm Publishes New Book on U.S. Encased Postage Stamps," *Coin World*, August 9, 1989, p. 46.

Foley, Kevin. *Catalog and Price List of Postage Stamp Envelopes*, May 24, 1985. 8 pages.

Folger, [Rober]t Gardner, "Fourth and Main: Corner Lot, $4," newspaper clipping, n.d. Cincinnati Historical Society.

Ford, John J. "U.S. Encased Postage Stamps: Background and Alterative Skullduggery," *The Numismatist*, XCVII (January 1984), pgs. 20-32.

———. "Numismatic Americana: The Confederate Cent," *The Coin Collector's Journal*, (January-February 1951), pgs. 9-14.

———. "The Story of the Confederate Cent," *Coin World*, January 19, 1962, pgs. 60-61. [The article was an updating of the similarly titled entry above.]

Forrer, L. "Bailey Banks and Biddle," *Biographical Dictionary of Medalists*. Vol. VII, Supplement A-L, pg. 40. New York: Burt Franklin, 1923, 1970.

"Fractional Currency Was Solution to Coin Shortage," *Bank Note Reporter*, January 1986, p. 12.

"Frederick Ayer," *America's Successful Men*. Henry Hall ed., pgs. 37-38. New York: New York Tribune, 1896.

"Frederick Ayer Dead," *The Numismatist*, XXXI (April 1918), p. 174.

Frey, Albert R. "Auction Records of the Encased Postage Stamps," *The Numismatist*, XV (May 1902), pgs. 139-142; (June 1902), pgs. 170-172.

———. "A Dictionary of Numismatic Names, Their Official and Popular Designations," *American Journal of Numismatics*, Vol. L (1916).

Fritz, Arthur. "Life of Noted Diesinker Reported by . . .," *Coin World*, June 14, 1963, p. 55.

———. Letter to the Token Editor, *Coin World*, September 6, 1963, p. 68.

Fuld, George. "Civil War Emergency Money Issues Total into Thousands," *Coin World*, March 23, 1961, p. 50.

Fuld, Melvin. "Scovill Manufacturing Company of Waterbury, Connecticut," *Journal of the Civil War Token Society*, II (Fall 1968), pgs. 3-6; (Winter 1968), pgs. 3-7; III (Spring 1969), pgs. 12-17.

Gale, David M., and Gale, Charlotte, "A Study and Catalog of 19th-Century Photographic Tokens," *The Numismatist*, XCVII (May 1984), pgs 912-932.

Gardner, Thomas P. "The Munn & Co. Shellcard," *TAMS Journal*, XXIX (June 1989), p. 89.

Gates, Paul Wallace. "Land and Credit Problems in Underdeveloped Kansas," *The Kansas Historical Quarterly*, XXXI (Spring 1965), pgs. 41-61.

"Genealogical [re. marriage of John I. Brown]," *Boston Evening Transcript*, August 2, 1905.

Gladfelter, David D. "Attribution: The Detective Work of Token Collecting," *Journal of the Civil War Token Society*, III (Summer 1969), pgs. 8-10.

———. "Civil War Die Sinkers and Their Cards," *Journal of the Civil War Token Society*, IV (Summer 1970), pgs. 7-12; (Fall 1970), pgs. 8-13.

———. "Civil War Die Sinkers and Their Cards: An Update," *Copperhead Courier*, XIV (Winter 1980), pgs. 94-103.

———. "The Largest Civil War Token." *Journal of the Civil War Token Society*, VIII (Summer 1974), pgs. 48-49.

———. "The Matthews Civil War Cardboard Check Hoard," *Journal of the Civil War Token Society*, VIII (Spring 1974), pgs. 12-14.

Glazer, Len. "Encased Postage Stamps," *Coin Prices*, No. 97 (July 1984), pgs. 87, 90-93.

———. "Encased Postage Stamps." *Standard Catalogue of U.S. Paper Money*, pgs. 177-183. Iola [WI]: Krause Publications, 1981.

Gould, Maurice. "Encased Postage Stamps Popular Necessity Money During Civil War," *Numismatic News Weekly*, April 26, 1975, p. 28.

Graham, Richard. "Stamps Served as Money During Civil War," *Linn's Stamp News*, August 22, 1988, p. 8.

Graham, Richard B. "Chicago Double Circle and Local Post Marks With Initials," in *Chicago Postal History*, edited by Harvey M. Karlen. Chicago: Collector's Club of Chicago, 1971.

"Green, Ben G.," *The Numismatist*, XIX (July 1906), p. 248.

"Green, Ben G." obituary, *The Numismatist*, XXVII (February 1914), pgs. 68-69.

"Green, Ben G. [Tribute To]," *The Numismatist*, XXVII (March 1914), p. 135.

Green, Ben G. "Encased Postage Stamps," *The Numismatist*, XXV (September 1912), p. 299-300.

———. "U.S. Necessity Money," *The Numismatist*, XVIII (October 1905), pgs. 307-311.

Gregory, Charles. "Encased Postage Stamps," *The Philatelic Gazette*, Vol. IV No. 46 (May 1888), p. 116.

———. "Encased U.S. Postage Stamps," *The American Philatelist*, Vol. II (October 1887-September 1888), unnumbered advertising pages bound in volume.

———. "The U.S. Encased Postage Stamps," *Philatelic Journal of America*, V (January 1889), pgs. 25-26, and (April 1889), pgs. 136-138.

Greve, Charles Theodore, "George Washington McAlpin," pgs. 525-527. *Centennial History of Cincinnati and Representative Citizens*. Vol. 2. Chicago: Biographical Publishing Co., 1904.

———. "John Shillito," pgs. 164-165. *Centennial History of Cincinnati and Representative Citizens*. Vol. 2. Chicago: Biographical Publishing Co., 1904.

Griffenhagen, George B. "Postage Stamps as an Advertising Medium for Drugs and Drug Sundries," *The Congress Book*, Thirty-Fifth American Philatelic Congress, October 31-November 2, 1969, pgs. 19-42. Federalsburg [MD]: American Philatelic Congress.

Gros, Julian. "The Joseph R. Carpenter Presentation Volume of Revenue Proofs, *The Essay-Proof Journal*, XXVI (Summer 1969), pgs. 128-129.

Hahn, Manuel. "U.S. Encased Postage Stamps," *Scott's Monthly Journal*, (October 1937).

Hammond, Bray. "The North's Empty Purse, 1861-1862," *American Historical Review*, LXVII (October 1961), pgs. 1-18.

Hall, Tom. "Once More into the Drake Dear Friends," *Chicago Tribune Magazine*, November 8, 1970, pgs. 36-44, 52, 55, 57.

Hardten, Dillie and Kimpler, Mary. "Recollections of Claflin," Great Bend [KS] *Daily Tribune*, July 15, 1962.

Hardten, Reta June. "Claflin is Healthy Industrial Town," Great Bend [KS] *Daily Tribune*, August 10, 1951.

Harris, Jon. "Store Card Chatter," *Journal of the Civil War Token Society*, IX (Summer 1975), p. 75.

Harris, R. Winston. "A Coin of A Different Stamp," *New Jersey Numismatic Journal*, Garden State Numismatic Association, IV (3rd Quarter 1978), p. 9.

[Haseltine, John]. "Address by Captain John W. Haseltine" to the 1908 American Numismatic Association Convention, *The Numismatist*, XXI (October-November 1908), pgs. 324-326.

Hatcher, Robert S. "Notes for U.S. Philatelists," *Philatelic Journal of America*, IV (April 1888), p. 121.

Henley, Helen. "Woman's Plea for Vanilla Starts A Business; Joseph Burnett Launched Firm 100 Years Ago," *Christian Science Monitor*, December 26, 1945.

Herst, Herman Jr. "Boston Machinist Devised Encased Postage Stamps," *Coin World*, July 24, 1974, pgs. 40-41.

———. "It Looks Like a Postage Stamp," *S.P.A. Journal*, XXXIV (June 1972), pgs. 591-598.

———. "Stamps Used As Money During Civil War," *Fractional Currency Collectors Board Newsletter*, March 1991. [reprint of article from *Linn's Stamp News*]

Hewitt, Lee F. "Contents of a Civil War Period Church Collection," *The Numismatist*, LV (November 1942), p. 792.

[Hewitt, Lee F.]. "Feuchtwanger Bid on Making Three Cent Nickel Blanks," *Numismatic Scrapbook Magazine*, XXIX (February 1963), p. 318.

Hickman, Russell K. "A Little Satire on Emigrant Aid," *The Kansas Historical Quarterly*, VIII (November 1939), pgs. 342-349.

———. "Speculative Activities of the Emigrant Aid Company," *The Kansas Historical Quarterly*, IV (August 1935), pgs. 235-267.

"High-Grade Encased Postage Stamps Change Hands in California Auction," *Bank Note Reporter*, December 1988, p. 19.

["A History of Claflin"], in "Kansas History as Published in the Press," *Kansas Historical Quarterly*, XV (November 1947), p. 408.

Holcombe, H. "Anglo-American Drug Co.," *Stamp and Cover Collectors Review*, I (April 1937), pgs. 91-93.

———. "Curtis & Brown Manufacturing Co.," *Weekly Philatelic Gossip*, XXXIII (February 14, 1942), pgs.

610-611.

------. "Demas S. Barnes & Company," *Weekly Philatelic Gossip*, XXXIV (April 25, 1942), pgs. 153-154, and (May 9, 1942), pgs. 202-207.

------. "J. C. Ayer & Company," *Scott's Monthly Journal*, XVIII (December 1937), pgs. 344-349, (January 1938), pgs. 394-398.

------. "Jeremiah Curtis & Son," *Weekly Philatelic Gossip*, XXXIII (February 14, 1942), pgs. 608-609.

------. "John F. Henry," *Scott's Monthly Journal*, XXIII (May 1942), pgs. 88-91, and (July 1942), pgs. 164-167.

------. "John I. Brown & Son," *Weekly Philatelic Gossip*, XXV (September 18, 1937), pgs. 5-6.

------. "Joseph Burnett & Company," *Weekly Philatelic Gossip*, XXIV (July 24, 1937), pgs. 653-654.

------. "Lyon Manufacturing Company," *Weekly Philatelic Gossip*, XXXIV (July 11, 1942), pgs. 417-418.

------. "P. H. Drake & Company," *Weekly Philatelic Gossip*, XXXIV (June 13, 1942), pgs. 321-324.

Holcombe, Henry W. "Match and Medicine Stamp History." *The Stamp Collectors' Round Table*. Edited by Foster W. Loso. New York: Frederick A. Stokes Co., 1937.

Holli, Melvin G., and d'A Jones, Peter [eds.]. "Christian H. Buhl" and "Frederick Buhl," pgs. 48-50. *Biographical Dictionary of American Mayors, 1820-1980*. Westport [CT]: Greenwood Press, 1981.

Holliday, Joseph E. "The Cincinnati Philharmonic and Hopkins Hall Orchestras, 1856-1868," *Bulletin of the Cincinnati Historical Society*, Vol. XXVI (April 1968), pgs. 169-173.

Holt, Glen E. "Private Plans for Public Spaces: The Origins of Chicago's Park System, 1850-1875," *Chicago History*, VIII (Fall 1979), pgs. 173-184.

Homren, Wayne. "Allegheny City: Gone But Not Forgotten," *Copperhead Courier*, XVIII (Summer 1984), pgs. 9 ff.

------. "Collecting Encased Postage Stamps," *Proceedings of the Western Pennsylvania Numismatic Society*, edited by E. Tomlinson Fort, I (June 1994), pgs. 47-57.

------. "Searching For Elusive Coin Books," *The Asylum* [Journal of the Numismatic Bibliomania Society], (Summer 1984), pgs. 14 ff.

Hoober, Richard T. "Enigma of the Confederate Cent," *The Numismatist*, LXIX (September 1956), pgs. 989-991

------. "Enveloped Postage Stamps," *The Numismatist*, LXXIV (April 1961), pgs. 457-460; (May 1961), 602-608.

Huff, Wayne. "Early Day History of Claflin," Claflin *Clarion*, July 12, 1956, p. D-2.

Hughes, Brent H. " Cardboard Currency," *Paper Money*, X (Fall 1971), pgs. 104-107; XI (Spring 1972), p. 28; (Fall 1972), p. 149.

"Indians Killed Pioneer Resident of Claflin Area," Great Bend [KS] *Daily Tribune*, May 7, 1961.

"Imitating Gault's Encased Postage Stamp Idea," *The Numismatist*, XXXIV (June 1921), p. 247.

Inbinder, Sheila. "The Drake: More than a Rehab . . . A Complete Rebirth," *Realty & Building*, April 27, 1985, pgs. 64-65.

Jacob, C. Albert. "Cardboard Money of the Civil War," *The Numismatist*, L (December 1937), pgs. 1097-1100.

"The James Collection Given to the Buffalo Historical Society," *American Journal of Numismatics*, XXVIII (October 1893), p. 48.

Jenney, Charles E. "Proprietary Cancellations," *The Adhesive*, II (March 1901), pgs. 43-44, (August 1901), pgs. 118-119, (October 1901), p. 145, (December 1901), p. 176.

------. "Stamps as Advertisers," *The American Collector*, II No. 6 New Series (October 1897), pgs. 111-112.

Johns, Roy W. "Philatelic Patents," *The American Philatelist*, LIII (November 1939), pgs. 124-127.

Johnson, D. Wayne. "Dearth in Literature: Civil War Numismatic Books Scarce," *Coin World*, March 23, 1961, p. 75.

Johnson, Samuel A. "The Emigrant Aid Company," The *Kansas Historical Quarterly*, I (November 1932), pgs. 429-441.

Jones, John F. "Encased Postage Stamps: A Necessity Money of the U. S.," *The Numismatist*, LII (August 1939), pgs. 627-635.

------. "Makers of Encased Postage Stamps," *The Numismatist*, LII (September 1939), pgs. 709-711.

------. "More Information on Encased Postage Stamps," *The Numismatist*, LII (September 1939), pgs. 726, 728.

------. "Supply and Demand for Postage Stamps in 1862," *The Numismatist*, LII (September 1939), p. 728.

"Joseph Burnett" in "Necrology of Historical Genealogical Society, 1895." *Proceedings of New England Historic Genealogical Society*, Vol. IL, (1895), p. 85.

"Journal Features Encased Stamps," *Coin World*, December 13, 1963, p. 90.

Kagin, Donald. "Quarterly Currency Market Review," various issues.

"Kagin's Presents . . . the Finest-Ever Collection of Encased Postage!" *Coin World*, September 2, 1987, p. 29.

"Kagin Auction Tops $1.6 Million Mark," *Coin World*, February 24, 1988, p. 15.

Kasten, Marie A. "Joseph Burnett," *Dictionary of American Biography*. Vol 2. pgs. 299-300. New York: Charles Scribner's Sons, 1944.

Kilpatrick, James J. "What Counts the Most for Those Who Live on the Road?" Syndicated Column, Universal Press Syndicate, in Fort Worth *Star-Telegram*, December 25, 1985, p. 18A.

Kincaid, Robert. "A Guide to Encased Postage Stamps,"

Currency Market Review, IV (March 1983), p. 1.
———. "Original Numismatic Research Possible," *Coin World*, June 22, 1983, p. 4.
Klein, Frederic Shriver. "The Civil War Was A Pitchman's Paradise," *Civil War Times Illustrated*, II (June 1963), pgs. 30-33.
Klein, Maury. "The North at War," pgs. 364-407. *Shadows of the Storm*. Vol. I of "The Image of War, 1861-1865." The National Historical Society, ed. by William C. Davis. Garden City [NY]: Doubleday & Co., 1981.
Konwiser, Harry M. "Encased Postage Stamps," and "Encased Stamps," *American Philatelic Dictionary*, p. 43. New York: Jacques Minkus, 1947.
Kubal, George. "Encased Postage and Postage Stamp Envelopes," *The Texas Philatelist*, XXXI (July-August 1983), pgs. 2-3.
La Marre, Thomas. "Feuchtwanger's Silver," *Coinage*, XX (December 1984), pgs. 82, 84.
———. "Gault's Better Idea," *Bank Note Reporter*, October 1988, p. 10.
Lemke, Bob. "Col. Drake's Bunkum Bank Note Strikes Again; Patent Medicine Promotion Makes Collector Ill," *Best of the Bank Note Reporter*, p. 11, insert in Bank *Note Reporter*, Issue No. 100 (May 1981). [Originally published November 1979, p. 10]
Limpert, Frank A. "The Necessity for Having Postage and Fractional Currency," *The Numismatist*, LX (January 1947), pgs. 10-15.
"Lot Owners in Forest Home Cemetery, Milwaukee, 1871," *Wisconsin State Genealogical Society Newsletter*, XIX (April 1973).
Lowe, David. "Greek Revival Architecture in Chicago," *Chicago History*, IV (Fall 1975), pgs. 157-166.
"Lowell of Today," Lowell *Daily Citizen*, 1893.
"Lower Court Confirms PNG Arbitration Award," *Coin World*, September 14, 1983, p. 13.
Mabbott, Thomas O. "Cardboard Scrip from Shushan, New York," *Numismatic Review*, III (October 1946), p. 124.
Malpass, George N. "Philadelphia's Part in the Civil War," *The Stamp Specialist*. Coral Book, pgs. 109-124. New York: H. L. Lindquist, 1945.
Markoff, Fred R. "Currency and Banking In Illinois Before 1865," *Journal of Illinois Historical Society*, LII (Autumn 1959), pgs. 365-418.
Mason, Eben [ed.]. *Coin Collector's Herald*, Vol. II (June 1880 to March 1881).
——— [ed.]. *Numismatic Visitor*, Vol. I (January, 1881).
"McAlpin's Department Store 100 Years Old; Modern Concern Had Start as Wholesaler," Cincinnati *Enquirer*, February 3, 1952.
["McAlpin, George W."] *The City of Cincinnati and Its Resources*, p. 36. Cincinnati: Cincinnati Times Star, 1891.
McCrea, Roswell Cheney. "John Washington Ellis," *Dictionary of American Biography*. Vol. IV, p. 106. New York: Charles Scribner's Sons, 1944.
Mehl, B. Max. "Encased Postage Stamps," *The Star Coin Encyclopedia and Premium Catalog*, pgs. 76-80, 184-185. Ft. Worth: The Numismatic Company of Texas, 1932.
———. "Encased Postage Stamps Used as Money, 1861-1865," *Star Coin Book Junior*. 15th edition. Ft. Worth: by the author, n. d.
"Miles Encased Postage Brings $1,950 Bid," *Coin World*, October 5, 1983, p. 76.
"Milwaukee Specialist Offers Postage Stamp Envelopes," *Coin World*, June 12, 1985, p. 72.
Munsey, Cecil. "Encased Postage Stamps," *The Western Collector*, VI (May 1968), pgs. 39-40.
Murray, William Bain [Col. Bill]. "Reed Feature Proves Enjoyable Reading," *Coin World*, November 23, 1977, p. 4.
"The N. & G. Taylor Co.," *The Numismatist*, XXIV (September 1911), pgs. 335-336.
Nelson, Frank. "A Different Way to Make Money," *Hobbies*, LXXXIX (February 1983), p. 69.
"New Galleries Opened in Shillito's Store, Reminiscent of Rotunda 40 Years Ago," Cincinnati *Commercial Tribune*, May 2, 1923.
Newman, Eric P. "Both History, Mystery Surround Confederate Half Dollar and Cent," *Coin World*, March 23, 1961, pgs. 6-7.
"Nine Cent Strip of Dubious Origin," *The Numismatist*, (July 1947), p. 519.
Norton, Robert E. "Scovill's Smart Locks Click," *Fortune*, CXX (September 17, 1984), pgs. 51-52.
"November Encased Auction Shows Buyers Waiting for Bigger, Better," *Bank Note Reporter*, January 1988, p. 8.
O'Bleness, Linley. "History of Claflin," Kiowa County [KS] *Signal*, July 11, 1973.
"Odd Paper Money Put on Exhibition," *The Philatelic West*, LXII (April 30, 1914), [no pagination].
"On the Memphis Scene," *Bank Note Reporter*, August 1986, p. 10.
"Our City Business," Cincinnati *Miscellany*, March 1846, pgs. 357-358.
Owen, David. "The Cigarette Companies: How They Get Away With Murder, Part II," *The Washington Monthly*, XVII (March 1985), pgs. 48-54.
"Parties Agree to a Delay," *Coin World*, March 23, 1983, p. 20.
"Parva Ne Pereant," *American Journal of Numismatics*, XIII (January 1879), p. 68.
Perl, Arnold. "Ingenius 'Metallic Currency' Patented Century Ago by Gault," *Coin World*, August 17, 1962 [n.b. centennary of patent], pgs. 68-69.
———. "Notes on U. S. Encased Postage," *The Numismatist*, LXXIX (June 1966), pgs. 707-716.
———. "On the Joys of Specialized Collecting," *Stack's Public Auction Sale*, December 5-6, 1969 [Arnold Perl collection, and others], pgs. 76-77.
Pilsbry, Henry August. "George Sewall Boutwell," *Dictionary of American Biography*. Vol. I, edited by

Allen Johnson, pgs. 489-490. New York: Charles Scribner's Sons, 1927, 1936.

President, Canadian Bankers' Association. "Address of... Delivered at the Eighth Annual Meeting of the Association," *Journal of the Canadian Bankers' Association*, VII (October 1899 to July 1900), pgs. 112-114. Toronto: Monetary Times Printing Co., 1900.

"Proof Book With Stamp Printing Dates," *Essay Proof Journal*, XII (October 1955), p. 212.

Puff, Richard A. (comp.). "Civil War Participation in the National Association," *Nineteenth Century Notes*, newsletter of the Nineteenth Century Committee, Society for American Baseball Research, December 1991, p. 1.

"Rare Encased Postage Stamps Highlight A.N.A. Paper Session," *Bank Note Reporter*, October 1981, p. 3.

"Rare U.S. Sets at San Diego Sale Include Complete EPS and Two Super Bowl Tickets," *Bank Note Reporter*, February 1988, p. 20.

Raymond, Wayte [ed.]. Editorial, *The Coin Collector's Journal*, New Series, VII (September 1940), p. 251. [re. fake encased stamps]

"Records of the Fort Street Presbyterian Church," *The Detroit Society for Genealogical Research Magazine*, Baptisms by R. R. Kellogg, XXI (Fall 1957), Membership List, XXI (Spring and Summer 1958).

Reed, Fred L. "Advertisers Quick to Use Lincoln Image: Sought to Use Portrait of 'Honest Abe' to Suggest Honesty," *Coin World*, March 7, 1990, pgs. 38, 41, 44. [Number 5 of the Lincoln series]

———. "Advertising, Hollywood Use Lincoln Portrait: Legendary Honesty Wins Lincoln Place on Checks, Advertisements," *Coin World*, March 14, 1990, pgs. 26, 34, 36, 40. [Number 6 of the Lincoln series]

———. "An Exercise in Removing History's Blinders," *Coin World*, November 3, 1976, p. 52.

———. "Berger-Burt Image of Lincoln Wide-Ranging: 'Universal Lincoln' Appearances Range from Stamps to Cards," *Coin World*, February 21, 1990, pgs. 24, 30, 34. [Number 3 of the Lincoln series]

———. *Civil War Encased Stamps: Auction Census Data, 1891-1988*. 2 vols. Part I: Aërated Bread – Drake; Part II: Ellis McAlpin – "Feuchtwanger." Dallas [TX]: Privately Printed, 1988. [n.b. containing 6,040 listings]

———. "Confederate Cent No Link to Confederacy: Researcher Believes Idler, Haseltine Commissioned Lovett," *Coin World*, October 18, 1989, pgs. 30, 38. [Number 3 of the Confederate Cent series, *n.b.* this unconventional view *is not* the one presented in the present work.]

———. "Cream City Lays Claim to Sands: Researcher Traces Encased Postage Stamps to Milwaukee Ale Brewers," *Coin World*, August 6, 1986 [American Numismatic Association Convention Special Issue], pgs. 1, 68, 90, 112. [This was the article which, misread by others, has led to the identification of the Sands' Ale piece with Milwaukee exclusive ly.]

———. "CSA Cent Remains Enigma to Collectors," *Coin World*, October 4, 1989, pgs. 1, 30, 48, 52. [Number 1 of the Confederate Cent series]

———. "Currency Riot Causes Change in Distribution: Officials Move to Chase Private Shinplasters from Circulation," *Coin World*, November 9, 1988, pgs. 70, 72-74. [Number 2 of the Postage Currency series. This article was reprinted in the *Fractional Currency Collector's Board Newsletter*, November, 1988, and again in May 1993. It was also excerpted in the *Two Hundred Year History of the Cincinnati Post Office*. Cincinnati: Bicentennial Committee U.S. Postal Service, 1994.]

———. "Doctor Feuchtwanger's Tokens," *Journal of the Civil War Token Society*, VIII No. 3 (Fall 1974), pgs. 96-98.

———. "Eastman's Token, Scrip Unlock Fascinating Tale," *Coin World*, August 18, 1976 [American Numismatic Association Convention Special Issue], pgs. 64, 70. [Number 1 of the Eastman series]

———. "Emergency Coinage Fulfills Civil War Needs," *Coin World*, August 4, 1976, pgs. 60, 62, 64, 66.

———. "Emergency Currency Fulfills Civil War Needs," *Copperhead Courier* [Journal of the Civil War Token Society], XI (Spring 1977), pgs. 18-22; (Summer 1977), pgs. 40-46; (Fall 1977), pgs. 91-94. [This series is a reprise of the 1976 *Coin World* article of a similar title.]

———. "Encased Postage Enigmatic Sign of Merchant: Pearce, Tolle & Holton Among Most Obscure of EPS Issuers," *Coin World*, July, 1988 [American Numismatic Association Convention Special Daily Issue No. 3], pgs. 26, 28.

———. "Encased Postage Stamps: The Collection of James F. Ruddy," in *The Collections of Admiral Oscar H. Dodson and Dr. Richard Collier*, Session Two. Lot Descriptions 2501-2531. Auctions by Bowers & Merena, Inc. June 19-21, 1984, pages 41-57. ["Thumbnail sketches and biographies of *all* the merchants who advertised [on] encased postage stamps . . . mark[ing] the *first time* such information has ever been found in one place," according to the catalog. Based on 11-page manuscript supplied the firm, February 1984.]

———. "Evans Encased Postage Becoming Clearer: Past Literature Often Misleading, Full of Incorrect Information," *Coin World*, August 9, 1989 [American Numismatic Association Convention Special Issue], pgs. 90, 96. [Number 1 of G. G. Evans series]

———. "Face Value: Lincoln Features Have Always Attracted Interest," *Coin World*, February 11, 1987, pgs. 1, 28, 30, 34, 38. [Number 1 of the Lincoln series]

———. "Gone With the Wind: Author's Attention to Details Clear in Novel About South," *Coin World*, August 26, 1987 [American Numismatic Association Convention Special Issue], pgs. 198, 200, 202, 208, 213. [Number 2 of the GWTW series]

———. "Gone With the Wind: Novel's Numismatic Reflections Accurate," *Coin World*, August 17, 1977 [American Numismatic Association Convention Special Issue], pgs. 98, 100. [Number 1 of the GWTW series]

———. "Hopkins Among Encased Postage Issuers; History Records Cincinnati Dry Goods Merchant As Risk Taker," *Coin World*, July, 1988 [American Numismatic Association Convention Special Daily Issue No. 2], pgs. 26, 28.

———. "Knowing Public's Book Tastes Key For Publisher: History of Mint Still Popular," *Coin World*, November 1, 1989, pgs. 108-111, 113. [Number 2 of the G. G. Evans series]

———. "Lincoln: Face of Lincoln an American Institution," *Coin World*, February 14, 1990, pgs. 1, 26, 30, 36, 42. [Number 2 of the Lincoln series]

———. "Lincoln Photos Fill Public's Need for Image: Universal Image Most Acceptable Photo of Martyred President," *Coin World*, March 21, 1990, pgs. 24, 28, 30. [Number 7 of the Lincoln series]

———. "Lincoln Popular Subject for Medallic Art: Commemorative Medals Frequently Use Universal Image," *Coin World*, March 28, 1990, pgs. 50, 52. [Number 8 of the Lincoln series]

———. "Lincoln Portrait Appears on Many Items: Early 19th Century Books Feature Illustrations Based on Portrait," *Coin World*, February 28, 1990, pgs. 54, 62. [Number 4 of the Lincoln series]

———. "Lovett Family Prolific Die Sinkers, Engravers: 'CSA Cent' Shares Designs With Robert Lovett Jr. Store Cards," *Coin World*, October 11, 1989, pgs. 1, 10, 12-14. [Number 2 of the Confederate Cent series]

———. "McAlpin, Cincinnati Virtually Synonymous: Early Merchant Leaves Behind Rich Numismatic Legacy," *Coin World*, July 20, 1988 [American Numismatic Association Convention Special Issue], pgs. 30, 38, 46, 52, 58, 78.

———. "Pliny Chase," *Journal of the Civil War Token Society*, IX No. 2 (Summer 1975), pgs. 40-48.

———. "Private Merchants Meet Cry for Small Change: Store Cards Fill Gap as Civil War Drives Coins Out of Circulation," *Coin World*, July, 1988 [American Numismatic Association Convention Special Daily Issue No. 1], pgs. 26, 28, 30.

———. "Rarest of the Rare: Claflin Encased Postage Stamps Deserve Special Place," *Coin World*, November 4, 1987, pgs. 1, 46, 52. [Original publication of this article was slated for issue No. 3 of the *New England Journal of Numismatics*, which unfortunately was never published.]

———. "Riot Erupts Over Shortage of Small Change: Storm Breaks in Cincinnati After Arrival of Postage Currency," *Coin World*, November 2, 1988, pgs. 16, 40, 48. [Number 1 of the Postage Currency series. This article was reprinted in the *Fractional Currency Collector's Board Newsletter*, November 1988, and again in May 1993. It was also excerpted in the *Two Hundred Year History of the Cincinnati Post Office*. Cincinnati: Bicentennial Committee U.S. Postal Service, 1994.]

———. "Shades of the Blue and Grey," *The Blue and the Grey* [Journal of the Civil War Philatelic Society]. IV (October 1964), p. 4; (November-December 1964), pgs. 8-9; V (January 1965), pgs. 5-6; (February 1965), p. 8.

———. "Shades of the Blue and Grey," *Linn's Weekly Stamp News*, April 26, 1965, p. 28.

———. "So What's New?" *Journal of the Civil War Token Society*, V (Spring 1971), pgs. 17-19.

———. "This One Thing I Do: Harvey Gridley Eastman's College Leaves Syngraphic Legacy," *Coin World*, June 17, 1987, pgs. 1, 26, 36, 60, 64, 66, 68, 69. [Number 2 of the Eastman series]

———. "Tokens Really Are History in Your Hands," *Coin World*, August 20, 1980 [American Numismatic Association Convention Special Issue], pgs. 122-123, 134.

"Reminiscences of James C. Ayer and the Town of Ayer," *New-England Historic Genealogical Register*, XXXIV (January 1880), p. 112.

Ressequie, Harry E. "A. T. Stewart's Marble Palace, the Cradle of the Department Store," *The New-York Historical Society Quarterly*, XLVIII (April 1964), 131-162.

Riley, Richard F. "Nostrum Wizard Cured Neither Disease Nor War," *American Philatelist*, IC (November 1985), pgs. 1008-1012.

Robertson, Jasper L. "United States Encased Postage Stamps," *The Essay-Proof Journal*, XX No. 2 (Whole No. 78, 1963), pgs. 71-79. [This is a reprint of an article which originally appeared in *Numismatic Scrapbook Magazine*, December 1959.]

"Robins buys Dr. Ouellet's Canadian Collection [re. Weir & Larminie encased stamps]," *Coin World*, April 23, 1975, p. 52.

Romain, Robert. "Private Mail Bid Very Scarce Early Americana [and] Encased Postage," *Coin World*, October 16, 1968, p. 61; October 23, 1968, p. 63; November 13, 1968, p. 63.

Rotundo, Barbara. "Mount Auburn Cemetery: A Proper Boston Institution," *Harvard Library Bulletin*, XXII (July 1974), pgs. 268-279.

Rulau, Russell. "Civil War Coins," *Coin World Guide to Coins*. Greenwich [CT]: Fawcett, 1964.

———. "Stock, Literature Scanty for Civil War Token Collectors," *Coin World*, March 23, 1961, pgs. 51, 54.

"San Diego Auction to Offer Unique 2-cent Experimental [encased stamp]," *Bank Note Reporter*, January 1988, p. 8.

Schell, J. Christopher. "Mary Livermore and the Great Northwestern Fair," *Chicago History*, IV (Spring 1975), pgs. 32-43.

Schreiber, Harry N. "Economic Change in the Civil War Era: An Analysis of Recent Studies," *Civil War History*, XI (December 1965), pgs. 396-411.

Schultz, William J. "Why the Feuchtwanger Composition Metal Coins Received Their Knockout Blow," *The Numismatist*, LI (November 1938), pgs. 949-950.

Schwan, Fred. "ANA Action Important," *Coin World*, April 10, 1985, p. 4

Schwartz, Ted. "Patriotic Postage: How Stamps Served the Nation," *Coins*, (February 1981); pgs. 62-68.

Sellers, James L. "An Interpretation of Civil War Finance," *American Historical Review*, XXX (January 1925), pgs. 282-297.

"75 Years Reputation, Brown's Bronchial Troches," *World Almanac and Book of Facts*. 44th ed. Edited by Robert Hunt Lyman, p. 914. New York: New York World, 1929.

Shafer, Neil. "Stamps Used As Coins Popular With Hobbyists," *Bank Note Reporter*, July 1993, pgs. 17-18.

"Shillito's 150th Anniversary Sale," special advertising supplement to the Cincinnati *Enquirer*, April 16, 1980, 8 pages.

"Shillito's Shows Rapid Growth," Cincinnati *Post*, February 16, 1950.

Shortt, Adam. "History of the Canadian Metallic Currency," *Money and Banking in Canada*. Edited by E. P. Neufeld, pgs. 116-131. Rep. from *Transactions of the Canadian Institute*, University of Toronto Press, 1911. Toronto: McClelland and Steward Ltd., 1964.

[Stern, Edward.] "Postage Stamp Envelopes Found," *Stamps*, LXXI (June 24, 1950), p. 562.

Sicker, John. "Fake Cases May Exist on Encased Stamps," *Linn's Stamp News*, August 8, 1983, p. 2.

"Since 1830, Shillito's Has Followed Growth of City to Become One of the Nation's Largest," Cincinnati *Enquirer*, February 13, 1950.

Sloane, George B. "Civil War Philatelic Currency," *Stamps*, LXXXII (January 24, 1953), p. 121.

Sloate, Barry, "Baseball's First Cards: Peck & Snyder Sporting Goods Trade Cards," *The Vintage and Classic Baseball Collector*, I (March 1995), pgs. 4-7.

Smith, Mary Ann. "John Snook and the Design for A. T. Stewart's Store," *New-York Historical Society Quarterly*, LVIII (January 1974), pgs. 18-33.

Socolofsky, Homer E. "How We Took the Land," Chapter XII in *Kansas, the First Century*, pgs. 281-306. Vol. I, edited by John D. Bright. New York: Lewis Historical Publishing Co., 1950.

Spinelli, Fred. "Calendar," *TLC*, IV (March 1983), p. 35.

———. "Calendar," *TLC*, IV (October 1983), p. 16.

———. "The Great Chicago Fire," *TLC*, IV (October, 1983), p. 2.

Springer, Sherwood. "Private Die Medicine Stamps Popular Among Physician-Collectors," *Clinical Pediatrics*, IV (March 1965), pgs. 186-189.

"Stamps Used as Money," *Hobbies*, XLV (September 1940), p. 84.

Steigerwalt, Charles. "Cheap Price List," of encased stamps, *Numismatic News*, Vol. II No. 6.

Steigerwalt, Charles [ed.]. *The Coin Journal*, Vol. III (February 1882 to July 1882).

——— [ed.]. *Numismatic News*, Nos. 1-3 (March 1895 to September 1895).

Stone, William C. et al. "[A Catalog of] Encased Postage Stamps, etc." *Philatelic Side Lines*. Springfield [MA]: Springfield Stamp Club, 1908.

Storer, Dr. Horatio R. "Dr. Lewis Feuchtwanger," in "The Medals, Jetons, and Tokens Illustrative of the Science of Medicine," *American Journal of Numismatics*, XXXI (October 1896), pgs. 44-45.

Sumner, William G. "Monetary Development," *The First Century of the Republic: A Review of American Progress*, Vol. 8. New York: Harper & Brothers, 1876.

Svensson, Robert H. "One Man's Answer to the Cash Crunch: Postage Stamps and Brass," *Civil War Times Illustrated*, XXI (December 1982), pgs. 26-27.

Talbot, Pat. An article on Frederick and C. H. Buhl, Buhl File, Burton Historical Collection.

Taylor, John M. "Representative Recruit for Abraham Lincoln," *Civil War Times Illustrated*, XVII (June 1978), pgs. 34-35.

Teachout, Terry. "Farewell, Dagny Taggart," *National Review*, XXXIV (May 14, 1982), pgs. 566-567.

Thorn, John and Rucker, Mark. "A Review of Baseball History," *The National Pastime*, III (Spring 1984), pgs. 27-31.

Thorp, Prescott Holden. "Change, Please!" *Scott's Monthly Journal*, X (January 1930), pgs. 340-342.

Thrall, Don. "Postage Stamps as Currency." *The MANA Journal*, XIV (No. 2 1970), pgs. 4-8.

Torres, David. "The Black Jack of 1863," *The Blue and the Grey* [Journal of the Civil War Philatelic Society], III (November-December 1963), pgs. 7-10.

"Tradesmen's Tokens, Other Than Those of the 'Copperhead Series' Issued in the State of New York," *The Coin Collector's Journal*, X (March 1885-February 1886), photocopy, 60 pages.

"Tricks of the Trade," Cincinnati *Miscellany*, July 1845, p. 72.

Trobaugh, Ken. "New Discovery," *Journal of the Civil War Token Society*, VIII (Winter 1974), p. 133.

———. "Postage Stamp Currency," *Copperhead Courier*, XIX (Winter 1985), p. 29.

———. "Robinson & Ballou, NY 890E, Cardboard Currency," *Copperhead Courier*, XV (Winter 1981), p. 5.

"Two-cent Black Jack Encasement Featured in Kagin's Auction," *Bank Note Reporter*, January 1988, p. 8.

"U. S. Postage Stamps as Necessity War Money," by Henry Russell Drowne, review of. *Mekeel's Weekly Stamp News*, XXXIII (December 6, 1919), p. 454.

Utter, William T. "John Burroughs Drake," *Dictionary of American Biography*. Vol. III. Edited by Allan Johnson and Dumas Malone, pgs. 430-431. New York: Charles Scribner's Sons, 1930.

Valentine, D. W. "Paper Fractional Money of the United States," *The Numismatist*, LXV (January 1952).

Wallace, W. Stewart. "Frank Weir" and "William Weir."

The MacMillan Dictionary of Canadian Biography, pgs. 788-789. Third Ed. London and Toronto: MacMillan, 1963.

Wells, Lisa. "Breakfasting: Early Risers Power Up in Posh Spots," *Advertising Age*, LVI No. 32 (April 25, 1985), p. 4.

"What Makes a Man . . . a Man?" Dallas *Morning News*, July 23, 1988.

"William Newton and Company," *Fractional Currency Collectors Board Newsletter*, April 15, 1989, unnumbered page reprinted from unnamed source.

Williams, Dale L. "At War With Itself: Coinage Crisis Occasions Emergency Substitutes," *Coin World*, November 3, 1976, pgs. 52, 68.

Williams, Henry. "U.S. Proprietary Stamps," Part II, *Philatelic Journal of America*, V (January 1889), p. 72.

Winter, Douglas. "Civil War Hysteria Triggers Financial Crisis," *Coin World*, May 15, 1985, pgs. 1, 28, 56.

———. "Many Factors in Postage Coinage Failure," *Coin World*, June 12, 1985, pgs. 1, 36, 40, 44.

———. "Mint Assayers Take Pattern Initiative," *Coin World*, May 22, 1985, pgs. 1, 62, 66.

Wylie, Wm. W. "An Informal History of the Collectors Club [of New York]." Reprinted from the *ANPHILEX 1971 Catalogue*.

York, Norton D. "The Reason for the Fiat 1861 Postage Stamps," *The American Philatelist*, LXXVIII (August 1965), pgs. 829-830.

———. "When Stamps Were Limited Legal Currency," *Weekly Philatelic Gossip*, LXVII (August 30, 1958), p. 14.

Zerbe, Farran. "Bits of Numismatic Wisdom," *The Numismatist*, XXXVI (July 1923), p. 313.

———. "Numismatic Papers at the ANA Convention," *The Numismatist*, XXXV (October 1922), pgs. 474-477.

Books (Secondary Sources)

Abbott, John S. C. *The History of the Civil War in America*. 2 vols. Springfield [MA]: Gurdon Bill, 1863, 1866.

Adams, James Truslow [ed.]. *Album of American History*. Vol. III (1853-1893). New York: Charles Scribner's Sons.

Adams, John W. *United States Numismatic Literature*. Vol. I. Mission Viejo [CA]: George Frederick Kolbe Publications, 1982.

Adams, Samuel Hopkins. *The Great American Fraud*. New York: P. F. Collier & Son, 1905, 1906.

Adelson, Howard L. *The American Numismatic Society, 1858-1958*. New York: The American Numismatic Society, 1958.

Albert, Alphaeus. *Record of American Uniform and Historical Buttons*, 1969.

Alexander, Charles. *Our Game: An American Baseball History*. New York: Henry Holt & Co., 1991.

Altick, Richard D. *Lives and Letters: A History of Literary Biography in England and America*. New York: Alfred A. Knopf, 1965.

Alvarez, Mark. *The Old Ball Game*. Alexandria [VA]: Redefinition Inc., 1992.

Amann, William Frayne [ed.]. *Personnel in the Union Army*. Vol. 2. New York: Thomas Yoseloff, 1962.

Ambrose, Stephen E. [ed.]. *A Wisconsin Boy in Dixie: The Selected Letters of James K. Newton*. Madison: University of Wisconsin Press, 1961.

American Medical Association. *Nostrums and Quackery*. "Articles on the Nostrum Evil and Quackery reprinted . . . from *The Journal of the American Medical Association*." Edited by Arthur Cramp. 2 vols. Second Edition. Chicago: American Medical Association Press, 1912, 1921.

American Numismatic Association. *Selected Articles on the Subject of American Tokens Reprinted from 'The Numismatist.' 1904-1938*. n.p.: Token and Medal Society, 1969.

———. *Selections from The Numismatist: U. S. Paper Money, Tokens, Medals and Miscellaneous*. Racine [WI]: Whitman Publishing Co., 1960.

Andreano, Ralph [ed.]. *The Economic Impact of the American Civil War*. Cambridge [MA]: Schenkman Publishing Co., Inc. 1962.

Andreas, A. T. *History of Cook County, Illinois*. 3 vols. Chicago: A. T. Andreas, 1884.

———. *History of the State of Kansas*. 2 vols. Chicago: A. T. Andreas, 1883.

Angle, Paul M. [ed.]. *Created Equal? The Complete Lincoln-Douglas Debates of 1858*. Chicago: University of Chicago Press, 1958.

Angle, Paul M. *The Great Chicago Fire*. Chicago: The Chicago Historical Society, 1971.

——— and Miers, Earl Schenck. *Tragic Years 1860-1865: A Documentary History of the American Civil War*. 2 vols. New York: Simon and Schuster, 1960.

Austen, Ferol. *Poor Man's Guide to Bottle Collecting*. Garden City: Doubleday, 1971.

Axon, Gordon V. *The California Gold Rush*. New York: Mason/Charter, 1976.

Ayer, Frederick Jr. *The Man in the Mirror*. Chicago: Henry Regnery Co., 1965. [He was the grandson of Frederick Ayer.]

———. *Yankee G-Man*. Chicago: Henry Regnery Co., 1957.

Bailey, Adrian. *The Blessings of Bread*. New York & London: Paddington Press Ltd., 1975.

Baker, William S. *Medallic Portraits of Washington*. Philadelphia: Lindsay, 1885. Revised and edited by George Fuld. Iola [WI]: Krause Publications, 1965.

Ball, Douglas B. *Financial Failure and Confederate Defeat*. Urbana and Chicago: University of Illinois Press, 1991.

Baringer, William E. *Lincoln Day By Day: A Chronology*. Vol. II. Ed. by Earl Schenck Miers. Washington, D.C.: Lincoln Sesquicentennial Commission, 1960.

Barrett, Don C. *The Greenbacks and Resumption of Specie*

Payments, 1862-1879. "Harvard Economic Studies," Vol. XXXVI. Cambridge: Harvard University Press, 1931.

Baron, Stanley. *Brewed in America*. New York: Arno Press & New York Times, 1972.

Bateman, Newton and Selby, Paul (eds.). *Historical Encyclopedia of Illinois, and History of Lake County*. Edited by Charles A. Partridge. Chicago: Munsell Publishing Co., 1902.

———. *Historical Encyclopedia of Illinois, and History of Peoria County*. 2 vols. Chicago and Peoria: William W. Munsell Publishing, 1901-1902.

Bauer, W. W. *Potions, Remedies and Old Wives' Tales*. Garden City: Doubleday & Co., 1969.

Beebe, Lucius, and Clegg, Charles. *San Francisco's Golden Era*. Berkeley: Howell-North, 1960.

Belknap, Henry Wyckoff. *The Burnap-Burnett Genealogy*. Salem [MA]: The Essex Institute, 1925.

Benner, Judith Ann. *Fraudulent Finance: Counterfeiting and the Confederate States, 1861-1865*. "Hill Junior College Monographs in Texas and Confederate History," No. 3. Hillsboro [TX]: Hill Junior College Press, 1970.

Benson, Michael. *Ballparks of North America: A Comprehensive Historical Reference to Baseball Grounds, Yards and Stadiums, 1845 to Present*. Jefferson [NC]: McFarland & Co., 1989.

Bierman, Stanley M. *The World's Greatest Stamp Collectors*. New York: Frederick Fell Publishers, n.d.

Bileski, Kasimir. *The First Philatelist?* Winnipeg: Privately Printed by the Author, 1973.

Birmingham, Nan Tillson. *Store*. New York; G. P. Putnam's Sons, 1978.

Black, Mary. *Old New York in Early Photographs*. New York: Dover Publications, 1973.

Black, George F. *The Surnames of Scotland, Their Origin, Meaning and History*. New York: New York Public Library and Readex Books, 1946.

Blakely Marsh Printing Co. *History of McHenry County, Illinois*. Chicago: Interstate Publishing Co., 1885.

Blumenson, Martin. *The Patton Papers, 1885-1940*. Boston: Houghton Mifflin Co., 1972.

------. *The Patton Papers, 1940-1945*. Boston: Houghton Mifflin Co., 1957.

Bowers, Q. David. *Adventures With Rare Coins*. Los Angeles: Bowers & Ruddy Galeries, 1979.

Bowman, Alan P. (comp.). *Index to the 1850 Census of the State of California*. Baltimore: Genealogical Publishing Co., 1972.

Bramwell, Ruby Phillips. *City on the Move: The Story of Salina*. Salina [KS]: Survey Press, 1969.

Branden, Nathaniel. *Who is Ayn Rand?* New York: Random House, 1962.

Breen, Walter. *Walter Breen's Complete Encyclopedia of U. S. and Colonial Coins*. New York: Doubleday, 1988.

Breton, P. Napoleon. *Illustrated History of Coins and Tokens Relating to Canada*. Montreal: British Amrican Bank Note Co., 1894.

-------. *Popular Illustrated Guide to Canadian Coins, Medals, &. &*. Montreal: L'Imprimerie Modele, 1912.

Brookman, Lester G. *The U. S. Postage Stamps of the 19th Century*. Vol. II. New York: H. L. Lindquist Publications Inc., 1966.

Brooks, Van Wyck. *The Flowering of New England*. New York: E. P. Dutton & Co., 1936, 1952.

———, and Bettmann, Otto L. *Our Literary Heritage, a Pictorial History of the Writer in America*. New York: E. P. Dutton & Co., 1956.

Brown, John Howard [ed.]. *Lamb's Biographical Dictionary of the United States*. Boston: James H. Lamb Co., 1900.

Buck, Wendell. *The Old Reliable: An Account of the First 100 Years of the Manhattan Life Insurance Company*. New York: Manhattan Life Insurance Co., 1950.

Buicki, Cecelia. *Metal, Minds and Machines: Waterbury at Work*. Waterbury [CT]: Mattatuck Historical Society, 1980.

Buley, Roscoe Carlyle. *The American Life Convention 1906-1952: A Study in the History of Life Insurance*. New York: Appleton-Century-Crofts Inc. 1953.

———. *The Equitable Life Assurance Society of the United States, 1859-1964*. 2 vols. New York: Appleton-Century-Crofts, 1967.

Bull, Donald, Friedrich, Manfred, and Gottschalk, Robert. *American Breweries*. Trumbull [CT]: Bullworks, 1984.

Burch, Lawrence D. *Kansas As It Is*. Chicago: C. S. Burch, 1878.

Burton, Clarence M. *The City of Detroit, Michigan, 1701-1922*. Vol. V. Detroit: S. J. Clark Publishing Co., 1922.

Carothers, Neil. *Fractional Money: A History of the Small Coins and Fractional Paper Currency of the United States*. A PhD dissertation, Department of History, Politics, and Economics, Princeton University, 1916. New York: John Wiley & Sons Inc., 1930.

Carson, Gerald. *One For a Man, Two For a Horse*. Garden City: Doubleday & Co., 1961.

———. *The Polite Americans: 300 Years of More or Less Good Behavior*. London and Melbourne: Macmillan, 1967.

Castenholz, B. J. *Field Guide to Revenue Stamped Paper: Part 6, New York State*. Pacific Palisades [CA]: Castenholz and Sons, 1991.

Catton, Bruce. *The Army of the Potomac: Glory Road*. Garden City [NY]: Doubleday, 1952.

———. *The Army of the Potomac: Mr. Lincoln's Army*. Garden City [NY]: Doubleday, 1952, 1962.

Chapman Brothers. *Portrait and Biographical Record of Dickinson, Saline, McPherson and Marion Counties, Kansas*. Chicago: Chapman Brothers, 1893.

Charlton, J. E. *Standard Catalogue of Canadian Coins, Tokens and Paper Money*. 26th ed. Toronto: Charlton International Publishing Inc., 1978.

———. *Standard Catalogue of Canadian Paper Money*.

Toronto: Charlton International Publishing Inc., 1980.

Chase, Carroll. *Classic U. S. Stamps*. Shrub Oak [NY]: Herman Herst Jr., 1962.

Chicago Historical Society. "Here's Chicago" exhibition at the historic Water Tower Museum and Chicago Pumping Station, 1985.

Cincinnati Times-Star. *The City of Cincinnati and Its Resources*. Cincinnati: Times-Star Publishing Co., 1891.

Clark, Howard. *The Mill on Mad River*. Boston: Little, Brown & Co., 1948.

Clark, Dwight L. *William Tecumseh Sherman: Gold Rush Banker*. San Francisco: California Historical Society, 1969.

Clayton, John. *The Illinois Fact Book and Historical Almanac, 1673-1968*. Carbondale: Southern Illinois University Press, 1970.

Clough, Shepard B. *A Century of American Life Insurance: A History of the Mutual Life Insurance Company of New York, 1843-1943*. New York: Columbia University Press, 1946.

Coburn, F. W. *History of Lowell and Its People*. 2 vols. Lowell [MA]: 1920.

Cochran, T. C. *The Pabst Brewing Company: The History of an American Business*. New York: University Press, 1948

Coffin, Margaret. *The History and Folklore of American Country Tinware, 1700-1900*. New York: Galahad Books, 1968.

Coggins, Jack. *Arms and Equipment of the Civil War*. Garden City: Doubleday & Co., 1962.

Cole, Arthur Charles. *The Era of the Civil War, 1848-1870*. Vol. III of "Centennial History of Illinois." Freeport [NY]: Books for Libraries Press, 1919, 1971.

Collet, Mark W., Hodge, J. Ledyard, and Taylor, Alfred B. *Catalogue of American Store Cards &c*. n.p. [Philadelphia]: Numismatic Society of Philadelphia, n.d. [1858].

Colson, Warren H. *The [Dr. William C.] Bowers' Collection*. "Postage Stamps and Their Collection: A Series of Handbooks Describing the Great Collectors and Collections of the World." No. 1. Boston: By the Author, 1909.

Colton, John W. *The First Century of the Connecticut Mutual Life Insurance Company, 1846-1946*. Hartford: Connecticut Mutual Life Insurance Co., 1946.

Commager, Henry Steele. *The Blue and the Gray: The Story of the Civil War as Told by the Participants*. 2 vols. Indianapolis and New York: Bobbs-Merrill, Inc. 1950.

Conwell, Col. Russell H. *History of the Great Fire in Boston*. Boston: B. B. Russell, 1873.

Cooper, John A. *Men of Canada*. Montreal and Toronto: Canadian Historical Co., 1901-02.

Copeland, Peter F., et al. *Round Shot and Rammers*. New York: Stackpole Books, 1969.

Criswell, Grover and Romerstein, Herb. *The Official Guide to Confederate Money and Civil War Tokens, Tradesmen & Patriotic*. New York: HC Publishers, Inc., 1971.

Cromie, Robert. *The Great Chicago Fire*. New York: McGraw-Hill, 1958.

Curl, Donald W. *Murat Halstead and the Cincinnati Commercial*. Boca Raton: University Presses of Florida, 1980.

Currier, Thomas Franklin. *A Bibliography of Oliver Wendell Holmes*. Edited by Eleanor M. Tilton for the Bibliographical Society of America. New York: Russell & Russell, 1953, 1971.

Curry, Leonard P. *Blueprint for Modern America: Non-military Legislation of the First Civil War Congress*. Nashville: Vanderbilt University Press, 1968.

Curto, James J. *Sutlers and Their Tokens, 1861-1866*. Reprinted from *The Numismatist*. Grosse Pointe [MI]: By the Author, 1962.

———, and Schwartz, Max M. *A Tentative List of Sutler Tokens and Scrip*. Reprinted from *The Numismatist*. Grosse Pointe [MI]: By the Authors, 1962.

Dary, David. *Entrepreneurs of the Old West*. New York: Alfred A. Knopf, 1986.

Dedmond, Emmett. *Fabulous Chicago*. Enlarged Edition. New York: Atheneum, 1981.

DeWitt, J. Doyle. *A Century of Campaign Buttons, 1789-1889*. Hartford [CT]: The Travelers Press, 1959.

Dick, Everett. *The Sod House Frontier, 1854-1890*. Lincoln [NE]: Johnsen Publishing Co., 1954.

Dickeson, Montroville Wilson. *The American Numismatical Manual of the Currency or Money of the Aborigines, and Colonial, State, and United States Coins. . . .* Philadelphia: J. B. Lippincott & Co., 1859.

Dickey, Thomas, and George, Peter C. *Field Artillery Projectiles of the American Civil War*. Atlanta: Arsenal Press, 1980.

Dickson, Paul. *The Dickson Baseball Dictionary*. New York and Oxford: Facts on File, 1989.

Dimitri, John. *Confederate Military History*. Vol. X. Edited by Clement A. Evans. Secaucus [NJ]: The Blue & Grey Press, n. d.

Donald, David [ed.]. *Inside Lincoln's Cabinet: The Civil War Diaries of Salmon P. Chase*. New York: Longmans, Green and Co., 1954.

Divers Hands (sic) [multiplicity of contributors]. *Illustrated History of Lowell and Vicinity*. Lowell: Courier-Citizen Co., 1897.

Doty, Richard G. *The Macmillan Encyclopedic Dictionary of Numismatics*. New York: Macmillan and Co., 1982.

Dunham, J. P. (comp.). *Map of the City of Salina*. n.p.: Northwest Publishing Co., 1903.

Dunham, William F. *Check List and Auction Record Prices of Encased Postage Stamps of the United States*. Chicago: By the Author, 1915

———. *Easy Finding List, Canadian and United States Coins. . .* [and] *Encased Postage Stamps*. Los Angeles: Bundy Quill & Press, n. d. [1929].

Dusinberre, William. *Civil War Issues in Philadelphia,*

1856-1865. Philadelphia: University of Pennsylvania Press, 1965.

Dyer, Frederick H. *A Compendium of the War of the Rebellion*. 3 vols. Des Moines: 1908. Reprint. 2 vols. Dayton [OH]: The National Historical Society and Morningside Press, 1979.

Early American Numismatics [Dana Linett]. *The Encased Postage Stamps of John Gault*. La Jolla [CA]: Privately Printed, 1988.

Edwards, William B. *Civil War Guns*. Harrisburg [PA]: The Stackpole Co., 1962.

Elliott, Joseph. P. *A History of Evansville and Vanderburgh County, Indiana*. Evansville: Keller Printing Co., 1897.

Ellis, David M. et al. *A History of New York State*. Ithaca: Cornell University Press in co-operation with the New York State Historical Association, 1957, 1967.

Ellis, Edward Robb. *The Epic of New York City*. New York: Coward-McCann, Inc., 1966.

Epstein, Diana. *Collectors' Blue Books: Buttons*. New York: Walker & Co., 1968.

Erdoes, Richard. *Saloons of the Old West*. New York: Alfred A. Knopf, 1979.

Evans, George G. *History of the United States Mint and Coinage*, Reprint ed. of Evans' *Illustrated History of the United States Mint*. New York: Sanford J. Durst Numismatic Publications, 1977.

Ewers, William et al. *Sincere's History of the Sewing Machine*. Phoenix: Sincere Press, 1970.

Falley, Margaret Dickson. *Irish and Scotch-Irish (sic) Ancestral Research*. Vol. 1. Evanston [IL]: By the Author, 1962.

Farago, Ladislas. *The Last Days of Patton*. New York: McGraw-Hill, 1981.

———. *Patton: Ordeal and Triumph*. New York: Dell Publishing Co., 1963.

Farmer, Silas. *The History of Detroit and Wayne County, Michigan*. 2 vols. Detroit: 1889.

Farr, Finis. *Chicago: A Personal History of America's Most American City*. New Rochelle [NY]: Arlington House, 1973.

Faulkner, Harold Underwood. *American Economic History*. XVII. 4th ed. New York: Harper and Brothers, 1938.

———. *Economic History of the United States*. VIII. Revised ed. New York: The MacMillan Co., 1937.

Fauver, L. B. *Exonumia Symbolism and Classification*. Menlo Park [CA]: Oak Grove Publications, 1982.

Feck, Luke. *Yesterday's Cincinnati*. Miami: E. A. Seemann Publishing Inc., 1975.

Ferraro, Pat and Ferraro, Bob. *A Bottle Collector's Book*. n. p.: Western Printing and Publishing Co., 1966.

Filby, P. William and Meyer, Mary K. (eds.). *Passenger and Immigration Lists Index*. 4 vols. with supplements. First edition. Detroit: Gale Research Co., 1981-1983.

Fischer, LeRoy H. *Lincoln's Gadfly, Adam Gurowski*. Norman: University of Oklahoma Press, 1964. [Dr. Fischer was this author's mentor on the Civil War and Reconstruction. This book was the 1963 Literary Award winner of the War Library and Museum and the Pennsylvania Commandery of the Military Order of the Loyal Legion.]

Fisher, Irving, et al. *Stamp Scrip*. New York: Adelphi Co., 1933.

Fite, Emerson David. *Social and Industrial Conditions in the North During the Civil War*. New York: The MacMillan Co., 1910.

Fite, Gilbert C. and Reese, Jim E. *An Economic History of the United States*. Boston: Houghton Mifflin Co., 1959.

Ford, Henry A. and Ford, Kate B. *History of Cincinnati, Ohio*. Cleveland: L. A. Williams & Co., 1881.

Foster, F. Apthorp (ed.). *Vital Records of Hopkinton, Massachusetts to the Year 1850*. Boston: New-England Historic Genealogical Society, 1911.

Foster, Genevieve. *Year of Lincoln, 1861*. New York: Charles Scribner's Sons, 1970.

Fowler, Chester A. "Counterfeiting," *Cyclopedia of Law and Procedure*, XI, pgs. 300-323. Ed. by William Mack. New York: The American Law Book Co., 1904.

Fractional Currency, Inc. [Len and Jean Glazer]. *Encased Postage Fixed Price Catalog* [Complete Merchant Set Collection with many additional varieties. Die cut with 2 color plates.] Forest Hills [NY]: Privately Printed, 1980.

Freeman, Larry. *Grand Old American Bottles*. Watkins Glen [NY]: Century House, 1964.

Friedberg, Milton R. *Catalog of Enveloped Postage*. Cleveland: By the Author, 1986, with supplements.

———. *The Encyclopedia of United States Fractional and Postal Currency*. Rockville Centre, L.I.: Numismatic and Antiquarian Service Corporation of America, 1978.

Friedberg, Robert. *Paper Money of the United States*. All editions. New York: The Coin and Currency Institute, various years.

Fuld, George and Fuld, Melvin. *A Guide to Civil War Store Card Tokens*. Racine [WI]: Whitman Publishing Co., 1962.

------. *Patriotic Civil War Tokens*, Racine [WI]: Whitman Publishing Co., 1960, 1965.

———. *Patriotic Civil War Tokens*. 4th ed. Jack Detwiler, editor; Fred L. Reed, et al. associate editors. Iola [WI]: Civil War Token Society, 1982.

———. *U. S. Civil War Store Cards*. Second Edition. Lawrence [MA]: Quarterman Publications Inc., 1973.

Furer, Howard B. [ed.]. *Cincinnati*. "American Cities Chronology Series." Dobbs Ferry [NY]: Oceana Publications, 1975.

Gale, Edwin O. *Reminiscences of Early Chicago and Vicinity*. Chicago: n.d.

Garland, Joseph E. *Boston's Gold Coast*. Boston: Little, Brown & Co., 1981.

Gershman, Michael. *Diamonds: The Evolution of the Ballpark*. Boston and New York: Houghton Mifflin

Co., 1993.

Gilbert, Paul and Bryson, Charles Lee. *Chicago and Its Makers*. Chicago: Felix Mendelsohn, 1929.

Gilchrist, David T. and Lewis, W. David [eds.]. *Economic Change in the Civil War Era*. "Proceedings of a Conference on American Economic Institutional Change, 1850-1873, and the Impact of the Civil War, March 12-14, 1964." Greenville [DE]: Eleutherian Mills-Higley Foundation, 1965.

Ginger, Ray. *Altgeld's America: The Lincoln Ideal Versus Changing Realities*. New York: New Viewpoints, 1973.

Glazier Ira A. [ed.]. *The Famine Immigrants Arriving at the Port of New York, 1846-1851*. 4 vols. Vol. III (July 1848-March 1849). Baltimore: Genealogical Publishing Co., 1984.

Gluckman, Arcadi. *Identifying Old U. S. Muskets, Rifles and Carbines*. Harrisburg [PA]: Stackpole Books, 1959, 1965.

Goodspeed, Weston A. and Healy, Daniel D. *History of Cook County, Illinois*. 2 vols. Chicago: Goodspeed Historical Association, 1909.

Grafton, John. *New York in the Nineteenth Century*. New York: Dover Publications, 1977.

Grant, Robert W. *The Handbook of Civil War Patriotic Envelopes and Postal History*. Vol. I. Hanover [MA]: Hugh Romano, Printer, 1977.

Green, Ben G. *The Numismatists' Reference and Check Book* [n.b. cover reads "Green's Numismatist's (sic) Reference and Check Book"]. Chicago: By the Author, 1902.

Green, C. E. *Mint Record and Type Table, U. S. Coins*. Chicago: Privately printed, 1936.

Gregory, Winifred [ed.]. *American Newspapers, 1821-1936: A Union List of Files Available in the U. S. and Canada*. New York: W. W. Wilson Co., 1937.

Griffenhagen, George B. *Private Die Proprietary Medicine Stamps*. Vol. 4, Medical Series, Handbook No. 66. Milwaukee: American Topical Association, 1969.

Griffing, B. N. *Griffing's Atlas of Vanderburg County, Indiana*. Philadelphia: D. J. Lake & Co., 1880.

Gudde, Erwin G. *California Gold Camps*. Berkeley: University of California Press, 1975.

Gurney, Gene and Gurney, Clare. *The United States Treasury, A Pictorial History*. New York: Crown Publishers Inc., 1978.

Hall, Henry [ed.]. *America's Successful Men of Affairs*. 2 vols. New York: New York Tribune, 1896.

Hamilton, Charles and Ostendorf, Lloyd. *Lincoln in Photographs: An Album of Every Known Pose*. Norman: University of Oklahoma Press, 1963.

Hammond, Bray. *Sovereignty and an Empty Purse: Banks and Politics in the Civil War*. Princeton: Princeton University Press, 1970.

Harlow, Alvin F. *Paper Chase: the Amenities of Stamp Collecting*. New York: Henry Holt & Co., 1940.

------. *The Serene Cincinnatians*. New York: E. P. Dutton & Co., 1950.

Harris, Leon. *Merchant Princes*. New York: Harper & Row, 1979.

Haskins, Charles Warren. *Libera Martina Spinazze's Index to the Argonauts of California*. New Orleans: Polyanthos, 1975.

[Hays, Reuben Benjamin]. *The First National Bank of Cincinnati: A Brief History*. n. p.: n. d. [a pamphlet]

Hays, Reuben Benjamin. *Through Wars, Panics and Periods of Prosperity: A Narrative of the First National Bank of Cincinnati*. New York: Newcomen Society in North America, 1963.

Hazlett, James C., Olmstead, Edwin, and Parks, M. Hume. *Field Artillery Weapons of the Civil War*. Newark: University of Delaware Press, 1983.

Headley, P. C. *Massachusetts in the Rebellion: A Record of the Historical Position of the Commonwealth*. Boston: Walker, Fuller & Co., 1866.

Hechtlinger, Adelaide. *The Great Patent Medicine Era*. New York: Grosset & Dunlap, 1970.

Hendrickson, Robert. *The Grand Emporiums: The Illustrated History of America's Great Department Stores*. New York: Stein and Day, 1979.

Hepburn, A. Barton. *A History of Currency in the United States*. Revised edition. New York: The MacMillan Co., 1915.

Herringshaw, Mae Felts. *Clark J. Herringshaw's City Blue Book of Current Biography*. Chicago: American Publishers' Association, 1913.

Hershkowitz, Leo. *Tweed's New York, Another Look*. Garden City: Anchor Press/Doubleday, 1977.

Herst, Herman Jr. *Stories to Collect Stamps By*. Boca Raton [FL]: Philatelic Book Publishers, 1968.

Hessler, Gene. *The Comprehensive Catalog of U. S. Paper Money*. Port Clinton [OH]: BNR Press, 1981.

Hetrich, George and Guttag, Julius. *Civil War Tokens and Tradesmen's Store Cards*. n. p.: By the Authors, 1924.

Hickman, John and Oakes, Dean. *Standard Catalog of National Bank Notes*. Iola [WI]: Krause Publications, 1982.

Historical and Descriptive Review of Kansas. Vol. III. Topeka: Jno. Lethem, 1891.

History of Peoria County, Illinois. Chicago: Johnson & Co., 1880.

History of the Young Men's Mercantile Library Association of Cincinnati, 1835-1935. Exhibit JJ Young Men's Mercantile Library. A pamphlet, 20 pages. Privately Printed, 1935.

Hoch, Al [ed.]. *Selected Articles on the Subject of American Tokens*, Reprinted from *The Numismatist* (1904-1938). n. p.: The Token and Medal Soceity, 1969.

Hodder, Michael J., and Bowers, Q. David. *The Standard Catalogue of Encased Postage Stamps*. Wolfeboro [NH]: Bowers and Merena Galleries, Inc., 1989.

Holbrook, Stewart H. *The Golden Age of Quackery*. New York: The MacMillan Co., 1959.

Holcombe, Henry W. *Patent Medicine Tax Stamps: A History of the Firms Using U. S. Private Die Proprietary Medicine Tax Stamps*. Lawrence [MA]: Quarterman Publications Inc., [1977].

Holliday, J. S. *The World Rushed In: The California Gold Rush Experience*. New York: Simon & Schuster, 1981.

Holt, Arthur G. *Handwriting in Psychological Interpretations*. Springfield [IL]: Charles C. Thomas, 1965.

Holzer, Harold. *Dear Mr. Lincoln, Letters to the President*. Reading [MA}: Addison-Wesley Publishing Co., 1993.

———, Boritt, Gabor S., and Neely, Mark E. Jr. *The Lincoln Image: Abraham Lincoln and the Popular Print*. New York: Charles Scribner's Sons, 1984.

Horan, James D. *Confederate Agent*. New York: The Fairfax Press, 1954.

Hornung, Clarence P. *New York, 1850-1890*. New York: Schocken Books, 1978.

———. *The Way It Was in the U.S.A.: A Pictorial Panorama of America, 1850-1890*. New York: Abbeville Press, 1978.

———. and Johnson, Fidolf. *200 Years of American Graphic Art*. New York: George Brazillier, 1976.

Howe, Octavius Thorndike. *Argonauts of '49: History and Adventures of the Emigrant Companies from Massachusetts, 1849-1850*. Cambridge: Harvard University Press, 1923.

Hoyt, Edwin P. *The Improper Bostonian*. New York: William Morrow & Co., 1979.

Hubbard, Freeman. *Great Days of the Circus*. New York: American Heritage Publishing Co., 1962.

Huff, Wayne. *Early History of Claflin, Kansas*. n. p.: Privately printed, 1982. A pamphlet, 11 pages.

Hurd, D. Hamilton. *History of Middlesex County, Massachusetts With Biographical Sketches of Many of Its Pioneers and Prominent Men*. 3 vols. Philadelphia: J. W. Lewis & Co., 1890.

Hutchinson, Clinton Carter. *Resources of Kansas, 1871*. Topeka: By the Author, 1871.

Ingalls, Sheffield. *History of Atchison County, Kansas*. Lawrence: Standard Publishing Co., 1916.

Insurance Year Book. New York: The Spectator Co., 1911.

The Interstate Exposition Souvenir, . . . [of the] Great Inter-State Exposition of 1873. Chicago: Van Arsdale & Massie, 1873.

Jackson, Donald Dale. *Gold Dust*. New York: Alfred A. Knopf, 1980.

Jackson, Joseph Henry [ed.]: *Gold Rush Album*. New York: Bonanza Books, 1949.

Jackson, Ronald Vern. *Iowa Census Records, 1841-1849*. Vol. II. Bountiful [UT]: Accelerated Indexing Systems Inc., 1981.

———, and Teeples, Gary Ronald [eds.]. *Maryland 1840 Census Index*. Bountiful [UT]: Accelerated Indexing Systems Inc., 1978.

———. *California 1850 Census Index*. Bountiful [UT]: Accelerated Indexing Systems Inc., 1978.

———. *New York 1850 Census Index*. Bountiful [UT]: Accelerated Indexing Systems, Inc., 1977.

———. *Pennsylvania 1860 Census Index*. Bountiful [UT]: Accelerated Indexing Systems Inc., 1979.

——— et al. *Early Michigan*. "Early American Series," Vol. 4. Bountiful [UT]: Accelerated Indexing Systems Inc., 1981.

Johnson, Robert U. and Buel, Clarence C. [eds.]. *Battles and Leaders of the Civil War*. 4 vols. New York: Century Co. Publishing, 1884-1888.

Johnson, William Weber. *The Forty-Niners*. New York: Time-Life Books, 1974.

Jones, Edgar R. *Those Were the Good Old Days: A Happy Look at American Advertising, 1880-1930*. New York: Simon and Schuster, 1959.

Jones [&] Lang [&] Wootton. *The Plaza*. An Investment Offering. Dallas: RM Graphics, n.d. [1994]. 42 pages.

Judd, J. Hewitt, Breen, Walter H., and Kosoff, Abe. *United States Patterns, Experimental and Trial Pieces*. Third Edition. Racine [WI]: Whitman Publishing Co., 1965.

Julian, R. W. *Medals of the United States Mint: The First Century, 1792-1892*. El Cajon [CA]: The Token and Medal Society, 1977.

Kagin, Donald H. *Private Gold Coins and Patterns of the United States*. New York: Arco Publishing, Inc., 1981.

Kauffman, Henry J. *Early American Ironware*. Rutland [VT]: Charles E. Tuttle Co., 1966.

———. *Early American Ironware, Cast and Wrought*. Rutland [VT]: Charles E. Tuttle Co., 1946.

Kay, Jane Holtz. *Lost Boston*. Boston: Houghton Mifflin Co., 1980.

Keller, Kenneth. *Sutler Paper Money*. Rockford [IL]: World Exonumia Press, 1994.

Kelly, Don C.. *National Bank Notes*. Oxford [OH]: The Paper Money Institute Inc., 1981.

Kemmerer, Edwin Walter. *Money: The Principles of Money and Their Exemplification in Outstanding Chapters of Monetary History*. New York: The MacMillan Co., 1935.

Kenngott, George F. *The Record of A City; A Social Survey of Lowell Massachusetts*. New York: The MacMillan Co., 1912.

Kerksis, Sydney C., and Dickey, Thomas. S. *Field Artillery Projectiles of the Civil War*. Atlanta: The Phoenix Press, 1968.

———. *Heavy Artillery Projectiles of the Civil War*. Kennesaw [GA]: Phoenix Press, 1972.

Kerrigan, Evans E. *American Badges and Insignia*. New York: The Viking Press, 1967.

King, Moses. *King's Handbook of New York City*. 2nd edition. Buffalo [NY]: Matthews-Northrup Co., 1893.

———. *Philadelphia and Notable Philadelphians*. New York: By the Compiler, 1901.

King, Robert. *Lincoln in Numismatics*. Reprinted from issues of *The Numismatist*, 1924, 1927, 1933. El Cajon [CA]: Token and Medal Society, 1966.

Kirkland, Moses. *History of Chicago*. 2 vols. Chicago: Munsell & Co., 1895.

Klamkin, Marian. *The Collector's Book of Bottles*. New York: Dodd, Mead & Co., 1971.

Knox, John Jay. *United States Notes: A History of the Various Issues of Paper Money by the Government of the United States*. New York: Charles Scribner's Sons, 1884.

———. *A History of Banking in the United States*. New York: 1900.

Kogan, Herman and Cromie, Robert. *The Great Fire, Chicago, 1871*. New York: G. P. Putnam's Sons, 1971.

——— and Wendt, Lloyd. *Chicago: A Pictorial History*. New York: E. P. Dutton & Co., 1958.

Konwiser, Harry M. *American Stamp Collector's Dictionary*. New York: Tudor Publishing Co., 1949.

Korn, Jerry. *War on the Mississippi*. Alexandria [VA]: Time-Life Books, 1985.

Kouwenhoven, John A. *Adventures of America, 1857-1900: A Pictorial Record from Harper's Weekly*. New York: Harper and Brothers, 1938.

———. *The Columbia Historical Portrait of New York*. New York: Harper and Row, 1972.

———. *Parnters in Banking: An Historical Portrait of a Great Private Bank, Brown Brothers Harriman & Co., 1818-1968*. Garden City: Doubleday & Co., 1968.

Kovel, Ralph M. and Kovel, Terry H. *A Directory of American Silver, Pewter and Silver Plate*. New York: Crown Publishers, 1961.

Krause, Chet and Lemke, Bob. *Standard Catalogue of U. S. Paper Money*. Iola [WI]: Krause Publications, 1981.

Kroll, Wayne L. *Badger Breweries, Past and Present*. Jefferson [WI]: By the Author, 1976.

Kroos, Herman E. *Documentary History of Banking and Currency in the United States*. 4 vols. Vol II. New York: Chelsea House Publishers, 1969.

Kunhardt, Dorthy Meserve and Kunhardt, Philip B. Jr. *Mathew Brady and His World*. Alexandria [VA]: Time-Life Books, 1977. [The authors are eminent Lincoln photographic authority Frederick Hill Meserve's daughter and grandson. The latter was the source for the Brady photograph which graces this volume's endpapers.]

Lane, Maryette B. *The Harry F. Allen Collection of Black Jacks: A Study of the Stamp and Its Use*. Federalsburg [MD]: American Philatelic Society and J. W. Stowell Printing Co., 1969.

Laugel, Auguste. *The United States During the Civil War*. Ed. by Allan Nevins. "Civil War Centennial Series." Bloomington: Indiana University Press, 1961.

Leeper, David Rohrer. *The Argonauts of 'Forty-Nine*. South Bend [IN]: J. B. Stoll & Co., Printer, 1894.

Lehman-Haupt, Hellmut. *The Book in America: A History of the Making and Selling of Books in the U. S.* New York: R. R. Bowker, 1952.

Liebers, Arthur. *United States Coins*. New York: G. P. Putnam's Sons, 1965.

Lodge, John C. *I Remember Detroit*. Detroit: Wayne University Press, 1949.

Longstreet, Stephen. *Chicago, 1860-1919*. New York: David McKay Co., 1973.

Looney, Robert F. *Old Philadelphia in Early Photographs, 1839-1914*. New York: Dover Publications Inc. 1976.

Lord, Francis A. *Civil War Collector's Encyclopedia*. 2 vols. New York: Castle Books, 1965, 1975.

———. *Civil War Sutlers and Their Wares*. New York: Thomas Yoseloff, 1969.

———. *They Fought for the Union*. New York: Bonanza Books, 1965.

Lossing, Benson John [ed.]. *Harper's Encyclopedia of American History*. 10 vols. New York: Harper & Brothers, 1907.

Lowe, David. *The Great Chicago Fire*. New York: Dover Publications, 1979.

Lowry, Philip J. *Green Cathedrals*. Revised ed. Reading [MA]: Addison-Wesley Publishing Co., 1986.

Luscomb, Sally C. *The Collector's Encyclopedia of Buttons*. New York: Crown Publishers Inc., 1967.

Luthin, Reinhard H. *The First Lincoln Campaign*. Cambridge: Harvard University Press, 1944.

Mahoney, Tom and Stone, Leonard. *The Great Merchants: America's Foremost Retail Institutions and the People Who Made Them Great*. New York: Harper and Row, 1974.

Map of Saline County Kansas. Salina: Salina Union, n.d. Salina Public Library Collections.

Marcus, Stanley. *Quest for the Best*. New York: The Viking Press, 1979.

Masters, Robert V., and Reinfeld, Fred. *Coinometry*. New York: Sterling Publishing Co., 1960.

Mathison, Richard R. *The Eternal Search: The Story of Man and His Drugs*. New York: G. P. Putnam's Sons, 1958.

Mayfield, Frank M. *The Department Store Story*. New York: Fairchild Publications Inc., 1949.

McCabe, James D. *Illustrated History of the Centennial Exposition*. Philadelphia: National Publishing Co., 1876.

------. *Lights and Shadows of New York Life*. Philadelphia: National Publishing Co., 1872.

McLachlan, Robert Wallace. *A Descriptive Catalogue of Coins, Tokens and Medals Issued in or Relating to the Dominion of Canada and Newfoundland*. Montreal: T. R. Marvin & Son, 1886.

McMaster, John Bach. *A History of the People of the United States During Lincoln's Administration*. New York: D. Appleton and Co., 1927.

Mearns, David C. *The Lincoln Papers*. Vol. 1. Garden City: Doubleday & Co., 1948.

Megura, Jim. *Official Price Guide* [to] *Bottles*. 11th edition. New York: House of Collectibles, 1991.

Meyer, Jerome S. *The Handwriting Analyzer*. New York: Simon & Schuster, 1927, 1953.

Miers, Earl Schenck [ed.]. *Lincoln Day By Day: A Chronology 1809-1865*. 3 vols. Washington, D. C.: Lincoln Sesquicentennial Commission, 1960.

Micarelli, Charles. *Manual and Identification Guide to the U.S. Regular Issues, 1847 through 1934*. Maitland [FL]: Adriatic Stamp Co., 1979.

Miller, Donald M. *A Catalogue of U. S. Store Cards or*

Merchants Tokens: The Money of the Merchants. Indiana [PA]: By the Author, 1962.

Miller, Nyle H. and Snell, Joseph W. *Great Gunfighters of the Kansas Cowtowns, 1867-1886.* Lincoln: University of Nebraska Press, 1963.

Mitchell, Wesley Clair. *Gold, Price & Wages Under the Greenback Standard.* Berkeley: University of California Press, 1908.

------. *A History of the Greenbacks, With special Reference to the Economic Consequences of Their Issue: 1862-1865.* "The Decennial Publications," Second Series, Vol. 9. Chicago: The University of Chicago Press, 1903.

Moore, Frank [ed]. *The Rebellion Record: A Diary of American Events, with Documents, Narratives, Illustrative Incidents, Poetry, etc.* 11 vols and supplements. New York: G. P. Putnam and Van Nostrand, 1861-1868.

Moors, J. F. *History of the Fifty-Second Regiment Massachusetts Volunteers.* Boston: George H. Ellis, 1893.

Morgan, Hal. *Symbols of America.* New York: Viking Penguin, 1986.

Morris, Lloyd. *Incredible New York.* New York: Random House, 1951.

Morse, John T. Jr. *Life and Letters of Oliver Wendell Holmes.* Vol. II. "American Men and Women of Letters Series," edited by Daniel Aaron. New York and London: Chelsea House, 1980.

Moulton, C. W. *References to the Coinage Legislation of the United States.* Cincinnati: Peter G. Thomson, 1877.

Munroe, R. C. (chairman). *Philatelic Massachusetts.* Springfield [MA]: Springfield Stamp Club, 1945.

Munsey, Cecil. *The Illustrated Guide to Collecting Bottles.* New York: Hawthorn Books, 1970.

Muscatine, Doris. *Old San Francsico: The Biography of A City.* New York: G. P. Putnam's Sons, 1975.

Muzzey, David Saville. *The United States of America.* Vol. 1. Boston: Ginn and Co., 1922.

Naisawald, L. Van Loan. *Grape and Canister: The Story of the Field Artillery of the Army of the Potomac.* Washington, D. C.: Zenger Publishing Co., 1960, 1983.

Names, Larry D. *Bury My Heart at Wrigley Field, The History of the Chicago Cubs.* Neshkoro [WI]: Sportsbook Publishing Co., 1990.

Nason, Elias. *A Gazetteer of the State of Massachusetts.* Boston: B. B. Russell, 1874.

Naylor, R. T. *The History of Canadian Business, 1867-1914.* Vol. I, "The Banks and Finance Capital." Toronto: James Lorimer & Co., 1975.

Needleman, Saul B. [ed.]. *Perspectives in Numismatics.* Chicago Coin Club. Chicago: Ares Publishers Inc., 1986.

Neeley, Mark E. Jr. *The Abraham Lincoln Encyclopedia.* New York: McGraw Hill Book Co., 1982.

Nelson, S. B. and Runk, J. M. *History of Cincinnati and Hamilton County.* 3 vols. Cincinnati: S. B. Nelson Co., 1894.

Nevins, Allan. *The Emergence of Lincoln.* Vol. 1. New York: Charles Scribner's Sons, 1950.

Newhall, Beaumont. *The Daguerreotype in America.* New York: Duell, Sloan and Pearce, 1961.

Nicolay, John G. and Hay, John. *Abraham Lincoln: A History.* 10 vols. New York: The Century Co., 1886.

——— [eds.]. *Complete Works of Abraham Lincoln.* New and enlarged ed. 12 vols. n. p.: Lincoln Memorial University, 1894.

Norton, Bettina A. *Edwin Whitefield: Nineteenth-Century North American Scenery.* Barre [MA]: Barre Publishing, 1977.

Oakes, Dean. *Iowa Obsolete Notes and Scrip.* Iola [WI]: Society of Paper Money Collectors, 1982.

Oberholtzer, Ellis Paxson. *Jay Cooke: Financier of the Civil War.* 2 vols. Philadelphia: George W. Jacobs and Co., 1907.

O'Connor, Richard. *Iron Wheels and Broken Men: The Railroad Barons and the Plunder of the West.* New York: G. P. Putnam's Sons, 1973.

O'Donnell, Terence. *History of Life Insurance in Its Formative Years.* Chicago: American Conservation Co., 1936.

The Official State Atlas of Kansas. Philadelphia: L. H. Everts & Co., 1887.

Palmer, Friend. *Early Days in Detroit.* Detroit: Hunt & June, 1906. Reprinted Detroit: Gale Research Co., 1979.

The Passavant House. Zelienople [PA]: Zelienople Historical Society, n. d. A brochure.

Perry, Dick. *Vas You Ever in Zinzinnati?* Garden City: Doubleday & Co., 1966.

Perry, Elliott. *Byways of Philately: Privately-Owned Posts and Early Locals.* Federalsburg [MD]: J. W. Stowell, 1966.

———. *Pat Paragraphs.* Compiled by George T. Turner and Thomas E. Stanton. Springield [VA]: Bureau Issues Association and Goetz Printing Co., 1981.

Peterson, Harold L. *Round Shot and Rammers.* Harrisburg: Stackpole Books, 1969.

Phillips, Charles J. *Stamp Collecting.* New York: H. L. Lindquist, 1936.

Phillips, John [comp.]. *The Composition of Certain Patent and Proprietary Medicines.* Chicago: 1917.

Pierce, Bessie Louise. *A History of Chicago.* Vol. III, "The Rise of a Modern City, 1871-1893." New York: Alfred A. Knopf, 1957.

Plat of Salina, Saline County, Kansas. n.p.: 1887. Salina Public Library Collections.

Pollock, Andrew W. III. *United States Patterns and Related Issues.* Wolfeboro [NH]: Bowers and Merena Galleries, Inc., 1994.

Power, John Carroll. *Abraham Lincoln. His Life, Public Services, Death and Great Funeral Cortege . . . .* Monumental edition. Springfield [IL]: Edwin A. Wilson & Co., 1875.

Powers, George W. *The Story of the Thirty-Eighth*

Regiment of Massachusetts Volunteers. Boston: Cambridge Press of Dakin and Metcalf, 1866.

Rainwater, Dorothy T. *Encyclopedia of American Silver Manufacturers.* New York: Crown Publishers, Inc., 1975.

Rand, Ayn. *Atlas Shrugged.* New York: Random House, 1957.

Randall, J. G., and Donald, David. *The Civil War and Reconstruction.* Second ed., revised. Lexington [MA]: D. C. Heath and Co., 1969.

Raphael, Morris. *The Battle in the Bayou Country.* Detroit: Harlo Press, 1976.

Rasmussen, Louis J. *San Francisco Ship Passenger Lists.* 4 vols. Columa [CA]: San Francisco Historic Record and Genealogy Bulletin, 1965.

Raymond, Wayte. *The Standard Catalog of United States Coins.* 11th ed. New York: Wayte Raymond, Inc., 1945.

Reed, Fred L. et al. *Basic Knowledge for the Coin Collector and Investor.* Edited by Fred Reed and Bill Gibbs. Sidney [OH]: Amos Press, 1981, 1982.

———. *Civil War Encased Stamps: Auction Census Data, 1891-1988.* 2 vols. Part I: Aërated Bread – Drake; Part II: Ellis McAlpin – "Feuchtwanger." Dallas [TX]: Privately Printed, 1988. [n.b. containing 6,040 listings]

———. *That New Metallic Currency – Civil War Encased Stamps, The Issuers and Their Times.* Dallas [TX]: Privately Printed, 1985. [A brochure, 6 panels, tri-fold, 8 X 14 inches. This promotional brochure was distributed to American Numismatic Association executive officers, board members, and interested parties February 20, 1985 in support of the research grant requested for the present work and approved by the board on that date.]

———, and DeLorey, Tom. *Price Guide for the Collector of Paper Money Errors.* 3rd and 4th editions. Sidney [OH]: Coin World, 1977, 1978.

Reichler, Joseph L. [ed.]. *The Baseball Encyclopedia.* Sixth edition. New York: Macmillan Publishing Co., 1985.

Reilly, Philip J. *Old Masters of Retailing.* New York: Fairchild Publications Inc., 1966.

Reinfeld, Fred. *The Story of Civil War Money.* New York: Sterling Publishing Co., 1959.

Revi, Albert Christian. *American Pressed Glass and Figure Bottles.* New York: Thomas Nelson & Sons, 1964.

Reynolds, Quentin. *The Fiction Factory: The Story of 100 Years of Publishing at Street & Smith.* New York: Random House, 1955.

Rhodes, James Ford. *History of the Unived States from the Compromise of 1850 to the End of the Roosevelt Advministration.* Vols. III-IV (1860-1866). New York: The MacMillan Co., 1928.

Ritchie, Carol M. *Rhymer By Chance.* Boston: Bruce Humphries Inc., 1939. [Written by a Gault family descendent.]

Riddle, Albert Gallatin. *Recollections of War Times: Reminiscences of Men and Events in Washington, 1860-1865.* New York: G. P. Putnam's Sons, 1895.

Ripley, Warren. *Artillery and Ammunition of the Civil War.* New York. Promontory Press, 1970.

Roberts G. and Tunnell, D. [eds.]. *Standard Dictionary of Canadian Biography,* Vol. II. [publication data unknown]

Rodgers, Arel and Rodgers, Carolyn. *Historical Atlas of Saline County, Kansas.* McPherson [KS]: American Atlas Co., 1972.

Rosenberg, Leon Joseph. *Sangers: Pioneer Texas Merchants.* Austin: Texas State Historical Association, 1978.

Ross, Ishbel. *Crusades and Crinolines.* New York: Harper & Row, 1963.

Ross, Robert B. and Catlin, George B. *Landmarks of Detroit: A History of the City.* Revised by Clarence W. Burton. Detroit: Evening News Association, 1898.

Rothert, Matt. *A Guide Book of United States Fractional Currency.* Racine [WI]: Whitman Publishing Co., 1963.

Rulau, Russell. *Hard Times Tokens, 1832-1844.* 4th edition. Iola [WI]: Krause Publications, 1992.

———. *U.S. Merchant Tokens, 1845-1860.* 3rd edition. Iola [WI]: Krause Publications, 1990.

———. *United States Trade Tokens, 1866-1889.* 2nd edition. Iola [WI]: Krause Publications, 1988.

Ryczek, William J. *Blackguards and Red Stockings: A History of Baseball's National Association, 1871-1875.* Jefferson [NC] and London [England]: McFarland & Co., 1992.

Rydjord, John. *Kansas Place-Names.* Norman: University of Oklahoma Press, 1972.

Sandburg, Carl. *Abraham Lincoln.* Vol II, "The War Years." New York: Dell Publishing Co., Inc., 1954.

Sandham, Alfred. *Coins, Tokens and Medals of the Dominion of Canada.* Montreal: Daniel Rose, Printer, 1869.

Sagendorph, Robb. *America and Her Almanacs.* Boston: Little, Brown and Co., 1970.

Schenkman, David E. *Civil War Sutler Tokens and Cardboard Scrip.* Bryans Road [MD]: Jade House Publications, 1983.

------ [ed.]. *A Survey of American Trade Tokens.* Lawrence [MA]: Quarterman Publications, 1975.

Scott Publishing Co. *Scott Specialized Catalogue of United States Stamps.* Various editions. New York and Sidney [OH]: Scott Publishing Co. and Amos Press, all years 1937 to date.

------. *Scott's Stamps in Color.* New York: Scott Publishing Co., n. d.

Scott Stamp & Coin Co. *Scott's Standard Catalogues, Copper Coins,* No. 5. 16th edition. New York: Scott Stamp and Coin Co., 1890.

———. *Scott's Standard Catalogues, Copper and Nickel,* 17th edition. New York: Scott Stamp and Coin Co., 1893.

Scull, Penrose. *From Peddlers to Merchant Princes: A History of Selling in America.* Chicago and New York:

Follett Publishing Co., 1967.

Sears, Roebuck and Co. *Sears, Roebuck and Co. Consumer Guide, Fall, 1900*. Rep. ed. Northfield [IL]: DBI Books, 1970.

Seymour, Harold. *Baseball: The Early Years*. New York: Oxford University Press, 1960.

Shannon, Fred Albert. *Economic History of the People of the United States*. New York: The MacMillan Co., 1934.

———. *The Organization and Administration of the Union Army, 1861-1865*. 2 vols. Cleveland: Arthur H. Clark Co., 1928.

Shaw, Albert. *Abraham Lincoln: The Year of His Election*. New York: The Review of Reviews Corp., 1930.

Sheahan, James W. and Upton, George P. *The Great Conflagration: Chicago – Its Past, Present and Future*. Chicago: Union Publishing Co., 1872.

Sheehan, Donald. *This Was Publishing: A Chronicle of the Book Trade in the Gilded Age*. Bloomington: Indiana University Press, 1952.

Silver, Nathan. *Lost New York*. New York: Houghton Mifflin Co., 1967.

Simon, Kate. *Fifth Avenue: A 'Very' Social History*. New York and London: Harcourt Brace Jovanovich, 1978.

Singer, Eric. *A Manual of Graphology*. Surrey [England]: Duckworth, 1969.

Slabaugh, Arlie. R. *U.S. and Foreign Encased Postage Stamps*. "Hewitt's Numismatic Information Series." [Two variant printings, distinguished principally by the appearance or absence of the Joseph L. Bates encased stamp illustration.] Chicago: Hewitt Brothers, n. d., and 1967.

Slaten, James W. *Antique American Sewing Machines: A Value Guide*. Oakland [CA]: Singer Dealer Museum, 1992.

Smith, Donald L. *The Twenty-Fourth Michigan: The Iron Brigade*. Harrisburg [PA]: The Stackpole Co. 1962.

Smith, Elsdon C. *New Dictionary of American Family Names*. New York: Harper & Row, 1973.

Smith, George Winston. *Medicines for the Union Army*. Madison [WI]: American Institute of the History of Pharmacy, 1962.

———, and Judah, Charles. *Life in the North During the Civil War – A Source History*. Albuquerque: The University of New Mexico Press, 1966.

Smith, H. P. *History of Broome County*. n. p.: 1885.

Smith, Pete. *American Numismatic Biographies*. Rocky River [OH]: Gold Leaf Press/The Money Tree, 1992.

Sobieszek, Robert A. and Appel, Odette M. *The Spirit of Fact: The Daguerreotypes of Southworth and Hawes, 1843-1862*. Boston: David R. Godine and Rochester: The International Museum of Photography, George Eastman House, 1976.

Spann, Edward K. *The New Metropolis: New York City, 1840-1857*. New York: Columbia University Press, 1981.

Spaulding, E. G. *A Resource of War: The Credit of the Government Made Immediately Available*. Reprint edition. Westport [CT]: Greenwood Press, 1971.

Stern, Philip Van Doren [ed.]. *Soldier Life in the Union and Confederate Armies*. "Civil War Centennial Series." Bloomington: Indiana University Press, 1961.

Stevens, Phillip H. *Artillery Through the Ages*. New York: Franklin Watts Inc., 1965.

Stone, Mildred F. *A History of the Mutual Benefit Life Insurance Company Since 1845*. New Brunswick: Rutgers University Press, 1957.

Stratton, Joanna L. *Pioneer Women: Voices from the Kansas Frontier*. New York: Simon and Schuster, 1981.

Sullivan, Edmund B. *America Political Badges and Medalets, 1789-1892*. Lawrence [MA]: Quarterman Publications Inc., 1981.

———. *Collecting Political Americana*. Hanover [MA]: Christopher Publishing House, 1991.

Sutphen, Dick. *The Mad Old Ads*. New York: McGraw-Hill Book Co., 1966.

Sutton, Felix. *Master of Ballyhoo: The Story of P. T. Barnum*. New York: G. P. Putnam's Sons, 1968.

Taft, Robert. *Photography and the American Scene: A Social History, 1839-1889*. New York: The MacMillan Co., 1938.

Tatham Stamp & Coin Co. *Coin Collector's Annual Catalogue*. Springfield [MA]: Tatham Stamp & Coin Co., 1955.

Taxay, Don. *The Comprehensive Catalogue and Encyclopedia of United States Coins*. Second edition. New York: Scott Publishing Co., 1975.

———. *Counterfeit, Mis-Struck and Unofficial U. S. Coins*. New York: Arco Publishing Co., 1963.

———. *The U. S. Mint and Coinage*. New York: Arco Publishing Co., 1966.

Tebbel, John. *A History of Book Publishing in the United States*. Vol. I, "The Creation of an Industry, 1630-1865." New York: R. R. Bowker, 1972.

———. *A History of Book Publishing in the United States*. Vol. II, "The Expansion of an Industry, 1865-1919." New York: R. R. Bowker, 1975.

Thompson, Bish. *St. Mary's Hospital, 1872-1972*. Evansville: Creative Press Inc., n. d. [1972]

Thorp, Prescott Holden [ed.]. *Bartel's Catalogue of the Stamped Envelopes and Wrappers of the U.S. and Possessions*. Fifth ed. Vol 1. Netcong [NJ]: Prescott Holden Thorp, 1943.

Tiffany, John K. *Postage Stamps of the United States of America*. St. Louis: C. H. Mekeel, Philatelic Publisher, 1887.

Todd, Richard Cecil. *Confederate Finance*. Athens: University of Georgia Press, 1954.

Toppan, George L., Deats, Hiram E., and Holland, Alexander. *The Boston Revenue Book*. [Reprint of *An Historical Reference List of the Revenue Stamps of the U. S. Including the Private Die Proprietary Stamps*. Boston: Boston Philatelic Society, 1899.] Lawrence [MA]: Quarterman Publications, Inc., n. d.

Turner, George T. *Essays and Proofs of U.S. Internal*

Revenue Stamps.

Van Rensselaer, Stephen. *Early American Bottles and Flasks*. Revised edition, edited by J. Edmund Edwards. Stratford [CT]: J. Edmund Edwards, Publisher, 1971.

Vexler, Robert I. *Cincinnati: A Chronological and Documentary History, 1676-1970*. "American Cities Chronology Series," ed. Howard B. Furer. Dobbs Ferry [NY]: Oceana Publications, 1975.

Waldsmith, John. *Stereoviews: An Illustrated History and Price Guide*. Radnor [PA]: Wallace-Homestead Book Co., 1991.

Walker, Robert H. *Everday Life in the Age of Enterprise, 1865-1900*. New York: G. P. Putnam's Sons, 1967.

Wallace, Irving. *The Fabulous Showman: the Life and Times of P. T. Barnum*. New York: Alfred A. Knopf, 1959.

Wallace, W. Stewart [comp.]. *A Dictionary of North American Authors Deceased Before 1950*. Toronto: The Ryerson Press, 1951. Rep. Detroit: Gale Research Co., 1968.

Warden, Robert B. *An Account of the Private Life and Public Services of Salmon Portland Chase*. Cincinnati: Wilstach, Baldwin & Co., 1874.

Ware, Eugene F. *The Indian War of 1864. Being a Fragment of the Early History of Kansas, Nebraska, Colorado and Wyoming*. New York: St. Martin's Press, 1960.

Watson, David Kemper. *History of American Coinage*. New York: G. P. Putnam's Sons, 1899.

Watson, Edward B. *New York Then and Now*. New York: Dover Publications, Inc., 1976.

Watson, Richard. *Bitters Bottles*. New York: Thomas Nelson & Sons, 1965.

Weeden, William B. *War Government: Federal and State in Massachusetts, New York, Pennsylvania and Indiana, 1861-1865*. Boston: Houghton, Mifflin and Co., 1906.

Weeks, Edward and Flint, Emily. *Jubilee: One Hundred Years of the Atlantic*. Boston: Little, Brown and Co., 1957.

West, Christopher. *United States Match and Medicine Stamps*. Pacific Palisades [CA]: Castenholtz and Sons, 1980.

Whitman, Walt. *Memoranda During the War & Death of Abraham Lincoln*. Roy P. Basler ed. Bloomington: Indiana University Press, 1962.

Wight, C. H. *Genealogy* [of the] *Claflin Family*. n.p.:Privately Printed, 1903. [Hopkinton Public Library]

Wilhite, Bob et al. 1983 *Auction Prices Realized, U. S. Paper Money*. Iola [WI]: Krause Publications Inc., 1983.

Williamson, Harold F. and Smalley, Orange A. *Northwestern Mutual Life: A Century of Trusteeship*. Evanston: Northwestern University Press, 1957.

Wilson, Mitchell. *American Science and Invention*. New York: Bonanza Books, 1954.

Winks, Robin W. *Canada and the United States, the Civil War Years*. Baltimore: The Johns Hopkins University Press, 1960.

Winsor, Justin [ed.]. *The Memorial History of Boston... 1630-1880*. Vol. IV, Pt. 2, "The Last Hundred Years." Boston: Ticknor & Fields, 1881.

Wolka, Wendell A., Vorhies, Jack M., and Schramm, Donald A. *Indiana Obsolete Notes and Scrip*. Iola [WI]: Krause Publications, 1978.

Wood, John C. [pres.]. *Fifty Years on Fifth*. New York: The Fifth Avenue Association and International Press, 1957.

Woodford, Frank B. *Father Abraham's Children*. Detroit: Wayne State University Press, 1961.

Woulfe, Rev. Patrick. *Irish Names and Surnames*. Dublin [Ireland]: M. H. Gill & Son, 1923.

Wright, Louis B. [ed.]. *Everyday Life in the Age of Enterprise*. New York: G. P. Putnam's Sons, 1967.

Wright, Lyle H. *American Fiction, 1851-1875*. San Marino [CA]: Huntington Library, 1965.

Yeoman, R. S. *A Guide Book of United States Coins*. Various editions. Racine [WI]: Whitman Publishing Co., various years.

Young, James Harvey. *The Toadstool Millionaires*. Princeton: Princeton University Press, 1961.

Yount, John T. *Bottle Collector's Hand Book and Pricing Guide*. Fullerton [CA]: Educator Publications, 1970.

Zartman, Lester W. *The Investments of Life Insurance Companies*. New York: Henry Holt & Co., 1906.

Ziegler, Gertrude Mohlin. *The Christian Buhl Family Story*. Zelienople [PA]: Zelienople Historical Society, 1980.

Zornow, William Frank. *Kansas: A History of the Jayhawk State*. Norman: University of Oklahoma Press, 1957.

Index

Colophon

This book is typeset in a digitized version of Goudy Old Style, a face originally designed in 1912 by American Frederic Goudy for a book on Abraham Lincoln. It is based on early Italian type designs and is one of the most popular designs by Goudy. Headings are typeset in Helvetica Condensed to contrast the body face. The book was composed in Microsoft Word 5.1a and produced by the author in QuarkXPress 3.31 on a Macintosh Centris 610 computer with Sony Trinitron Multiscan HG video display monitor. Images were scanned in Adobe Photoshop 3.0 software on a Pixel Craft Pro Imager 7650 scanner. Some three-dimensional artwork was digitized on a Kodak DCS 200 digital camera mounted on a Nikon AF equipped with a 28 mm Nikon lens. Gray scale enhancement was performed in Intellihance Pro GS software. Illustrations were done in Adobe Illustrator 5.5. System software was Apple 7.1. Pages were proofed on a Hewlett Packard Laser Jet 4si. It is printed on Cross Pointe (Mfg.), Halopaque Vellum, Cream White 60# Text, supplied by Olmsted Kirk Paper Co. Dallas. This book is printed on 100% recycled fiber paper.

Designed by Therese Bellar
Printed and bound by Haddon Craftsmen, Inc., Bloomsburg, Pennsylvania
An R. R. Donnelley & Sons Company

Endpapers photograph by Mathew Brady, 1862
"Broadway Looking North at City Hall Park
From the Balcony of Barnum's Museum"

Looking north from Barnum's American Museum, corner of Broadway and Park Row. Flag flying at right is at the U.S. Army recruiting station. Trees behind it are in City Hall Park. The Astor House is at left with carriages picking up and dropping off guests. St. Paul's Church and Brady's Gallery are one and two buildings to the left, out of photograph. Barclay, Park Place and Murray are the streets merging with Broadway at left. Vendor in foreground is offering sarsaparilla or beer for three cents a glass, likely paid with a stamp.

APPLICATION FOR ANA MEMBERSHIP

❑ Regular ❑ Senior ❑ 3- or 5-Year ❑ Club ❑ Life
❑ Mr. ❑ Mrs. ❑ Ms. ❑ Club

Name (please print)

Street

City State Zip

Birth Date (For senior discount)

ANA Bylaws require the publication of each applicant's name and state.

❑ **Check here if you DO NOT want your name and address forwarded to the ANA Representative in your area.**

❑ **Check here if you would like your name provided to companies with offers we feel may interest you.**

I herewith make application for membership in the American Numismatic Association, subject to the Bylaws of said Association. I also agree to abide by the Code of Ethics adopted by the Association.

Signature of Applicant Date

Signature of Sponsor Member Number

ANA No.

❑ Check ❑ Money Order ❑ MasterCard ❑ Visa ❑ AmExpress

Credit Card No. Expires

DUES

Regular (age 18 to 64)	$29 *
Outside U.S.	36 *
Senior Citizen (age 65 or older)	25 *
3-Year (individual)	79
5-Year (individual)	130
Club (any country)	33 *
Life (individual)	750 ‡
Life (senior citizen)	500 ‡

* Plus $6 application fee, first year only.

‡ Installment plan available. Call for details.

Forward completed application and payment to:

ANA • 818 N. Cascade Ave. • Colorado Springs • CO 80903-3279

Telephone 1-800-367-9723 • FAX 719-634-4085

Foreign applications must be accompanied by U.S. funds drawn on a U.S. bank.

S. HATFIELD